Lecture Notes in Artificial Intelligence   2198

Subseries of Lecture Notes in Computer Science
Edited by J. G. Carbonell and J. Siekmann

Lecture Notes in Computer Science
Edited by G. Goos, J. Hartmanis, and J. van Leeuwen

Springer
Berlin
Heidelberg
New York
Barcelona
Hong Kong
London
Milan
Paris
Tokyo

Ning Zhong   Yiyu Yao
Jiming Liu   Setsuo Ohsuga (Eds.)

Web Intelligence:
Research and Development

First Asia-Pacific Conference, WI 2001
Maebashi City, Japan, October 23-26, 2001
Proceedings

Springer

Volume Editors

Ning Zhong
Maebashi Institute of Technology
Department of Systems and Information Engineering
460-1 Kamisadori-Cho, Maebashi-City 371-0816, Japan
E-mail: zhong@maebashi-it.ac.jp

Yiju Yao
University of Regina, Department of Computer Science
Regina, Saskatchewan, Canada S4S 0A2
E-mail: yyao@cs.uregina.ca

Jiming Liu
Hong Kong Baptist University, Department of Computer Science
224 Waterloo Road, Kowloon, Hong Kong, China
E-mail: jiming@comp.hkbu.edu.hk

Setsuo Ohsuga
Waseda University, Department of Information and Computer Science
3-4-1 Okubo Shinjuku-Ku, Tokyo 169, Japan
E-mail: ohsuga@fd.catv.ne.jp

Cataloging-in-Publication Data applied for

Die Deutsche Bibliothek - CIP-Einheitsaufnahme

Web intelligence : research and development ; first Asia Pacific conference ;
proceedings / WI 2001, Maebashi City, Japan, October 23 - 26, 2001.
Ning Zhong ... (ed.). - Berlin ; Heidelberg ; New York ; Barcelona ; Hong Kong ;
London ; Milan ; Paris ; Tokyo : Springer, 2001
    (Lecture notes in computer science ; Vol. 2198 : Lecture notes in
    artificial intelligence)
    ISBN 3-540-42730-9

CR Subject Classification (1998): H.3, C.2, H.4, H.5, J.1, I.2

ISBN 3-540-42730-9 Springer-Verlag Berlin Heidelberg New York

This work is subject to copyright. All rights are reserved, whether the whole or part of the material is
concerned, specifically the rights of translation, reprinting, re-use of illustrations, recitation, broadcasting,
reproduction on microfilms or in any other way, and storage in data banks. Duplication of this publication
or parts thereof is permitted only under the provisions of the German Copyright Law of September 9, 1965,
in its current version, and permission for use must always be obtained from Springer-Verlag. Violations are
liable for prosecution under the German Copyright Law.

Springer-Verlag Berlin Heidelberg New York
a member of BertelsmannSpringer Science+Business Media GmbH

http://www.springer.de

© Springer-Verlag Berlin Heidelberg 2001
Printed in Germany

Typesetting: Camera-ready by author, data conversion by PTP-Berlin, Stefan Sossna
Printed on acid-free paper   SPIN: 10840672   06/3142   5 4 3 2 1 0

Preface

This volume contains the papers selected for presentation at *the First Asia-Pacific Conference on Web Intelligence* (WI 2001) held in Maebashi TERRSA, Maebashi City, Japan, October 23-26, 2001. It was sponsored by ACM SIGART and Maebashi Institute of Technology, in cooperation with ACM SIGCHI, ACM SIGWEB, the Japanese Society for Artificial Intelligence (JSAI), JSAI SIGFAI, JSAI SIGKBS, and IEICE SIGKBSE. The conference was held jointly with the Second Asia-Pacific Conference on Intelligent Agent Technology (IAT 2001).

WI 2001 was the first conference on a new and emerging subfield of computer science known as *Web Intelligence*. It provided an international forum for researchers and practitioners to present the state of the art in the development of Web intelligence, to examine performance characteristics of various approaches in Web-based intelligent information technology, and to cross-fertilize ideas on the development of Web-based intelligent information systems among different domains. By idea-sharing and discussions on the underlying foundations and the enabling technologies of Web intelligence, we hoped to stimulate the future development of new models, new methodologies, and new tools for building a variety of embodiments of Intelligent Web Information Systems (IWIS).

In spite of its name, WI 2001 was truly an international conference that attracted 153 full-length research paper submissions from 31 countries and regions of all continents. Each submitted paper was reviewed by at least three experts on the basis of technical soundness, relevance, originality, significance, and clarity. Based on the review reports, 28 regular papers and 45 short papers were accepted for presentation and publication. Seven technical sessions were organized, namely: Web Information System Environment and Foundations; Web Human-Media Engineering; Web Information Management; Web Information Retrieval; Web Agents; Web Mining and Farming; Web-Based Applications.

We wish to express our gratitude to all members of the Conference Committee and the International Advisory Board for their instrumental and unfailing support. WI 2001 had a very exciting program with a number of features, ranging from technical sessions, invited talks, demos, and social programs. All of this work would not have been possible without the generous dedication of the Program Committee members and the external reviewers, of our keynote speakers, Edward A. Feigenbaum and Benjamin Wah, and invited speakers, Nick Cercone, James Hendler, W. Lewis Johnson, Riichiro Mizoguchi, Prabhakar Raghavan, and Patrick S. P. Wang, who prepared and presented very stimulating talks, and of Yiming Ye (Demos & Exhibits Chair) who solicited demo proposals and set up the program. We thank them for their strong support.

The conference Web support team at the Knowledge Information Systems Laboratory, Maebashi Institute of Technology did a terrific job of putting together and maintaining the home page for the conference as well as building a software, *cyber-chair*, which is an intelligent agent and interface among organizers, program committee members, and authors/attendees. We would like to thank Juzhen Dong, Muneaki Ohsima, and Norichika Hayazaki of the conference Web support team for their dedication and hard work.

WI 2001 could not have taken place without the great team effort of the Local Organizing Committee and the support of Maebashi Institute of Technology and Maebashi Convention Bureau. Our special thanks go to Nobuo Otani (Local Organizing Chair), Sean M. Reedy, Masaaki Sakurai, Kanehisa Sekine, and Yoshitsugu Kakemoto (the Local Organizing Committee members) for their enormous efforts in planning and arranging the logistics of the conference from registration/payment handling, venue preparation, accommodation booking, to banquet/social program organization. Our sincere gratitude goes to all of the authors who submitted papers. We are very grateful to the WI 2001 corporate sponsors: Maebashi Convention Bureau, Maebashi City Government, Gunma Prefecture Government, The Japan Research Institute, Limited, United States Air Force Office of Scientific Research, Asian Office of Aerospace Research and Development, United States Army Research Office in Far East, and Web Intelligence Laboratory, Inc. for their generous support. Last but not the least, we thank Alfred Hofmann of Springer-Verlag for his help in coordinating the publication of the proceedings.

October 2001

Ning Zhong, Yiyu Yao
Jiming Liu, Setsuo Ohsuga

WI 2001 Conference Committee

General Chairs:

Jiming Liu   Hong Kong Baptist University
Setsuo Ohsuga   Waseda University, Japan

Program Chairs:

Ning Zhong   Maebashi Institute of Technology, Japan
Yiyu Yao   University of Regina, Canada

Demos and Exhibits Chair:

Yiming Ye   IBM T.J. Watson Research Center, USA

Local Organizing Chair:

Nobuo Otani   Maebashi Institute of Technology, Japan

Advisory Board:

Nick Cercone   University of Waterloo, Canada
Edward A. Feigenbaum   Stanford University, USA
T.Y. Lin   San Jose State University, USA
Jiming Liu   Hong Kong Baptist University
Setsuo Ohsuga   Waseda University, Japan
Ryuichi Oka   Real World Computing Partnership, Japan
Nobuo Otani   Maebashi Institute of Technology, Japan
Zbigniew W. Ras   University of North Carolina, USA
Andrzej Skowron   Warsaw University, Poland
Xindong Wu   Colorado School of Mines, USA
Yiyu Yao   University of Regina, Canada
Philip Yu   IBM T.J. Watson Research Center, USA
Ning Zhong   Maebashi Institute of Technology, Japan

Local Organizing Committee:

Masahiko Satori	Maebashi Institute of Technology, Japan
Tadaomi Miyazaki	Maebashi Institute of Technology, Japan
Nobuo Otani	Maebashi Institute of Technology, Japan
Sean M. Reedy	Maebashi Institute of Technology, Japan
Ning Zhong	Maebashi Institute of Technology, Japan
Masaaki Sakurai	Maebashi Convention Bureau, Japan
Toshio Kawamura	Maebashi Convention Bureau, Japan
Kanehisa Sekine	Maebashi Convention Bureau, Japan
Midori Asaka	Information Technology Agency, Japan
Yoshitsugu Kakemoto	Japan Research Institute, Limited, Japan

Program Committee

Sarabjot Singh Anand	MINEit Software Limited, USA
Hendrik Blockeel	Katholieke Universiteit Leuven, Belgium
Peter Bollmann-Sdorra	Technische Universität Berlin, Germany
Cory Butz	University of Ottawa, Canada
Keith Chan	Hong Kong Polytechnic University
Hsinchun Chen	University of Arizona, USA
Ming-Syan Chen	National Taiwan University
Jingde Cheng	Saitama University, Japan
David Cheung	Hong Kong University
Robert Cooley	University of Minnesota, USA
Stefan Decker	Stanford University, USA
Liya Ding	National University of Singapore
Dieter Fensel	Vrije Universiteit Amsterdam
Benjamin Grosof	Massachusetts Institute of Technology, USA
Jiawei Han	Simon Fraser University, Canada
James Hendler	DARPA/ISO, USA
Bernardo A. Huberman	Xerox Palo Alto Research Center
W. Lewis Johnson	University of South California, USA
Tomonari Kamba	NEC Human Media Research Lab., Japan
Yasuhiko Kitamura	Osaka City University, Japan
Ramamohanarao Kotagiri	University of Melbourne, Australia
Bing Liu	National University of Singapore
Chunnian Liu	Beijing Polytechnic University, China
Jiming Liu	Hong Kong Baptist University
Brien R. Maguire	University of Regina, Canada
Akira Namatame	National Defense Academy, Japan
Jian-Yun Nie	Université de Montréal, Canada
H-O Nyongesa	Sheffield Hallam University, UK
Yukio Ohsawa	University of Tsukuba, Japan
Terry R. Payne	Carnegie Mellon University, USA
Gregory Piatetsky-Shapiro	Knowlegde Stream, USA
Mohamed Quafafou	University of Nantes, France
Vijay V. Reghavan	University of SW Louisiana, USA
Qiang Shen	University of Edinburgh, UK
Timothy K. Shih	Tamkang University, Taiwan
Myra Spiliopoulou	University of Magdeburg, Germany
Jaideep Srivastava	University of Minnesota, USA
Yasuyuki Sumi	ATR Laboratory Japan
Einoshin Suzuki	Yokohama National University, Japan
Roman W. Swiniarski	San Diego State University, USA
Atsuhiro Takasu	National Institute of Informatics, Japan

Pierre Tchounikine   University of Maine, France
Hiroshi Tsukimoto   Toshiba Corporation, Japan
Shusaku Tsumoto   Shimane Medical University, Japan
Gottfried Vossen   University of Munster, Germany
Lipo Wang   Nanyang Technology University,
    Singapore
Takashi Washio   Osaka University, Japan
Michael S.K. Wong   University of Regina, Canada
Graham Williams   CSIRO, Australia
Seiji Yamada   Tokyo Institute of Technology
Yoneo Yano   Tokushima University, Japan
Yiyu Yao   University of Regina, Canada
Yiming Ye   IBM T. J. Watson Research Center,
    USA
Tetuya Yoshida   Osaka University, Japan
Ning Zhong   Maebashi Institute of Technology,
    Japan
Lizhu Zhou   Tsinghua University, China
Wojciech Ziarko   University of Regina, Canada

Table of Contents

Web Human-Media Engineering

Web Information Management

Web Information Retrieval

Web Agents

Web Mining and Farming

Web-Based Applications

Author Index

Web Intelligence (WI)

Research Challenges and Trends in the New Information Age

Y.Y. Yao[1], Ning Zhong[2], Jiming Liu[3], and Setsuo Ohsuga[4]

[1] Department of Computer Science, University of Regina
Regina, Saskatchewan, Canada, S4S 0A2
yyao@cs.uregina.ca
[2] Department of Information Engineering, Maebashi Institute of Technology
Japan
zhong@maebashi-it.ac.jp
[3] Department of Computer Science, Hong Kong Baptist University
Hong Kong
jiming@Comp.HKBU.Edu.HK
[4] Department of Information and Computer Science, Waseda University
Japan

Abstract. This paper is about a new research field called *Web Intelligence* (WI for short). We try to explain the needs for coining the term as a sub-discipline of computer science for systematic studies on advanced Web related theories and technologies, as well as the design and implementation of Intelligent Web Information Systems (IWIS). Background information and related topics are discussed in an attempt to demonstrate why we consider WI to be a subject worthy of study and, at the same time, to establish a starting point for the further development of WI.

1 Introduction

With the rapid growth of Internet and World Wide Web (WWW), we have now entered into a new information age. The Web provides a total new media for communication, which goes far beyond the traditional communication medias, such as radio, telephone and television. The Web has significant impacts on both academic research and ordinary daily life. It revolutionizes the way in which information is gathered, stored, processed, presented, shared, and used. The Web offers new opportunities and challenges for many areas, such as business, commerce, marketing, finance, publishing, education, research and development. For computer scientists, the Web introduces many new research topics and provides a new platform to reconsider old problems. It might be high time to create a new sub-discipline of computer science covering theories and technologies related to the Web. *Web Intelligence* is our proposal for this purpose.

The authors of this paper conceived *Web Intelligence* (WI for short) in late 1999. We felt that although a number of conferences and journals publish or

N. Zhong et al. (Eds.): WI 2001, LNAI 2198, pp. 1–17, 2001.
© Springer-Verlag Berlin Heidelberg 2001

cover Web or Internet related topics, there was no conference and journal devoted to intelligence aspects in the design and implementation of Web information systems. We suspected that there exists a need for a conference devoted to Web Intelligence. At the 24th Annual International Computer Software and Applications Conference (IEEE COMPSAC) in 2000, we first introduced Web Intelligence and formally announced the new *Web Intelligence* conference in a position paper at a Panel on Data Mining and Web Information Systems [49]. We are impressed by the quick and vast responses, as well as kind support, from research community and reputable publishers.

The main objective of this paper is to formally initiate a sub-discipline of computer science by coining the term Web Intelligence, into which Web related research can be fitted. It is more a proposal and an appeal for the creation of WI on its own rights, rather than a precise definition of what is exactly WI. We are more concerned with the necessity and benefits of WI, as well as research topics of WI. It is our intention to create further discussion and critical examination of WI among researchers working on Web related topics.

The rest of the paper is organized as follows. In Section 2, we provide a definition of Web Intelligence. In Section 3, we argue that it is necessary and beneficiary to have a new sub-discipline of computer science labelled by WI. In Section 4, we present an overview of Artificial Intelligence and show its relevance to WI. In Section 5, we provide a list of topics of WI. In Section 6, we discuss trends and challenges of WI related research and development. Section 7 is devoted to intelligent Web Agents (WA). Finally, Section 8 introduces the Web Intelligence conference, and Section 9 gives conclusion, respectively.

2   What Is Web Intelligence?

At this very early stage, we are not sure if a formal definition of Web Intelligence is useful or desirable. Nevertheless, we suggest the following definition:

> "Web Intelligence (WI) exploits Artificial Intelligence (AI) and advanced Information Technology (IT) on the Web and Internet."

This definition has the following implications. The basis of WI is AI and IT. The "I" happens to be shared by both "AI" and "IT", although with different meanings in them, and "W" defines the platform on which WI research is carried out. The goal of WI is the joint goals of AI and IT on the new platform of the Web. That is, WI applies AI and IT for the design and implementation of Intelligent Web Information Systems (IWIS). An IWIS should be able to perform functions normally associated with human intelligence, such as reasoning, learning, and self improvement.

There perhaps might not be a standard and non-controversial definition of WI, as the case that there is no standard definition of AI. One may argued that our definition of WI focuses more on the software aspects of the Web. It is not our intention to exclude any research topic using the proposed definition. The term, Web Intelligence, should be considered as an umbrella or a label of a new branch of research centered on the Web. Our definition simply states the scopes and goals of WI. This allows us to include any theories and technologies that either fall in the scopes or aim at the same goals. To complement the formal definition, we try to make the picture clearer by listing topics to be covered by WI.

WI will be an ever-changing research branch. It will be evolving with development of the Web as new media for information gathering, storage, processing, delivery and utilization. It is our expectation that WI will be evolved into an inseparable research branch of computer science. Although no one can predict the future in detail and without uncertainty, it is clear that WI would have huge impacts on the application of computers, which in turn will effect our everyday lives.

3   Motivations and Justifications for WI

The introduction of Web Intelligence (WI) can be motivated and justified from both academic and industrial perspectives.

Two features of the Web make it a useful and unique platform for computer applications and research, the size and complexity. The Web contains a huge amount of interconnected Web documents known as Web pages. For example, the popular search engine Google claims that it can search 1,346,966,000 pages as of February 2001. The sheer size of the Web leads to difficulties in the storage, management, and efficient and effective retrieval of Web documents. The complexity of the Web, in terms of connectivity and diversity of Web documents, forces us to reconsider many existing information systems, as well as theories, methodologies and technologies underlying those systems. One has to deal with a heterogeneous collection of structured, unstructured, semi-structured, inter-related, and distributed Web documents consisting of texts, images and sounds, instead of homogeneous collection of structured and unrelated objects. The latter is the subject of study of many conventional information systems, such as databases, information retrieval, and multi-media systems. To accommodate the needs of the Web, one needs to study issues on the design and implementation of the Web-based information systems by combining and extending results from existing intelligent information systems. Existing theories and technologies need to be modified or enhanced to deal with complexity of the Web. Although individual Web-based information systems are constantly being deployed, advanced issues and techniques for developing and for benefiting from the Web remain to be systematically studied. The challenges brought by the Web to computer scientists may justify the creation of the new sub-discipline, WI, for carrying out Web-related research.

The Web increases the availability and accessibility of information to a much larger community than any other computer applications. The introduction of Personal Computers (PCs) brought the computational power to ordinary people. It is the Web that delivers more effectively information to everyone at finger tips. The Web, no doubt, offers a new means for sharing and transmitting information unmatchable by other media. The revolution started by the Web is just beginning. New business opportunities, such as e-commerce, e-banking, and e-publication, will increase with the maturity of the Web. It can hardly overemphasize more impacts of the Web on the business and industrial world. The creation of a new sub-discipline devoted to Web related research and applications might has a significant value in the future.

The needs for WI may be further illustrated by the current fast growing research and industrial activities centered on it. We searched the Web by using the keyword "Web Intelligence" through several search engines in February 2001. The results are summarized in Table 1.

Table 1. A Statistics on WI

Search Engine	Number of hits
Lycos (http://search.lycos.com/)	1,102,279
Google (http://www.google.com/)	1,080,000
Excite (http://www.excite.com)	223,825
AltaVista (http://www.AltaVista.com/)	1,271
Netscape (http://Netscape.com/)	77
Yahoo (http://www.yahoo.com/)	74
LookSmart (http://www.looksmart.com/)	62

There are some interesting observations from the search results. The Web pages returned by most search engines contain both keywords "Web" and "Intelligence", although they may not appear as a phrase in many pages. The co-occurrences of the two keywords show their strong association. This provides a piece of convincing empirical evidence supporting WI. The identification of this association may lead to the recognition of the importance of WI. We also used advanced search option of Google to search for the exact phrase "Web Intelligence". We obtained 3,660 hits. We found that many companies concentrate on WI to provide intelligent solutions to business in the new Web-based information age. In fact, the majority of the top 40 pages returned by Google is industry related. For comparison, we search ResearchIndex (the NECI Scientific Literature Digital Library, http://citeseer.nj.nec.com/cs) containing an extreme large collection of scientific papers on-line. We found only one paper contains the phrase "Web Intelligence". A further search of "Web" and "Intelligence" within two words results in 12 documents. They deal with topics such as Web browser intelligence, artificial intelligence for Web search, and Internet marketing intelligence through Web log mining. We also used "Web Intelligence" to query Ask Jeeves (http://www.ask.com/) and obtained related topics, such as intelligent Web systems, Web artificial intelligence, Web business intelligence, intelligent Web agents, intelligent Web robots, intelligent user interfaces, and Web user interfaces. Those topics clearly fit the proposed research areas of WI. From the search results, we also noticed that the Call for Papers of this conference (WI'01) was either archived on, or linked by many Web sites.

In summary, we can conclude that there is an interest and a need for WI. It seems that academic research needs to speed up to be in pace with the industrial demands. The introduction of WI sub-discipline may be helpful in bridging the gap between industry demands and academic research.

4   Perspectives of WI

As a new branch of research, Web Intelligence exploits Artificial Intelligence (AI) and Information Technology (IT) on the Web. On the one hand, it may be viewed as applying results from these existing disciplines to a totally new domain. On the other hand, WI may also introduce new problems and challenges to the established disciplines. WI may also be viewed as an enhancement or an extension of AI and IT. It remains to be seen if WI would become a sub-area of AI and IT or a child of a successful marriage of AI and IT. However, no matter what happens, studies on WI can benefit a great deal from the results, experience, success and lessons of AI and IT.

In their very popular textbook, Russell and Norvig [38] examined different definitions of artificial intelligence from eight other textbooks, in order to decide what is exactly AI. They observed that the definitions vary along the two dimensions. One dimension deals with the functionality and ability of an AI system, ranging from thought processes and reasoning ability of the systems to the behavior of the systems. The other dimension deals with the designing philosophy of AI systems, ranging from intimating human problem solving to making rational decision. The combination of the two dimensions results in four categories of AI systems adopted from Russell and Norvig [38]:

Systems that think like humans.	Systems that think rationally.
Systems that act like humans.	Systems that act rationally.

This classification provides a basis for the studies of various views and approaches for AI. It also clearly defines goals in the design of AI systems. According to Russell and Norvig [38], they correspond to four approaches, the cognitive modeling approach (thinking humanly), the Turing test approach (acting humanly), the the laws of thought approach (thinking rationally), and the rational agent approach (acting rationally).

The two rows for separating AI systems in terms of thinking and acting may not be a most suitable classification. Action is normally the final result of a thinking process. One may argue that the class of systems acting humanly is a super set of the class of system thinking humanly. In contrast, the separation of human-centered approach and rationality-centered approach may have a significant implications in the studies of AI. While earlier research on AI was focus more on human-centered approach, rationality-centered approach received more attention recently [38].

The first column is centered around humans and leads to the treatment of AI as an empirical science involving hypothesis and experimental confirmation. A human-centered approach represents the descriptive view of AI. Under this view, a system is designed by intimating the human problem solving. This implies that a system should have the usual human capabilities such as knowledge representation, natural language processing, reasoning, planning and learning. The performance of an AI system is measured or evaluated through the Turing test. An system is said to be intelligent if it provides human level performance. Such a descriptive view dominates the majority of earlier studies of expert systems, a special type of AI systems.

The second column represents the prescriptive or normative view of AI. It deals with theoretical principles and laws that an AI system must follow, instead of intimating humans. That is, a rationalist approach deals with an ideal concept of intelligence, which may be independent of human problem solving. An AI system is rational if it does the right thing and makes the right decision. The normative view of AI based on the well established disciplines such as mathematics, logic, and engineering.

The descriptive and normative views also reflect the experimental and theoretical aspects of AI research. The experimental study represents the descriptive view. It covers theories and models for the explanation of the workings of the human mind, and applications of AI to solving problems that normally require human intelligence. The theoretic study aims at the development of theories of rationality, and focuses on the foundations of AI. The two views are complementary to each other. Studies in one direction may provide valuable insights into the other.

Web Intelligence concerns the design and development of intelligent Web information systems. The previous framework for the study of AI can be immediately applied to that of Web Intelligence. More specifically, we can cluster research in WI into the prescriptive approach and the normative approach, and cluster Web information systems in terms of thinking and acting. Various research topics can be identified and grouped accordingly.

Like AI, a foundation of WI can be established by drawing results from the following many related disciplines:

Mathematics:
computation, logic, probability.

Applied Mathematics and Statistics:
algorithms, non-classical logics, decision theory, information theory, measurement theory, utility theory, theories of uncertainty, approximate reasoning.

Psychology:
cognitive psychology, cognitive science, human-machine interaction, user interface.

Linguistics:
computational linguistics, natural language processing, machine translation.

Information Technology:
information science, databases, information retrieval systems, knowledge dis-

covery and data mining, expert systems, knowledge-based systems, decision support systems, intelligent information agents.

The topics under each entry are only intended as examples. They do not form an exhausted list.

In the development of AI, we have witnessed the formulation of many of its new sub-branches, such as knowledge-based systems, artificial neural networks, genetic algorithms, and intelligent agents. Recently, non-classical AI topics have received much attentions under the name of computational intelligence. Computational intelligence focuses on the computational aspect of intelligent systems [7, 52]. The application of AI in other disciplines also leads to new techniques in the corresponding fields. For instance, Business Intelligence (BI) is a result of applying artificial intelligence to the business domain. Artificial Intelligence in Medicine also proved to be a successful application. When viewing WI in such settings, we can identify at least two of its roles. WI may be interpreted "Web based Artificial Intelligence" as the study of particular aspects of AI in the context of the Web, in parallel to the study of computational intelligence. WI may also be interpreted as "Artificial Intelligence on the Web" which regards it as a new application of AI.

A more practical goal of WI is the design and implementation of intelligent Web information systems (IWIS). It should be realized that an IWIS is an integrated system containing many sub-systems. To design such a system, it is necessary to apply a variety of theories and technologies.

In his work on vision, Marr [36] convincingly made the point that a full understanding of an intelligent system involves explanations at various levels. The same argument is applicable to the development of an IWIS. We can identify at least two levels, the conceptual formulation and physical implementation. The conceptual formulation deals with foundations of IWIS, while physical implementation concerns with construction of an IWIS. The former depends on mathematics and logic, and the latter depends on algorithms and programming. Each level may be further divided into more sub-levels. Research in WI should include any topics at different levels.

5   Topics Covered by WI

In order to study advanced Web technology systematically, and develop advanced Web-based intelligent information systems, we list several major subtopics in each topic below.

- Web Information System Environment and Foundations:
  - competitive dynamics of Web sites,
  - emerging Web technology,
  - network community formation and support,
  - new Web information description and query languages,
  - the semantic Web,
  - theories of small world Web,

- Web information system development tools,
- Web protocols.
- Web Human-Media Engineering:
  - the art of Web page design,
  - multimedia information representation,
  - multimedia information processing,
  - visualization of Web information,
  - Web-based human computer interface.
- Web Information Management:
  - data quality management,
  - information transformation,
  - Internet and Web-based data management,
  - multi-dimensional Web databases,
  - OLAP (on-line analytical processing),
  - multimedia information management,
  - new data models for the Web,
  - object oriented Web information management,
  - personalized information management,
  - semi-structured data management,
  - use and management of metadata,
  - Web knowledge management,
  - Web page automatic generation and updating,
  - Web security, integrity, privacy and trust.
- Web Information Retrieval:
  - approximate retrieval,
  - conceptual information extraction,
  - image retrieval,
  - multi-linguistic information retrieval,
  - multimedia retrieval,
  - new retrieval models,
  - ontology-based information retrieval,
  - automatic Web content cataloguing and indexing.
- Web Agents:
  - dynamics of information sources,
  - e-mail filtering,
  - e-mail semi-automatic reply,
  - global information collecting,
  - information filtering,
  - navigation guides,
  - recommender systems,
  - remembrance agents,
  - reputation mechanisms,
  - resource intermediary and coordination mechanisms,
  - Web-based cooperative problem solving.
- Web Mining and Farming:

- data mining and knowledge discovery,
- hypertext analysis and transformation,
- learning user profiles,
- multimedia data mining,
- regularities in Web surfing and Internet congestion,
- text mining,
- Web-based ontology engineering,
- Web-based reverse engineering,
- Web farming,
- Web-log mining,
- Web warehousing.
- Web-Based Applications:
  - business intelligence,
  - computational societies and markets,
  - conversational systems,
  - customer relationship management (CRM),
  - direct marketing,
  - electronic commerce and electronic business,
  - electronic library,
  - information markets,
  - price dynamics and pricing algorithms,
  - measuring and analyzing Web merchandising,
  - Web-based decision support systems,
  - Web-based distributed information systems,
  - Web-based electronic data interchange (EDI),
  - Web-based learning systems,
  - Web marketing,
  - Web publishing.

It should be pointed out that WI researches are not limited to the topics listed above. We expect that new topics will be added, and existing topic will be regrouped or redefined.

In summary, we can observe two ways in which WI research can be characterized. The first one is by adding "Web" as a prefix to an existing topic. For example, from "digital library", "information retrieval", and "agents", we can obtain "Web digital library", "Web information retrieval", and "Web agents". On the other hand, we can add "on the Web" as a postfix. For example, we can obtain "digital library on the Web", "information retrieval on the Web", and "agent on the Web". Our list of research topics is given by the prefix method. However, we must avoid mistakes of seductive semantics as discussed by Bezdek [5]. That is, "words or phrases which convey, by being interpreted in their ordinary (non-scientific) usage, a far more profound and substantial meaning about an algorithm or computational architecture than can be readily ascertained from the available theoretical and/or empirical evidence." For a healthy development of Web Intelligence, we have to be more realistic about our goals and try to avoid over-selling of the subject.

6   Trends and Challenges of WI Related Research and Development

Web Intelligence presents excellent opportunities and challenges for the research and development of new generation Web-based information processing technology, as well as for exploiting business intelligence. With the rapid growth of the Web, research and development on WI have received much attention. We expect that more attention will be focused on WI in the coming years. Many specific applications and systems have been proposed and studied. Several dominant trends can be observed and are briefly reviewed in this section.

E-commerce is one of the most important applications of WI. The e-commerce activity that involves the end user is undergoing a significant revolution [41]. The ability to track users' browsing behavior down to individual mouse clicks has brought the vendor and end customer closer than ever before. It is now possible for a vendor to personalize his product message for individual customers at a massive scale. This is called *targeted marketing* or direct marketing [25]. Web mining and Web usage analysis play an important role in e-commerce for customer relationship management (CRM) and targeted marketing. Web mining is the use of data mining techniques to automatically discover and extract information from Web documents and services [23,41,47]. Zhong *et al.* proposed a way of mining peculiar data and peculiarity rules that can be used for Web-log mining [51]. They also proposed ways for targeted marketing by mining classification rules and market value functions [43,48]. A challenge is to explore the connection between Web mining and the related agent paradigm such as Web farming that is the systematic refining of information resources on the Web for business intelligence [14].

Text analysis, retrieval, and Web based digital library is another fruitful research area in WI. Topics in this area include semantics model of the Web, text ming, automatic construction of citation. Abiteboul *et al.* systematically investigated the data on the Web and the features of semistructured data [1]. Zhong *et al.* studied text mining on the Web including automatic construction of ontology, e-mail filtering system, and Web-based e-business systems [46,50].

Web based intelligent agents are aimed at improving a Web site or providing help to a user. Liu *et al.* worked on e-commerce agents [28]. Liu and Zhong worked on Web agents and KDDA (Knowledge Discovery and Data Mining Agents) [30, 31]. We believe that Web agents will be a very important issue. It is therefore not surprising that we decide to hold the WI conference in parallel to the Intelligent Agents conference. In the next section, we provide a more detailed description of intelligent Web agents.

The Web itself has been studied from two aspects, the structure of the Web as a *graph* and the *semantics* of the Web. Studies on Web structures investigate several structural properties of graphs arising from the Web, including the graph of hyperlinks, and the graph induced by connections between distributed search servants. The study of the Web as a graph is not only fascinating in its own right, but also yields valuable insight into Web algorithms for crawling, searching and community discovery, and the sociological phenomena which characterize its evolution [6]. Studies of the *semantics* of the Web were initiated by Tim Berners-Lee, the creator of the World Wide Web [4]. The Web is referred to as the "semantic Web", where information will be machine-processible in ways that support intelligent network services such as information brokers and search agents [11,12]. The semantic Web requires interoperability standards that address not only the syntactic form of documents but also the semantic content. A semantic Web also lets agents utilize all the data on all Web pages, allowing it to gain knowledge from one site and apply it to logical mappings on other sites for ontology-based Web retrieval and e-business intelligence. Ontologies and agent technology can play a crucial role in enabling such Web-based knowledge processing, sharing, and reuse between applications. A new DARPA program called DAML (DARPA Agent Markup Languages) is a step toward a "semantic Web" where agents, search engines and other programs can read DAML mark-up to decipher meaning rather than just the content on a Web site [16].

7   Intelligent Web Agents

Intelligent agents are computational entities that are capable of making decisions on behalf of their users and self-improving their performance in dynamically changing and unpredictable task environments [26,30,31,32,33]. In [27], Liu provided a comprehensive overview of related research work in the field of autonomous agents and multi-agent systems, with an emphasis on its theoretical and computational foundations as well as in-depth discussions on the useful techniques for developing various embodiments of agent-based systems, such as autonomous robots, collective vision and motion, autonomous animation, and search and segmentation agents. The core of those techniques is the notion of synthetic or emergent autonomy based on behavioral self-organization.

Intelligent Web Agents (WA) are software programs that primarily serve two important roles: a). autonomous entities for exploring and exploiting Web-based services, and b). prototype entities for exhibiting and explaining Web-generated regularities. These two roles are summarized below.

7.1   From WA to Web-Based Services

The first role for WA can be readily described and appreciated by examining the following typical scenarios in which various tasks and objectives are achieved [9, 28,44,45].

1. **Personalized Multimodal Interface.**   WA can provide users with a user-friendly style of presentation that personalizes both the interaction with users and the content presentation. This activity involves the creation of various cognitive aids, including tables, charts, executive summaries, indices, and personalized visual assistants (*e.g.,* graphically animated personas and virtual-reality avatars). WA as interfaces must offer the ease of using electronic services. The provided cognitive aids must be concise (*i.e.,* accessible

with as fewer manipulations as possible and as less memorization as possible) and consistent (*i.e.*, understandable based on users' previously customized cognitive styles).

2. **Push and Pull.** WA can play an important role in dynamically creating pull-and-push advertising. Here, by pull-and-push advertising we mean that a user expresses his or her favorites during the interaction with the agents (pull advertising) and in return the agents search and deliver the information about the favorite items dynamically to the user (push advertising). Such agents can also increase the positive externality of products, that is, the better people are informed about certain products, the more likely the products will be sold.

3. **Pattern Discovery and Self-Organization.** WA will enable to detect what users' buying patterns are forming and how they are structured, and hence effectively manage the online commerce. Collaborative recommendation agents can help individual users aggregate into groups, which can in turn form a dynamical marketplace (for example, see [13]).

4. **Information Gateway.** WA can provide users with immediate access to the most relevant information. This support encompasses a wide spectrum of information filtering and delivery activities by manipulating various heterogeneous Web sources including databases, data warehouses, newswire, financial reports, newsletters, newsgroups, outbound emails, electronic bulletin boards, and hypermedia documents, and based on users' profiles, tailoring and delivering the retrieved information to the users. The provided summary information must be just-in-time (*i.e.*, delivered whenever is needed), relevant (*i.e.*, focused on whichever topics the users are concerned with), and up-to-minute (*i.e.*, refreshed whenever a new piece of information arrives). An example of applications with this type of agent support is comparison shopping that utilizes WA with mobile and filtering capabilities. Some related experiences have been reported in [24,34,40].

5. **Reward.** WA can motivate users to enter and re-enter a certain electronic service. While an ever-greater proliferation of content continues to consume individuals' attention, *e.g.*, through push technology to sell something or to support users, WA can play a crucial role in creating a captive audience, in educating it constantly, and even in removing away users' old purchase habits. To be rewarding is to add value. The motivational rewards or incentives can be created by offering free access to certain information and utility resources (*e.g.*, free software download), opportunities to participate in multi-user information/commodity exchange activities (*e.g.*, collaborative recommendation, chat, bidding, and auction), and scheduled plans for promotional deals.

6. **Matchmaking.** WA can serve as a new means for trading commodities. Since the interests of users as well as the availability of products from dealers can change dynamically from time to time, what usually happens in present day electronic commerce is: (1) a dealer sells his or her items simply because these are the *only* items that he or she has at the moment, or (2) a user buys a certain item simply because it is the *last* item that he or she can find

that partially fits his or her need. WA-based customized business attempts to change the existing online buying and selling into the following new scenarios: (1) a dealer identifies and offers what exactly users are interested in, and (2) a user finds and purchases what he or she really loves – some technical issues related to matchmaking have been addressed in [8,22,35].

7. **Decision.** WA can assist Web users in making decisions. Such decision support may be in the forms of evaluations or recommendations on the various features of certain specific items, cost-benefit analysis, inference support for optimizing utility and resources with respect to functional, time, and cost requirements, and model-based trend analysis and projections concerning new patterns of demand (for example, see [19,39]).

8. **Delegation.** WA can act on behalf of Web users in online activities. The tasks that WA may delegate to achieve include matchmaking, server monitoring, negotiation, bidding, auction, transaction, transfer of goods, and follow-up support. This scenario will empower a new paradigm shift from user-centric to user-delegated electronic business. The delegations of these tasks may be carried out in either semi-autonomous (with users' intervention on decisions) or fully autonomous manners. To this end, various computational theories and models have been proposed and reported in [15,18,37, 42]).

9. **Collaborative Work Support.** WA can offer the infrastructure support as well as the necessary function for collaboratively solving problems and managing workflow activities (for related examples, see [10,19,42]).

7.2   From WA to Web-Generated Regularities

The World Wide Web has evolved into a dynamic, distributed, heterogeneous, complex network, which is hard to control [2,20]. To many people, whether Web developers or researchers who are concerned about the dynamics of complex systems [17] such as Internet, human community, and ecology, it has become imperative to truly understand and interpret (in addition to merely observe) the strong regularities emerged from the 'messy' universe of the World Wide Web. Up till now, there have been few efforts on describing different aspects of the orders in the World Wide Web [20,21,3]. However, as an entire system, the origin and interrelated elements of the regularities still remain unknown.

Liu and Zhang [29] have designed and validated an agent-based model that takes into account Web topology, information distribution, and user interest profile to simulate user surfing behavior and explore the origin of regularities on the World Wide Web surfing. In their experiments, they have discovered that it is the unique distribution of user interest that leads to the regularities in user surfing behavior, i.e., a power law distribution of user surfing depth. The Web topology can only influence the shape parameters of the distribution without changing the nature of the distribution. Also discovered is that the power law of link click frequency is largely due to user purposeful surfing behavior. Their work shows that the regularities in the Web are interrelated and not artifacts of a particular surfing process.

Also in their studies, they have studied three categories of users, according to their interest and familiarity with the Web: Random users who have no obvious intention in Web surfing, rational users who have certain goals to achieve but are not familiar with the Web structure, recurrent users who have certain specific intents and are very familiar with the Web structure. The ability to predict the content at the next-level nodes becomes stronger when moving from random to recurrent users. The result of simulations with respect to the three user categories unveiled that the regularities of user surfing depth on pages and domains still remain the same, while a power law of link click frequency distribution will disappear as we move from recurrent users to random users. This result shows that the order existing in link click frequency comes from user's content-prediction ability, that is whether or not a user can determine his/her next step according to his/her own interest and names of the hyperlinks.

8   Web Intelligence Conference

In order to meet the challenges of WI in the new information age, a new high-quality, high-impact international conference series, namely the Asia-Pacific Conference on Web Intelligence (WI) is initiated. WI-2001 is the first meeting in this new series (http://kis.maebashi-it.ac.jp/wi01). It is an international forum for researchers and practitioners to present the state-of-the-art in the development of Web intelligence, to examine performance characteristics of various approaches in Web-based intelligent information technology, and to cross-fertilize ideas on the development of Web-based intelligent information systems among different domains. By idea-sharing and discussions on the underlying foundations and the enabling technologies of Web intelligence, we hope to stimulate future development of new models, new methodologies, and new tools for building a variety of embodiments of Intelligent Web Information Systems. By jointly holding WI conference and Intelligent Agents conference, we expect a close interaction between the two groups.

The title "Web Intelligence" of the conference was chosen to reflect the distinct feature that the conference is focused on intelligence aspects of Web and Web information systems. The name is short enough to catch attention to this important subfield. It is also general enough to attract contributions from all Web related research.

9   Conclusion

While it may be difficult to define what is exactly Web Intelligence (WI), one can easily argue for the need and necessity of creating such a subfield of study in computer science. With the rapid growth of the Web, we foresee a fast growing interest in Web Intelligence.

Roughly speaking, we define Web Intelligence as a field that "exploits Artificial Intelligence (AI) and advanced Information Technology (IT) on the Web and Internet." It may be viewed as a marriage of artificial intelligence and information technology in the new setting of the Web. By examining the scope and historical development of artificial intelligence, we discuss some fundamental issues of Web Intelligence in a similar manner. There is no doubt in our mind that results from AI and IT will influence the development of WI.

Instead of searching for a precise and non-controversial definition of WI, we list topics that might be interested by a researcher working on Web related issues. In particular, we identify some challenging issues of WI, including e-commerce, studies of Web structures and Web semantics, Web information storage and retrieval, Web mining, and intelligent Web agents.

We advocate for a new conference devoted to WI, namely, the Asia-Pacific Conference on Web Intelligence. The conference will be an international forum for researchers and practitioners to present the state-of-the-art in the development of Web intelligence, to examine performance characteristics of various approaches in Web-based intelligent information technology, and to cross-fertilize ideas on the development of Web-based intelligent information systems among different domains.

References

1. Abiteboul, S., Buneman, P., and Suciu, D. *Data on the Web*, Morgan Kaufmann, 2000.
2. Albert, R., Jeong, H. and Barabasi, A.-L., Diameter of the World-Wide Web, *Nature*, **410**, 130-131, 1999.
3. Barabasi, A.-L. and Albert, R., Emergence of scaling in random networks, *Science*, **286**, 509-512, 1999.
4. Berners-Lee, T., Hendler, J., and Lassila, O. The semantic Web, *Scientific American*, 29-37, May 2001.
5. Bezdek, J.C. What is computational intelligence? in: *Computational Intelligence: Imitating Life*, Zurada, J.M., Marks II, R.J. and Robinson, C.J. (Eds.), IEEE Press, 1-12, 1994.
6. Broder, A., Kumar, R., Maghoul, F., Raghavan, P., Rajagopalan, S., Stata, R., Tomkins, A. and Wiener, J.L. Graph structure in the web, *Computer Networks*, **33**, 309-320, 2000.
7. Cercone, N. and McCalla, G. (eds.) *Computational Intelligence*, **1**, iii-vi, 1985.
8. Chavez, A. and Maes, P., Kasbah: an agent marketplace for buying and selling goods, *Proceedings of the First International Conference on the Practical Application of Intelligent Agents and Multi-Agent Technology (PAAM'96)*, 1996.
9. Cheung, K. W., Li, C. H., Lam, E. C. M., and Liu, J., Customized electronic commerce with intelligent software agents, in: *Internet Commerce and Software Agents - Cases, Technologies and Opportunities*, Rahman, S.M. and Bignall, R.J. (Eds.), IDEA Group Publishing, 150-176, 2001.
10. Clearwater, S. (ed.) *Market-Based Control: A Paradigm for Distributed Resource Allocation*, World Scientific, 1995.
11. Decker, S., Melnik, S. et al. The semantic web: the roles of XML and RDF, *IEEE Internet Computing*, **4:5**, 63-74, 2000.
12. Decker, S., Mitra, P., and Melnik, S. Framework for the semantic web: an RDF tutorial, *IEEE Internet Computing*, **4:6**, 68-73, 2000.

13. Guttman, R., Moukas, A., and Maes, P., Agent-mediated electronic commerce and consumer buying behavior, *Knowledge Engineering Review Journal*, **13**, June, 1998.
14. Hackathorn, R.D. *Web Farming for the Data Warehouse*, Morgan Kaufmann, 2000.
15. Hausch, D., Multi-object auctions: sequential vs. simultaneous sales, *Management Science*, **32**, 1599-1610, 1986.
16. Hendler, J.A. Agents and the semantic Web, *IEEE Intelligent Systems*, **16:2**, 30-37, 2001.
17. Helbing, D., Huberman, B. A., and Maurer, S. M, Optimizing traffic in virtual and real space, in: *Traffic and Granular Flow '99: Social, Traffic, and Granular Dynamics*, Helbing, D., Herrmann, H. J., Schreckenberg, M., and Wolf, D. E. (Eds.), Springer-Verlag, 2000.
18. Hon-Snir, S., Monderer, D. and Sela. A., A learning approach to auctions, *Journal of Economic Theory*, **8**, 65-88, 1998.
19. Hu, J. and Wellman, M., Online learning about other agents in a dynamic multi-agent system, *Proceedings of the Second International Conference on Autonomous Agents*, 1998.
20. Huberman, B. A. and Adamic, L. A., Growth dynamics of the World-Wide Web, *Nature*, **410**, 131, 1999.
21. Huberman, B. A., Pirolli, P. L. T., Pitkow, J. E., and Lukose, R. M., Strong regularities in World Wide Web surfing, *Science*, **280**, 96-97, 1997.
22. Jennings, N., Faratin, P., Johnson, M., Norman, T., O'Brien, P., and Wiegand, M., Agent-based business process management, *International Journal of Cooperative Information Systems*, **5**, 105-130, 1996.
23. Kosala, R. and Blockeel, H. Web mining research: a survey, *ACM SIGKDD Explorations Newsletter*, **2**, 1-15, 2000.
24. Kushmerick, N., Weld, D., Doorenbos, R., Wrapper induction for information extraction, *Proceedings of the 16th International Joint Conference on Artificial Intelligence (IJCAI'97)*, 1997.
25. Ling, C.X. and Li, C. Data mining for direct marketing: problems and solutions, *Proceedings of KDD'98*, 73-79, 1998.
26. Liu, J. Self-organized intelligence, in: *Agent Engineering*, Liu, J., Zhong, N., Tang, Y. Y., and Wang, P. S. P. (Eds.), World Scientific, 2001.
27. Liu, J., *Autonomous Agents and Multiagent Systems*, World Scientific, 2001.
28. Liu, J. and Ye, Y. E-commerce agents: marketplace solutions, security issues, and supply and demand, in: *E-Commerce Agents: Marketplace Solutions, Security Issues, and Supply and Demand*, Liu, J. and Ye, Y. (Eds.), Springer-Verlag, 2001.
29. Liu, J. and Zhang, S. W., Unveiling the origins of Internet use patterns, *Proceedings of INET 2001, The Internet Global Summit*, 2001.
30. Liu, J. and Zhong, N. (Eds.) *Intelligent Agent Technology: Systems, Methodologies, and Tools*, World Scientific, 1999.
31. Liu, J., Zhong, N., Tang, Y.Y., and Wang, P.S.P. (Eds.) *Agent Engineering*, World Scientific, 2001.
32. Liu, J., Zhong, N., Tang, Y. Y., and Wang, P. S. P., *Special Issue on Agent Technology, International Journal of Pattern Recognition and Artificial Intelligence*, World Scientific, 2001.
33. Liu, J., Zhong, N., Tang, Y.Y., and Wang, P.S.P., Introduction to agent engineering, in: *Agent Engineering*, Liu, J., Zhong, N., Tang, Y.Y., and Wang, P.S.P. (Eds.), World Scientific, 2000.
34. Maes, P., Agents that reduce work and information overload, *Communications of the ACM*, **37**, 31-40, 1994.

35. Maes, P., Guttman, R., Moukas, A., Agents that buy and sell, *Communications of the ACM*, 1999.
36. Marr, D. *Vision*, Freeman, 1982.
37. Rosenschein, J. and Zlotkin, G., *Rules of Encounter: Designing Conventions for Automated Negotiation among Computers*, MIT Press, 1994.
38. Russell, S. and Norvig, P. *Artificial Intelligence, A Modern Approach*, Prentice Hall, 1995.
39. Sandholm, T., An implementation of the contract net protocol based on marginal cost calculations, *Proceedings of the 11th National Conference on Artificial Intelligence (AAAI'93)*, 1993.
40. Shardanand, U. and Maes, P., Social information filtering: algorithms for automating 'Word of Mouth', *Proceedings of the CHI-95 Conference*, ACM Press, 1995.
41. Srivastava, J. Cooley, R., Deshpande, M. and Tan, P. Web usage mining: discovery and applications of usage patterns from web data, *SIGKDD Explorations, Newsletter of SIGKDD*, 1, 12-23, 2000.
42. Tesauro, G. J. and Kephart, J. O., Foresight-based pricing algorithms in an economy of software agents, *Proceedings of the International Conference on Information and Computation Economies*, 1998.
43. Yao, Y.Y. and Zhong, N. Mining market value functions for targeted marketing, *Proceedings of the 25th IEEE Computer Society International Computer Software and Applications Conference (COMPSAC 2001)*, 2001.
44. Ye, Y., Liu, J., and Moukas, A., *Special Issue on Intelligent Agents in E-Commerce, Electronic Commerce Research Journal*, Baltzer Science Publishers, The Netherlands, 2001.
45. Ye, Y., Liu, J., and Moukas, A., Agents in electronic commerce, in: *Special Issue on Intelligent Agents in Electronic Commerce, Electronic Commerce Research Journal*, 2001.
46. Zhong, N. *A Study on E-mail Filtering by Uncertainty Sampling and Relation Learning*, Technical Report, Yamaguchi University, 2000.
47. Zhong, N. Knowledge discovery and data mining, *The Encyclopedia of Microcomputers*, **27**, Supplement 6, 235-285, Marcel Dekker, 2001.
48. Zhong, N., Dong, J.Z., and Ohsuga, S. Rule discovery by soft induction techniques, *Neurocomputing, An International Journal*, **36:1-4**, 171-204, Elsevier, 2000.
49. Zhong, N., Liu, J., Yao, Y.Y. and Ohsuga, S. Web Intelligence (WI), *Proceedings of the 24th IEEE Computer Society International Computer Software and Applications Conference (COMPSAC 2000)*, 469-470, 2000.
50. Zhong, N., Yao, Y.Y., and Kakemoto, Y. Automatic construction of ontology from text databases, N. Ebecken and C.A. Brebbia (Eds.) *Data Mining*, **2**, WIT Press, 173-180, 2000.
51. Zhong, N., Yao, Y.Y., and Ohsuga, S. Peculiarity oriented multi-database mining, J. Zytkow and Jan Rauch (eds.) *Principles of Data Mining and Knowledge Discovery*, LNAI 1704, Springer-Verlag, 136-146, 1999.
52. Zurada, J.M., Marks II, R.J. and Robinson, C.J. (Eds.) *Computational Intelligence: Imitating Life*, IEEE Press, 1994.

Knowledge Is Power: The Semantic Web Vision

James Hendler[1] and Edward A. Feigenbaum[2]

[1] Director, Semantic Web and Agent Technologies
Maryland Information and Network Dynamics Laboratory
University of Maryland

[2] Kumagai Professor of Computer Science, Emeritus
Stanford University

Abstract. Good science periodically revisits old results in the context of new discoveries and technologies. In this way, new understanding is gained of the earlier results and, sometimes, new insights can be gained into current work. This in turn can lead to new discoveries, and so the process continues. In this paper, we revisit the generalization known as the "knowledge principle," introduced more than twenty years ago to explain the source of power of expert systems. We show that in a new context, the power of knowledge will come from the distribution and decentralization of knowledge that is ubiquitously developed and applied. In the new semantic web concept, tools are provided to the large population of WWW users that allow those individuals (perhaps millions of them) to encode small bodies of knowledge that can be integrated into an effective large knowledge base. The metaphor of "knowledge is power" thus changes from one of the centralized power to one of distributed power.

1 Introduction

In 1963, Feigenbaum and Feldman [1] edited the first major collection of papers in the Artificial Intelligence (AI) field. The book divided AI into two big parts. One part, called "Artificial Intelligence", had an engineering motivation to construct intelligent computer programs, but was not concerned about whether the programs behaved in the same way that people behave intelligently. The second part, called "Simulation of Cognitive Processes," reported work that had a motivation in Psychology, where the concern was to model accurately the processes that people used to behave intelligently. Both kinds of work have been present in the field over the past four decades. The work has brought great changes to both information technology and to psychology.

N. Zhong et al. (Eds.): WI 2001, LNAI 2198, pp. 18–29, 2001.
© Springer-Verlag Berlin Heidelberg 2001

2 Previous Results about Knowledge in AI Systems

The application of artificial intelligence led to a number of areas of AI research. Expert Systems made the transition from university research to industry in the late 1970s and early 1980s. These programs generalized the approach developed in MYCIN and other early systems. Most of them used sets of rules about a limited domain to provide specific advice or offer diagnoses of the malfunction of complex devices and processes. A key insight from the work of the past forty years is that computers have been able to achieve human-like behavior at world-class levels of performance, but only in limited domains. One of the most impressive demonstrations of this occurred in 1997, when the computer Deep Blue beat the world chess champion, Gary Kasparov. Kasparov remarked in an interview that the computer move that upset him most was "almost human." Of course the subject matter of the chess game was not general, and the discourse was stylized to chess notation, a specific jargon of the chess domain. Deep Blue is unique only in that it arrived thirty years later than predicted famously by Professor Herbert Simon (one of the founders of AI) and was therefore eagerly awaited.

Much earlier however, other AI programs were already behaving at world-class levels of performance. For example, as early as the mid-1970s, a computer program at Stanford University—the MYCIN program—was interacting with physicians about blood infections, asking questions about patient signs and symptoms, offering diagnoses, recommending antibiotic therapy, explaining both diagnosis and therapy recommendation in the stylized English and jargon that doctors speak to each other. MYCIN's behavior was evaluated in a test that involved judgments by dozens of infectious disease experts around the country. Its behavior was formally evaluated as essentially the same as that of the best doctors. MYCIN was an early example of a type of AI program called Expert Systems, so called to indicate that their behavior ranked them with experts in their field.

3 Commercialization of AI as Expert Systems

The application of artificial intelligence led to a number of areas of AI research. Expert Systems made the transition from university research to industry in the late 1970s and early 1980s. These programs generalized the approach developed in MYCIN and other early systems. Most of them used sets of rules about a limited domain to provide specific advice or offer diagnoses of the malfunction of complex devices and processes.

Expert Systems used reasoning processes for inference, setting them apart from most other computer programs, which used arithmetic processes for calculation. The reasoning of expert systems was typically done with some form of logic. The program generally reasoned from collections (called knowledge bases) of knowledge acquired from people who were expert in the domain.

Knowledge Bases (KB) contained a combination of:
- Facts (a set of ground assertions that were assumed to be true in some domain), and
- Heuristics (rules of good judgment, rules of "good guessing", acceptable shortcuts), which could be used to combine these facts in ways that provided inferential power.

This knowledge was typically represented as logic expressions or logic production rules (IF…THEN…), and a program, often called an inference engine, was used to manage the process of combining rules and facts to reach conclusions.

Expert System technology has been absorbed into the mainstream of commercial software development. In practical applications, they are often embedded into large software systems. For example, an equipment configuration expert system is embedded within a larger software system for helping salespeople sell complex equipment ("Salesbuilder" from Trilogy).

Tens of thousands of Expert Systems were built worldwide during the past twenty years. As well as those mentioned above, other notable cases include:

- Shopping advisors on the WWW
- Microsoft hardware troubleshooting wizards and user-help wizards.
- Tools for diagnosis of system failures and equipment failures
- Decision aids for financial analysis and transactions
- Tools for scheduling and planning of operations and manufacturing logistics

In universities, research into new technologies for expert reasoning is also being pursued. On important technology is used for reasoning directly about probabilities and uncertainties using decision theory. There are hybrids of logic and probabilistic reasoning (called Bayes nets or belief nets). The technology called "qualitative physics for device modeling" seeks methods for symbolic modeling of the physics and engineering of devices. Perhaps the best example of this was the experimental system, deployed on the NASA spacecraft Deep Space 1, that was allowed to control the entire spacecraft autonomously for a period of several days.

What powered the Expert Systems to expert-level performance?

In all of these systems, the most important part of the software is the Knowledge Base -- the model of human expertise in the domain of discourse captured in a form suitable for reasoning by programs. Thus, the successful construction of an Expert System is an exercise in expertise modeling, and as such it is much more an exercise in epistemology than technology. This work is quintessentially (in fact, almost by definition) interdisciplinary. For every system built, it was the knowledge from the domain of discourse, knowledge outside of Computer Science, that allowed the program to behave at expert levels of performance. In each case, the knowledge deployed was more important than the logical or probabilistic reasoning method employed.

4 The Knowledge Principle

One can view the many Expert System developments as a large number of experiments in the building of individual specialized AIs, each tailored to a particular domain. Given this view, what principles can be extracted from this body of experimentation?

The most important scientific generalization is that the power of an AI program to behave at high levels of intelligent performance lies in a systematic and extensive encoding of the knowledge of experts of the domain of performance.

This is known as the knowledge-is-power hypothesis or the knowledge principle [2]. Stated succinctly, this principle states that

Knowledge is the primary source of the intellectual power of intelligent agents, both human and computer.

Knowledge supplies the semantic basis for performance in all tasks requiring understanding. That includes natural language understanding or any kind of situation understanding or sensory understanding. The primary lesson learned from this principle is that, practically speaking, there is no shortcut via the elegant logical machinery of AI-- that is, most of the time one cannot derive what one needs to know for adequate performance. The intelligent agent (human or computer) must have an encoding of the practical knowledge needed to reason about a given domain.

5 Semantics

Unfortunately, the knowledge principle comes with a corollary that is difficult for many in AI to accept. If we want to have significant levels of computational intelligence, we need significant bodies of knowledge in knowledge bases. Each domain of reasoning for which we want expert performance requires much engineering of the knowledge and much time spent in the acquisition of this knowledge from those who know the domain well. There is no "magic bullet" – significant performance requires significant knowledge engineering and the capture of many domain specific rules.

There have been other AI approaches explored to overcome this so-called "knowledge acquisition bottleneck." Symbolic machine learning, numerical learning approaches (such as those in neural networks) and "evolutionary" computing approaches have all been shown to have niches in which they perform well. In most cases, however, these approaches have either not had the impact of the expert systems produced by the usual knowledge engineering methods; or they have required significant domain expertise for the design of the algorithms, training sets, etc. Nothing to date has weakened the knowledge principle and its corollary of the need for significant knowledge engineering effort.

The knowledge acquisition bottleneck becomes particularly troubling in the era of the World Wide Web. The ubiquity of (human readable) information accessible at the fingertips of millions of users drives a relentless demand for more intelligent computer assistance—to find, filter, integrate and visualize computer-retrievable data. If we must have a time-consuming and centralized knowledge engineering for each domain of discourse, the ubiquity of intelligent computer assistance for WWW users will not happen because of the enormity of the effort needed.

6 The Semantic Web

In a recent article [3], Berners-Lee, Hendler, and Lasilla discuss how we can get ubiquitous semantic knowledge out into the world of the WWW in a way that it can be harnessed to allow better human access to, and use of, information. This need is being forced by the huge size and penetration of the World Wide Web – which drives an enormous economic pressure to deliver more meaningful WWW behavior to customers and users. Users need what the researchers at Xerox PARC call "sense-making" — semantic processes that aid the average computer user in turning information on the WWW into human accessible knowledge.

The knowledge principle applies to this issue. Since knowledge is the basis for the semantics and supports all understanding, we need knowledge bases to match the large scope of user needs. Thus, the construction of very large knowledge bases, and probably the networking of many knowledge bases, is the number one task for AI, for the information industry, or possibly for a consortium of universities and non-profits organizations. Much actually has been done toward answering this need, but very little has been made robust and integrated into practice to date.

7 Research on Very Large Knowledge Bases

The idea of building very large knowledge bases is not new. The progenitor of all of these efforts is the so-called semantic network, a research topic of the 1960s and 1970s. One strand of this research, and the one we focus on, was the building, by hand, of semantic networks representing very large amounts of knowledge in broad areas.

7.1 EDR

In Japan there was a ten-year national research initiative in the 1980s and 1990s called Electronic Dictionary Research (EDR) to support research in natural language processing (http://www.iijnet.or.jp/edr/). One of EDR's products was the Concept Dictionary, a very large and carefully done semantic network (the language was Japanese but the concepts of course were largely universal). This excellent product was not transferred to commercial use, nor has it been made available in any language other than Japanese.

7.2 CYC

The major US project to build a very large knowledge base is the CYC project. CYC's goal has been to encode in logical expressions a very large body of common sense knowledge. Started by an industrial consortium in 1984, its development is being continued today by CYC Corporation. The CYC knowledge base now encodes millions of assertions and is clearly the best practical example of a very large knowledge base generated by a knowledge engineering process.

CYC's knowledge is layered from most general to most specific. The most general levels contain generic knowledge about such concepts as (these are examples) time, space, causality, intention, belief, emotions, substances, physical actions, and human capabilities (both physical and mental). There are about half a million assertions of this type.

Other knowledge is somewhat more specialized, e.g. occupations, clothing, human-occupied dwellings, and information about specific humans. In addition, CYC contains a number of facts relating to specialty knowledge. These could be as diverse as the engineering of metal parts to how to perform various military maneuvers. CYC goes well beyond all other semantic networks in the detail and richness with which the knowledge is encoded.

7.3 Word Net

A massive semantic net project that is similar in motivation and methodology to the Japanese EDR project is Word Net. Word Net was started at Princeton University and has been built with the help of many American and European researchers. Word Net is a semantic net of terms, synonyms and relationships. To date it is a research tool and, like EDR and CYC, has received little application in the information industry. Other major projects involving semantic encoding have been done by the US National Library of Medicine), by the IEEE, and by NASA.

7.4 HPKB and RKF

The American organization DARPA, The Defense Advanced Research Projects Agency, has been sponsoring the two largest American projects of AI research and development in recent years: the High-Performance Knowledge Base (HPKB) initiative and the ongoing Rapid Knowledge Formation (RKF) project (http://reliant.teknowledge.com/RKF/).

In HPKB, DARPA hoped to stimulate new and different technology in the spirit of CYC's large knowledge base. Issues explored included the technology for scaling up the size of knowledge bases; the systematic encoding of more knowledge (in the spirit of CYC's motivation); and the application of large knowledge bases to interesting classes of military "crisis management" problems (supporting intelligence analysts or their automated agents in interpreting international events and providing a corporate memory about past international crises). The HPKB project was successful, but the applications showed that the limiting factor for success was the speed at which people could encode knowledge accurately into the knowledge bases. This is the same "knowledge acquisition bottleneck" that was described by one of this paper's authors as long ago as 1977!

DARPA launched a successor project. The RKF project has as its goal increasing the speed of knowledge engineering and perhaps automating part or all of the process. More importantly, RKF focuses on the building of tools and processes to make it possible for subject matter experts to author their own very large knowledge bases, instead of requiring AI researchers to do the knowledge engineering. For example, a test problem used in RKF is for students in biology to be able to use the tools themselves to encode the knowledge encapsulated in a standard university biology textbook.

Despite these efforts, it is clear that the development and deployment of very large knowledge bases is not helping the engineering of semantic web assistants – making knowledge of a great variety of domains, across a great variety of applications, available to a great variety of users. The design of large and correct knowledge bases, requires effort that simply cannot cope with the scope, complexity, and exponential growth speed of the WWW and modern information sources.

8 Web Ontology Languages

Until now, the approach to building the very large knowledge base that is needed has been mainly a centralized approach (as exemplified by CYC and EDR). Word Net uses a more decentralized approach. It is probably the case that a much more decentralized approach is needed to recruit the effort of a large number of people in helping to build the knowledge base(s) to support intelligent assistance for WWW applications.

Such an approach has been emerging. In this approach, users of the WWW are given the languages and tools to encode conceptual content by themselves. Just as giving the users tools (based on HTML) to encode document format descriptions led to an immense and unexpected explosion of the number of web pages, we believe tools can be developed that will let users develop and use knowledge bases on the web. Current web languages, such as XML and RDF, are starting to provide the basis on which such new tools can be developed. Though it is early in the exploration of this approach, some users are beginning to have an ability to encode content and concept. In this way, XML and its later extensions have the potential to trigger an explosion of computer-encoded knowledge. XML itself has been widely and rapidly appreciated by the information technology industry. Yet XML is just the first simple step down a long and very important path.

A critical starting place for this explosion of knowledge encoding is the creation of web languages for ontologies. In today's networked world, ontologies are usually just taxonomies of terms linked by relationships to give logical order to a large set of concepts and objects. Because ontologies have a formal logical structure with which they index their world of symbols, they can be used as a framework for making inferences about these symbols.

8.1 Commercial Ontologies

Within the e-commerce world, ontologies are beginning to become important corporate IT tools. What was in 1990 just an arcane topic in the AI research community is now a thriving industrial activity among portal companies and the corporate web sites of large companies. In each case, the need is to give logical organization to a large amount of information on web pages, and to aid search engines to produce more relevant and categorized results.

The first, and still probably the largest, such ontology is the one that launched Yahoo as a business. Yahoo was first a personal project of two Stanford University graduate students, then later a business. One of Yahoo's first technical employees had the title of "Chief Ontologist." Other industry efforts include "vertical industry portals" which use ontologies that are specific to an industry (such as steel or chemicals).

8.2 The Language SHOE

In the AI community, the need to represent ontological information in a web-embedded form was realized a number of years ago with the advent of the language SHOE, developed at the University of Maryland [4]. It extended HTML to allow users to specify class and subclass relations, properties of classes, and a limited set of inference rules. A tool set for manipulating and using ontologies on the web was also designed. SHOE was used in a number of academic efforts in the US and abroad, but was not widely accepted, in part because the HTML basis of the language didn't have quite the power needed for building web tools that could easily coexist within existing browsers.

With the advent of XML and RDF, web languages could more naturally encode the predicates and relationships needed for ontologies. RDF-Schema, a proposed "web recommendation", added some SHOE-like properties to RDF. The European language OIL, is also built on RDF to allow ontological design (using a description logic approach). In the USA, DARPA is supporting the design of the "DARPA Agent Markup Language" (DAML) and sponsors researchers to develop tools and applications that would exhibit and demonstrate the power of semantics on the WWW. Recently, a unification of DAML and OIL has occurred, and the resulting DAML+OIL language is now being considered as the basis of a "web recommendation" for a web ontology language. (DAML+OIL uses a proper XML encoding, thus allowing it easily to build on existing XML browsing tools, style sheets, etc. See http://www.daml.org/ for language details, tools, etc.)

8.3   DAML+OIL

The DAML effort and DAML+OIL language can be considered the first in a modern series of experiments with a more distributed and diverse approach to knowledge bases and knowledge engineering. As of June, 2001, a repository of DAML+OIL ontologies holds over 150 contributions (with a total of 3400 properties expressed about 17,500 classes). In addition, a new semantic web crawler (http://www.daml.org/crawler) has collected 2,450,000 DAML statements that describe documents on the WWW, and the number is increasing constantly. We see that the idea of enabling many users to create and edit small individual knowledge bases is starting to create a new kind of very large knowledge base. Importantly, the distribution of effort over many people will allow this knowledge base to become very large very quickly.

The knowledge principle of course will still apply. An investigation of the ontologies in the DAML repository reveals that many are very incomplete (containing only a small amount of facts about a wide range of topics) and that there are inconsistencies between them. Thus, a term such as "person" appears in many different ontologies, but in some may contain no properties other than an identifier, while in others may contain a larger set of restricted features. The super classes of person include items like agent, entity, primate and thing while subclasses include employee, researcher, project-leader among others. Thus, a user coming to the semantic web, wishing to use it for a more complex reasoning task, will either need mechanisms for collecting and merging definitions, or will be unable to use it for any sophisticated problem solving. In short, the lack of engineered knowledge is felt, even though the quantity and variety of terms is growing at a rapid rate.

9   Bridging between Knowledge Bases, Large and Small

Several research efforts, still very much in their infancy, seem to us to hold a very exciting direction for the future of the semantic web. These efforts focus on using large knowledge bases, such as Word Net and CYC, to provide the semantics for providing mappings between smaller ontologies. In short, the large carefully engineered ontologies may hold the key to providing significant computational power in the use of the more distributed and localized ontologies. Small communities can develop their own ontologies and terms. The larger knowledge bases can be used to help (in automated or semi-automated ways) in the discovery of common terms and the development of "articulation" ontologies [5]. Term "dictionaries" can provide a mapping, full or partial, between ontologies. For example, an articulation rule located on the web page http://www.cs.umd.edu/users/hendler/jhendler.daml asserts that the term "project" defined in an ontology called "atlas-cmu" is EquivalentTo (i.e. has the same meaning as) the term "organization" located in a general ontology developed at the University of Maryland.

10   Another Look at the Metaphor of Power

We can now see a new way to think about "knowledge is power". In the earlier Expert System experiments, where reasoning was restricted to relatively small specialty domains, a single centralized knowledge base provided major leverage. In this "centralized" sense, the power of the knowledge is analogous to that of a centralized electric dynamo in a power plant. From the emerging semantic web experiments, we foresee that knowledge will be much more distributed, and in smaller packages. In the analogy, this is the power found in electrical batteries. Knowledge is power, but in small amounts of power.

We foresee a unification of large and small -- using distributed ontology creation and tools for the creation of a wide range of small efforts, coupled with a few larger efforts to provide large and powerful knowledge bases. In the analogy, the dynamos are Word Net, CYC, etc. The distribution is accomplished using tools for distribution, such as the DAML ontologies. The WWW provides the "wires" to connect.

The analogy leads to a vision similar to the early days of the coming of electrical power, and the evolution of this into the current large-scale power grids. The metaphor of "knowledge is power" thus changes from one of centralized power of the dynamo to the distributed power of the modern electrical grid, which can deliver electricity into an extremely wide range of small things. These small things, since they can rely on a plentiful supply of widely accessible electricity, can have more power than could be provided simply by individual batteries, and the batteries themselves can be "recharged" when connected to the grid.

10.1   A Vision of the Knowledge-Connected Portable

The idea of "recharging" is starting to be explored in several small experimental efforts. The PalmDAML application described at http://www.daml.org/PalmDAML is a good example. A tool was developed to download DAML ontologies and instances on to a PalmPilot™. When connected to the web, the user can choose from a large variety of types of information to load. The complete set of ontologies, however, is far too large to fit on the small device. The user chooses what libraries to download based on current preferences. Demonstration examples include the genealogy of the British Royal family, the military term ontology used by the US Center for Army Lessons Learned, and several others. A Palm application can then be used to browse this ontological information, which can be used when uncoupled from the WWW.

This sort of application is still primitive compared to others currently envisioned. However, it shows the tremendous potential possible in the distribution of knowledge and its use in localized applications. Coupled with the term mapping and merging and the more sophisticated rule sets proposed for the larger WWW Knowledge Base efforts, we can envision the potential for the future semantic-web based "knowledge grid."

11   A Challenge for Twenty-First Century AI Research

The Semantic Web, as we envision it evolving, will not primarily be comprised of carefully groomed ontologies that skilled knowledge engineers have constructed. Instead, we envision a complex Web of semantics ruled by the same sort of anarchy that rules the rest of the Web. Instead of a few large, complex, consistent ontologies that great numbers of users share, we may see a world in which a great number of small ontological components exist, often consisting of pointers to other Web ontologies. Web users will develop these components in much the same way that Web content is created – via tools that make it easy to do layout and web design, while capturing knowledge in the background.

The challenge to AI researchers is to create knowledge development tools that are usable by non-experts without a strong knowledge engineering background. These tools are a precondition for recruiting the millions of web page contributors into the effort to build the enormous Knowledge Base that will be needed to bring intelligence to the Web. With a spiral development of such tools, with content created automatically, and with techniques that use that knowledge to do new and exciting things for users of the Web, we may yet reach the long-range goal of Web intelligence.

References

1. Feigenbaum, E. and J. Feldman (eds.), Computers and Thought, New York: McGraw-Hill, 1963
2. Feigenbaum E.A., How the "what" becomes the "how", Communications of the ACM, Vol. 39, 5, pp.97 – 104 (1996)
3. Berners-Lee, T., Hendler, J., and Lassila, O., The Semantic Web, Scientific American, Vol. 284, 5, pp.34-43 (2001)
4. Heflin, J. and Hendler, J. Dynamic Ontologies on the Web. Proceedings of the Seventeenth National Conference on Artificial Intelligence (AAAI-2000). AAAI/MIT Press, pp. 443-449 (2000).
5. Mitra, P., Wiederhold, G., and Kersten, M., A graph oriented model for articulation of ontology interdependencies, Extending Data Base Technologies 2000, Springer-Verlag Lecture Notes in Computer Science (2000)

From Computational Intelligence to Web Intelligence: An Ensemble from Potpourri

Nick Cercone

Department of Computer Science, University of Waterloo
Waterloo, Ontario N2L 3g1 Canada
ncercone@uwaterloo.ca

Abstract. The advent of the internet has changed the world in possibly more significant ways than any other event in the history of humanity. Is internet access and use beyond the reach of ordinary people with ordinary intelligence? Ignoring for the moment economic issues of access for all citizenry, what is it about internet access and use that hinders more widespread acceptability? We explore several issues, not exclusive, that attempt to provoke and poke at answers to these simple questions. Largely speculative, as invited talks ought to be, we explore 3 topics, well studied but as yet generally unsolved, in computational intelligence and explore their impact on web intelligence. These topics are machine translation, machine learning, and user interface design. Conclusion will be mine; readers will draw general conclusions.

Keywords: Computational Intelligence, Web Intelligence, Data Mining, User Interfaces, Natural Language Processing, Machine Translation, Machine Learning.

1. Introduction

By the time you have completed reading this sentence you will have understood its meaning. Your achievement and success in understanding is most impressive. The speaker's task is much simpler - to generate an utterance which conveys a presumably preexisting thought. Your task as listener is to decide what the speaker must have been thinking in order to motivate his utterance in the particular context in which he uttered it. In general, understanding a natural language (NL) is simply miraculous.

NL represents an important modality for human computer interactions, from simple NL interfaces to databases to machine translation to more general answer-extraction and question answering systems. Other important modalities, e.g., speech, pointing devices, graphical user interfaces, etc. remain. The perfection and integration of multimodal systems takes on new importance when we transpose previous solutions to the internet. Systems which can communicate in natural ways and can learn from interactions are key to long term success transferring *computational to web intelligence.*

Although this talk will be somewhat speculative, as invited talks ought to be, we consider three aspects, well studied but as yet generally unsolved, in computational intelligence and we explore the impact of these topics for web intelligence. These

N. Zhong et al. (Eds.): WI 2001, LNAI 2198, pp. 30–42, 2001.
© Springer-Verlag Berlin Heidelberg 2001

three topics include natural language processing (particularly machine translation), machine learning, and user interface design.

2. Natural Language Interfaces

In the 1990's Simon Fraser University researchers were engaged in a long-term project entitled "Assessing Information with Ordinary Language" which has found its realization in several versions of SystemX. Initial SystemX NL interface prototypes were modularly designed utilizing proven technologies, e.g., augmented transition network grammars. SystemX served as an umbrella project for new ideas and technologies to be incorporated [1], as a testbed for various techniques espoused by graduate students [2] and for experimenting with nonstandard or incompletely specified theories [3].

Subsequent to these early experiments, the use of techniques pioneered in SystemX led to research into NL access to internet search engines. This effort was designed to make access to relevant information on the internet more easily accessible to ordinary users without the need for sophisticated knowledge of appropriate keyword selection or complicated Boolean expression evaluation. This research led to two interesting NL systems for internet information access [4,5].

We briefly illustrate these systems with examples in order to track the progression of research and the directions of change imposed by the advent of the internet.

2.1 SystemX

At Roger's Cablesystems Ltd., the vice president for customer service enters the following into his computer terminal, "Give me the Western region outage log for June". Within seconds SystemX presents him with a neatly formatted table (or graph) of the data retrieved from Rogers' relational database. He could have said, "What's the outage log for the Western region for June?", or "Tell me the June regional outage log for the West." or "Find the Western outages for June.", etc. SystemX can determine that whichever phrase he uses, he means the same thing. Such flexibility in parsing, applying the logical rules of grammar to determine meaning, is nontrivial. SystemX's parsing techniques are described in [6]. After parsing, SystemX reformulates the question in SQL (structured query language) and data is extracted for presentation from Roger's large central database.

The nontrivial problem described in the preceding paragraph is but one of a large number of very difficult problems of understanding NL by computer. Fortunately, a NL interface is simpler to comprehend. Although one ultimately encounters problems comparable to the unconstrained NL understanding situation, the domain of discourse, and thereby the context, is highly constrained by the database schema. General analysis of language phenomena and much of the ambiguity inherent in NL understanding is limited but complexities arise when building NL capabilities into database interfaces. One quickly comes to realize that domain knowledge is required in order to interpret queries, in order to answer queries, and that modeling the user is important as well [7].

We present an example of SystemX accepting an English query from Rogers' vice president, translating the query into SQL, retrieving data from Rogers' database and displaying the data in the format (table or graphical trend) specified by the user in the query. SystemX permits the user to generate printed copy of the data. This functionality is currently accessed by way of a menu interface, see Figure 1. The user may examine the SQL generated in order to assure himself of the validity of the response.

SystemX is able to display responses to requests for trends in statistical data graphically. The user has the choice of inputting his trend request using English, using menus (in the case of "canned" trends) or using a combination of English and menu responses. Various input modalities are provided as a convenience to users. The "canned" trends display data that is predictably desired on a reasonably frequent basis. They may be accessed for a minimum of keystrokes. The "canned" trends are those available through the first eight menu items in the Trend Menu in Figure 1.

Specifying a request for a trend in English may become quite cumbersome if default parameters (specifying timing and so forth) are not employed. The complex statements required are difficult to formulate and demand patience on the part of the users while waiting parsing. The system therefore allows the users to request ad-hoc trends using a combination of English and responses to menus. This combination of modality reduces the task of specifying a complex query into a set of simple tasks that are accomplished in sequence. The system accesses the database in order to be able to present tasks to users in as helpful a manner as possible.

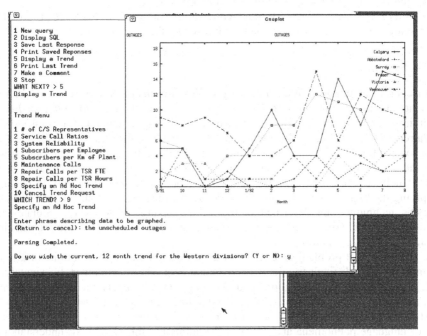

Fig. 1. The SystemX main menu and a trend menu.

2.2 NLAISE and MATISE

Despite the many search engines available, searching for a relevant site remains difficult. One major reason for this difficulty is that search engines do not analyze queries semantically; in contrast, most search engines perform keyword matching.

How can our use of NL semantics improve internet searching? There have been many applications of automated NL understanding such as speech understanding, information retrieval, question-answering systems, machine translation etc. One common application provides a NL "front-end", which enables users to access database information without any need to know database structure or any query language, and with no need for query transformation to some other representation, [1]. Our NL "front-end" to Internet search engines, which allows users to utilize search engines without finding appropriate search terms, is presented in [4,5]. For a search for: "I want to book a flight ticket" or "Show me some sites on online reservation of flight tickets" or phrases like "online reservation of flight tickets", these queries would yield the same search results.

Figure 2 shows the representation of existing search engines compared with the NL "front-end" we provide. Using search engines, the user must study various options provided and transform the query into a form suitable for the specific search engine. The NL "front-end" analyses the NL query of the user and transforms it into appropriate search terms.

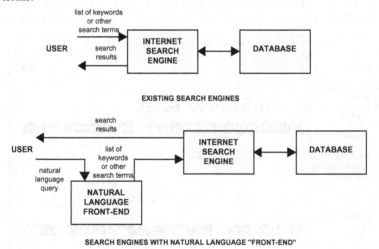

Fig. 2. Representation of Search Engines.

NLAISE allows users to choose the search engine best suited for their search and enter the query in English. The NL query is analyzed both syntactically and semantically in order to select the most appropriate keywords describing sought information. Keywords are interpreted to provide more meaningful search terms by using keyword synonyms in conjunction with Boolean operators supported by specific search engines.

Figure 3 illustrates the architecture of NLAISE. The NL query, along with the choice of search engine, is pre-processed in order to transform the query into a form suitable for input to the parser. The parser, in turn, has a description of grammar rules

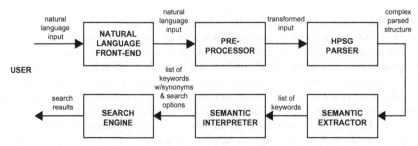

Fig. 3. Natural Language Access to Internet Search Engines (NLAISE).

for capturing the constraints of English and a lexicon that contains the words permitted as input. The Head Driven Phrase Structure (HPSG) parser generates a complex feature structure representing the query, [3]. The semantic content of such a complex feature structure is extracted, interpreted and transformed into a form suitable for the search engine that was selected. Figure 4 shows the output from asking NLAISE to parse the phrase "I want to schedule a trip to Japan" and generate appropriate keywords for search engine examination. NLAISE was also requested to use Infoseek as the search engine. Inspection of the 1,473 web pages returned verified that 80% were relevant. Note the choice of keywords "Japan" and "travel" which indicates the level of sophistication of NLAISE's semantic interpretation of the original input phrase.

Fig. 4. Inforseek output for "I want to schedule a trip to Japan" using NLAISE.

EMATISE extended NLAISE in 3 user-oriented ways: (1) whereas NLAISE was tied to a single "travel" domain, EMATISE greatly enhanced semantic interpretation to eliminate much ambiguity and toil over multiple domains; (2) EMATISE sent out term expanded queries to multiple search engines in parallel and reranked results returned from these search engines into a single relevant high precision list for the user; and (3) EMATISE's higher level of abstraction above conventional search services presented the user with a single, central and natural search interface with which to interact.

Figure 5 shows the results of EMATISE after a simple translation of the sentence "I want to visit the homepage of IBM product review" into search engine neutral search terms, term expanded by the drivers for particular search engines. Figure 5 illustrates the results of this query after the aggregation engine assembles the results.

3. Generate and Repair Machine Translation (GRMT)

Imagine picking up the phone in Toronto, dialing your Japanese program co-chairman in Tokyo to explain several papers lost in the shuffle of email systems. You speak English and she speaks Japanese. Fortunately it is 2010 and the English you speak in Toronto is automatically translated into Japanese in the time it takes to transfer your words over the phone lines. Impossible, - probably not. The world of machine translation has both fascinated and frustrated researchers for over 50 years. More recent successes in statistical, nonlinguistic and hybrid systems have given hope that we will not be confined to the traditional direct, transfer and intralingual approaches that have dominated in the past. An informative critique of these traditional approaches is given in [8]. We provide another approach following from computer science methodology: generate and repair machine translation. (GRMT).

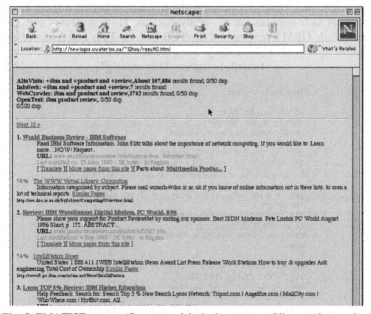

Fig. 5. EMATISE output -"I want to visit the homepage of ibm product review".

GRMT (Figure 6) is composed of 3 phases: "Quick and Dirty MT", "Translation Candidate Interpretation (TCI)" and "Repair and Iterate (RI)". "QDMT" generates translation candidates (TC) by considering syntactic and semantic differences between language pairs without performing any sophisticated analysis. This ensures that the TC can be generated quickly, simply and efficiently. Next, the system interprets the TC to see if it retains the meaning of the SL. If so, that TC will be considered a translation. If not, that TC will be repaired based on the diagnosis that is indicated in the second phase, TCI. Subsequently the repaired TC will be re-interpreted to determine if it still has a different meaning from the SL. These two processes iterate until the TC conveys the same meaning as the SL. The TCI and RI stages ensure the accuracy of the translation result. They also guarantee the accuracy of the translation back from the TL to SL.

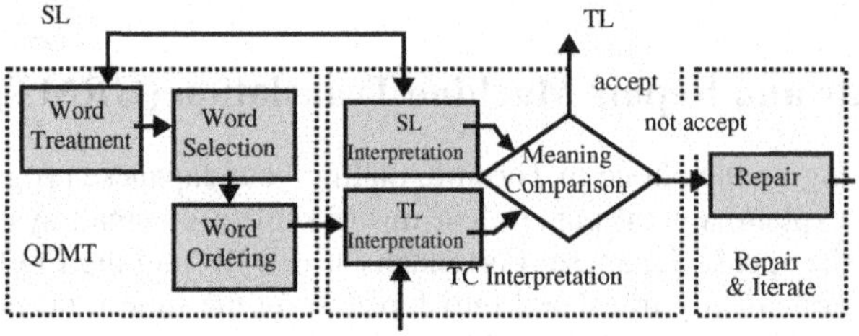

Fig. 6. GRMT Architecture

GRMT treats SL and TL separately and is aware of the differences between languages. Therefore, if languages can be grouped according to various characteristics, e.g., auxiliary verb, continuous tenses, passive voice, etc., which they have in common, then the translation between groups can be performed more simply by GRMT. For example: Group 1 consists of English, French and Spanish, Group 2 consists of Chinese, Japanese and Thai. To perform the translation between these two groups, the transfer approach requires six SL analyzers, six TL generations and 18 sets of transfer rules while GRMT requires six SL TCIs, six TL TCIs and 2 sets of constraint applications.

Table 1. Examples of Generated TC

1. The wheat was yellow. TC: ¢È“« “≈’ π—Èπ ’‡À≈◊Õß CT: ¢È“« “≈’ π—Èπ ’‡À≈◊Õß
2. Five days before the trout are released. TC: ÀÈ“ «—π °ËÕπ ∑’Ë ª≈“‡∑√“∑Ï π—Èπ ®– ∂Ÿ° ª≈ËÕ¬ CT: ÀÈ“ «—π °ËÕπ ∑’Ë ª≈“‡∑√“∑Ï π—Èπ ®– ∂Ÿ° ª≈ËÕ¬
3. You can take a fish to school but you can not make them think. TC: §ÿ≥ “¡“√∂ ‡Õ“ ª≈“ µ—«Àπ÷Ëß ‰ª ΩŸß ·µË §ÿ≥ ‰¡Ë “¡“√∂ ∑”„ÀÈ æ«°‡¢“ §‘¥ CT: §ÿ≥ “¡“√∂ ‡Õ“ ª≈“ µ—«Àπ÷Ëß ‰ª ‚√ß‡√’¬π ·µË §ÿ≥ ‰¡Ë “¡“√∂ ∑”„ÀÈ æ«°‡¢“ §‘¥
4. When I was an ugly duckling he thought I never dreamed I could be so happy. TC: ‡¡◊ËÕ ©—π ‡ªÁπ ≈Ÿ°‡ªÁ¥ µ—«Àπ÷Ëß ‡¢“ §‘¥ ©—π ‰¡Ë‡§¬ Ω—π ©—π “¡“√∂ ‡ªÁπ §«“¡ ÿ¢ ¢’È‡À√Ë ¡“° CT:‡¡◊ËÕ ©—π ‡ªÁπ ≈Ÿ°‡ªÁ¥ ¢’È‡À√Ë µ—«Àπ÷Ëß ‡¢“ §‘¥ ©—π ‰¡Ë‡§¬ Ω—π ©—π “¡“√∂ ¡’ §«“¡ ÿ¢ ¡“°

Initial experiments of QDMT (English to Thai) indicate that TCs can be generated with relative accuracy. Table 1 shows example results. Generated TCs of Examples 1 & 2 can be the translation results of each without the need of the RI stage because they are exactly the same as the correct translations(CT). There is one inappropriate word (underlined word) in the TC of Example 3. However, this inappropriately selected word can be diagnosed and replaced in TCI and RI stages. In example 4, There is one inappropriate selected word and one misordered word that can be simply repaired.

4. Machine Learning: Rule Induction and Classification

Research into data classification and rule induction carried out at the University of Waterloo, has resulted in the development of the ELEM2 system. ELEM2 outperforms existing rule induction methods and has many potential applications, including the data classification and rule induction application role for a molecular compound database used by GlaxoKleinSmith. For a detailed description of the ELEM2 system, see [9-11].

ELEM2 induces decision rules from a set of observed data and classifies new examples by applying the induced rules [9]. ELEM2 is distinguished from other rule induction systems in that it employs several new strategies in the induction and classification processes. First, ELEM2 uses a new heuristic function for evaluating attribute-value pairs in the induction process. The function reflects the degree of relevance of an attribute-value pair to a target concept and leads to selection of the most relevant pairs for formulating rules. Second, ELEM2 handles inconsistent training examples by defining an unlearnable region of a concept based on the probability distribution of that concept in the training data. The unlearnable region is used as a stopping criterion for the concept learning process, which resolves conflicts without removing inconsistent examples before rule induction. Third, ELEM2 employs several methods for the discretization of continuous attributes for learning classification rules, thus providing a choice to the user of the best method. In addition to the traditional equi-distant interval and equi-density methods, ELEM2 provides a new measure based on information entropy [10]. Fourth, ELEM2 employs a new rule quality measure for the purpose of handling imperfect data by post-pruning generated rules [11]. The measure is defined according to the relative distribution of a rule with respect to positive and negative examples and is chosen from 4 alternatives that represent different kinds of distributions.

All four strategies reported above provide ELEM2 with its unique character that has imbued ELEM2 with incremental improvement over competing systems and tested over a wide variety of datasets. We have tested ELEM2 using over 50 different datasets from the UCI Repository and with several commercial datasets provided by Knowledge-Junction Systems, GlaxoKleinSmith, etc. It is perhaps the rule quality measures that hold promise for the greatest overall performance enhancement.

A rule induction system generates decision rules from a set of training data. The set of decision rules determines the performance of a classifier that exploits the rules to classify unseen objects, for example unknown words in text. It is therefore important for a rule induction system to generate decision rules that have high predictability or reliability. These properties are commonly measured by a function called rule quality. A rule quality measure is needed in both the rule induction and classification processes. A rule induction process is usually considered as a search over a hypothesis space of possible rules for a decision rule that satisfies some criterion. The possible rules, in this case, are those rules that are defined by a concept description language, such as prepositional rules. In the rule induction process that is based on general-to-specific search (such as CN2 [12]) a rule quality measure can be used as an evaluation heuristic to select attribute-value pairs in the rule specialization process; and/or it can be employed as a significance measure to stop further specialization. The main reason to focus special attention on the stopping criterion can be found in the studies on small *disjunct problems* [13]. The studies indicated that small disjuncts, which cover a small number of training examples, are much more error prone than large disjuncts that cover a large amount of training examples. To prevent small disjuncts, a stopping criterion based on rule consistency (i.e., the rule is consistent with the training examples) is not suggested for use in rule induction. Other criteria, such as the G2 likelihood ratio statistic as used in CN2 and the degree of logical sufficiency have been proposed to *pre-prune* a rule to avoid overspecialization of the rule. Some rule induction systems, such as C4.5 [14] and ELEM2, use an alternative strategy to prevent the small disjunct problem. In these systems, the rule specialization process is allowed to run to completion (i.e., it forms a rule that is consistent with the training data or as nearly consistent as possible) and *post-prunes* overfitted rules by removing components that are deemed unreliable. Similar to pre-pruning, a criterion is needed in post-pruning to determine when to stop this generalization process.

A rule quality measure is also needed in the classification process. It is possible that in the decision making process an unseen example satisfies multiple decision rules that are assigned to different classes. In this situation, some conflict resolution scheme must be applied to assign the unseen object to the most appropriate class. It is therefore useful for each rule to be associated with a numerical factor which can represent its classification power, its reliability, etc.

5. Brainstorms

Successes mentioned in sections 2-4, and others like them, represent contemporary computational intelligence solutions. How do we adapt them to represent web intelligence solutions? We briefly describe current work designed to make useful solutions to computational intelligence problems amenable to web intelligence. Some of this work takes advantage of newer technologies already beginning to show up in web applications (agent architectures. recommender systems, information extraction tools, etc.). This curren work represents an intermediate step along the way to web intelligence. It necessarily leads to the realization that more adaptable and more general machine learning strategies need developed and incorporated into every aspect of web intelligence. One glaring example would be learning the meaning of unknown or undefined words, for machine translation and general speech and NL processing.

5.1 Java Parsers, Just-in-Time Subgrammar Extraction, Modular HPSG's

Stefy is a NL parser implemented in Java, based on HPSGs [15], It is part of a larger project to implement a NL processing system for Internet information retrieval (IR).

This IR task requires Java applets capable of parsing a NL. Earlier we discussed work on developing HPSG parsers. However, Stefy is one of the first implemented in Java. Java was chosen for two reasons. Java supports dynamic class loading and object serialization, which are important features necessary for our concept of distributed NL processing. Java is a good prototyping language, compared to C++ for example, and facilitates easy experimentation with various approaches, which makes this shift in programming language paradigm less drastic.

A drawback of our implementation is that it is not suitable for development of the grammar and lexical resources. Other systems, like ALE [19] and LKB [20], are more appropriate for this task. After a grammar or a lexicon is developed in one of those systems, it is translated into a Java description and used in Stefy.

Stefy represents a new precise and compact description of the HPSG formalism, which is especially suitable for implementation of HPSG parsers in low-level languages. Stefy represents an important step towards applying HPSG formalism in the area of distributed NLP and answer extraction.

Stefy's approach is similar to the filtering techniques, which are a recognized way to improve parser's performance. However, Stefy is different because we insist that the filtered, i.e., extracted, knowledge is in the form of a grammar. This approach is theoretically sound, and in practice it provides a clean interface between subgrammar-extraction part and the parser. More arguments for this separation of the subgrammar extraction and parsing are given in [17].

An important part of the HPSG subgrammar extraction is the extraction of the corresponding type sub-hierarchy out of the original hierarchy. Efficient type operations and representation of the types are used in approximate algorithm for subgrammar extraction for HPSGs.

Recently, there has been a lot of research activity in the area of grammar modularity. Some of the motivational factors for this work are the following:

- *managing complexity.* The NL grammars used in NL processing are large and complex. The difficult problems are designing, creating, testing, and maintaining them. Using smaller modules that are combined into larger grammars addresses the complexity problem.
- *parsing efficiency.* Parsing with a large, wide-coverage grammar is typically not efficient. Quickly extracting a small subgrammar module, and then using it to parse the text can reduce the running-time and space requirements.
- *context-based disambiguation.* By having a larger grammar we achieve a better coverage, but in the same time it becomes susceptible to ambiguities. Any NL is very ambiguous, and it is well known that humans use world-knowledge and contextual knowledge to do disambiguation. Extracting a subgrammar based on the text to be processed can be viewed as creating a context that can improve disambiguation.

5.2   Recommender Systems Using ELEM2

Recommender systems suggest information sources, products, services, etc., to users based on learning from examples of their preferences, dislikes, etc. There are two predominant methodologies employed in such systems. *Collaborative (social) filtering methods* base recommendations on other users preferences, e.g., when you order books from Amazon.com, the recommender system may detect other customers who ordered the same books and determine other orders placed by these customers to then enquire whether you may also be interested in acquiring similar material. *Content-*

based methods use information about the item ordered/specified in order to make further suggestions to the user. Advantages of content-based methods include the ability to recommend previously unrelated items to users with unique interests and to also provide explanations for recommendations.

For collaborative (social) filtering, we plan to merge information sources to permit more fine-grained analysis and subsequent recommendations. For example, use of the Statistics Canada database on wealth demographics in Canada, which they categorize from richer to poorer by postal code, could conceivably recommend products/services based not only on social preference but also by wealth demographics at the same time.

We especially wish to develop content-based methods since this will provide a new application for ELEM2. Content-based recommender systems provides another unique application for embedded ELEM2. Briefly, a set of documents (web pages, newsgroup messages, etc.) would have information extracted from an information extraction (word extraction) phase to develop a set of examples. We randomly select a set of examples and choose a subset of these examples from which we determine from a user, positive and negative examples. These positive and negative examples serve as a training set for the user. We apply ELEM2 rule induction process to extract a "user's profile" and then rank the rest of the examples accordingly. The top ranked examples then serve as a list of items for recommendation.

5.3   Agents and Agent Architectures

The internet is a large, distributed, and heterogeneous source of information primarily consisting of on-line World Wide Web documents. It is perceived through a set of applications based on the point-to-point communication links provided by the TCP/IP protocol. Many applications frequently end up with the problem that we want to find a relevant document, relevant item, or, generally, a relevant point in the information space consisting of Telnet sites, news groups, news group postings, FTP (File Transfer Protocol) sites, and WWW documents (pages, movies, radio broadcasts). How can we find out if someone has an e-mail address and how can we find that address? Finding interesting mailing lists is a still better example.

The internet can be imagined as a low-level structure activated with considerable manual (human) participation. Such an intelligence-assuming environment requires computational intelligence management techniques. The most obvious example is a simple Web page. If we want to automatically use its content in a fashion more sophisticated than collecting keywords, or collecting embedded links for further navigation, then the most flexible, robust, and appropriate way to do this is to understand some of its content and to reason about it. This is the realm of computational intelligence.

"Agent" has become a computational intelligence term, and a frequent buzzword having a wide range of definitions. Nevertheless, there are some common characteristics that describe an agent. An agent is anything that can be viewed as perceiving its environment through sensors and acting upon that environment. Furthermore, the development of multi-agent systems is based on work in two areas artificial intelligence and distributed systems.

The combination of NL processing and multi agent system's is still quite novel and often the terms are used independently. Consider the use of NL processing for information retrieval (IR) over the internet. This is an attempt to match the meaning of the user's query to the meaning of retrieved documents. Since this approach relies on higher levels of NL processing, it is difficult to implement. Issues include deciding what is a concept, how to extract concepts from NL texts, and how to do concept matching. The inefficiency of existing NL processing systems is a major obstacle to using them in IR. If we want to use an NLP system to analyze the documents in a large document collection, it has to be efficient and robust to be useful in practice.

A positive approach is to implement distributed NL processing so that the processing cost is widely distributed in the same way as are internet resources. Multi agent systems are appropriate for this task, see [16].

6. Concluding Remarks

Web intelligence requires further research and development into the technologies discussed above and other technologies as well. Adapting existing computational intelligence solutions may not always be appropriate for web intelligence for a number of reasons, e.g., the magnitude of information available on the internet and the additional requirements for speedy processing. Computational intelligence solutions which may be adapted must incorporate a more robust notion of learning in order for these solutions to scale to the web, in order for these solutions to adapt to individual user requirements, and in order for these solutions to personalize interfaces.

We have only briefly touched on a few, albeit important, issues that will be the mainstay of web intelligence in the near term future. Users will demand access to the internet that is simple (multimodal interfaces), with language/speech capabilities – both comprehension and, when needed, translation – and personalized (multi agent architectures) internet use which "learns".

How soon might we expect to see breakthroughs? One way of considering this question is to recognize that research progress is highly incremental, thus, we are seeing progress every day. I, for one, have great hopes for the future of web intelligence.

Acknowledgements. I would like to thank my many fine students and colleagues over the years for contributing to many of the ideas, prototypes, and systems briefly described in is paper and for the opportunity to learn from each and every one of them. For that I am truly blessed. I am a member of the Institute for Robotics and Intelligent Systems (IRIS) and wish to acknowledge the support of the Networks of Centers of Excellence Program of the Government of Canada, the Natural Sciences and Engineering Research Council, and the participation of PRECARN Associates Inc.

References

1. McFetridge, P., & Cercone, N. (1991) Installing an HPSG Parser in a Modular NL Interface, Computational Intelligence III, North Holland, Amsterdam, 169-178.
2. Cercone, N., Hall, G., Joseph, S., Kao, M., Luk, W., McFetridge, P., & McCalla, G. (1990) Natural Language Interfaces: Introducing SystemX. Advances in Artificial Intelligence in Software Engineering. T. Oren (ed.), JAI Press, Greenwich, CT, 169-250.

3. Pollard, C. and Sag, I. (1987) Information-based Syntax and Semantics: Fundamentals. Stanford: Center for the Study of Language and Information.
4. Mahalingam, G. (1997) Natural Language Access to Internet Search Engines, M.Sc. Thesis, Computer Science Department, University of Regina, Regina, Saskatchewan.
5. Hou, L. (1999) EMATISE: English Meta Access to Internet Search Enginesd. M.Math Thesis, Computer Science Department, University of Waterloo, Waterloo, Ontario.
6. Cercone, N., McFetridge, P., Hall, G., and Groeneboer, C. (1991) An unnatural natural language interface. Research in Humanities Computing, Hockey, S. and Ide, N (eds), Oxford Univ. Press, 285-306, also appearing in 16th ALLC/9th ICCH, Toronto.
7. Cercone, N, and McCalla, G. (1986) Accessing Knowledge Through Natural Language. Invited chapter for M.Yovits Advances in Computers series, Academic Press, 1-99.
8. Naruedomkul, K. (2000) Generate and Repair Machine Translation, Ph.D. Thesis, Computer Science Department, University of Regina, Regina, Saskatchewan.
9. An, A. and Cercone, N. (1998). "ELEM2: A Learning System for More Accurate Classifications", Proceedings of the 12th Canadian Conf. on Artificial Intelligence (Lecture Notes in Artificial Intelligence 1418), 426-441.
10. An, A., and Cercone, N. (1999). Discretization of Continuous Attributes for Learning Classification Rules, PAKDD'99, Lecture Notes in Artificial Intelligence 1574, Springer, Beijing, 509-514.
11. An, A., and Cercone, N. (1999). An Empirical Study on Rule Quality Measures, RSFDGrC'99, Yamaguchi, Japan, 482-491.
12. Quinlan, J.R. (1993) C4.5: Programs for Machine Learning, Morgan Kaufmann, San Mateo, CA.
13. Holte, R., Acker, L. and Porter, B. (1989). Concept Learning and the Problem of Small Disjuncts". Proceedings of 11th IJCAI, Detroit, Michigan.
14. Clark, P. and Boswell, R. (1991) Rule Induction with CN2: Some Recent Improvements. Procs of European Working Session on Learning, Porto, Portugal, 151-163.
15. Keselj, V. (2000) Stefy: Java Parser for HPSGs, Version 0.1, Technical Report CS-99-26, Department of Computer Science, University of Waterloo, Waterloo, Canada
16. Keselj, V. (1998).Multi-agent systems for Internet information retrieval using natural language processing, M. Math Thesis, Computer Science, University of Waterloo, Waterloo, Canada
17. Keselj, V. (2001).Just-in-time subgrammar extraction for HPSG, Technical Report CS-2001-08, Computer Science, University of Waterloo, Waterloo, Canada.
18. Carpenter, B and Penn, G.(1999) ALE, the attribute logic engine, user's Guide,: //www.sfs.nphil.uni-tuebingen.de/~gpenn/ale.html.
19. Copestake, A. (1999) The (new) LKB system, Version 5.2, http://www-csli.stanford.edu/~aac/lkb.html .

Pedagogical Agents for Web-Based Learning

W. Lewis Johnson

University of Southern California, USA

Abstract. This presentation will discuss techniques for incorporating "guidebots," or animated pedagogical agents, into Web-based learning environments. Guidebots help keep learning on track; they offer students advice and guidance as appropriate in order to get the most out on-line learning experiences. Guidebots build on research in intelligent tutoring systems, but go further by engaging the learner in natural face-to-face interaction. Guidebots can stand on the side and discuss learning objectives with the learners; they also can work together with learners as teammates, and can play roles within interactive educational stories. They help bring the aesthetics of animated entertainment to interactive educational experiences. This talk will present recent developments in guidebot technology, and outline challenges for current research.

N. Zhong et al. (Eds.): WI 2001, LNAI 2198, p. 43, 2001.
© Springer-Verlag Berlin Heidelberg 2001

Ontological Engineering: Foundation of the Next Generation Knowledge Processing

Riichiro Mizoguchi

ISIR, Osaka University
8-1 Mihogaoka, Ibaraki, Osaka 567-0047 Japan
miz@ei.sanken.osaka-u.ac.jp

Abstract. Ontological engineering as a key technology of the next generation knowledge processing is discussed. After a brief introduction to ontological engineering with my speculation about its potential contribution, three major results of the practice of ontological engineering in my lab are presented. Then, paradigm shift in information processing is discussed followed by a future directions in the Web intelligence context.

1 Introduction

In AI research history, we can identify two types of research. One is "Form-oriented research" and the other is "Content-oriented research". The former investigates formal topics like logic, knowledge representation, search, etc. and the latter content of knowledge. Apparently, the former has dominated AI research to date. Recently, however, "Content-oriented research" has attracted considerable attention because a lot of real-world problems to solve such as knowledge sharing, facilitation of agent communication, meta-data, semantic web, large-scale knowledge bases, etc. require not only advanced formalisms but also sophisticated treatment of the content of knowledge before it is put into a formalism.

Formal theories such as predicate logic provide us with a powerful tool to guarantee sound reasoning and thinking. It even enables us to discuss the limit of our reasoning in a principled way. However, it cannot answer any of the questions such as what knowledge we should prepare for solving the problems given, how to scale up the knowledge bases, how to reuse and share the knowledge, how to manage knowledge and so on. In other words, we cannot say it has provided us with something valuable to solve real-world problems.

In expert system community, the knowledge principle [Feigenbaum, 77] proposed by Feigenbaum has been accepted and a lot of development has been carried out with a deep appreciation of the principle, since it is to the point in the sense that he stressed the importance of accumulation of knowledge rather than formal reasoning or logic. This has been proved by the success of the expert system development and a lot of research activities have been done under the flag of "knowledge engineering". However, the author is not claiming the so-called rule-base technology is what we need for future knowledge processing. Rather, in order to adapt to the rapid change of the situation, treatment of knowledge should be in-depth analyzed. Advanced

N. Zhong et al. (Eds.): WI 2001, LNAI 2198, pp. 44–57, 2001.
© Springer-Verlag Berlin Heidelberg 2001

knowledge processing technology should cope with various knowledge sources and elicit, transform, organize, and translate knowledge to enable the agents to utilize it.

Although importance of such "Content-oriented research" has been gradually recognized these days, we do not have sophisticated methodologies for content-oriented research yet. In spite of much effort devoted to such research, major results were only development of KBs. We could identify the reasons for this as follows:

a)   It tends to be ad-hoc, and
b)   It does not have a methodology which enables knowledge to accumulate.

It is necessary to overcome these difficulties in order to establish the content-oriented research or content technology. Ontological Engineering has been proposed for that purpose. It is a research methodology which gives us design rationale of a knowledge base, kernel conceptualization of the world of interest, semantic constraints of concepts together with sophisticated theories and technologies enabling accumulation of knowledge which is dispensable for knowledge processing in the real world. The author believes knowledge management essentially needs content-oriented research. It should be more than information retrieval. The content technology should be more sophisticated and powerful to realize the true knowledge management.

The objective of this paper is to discuss how ontological engineering[Mizoguchi 97] has emerged and how it will contribute to the future knowledge processing together with a brief history of the author's research activities on those topics.

2   What Is an Ontology and What Is Ontological Engineering?

Ontological engineering is a successor of knowledge engineering which has been considered as a technology for building knowledge-intensive systems. Although knowledge engineering has contributed to eliciting expertise, organizing it into a computational structure, and building knowledge bases, AI researchers have noticed the necessity of a more robust and theoretically sound engineering which enables knowledge sharing/reuse and formulation of the problem solving process itself. Knowledge engineering technology has thus developed into "ontological engineering" where "ontology" is the key concept to investigate. Roughly speaking, ontology consists of **task ontology**[Mizoguchi 95a] which characterizes the computational architecture of a knowledge-based system which performs a task and **domain ontology** which characterizes the domain knowledge where the task is performed. By a task, we mean a problem solving process like diagnosis, monitoring, scheduling, design, and so on. The idea of task ontology which serves as a theory of vocabulary/concepts used as building blocks for knowledge-based systems might provide us with an effective methodology and vocabulary for both analyzing and synthesizing knowledge-based systems.

An ontology is understood to serve as a kernel theory and building blocks for content-oriented research. Definitions of an ontology are presented below:

a)   In philosophy, it means *theory of existence*. It tries to explain what exists in the world and how the world is configured by introducing a system of critical categories to account for things and their intrinsic relations.
b)   From an AI point of view, an ontology is defined as "explicit specification of conceptualization" [Gruber].

c) From a knowledge-based systems point of view, it is defined as "a theory (system) of concepts/vocabulary used as building blocks of information processing systems" [Mizoguchi 95a].

d) Another definition [Gruber]: Ontologies are agreements about shared conceptualizations. Shared conceptualizations include conceptual frameworks for modeling domain knowledge; content-specific protocols for communication among inter-operating agents; and agreements about the representation of particular domain theories. In the knowledge sharing context, ontologies are specified in the form of definitions of representational vocabulary.

e) A compositional definition: An ontology consists of concepts with definitions, hierarchical organization of them, relations among them (more than *is-a* and *part-of*), and axioms to formalize the definitions and relations.

f) Yet another definition: An ontology is an explicit specification of objects and relations in the target world intended to share in a community and to use for building a model of the target world.

Why ontology instead of knowledge? Knowledge is domain-dependent, and hence knowledge engineering which directly investigates such knowledge has been suffering from rather serious difficulties, such as domain-specificity and diversity. Further, much of the knowledge dealt with in expert systems has been heuristics that domain experts have, which makes knowledge manipulation more difficult. However, in ontological engineering, we investigate knowledge in terms of its origin and elements from which knowledge is constructed. An ontology reflects what exists out there in the world of interest or represents what we should think exists there. An ontology is essentially designed to be objective and shared by many people. Hierarchical structure of concepts and decomposability of knowledge enable us to identify portions of concepts sharable among people. Exploitation of such characteristics makes it possible to avoid the difficulties knowledge engineering has faced with. The following is a list of the merits we can enjoy from an ontology:

a) *A common vocabulary.* The description of the target world needs a vocabulary agreed among people involved.

b) *Explication* of what has been often left implicit. Any knowledge base built is based on a conceptualization possessed by the builder and is usually implicit. An ontology is an explication of the very implicit knowledge. Such an explicit representation of assumptions and conceptualization is more than a simple explication. Its contribution to knowledge reuse and sharing is more than expectation considering that the implicitness has been one of the crucial causes of preventing knowledge sharing and reuse.

c) *Systematization* of knowledge. Knowledge systematization requires well-established vocabulary/concepts in terms of which people describe phenomena, theories and target things under consideration. An ontology thus contributes to providing a backbone for the systematization of knowledge.

d) *Standardization.* The common vocabulary and knowledge systematization bring us more or less standardized terms/concepts. Standardization has to be taken not as restriction of free exploration of research mind but as a minimum set of shared terms/concepts among human and computer agents who can communicate with each other thanks to them.

e)   *Meta-model functionality.* A model is usually built in the computer as an abstraction of the real target. And, an ontology provides us with concepts and relations among them which are used as building blocks of the model. Thus, an ontology specifies the models to build by giving guidelines and constraints which should be satisfied. This function is viewed as that at the metalevel. This functionality suggests us the possibility of an "ontology-aware" authoring tool which can be very intelligent in the sense that it knows what model it is going to help authors build.

3   Some Experiences in Ontological Engineering

3.1   Functional Ontology and Knowledge Systematization

The first topic is on systematization functional knowledge in computer-aided design(CAD)[Mizoguchi 00a]. Knowledge systematization is indeed a topic of content-oriented research and is not that of a knowledge representation such as production rule, frame or semantic network. Although knowledge representation tells us how to represent knowledge, it is not enough for our purpose, since what is necessary is something we need before the stage of knowledge representation, that is, knowledge organized in an appropriate structure with appropriate vocabulary. This is what the next generation knowledge base building needs, since it should be principled in the sense that it is based on well-structured vocabulary with an explicit conceptualization of the assumptions. This nicely suggests ontological engineering is promising for the purpose of our enterprise.

While any scientific activity which has been done to date is, of course, a kind of knowledge systematization, it has been mainly done in terms of analytical formulae with analytical/quantitative treatment. As a default, the systematization is intended for human interpretation. Our knowledge systematization adopts another way, that is, ontological engineering to enable people to build knowledge bases on the computer as a result of knowledge systematization. The philosophy behind our enterprise is that ontological engineering provides us with the basis on which we can build knowledge and with computer-interpretable vocabulary in terms of which we can describe knowledge systematically in a computer-understandable manner.

By building a framework for knowledge systematization using ontological engineering, we mean identifying a set of backbone concepts with machine understandable description in terms of which we can describe and organize design knowledge for use across multiple domains. The system of concepts is organized as layered ontologies as is seen in Figure 1.

3.1.1   Functional Modeling

No one would disagree that the concept of function should be treated as a first class category in design knowledge organization. That is, function is an important member of a top-level ontology of design world. One of the key claims of our knowledge systematization is that the concept of function should be defined independently of an object that can possess it and of its realization method. If functions are defined depending on objects and their realization, few functions are reused in different domains. As is well understood, innovative design can be facilitated by flexible application of knowledge or ideas across domains.

Functional representation has been extensively investigated to date [Sasajima 95] [Chandrasekaran 00] and a lot of functional representation languages are proposed with sample descriptions of functions of devices. However, because it is not well understood how to organize functional knowledge in what principle in terms of what concepts, most of the representation are ad-hoc and lack generality and consistency, which prevents knowledge from being shared. One of the major causes of the lack of consistency is the difference between the ways of how to capture the target world. For example, let us take the function of a super heater of a power plant, *to heat steam* and that of cam of cam&shaft pair, *to push up the shaft*. The former is concerned with something that comes in and goes out of the device but the latter with the other device that cannot be either input or output of the device. This clearly shows the fact that there is a difference in how to view a function according to the domain. The difference will be one of the causes of inconsistency in functional representation and non-interoperability of the knowledge when functional knowledge from different domains is put into a knowledge base.

The above observation shows that we need a framework which provides us with a viewpoint to guide the modeling process of artifacts as well as primitive concepts in terms of which functional knowledge is described in order to come up with consistent and sharable knowledge.

3.1.2 Hierarchy of Functional Knowledge and Ontology

Figure 1 shows a hierarchy of functional knowledge built on top of fundamental ontologies. The lower layer knowledge is in, the more basic. Basically, knowledge in a certain layer is described in terms of the concepts in the lower layer. Top-level ontology defines and provides very basic concepts such as time, state, process and so on. Causal ontology specifies actions and causality against teleology. Physical world ontology specifies 3D space and entity to give axiomatic physical world with a state-based modeling reflecting a special world of design in which an entity(artifact) is created from nothing. These two ontologies contribute to "Symbol grounding" of higher-level concepts, that is, functional concepts. On top of these three, process ontology is introduced to specify natural processes or phenomena. Every device utilizes several natural phenomena to realize its functions.

Device ontology imposes a frame or viewpoint on an event to introduce a more engineering perspective. That is, it introduces the concepts of a black box equipped with input and output ports. Device ontology defines fundamental roles such as *agent, object, conduit and medium*. Although process ontology is more fundamental than device ontology, there are some cases where process ontology is directly employed to model real world events/phenomena instead of device ontology. Typical cases are found in modelling chemical processes for which device ontology is not appropriate. In summary, five ontologies(Top-level, causality, physical world, process and device ontologies) collectively work as a substrate on which we can build consistent knowledge in layers.

Functional concept ontology specifies functional concepts as an instance of *function* defined in device ontology. The definitions are scarcely depends on the device, the domain or the way of its implementation so that they are very general and usable in a wide range of areas. Theories and principles of physics and abstract part library also belong to this class of knowledge called *general concept layer*.

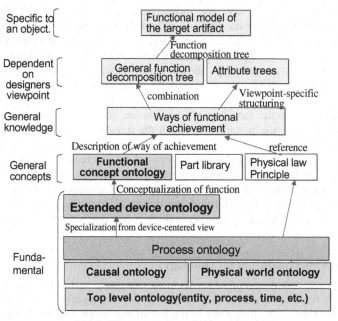

Fig. 1. Hierarchy of ontology and knowledge.

Functional achievement way knowledge is such knowledge that represents various ways of achievement of a function. This knowledge is about *how*(in what way) a function is achieved, whereas the functional concept is about *what* the function is going to achieve. In other words, the former is formulated in terms of *whole-part relation* and the latter in terms of *is-a relation*. Although functional achievement way knowledge looks similar to functional decomposition like that discussed in [Pahl 88], the former is much richer than the latter in that it consists of four kinds of hierarchies of different roles and principles(*is-a* hierarchy, attribute tree, functional decomposition tree and general functional decomposition tree). The inherent structure of such knowledge is organized in an *is-a* hierarchy from which the other three structures are derived according to the requirement. The *is-a* structure is carefully designed identifying inherent property of each *way* to make it sharable and applicable across domains. One of the key issues in knowledge organization is clear and consistent differentiation of *is-a relation* from other relations such as *part-of*, *is-achieved-by*, etc. keeping what is the inherent property of the target thing in mind.

3.1.3 Roles and Effects of Functional Ontology

The extended device ontology views an artifact as something that inputs, process and outputs *objects*. The *object* is something processed by the device during it goes through a device and hence it never be another device that cannot go through a device. This ontology imposes a proper viewpoint from which one can successfully model a mechanical system in a way consistent with those models of engineering artifacts produced in other domains. It is not an easy task to build models of a lot of artifacts in a consistent way. "A gear pair changes torque", "A cam shrinks a spring" and "A cam pushes up a rod" are inconsistent with each other in the hidden computational models. While the first one is based on the extended device ontology, the latter two are based on a different ontology, say, inter-device operation ontology. The organization of knowledge including these models will lose consistency.

The extended device ontology allows us to build interoperable models and provides us with a guideline for modelling process by its *role-assignment* functionality which is the very source of consistency in functional knowledge organization. For example, the concept of a *conduit* helps us consistently recognize devices by taking it as the boundary between the devices. In the mechanical system domain, a shaft and a wire, which play the role of *conduit* in the mechanism level, enable us to identify each mechanism composed of mechanical elements. Models designed based on the extended device ontology has a high composability thanks to its localized description, that is, its independence of neighboring devices that are connected to each other only through attributes of an *object*. On the contrary, composability of inter-device operation ontology is low due to its high dependence on neighboring devices.

3.1.4   Use of Functional Concept Ontology

Functional concept ontology provides us with necessary and sufficient operational terms used for representing functional knowledge/model together with constraints to be satisfied by them. The following is the list of our work on use of the ontology through to evaluate it. All the activities are of new type and different from the conventional knowledge base technology. No problem solving knowledge is treated. Instead, objective and fundamental knowledge is analyzed and modeled to enable a knowledge-based system to articulate the domain and hence to in-depth understand the fundamental knowledge to provide useful knowledge with designers. This is what we need intelligent functional knowledge management in CAD community.

a)   **Explanation generation** at the functional level[Sasajima 95].
b)   **Functional model description** of specific artifacts of many kinds[Kitamura 99a]
c)   **Description of ways of functional achievement**: 104 ways for 26 functions found in five different artifacts(a washing machine, a printing device, slicing machines for ingot of semiconductors (using wire or rotating blade), and an etching device)
d)   **Specification of the inference space** for functional reasoning[Kitamura 99b,00].
e)   **Way knowledge server** for designer support.

3.2   Plant Ontology for Multi-agent Plant Operator Support System

This section describes an activity of ontology construction and its deployment in Oil-refinery plant which has been done under the umbrella of Human-Media Project for five years, which is a MITI(Japanese Ministry of International Trade and Industries) funded national project, is intended to invent an innovative media technology for happier human life in the coming information society. Our ontology construction activities have been done in the project named "Development of a human interface for the next generation plant operation" running as a subproject of Human Media project[Mizoguchi 99, 00b].

The interface for oil-refinery plant operation has been developed intended to establish a sophisticated technology for advanced interface for plant operators and consists of Interface agent: IA, Virtual plant agent: VPA, Semantic information presentation agent: SIA, Ontology server: OS and Distributed collaboration infrastructure: DCI. The last two are mainly for issues related to system building, while the first three are related directly to interface issues. OS has been developed employing ontological engineering.

3.2.1 The Role of a Plant Ontology

Any intelligent system needs a considerable amount of domain knowledge to be useful in a domain. The amount of knowledge necessary often goes large, which sometimes causes difficulties in the initial construction and maintenance phases. As described above, one of the methods we adopted to cope with such problems is ontological engineering. Roughly speaking, the essential contribution of the plant ontology is making shared commitment to the target plant explicit, and hence terminology is standardized within the community of agents. By agents, we also mean human agents, operators, to share such a fundamental understanding about the plant. This enables the system to communicate with operators using the terms stored in Ontology server: OS. It is the second major role of OS in the current implementation of the interface system which is discussed below.

In message generation, we need to pay maximal attention to word selection to make operators' cognitive load minimum in message understanding. After an intensive interview with domain experts, we found human operators use different terms to denote the same thing depending on context. When we first noticed this fact, domain experts apologized for this seemingly random fluctuation of word usage, since they did not know the reason why they use terms that way and they were used to collaboration with computer engineers who do not like neat adaptation and tend to compel their idea of "this is what a computer can do, so accept it". They kindly declared that they would soon determine a unique label for each thing. But, we were different from such computer engineers. Instead of accepting their proposal, we carefully analyzed the way of their word usage and finally came up with that it is not random except a few cases. Many of the wording have good justifications which have to be taken care of in the message generation.

The reasons why we employed distributed collaboration architecture with multiple agents include making the whole system robust and easy to maintain. As is well known, however, these merits are not free. We need a well-designed vocabulary for describing message content as well as a powerful negotiation protocol. Although the latter is of importance, it is out of the scope of this article. DCI is responsible for enabling collaborative problem solving by multiple agents with the help of OS. It is one of the key factors that domain-dependent knowledge be isolated in OS so that DCI can be as general as possible.

3.2.2 Plant Ontology

The plant ontology we built consists of several hierarchical organizations of concepts such as *operation task*, *plant components*, *plant objects*, *basic attributes* and *ordinary attribute*. Because of the space limitation, only domain ontology is discussed here. The key issue in the design of an ontology is clear distinction essential categories from view-dependent concepts.

There exist two major things in the plant domain: ***Plant components(devices)*** and ***plant objects*** to be processed by the ***devices***. Domain concepts also have role concepts like task ontology does. To say precisely, many of the domain concepts are role concepts. The first things we have to do when designing a domain ontology is discrimination of roles concepts from essential categories (or basic concepts), i.e., view- or context-independent concepts. Let us first take ***plant object***. The top-level categories of ***plant object*** are ***view-independent object*** and ***view-dependent object***. The former includes LP gas, gasoline, naphtha, etc. which are categories persistent in any situation. The latter includes ***tower-head ingredient, liquid, distillate, input, intermediate product, raw material, fuel***, etc. All are view- or context-dependent. The major task needed was categorization of such dependency. Figure 2 shows a portion of ***plant object*** *is-a* hierarchy. The major categories of ***view-dependent plant object*** are ***state-dependent, location-dependent, history-dependent*** and ***role-dependent*** objects. ***state-dependent*** objects has ***inherent state-dependent*** and ***relative***

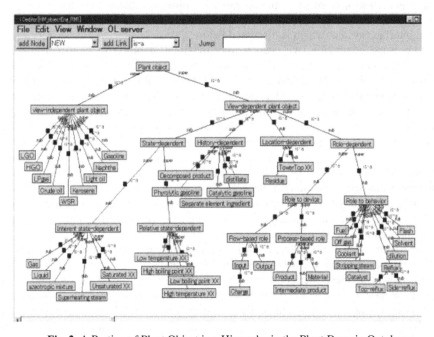

Fig. 2. A Portion of Plant Object is-a Hierarchy in the Plant Domain Ontology

state-dependent objects as its sub-concepts. The former includes ***liquid, gas, superheating steam*** etc. and the latter ***low temperature ingredient, low boiling point ingredient***, etc.

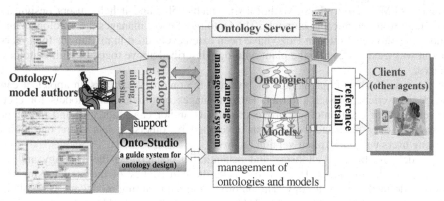

Fig. 3. The architecture of Hozo.

Attribute also needs careful treatment. Most of the attributes people think so are not true attribute but role attribute. Let us take an example of height. It is a role attribute whose basic attribute is length. Height, depth, width and distance are role attributes. Just like a man is called a husband when he has got married. The true attribute is called basic attribute. Examples of basic attribute include length, area, mass, temperature, pressure, volt, etc. Role attribute includes height, depth, input pressure, maximum weight, area of cross section, etc. Needless to say, these attributes are also decomposed into several sub-concepts.

We finally built an ontology which contains about 400 concepts which are approved by the domain experts and the coverage is around the normal pressure fractionator of a full-scale refinery plant. The model of the target refinery plant is built by instantiating the appropriate concepts in the ontology and connect them. The number of instances generated is about 2000. The ontology and the model of the target plant is stored in OS and served to other agents in the total prototype system. Evaluation was done by experts and we have got a favorable result.

3.3 Hozo: An Integrated Ontology Development/Use Environment

Building an ontology requires a clear understanding of what can be concepts with what relations to others. An ontology thus focuses on "concepts" themselves rather than "representation" of them. Although several systems for building ontologies have been developed to date, they were not based on adequate consideration of an ontological theory which is why most of them are yet another KR languages. We believe that a fundamental consideration of ontological theories is needed to develop an environment for developing ontologies. We discuss mainly "role concept" and "relationship", and consider how these ontologically important concepts should be treated in our environment. On the basis of the consideration we have designed and have developed an environment for building and using ontologies, named "Hozo".

"Hozo"[Kozaki 00] is composed of "Ontology Editor", "Onto-Studio" and "Ontology Server"(See Figure 3). The Ontology Editor provides users with a graphical interface, through which they can browse, build and modify ontologies by simple mouse operations. This system manages attributes between concepts organized in an *is-a* hierarchy. The Onto-Studio is based on a method of building ontologies, named AFM (Activity-First Method)[Mizoguchi 95b], and it helps users design an ontology from technical documents. The Ontology Server manages the ontologies and models. Ontology Editor in Hozo have been extensively used in my lab for four years and it was used to develop the plant ontology described above together with Ontology Server.

Because Hozo is implemented in Java and the ontology editor is an applet, it can work as a client through Internet. Hozo manages ontologies and models for each developer. For each ontology in Hozo, only its author can modify it, and the other users can only read and copy those developed by others. It lets share ontologies among users without explicit version control.

Models are built by choosing and instantiating concepts in the ontology and by connecting the instances. Hozo also checks the consistency of the model using the axioms defined in the ontology. The ontology and the resulting model are available in different formats (Lisp, Text, XML/DTD) that make them portable and reusable. The axiom contains constraints which part-concepts or attributes should satisfy, and relations among the part-concepts. For example, these are constraints on the part-concept such as "any teachers must have a teaching certificate" in a "school", and "the size of wheels are from 10 inch to 30 inch" in a "bicycle". Another example is a constraint on the relation such as there must be a connection relation between a wheel and a frame in a "bicycle". Figure 4 depicts a snapshot of plant ontology definition using Ontology editor where *Flow controller* as a subclass of *controller* is defined. A string above a blank rectangle represents a role name of an instance which should be put in the rectangle followed by colon and an dark rectangle which is a class constraints of the instance.

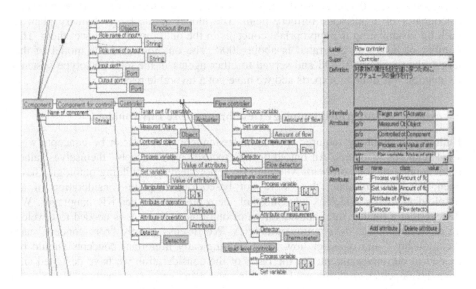

Fig. 4. A snapshot of the plant ontology definition.

4 Paradigm Shift

At the expert system time, people's expectation was to build a stand-alone problem solving system which has a knowledge base of a domain expert's heuristics to perform a specific task with similar or higher performance than that of the expert. That is, the main focus was put on dealing with subjective and specific knowledge for problem solving. However, situation has been changing. Most of the salient activities such as Web document search in the internet, Electronic commerce(EC), Electronic Data Interchange(EDI), Knowledge management(KM), STEP, XML tag design, etc. do require almost opposite characteristics to *knowledge*, that is, objective, general and sharable *knowledge* which is not necessarily tuned to problem solving.

We can summarize the major trends in the following four kinds of paradigm shifts in computer technology:

a) From Computer-centered to Human-centered
b) From Processing-centered to Information-centered
c) From Form-oriented to Content-oriented
d) From Centralized control to Distributed control

The first is based on deep reflection on the long history of computer-centered research which have never been good in human-computer interaction aspects, since such technology forces a human to approach machines/systems or allow, at best, addition of an ad-hoc interface on top of each system. We need to change paradigmatically to come up with an innovative and essentially better human interface technology. The concepts of Human-centered and Information-centered technologies are key concepts of such an enterprise. The true man-machine systems which are what we need in the coming information age do require an open architecture involving humans who need computers to help them facilitate their daily activities.

The second reflects what we learned from expert system development in which *processing-centered* approach has been dominant. That is, an expert system tries to solve a problem instead a human. The problem was it is not what people really need. What people need is an intelligent life-long partner who helps them in many aspects to amplify their capability.

The third is a topic related to artificial intelligence(AI) research where so-called form-oriented basic research has been extensively conducted. It has been trivial from the beginning that no intelligent system can function without a reasonable amount of knowledge. Nevertheless, form-oriented research has dominated AI research. Content-related activities are mainly knowledge base construction. Although huge amount of such activities have been conducted to date, they are "development" rather than "Research", since they are ad hoc, heavily domain-specific and hardly accumulatable. We need content-oriented "Research" to make an essential contribution to intelligent system building.

The fourth is related to system architecture issues. It is an infrastructure of building a large-scale robust system which is often difficult to build and maintain. Typical distributed control systems include a multi-agent system in which agents collaborate with each other without a priori specification of interaction between them unlike the conventional centralized control systems. This paradigm of system design makes it easier to build a large-scale system provided a powerful negotiation protocol.

Web Intelligence, or Web-based intelligent systems should be something like a partner of a human by being compliant with the above paradigm shift.

5 Web Intelligence and Ontological Engineering

When we accept the paradigm shift, WWW technology is going to bring us a kind of revolution to a knowledge base building. Conventionally, a knowledge base has been something to design and build upon request. However, WWW and semantic web technologies facilitate automatic building of knowledge resources so that a huge knowledge base virtually exists out there, and hence the problem to solve has become not to build a knowledge base from scratch but to collect appropriate web pages out of already existing WWW knowledge resources, to reorganize and to merge them. Enabling technologies are XML, RDF(S) and DAML+Oil in Semantic Web[SW].

Semantic web has been devised to make web pages machine interpretable and hence to change the WWW from flood of irrelevant information to a huge useful knowledge source. The goal is good. The problem, however, is how we can make use of the web pages retrieved which still include irrelevant pages and need more elaboration for use of specific purposes. Although ontology will be extensively used in Semantic web activities, the major use is limited to exploiting super-sub relation between concepts for the purpose of the intelligent retrieval of relevant web pages. It is true that retrieval is one of the key technologies in Semantic web. We look further ahead and envision critical contribution of ontological engineering to the next generation knowledge processing. That is, systematic development and sophisticated processing of semantic tags which will definitely overflow all over the world and will need sophisticated ontologies that are something more than a hierarchical organization of concepts to process them appropriately.

6 Conclusions

We have discussed the ontological engineering, its successful applications and future directions to go mostly from the application-oriented viewpoint. Academic perspectives of ontological engineering include fundamental theories and common top-level ontology. Both perspectives suggest ontological engineering will play a critical role as content technology for the next generation knowledge processing.

Acknowledgement. The author is grateful to Dr. Yoshinobu Kitamura and Mr. Kouji Kozaki for their contributions.

Reference

[Feigenbaum, 85] Feigenbaum, E.A.: "The art of artificial intelligence – Themes and case studies of knowledge engineering" Proc. of 5th IJCAI, pp.1014-1029, 1977.
[Gruber] Gruber, T., *What-is-an-ontology?*.
    http://www-ksl.stanford.edu/kst/what-is-an-ontology.html.

[Chandrasekara 2000] Chandrasekaran, B. and John R. Josephson, "Function in Device Representation," to appear in *Journal of Engineering with Computers*, Special Issue on Computer Aided Engineering. http://www.cis.ohio-state.edu/~chandra/Function-in-device-representation.pdf

[Kitamura 99a] Kitamura, Y., and Mizoguchi, R., Meta-functions in Artifacts, Papers of 13th International Workshop on Qualitative Reasoning (QR-99), 136-145, 1999

[Kitamura 99b] Kitamura, Y., and Mizoguchi, R., Towards Redesign based on Ontologies of Functional Concepts and Redesign Strategies, Proc. of the 2nd International Workshop on Strategic Knowledge and Concept Formation, pp.181-192, 1999

[Kitamura 00] Kitamura, Y., Sano, T., Mizoguchi, R., Functional Understanding based on an Ontology of Functional Concepts, The Sixth Pacific Rim International Conference on Artificial Intelligence (PRICAI 2000), pp.723-733, Springer-Verlag, 2000

[Kozaki 00] Kozaki, K. et al.: Development of an Environment for Building Ontologies which is based on a Fundamental Consideration of "Relationship" and "Role": Proc. of the Sixth Pacific Knowledge Acquisition Workshop (PKAW2000), pp.205-221 ,Sydney, Australia, December 11-13, 2000.

[Mizoguchi 95a] Mizoguchi R. et al., Task Ontology for Reuse of Problem Solving Knowledge Knowledge Building & Knowledge Sharing 1995(KB&KS'95) (2nd International Conference on Very Large-Scale Knowledge Bases), Enschede, The Netherlands, pp.46-59.

[Mizoguchi 95b] Mizoguchi, R., et al.: Ontology for Modeling the World from Problem Solving Perspectives Proc. of IJCAI-95 Workshop on Basic Ontological Issues in Knowledge Sharing, pp. 1-12, 1995.

[Mizoguchi 97] Mizoguchi, R., and Ikeda, M. 1997, Towards ontology engineering. In *Proc. of PACES/SPICIS '97*, 259-266.

[Mizoguchi 99] Mizoguchi, R., et al.: Human media interface system for the next generation plant operation, Proc. of the IEEE SMC99, IEEE Systems, Man and Cybernetics Society, V-630-635, 1999.

[Mizoguchi 00a] Mizoguchi, R., and Kitamura, Y., Foundation of Knowledge Systematization: Role of Ontological Engineering, Industrial Knowledge Management - A Micro Level Approach, Rajkumar Roy Ed., Chapter 1, pp.17-36, Springer-Verlag, London, 2000

[Mizoguchi 00b] Mizoguchi, R. et al., Construction and Deployment of a Plant Ontology, The 12th International Conference on Knowledge Engineering and Knowledge Management - Methods, Models and Tools -, EKAW2000, pp.113-128, 2000.

[Pahl 88] Pahl, G., and Beitz, W., Engineering design - a systematic approach, The Design Council, 1988.

[Saasajima 95] Sasajima, M.; Kitamura, Y.; Ikeda, M.; and Mizoguchi, R. FBRL: A Function and Behavior Representation Language. Proc. of IJCAI-95, 1830-1836, 1995.

[SW] http://www.semanticweb.org/

Social Networks on the Web and in the Enterprise

Prabhakar Raghavan

Verity, Inc. 892 Ross Drive, Sunnyvale, CA 94089, USA,
pragh@verity.com,
http://theory.stanford.edu/ raghavan

Abstract. The subject of this talk is the use of ideas from social network theory on the web and in the enterprise. We begin by reviewing a number of empirical observations on the web, concerning various measures of popularity of websites. Next, we describe how these observations can be used in algorithms for searching and mining on the web. We develop mathematical models for these phenomena. Finally, we discuss how these ideas and phenomena change as one goes from the public web to the confines of enterprises.

1 Overview

The internet, and its particular manifestation as the World-Wide Web, have led to a rich interplay between hundreds of millions of people and billions of pages of web content. This represents a social network unprecedented in history. We begin by reviewing several empirical observations on this network, followed by a listing of web search and mining algorithms built on the network. We give pointers to models of the web as a random graph, and finish with a brief discussion of how these phenomena differ in enterprises.

2 Structure in the Web Graph

The web may be viewed as a directed graph in which each vertex is a static html web page, and each edge is a hyperlink from one web page to another. Current estimates suggest that this graph has well over a billion vertices, and an average degree of about 7. We begin by reviewing a series of empirical observations on the web graph [5,11].

A striking, fairly consistent observation on the web is the distribution of vertex in-degrees: they follow a power law [16], with the fraction of web pages having in-degree k being proportional to $k^{-2.1}$ across a variety of measurements by various researchers. Other power laws observed on the social network of the web include the frequency of visits to websites. Clearly these statistics would not be observed if the actions of various users (which sites they visit, which pages they link to) are statistically independent. These and other phenomena (e.g., the connectivity structure of the web [5]) demand the development of new graph

N. Zhong et al. (Eds.): WI 2001, LNAI 2198, pp. 58–60, 2001.
© Springer-Verlag Berlin Heidelberg 2001

models. Work to date in this area [2,13] seems to suggest that random copying is a phenomenon that helps explain some of the observed statistics. Another important aspect of the new models is that they capture an *evolving* graph in which new nodes and edges appear over time.

3   Exploiting the Structure

Perhaps the best know use of the link structure of the web is the google search engine [3] (www.google.com). The google engine uses the link structure of the web to induce a total ordering on the pages of the web, assigning to each page a number called the PageRank. A different approach to using link structure for web search is the HITS method of Kleinberg [10]. Here the ordering of pages is topic-dependant, and invokes a particular insight into the way web content creators behave: they congregate into groups of self-styled experts on a topic. Interestingly, this phenomenon is also captured by the new random graph models that embody random copying [13]. These ideas have their origins in work from citation analysis [6,8,9]. Finally, we mention that it is possible to enumerate these congregations of experts, mining the web for interesting topics [12] and other structures.

4   Social Networks in the Enterprise

The web has been a tremendously exciting and instructive test bed for experimenting with ideas from social networks. However, most of the content on the web is, we believe, "low quality" – it consists primarily of unfiltered marketing information and annotation. The truly valuable unstructured information resides inside enterprises (by "enterprise", we mean not just profit-making corporations, but also governments, academic institutions, and so on). The very fact that these enterprises limit access to their information means they place a significant value on this information. How can we use ideas from social networks to these settings?

Preliminary investigations suggest that a number of the ideas that are honed to the web will have to be adapted to the enterprise. For instance, the structure of hyperlinks in the enterprise is likely to be very different from the web: content creation in enterprises is typically less free-form and more templated, with a lot more navigational links and a lot fewer annotative/expressive links. As for connectivity, it appears that a large enterprise such as IBM may behave more or less like the web, but small enterprises are likely to be very different. We are performing more experiments on this front, and only a detailed study will reveal how the scope and scale of an enterprise affect its link structure.

Beyond hyperlinks, there is a great deal more to the social network of an enterprise: what documents do employees tend to access, how are these related to their roles in the enterprise, and what navigational assistance can an enterprise portal derive from these patterns? The challenge ahead, we believe, is to tap into these patterns and use them to help search, navigate, classify and personalize information access within the enterprise, much as we have had successes on these fronts in the web.

References

1. R. Albert, H. Jeong, and A.-L. Barabasi. Diameter of the World Wide Web. *Nature* 401:130–131, 1999.
2. W. Aiello, F. Chung, and L. Lu. A random graph model for massive graphs. *Proc. ACM Symp. on Theory of Computing*, pp. 171–180, 2000.
3. S. Brin and L. Page. The anatomy of a large-scale hypertextual Web search engine. *Proc. 7th WWW Conf.*, 1998.
4. B. Bollobás. *Random Graphs*. Academic Press, 1985.
5. A. Z. Broder, S. R. Kumar, F. Maghoul, P. Raghavan, S. Rajagopalan, R. Stata, A. Tomkins, and J. Wiener. Graph structure in the web: experiments and models. *Proc. 9th WWW Conf.*, pp. 309–320, 2000.
6. L. Egghe and R. Rousseau. *Introduction to Informetrics*. Elsevier, 1990.
7. W. Feller. *An Introduction to Probability Theory and its Applications: I*, John Wiley, 1950.
8. E. Garfield. Citation analysis as a tool in journal evaluation. *Science*, 178:471–479, 1972.
9. N. Gilbert. A simulation of the structure of academic science. *Sociological Research Online*, 2(2), 1997.
10. J. Kleinberg. Authoritative sources in a hyperlinked environment. *J. of the ACM*, 1999, to appear. Also appears as IBM Research Report RJ 10076(91892) May 1997.
11. S. R. Kumar, P. Raghavan, S. Rajagopalan, and A. Tomkins. Trawling the web for emerging cyber-communities. *Proc. 8th WWW Conf.*, 403–416, 1999.
12. S. R. Kumar, P. Raghavan, S. Rajagopalan, and A. Tomkins. Extracting large-scale knowledge bases from the web. *Proc. VLDB*, pp. 639–650, 1999.
13. S.R. Kumar, P. Raghavan, S. Rajagopalan, D. Sivakumar, A. Tomkins and E. Upfal. Stochastic models of the web graph. *Proc. IEEE Symposium on Foundations of Computer Science*, 57–65, 2000.
14. R. Larson. Bibliometrics of the World Wide Web: An exploratory analysis of the intellectual structure of cyberspace. *Ann. Meeting of the American Soc. Info. Sci.*, 1996.
15. A. J. Lotka. The frequency distribution of scientific productivity. *J. of the Washington Acad. of Sci.*, 16:317, 1926.
16. G. K. Zipf. Human behavior and the principle of least effort. *New York: Hafner*, 1949.

3D Object Recognition and Visualization on the Web

Professor Patrick S.P. Wang *Ph.D.* and IAPR Fellow

College of Computer Science
Northeastern University
Boston, MA 02115
(617)373-3711(O), (617)373-5121(fax)
pwang@ccs.neu.edu
http://www.ccs.neu.edu/home/pwang/

Abstract. This research deals with state-of-the-art novel ideas in high level visualization, understanding and interpretation of line-drawing images of 3D patterns, including articulated objects. A new structural approach using *linear combination* and *fast two-pass parallel matching techniques* is presented. It is aimed at learning, representing, visualizing, and interpreting 2D line drawings as 3D objects, with only very few learning samples. It solves one of the basic concerns in *diffusion tomography* complexities, i.e. patterns can be *reconstructed* through fewer *projections*, and 3D objects can be recognized by a few *learning* samples views. It can also strengthen advantages of current key methods while overcome their drawbacks. Furthermore, it will be able to distinguish objects with very similar properties and is more accurate than other methods in the literature. In addition, an expsrimental system using JAVA and user-friendly interative platform has been established for testing large volume of image data in virtual environment on the web, for learning, and recognition. Several illustrative examples are demonstrated, including learning, recognizing, visualization and interpretation of 3D line drawing polyhedral objects. Finally, future research topics are outlined.

Keywords: visualization and interpretation, 3D articulated objects, learning, pattern recognition, linear combination, diffusion tomography, finite representation, interactive learning, on-line virtual environment

1 Introduction and Objectives

Recently, there has been a growing interest in the research of 3D object recognition. Not only it is interesting and challenging, but also it can be applied to many fields, including industrial parts inspection, military target recognition, CAM/CAD engineering design, image understanding, and document image analysis [5,11,18,22,33,41,44,45]. However, most work tackled rigid objects only, with large learning sample size, low speed, and can not distinguish similar patterns [2,25,44]. Recently, with rapid development of modern computer technologies,

N. Zhong et al. (Eds.): WI 2001, LNAI 2198, pp. 61–74, 2001.
© Springer-Verlag Berlin Heidelberg 2001

there is an increasing interest and need to recognize *articulated* objects. Many 3D objects including military targets fall into this category. In this research, a novel strategy is proposed aimed at faster, more accurate and needs fewer learning samples for high level visualization, understanding, and interpretation of 3D articulated objects.

A Brief Historical Background. Line drawing images, also known as "noble class of images" [31] in which many important and essential phenomena of 3D objects hold in the real world, provide an effective and practical method to describe the 3D shape of an object. These drawings normally can be organized into two or more distinct views, known as characteristic views or aspects in which no one view by itself is sufficient to completely characterize the object being represented [20]. One of the most challenging and difficult problems is : how can we visualize and interpret a line drawing image of 3D object? How a 3D object in various rotations and topological scalings can be properly represented and recognized? There have been several developments in engineering drawing interpretation over the past twenty years. Earlier work was reported in 1971 [12]. Later, a bottom-up approach to interpretation was developed [42], and was extended to include objects with curved surfaces [29]. Recently, it has applied the bottom-up technique to interpret paper-based drawings [24]. An alternative approach was presented in [43], using a rule-based method to produce a wire frame interpretation, but only for simple polyhedral objects. In 1988, Nagendra and Gujar did a comprehensive survey on various methodologies in the literature[23]. However, all of these methods appear to require a rigidly controlled drawing layout as there is no mechanism to determine relative viewing directions between the various views. Also, there is no provision for any error in the alignment of the views or in the location of point features other than those that can be accommodated by a simple distance threshold. In 1984, a method was developed for correcting misalignments in single-view drawings with a non-special view point; yet it does not appear to be extensible to multiple views with special view points [31].

Almost simultaneously, there have been various methods in computer vision and object recognition. An interesting approach was presented for recognizing 3D objects using a set of 72 x 72 = 5184 sample views from learning [32]. Further effort has reduced it to 100 views [25]. More recently, a powerful new computational method called linear combinations (LC) using alignment techniques was developed at MIT [2,34,35]. It involves easy computations and needs fewer learning sample views, in contrast to other methods that required a huge set of learning samples even for describing and recognizing only one single object [8,9,14,17], and some other methods which require more complicated primitive structures such as ellipsoid and bent cylinder [10]. Yet, it has many limitations and may misrecognize invalid objects and reject valid ones. Such difficulties were overcome by another approach using parallel graph matching by Wang [39] with several explicit rules for learning and recognition of concave rigid objects with very few sample views. Other recent developments and surveys can be found in [4,7,24].

Now we will tackle a more general problem involving *articulated* objects. This class of objects is of special interests and importance since it includes most of the industrial robots and man made factory tools as well as military targets. For example, in recognizing a tank, it will involve different views of the model and various status/range of how far each component, e.g. cannon can rotate. How can such process be automated by using computer to visualize, understand and interpret such images? Though interesting and important, yet recognizing such objects by computers is more difficult and challenging. An earlier attempt to tackle such problems was in [6] using symbolic reasoning in ACRONYM system. An interpretation tree approach to deal with 2-d objects with rotating subparts was introduced in [16] and extended to handle 3D articulated objects such as staplers [15]. In [3], different aspects in this area were reviewed and generalized the generalized Hough Transform (GHT) to recognize single joint articulated objects such as pairs of scissors. Yet, it remains to be seen how to overcome the added limitations of the GHT method, as usually happens when an existing object recognition technique is extended to handle articulated objects [3,13]. The method proposed in [37,40] uses very few learning samples and can handle articulated objects but only works for wire-frames, and needs 3D coordinates of the objects.

Our main goal is to present a new approach to overcome the above mentioned drawbacks, while maintaining advantages of key methods, and a system is constructed using JAVA for testing various 3D articulated pbjects in virtual environment on the web [1,14,19,21,23,27,28,36,41-45].

2   Linear Combination Method (LC)

Linear combination method is based on the observation that novel views of objects can be expressed as linear combination of the stored views (from learning). It identifies objects by contructing custom-tailored templates from stored two-dimensional image models. The template-construction procedure just adds together weighted coordinate values from corresponding points in the stored two-dimensional image models. Here, a model is a representation in which

* an image consists of a list of feature points observed in the image
* the model consists of several images – minimally three for polyhedra.

An unknown object is matched with a model by comparing the points in an image of the unknown object with a template-like collection of points produced from the model. In general, an unknown object can be arbitrarilly rotated, arbitrarily translated and even arbitrarilly scaled relative to an arbitrary original position. From the basis graphic knowledge, an arbitrary rotation and translation of an object transforms the coordinate value of any point on that object according to the following equations:

$$X_\theta = r_{xx}(\theta)X + r_{yx}(\theta)Y + r_{zx}(\theta)Z + t_x$$
$$Y_\theta = r_{xy}(\theta)X + r_{yy}(\theta)Y + r_{zy}(\theta)Z + t_y$$
$$Z_\theta = r_{xz}(\theta)X + r_{yz}(\theta)Y + r_{zz}(\theta)Z + t_z$$

where $r_{ij}(\theta)$ (i,j=x,y,z) is the parameter that shows how much the i coordinate of a point, before rotation, contributes to the j coordinate of the same point after rotation, and t_s(s=x,y,z) is the parameter that is determined by how much the object is translated.

Based on S. Ullman's concept that three images , each showing four corresponding vertexes, are almost enough to determine the vertexes' relative positions, therefore, at least three model images are needed and these three model images yield the following equations relating models and unknown object coordinate values to unrotated, untranslated coordinate value, x,y,z.

$$X_{I_1} = r_{xx}(\theta_1)X + r_{yx}(\theta_1)Y + r_{zx}(\theta_1)Z + t_x(\theta_1)$$
$$X_{I_2} = r_{xx}(\theta_2)X + r_{yx}(\theta_2)Y + r_{zx}(\theta_2)Z + t_x(\theta_2)$$
$$X_{I_3} = r_{xx}(\theta_3)X + r_{yx}(\theta_3)Y + r_{zx}(\theta_3)Z + t_x(\theta_3)$$
$$X_{I_0} = r_{xx}(\theta_0)X + r_{yx}(\theta_0)Y + r_{zx}(\theta_0)Z + t_x(\theta_0)$$

These equations can be viewed as four equations in four unknowns, X, Y, Z and X_{I_0}, and can be solved to yield X_{I_0} in term of $X_{I_1}, X_{I_2}, X_{I_3}$ and a collection of four constraints,

$$X_{I_0} = \alpha_x X_{I_1} + \beta_x X_{I_2} + \gamma_x X_{I_3} + \delta_x$$

where $\alpha_x, \beta_x, \gamma_x$ and δ_x are the constraints required for x-coordinate-value prediction, each of which can be expressed in term of r_s and t_s. In order to determine the constraints value, a few corresponding points are needed, here there are four constraints, therefore, four equations are needed, furthermore, four feature points are required in every image.

The four equations are described as follows:

$$X_{P_1 I_0} = \alpha_x X_{P_1 I_1} + \beta_x X_{P_1 I_2} + \gamma_x X_{P_1 I_3} + \delta_x$$
$$X_{P_2 I_0} = \alpha_x X_{P_2 I_1} + \beta_x X_{P_2 I_2} + \gamma_x X_{P_2 I_3} + \delta_x$$
$$X_{P_3 I_0} = \alpha_x X_{P_3 I_1} + \beta_x X_{P_3 I_2} + \gamma_x X_{P_3 I_3} + \delta_x$$
$$X_{P_4 I_0} = \alpha_x X_{P_4 I_1} + \beta_x X_{P_4 I_2} + \gamma_x X_{P_4 I_3} + \delta_x$$

The solutions of $\alpha_x, \beta_x, \gamma_x$ and δ_x values can be used to predict the x coordinate value of any point in the unknown image from the corresponding points in the three model images. Then these predicted values can be used to compare to the original x coordinate values in unknown image. If the difference between them is less than a certain threshold, these two points match with each other and if all feature points match, the conclusion can be made that the unknown image matches the image models.

Similarly, we can build equations for y coordinate, by using same method as that used for x coordinate, producing another set of constraints: $\alpha_y, \beta_y, \gamma_y$ and δ_y to predict the y coordinate value of any point in the unknown image.

Each input image is partitioned to two portions, i.e. the *main* and *articulated* portion. The rationale is to use as few projections as possible for *learning* and *recognition*, use *graph* for *pattern representation*, and gain faster speed by *parallel matching*. Each portion needs projections from two directions for every characteristic view in *learning*. Only one view is needed for *recognition*, though. If each portion of an input is a linear combination of some object models, it is accepted, else rejected. Human interactions are involved in *learning/*

recognition. In 2D space, the values of z axis of orthographic projection of a 3D image are all set to 0 or a constant. A linear combination (LC) scheme uses two images in the same characteristic view class to see if an input is acceptable.

If the input image is an LC of two images in the model-base, then it is accepted, else rejected. In a way, it is equivalent to solving simultaneous equations of the following two vectors :

$$\hat{\mathbf{x}} = a_1\mathbf{x}_1 + a_2\mathbf{y}_1 + a_3\mathbf{x}_2 \text{ and } \hat{\mathbf{y}} = b_1\mathbf{x}_1 + b_2\mathbf{y}_1 + b_3\mathbf{x}_2$$

We therefore propose the following method for recognizing line drawings of 3D objects. Learning and recognition. The recognition phase consists of : (i)extracting of articulated portions and (ii) determining its status, both based on the knowledge obtained from learning.

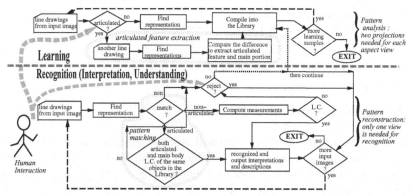

Fig. 2.1 Interactive object recognition/understanding(in virtual environment on web)

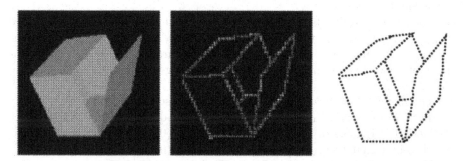

Fig. 2.2 An example of hough transform of an input image (3D articulated object) to line drawing and skeleton. In this article, smoothed and thinned lines such as those shown below will be used for illustrations.

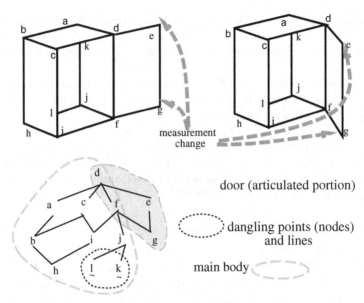

Fig. 2.3 An example of articulated feature extraction

3   Some Experimental Results

Some of the examples and experimental results are given in this section. As it is mentioned before, the Linear Combination Method applies to both rigid objects, which include both convex and concave objects, and articulated objects with visible and invisible hinges. This will cover a large amount of objects in real world and that is why this method is so useful.

The following gives two kinds of articulated objects and shows how the LCM works on them according to the experimental data.

Articulated Objects

The objects in fig. 3.1 are kinds of closets and their doors can be rotated along their hinges. The three model images in (i), (ii) and (iii) are set up by rotating both main part and articulated part separately. Fig 3.1(iv) shows the different view of the same object and the following data verify that it matches the model images.

The match procedures on the main part are described as follows:

The feature points on the main parts of the model images are as belows:

Model1: (-1.90,0.40), (1.00,-0.20), (1.70,-1.10), (0.70,-2.10)
Model2: (-2.00,0.60), (0.70,-0.50), (1.70,-1.20), (0.30,-2.20)
Model3: (-2.00,0.70), (0.40,-0.70), (1.70,-1.30), (-0.00,-2.40)

and the selected feature points on the main part of this unknown image are

(-2.0,0.8), (0.3,-0.8), (1.7,-1.3), (-0.2,-2.4), and (-2.3,-0.8).

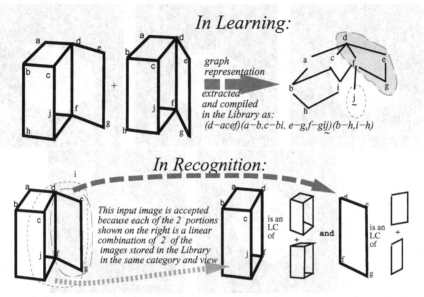

Fig. 2.4 An example of pattern matching (learning and recognition)

After the equations are solved, the constrain values are as follows:
$\alpha_x = -1.12, \beta_x = 1.78, \gamma_x = 0.31, \delta_x = 0.05$
$\alpha_y = -0.32, \beta_y = 0.09, \gamma_y = 1.21, \delta_y = 0.03$
the predicted x and y coordinate values are -2.4030 and -0.7106 and the absolute differences between the predicted value and the original one are 0.1030 and 0.0894. If we select threshold to be 0.6, both the differences are less than threshold, so far the main part of this unknown image matches those of the model images.

The match procedures on the articulated portion are described as follows:

The feature points on the articulated portion of the model images are as follows:

Model1: (-1.90,0.40), (1.00,0.30), (2.00,1.20), (-0.80,1.30)
Model2: (-2.00,0.60), (0.70,0.60), (2.10,1.40), (-0.40,1.40)
Model3: (-2.00,0.70), (0.40,0.80), (2.20,1.70), (-0.10,1.60)
and The feature points on the articulated portion of this unknown image are (-2.0,0.8), (0.1,1.2), (2.2,2.1), (0.0,1.7), and (-0.95,1.0).

After calculation, the constrain values are as follows:
$\alpha_x = 0.62, \beta_x = -2.00, \gamma_x = 2.38, \delta_x = -0.07$
$\alpha_y = 0.33, \beta_y = 0.67, \gamma_y = 1.00, \delta_y = 1.60$
the predicted x and y coordinate values are -1.4835 and 1.2656 and the absolute differences between the predicted value and the original one are 0.5335 and 0.2656 . If we select threshold to be 0.6, both the differences are less than threshold, so far the articulated portion of this unknown image also matches those of the model images.

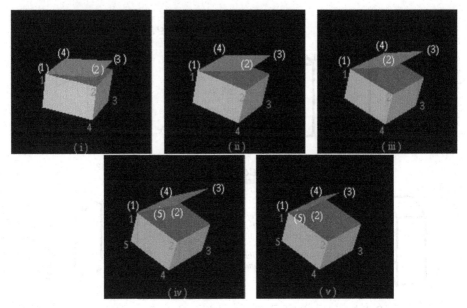

Fig. 3.1 Articulated object recognition. (i), (ii) and (iii) are model images of the closet, (iv) is another view of the same closet,and (v) is the image of a different closet

Therefore, the conclusion can be made that this unknown image matches the model images.

Figure 3.1 (v) is a closet which has the same main part as that of model object, however, its door is different from that of the model one: it has a various size. Therefore, when this input image is recognized, the main part should match the models and the articulated portion should not. Hence, the entire image will not match model images. The followings are the recognization data which demonstrate the above statement.

Because the main part of this unknown image is the same as that in (iv) and from the above calculation, we know that it matches the main parts of the model images.

Next, let us focus on the articulated portion recognition.

The feature points on the articulated portion of this unknown image are (-2.0,0.8), (-1.0,1.0), (1.1,1.9), (0.0,1.7), and (-1.5,0.9).

After calculation, the constrain values are as follows:

$\alpha_x = 0.26, \beta_x = -1.68, \gamma_x = 2.62, \delta_x = -0.61$

$\alpha_y = 0.50, \beta_y = -0.92, \gamma_y = 0.67, \delta_y = 0.40$

the predicted x value is -0.0273 and the absolute difference between the predicted value and the original one is 1.4727 . If we select threshold to be 0.6, both the difference is much greater than threshold. Since the articulated portion of this unknown image does not match that of the model images, therefore, one can cluclude this unknown image does not match the model images, as stated before.

4   Discussions, Conclusions, and Future Research

Through our interactive on-line system of testing, it is observed that the ability to open the lid gives us the extra possibility to test the result of the recognition. As in Figure[4.1], the interactive web platform has two portions for correspondence points selection: Learning on left, and target object to be recognized on right. The upper two and lower left objects are learning samples from various angles of the same object, while the lower right object is the target to be tested. Figure [4.1(3)] shows computedr distance values against threshhold values, and the Figure[4.1(4)] shows their relations on curve.

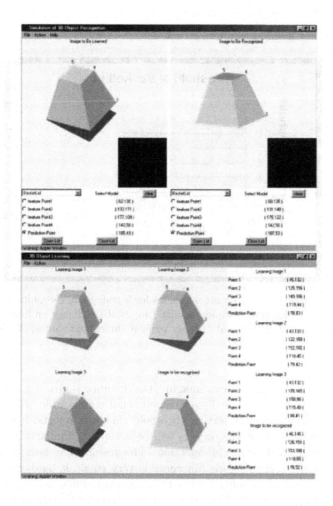

The lid can be opened every 5 degrees. So we can use it to create a set of continuously changed objects. It is interesting to see how the angle of opening is

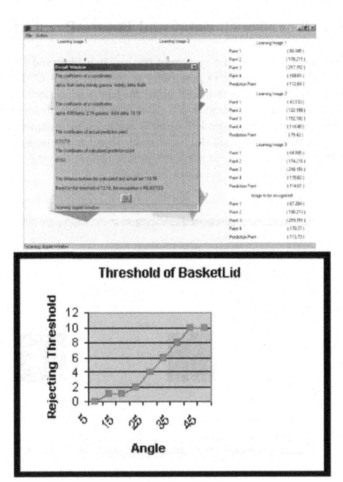

Fig. 4.1 (1) Correspondence points selections for learning and recognition target input object image, (2) 3 learning samples against 1 input object image on lowwer right corner, (3) some computed values of distance against threshhold values, (4) their relation curves

related with distance. As we can imagine, the distance is growing with the angle of opening getting larger. The distance itself is not comparable between different object, so we use the characteristic threshold that just rejects. If the threshold is set to below this value, the objects will be accepted. Similarly, any threshold above this value will result in rejection. The result of it is a monolithically increasing function. If the angle difference is very small, it tends to accept (i.e., small characteristic threshold). By the time the angle difference growing, it tends toward rejecting. At about 35 degree, even the largest threshold can recognize it (i.e., reject it). This result shows how the recognition is related with the difference of objects. It is a continuous procedure that the distance recognized by computer is changed with the difference of objects.

It is also interesting to see that how the selection of feature points affects the result. Previously the affection of selection of feature points is hard to observe because of the lack of comparison basis, i.e., the selection is restricted by the prerequisite that all points be visible. And the objects are either too different or too same to make selection. Here we can make selection and make change by demand, so it's easy to see the change.

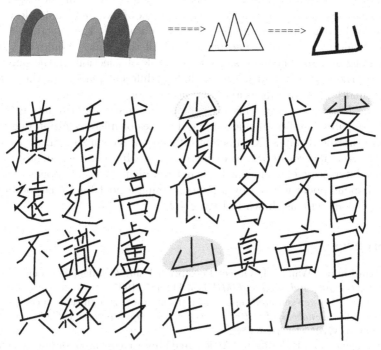

Looking from one side, mountains, from the other side, ranges
Far, near, high, low, all different
I can hardly recognize the true face of the Lu Shan mountain
Simply because I am in the middle of it

Written by Su Dong-po, 11th Century, Translated by P. Wang, 1997

Fig. 4.2 A famous poem by a well known Chinese poet Su Dong-po (11th Century), translated to English by the author.

If opening the lid doesn't change all the selected points (i.e., no selection on the lid point), then the result is the same as same object recognition. This is what we expected: the computer still need human to provide the knowledge of selections. If opening the lid changes some of the points (i.e., there are some points selected on the lid), then the objects can be recognized differently. If we select the points that are across the opening, the distance will be obvious enough in any threshold. The reason is that when two points are across the opening, they have more relative distance than other cases, in the extreme example, in one object the two points are separate and in the other object these two points are combined together. So their relative distance will be much more than other selections.

Human eyes have similar phenomenon. We can hardly tell the difference between two lines with length 1 inch and 1.05 inch, but we can easily tell whether there is a 0.05 inch line or not.

However, there are some exceptions or occluded areas in the experiments. To calculate the matrix transformation, the rank of 3x3 matrix should be 3 and should not be degraded during the series of rotation. So the selection of feature points shouldn't be in the same plane, and all the points should be visible in the learning images. The folders are the example of selections in the same plane. (Actually the points in folders are in slightly different plane, but the difference is very small) Their distances are large because of this reason.

In the future, we would like to explore automatic determination of *correspondence points*, and overcome some difficulties of misrecognition due to poor choice of threshold values. An inherent difficulty of recognizing 3D objects seems due to its so many *variations*, as many as *infinite*, from various angles, sizes and statuses. Interesting enough, this basic natural phenomenon happens to coincide with a famous poem written by a famous Chinese poet Su Dong-po about one thousand years ago, as shown in Figure 4.2.

References

1. L.Baird and P.Wang, "3D Object Perception Using Gradient Descent", *Int. J. of Math. Imaging and Vision (IJMIV)*, 5, 111-117, 1995
2. R. Basri, "Viewer-centered representations in object recognition - a computational approach", *Handbook of Pattern Recog. and Comp. Vision* (eds C.Chen,L.Pau and P.Wang), WSP, (1993) 863-882
3. A. Beinglass and H. Wolfson, "Articulated object recognition, or how to generalize the generalized Hough transform", *Proc. ICCVPR*, 461-466, 1991
4. P. Besl and R.Jain, "3-d object recognition", *ACM Computing Survey*, 17(1): 75-154, 1985
5. A.F.Bobick and R.C.Bolles, "The representation space paradigm of concurrent evolving object descriptions", *IEEE-PAMI*, v14 n2 (1992) 146-156
6. R. Brooks, "Symbolic reasoning around 3-d models and 2-d images", *Arti. Int.*, 17, 285-348, 1981
7. I. Chakravarty and H. Freeman, "Characteristic views as a basis for 3-d object recognition", *SPIE: Robot Vision*, 336, 37-45, 1982
8. C.Chien and J. Aggarwal, "Shape recognition from single silhouette", *ICCV*, 481-490, 1987
9. R.T.Chin and C.R.Dyer, "Model-based recognition in robot vision", *ACM Computing Survey*, 18(1), 67-108, 1986
10. S.I.Dickinson, A.P. Pentland and A. Rosenfeld, "3-D Shape Recovery Using Distributed Aspect Matching", *IEEE-PAMI*, v14, n2, 174-197 (1992)
11. D.Dori, "Self-structured syntax-directed pattern recognition of dimensioning components in engineering drawing", *Structured Document Analysis* (ed. H.Baird, H.Bunke, K.Yamamoto), Springer Verlag, (1992) 359-384

12. M.Ejiri, T.Uno, H.Yoda, T.Goto and K.Takeyasu, "An intelligent robot with cognition and decision-making ability", *Proc. 2nd IJCAI*, pp350-358, 1971

13. J.R.Engelbracht and F.M.Wahl, "Polyhedral object recognition using hough-space features", *PR*, v21 n2 (1988) 155-167

14. B. Girod and S. Scherock, "Depth from defocus of structured light", *SPIE Proc. Optics, Illumination and Image Sensing for Machine Vision IV* (1989), v1194, 129-146

15. R.Goldberg and D.Lowe, "Verification of 3-d parametric models in 2-d image data", *Proc. IEEE Workshop on Computer Vision*, 255-267, 1987

16. W.E.L.Grimson and T. Lozano-Perez, "Localizing overlapping parts by searching the interpretation tree", *IEEE-PAMI*, 9(4), 469-482, 1987

17. T.S.Huang and C.H.Lee, "Motion and structure from orthographic projections", *IEEE-PAMI*, 2(5), 536-540, 1989

18. M.Karima, K.S.Sadhal and T.O.McNeil, "From paper drawing to computer aided design", *IEEE Trans. on Computer Graphics and Appl.*, pp27-39, Feb., 1985

19. R.Kasturi, S.T.Bow, W. El-Masri, J.R. Gattiker, U.B. Mokate, "A system for interpretation of line drawings", *IEEE-PAMI*, PAMI-12, 10, October 1990, pp978-992

20. B. Liu and P.S.P. Wang, "3D Articulated Object Recognition - A Case Study", SPIE'96, v. 2904 *Robotics and Computer Vision*, Boston, November 1996, pp14-24

21. T. Marill. "Emulating the human interpretation of line-drawings as 3-d objects", *IJCV*, v6-2, (1991) 147-161

22. E.Marti, J.Regincós, J. López-Krahe and J.Villanueva, "A system for interpretation of hand line drawings as 3-d scene for CAD input", *Proc. ICDAR'91*, Saint-Malo, France, September 1991, pp472-481

23. I.V.Nagendra and U.G. Gujar, "3-D objects from 2-D orthographic views - a survey", *Computers and Graphics*, v12, no 1, pp 111-114, 1988

24. S. Negahdaripour and A.K. Jain, "Challenges in computer vision: future research directions", *IEEE-CVPR'92*, 189-198

25. T.Poggio and S. Edelman, "A network that learns to recognize 3D objects", *Nature*, (1990), 343: 263-266

26. T.Poggio, "3d object recognition: on a result by Basri and Ullman", TR 9005-03, IRST, Italy, 1990

27. R. N. Shepard and J.Metzler, "Mental rotation: effects of dimensionality of objects and type of task", *I. Exp. Psychol. : Human Perception and Performance*, 14 : 3-11 (1988)

28. L.Stark and K.W.Bowyer, "Achieving generalized object recognition through reasoning about association of function to structure", *IEEE-PAMI*, v13 (1991) 1097-1104

29. H.Sakurai and D.C.Gossard, "Solid model input through orthographic views", *Computer Graphics*, v 17, no 3, pp243-252, 1983

30. C.Y. Suen and P.S.P. Wang (eds), *Advances of Thinning Methologies in Pattern Recognition*, WSP, 1994

31. K. Sugihara, *Machine interpretation of line drawings*, MIT Press, Cambridge (1986)

32. Y.Y.Tang, C.D.Yan, M.Cheriet and C.Y.Suen, "Automatic analysis and understanding of documents", *Handbook of Pattern Recog. and Comp. Vis.*, (C.H.Chen, L.Pau and P.S.P.Wang eds), WSP, 1993, 625-654

33. D.W. Thompson and J.L. Mundy, "3D model matching from an unconstrained viewpoint", *Proc. IEEE Int. Conf. on robotics and automation*, Raleigh, NC, (1987) 208-220

34. S. Ullman and R. Basri, "Recognition by Linear Combinations of Models", *IEEE-PAMI*, v13, no 10, (1991) 992-1006
35. S. Ullman, "Aligning pictorial descriptions: an approach to object recognition", *Cognition*, 32(3):193-254, 1989
36. D. Waltz, "Understanding line drawings of scenes with shadows", in *The Psychology of Computer Vision*(ed. by P. Winston), McGraw-Hill, 1975, 19-92
37. P.S.P.Wang,"3D Object recognition with Learning", *IJPRAI* v14, n8, Dec 2000
38. P.S.P.Wang,"High Level Visualization, Representation, Understanding, and Recognition of 3D Articulated Objects" *The Encyclopedia of Microcomputers,* (ed. A. Kent, J. Williams), Marcer Dekker Pub. Co., 1999
39. P.S.P.Wang and Y.Y.Zhang, "A fast and flexible thinning algorithm", *IEEE-Computers*, v 38, no 5, (1989) 741-745
40. P.S.P.Wang, http://www.ccs.neu.edu/home/pwang/3dpr/ (1999-2001)
41. P.S.P.Wang, "A heuristic parallel algorithm for line-drawing object pattern representation and recognition", in *Advances in Image Processing*, ed by E. Dougherty, Marcel Dekker, (1994) 197-222
42. P.S.P.Wang, "3D Line Image Analysis - A Heuristic Parallel Approach", *Int. J. of Information Science*, 81/3-4, 155-175, 1994
43. M.A.Wesley and G.Markowsky, "Fleshing out projections", *IBM J. Res. Deve.* v25, n6, 934-954, 1981
44. E.T. Whitaker and M.N. Huhns, "Rule-based geometric reasoning for the interpretation of line drawings", *Appl. of A.I. III, Proc. SPIE*, v635, pp 621-627, 1986
45. E.K.Wong, "Model matching in robot vision by subgraph isomorphism", *Pattern Recognition*, v25 no3,287-303, 1992

A Web Proxy Cache Coherency and Replacement Approach

Jose Aguilar[1] and Ernst Leiss[2]

[1] CEMISID, Dpto. de Computacion, Facultad de Ingenieria, Universidad de Los Andes,
Merida 5101, Venezuela
aguilar@ing.ula.ve

[2] Department of Computer Science, University of Houston, Houston, TX 77204-3475, USA
coscel@cs.uh.edu

Abstract. We propose an adaptive cache coherence-replacement scheme for web proxy cache systems that is based on several criteria about the system and applications, with the objective of optimizing the distributed cache system performance. Our coherence-replacement scheme assigns a replacement priority value to each cache block according to a set of criteria to decide which block to remove. The goal is to provide an effective utilization of the distributed cache memory and a good application performance.

1 Introduction

Many studies have examined policies for cache replacement and cache coherence; however, these studies have rarely taken into account the combined effects of policies [2, 6]. In this paper we propose an adaptive cache coherence-replacement scheme for web proxy cache systems. This work is based on previous work we have done on cache replacement mechanisms which have shown that adaptive cache replacement policies improve the performance of computing systems [1]. Our approach combines classical coherence protocols (write-update and write-invalid protocols) and replacement policies (LRU, LFU, etc.) to optimize the overall performance (based on criteria such as network traffic, application execution time, data consistence, etc.). The cache coherence mechanism is responsible for determining whether a copy in the distributed cache system is stale or valid. At the same time, it must update the invalid copies when a given site requires a block. Because a cache has a fixed amount of storage, when this storage space becomes full, the cache must choose a set of objects (or a set of victim blocks) to evict to make room for newly requested objects/blocks. The replacement mechanism is used for this task. Our approach attempts to improve the performance of the distributed cache memory system by assigning a replacement priority value to each cache block according to a set of criteria to select the block/object to remove. To fix this priority, we take into account the state of the cache block. In addition, our scheme uses an adaptive replacement strategy that looks at the

N. Zhong et al. (Eds.): WI 2001, LNAI 2198, pp. 75–84, 2001.
© Springer-Verlag Berlin Heidelberg 2001

information available to make the decision what replacement technique to use, without a proportional increase in the space/time requirements.

2 Theoretical Aspects

2.1 Coherence Problem

Distributed cache systems provide decreased latency at a cost: every cache will sometimes provide users with *stale* pages. Every local cache must somehow update pages in its cache so that it can give users pages which are as fresh as possible. Indeed, the problem of keeping cached pages up to date is not new to cache systems: after all, the cache is really just an enormous distributed file system, and distributed file systems have been with us for years. In conventional distributed systems terminology, the problem of updating cached pages is called *coherence* [2, 3, 5, 6, 8, 11, 14]. Specifically, the cache coherence problem consists of keeping a data element found in several caches current with each other and with the value in main memory (or local memories). A *cache coherence protocol* ensures the data consistency of the system: the value returned by a read must always be the last value written to that location. There are two classes of cache coherence protocols [14]: write-invalidate and write-update. In a *write-invalidate* protocol, a write request to a block invalidates all other shared copies of that block. If a processor issues a read request to a block that has been invalidated, there will be a coherence miss. In a *write-update* protocol on the other hand, each write request to shared data updates all other copies of the block, and the block remains shared. Although there are fewer read misses for a write-update protocol, the write traffic on the bus is often so much higher that the overall performance is decreased. A variety of mechanisms have been proposed for solving the cache coherence problem. The optimal solution for a multiprocessor system depends on several factors, such as the size of the system (i.e., the number of processors), etc.

2.2 Replacement Policy Problem

A replacement policy specifies which block should be removed when a new block must be entered into an already full cache; it should be chosen so as to ensure that blocks likely to be referenced in the near future are retained in the cache. The choice of replacement policy is one of the most critical cache design issues and has a significant impact on the overall system performance. Common replacement algorithms used with such caches are [1, 4, 7, 9, 10, 15]:

- *First In-First Out (FIFO):* this is the simplest scheme; it is easily managed with a FIFO queue. When a replacement is necessary the first block entered at the cache memory (at the head of the queue) must be removed.

- *Most Recent Used (MRU):* Replaces the block in the cache, which has been more recently used. This is not used frequently on cache memory system because it has bad temporal locality. It is a typical property of the memory reference patterns of processors, page reference patterns in virtual memory patterns, etc.
- *Least Recently Used (LRU):* Replaces/evicts the block/object in the cache that has not been used for the longest period of time. The basic premise is that blocks that have been referenced in the recent past will likely be referenced again in the near future (temporal locality). This policy works well when there is a high temporal locality of references in the workload. There is a variant, called Early Eviction LRU (EELRU), proposed in [7]. EELRU performs LRU replacement by default but diverges from LRU and evicts pages early when it notes that too many pages are being touched in a roughly cyclic pattern that is larger than the main memory.
- *Least Frequently Used (LFU):* It is based on the frequency with which a block is accessed. LFU requires that a references count be maintained for each block in the cache. A block/object's referenced count is incremented by one with each reference to it. When a replacement is necessary, the LFU replaces/evicts the blocks/objects with the lowest reference count. The motivation for LFU and other frequency based algorithms is that the reference count can be used as an estimate of the probability of a block being referenced. In [7], Lee et al. show that there exists a spectrum of block replacement policies that subsumes both the LRU and LFU policies. The spectrum is formed according to how much more weight is given to the recent history over the older history and is referred to as the LRFU (Least Recently/Frequently Used) policy.
- *Least Frequently Used (LFU)-Aging*: The LFU policy can suffer from cache pollution (an effect of temporal locality): if a formerly popular object becomes unpopular, it will remain in the cache for a long time, preventing other newly or slightly less popular objects from replacing it. *LFU-Aging* addresses cache pollution when it considers both a block/object's access frequency and its age in cache. One solution to this is to introduce some form of reference count "aging". The average reference count is maintained dynamically (over all blocks currently in the cache). Whenever this average counts exceeds some predetermined maximum value (a parameter to the algorithm) every reference count is reduced. There is a variant, called LFU with Dynamic Aging (LFUDA), that uses dynamic aging to accommodate shifts in the set of popular objects.
- *Greedy Dual Size (GDS):* It combines temporal locality, size, and other cost information. The algorithm assigns a *cost/size* value to each cache block. In the simplest case the cost is set to 1 to maximize the hit ratio, but costs such as latency, network bandwidth can be explored. GDS assigns a key value to each object. The key is computed as the object's reference count plus the cost information divided by its size. The algorithm takes into account recency for a block by inflating the key value (*cost/size* value) for an accessed block by the least value of currently cached blocks. The *GDS-aging* version adds the cache age factor to the key factor. By adding the cache age factor, it limits the influence of previously popular documents. The algorithm is simple to implement with a priority queue. There are several variations of the GDS algorithm each of which takes into ac-

count coherency information and the expiration time of the cache (*GDSlifetime*). The second variation uses the observation that different types of applications change their references at different rates (*GDStype*). A last GDS variation is *GDSlatency*, which uses as key value for an object the quantity *latency/size* where latency is the measured delay for the last retrieval of the object.

- *Frequency Based Replacement (FBR):* This is a hybrid replacement policy, attempting to capture the benefits of both LRU and LFU without the associated drawbacks. FBR maintains the LRU ordering of all blocks in the cache, but the replacement decision is primarily based upon the frequency count. To accomplish this, FBR divides the cache into three partitions: a new partition, a middle partition and an old partition. The new partition contains the most recent used blocks (MRU) and the old partition the LRU blocks. The middle section consists of those blocks not in either the new or the old section. When a reference occurs to a block in the new section, its reference count is not incremented. References to the middle and old sections do cause the reference counts to be incremented. When a block must be chosen for replacement, FBR chooses the block with the lowest reference count, but only among those blocks that are in the old section.
- *Priority Cache (PC):* Uses both runtime and compile-time information to select a block for replacement. PC associates a data priority bit with each cache block. The compiler, through two additional bits associated with each memory access instruction, assigns priorities. These two bits indicate whether the data priority bit should be set as well as the priority of the block, i.e., low or high. The cache block with the lowest priority is the one to be replaced.

In general, the policies anticipate future memory references by looking at the past behavior of the programs (program's memory access patterns). Their job is to identify a line/block (containing memory references) which should be thrown away in order to make room for the newly referenced line that experienced a miss in the cache.

3   An Adaptive Coherence-Replacement Policy

The growth of the Internet and the WWW has significantly increased the amount of online information and services available. However, the client/server architecture employed by the current Web-based services is inherently unscalable. Web caches have been proposed as a solution to the scalability problem [4, 5, 6, 8, 12, 16]. Web caches store copies of previously retrieved objects to avoid transferring those objects in response to subsequent requests. Web caches are located throughout the Internet, from the user's browser cache through local proxy caches and backbone caches, to the so-called reverse proxy caches located near the origin of the content. Client browsers may be configured to connect to a proxy server, which then forwards the request on behalf of the client. All Web caches must try to keep cached pages up to date with the master copies of those pages, to avoid returning stale pages to users. There are strong benefits for the proxy to cache popular requests locally. Users will receive cached documents more quickly. Additionally, the organization reduces the amount of traffic imposed on its wide-area Internet connection.

Because a cache server has a fixed amount of storage, the server needs a cache replacement mechanism [4, 6]. Recent studies on web workload have shown tremendous breadth and turnover in the popular object set-the set of objects that are currently being accessed by users [16]. The popular object set can change when new objects are published, such as news stories or sports scores, which replace previously popular objects. We should define cache replacement policies based on this workload characterization. In addition, a cache must determine if it can service a request, and if so, if each object it provides is fresh. This is a typical question to be solve with a cache coherence mechanism. If the object is fresh, the cache provides it directly, if not, the cache requests the object from its origin server.

Our adaptive coherence-replacement mechanism for Web caches is based on systems like Squid [13], which caches Internet data. It does this by accepting requests for objects that people want to download and by processing their requests at their sites. In other words, if users want to download a web page, they ask Squid to get the page for them. Then Squid connects to the remote server and requests the page. It then transparently streams the data through itself to the client machine, but at the same time keeps a copy. The next time someone wants that same page, Squid simply reads it from its disks, transferring the data to the client machine almost immediately (Internet caching). Normally, in Internet caching cache hierarchies are used. The Internet Cache Protocol (ICP) describes the cache hierarchies. The ICP's role is to provide a quick and efficient method of intercache communication, offering a mechanism for establishing complex cache hierarchies. ICP allows one cache to ask another if it has a valid copy of a object. Squid ICP is based on the following procedure [13]:

1. Squid sends an ICP query message to its neighbors (URL requested)
2. Each neighbor receives its ICP query and looks up the URL in its own cache. If a valid copy exists, the cache sends ICP_HIT, otherwise ICP_MISS
3. The querying cache collects the ICP replies from its peers. If the cache receives several ICP_HIT replies from its peers (neighbors), it chooses the peer whose reply was the first to arrive in order to receive the object. If all replies are ICP_MISS, Squid forwards the request to the neighbors of its neighbors, until to find a valid copy.

Neighbors refer to other caches in a hierarchy (a parent cache, a sibling cache or the origin server). Squid offers numerous modifications to this mechanism, for example:

- Send ICP queries to some neighbors and not to others
- Include the origin sever in the ICP "ping" so that if the origin servers reply arrives before any ICP-hits, the request is forward there directly.
- Disallow or require the use of some peers for certain requests.

In this case, each cache block is in the following state:
   Invalid: a stale copy.

Normally, there is only one state because the users typically do not write. Then, the adaptive cache coherence-replacement mechanism is as follows:

1. If *read miss* then
   1.1 Search for a valid copy (using the ICP). A read-miss request is sent using the ICP
   1.2 If cache is full, choose a replacement policy according to a *decision system*
   1.3 Receive a valid copy
   1.4 Read block
2. If *read hit* then
   2.1 Read block

3.1 The Replacement System

Normally, user cache access patterns affect cache replacement decisions while block characteristics affect cache coherency decisions. Therefore, it is reasonable to consider replacing cache blocks that have expired or are closed to expiring because their next access will result in an invalidation message. In this way, we propose a cache coherence-replacement mechanism that incorporates the state information into an adaptive replacement policy. The basic idea behind the proposed mechanism is to combine a coherence mechanism with our adaptive cache replacement algorithm [1, 2]. Our adaptive cache coherence-replacement mechanism exploits semantic information about the expected or observed access behavior of particular data shared objects on the size of the cache items, and the replacement phase employs several different mechanisms, each one appropriate for a different situation. Since our coherence-replacement is provided in software, we expect the overhead of providing our mechanism to be offset by the increase in performance that such a mechanism will provide. That is, in our approach we examine if the overall performance can be improved by considering coherency issues as part of the cache replacement decision. We incorporate the additional information about a program's characteristics, which is available in the form of the cache block states, in our replacement system. Thus, we define a set of parameters that we can use to select the best replacement policy in a dynamic environment:

A) Information about the system
- Workload, Bandwidth, Latency, CPU Utilization.
- Type of system (Shared memory, etc.)

B) Information about the application
- Information about the data and cache block or objects (Frequency, Age, Size, Length of the past information (patterns), State (invalid, shared, etc.)).
- Type an degree of access pattern on the system (High or low spatial locality (SL), High or low temporal locality (TL)).

C) Other information
- Cache conflict resolution mechanism
- Pre-fetching mechanism

An optimal cache replacement policy would know the future workload. In the real world, we must develop heuristics to approximate ideal behavior. For each of the policies we discussed in section 2.2, we list the information that is required by them:

- LFU: reference count.
- LRU: the program's memory access patterns.
- Priority Cache: information at runtime or compile time (data priority bit by cache/block).
- Prediction: a summary of the entire program's memory access pattern.
- FBR: the program's memory access patterns and organization of the cache memory.
- MRU: the program's memory access patterns.
- FIFO: the program's memory access patterns.
- GDS: size of the objects, information to calculate the cost function, reference count.
- Aging approaches: GDS-aging: GDS age factor; LFU-aging: LFU age factor.

We define one expression, called the *key value*, to define the priority of replacement of each block/object. According to this value, the system chooses the block with higher priority to replace (low key value). The key value is defined as:

$$\text{Key-Value} = (CF+A+FC)/S + \text{cache factor} \qquad (1)$$

where, - FC is the frequency/reference count, that is the number of times that a block has been referenced,
- A is the age factor,
- S is the size of the block/object,
- CF is the cost function that can include costs such as latency or network bandwidth.

The first part of Equation (1) is typical for the GDS, LRU and LFU policies (using information about objects to reference and not about cache blocks). The cache factor is defined according to the replacement policy used:

- LFU: blocks with a high frequency count have the highest cache factor.
- LRU: the least recently used block has the highest cache factor.
- Priority Cache: defined at runtime or compile-time.
- Prediction: the least used block in the future has the highest cache factor.
- FBR: the least recently used block has the highest cache factor.
- MRU: the most recently used block has the highest cache factor.
- FIFO: the block at the head of the queue has the highest cache factor.
- GDS: not applicable.
- Aging approaches: FC/A, with a reset factor that restarts this value after a given number of ages or when the age average is more than a given value.

The coherence-replacement policy defines the cache factor so that: blocks in invalid state have the highest priority to be chosen to replace. Otherwise, blocks in shared states must be chosen to replace, then blocks in exclusive states, and finally, blocks in modified states. If there are several blocks in a particular state, we use the replacement policy specified in our *decision system* [1]. The *decision system* is composed of a set of rules to decide the replacement policy to use. Each rule selects a replacement policy to apply according to different criteria:

If *TL is high and the system's memory access pattern is regular* then
    Use a LRU replacement policy
If *TL is low and the system's memory access pattern is regular* then
    Use a LFU replacement policy
If *TL is low and the system's memory access pattern is large* then
    Use a MFU replacement policy
If *we require a precise decision using a large system's memory access pattern
        history* then
    Use a Prediction replacement policy
If *objects/blocks have variable sizes* then
    Use a GDS replacement policy
If *a fast decision is required* then
    Use a RAND replacement policy
If *there is a large number of LRU candidate blocks* then
    Use a FBR replacement policy
If *SL is high* then
    Use a hybrid FBR + GDS replacement policy
If *the system's memory access pattern is irregular* then
    Use an age replacement policy

4   Result Analysis

We constructed a trace-driven simulation to study our approach using a set of client traces from Digital Equipment Corporation [6]. We compare our approach with [6]. These traces are distinguished from many proxy logs in that they contain last modification time. We use four evaluation criteria: response latency, bandwidth, hit rates and number of request. We use a normalized cost model for each of these criteria where each of these costs is defined 0 if a "get request" can be retrieved from the proxy cache, or 1 for a "get request" to a server. The total cost for a simulation is the average of these normalized costs. Figure 1 shows the average costs of the best policy proposed on [6] and of our work. The approach proposed on [6] has the highest cost. For a 10 GB cache, the cost saving is 4%. Our results indicate that for caches where the cache space is small, the cache replacement policy primarily determines the costs. For cache operating in configurations with large amounts of cache space, the cache coherency policy primarily determines the overall costs. To reduce the overhead of our approach, we can make an appropriate inclusion of coherency characteristics on the replacement policy.

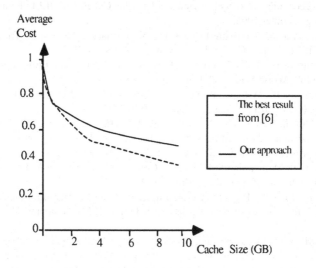

Fig. 1. Average Cost vs. Cache Size

5 Conclusions

The goal of this research was to formulate an overarching framework subsuming various cache management strategies in the context of different distributed platforms. We have proposed an adaptive coherence-replacement policy. Our approach includes additional information/factors such as frequency of block use, state of the blocks, etc., in replacement decisions. It takes into consideration that coherency and replacement decisions affect each other. This adaptive policy system has been validated by experimental work. Our majors results are: a) cache replacement and coherency are both important in reducing the costs for a proxy cache, b) direct inclusion of cache coherency issues maybe can reduce the overhead of our approach but doesn't guarantee a better performance.

References

1. Aguilar J., Leiss E. A Proposal for a Consistent Framework of Dynamic/Adaptive Policies for Cache Memory Management, Technical Report, Department of Computer Sciences, University of Houston, (2000).

2. Cho S., King J., Lee G. Coherence and Replacement Protocol of DICE-A Bus Based COMA Multiprocessor, Journal of Parallel and Distributed Computing, Vol. 57 (1999) 14-32.
3. Choi L. Techniques for compiler-directed Cache Coherence. IEEE Parallel Distributed Technology, Winter 1996.
4. Dilley J., Arlitt M. Improving Proxy Cache Performance: Analysis of Three Replacement Policies, IEEE Internet Computing, November, (1999) 44-50.
5. Krishnamurthy B., Wills C. Piggyback Server Invalidation for Proxy Cache Coherency, Proc. 7th Intl. World Wide Web Conf., (1998) 185-193.
6. Krishnamurthy B., Wills C. Proxy Cache Coherency and Replacement-Towards a More Complete Picture, IEEE Computer, Vol. 6, (1999) 332-339.
7. Lee D., Choi J., Noh S., Cho Y., Kim J., Kim C. On the Existence of a Spectrum of Policies that Subsumes the Least Recently Used (LRU) and Least Frequently Used (LFU) Policies, Performance Evaluation Review, Vol. 27 (1999). 134-143.
8. Liu C., Cao P. Maintaining Strong Cache Consistency in the WWW, Proc. 17th IEEE Intl. Conf. on Distributed Computing Systems, (1997).
9. Mounes F., Lilja D. The Effect of Using State-based Priority Information in a Shared-Memory Multiprocessor Cache Replacement Policy, IEEE Computer, Vol. 2 (1998) 217-224.
10. Obaidat M., Khalid H. Estimating NN-Based Algorithm for Adaptive Cache Replacement, IEEE Transaction on System, Man and Cybernetic, Vol. 28 (1998) 602-611.
11. Sandhu H., Sevcik; K. An Analytic Study of Dynamic Hardware and Software Cache Coherence Strategies. Proc.1995 ACM SIGMETRICS Intl. Conf. on Measurement and Modeling of Computer Systems , pp. 167 - 177, 1995.
12. Shim J., Scheuermann P., Vingralek R. Proxy Cache Design: Algorithms, Implementation and Performance, IEEE Trans. on Knowledge and Data Engineering, (1999).
13. Squid Internet object cache. http://squid.nlanr.net/Squid.
14. Stenstrom P. A Survey of Cache Coherence Schemes for Multiprocessors. IEEE Computer, (1990) 12-24.
15. G. Tyson, M. Fonrens, J. Matthews and A. Pleczkun, "Managing Data Caches Using Selective Cache Lien Replacement", International Journal of Parallel Programming, (1997) 25(3) 213-242.
16. Wills C., Mikhailov M. Towards a better Understanding of Web Resources and Server Responses for Improved Caching, Proc. 8th Intl. World Web Conf., (1999).

Content Request Markup Language (CRML): A Distributed Framework for XML-Based Content Publishing

Chi-Huang Chiu, Kai-Chih Liang, and Shyan-Ming Yuan

Dept. of Computer & Information Science, National Chiao Tung University,
1001 TaHsueh Rd, HsinChu 300, Taiwan
{chchiu, kcliang, smyuan}@cis.nctu.edu.tw

Abstract. Construct web applications to provide dynamic, personalized web contents with high scalability and performance is a challenge to the software industry in the next century. In most available solutions, load balancing and caching mechanisms are introduced in front of web servers to reduce workload. In this paper we present Content Request Markup Language (CRML), an enabling technique for distributed XML processing at the content level. CRML is a language based on emerging XML standards, XSLT and XPATH, to publish XML-based content over HTTP protocol. It provides hints to construct a distributed framework to support parallel XML-based content publishing. In addition, the content from databases or other sources could be cached before or after processing in block or page level. With the parallel content publishing and the caching mechanism, the CRML could provide a high performance platform for fully customized web service.

1 Introduction

While Tim Berners-Lee created the first web site to provide hypermedia information at the distributed environment, nobody believed that he would change the world. However, he did. The invention changes the way people communicate, learn, and even live. In the end of twenty century, the old economy was replaced by the e-commerce, we called it new economy, which is mostly built on the World Wide Web technologies.

1.1 Building a Web Application

The explosive growth of the World Wide Web over the last few years continues unabated. The Web has evolved from sites that serve static HTML pages to a global arena for recreation, information, and business transactions.

Web applications use enabling technologies to make their content dynamic and to allow users of the system to affect business logic on the server. To support the web applications, web servers start to provide the extension mechanisms. Developers of

N. Zhong et al. (Eds.): WI 2001, LNAI 2198, pp. 85–94, 2001.
© Springer-Verlag Berlin Heidelberg 2001

the web applications use these mechanisms to connect the business logics and web applications. The first & most popular approach is Common Gateway Interface (CGI).

The CGI has a lot of disadvantages such as hard-to-write and forking processes, and some solutions are presented to the public to replace its position. The most famous solution is the Active Server Pages from Microsoft. It uses the simple script language embedded in the HTML to process the data. Besides, the Java Servlet & Java Server Pages on Java Platform provide similar solutions but based on the Java programming language.

No matter what solution to use, the web applications always do the two jobs:

- Retrieve the Content
- Present the Content to the users.

The web applications retrieve the content from databases, files, or the enterprise information systems, and the retrieved content will be formatted to HTML and sent to users. Sometimes, the update of the content will be sent to the date sources.

1.2   Caching & Load Balancing

When the number of Internet users is increasing, the web servers get incredible heavy traffic on their service. The caching is applied to reduce the load of the web server. Usually, the caching system is placed in front of the web server to cache each request with matched parameters. Such system has a big problem on the fully customized web-service because each user may get different page on the same content, which is generated by his preference. Some solutions put the cache in the back of the web applications, which cache the data from the databases.

The Load Balancing is used to increase the capacity to handle the traffic. The common solution is using duplicated machine to provide the same service. The problem is that some resources may be allocated in each machine and some information such as session information is not easy to be migrated.

1.3   The CRML Framework

The CRML Framework is introduced based on the idea on the previous discussion. First, it separates the two job of the web application. The Retrieving of the Data is made by some Content Request Blocks. Second, then the XSL Transformation is used to present the data to the users. The strategy is "Divide and Conquer". The content used to generate a requested page is separated to several Content Request Blocks, which describe the data source and how to retrieve the data. When all required data is ready to process, the XSL Transformation is used to process the data.

Each XML file with CRML Content Request Blocks should be saved in a file with the extension name ".sxml" to tell the web server process the file with CRML Engine. Such XML files are named "CRML Source Files".

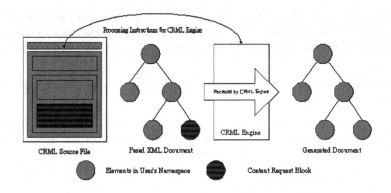

Fig. 1. Diagram for processing a CRML Source File

The whole concept of this section could be represented in the Figure 1. A CRML Source File is an XML file in user-assigned namespace with one or more Content Request Blocks. The CRML Engine can process the elements in the CRML's namespace and generate the contents in user-assigned namespace. Besides, the developer of the CRML Source File could add some special Processing Instructions for CRML Engine. These Processing Instructions could setup some page-level properties for CRML Engine.

2   The Content Request Block

In previous section, we introduce that the core strategy of this framework is "Divide and Conquer". The pages requested by users are composed of some data sources. Each data source should be described to a Content Request Block: CRB. A CRB could describe a data source from database, file, XML database, and the only requirement is that the data should be modeled into a XML document. The requirement is due to the processing of the content is based on XML as a data type.

2.1   The Data Source & Transformation

The data sources in a requested web page are various. A page could be composed of the information from databases, files, or remote service provider. The following example access the content in the SQL databases.

```
<crml:content id="query2"
    xmlns:we="http://www.nctu.edu.tw/2000/CRML">
<crml:source type="sql">
 <crml:attr name="db" value="jdbc:db2:sample"/>
   [!CDATA[select id, name from users]]
 </crml:source>
 <crml:transformation apply="table.xsl"
     cache="before"/>
</crml:content>
```

The data from a SQL database should not be represented in the form of XML because the CRML need the result of the data in XML. The data in a previous example should be transformed to a XML document like following code fragment.

```
<RESULT>
 <ROW><id>chchiu</id><name>Chi-Huang Chiu</name></ROW>
</RESULT>
```

A XSL Transformation could be invoked after the data is acquired. The above example just shows the usage and capability of the data sources in CRML. Although the CRB is a fundamental of the CRML but the source of the CRB is independent of the rest processes to handle the whole document. The only requirement is XML. The CRML create the possibility to adapt the all kind of data sources in to the CRML if the processor of the CRML could handle the kind of the source.

2.2   Caching

In order to improve the efficiency of processing a requested page, the caching is required. Unlike the mechanism provide by most existing publishing framework which cache each page of data. The CRML provides a caching mechanism in CRB-level to cache the content before processing them. The concept is simple that a CRB should be requested with some parameters. The CRML assumes that the results of the CRBs with the same parameters should be the same. In this assumption, the processor could reduce the effort to retrieve the data if the parameters are matched. The following code gives an example of caching a CRB:

```
<crml:content id="query2">
 <crml:cache keys="div,dept" />
 <crml:source type="sql">
  <crml:attr name="db" value="jdbc:db2:sample"/>
  [!CDATA[select id from users where div='@{div}' and
          dept='@{dept}']]
 ........1
```

In above CRB, the content is from the SQL databases and the div and dept are the variables passed as the parameters. The <crml:cache> tag provide the caching information of the block that if two requests with the same div and dept value should get the same result. Besides, the keys could be a time-variation variable like following example that could delay the request in assigned time:

```
<crml:content id="query2">
 <crml:cache name="userquery" keys="~{#{min}/5}" />
 <crml:source type="sql">
  <crml:attr name="db" value="jdbc:db2:sample"/>
   [!CDATA[select id from users where div='@{div}' and
          dept='@{dept}']]
 ......
```

---

[1] To reduce the space, some tags and attributes are ignored.

The example shows a notation of Expression Variable, which could enclose an expression as a variable. In such example, the variable ~{#{min}/5} represent the value of the numbers of minutes from 1970 divide 5. The variable has the same value in the same block of 5 minutes and could reduce the effort of processing. Besides, the name of the cached element could let the CRBs in different CRML document share the same cache data. The scheme is suitable for the CRB, which is accessed frequently, but the real-time accuracy is not pretty important.

In fact, the cache should be invalidated when the data in the data source is changed. The fourth section of the paper will discuss the way of cache invalidation to insure the accuracy of the content.

3   Inter-CRB Communication and CRB Merging

The CRB is the content provider of the requested page, and the CRML processor will merge one or more CRBs into a complete document. A CRML document has its owned Document Type such as XHTML and the CRBs will replace some nodes in the document, which information is dynamic. The CRML not only define the CRB to reference the dynamic data sources but also define some Processing Instructions to provide some hints to processing the document.

3.1   Variables

The variables play an important role on generating dynamic content like some examples in previous section. In CRML framework, the only supported data type is string. The reason for this restriction is that both HTTP parameters and XML documents use string as their data type. The initial set of variables is from the HTTP request. All CRBs in the document could use the variables in the form of "@{variable name}". If a CRB want to pass some information to another CRB, it could change the value of the variables using the "crml:variable" tag like the following example:

```
<crml:content id="query2"
   xmlns:we="http://www.nctu.edu.tw/2000/CRML">
 <crml:source type="sql">
  <crml:attr name="db" value="jdbc:db2:sample"/>
   [!CDATA[select name from users where id='@{id}']]
 </crml:source>
 <crml:variable name="name" catch="RESULT/ROW[0]/id"/>
</crml:content>
```

The catch attribute use XPATH to specify the data to catch from the data from the data sources. If the result of the XPATH is a XML document, only the character part of the document will be used as the value of the variable. In addition to the substitution in CDATA section, the variables will be pass to XSLT processors and each CRB processor. The Expression Variable in section 2.2 is used to modify the variable before using them and reduce the complex of the framework. The System Variable started with pond symbol is used to reference some system variable like system time, which is read-only. If there is any error on retrieving the value of the variable, a string with zero length will be returned or set.

3.2   Concurrency Control

A CRB may need to wait another CRB to store its result in the variable. Another situation is that a CRB could not be processed safely when another CRB in the same CRML document is processing. Because the concurrent access to the same resources may lead to data inconsistency. In the first CRB in next example, the authorization is checked by the first CRB and the other CRB needs to wait the CRB, which do the authorization.

```
<crml:content id="auth">
<crml:concunrrency threadsafe="no"/>
 <crml:source type="sql">
  <crml:attr name="db" value="jdbc:db2:sample"/>
   [!CDATA[select name from users where id='@{id}' and
          password='@{PASSWD}']]
 </crml:source>
 <crml:variable name="name" catch="RESULT/ROW[0]/id"/>
 <crml:exception code="100" type="page">
  <?xml-stylesheet href="error.xsl" type="xsl"?>
  <error type="autherror">
   The User/Password you inputted is not correct !
  </error>
 </crml:exception>
</crml:content>

<crml:content id="secdata">
 <crml:concunrrency threadsafe="no" wait="auth"/>
 ......
</crml:content>
```

The threadsafe attribute in the "crml:concurrency" tag is used to specify if the CRB could be processed with another CRB. The wait attribute obviously is used to specify the CRBs to wait before process it. The default values of "threadsafe" and "wait" are "yes" and an empty list.

3.3   Exception Handling

Each data source may throw exceptions to CRML Processor when some errors rise. The "crml:exception" tag is used to handle the exception from CRML Processor. In the designed of CRML, each exception is identified by an integer. Like previous example, the exception code 100 will be caught and whole requested page will be replaced. If the value of the "type" is "crb" not "page", only the result of the CRB will be replaced.

When a page exception is raised and caught, all waiting CRBs will be canceled and the result of CRBs, which is done, will be discarded. The sequence of processing CRBs is undefined if the "crml:concurrency" tag is not specified and the first page exception will replace the whole result. In previous example, the waiting of authorization CRB could be removed since the fail of authorization will replace the secured data.

4   The Caching Mechanism

In the second section, how to cache a CRB is introduced but the assumption, that the content is not change, is made which is not reasonable for a dynamic web site. Usually, web server is just a part of the whole information system; the content may retrieve from database, which could be updated via other interfaces. To avoid return out-of-date information, we try to invalidate the entries that are updated.

4.1   Buffer Pool

In the CRML, each cache tag will reference to a named buffer pool, which contains a map from keys to XML document fragments. In the default, each buffer pool has a name generated by the CRML processor but the name could also be assigned by the CRML which may let different CRML source files access the same buffer pool.

4.2   Self-Invalidation

Some content has the information about modification date or expiration information, which could be used to invalidate the buffer. When the buffer pool is requested to provide the content with such information, the buffer pool will try to check the date between the original and the cached content to determinate that if the access to original is required.

The well-known content has such capability is file. A file contains the timestamp of the last modification, which could be used to verify the correctness of the information in the buffer pool. The effort to do the self-invalidation is much less than opening a file and processing it.

4.3   Event-Driven Invalidation

Another solution to insure the real-time content is Event-driven Invalidation. The method based on an event-driven bus on which the other part of the whole information system could broadcast the event. The buffer pools adapted for the bus could subscribe the event to invalidate the entries in the buffer pools.

The Fig. 2 is an example of the scenario, which the event source is a DBMS. An event generator could be set via the replication module on the DBMS to publish the event. The buffer pool will invalidate the buffer when it gets the event from the database, which indicates the modification of the data.

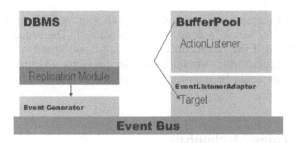

Fig. 2. Event-driven Invalidation

Such passive invalidation is not real-time accuracy but useful because the buffer pool don't need to check before response that may increase the response time. The time to trigger the modification could vary depended on the source. Usually, the replication module will fire the modification of the data each five to twenty minutes. If the applications, which modified the data could also fire the event, the time need to wait the correct information could less than five second.

5   Implementation for Parallel Processing

The CRML doesn't include the detail information about how to process a CRML source file and could be vary depended on the implementation. In this section, the implementation for parallel processing will be discussed to show the capability of the CRML.

5.1   The CRML Engine

The CRML Engine is the component to process a whole request. The architecture of the Engine is shown on Figure 3. The request will be associated with a CRML source file and be passed to the Engine with request parameters. The engine will try to use the page-level cache before process the CRML source file. If the cache is missed the engine will start to process the file.

First, the XSLT processor will be used if the pre-formatter or the post-formatter is assigned. Second, the compiler of the CRML will be invoked to compile the CRML source file and generate the access plan of the request. The access plan will be sent to the runtime and executed. Finally, if the result from the runtime contains other CRBs to process, the compiler will try to generate a access plan for next round.

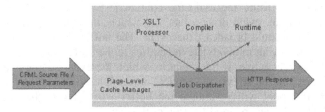

Fig. 3. The Architecture of the CRML Engine

The Access Plan

The Access Plan is some link-lists generated from the Compiler. According to the "concurrency" tag of each CRB, related CRBs will be put in the same link-list and in correct sequence. The plan will give the CRML runtime some information about how to execute the whole CRML file in a correct way.

The CRML Runtime

Like the Fig. 4, the access plan will be dispatched to several threads to execute. The CRB Executor is the core of each thread that executes the CRBs by the help of CRB Processors and Buffer Pools. The Result Collector could collect and manage the results and exceptions from each thread. The semaphores in the Result Collector also do the concurrency control.

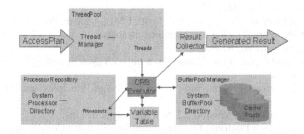

Fig. 4. The internal design of a CRML Runtime

5.2   Configuration for Distributed Environment

The previous focus of the Parallel Processing is the multi-thread processing in a single machine. This is helpful to decrease the response time because retrieving the data, such as a SQL query, needs to wait. If the multi-thread processing is applied, the CRB, which doesn't need to wait other CRB, could be processed together. If each thread could be separated to different machine, the benefit not only reduces the response time but also increases the capacity of the system.

6   Conclusions and Future Works

In this paper, we have presented the core of CRML, a distributed framework for XML-based Content Publishing. Comparing with other publishing framework or tools, CRML: 1) stresses the distributed architecture which could be used either to do the load balancing for a heavy traffic website or to perform multithread processing in a single machine to improve performance; 2) provides the block-level and content-independent cache for the data before processing which is a great improvement for fully-customized web service; 3) uses the emerging XML standards to process the XML-based data without any sequential programming language.

CRML is a part of WebEngine, a developing project of Web Content Management System. The concept of WCMS is like the DBMS, which both manage the data and handle the request. As the role of SQL in DBMS, the CRML is designed to describe what user wants to request not how to handle the request. Such spirit could let WebEngine improve the performance using a lot of techniques without change the original CRML source file. Since the CRML is used to request the content, the transaction management is not mentioned in the first version of design, which may be improved as future works.

References

1. John Akerley, Murtuza Hashim, Alexander Koutsoumbos, Anegelo Maffione: "Developing an e-business Application for the IBM WebSphere Application Server", IBM International Technical Support Organization (1999)
2. Tony Beveridge, Paul McGlashan: High Performance ISAPI/NSAPI Web Programming, Coriolis Group Books (1997)
3. Jim Conallen: Building Web Applications with UML, Addison Wesley (1999)
4. Bert Bos: XML representation of a relational database, http://www.w3.org/XML/RDB.html.
5. Eduardo Pelegri-Llopart, Larry Cable: Java Server Pages Specification Version 1.1, Sun Microsystems, Inc.
6. Doug Lea: Concurrent Programming in Java - Design Principles and Patterns, Addison-Wesly (2000)
7. Java Servlet Specification Version 2.2, Sun Microsystems, Inc.
8. Anne Thomas: Java 2 Platform, Enterprise Edition: Ensuring Consistency, Portability, and Interoperability, Patricia Seybold Group (1999)
9. XML Path Language Version 1.0, World Wide Web Consortium, November 1999, http://www.w3.org/TR/xpath.
10. Extensible Stylesheet Language (XSL) Version 1.0, World Wide Web Consortium, Mach 2000, http://www.w3.org/TR/xsl.
11. XSL Transformations (XSLT) Version 1.0, World Wide Web Consortium, November 1999. http://www.w3.org/TR/xslt.

A Rough Set-Aided System for Sorting WWW Bookmarks

Richard Jensen and Qiang Shen

Institute for Representation and Reasoning
Division of Informatics
The University of Edinburgh
Edinburgh EH1 1HN, UK

Abstract. Most people store 'bookmarks' to web pages. These allow the user to return to a web page later on, without having to remember the exact URL address. People attempt to organise their bookmark databases by filing bookmarks under categories, themselves arranged in a hierarchical fashion. As the maintenance of such large repositories is difficult and time-consuming, a tool that automatically categorises bookmarks is required. This paper investigates how rough set theory can help extract information out of this domain, for use in an experimental automatic bookmark classification system. In particular, work on rough set dependency degrees is applied to reduce the otherwise high dimensionality of the feature patterns used to characterize bookmarks. A comparison is made between this approach to data reduction and a conventional entropy-based approach.

1 Introduction

As the use of the Web becomes more prevalent and the size of personal repositories grows, adequately organising and managing bookmarks becomes crucial, somewhat analogous to the need to organise files in a private disk. Several years ago, in recognition of this problem, web browsers included support for tree-like folder structures for organising bookmarks. These enable the user to browse through their repository to find the necessary information. However manual URL classification and organisation can be difficult and tedious when there are more than a few bookmarks to classify - something that goes against the whole grain of the bookmarking concept.

An empirical study on users' World Wide Web page revisitation patterns (as reported in [1]) found that 58% of pages viewed are revisits. So over half of the instances where a user accesses a page, they are revisiting it (probably via their bookmark database). Another survey was carried out by the GVU's WWW Surveying Team [2] to determine which bookmarking activities are performed by different groups of people. Most respondents create entries (86%), delete entries (74%), create folders (70%) and rearrange entries (63%), with only 4% saying that they do not use them at all. Those creating sub-folders, however, were comparatively low.

N. Zhong et al. (Eds.): WI 2001, LNAI 2198, pp. 95–105, 2001.
© Springer-Verlag Berlin Heidelberg 2001

This suggests that although people spend time creating and rearranging their bookmarks, the hierarchy tends to have a shallow tree-like structure. This could be for the following reasons:

- Many usability studies, for example [3], indicate that a deep hierarchy results in less efficient information retrieval as many traversal steps are required, so users are more likely to make mistakes.
- Users do not have the time/patience to arrange their collection into a well-ordered hierarchy. Also, if the tree has been ordered and is quite deep, it can take too long to traverse the sub-folders to reach the desired bookmark.

It seems, then, that there is a need for a tool that can automatically create folders and sub-folders and classify bookmarks into them. Surprisingly, few such systems are in existence; two worth noting are the BOOKMARK ORGANISER [4] and POWERBOOKMARKS [5]. However, these approaches rely on information other than that contained in the bookmark databases. Both applications use the information contained in the documents pointed to by the URLs in order to generate classifications.

Many classification problems involve high dimensional descriptions of input features. It is therefore not surprising that much research has been done on dimensionality reduction. However, existing work tends to destroy the underlying semantics of the features after reduction (e.g. transformation-based approaches [6]) or require additional information about the given data set for thresholding (e.g. entropy-based approaches [7]). A technique that can reduce dimensionality using information contained within the data set and preserving the meaning of the features is clearly desirable. Rough set theory can be used as such a tool to discover data dependencies and reduce the number of attributes contained in a dataset by purely structural methods.

The rest of this paper is structured as follows. Section 2 introduces the main approach to dimensionality reduction, namely *Rough Set Attribute Reduction* and also highlights the operation of an additional technique, *Entropy-based Reduction*. The modular design of the bookmark classification system is described in section 3; each module involved is detailed. Section 4 presents the experimental results obtained and section 5 concludes the paper and mentions some important future work.

2   Dimensionality Reduction

The datasets generated in Information Retrieval systems tend to be extremely large, rendering most classifiers intractable. This results in the need for a mechanism that will greatly reduce the dimensionality of these datasets, whilst retaining important information. To be self-contained, this section presents those techniques that have been developed for this purpose.

2.1   Rough Set-Based Reduction

A rough set [8] is an approximation of a vague concept by a pair of precise concepts, called lower and upper approximations (which are a classification of the domain of interest into disjoint categories). The classification formally represents knowledge about the problem domain. Objects belonging to the same category characterized by the same attributes (or features) are not distinguishable.

Central to Rough Set Attribute Reduction (RSAR) is the concept of indiscernibility. Let $I = (U, A)$ be an information system, where $\mathbf{U}$ is a non-empty set of finite objects (the universe). A is a non-empty finite set of attributes such that $a : \mathbf{U} \to V_a$ for every $a \in A$; V_a is the value set for attribute a. In a decision system, $A = \{C \cup D\}$ where C is the set of conditional attributes and D is the set of decision attributes. With any $P \subseteq A$ there is an associated equivalence relation $IND(P)$:

$$IND(P) = \{(x, y) \in U^2 \mid \forall a \in P \, a(x) = a(y)\} \tag{1}$$

If $(x, y) \in IND(P)$, then x and y are indiscernible by attributes from P. The equivalence classes of the P-indiscernibility relation are denoted $[x]_P$. Let $X \subseteq U$, the P-*lower* approximation of a set can now be defined as:

$$\underline{P}X = \{x \mid [x]_P \subseteq X\} \tag{2}$$

Let P and Q be equivalence relations over $\mathbf{U}$, then the positive region can be defined as:

$$POS_P(Q) = \bigcup_{X \in \mathbf{U}/Q} \underline{P}X \tag{3}$$

The positive region contains all objects of $\mathbf{U}$ that can be classified to classes of $\mathbf{U}/Q$ using the knowledge in attributes P.

An important issue in data analysis is discovering dependencies between attributes. Intuitively, a set of attributes Q depends totally on a set of attributes P, denoted $P \Rightarrow Q$, if all attribute values from Q are uniquely determined by values of attributes from P. If there exists a functional dependency between values of Q and P, then Q depends totally on P. Dependency can be defined in the following way:

For $P, Q \subset A$, Q depends on P in a degree k $(0 \leq k \leq 1)$, denoted $P \Rightarrow_k Q$, if

$$k = \gamma_P(Q) = \frac{|POS_P(Q)|}{|\mathbf{U}|} \tag{4}$$

If $k = 1$ Q depends totally on P, if $k < 1$ Q depends partially (in a degree k) on P, and if $k = 0$ Q does not depend on P.

By calculating the change in dependency when an attribute is removed from the set of considered conditional attributes, a measure of the significance of the attribute can be obtained. The higher the change in dependency, the more significant the attribute is. If the significance is 0, then the attribute is dispensable. More formally, given P, Q and an attribute $x \in P$,

$$\sigma_P(Q, x) = \gamma_P(Q) - \gamma_{P-\{x\}}(Q) \tag{5}$$

The reduction of attributes is achieved by comparing equivalence relations generated by sets of attributes. Attributes are removed so that the reduced set provides the same quality of classification as the original. A *reduct* is defined as a subset R of the conditional attribute set C such that $\gamma_R(D) = \gamma_C(D)$. A given dataset may have many attribute reduct sets, so the set R of all reducts is defined as:

$$\mathsf{R} = \{X : X \subseteq C, \gamma_X(D) = \gamma_C(D)\} \tag{6}$$

The intersection of all the sets in R is called the *core*, the elements of which are those attributes that cannot be eliminated without introducing more contradictions to the dataset. In RSAR, a reduct with minimum cardinality is searched for; in other words an attempt is made to locate a single element of the minimal reduct set $\mathsf{R}_{min} \subseteq \mathsf{R}$:

$$\mathsf{R}_{\mathsf{min}} = \{X : X \in \mathsf{R}, \forall Y \in \mathsf{R}, |X| \leq |Y|\} \tag{7}$$

A basic way of achieving this is to calculate the dependencies of all possible subsets of C. Any subset with $\gamma(D) = 1$ is a reduct; the smallest subset with this property is a minimal reduct. However, for large datasets this method is impractical and an alternative strategy is required.

1. $R \leftarrow \{\}$
2. do
3. $T \leftarrow R$
4. $\forall x \in (C - R)$
5.   if $\gamma_{R\cup\{x\}}(D) > \gamma_T(D)$
6. $T \leftarrow R \cup \{x\}$
7. $R \leftarrow T$
8. until $\gamma_R(D) = \gamma_C(D)$
9. return R

Fig. 1. The QUICKREDUCT Algorithm

The QUICKREDUCT algorithm [9] attempts to calculate a minimal reduct without exhaustively generating all possible subsets. It starts off with an empty set and adds in turn those attributes that result in the greatest increase in $\gamma_P(Q)$, until this produces its maximum possible value for the dataset (usually 1). However, it has been proved that this method does not always generate a *minimal* reduct, as $\gamma_P(Q)$ is not a perfect heuristic. It does result in a close-to-minimal reduct, though, which is still useful in greatly reducing dataset dimensionality.

An intuitive understanding of QUICKREDUCT implies that, for a dimensionality of n, $n!$ evaluations of the dependency function may be performed for the worst-case dataset. From experimentation, the average complexity has been determined to be approximately O(n).

2.2 Entropy-Based Reduction

To support the comparative study of the performance of RSAR for use in bookmark classification, the Entropy-based Reduction (EBR) technique is summarised here. This approach is based on the entropy heuristic employed by machine learning techniques such as ID3 [10]. A similar approach has been adopted in [11] where an entropy measure is used for ranking features.

EBR is concerned with examining a dataset and determining those attributes that provide the most gain in information. The entropy of attribute A (which can take values $a_1...a_m$) with respect to the conclusion C (values $c_1...c_n$) is defined as:

$$E(A) = - \sum_{j=1}^{m} p(a_j) \sum_{i=1}^{n} p(c_i|a_j) \; log_2 \; p(c_i|a_j) \qquad (8)$$

Using this function, the entropy of each conditional attribute appearing in a decision table can be calculated. The attribute with the lowest entropy is deemed to be the one that has the highest information gain, and so is the most useful determiner. By selecting only a certain number of attributes with the lowest entropies, a reduct[1] for the dataset can be constructed. Note that the determination of the number of attributes required to construct the reduct needs additional information other than given in the dataset.

In this work, for comparison, such a number is decided on by the size of a reduct produced by the rough set-based approach (which is solely determined by the dataset itself).

3   Bookmark Classification System Design

The application of rough sets to the domain of text classification has been attempted previously with some success [12], but has not yet been applied to bookmark classification. Bookmark databases are very information-poor, the useful information can only be found in the URL and title fields. Therefore, steps must be taken to ensure that all relevant information is used in the classification process, with any misleading or useless data removed.

The sorting system developed here is modular in structure, allowing various sub-components to be replaced with alternative implementations if the need arises. The main modules are *Keyword Acquisition*, *Dimensionality Reduction* and *Classification*.

---

[1] The term 'reduct' is used loosely here.

To clarify the operation of the system, an example is included. The following bookmark is one of many contained in a database under the category *Programming/Java*:

<A HREF="http://java.sun.com/Performance/">
Ways to Increase Java Performance</A>

3.1   Keyword Acquisition

In order to compare the similarity of bookmarks, a suitable representation must be chosen. Each bookmark is considered to be a vector where the ith element is the weight of term i according to some weighting method (a metric). The size of the vector is equal to the total number of keywords determined from the training documents.

This module produces weight-term pairs given a dataset. Each encountered word in a URL or title field is assigned a weight according to the metric used. Several metrics were implemented for this purpose:

- *Boolean Existential Metric.* All keywords that exist in the document are given a weight of 1, those that are absent are assigned 0 [15].
- *Frequency Count Metric.* The normalized frequency of the keywords in the document is used as the weight [14].
- *TF-IDF.* The Term Frequency-Inverse Document Frequency Metric [16] assigns higher weights to those keywords that occur frequently in the current document but not in most others. It is calculated using the formula: $w(t,i) = F_i(t) \times log\frac{N}{N_t}$ where $F_i(t)$ is the frequency of term t in document i, N is the number of documents in the collection, and N_t is the total number of documents that contain t.

For the example bookmark, the keywords {*java,sun,com,performance*} are obtained from the URL, and the keywords {*ways,increase,java,performance*} from the title field. Using the simple boolean existential metric, the vector elements relating to these keywords will each contain the value 1, the remainder 0.

The resulting sets of weight-term pairs, no matter which keyword acquisition metric is adopted, are large in size and need to be greatly reduced to be of any practical use for classification. Hence, the next step: *Dimensionality Reduction.*

3.2   Dimensionality Reduction

Given the weight-term sets, this module aims to significantly reduce their size whilst retaining their information content and preserving the semantics of those remaining keywords. As mentioned earlier, two approaches have been developed for this purpose, namely *RSAR* and *EBR*. Once a reduct has been calculated, the dataset can then be reduced by deleting those attributes that are absent from the reduct. The reduced dataset is now in a form that can be used by the classification module.

Returning to the example, it may be decided by this module that the term "com" provides little or no useful information. The column relating to this term is removed from the main dataset. This process is repeated for all keywords deemed to be information-poor.

3.3   Classification

This module attempts to classify a given bookmark or bookmarks using the reduced keyword datasets obtained by the dimensionality reduction stage. Each bookmark has been transformed into a weight-term vector by the keyword acquisition process. For comparison purposes, three different inference techniques were implemented to perform classification:

- *Boolean Inexact Model* [15]. This uses Boolean matching and scoring techniques. If a term exists in a document and is also present in the corresponding rule, then the score for that rule is increased; the rule with the highest score classifies the document.
- *Vector Space Model*. The vector space model [17] procedure can be divided in to three stages. The first stage is document indexing, where content bearing terms are extracted from the document text. The second stage is the weighting of the indexed terms to enhance retrieval of documents relevant to the user. The last stage ranks the document with respect to the query according to the similarity measure. The similarity measure used here is the cosine coefficient, which measures the angle between the rule vector and the query vector, and is defined as:

$$Sim(X, Y) = \frac{|X \cap Y|}{\sqrt{|X|}\sqrt{|Y|}} \qquad (9)$$

- *Fuzzy Reasoner*. This follows the usual approach for the construction of fuzzy rule-based systems [18]. Reasoning is carried out by the fuzzy classifier using the dataset generated previously. All precondition memberships are evaluated, and the necessary logical conjunctions integrated (using the conventional minimum operator in the present implementation of the system). The rule with the highest score classifies the document.

4   Results

A large set of bookmarks was used as the training dataset. This database was generated by collating various online bookmark lists into one uniform collection. Each bookmark is pre-classified into a relevant category (for example, "Sports" or "Computing/Java"). An additional testing dataset of "unseen" bookmarks was also compiled from online resources.

The experiments presented here attempt to test whether RSDR is a useful tool for reducing data whilst retaining the information content. Additionally, experiments are carried out that compare the performance of RSDR with that of using EBR. Random-reduct (RR) generation (i.e. generating reducts randomly) was also used to compare the results. This method deletes random attributes from the dataset, but is constrained to leave the same number of attributes present as the RSAR method. The results of these approaches can be found in table 2.

The classification modules (vector space model (VSM), boolean inexact model (BIM) and the fuzzy reasoner (FR)) are combined in order to improve the accuracy of the system; each combination is investigated.

Table 1. Comparison of Unreduced and RS-reduced classification accuracy

Dataset	Attributes (URL)	Attributes (Title)
Unreduced	1397	1283
RS-reduced	514	424

From table 1 it can be seen that using rough set theory, the amount of attributes was reduced to around 35%. For email classification, the average reduction of attributes was 3.5 orders of magnitude. This demonstrates that there is much less redundancy in the original datasets for the bookmark domain, which is intuitive as there is much less information in a bookmark than a document.

Table 2. Comparison of reduction strategies with unreduced dataset

Dataset	VSM + BIM	VSM + FR	FR + BIM
Unreduced	55.6%	49.7%	45.0%
RS-reduced	49.1%	47.3%	42.0%
EBR-reduced	50.9%	52.7%	43.2%
RR-reduced	37.3%	34.9%	26.3%

A comparison of the performance of the dimensionality reduction techniques is presented in table 2. The table shows that the overall accuracy is poor (obviously, the random reduction gives worst results). The main point to make here is that the ability of the system to classify new data depends entirely on the quality (and to a certain extent the quantity) of the training data. It cannot, in general, be expected that the RS-reduced or the EBR-reduced experiments should perform much better than the original unreduced dataset, which itself only allows a rather low classification rate.

In light of the fact that bookmarks contain very little useful information, the results are unsurprising and perhaps a little better than anticipated. As stated earlier, the goal is to investigate how useful rough set theory is in reducing the training dataset. For this, it is interesting to compare how well the rough set-reduced approach fares against the unreduced dataset. Consider the unreduced dataset results to be the optimum, the table can then be rewritten as:

Table 3. Comparison of reduction strategies

Dataset	VSM + BIM	VSM + FR	FR + BIM
RS-reduced	88.3%	95.2%	93.3%
EBR-reduced	91.5%	106%	96.0%
RR-reduced	67.1%	70.2%	58.4%

Viewed this way, it can be seen that EBR has the best results for each classifier pair, and is in fact better than the unreduced dataset in one instance. This could be due to the fact that EBR selects those attributes that provide the largest gain in information. This process might ignore otherwise misleading attributes that the unreduced dataset contains. The RS-reduced dataset can be thought of as a smaller version of the original dataset, and so this will fall prey to the same mistakes.

Importantly, the performance of the RS-reduced dataset is almost as good. Although a very small amount of important information may have been lost in the rough set reduction approach, this information loss is not significant enough to reduce classification accuracy significantly, while the reduction of dimensionality is substantial.

The success of EBR in generating useful reducts is a little surprising, due to its straightforward approach. As an alternative data reduction technique, it fares well against RSDR. However, with EBR a threshold needs to be specified beforehand. With no RSDR reducts to estimate this value, there is no method available for discovering the appropriate number of attributes that should appear. Another drawback with EBR is that it cannot find more than one possible reduct, which is perfectly fine for applications such as this, but may not be for more theoretical investigations.

5 Conclusion

Results clearly show that rough set theory can be used to significantly reduce the dimensionality of the training dataset without much loss in information content. The measured drop in classification accuracy was between 0.6% and 4% for the training dataset, which is within acceptable bounds.

The main limitation of this system is that it will only be as good as the training dataset itself. Ideally, a much larger database of bookmarks would have been used, but this would have required far too much time. It is not known how long it would take the QUICKREDUCT algorithm to find a reduct for such a large dataset as it takes many hours to find one for the existing training dataset. A related problem is how to effectively handle the dynamic aspect of bookmarking. Typically, a user's collection changes gradually over time, so an interesting extension to this work would be to incorporate these types of changes into the the learning framework.

It has already been mentioned that the QUICKREDUCT algorithm is not always guaranteed to find a minimal reduct. One potential solution to this problem is to include an N-lookahead step before choosing the next attribute. This and other approaches are being investigated, including the use of distinction tables to determine the choice of attribute. Work is also being carried out that focuses on improving the speed and efficiency of QUICKREDUCT. A promising research area being investigated is that of fuzzifying reducts [19]. This could be achieved by fuzzifying the dependency degree (the γ function), using fuzzy-rough sets.

Acknowledgements. The authors are grateful to the UK EPSRC for their support of this research, under grant 99407338 and 00317404. They are also very grateful to Alexios Chouchoulas for helpful discussions and contributions, whilst taking full responsibility of the views expressed in this paper.

References

1. L. Tauscher and S. Greenberg, Revisitation patterns in World Wide Web navigation, in: Proc. 1997 ACM CHI Conference, Atlanta, GA, March 1997.
2. Georgia Tech Research Corporation, GVU's 8th WWW User Survey, 1997, information available at http://www.gvu.gatech.edu/user_surveys/survey-1997-10/
3. K. Larson and M. Czerwinski, Web page design: implications of memory, structure and scent for information retrieval, in: Proc. 1998 ACM SIGCHI Conf. on Human Factors in Computing Systems, Los Angeles, CA, April 1998, pp. 25-32.
4. Y. S. Maarek, I. Z. Ben Shaul. Automatically Organizing Bookmarks per Contents. Fifth International World Wide Web Conference 1996, Paris, France. http://www5conf.inria.fr/fich_html/papers/P37/Overview.html
5. W. Li, Q. Vu, D. Agrawal, Y. Hara, H. Takano. PowerBookmarks: a system for personalizable Web information organization, sharing, and management. Proceedings of the Eighth International World Wide Web Conference, Toronto, Canada, 11-14 May 1999, ISBN 0-444-50264-5.
6. P. Devijver and J. Kittler, (1982) *Pattern Recognition: A Statistical Approach.* Prentice Hall.
7. T. Mitchell (1997) *Machine Learning.* McGraw-Hill.
8. Z. Pawlak. Rough Sets: Theoretical Aspects of Reasoning About Data. Kluwer Academic Publishing, Dordrecht, 1991.
9. Q. Shen and A. Chouchoulas. A Modular Approach to Generating Fuzzy Rules with Reduced Attributes for the Monitoring of Complex Systems. Engineering Applications of Artificial Intelligence, 13(3):263-278, 2000.
10. J.R. Quinlan. Induction of Decision Trees. Machine Learning 1(1), pp. 81-106. 1986.

11. M. Dash, H. Liu, J. Yao. Dimensionality Reduction of Unsupervised Data. Proceedings of the 9th International Conference on Tools with Artificial Intelligence (ICTAI'97).
12. A. Chouchoulas and Q. Shen. Rough set-aided keyword reduction for text categorisation. Applied Artificial Intelligence, 2001.
13. H. S. Heaps, Information retrieval, computational and theoretical aspects. Academic Press, 1978.
14. G. Salton, Introduction to Modern Information Retrieval. McGraw-Hill, 1983.
15. G. Salton, E. A. Fox, and H. Wu, (Cornell Technical Report TR82-511) Extended Boolean Information Retrieval. Cornell University. August 1982.
16. G. Salton, and C. Buckley. Term Weighting Approaches in Automatic Text Retrieval. Technical Report TR87-881, Department of Computer Science, Cornell University, 1987. Information Processing and Management Vol.32 (4), p. 431-443, 1996.
17. C.J. van Rijsbergen. Information Retrieval. Butterworths, London, United Kingdom, 1979. http://www.dcs.gla.ac.uk/Keith/Preface.html.
18. W. Pedrycz, and F. Gomide. An Introduction to Fuzzy Sets: Analysis and Design. The MIT Press, 1998.
19. R. Jensen. Rough-Fuzzy Methods for Determining Fuzzy Reducts. Project Report. The University of Edinburgh, 2001.

Average-Clicks: A New Measure of Distance on the World Wide Web

Yutaka Matsuo[1,2], Yukio Ohsawa[2,3], and Mitsuru Ishizuka[1]

[1] University of Tokyo, Hongo 7-3-1, Bunkyo-ku, Tokyo 113-8656, JAPAN,
matsuo@miv.t.u-tokyo.ac.jp,
http://www.miv.t.u-tokyo.ac.jp/ matsuo/
[2] TOREST, Japan Science and Technology Corporation,
Tsutsujigaoka 2-2-11, Miyagino-ku, Sendai, Miyagi, 983-0852 Japan,
[3] University of Tsukuba, Otsuka 3-29-1, Bunkyo-ku, Tokyo 113-0012, JAPAN

Abstract. The pages and hyperlinks of the World Wide Web may be viewed as nodes and edges in a directed graph. In this paper, we propose a new definition of the distance between two pages, called *average-clicks*. It is based on the probability to click a link through random surfing. We compare the average-clicks measure to the classical measure of clicks between two pages, and show average-clicks fits better to the users' intuitions of distance.

1 Introduction

The World Wide Web provides considerable auxiliary information on top of the text of the Web pages, such as its link structure. There has been a fair amount of recent activity on how to exploit the link structure of the Web. Kleinberg distinguished between two types of Web sites which pertain to a certain search topic: *hubs* and *authorities*. A good hub is a page that points to many good authorities and a good authority is a page that is pointed to by many good hubs [8]. The hub scores and authority scores are determined by an iterative procedure. The pages with the highest scores are returned as hubs and authorities for the search topic.

The Google[1] search engine uses the link structure for ranking Web pages, called PageRank [4]. A page has high rank if the sum of the ranks of its backlinks is high. And the rank of a page is divided among its forward links evenly to contribute to the ranks of the pages they point to. PageRank is a global ranking of all Web pages, regardless of their content, based solely on their location in the Web's graph structure.

Most of these works, which analyze the structure of the Web graph, assume the length of each link to be 1 (unit), and the clicks between two pages are counted to measure the distance. For example, [8] finds the bipartite core, which is a densely linked community consisting of a set of authorities and a set of hubs within 1 click. [1] shows that two randomly chosen documents on the web are

---

[1] http://google.com

N. Zhong et al. (Eds.): WI 2001, LNAI 2198, pp. 106–114, 2001.
© Springer-Verlag Berlin Heidelberg 2001

on average 19 clicks away from each other. However, the distance measured by the number of clicks doesn't reflect well the users' intuition of distance. Some pages have incredibly large amount of links, while most pages have 10 or less links [5]. For users, it requires a great effort to find and click a link among a large number of links than a link among a couple of links. If we count a minimal clicks to measure the distance between two pages, the path is likely to include link collections, such as Yahoo![2] directories.

In this paper, we propose a new definition of the distance between two pages, called *average-clicks* instead of the classical "clicks" measure. This measure reflects how many "average clicks" are needed from a page to another page. An average-click is one click among n links[3]. And two average-clicks is a distance of two successive clicks among n links for each, or one click among n^2 links. The average-click is defined on the probability for a "random surfer" to reach the page, based on the same idea as PageRank: A random surfer keeps clicking on successive links at random. The probability for a random surfer in page p to click one of the links in page p is considered as $1/OutDegree(p)$ in this model, (ignoring the damping factor). We annotate the link in page p with the length of $-log_n(1/OutDegree(p))$, so that summing lengths is akin to multiplying probabilities. An average-click is a unit distance of this measure.

If we measure the distance by average-clicks, the path through a large link collection can be considered long even if it takes only a couple of clicks. On the contrary, the path in a lines of pages is considered short even if many clicks are necessary. This fits very well to the users' intuition of distance. We show by questionnaires that our average-clicks is a better model to approximate the users' intuition than the classical clicks measure.

In the following section, the definition of average-clicks is explained in detail. In Section 3, we show some examples and a questionnaire data analysis on the user's concept of distance. We discuss related works and the possible application of average-clicks in Section 4, and conclude the paper.

2   Average-Clicks

When analyzing the Web as a graph, we are confronted by the diversity of the links. There are not only topic related links, but also intra domain links, commercial/sponsor links, and so on. Some pages have more than a hundred of links, while others have a few or no links. The variety is so wide that we want to classify these links by some means. Here we define the length of a link using only the number of the links in a page, inspired by the PageRank algorithm.

PageRank makes a probability distribution over Web pages, based on the simple idea that a "random surfer" keeps clicking on successive links at random. The probability to click each link in page p is $\alpha/OutDegree(p)$, where α is a

---

[2] http://www.yahoo.com

[3] In this paper, we set n to be 7 due to the fact that the average page has roughly seven hyperlinks to other pages.

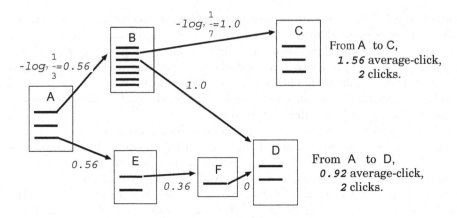

Fig. 1. Average-clicks and clicks.

damping factor and $OutDegree(p)$ is the number of links page p has. In probability $1 - \alpha$, a random surfer jumps to a random Web page. Following [10] α is usually set to be 0.85, however, we set $\alpha = 1$ below for simplicity[4].

We annotate a link with the length as negative logarithm of probability, so that summing lengths is akin to multiplying probabilities.

Definition 1. *A length of a link in page p is defined as*

$$-log_n(\alpha/OutDegree(p)).$$

We set the base of the logarithm n to be 7 in this paper, due to the fact that the average page has roughly seven hyperlinks to other pages [2][5]. We call a unit of the length an *average-click*.

The distance between two pages p and q is defined by the shortest path. From a probabilistic point of view, this is equivalent to focus only on the path with the largest probability for a random surfer to get from page p to page q.

Definition 2. *The* distance *from p to q is the sum of the length of the shortest path from p to q.*

Fig. 1 illustrates some pages and the links between them. Page A has three links, thus the length of each link is $-\log_7(1/3) \approx 0.56$ average-click. As page B has seven links, the length is each 1 average-click. Summing 0.56 and 1, the distance from A to C is 1.56 average-click. In the case of page D, there is two paths from page A to D. The average-clicks is smaller in the lower path, though it takes three clicks. The shortest path in terms of average-clicks is the lower

---

[4] We are aware that setting $\alpha = 1$ means that the users always click on a page. A more realistic assumption is that there is some probability α of following a link. However, since we don't have enough statistical results yet to decide α, we set simply $\alpha = 1$.

[5] The latest survey shows the average page has 1 external link and 4 internal links [9].

path, while the path with minimal clicks is the upper path. Note that if a page has only one link, as page F, the length of the link is 0 average-click.

This model offers a very good approximation to our intuitive concept of distance between Web pages. For example, Yahoo! top-page has currently more than 180 links. In our definition, the length from the top-page to each sub-page is very far, as the upper path in Fig. 1. On the other hand, the path length by the local relation, such as the link to one's friends or the link to one's interests, is estimated rather short, as in the lower path of the figure. Intuitively we think the path through the Yahoo! top-page is longer than the path along the acquaintance chain with the same clicks. In our model, page C is more distant from page A than page D, and this fits very well to our intuition.

3   Case Study and Experimental Results

3.1   Examples of the Distance

In this section, we show some examples of the distance between two pages by the average-clicks measure. We first implement the best-first algorithm to search the shortest path from page s (stated as *start page*) to page t (stated as *target page*), as shown in Fig.2.

```
function SEARCH_SHORTEST_PATH (start_page, target_page, d_thre)
    α ← 1.0,    n ← 7.
    list ← ADD_LIST(start_page, empty),   d(start_page) ← 0.
    p ← start_page
    while p ≠ target_page
        Fetch page p and extract links which points to page p_k (k = 1,...,n_p)
        for k ← 1 to n_p
            d(p_k) ← d(p) − log_n(α/n_p)
            if d(p_k) > d_thre then next
            list ← ADD_LIST(p_k, list)
        end
        if list is empty return failure
        p ← CHOOSE_MINIMAL(list, d)
    end
    return d(target_page)
```

ADD_LIST($a, list$) is a function which add a to $list$.
CHOOSE_MINIMAL($list, d$) is a function which choose $a \in list$ minimizing $d(a)$.
d_{thre} is the range of the search space.

Fig. 2. The best first search for the shortest path.

Table 1 shows an example of the distance from one of the author's homepage. This homepage, "www.miv.t.u-tokyo.ac.jp/ matsuo," stated below as page a,

Table 1. The distance measured by average-clicks from page a.

To URL Shortest path	Cumulative distance (average-clicks)
One of the author's colleagues	
http://www.miv.t.u-tokyo.ac.jp/~matumura/	1.62
http://www.miv.t.u-tokyo.ac.jp/JAICO/	1.13
http://www.miv.t.u-tokyo.ac.jp/ matsuo	0.0
Yahoo! (Japanese site)	
http://www.yahoo.co.jp/	3.02
http://www.geocities.co.jp/Athlete-Athene/6353/whatsnew.html	2.67
http://www.geocities.co.jp/Athlete-Athene/6353/	1.13
http://www.miv.t.u-tokyo.ac.jp/ matsuo	0.0
Japanese Society of Artificial Intelligence homepage	
http://www.nacsis.ac.jp/jsai/	4.69
http://www.miv.t.u-tokyo.ac.jp/ yabuki/	2.54
http://www.miv.t.u-tokyo.ac.jp/member/present-mem.htm	1.13
http://www.miv.t.u-tokyo.ac.jp/ matsuo	0.0
International Joint Conference on AI homepage	
http://ijcai.org/	5.39
http://w3.sys.es.osaka-u.ac.jp/ osawa/AIlinks.html	3.33
http://www.gssm.otsuka.tsukuba.ac.jp/staff/osawa	1.97
http://www.miv.t.u-tokyo.ac.jp/ matumura/research.html	1.62
http://www.miv.t.u-tokyo.ac.jp/JAICO/	1.13
http://www.miv.t.u-tokyo.ac.jp/ matsuo	0.0
WI-2001 homepage	
http://kis.maebashi-it.ac.jp/wi01	10.40
http://internet.aist-nara.ac.jp/research/security/	8.14
http://iplab.aist-nara.ac.jp/research.html.en	7.06
http://iplab.aist-nara.ac.jp/	5.80
http://shika.aist-nara.ac.jp/	4.13
http://www.miv.t.u-tokyo.ac.jp/ santi/oohm.html	2.54
http://www.miv.t.u-tokyo.ac.jp/member/present-mem.htm	1.13
http://www.miv.t.u-tokyo.ac.jp/ matsuo	0.0

is located on the server at Tokyo University in Japan. The results showed the following:

- The search is not trapped into the link collection.
- The distance by average-clicks seems to fit well to our intuitive concept of distance. In other words, pages familiar to the author of page a are estimated to be near, and unfamiliar pages are estimated to be distant.
- The shortest path is very informative for the author in that it provides the indirect relation of two pages.

For example, the distance to one of the author's colleagues or Yahoo! is small, and they are very familiar to the author. The IJCAI homepage is more distant than the JSAI homepage. In fact, we participate in JSAI events more. The distance to WI-2001 is very far now, however, it might get shorter in the future for the very reason that we are submitting this paper to WI-2001.

3.2 Evaluation by Questionnaires

This section shows a preliminary report on the quantitative evaluation using questionnaires. We asked five participants to rank the pages according to their perceived familiarity.

First we pick up 30 pages randomly which we can obtain within a few clicks from each participant's homepage. Then, we asked him/her to answer how familiar each URL of the page is, without providing the contents of the pages or any distance measures. Answers to the questions were made on a 5-point Likert-scale from 1 (very familiar) to 5 (very distant). After the questionnaires, we compared the rating with the distance measure of clicks and average-clicks.

Fig. 3 and 4 shows the scatter plot of the results by participant 1. We can see very clearly that the rating is correlated with the average-clicks measure. On the other hand, the classical clicks measure doesn't seem to have a strong correlation with the ratings. The statistical results of five participants are shown in Table 2, which shows correlation coefficients: If the correlation coefficient is close to 1, there is a strong positive correlation between two sets of data, and if the correlation coefficient is 0, there is no relationship. We can see from the table that the average-clicks have stronger correlation with the users' rating.

4 Discussion

In [6], the weight of a link is defined by referring to the text of the page: if the text in the vicinity of the "href" contains text descriptive of the topic at hand, the weight of the link is increased. This weighing algorithm requires the text analysis of a page, while our average-clicks measure requires only the number of links.

The average-clicks measure is another usage of the probability distribution by a random surfer model. To transform the probability into the length of a link, we can imagine more precisely the structure of the graph. This type of length (or cost) assignment is very common in the context of cost-based abduction, where finding the MAP (maximum a posteriori probability) solution is equivalent to finding the minimal cost explanation for a set of facts [7].

Many researchers now employ clicks as the measure of distance, however, it seems reasonable to use average-clicks instead. For example, when finding a

Table 2. The correlation coefficient of participants' rating and clicks/average-clicks.

Participant	Clicks	Average-clicks
1	0.524	0.836
2	0.696	0.715
3	0.517	0.699
4	0.325	0.804
5	0.471	0.685

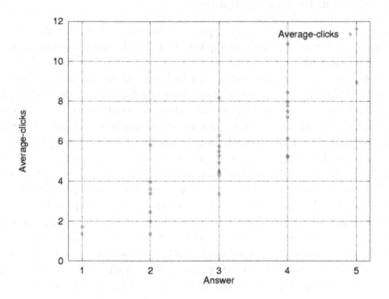

Fig. 3. Scatter plot of answers and average-clicks by participant 1.

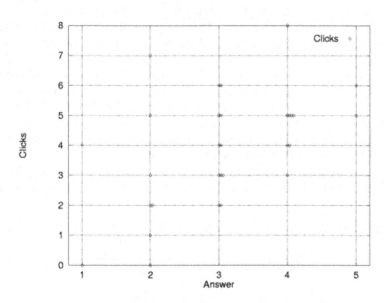

Fig. 4. Scatter plot of ansers and clicks by participant 1.

community on the Web, the general topics pages are likely to be included [3]. However, employing the average-clicks measure, the general topics pages are considered to be distant and can be filtered out, because such pages have usually many links[6]. Fetching the neighboring pages is a common procedure in many algorithms. We should fetch the pages within a given threshold of average-clicks, not within a given threshold of clicks. A given threshold of clicks means sometimes an incredibly large range of the search. Average-clicks measure provides a good justification of the practical search, such as "if there are few links, fetch the pages, but if there are many links, give up."

The classical clicks measure is intuitively understandable for all Internet users, while the distance based on the probability is relatively difficult to understand. That's why we bring semantics by setting the base of the logarithm to the average number of links in a page: The distance shows how many "average clicks" are needed from one page to another page.

5   Conclusion

In this paper, we have proposed a new measure, called average-clicks, and evaluate it by measuring the users' intuition of distance. By modelling the Web structure more precisely, many research fields will benefit from search engines to customized browsers. One of our future works is to estimate the value of a link using the average-clicks measure.

References

1. L. A. Adamic. The small world web. In *Proc. ECDL'99*, pages 443–452, 1999.
2. K. Bharat and A. Broder. A technique for measuring the relative size and overlap of public web search engines. In *Proc. 7th WWW Conf.*, 1998.
3. K. Bharat and M. R. Henzinger. Improved algorithms for topic distillation in a hyperlinked environment. In *Proc. 21st ACM SIGIR conf.*, pages 104–111, 1998.
4. S. Brin and L. Page. The anatomy of a large-scale hypertextual web search engine. In *Proc. 7th WWW Conf.*, 1998.
5. A. Broder, R. Kumar, F. Maghoul, P. Raghavan, S. Rajagopalan, R. Stata, A. Tomkins, and J. Wiener. Graph structure in the web. In *Proc. 9th WWW Conf.*, 2000.
6. S. Chakrabarti, B. Dom, P. Raghavan, S. Rajagopalan, D. Gibson, and J. Kleinberg. Automatic resource compilation by analyzing hyperlink structure and associated text. In *Proc. 7th WWW Conf.*, 1998.
7. E. Charniak and S. E. Shimony. Cost-based abduction and MAP explanation. *Artificial Intelligence*, 66:345–374, 1994.

---

[6] The power law distribution on the Web says that the number of nodes with high out degrees is much less than the number of nodes with low degrees[5]. However we can't ignore these pages with high out degrees because they sometimes recieves many links.

8. J. M. Kleinberg, R. Kumar, P. Raghavan, S. Rajagopalan, and A. S. Tomkins. The web as a graph: measurements, models, and methods. In *Proc. of the International Conference on Combinatorics and Computing*, 1999.

9. B. Murray and A. Moore. Sizing the internet (a white paper). White paper, Cyveillance, Inc., 2000. (http://www.cyveillance.com).

10. L. Page, S. Brin, R. Motwani, and T. Winograd. The PageRank citation ranking: Bringing order to the web. In *Techinical Report*, 1998. (http://www-db.stanford.edu/backrub/pageranksub.ps).

Autonomy Oriented Load Balancing in Proxy Cache Servers

Kwok Ching Tsui, Jiming Liu, and Hiu Lo Liu

Department of Computer Science, Hong Kong Baptist University
Kowloon Tong, Kowloon, Hong Kong
{tsuikc,jiming,c8002287}@comp.hkbu.edu.hk

Abstract. Proxy cache servers are used to deal with the increasing demand for information on the Internet by caching the frequently referenced web objects. It is common to have more than one proxy cache servers being installed in one local network. The problem of load balancing then arises as organizations want to utilise the resources in the best way. This article proposes two methods to tackle the load balancing problem. The two methods are based on the notion of autonomy oriented computation where entities in the model are allowed to make local decisions and they only need to interact with local neighbors.

1 Introduction

It is well known that the size of the Internet is increasing everyday. This can be measured both in terms of the number of web pages being put online, the number of people 'connected' to the global network, or the number of web servers being put online. All of these factors together contributed to one single phenomenon - traffic on the Internet is getting heavier and heavier. This has already put great stress on the networks that support all these requests for web objects.

One of the solutions to alleviate this problem is to store some frequently referenced web objects in a local machine so that the need to retrieve the same object from its host web site is reduced [3]. The Internet traffic is expected to be reduced and the response to user request is expected to be improved. The local machine is commonly known as the proxy cache server. It has a cache of considerable size for storing frequently used web objects. With the increasing demand for information from the Internet, multiple proxy cache servers in one site is commonly seen. The question now is what is the best strategy for assigning requests to these proxy cache servers. This is commonly known as the load balancing problem.

This article proposes two methods to tackle this load balancing problem. These methods are based on the notion of *autonomy oriented computation* (AOC). The basic idea is to allow the elements of a system to make decisions based on some simple local behavoir model that only need limited information about the system. A central control unit is definitely absent from algorithms following the AOC approach. This article will first describe some work related to

N. Zhong et al. (Eds.): WI 2001, LNAI 2198, pp. 115–124, 2001.
© Springer-Verlag Berlin Heidelberg 2001

the proxy cache server load balancing problem. A brief introduction to autonomy oriented computation follows, which will form the background to understand the two proposed methods. The next section is then devoted to describe the methods together with some experimental results. The article concludes with discussions on some interesting observations and future research directions.

2   Related Work

Proxy cache servers help to lower the demand on bandwidth and improve request turnaround time by storing up frequently referenced web objects in their local cache. However, the cache still has a limit to its physical capacity and objects in the cache need to be replaced so as to make room for new objects that need to be stored in the cache. A commonly used strategy is least recently used (LRU) where the oldest object in the cache is replaced first. There are a lot of work on improving this base strategy.

Another approach to alleviate the bandwidth load problem is by prefetching. As web usage patterns have peaks and troughs, this approach tries to spread the workload across the usage cycle. Hence, the average turnaround time per user request is lower. This approach relies heavily on reguarities in web usage pattern but cannot adapt well to daily variations as well as sudden changes in the network environment. See [9] for a more deailed discussion on the limitations of this approach.

Others have worked on structuring the proxy cache servers so as to improve the chance of locating the required object in one of the proxy cache servers. A common technique is to arrange a host of proxy cache servers in a hierarchical manner so that some proxy cache server, not necessarily on the same local area network, is the proxy of many other proxy cache servers while serving as the proxy of some local users [12]. This approach shortens the distance between the web server and the user who requests the object. However, some work has to be done on the design of the proxy hierarchy.

Besides caching web objects in local servers, they can be cached on the other side of the network closer to the web server [2]. In relation to this, adaptive web caching suggests arranging some proxy cache servers into overlapping clusters [15,16]. Note the need of a self-configuring cluster grouping and some algorithms has been proposed. Adaptive web cache concerns the restructuing of the Internet for sharing caching capability while we concerns the self-organisation of proxy cache servers within an organization, which might span over more than one physical location, where cooperation is a matter of strategy rather than relying on global concensus.

This article proposes two approaches based on the idea of self-organization of autonomous entities, or autonomy oriented computation. The main different between the AOC methods and the above approaches is that the architecture of the proxy cache servers is not predefined. The algorithms help the proxy cache servers to find the best distribution of load between them. Therefore, minimal human intervention is required and the system adapts well to rapid changes in usage requirement and network conditions.

3   Autonomy Oriented Computation

Autonomy oriented computation (AOC) [10] refers to computation algorithms that employ autonomy as the core model of any complex system. They aim at modeling, explaining and predicting the behavior of such systems, which are hard to model using top down approaches. Local interaction between the autonomous entities is the primary driving force of AOC. An abstracted version of some natural phenomenon is the starting point of AOC so that the problem at hand can be recasted. There are three different approaches to AOc and are applicable in different circumstances.

AOC-by-fabrication aims at replicating certain self-organized collective behavior observable in the real world. The operating mechanism is more or less known and may be simplified during the modeling process. Research in the Artificial Life community falls well into this approach. The natural application of this type of AOC algorithms is as a problem solving technique, such as optimization algorithm. Nature-inspired techniques such as Genetic Algorithm [8] and Ant system [4] are typical examples of such extension.

AOC-by-prototyping aims at understanding the operating mechanism underlying the system to be modeled by simulating the observed phenomenon, through modeling a society of autonomous entities. Examples include the study of traffic jams [7], crowd control [6,13] and web log analysis [11]. This approach to AOC relates to multiagent approach to complex system in Distributed Artificial Intelligence.

AOC-by-self-discovery aims at the discovery of a solution by employing autonomy. The trial-and-error process of the AOC-by-prototyping AOC is replaced by autonomy in the system. In other words, the distance measure between the desired emergent behavior and the current emergent behavior of the system in question becomes part of the environmental information used by the autonomy. Some evolutionary algorithms that exhibit self-adaptive capability are examples of this approach [1,5].

4   Self-Organized Approaches

The performance of a proxy cache server depends on the configuration of the machine, especially the cache size, the bandwidth of the connection dedicated to it, and its current workload, among others.

In the two self organized approaches to proxy cache servers selection, a centralized proxy virtual manager (VM) sits between users on the local network and the proxy cache servers. It is the proxy cache server known to the users. However, its real job is to route the user requests to the appropriate proxy cache server based on some knowledge learned from the proxy cache server. The following is a brief summary of the two approaches and details of them are given in the following two sections.

The first approach to load balancing is based on the likelihood that a particular server delivering an above average service. The likelihood is estimated from past job history and the average system performance. A reinforcement learning process ensures that good performers are credited while poor performers are suppressed. Note that one proxy cache server's chance of being chosen is a relative quality, depending on the actual performance of the other proxy cache servers.

The second approach to load balancing is learned from each user request. Specially, the system learns the characteristics of traffic pattern between the local network and the destination in relation to time. With this information, the proxy VM will try to find the best proxy cache server that can best serve the request on hand. A lattice of vetcors similar to a self-organized map is used to encode the traffic patterns and used to select an appropriate server.

4.1   Server Performance History Method

Each proxy cache server in this setup are initialized with a performance score, say 100. The objective of this approach is to adjust this score to reflect the current performance of the proxy cache servers. This score is bounded between 50 to 1000. The discussion of the score update rules will justify the need to have these boundaries. Formally, let $S_i(y_i)$ be the performance score of proxy cache server i after y_i requests have been completed, then $S_i(0) = 100$, and $50 \leq S_i(y_i) \leq 1000$.

When the system first start to function, jobs are assigned to the proxy cache servers randomly until all proxy cache servers have been used at least oncce. The proxy VM then starts to use the performance score to assign requests. Specifically, the probability $(P(i))$ of a proxy cache server being selected is:

$$P(i) = \frac{S_i'}{\sum_{j=1}^{n} S_j'}, S_i' = S_i + \delta \tag{1}$$

where n is the number of proxy cache servers available and $\delta \leq \pm 0.05$ is a random number added to avoid the system from being stuck in a sub-optimal condition. In other words, some random noise is added to the selection process to avoid the dominance of a super-fit server.

When a request is completed, the proxy VM updates the system average transfer rate $T(x)$ and proxy cache server transfer rate $T_i(y_i)$, where x is the total number of requests served by all proxy cache servers alltogether and y_i is the total number of requests served by proxy cache server i. All transfer rates are measured in bytes per second.

$$T(x) = \frac{T(x-1) \times (x-1) + \text{transfer rate for } x\text{th job}}{x} \tag{2}$$

self-organize-by-history:
begin
initialize: **for** each proxy cache server i **do** (*initialize*)
                    $score_i \leftarrow 100$
                enddo
main-loop   **while** there is user request **do** (*main-loop*)
                    if not all servers are assigned a job once **then**
                        randomly select a server
                    else
                        select server s based on $\frac{score_s}{\sum_j score_j}$
                    endif
                    assign job to server s
                    calculate server transfer rate T_s
                    calculate system transfer rate T
                    $score_s \leftarrow score_s + (score_{max} - score_s) \times (\frac{T_s}{T-1})$
                    if $score_s < 50$ **then**
                        $score_s \leftarrow 50$
                    endif
                enddo
end

Fig. 1. The algorithm for loan balancing based on history

$$T_i(y_i) = \frac{\text{size of the file received}}{\text{time used}} \tag{3}$$

The above transfer rate are used to update the performanace score of the proxy cache servers as follows:

$$S_i(y_i) = S_i(y_i - 1) + (S_{max} - S_i(y_i - 1)) \times (\frac{T_i(y_i)}{T(x)} - 1) \tag{4}$$

The general idea of the above upate rule is that if the transfer rate achieved by the proxy cache server processing the current request is higher than the system average transfer rate, then its score should be increased. The increment is proportional to the distance between the proxy cache server's score and the maximum allowable score. Otherwise, it should be decreased to lower its likelihood of being chosen. Note that the transfer rate is an aggregated represention of a proxy cache server's overall performance and workload. As a busy proxy cache server will have a corresponding lower transfer rate. A lower bound is needed in this update rule in order to prevent the performance score from falling below zero, which will make the selection probability (equation 1) becomes negative. The upper bound is there to insure that a 'super-fit' proxy cache server will not have its score increased indefinitely and dwarfing the rest proxy cache servers. The update rule is used every time a request is completed and will be used for the whole lifetime of the system. Figure 1 presents an overview of the algorithm.

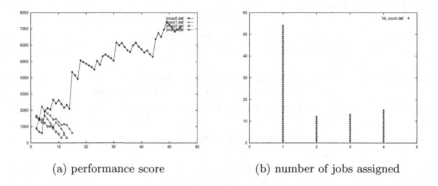

(a) performance score   (b) number of jobs assigned

Fig. 2. Changes in proxy cache server performance score and number of job assignments. proxy cache server 1 has the best configuration and hence has highest score and have been assigned the largest number of requests

Experimental Results. Some artificially generated data has been used which will generate a maximum of 2 requests per second to a randomly selected destination. A total of 21 days of traffic and four proxy cache servers are simulated in the experiments. The difference in perfromance is simulated by adding delays to the roundtrip time for each request. Figure 2a shows that strength of the four proxy cache servers over time. It shows that the performance strength reinforcement algorithm is able to help the proxy VM to differentiate between fast and slow servers. In figure 2b, it can be observed that proxy cache server with highest specification (1 in this case) is given the most number of job.

4.2   Route Transfer Pattern Method

It is well known that traffic on the Internet has peak access times within a day and within a month. Therefore, apart from the hardware limitations of the proxy cache server, the traffic on the Internet, particularly the traffic on a certain zone from which a local user wants to get information, will greatly affect the overall transfer rate achievable by a proxy cache server. The load balancing method based on route transfer rate attempts to address this issue.

Assuming there are N major nodes the Internet. The proxy VM maintains an array of size N, one entry for each node, which contains a pointer to the a 10 by 10 map of vectors (MOV). They are used to learn the traffic pattern of each route between the local network and the major nodes. Each vector contains the following information:

- time of the day
- an array of length equal to the number of proxy cache servers, each containing the latest transfer rate of the corresponding proxy
- the best proxy cache server
- a 'ready' flag, which is set to false initially

All vectors in all the maps are initialized with randomized data and all *ready* flags are set to false, signifying that the vector should not be used for decsision making. Therefore, the proxy VM will have to make some random decision while building up the MOV. When a request is received by the proxy VM, it locates the MOV using the requested URL. The *time* entry in all vectors in the chosen MOV are then searched to find the *closest* one (the winner) that match the time of the request. If the winner is ready to be used, the proxy cache server number contained in the best *proxy cache server slot* will be assigned the job. The transfer rate of the chosen proxy cache server is then updated when the completed. The time is also set as follows:

$$time_w = time_w + \alpha \times (time_{req} - time_w) \qquad (5)$$

where the subscripts w and req represents the winner and request respectively and $0 < \alpha < 1$. This time update rule modifies the chosen vector to the time of the request with some noise. When all the transfer rates of the proxy cache servers are available, the ready flag is set to true and the best proxy cache server slot is updated.

The next round of update concerns the neighbors of the vector. Vectors that are one and two positions away from the current vector in the 10 by 10 grid are considered as neighbours. Their time and transfer rate are then updated according to the following rule:

$$time_n = time_n + K^{distance_n} \times \alpha \times (time_{req} - time_{win}) \qquad (6)$$

where the subscript n represents neighbor, $K < 1$ is a contant and $distance_n$ is the distance of the neighbor from the winner. The transfer rate, best proxy cache server and ready flag are updated in the same manner as the winner. Note that the neighbors recieve a discounted time change proportional to its distance from the winner. This effectively help to build up the MOV with localized time information. This update process runs continuously so that the MOV can adapt to the traffic pattern quickly. Figure 3 presents the overall algorithm of this method.

Experimental Results. An artficial world with 100 randomly located nodes is set up to test the effectiveness of the route traffic pattern method. The exis-tence of a link between any two nodes u and v is determined by the following probability [14]:

$$P(u, v) = \alpha e^{\frac{-d}{\beta L}} \qquad (7)$$

where d is the Euclidean distance between nodes u and v, L is the maximun distance between any two nodes, and $0 \leq \alpha, \beta \leq 1$. In addition, traffic of each link is characterised by one of the following functions are $y = ((sin(x)/x) + 0.3)/1.3$, $y = (x * sin(x) + 5)/7$, $y = (x * sin(x) + 3.5)/7$ and $y = (sin(x) + 1.1)/2.1$. Furthermore, the discount factor α in equation 5 is set at 0.95. User requests are generated in the similar way as in the previous experiment.

self-organize-by-route-traffic-pattern:
begin

initialize: **for** each 10 by 10 map in the MOV **do**

    for each vector in the map **do**

      time ← random value between 0000 and 2400

      ready ← false

    enddo

  enddo

main-loop: **while** there is user request **do**

    locate the MOV corresponding to the requested URL

    if ready flag = false **then**

      randomly select a server s

    else

      select server s from *best_server* slot

    endif

    assign job to server s

    calculate server transfer rate T_s

    update-server

    update-neighbor

  enddo

update-server: update corresponding *server_transfer_rate* slot

  if all *server_transfer_rate* slots are filled **then**

    find the best transfer rate

    update *best_server* slot

  endif

  end

update-neighbor: **while** no all neighbor are updated **do**

    time ← time + distance $\times \alpha \times$ (request_time - time)

  update-server

  enddo

  end

end

Fig. 3. The algorithm for the route traffic pattern method

In order to verify the success rate of the proposed method, the experiment is run 6 times, one with the proxy VM equiped with the propsoed method and five others are run with only one of the five proxy cache servers present. The same set of test data is used throughout. The controlled experiments allow us to find the best proxy cache server, i.e. with the fastest transfer rate, to be identified. A baseline is established by assigning job randomly to one of the five proxy cache servers. These results are shown in figure 4.

Figure 4a shows the difference in transfer rate between the best case (found by the control experiments) and that achieved by the proposed method (lower line), and between the best case and the baseline (upper line). It can be noted that the proposed method tracks the best case performance closely after only a brief learning period. Figure 4b is another view of how successful the proposed method. This figure shows a 'hit rate' achieved by the proposed method. A 'hit'

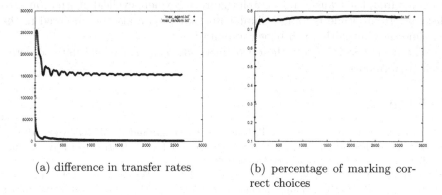

(a) difference in transfer rates

(b) percentage of marking correct choices

Fig. 4. Peformance of the route traffic pattern method. (a) shows the difference in transfer rate between the proposed method and hte ideal case, and between the random choice and the ideal case. (b) shows the percentage of times when the proposed method has chosen the best proxy cache server as determined by the control experiments.

is counted everytime the proposed method selects the same proxy cache server as the best case. The proposed method managed to make the right choice more than 75% of the time. We can confidently conclude that the proposed method can quickly learn the characteristics of the traffic on the Internet.

5   Discussion and Future Research

Two autonomy oriented load balancing methods have been proposed and described in this article. Experimental results on some artificially generated traffic and network setup are encouraging.

The first load balancing method based on server performance history makes decision is able to distinguish between the good and bad performer and allocate jobs accordingly. However, in the event of a proxy cache server failure of link problem, the proxy VM will not be able to stop sending job to the faulty server unless it is aware of the situation. One possible action is to stop sending jobs to this server suspected to be faulty. An alternative is to add a time-out condition to the transfer rate update mechanism. When a time-out is triggered, the proxy VM will just assume a very low transfer rate and update the statistics. If the problem persists, the server selection rule (equation 1) can provide a means to lower the priority of the faulty servers after a small number of job assignments. This would allow the system to respond to the disaster gracefully.

For the load balancing method based on learning the Internet traffic pattern, the algorithm can successfully learning the traffic characteristics by updating the information on the map of vectors (MOV). The neighborhood update mechanism allows the system to learn from one data point and extrapolate into areas in close proximity. The side-effect is that every vector will be modified and some previously learned information will be 'un-learned' in some sense. This can be observed from the transfer rate graph (figure 4.2) where cyclical fluctuation with decreasing amplitude is found. Similar fluctuation can also be observed in the baseline case but with much bigger amplitude.

The next step is to test these two methods using some real data to verify their performance.

References

1. T. Bäck. Self-adaptation. In T. Bäck, D. B. Fogel, and Z. Michalewicz, editors, *Handbook of Evolutionary Computation*, pages C7.1:1–15. Institute of Physics Publishing and Oxford University Press, 1997.
2. R. B. Bunt, D. L. Eager, G. M. Oster, and C. L. Williamson. Achieving load balance and effective caching in clustered web servers. In *Proceedings of the Fourth International WWW Caching Workshop*, 1999.
3. R. Caceres, F. Douglis, A. Feldmann, G. Glass, and M. Rabinovich. Web proxy caching: The devil is in the details. *Performance Evaluation Review*, 26(3):11–15, December 1998.
4. M. Dorigo, V. Maniezzo, and A. Colorni. The ant system: Optimization by a colony of cooperative agents. *IEEE Transactions on Systems, Man, and Cybernetics, Part B*, 26(1):1–13, 1996.
5. B. Freisleben. Metaevolutionary approaches. In T. Bäck, D. B. Fogel, and Z. Michalewicz, editors, *Handbook of Evolutionary Computation*, pages C7.2:1–8. Institute of Physics Publishing and Oxford University Press, 1997.
6. D. Helbing, I. Farkas, and T. Vicsek. Simulating dynamic features of escape panic. *Nature*, 407:487–490, 28 September 2000.
7. D. Helbing and B. A. Huberman. Coherent movng states in highway traffic. *Nature*, 396:738–740, 24/31 December 1998.
8. J. H. Holland. *Adaptation in Natural and Artificial Systems*. MIT Press, Cambridge, 1992.
9. Q. Jacobson and P. Cao. Potential and limits of web prefetching between low-bandwidth clients and proxies. In *Proceedings of Third International WWW Caching Workshop*, 1998.
10. J. Liu and K. C. Tsui. Introduction to autonomy oriented computation. In *Proceedings of 1st International Workshop on Autonomy Oriented Computation*, pages 1–11, 2001.
11. J. Liu and S. Zhang. Unveiling the origin of web surfing regularities. In *Proceedings of the INET 2001 Conference*, June 5-8 2001.
12. P. Rodriguez, C. Spanner, and E. W. Biersack. Web caching architectures: Hierarchical and distributed caching. In *Proceedings of the Fourth International WWW Caching Workshop*, 1999.
13. G. K. Still. *Crowd Dynamics*. PhD thesis, Mathematics Department, Warwick University, August 2000.
14. E. Zegura, K. Calvert, and S. Bhattacharjee. How to model an internetwork. In *Proceedings of INFOCOM 96*, 1996.
15. L. Zhang, S. Floyd, and V. Jacobson. Adaptive web caching. In *Proceedings of the Second International WWW Caching Workshop*, 1997.
16. L. Zhang, S. Michel, K. Nguyen, and A. Rosenstein. Adaptive web caching: Towards a new global caching architecture. In *Proceedings of the Third International WWW Caching Workshop*, 1998.

Emerging Topic Tracking System

Khoo Khyou Bun and Mitsuru Ishizuka

Dept. of Information and Communication Engineering
The University of Tokyo
7-3-1 Hongo, Bunkyo-ku, Tokyo 113-8656, JAPAN
{kbkhoo,ishizuka}@miv.t.u-tokyo.ac.jp

Abstract. Due to its open characteristic, the Web is being posted with vast amount of new information dynamically. Consequently, at any time, there will be hot issues emerge in any information area which may interest the users. However, it is not practical for users to browse the Web all the time for the updates. Thus, we need this Emerging Topic Tracking System (ETTS) as an information agent, to detect the changes in the information area of our interest and generate a summary from the changes back to us from time to time. This summary of changes will be the latest most discussed issues and it may reveal an emerging topic.

1   System Architecture

Figure 1 illustrates the system architecture of ETTS. ETTS consists of three main components: Area View System (AVS), Web Spider and Changes Summarizer. After taking in a keyword from the user, AVS will direct the keyword to the commercial search engine Google [6]. Then, AVS will analysis the returned hits and derive a number of domains that are most related to the keywords. These domains are grouped together to form an information area devoted to the keyword. Then, the Web Spider will dispatch to the Web to scan all the html files in these domains regularly, in order to collect all the modified and newly added html pages. Then, the Changes Summarizer will extract all the Changes (newly added sentences) from the collected html files by comparing the old and new database. Then, a new algorithm TF*PDF (Term Frequency * Proportional Document Frequency) (Equation 2) will be used to count the weight of the terms in the Changes. This new algorithm is innovated in a way to give more weight to the terms that deem to explain the most discussed issues in the Changes. Lastly, sentences with the highest average weight will be extracted to construct a summary for the user.

1.1   Area View System

Area View System will direct the user input keyword to the search engine Google and collect up to 500 hits. Each hit has a unique URL that may consists of a domain URL, a path, and a file name together. For example, the page http://www.cns.miis.edu/research/nuclear.html has a domain URL

N. Zhong et al. (Eds.): WI 2001, LNAI 2198, pp. 125–130, 2001.
© Springer-Verlag Berlin Heidelberg 2001

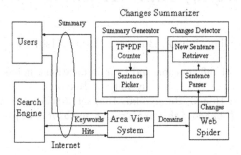

Fig. 1. ETTS System Architecture

of `http://www.cns.miis.edu/`, a path of research/ and a file name of nuclear.html. From the 500 hits, AVS will further derive 50 salient pages with their domain URL occur most frequently. Salient page is the top page of a domain if the domain has its overall contents relevant to the keyword. But some of the domains have only a sub-directory devoted to the keyword. In this case, the salient page will be the top page of the sub-directory. AVS determines this salient page as whether the top page of a domain or the top page of a sub-directory in the domain by analyzing the shortest common path of the hits originated from the domain. If all the hits originated from a domain have a shortest common path, then the salient page is the top page of the sub-directory with the name of the path. The principles on how AVS can determine the salient page is illustrated in Figure 2.

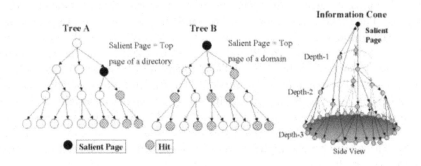

Fig. 2. Domain Tree and Information Cone

Figure 2 illustrates two different trees representing two domains. Each node represents a web page in the domain. In tree A, all the hits have a common path that is a top page of a sub-directory. In this case, the top page of the sub-directory is the salient page. While in Tree B, there is no shortest common path, so the salient page is the top page of the domain. Now, we can imagine that the combination of a salient page and all the pages under it shape an information cone (Figure 2). This cone provides a more comprehensive struture represenation than a tree. Salient page is always at the tip of the information cone.

However, by just analyzing the URL's frequency in determining the domains for tracking usage is insufficient. Hence, AVS will do a more detail analysis on the information cones in order to identify the real information cones with high suitability. The suitability of an information cone will be determined by Equation 1. All the information cones with suitability more than a certain trigger level will be added into the list of information cones used for tracking purpose.

$$Suitability = \frac{number\ of\ outer\ links\ pointing\ into\ other\ information\ cones}{total\ outer\ links}$$
$$+ \frac{number\ of\ pages\ containing\ keyword}{total\ number\ of\ pages} \tag{1}$$

1.2   Web Spider

Web Spider is an autonomous robot that dispatches to the Web regularly to scan all the qualified information cones for new and updated html pages. Basically, Web Spider adapts Breath-first search algorithm [5] to traverse through the information cones.

1.3   Changes Summarizer

Changes Summarizer is designed to analyze the updated and new pages collected by the Web Spider, derive the Changes and generate a summary of emerging topic from the Changes. Changes Summarizer consists of two major components:Changes Detector and Summary Generator (Figure 1). Changes Detector is designed to derive the Changes from the collected HTML pages. Changes is defined as a collection of text files containing all the sentences appear in the new pages but not in the old pages. Changes Detector will first wipe out all the html tags and parse the html pages in sentences text file. Then, it will compare the old and new version of sentences text file in order to derive the Changes. Then, Summary Generator will be used to generate a summary from the Changes. Summary Generator consists of two components: TF*PDF Counter and Sentence Picker. TF*PDF Counter will count the significance (weight) of the terms in the Changes by the new TF*PDF algorithm. Terms are normally content words. Stop words like prepositions (i.e. in, from,to, out) and conjuctions (i.e. and, but, or) are eliminated via a general stop word list. Different from the famous TF*IDF [7] algorithm, in TF*PDF, the weight of a term in a domain is linearly proportional to the term's within-domain frequency, and exponentially proportional to the ratio of document containing the term in the domain. The total weight of a term will be the summation of term's weight from each domain.

$$W_j = \sum_{d=1}^{d=D} |F_{jd}| \exp(\frac{n_{jd}}{N_d}) \tag{2}$$

$$|F_j| = \frac{F_j}{\sqrt{\sum_{k=1}^{k=K} F_k{}^2}} \qquad (3)$$

W_j=Weight of term j; F_{jd}=Frequency of term j in domain d; n_{jd}=Number of document in domain d where term j occurs; N_d=Total number of document in domain d; K=Total number of terms in a domain; D=number of domains under tracking.

In the final stage, Sentences Picker will calculate the average weight of each sentence in the Changes. The sentences with highest average weight will be used to construct a summary.

Table 1. First Experiment Salient Pages

Salient Page	Suitability	
	Content Page Ratio	**Outer Link Ratio**
http://www.acronym.org.uk/	0.856	0.256
http://www.ananuclear.org/	1.000	0.000
http://www.armscontrol.org/	0.767	0.018
http://www.basicint.org/	0.825	0.120
http://www.bullatomsci.org/	0.982	0.056
http://www.ccnr.org/	0.643	0.012
http://www.ceip.org/programs/npp/	0.520	0.073
http://www.cfcsc.dnd.ca/link/peace/	0.457	0.086
http://www.clw.org/coalition/	0.902	0.018
http://www.cns.miis.edu/	0.605	0.088
http://www.dtra.mil/nuclear/	0.909	0.000
http://www.fas.org/nuke/	0.583	0.036
http://www.hookele.com/abolition2000/	0.696	0.038
http://www.igc.org/disarm/	0.973	0.084
http://www.ippnw.org/	0.622	0.000
http://www.napf.org/	0.952	0.370
http://www.nci.org/	0.817	0.001
http://www.nuclearfiles.org/	0.994	0.225
http://www.nukefix.org/	0.816	0.042
http://www.stimson.org/policy/	0.988	0.063
http://www.un.org/Depts/dda/	0.512	0.000
http://www.wagingpeace.org/	0.952	0.186

2   Experimental Results

A keyword of "nuclear weapons" was used. In table 1, there were 22 information cones used for tracking. Changes happened during the time interval between Apr

23, 2000 and Apr 30, 2000 was collected. Size of the Changes (new sentences) was 3.61 Megabytes. The suitability of the cones ranges from 0.512 to 1.322.

Table 2. TF*PDF Term Weight

Term	Weight	Term	Wt	Term	Wt	Term	Wt	Term	Wt
nuclear	29.002	disarmament	3.364	world	2.400	weapons	11.598	2000	3.356
national	2.351	states	9.726	defense	2.919	power	2.349	treaty	8.315
review	2.735	like	2.288	conference	4.964	u.n.	2.680	war	2.237
united	4.762	npt	2.572	russian	2.216	missile	4.371	u.s.	2.559
plutonium	2.114	international	4.103	arms	2.518	use	1.959	peace	3.699
security	2.494	fuel	1.938	new	3.526	russia	2.411	global	1.911

Table 2 shows the 30 most weighted terms in the Changes. The result summary is showed in Table 3. The highlighted terms in the sentences are the terms that appear in the list of 30 most weighted terms. The first sentence contains nine terms (highlighted) that appear in the top 20 most weighted terms. This sentence tells that The United States of America is about to deploy a national missile defense system. The second sentence tells that Russia objects to this deployment since it is again the ABM (Anti Ballistic Missile) treaty signed between USA and Russia 30 years ago. In the third sentence, there are dangling anaphors that make the sentence unclear because it don't tell who are the two nuclear weapon states and potential enemy states. But if we are aware of the international military movements, we should be able to know that the two largest nuclear weapon states are USA and Russia; whereas one of the emphasized potential enemy states is North Korea which is believed having the ability to penetrate long range missile with nuclear warhead. Thus, American peoples are in argument whether to build a national missile defense system that can counter attack incoming missile.

3   Related Work and Discussion

There are quite a number of commercial tracking tools [1] have become available for online services. Basically, when users want to track a particular html page on the Web, they need to register the URL of the page with the system. And upon any changes happen on the page, they will be acknowledged through email. However, output from concurrent tracking systems always show little or no information on how the pages have changed. Thus, the AT&T Internet Difference Engine (AIDE) [2] has been contributing in solving this problem by automatically compares two html pages and creates a "merged" page to show the differences with special HTML markups. Other than tracking some specified URLs, some systems (Informant [3], Netmind [4]) are featured to detect the new pages containing the user input keywords.

Table 3. Result Summary

Top Sentences	Average Weight
As **world** leaders gather for the **2000** Non-Proliferation **Treaty** Review **Conference** at the **United** Nations , the **United States** is on the verge of deploying a National **Missile Defense** system.	3.151
If **Russia** objects to the **United States** defending itself against the offensive efforts of other **states** that were not even conceivable threats when the ABM **Treaty** was signed nearly 30 years ago, then the **United States** must make it clear that it is no longer bound by the ABM **Treaty**.	2.630
Leaders of both the nuclear weapon **states** and potential enemy **states** know these facts and know that the **United States**, in response to a **missile** attack, could wipe out their regimes, if not their countries.	2.588

In general, the conventional page trackers only tell that some pages have been updated or some pages are new. Users are left alone to figure out themselves what are the main topics behind the changes. At this point, we still lack of a tool that can track a particular information area of user's interest, collect the Changes regularly, and generate a summary of the most discussed issues from the Changes back to the user regularly.

4   Conclusion

In this paper, we have proposed a novel system, ETTS, and evaluated it by putting a proper experiment in place. To have this system reporting us the most updated topics related to our keywords regularly, we are "all time aware" of the latest trends in the information area of our interest.

References

1. Santi Saeyor and Mitsuru Ishizuka: WebBeholder: A Revolution in Tracking and Viewing Changes on the Web by Agent Community, in proceedings of WebNet98, 3rd World Conference on WWW and Internet, Orlando, Florida, USA, Nov. 1998.
2. Fred Douglis, Thomas Ball, Yih-Farn Chen and Eleftherios Koutsofios. The AT&T Internet Difference Engine (AIDE): Tracking and Viewing Changes on the Web, World Wide Web Volume 1 Issue 1, 1998. page 27-44.
3. http://informant.dartmouth.edu/
4. http://www.netmind.com/
5. Stuart J. Russell and Peter Norvig (1995). Artificial Intelligence: A Modern Approach, Prentice Hall
6. http://www.google.com/
7. Salton, G. and Buckley, C.: Term-Weighting Approached in Automatic Text Retrieval, Information Processing and Management, Vol.14, No.5, 1998

On Axiomatizing Probabilistic Conditional Independencies in Bayesian Networks

C.J. Butz

School of Information Technology & Engineering
University of Ottawa, Ottawa, ON, K1N 6N5, Canada

Abstract. Several researchers have suggested that *Bayesian networks* (BNs) should be used to manage the inherent uncertainty in information retrieval. However, it has been argued that manually constructing a large BN is a difficult process. In this paper, we obtain the only *minimal complete* subset of the semi-graphoid axiomatization governing the independency information in a BN. This result may be useful in developing an automated BN construction procedure for information retrieval purposes.

1 Introduction

Probability theory provides a rigorous foundation for the management of uncertain knowledge [4]. We may assume that knowledge is represented as a joint probability distribution. The probability of an event can be obtained (in principle) by an appropriate marginalization of the joint distribution. Obviously, it may be impractical to obtain the joint distribution directly: for example, one would have to specify 2^n entries for a distribution over n binary variables. However, Bayesian networks utilize probabilistic conditional independencies that are assumed to hold in the problem domain to indirectly obtain the required joint probabilities. A *Bayesian network* (BN) [4] consists of a *directed acyclic graph* (DAG) and a corresponding set of conditional probability distributions. The DAG encodes all of the probabilistic conditional independencies satisfied by a particular joint distribution. Thus, BNs provide a semantic modeling tool which facilitate the acquisition of probabilistic knowledge. Several researchers have suggested that BNs should be used to manage the inherent uncertainty in information retrieval. For instance, it was recently shown [5] how retrieval performance can be improved by using BNs to combine document content with the link structure of the Web. However, it has been argued that manually constructing a large BN is a difficult process [3]. Thereby, it would be desirable if an automated procedure could be developed for constructing a BN for information retrieval.

The *semi-graphoid axiomatization* is a set $\{(SG1), (SG2), (SG3), (SG4)\}$ of four inference axioms respectively called symmetry, decomposition, weak union, and contraction. Dawid [2] originally showed that these axioms were *sound* for the implication of probabilistic conditional independence. Pearl [4] realized that these axioms were in fact *complete* for inferring all conditional independencies in

N. Zhong et al. (Eds.): WI 2001, LNAI 2198, pp. 131–135, 2001.
© Springer-Verlag Berlin Heidelberg 2001

a BN. However, Pearl [4] incorrectly conjectured that the semi-graphoid axiomatization was complete for probabilistic conditional independence. This conjecture
sparked a flurry of studies into the completeness problem, including [6,7,11] to
name but a few. To the best of our knowledge, however, no investigation has ever
questioned the claim that the semi-graphoid inference axioms are *independent*.

In this paper, we obtain the only minimal complete subset of the semi-
graphoid axiomatization. The symmetry axiom (SG1) is stated as an iff inference axiom, while decomposition (SG2), weak union (SG3), and contraction
(SG4) are all stated as if-then inference axioms. Pearl's claim that the semi-
graphoid axioms are independent (see Theorem 1 in [4]) needs to be somewhat
qualified. The key observation in this exposition is that the contraction axiom (SG4), like the symmetry axiom (SG1), is *not* an if-then axiom but is in
fact an iff inference axiom $(SG4)'$. This means that the semi-graphoid axiomatization, traditionally written as $\{(SG1), (SG2), (SG3), (SG4)\}$, can be written as $\{(SG1), (SG2), (SG3), (SG4)'\}$. It immediately follows that the decomposition axiom (SG2) and the weak union axiom (SG3) can be removed from
$\{(SG1), (SG2), (SG3), (SG4)'\}$, since any probabilistic conditional independence
obtained by an application of $(SG2)$ or $(SG3)$ can be obtained by an application of $(SG4)'$. In other words, $\{(SG1), (SG4)'\}$ is a minimal complete subset
of the semi-graphoid axiomatization. We also show that $\{(SG1), (SG4)'\}$ is the
only subset enjoying this property. The important point to remember, however,
is that the set $\{(SG1), (SG4)'\}$ *completely* characterizes all of the probabilistic
conditional independencies holding in a BN.

This paper is organized as follows. The complete minimal subset of the semi-
graphoid axiomatization is given in Section 2. The conclusion is presented in
Section 3.

2   A Minimal Complete Subset of the Semi-graphoid Axiomatization

We first introduce the fundamental notion of *probabilistic conditional independency*. Let X, Y and Z be disjoint subsets of variables in R. Let x, y, and z
denote arbitrary values of X, Y and Z, respectively. We say Y and Z are *condi-
tionally independent* given X under the joint probability distribution p, denoted
$I_p(Y, X, Z)$, if

$$p(y \mid x, z) = p(y \mid x), \tag{1}$$

whenever $p(x, z) > 0$. This conditional independency $I_p(Y, X, Z)$ can be equiva-
lently written as

$$p(y, x, z) = \frac{p(y, x) \cdot p(x, z)}{p(x)}. \tag{2}$$

We write $I_p(Y, X, Z)$ as $I(Y, X, Z)$ if the joint probability distribution p is understood.

Let $\sum$ be a set of probabilistic conditional independencies and σ be a single independency. We say $\sum$ *logically implies* σ, written $\sum \models \sigma$, if every distribution which satisfies $\sum$ also satisfies σ. That is, there is no counter-example distribution such that all of the independencies in $\sum$ are satisfied but σ is not. The *implication problem* [9] is to test whether a given set $\sum$ of independencies logically implies another independency σ, namely, $\sum \models \sigma$.

An *inference axiom* gives conditions as to when certain probabilistic conditional independencies must be satisfied by a distribution, provided that the distribution satisfies other given independencies. Given a set $\sum$ of independencies and a set of inference axioms, the *closure* of $\sum$, written $\sum^+$, is the smallest set containing $\sum$ such that the inference axioms cannot be applied to the set to yield a independency not in the set. More specifically, the set $\sum$ *derives* a independency σ, written $\sum \vdash \sigma$, if σ is in $\sum^+$. A set of inference axioms is *sound* if whenever $\sum \vdash \sigma$, then $\sum \models \sigma$. A set of inference axioms is *complete* if the converse holds, that is, if $\sum \models \sigma$, then $\sum \vdash \sigma$. In other words, saying a set of axioms are complete means that if $\sum$ logically implies the independency σ, then $\sum$ derives σ.

The semi-graphoid inference axioms are [4]:

$(SG1) : I(Y, X, Z)$ if and only if $I(Z, X, Y)$;   [symmetry]

$(SG2) :$ If $I(Y, X, ZW)$, then $I(Y, X, Z)$;   [decomposition]

$(SG3) :$ If $I(Y, X, ZW)$, then $I(Y, XW, Z)$;   [weak union]

$(SG4) :$ If $I(Y, X, Z)$ and $I(Y, XZ, W)$, then $I(Y, X, ZW)$.   [contraction]

These inference axioms were shown *sound* by Dawid [2]. This means that if a conditional independency σ is derived from an input set $\sum$ of conditional independencies using the semi-graphoid axiomatization, then $\sum$ logically implies σ. Pearl [4] realized that the converse was true, provided that $\sum$ is a causal input list. In other words, if the conditional independencies in $\sum$ define a BN, then the semi-graphoid axioms will derive every conditional independency logically implied by $\sum$. It should be emphasized that if $\sum$ is an arbitrary set of independencies, then the semi-graphoid axioms may not derive *every* independency logically implied by $\sum$. An example of such a case can be found in [6].

Pearl has stated that the semi-graphoid inference axioms are independent (see Theorem 1 in [4]). In other words, no inference axiom in $\{(SG1), (SG2), (SG3), (SG4)\}$ is redundant. This remark needs to be somewhat qualified.

Consider again the semi-graphoid axiomatization. Notice that the symmetry (SG1) is an iff inference axiom, while decomposition (SG2), weak union (SG3), and contraction (SG4) are all if-then inference axioms. The following result indicates that the contraction axiom (SG4), like the symmetry axiom (SG1), is in fact an iff inference axiom.

Theorem 1. *The contraction axiom (SG4) in Pearl's semi-graphoid axioms [4] is bidirectional, namely:*

$(SG4)' : I(Y, X, Z)$ and $I(Y, XZ, W)$ *if and only if* $I(Y, X, ZW)$.   [contraction]

Proof. In [2], Dawid showed that $\{I(Y,X,Z),\ I(Y,XZ,W)\} \models I(Y,X,ZW)\}$, $\{I(Y,X,ZW)\} \models I(Y,X,Z)$, and $\{I(Y,X,ZW)\} \models I(Y,XZ,W)$ all hold.   □

Theorem 1 is significant since it means that Pearl's semi-graphoid axioms $(SG1),(SG2),(SG3),(SG4)$ can be written as $\{(SG1),\ (SG2),\ (SG3),\ (SG4)'\}$:

$(SG1)$: $I(Y,X,Z)$ if and only if $I(Z,X,Y)$;   [symmetry]
$(SG2)$: If $I(Y,X,ZW)$, then $I(Y,X,Z)$;   [decomposition]
$(SG3)$: If $I(Y,X,ZW)$, then $I(Y,XW,Z)$;   [weak union]
$(SG4)'$: $I(Y,X,Z)$ and $I(Y,XZ,W)$ if and only if $I(Y,X,ZW)$. [contraction]

Our objective now is to determine whether we can obtain a set with *fewer* inference axioms without changing the closure, i.e., obtain an equivalent set of inference axioms by removing any redundant axioms. Clearly, axioms (SG2) and (SG3) are redundant, since any conditional independency obtained using (SG2) and (SG3) can be obtained by the new contraction axiom $(SG4)'$. Thus, we obtain the following result.

Theorem 2. *The following two inference axioms $(SG1)$ and $(SG4)'$ are a minimal complete subset of Pearl's semi-graphoid axiomatization:*

$(SG1)$: $I(Y,X,Z)$ if and only if $I(Z,X,Y)$;   [symmetry]
$(SG4)'$: $I(Y,X,Z)$ and $I(Y,XZ,W)$ if and only if $I(Y,X,ZW)$. [contraction]

Proof. Clearly, $\{(SG4)'\}$ is equivalent to $\{(SG2),(SG3),(SG4)\}$. It immediately follows that $\{(SG1),(SG4)'\}$ is *equivalent* to $\{(SG1),(SG2),(SG3),(SG4)\}$.

We now show that $\{(SG1),(SG4)'\}$ is minimal. Again using the fact that $\{(SG4)'\}$ is equivalent to $\{SG2,SG3,SG4\}$, it immediately follows that $(SG1)$ is not redundant in $\{(SG1),(SG4)'\}$ since $(SG1)$ is not redundant in the semi-graphoid axioms $\{(SG1),(SG2),(SG3),(SG4)\}$ [4]. Obviously $(SG4)'\}$ is not redundant in $\{(SG1),(SG4)'\}$. Thus, $\{(SG1),(SG4)'\}$ is *minimal.*   □

Theorem 2 is important since it indicates that a conditional independency σ can be obtained from a given set $\sum$ using $\{(SG1),(SG2),(SG3),(SG4)\}$ if and only if σ can be obtained from $\sum$ using $\{(SG1),(SG4)'\}$. This means that the set $\{(SG1),(SG4)'\}$ of inference axioms *completely* characterizes all of the probabilistic conditional independencies holding in a BN. It can be easily verified that $(SG2)$ and $(SG3)$ cannot be written as iff axioms.

Corollary 3. $\{(SG1),(SG4)'\}$ *is the only minimal complete subset of the semi-graphoid axiomatization* $\{(SG1),(SG2),(SG3),(SG4)'\}$.

3   Conclusion

The key observation in this paper is that the contraction axiom $(SG4)$, like the symmetry axiom $(SG1)$, is in fact an iff inference axiom $(SG4)'$. This means that the Pearl's [4] semi-graphoid axiomatization $\{(SG1), (SG2), (SG3), (SG4)\}$, can be succinctly written as $\{SG1, SG4'\}$. In fact, we have shown that this is the *only* minimal complete subset of the semi-graphoid axiomatization. This is important since it means that the set $\{(SG1), (SG4)'\}$ *completely* characterizes all probabilistic conditional independencies holding in a BN.

A study of axiomatization is not only important from a theoretical point of view. On the contrary, a complete axiomatization provides an algorithmic approach to the design of relational databases [1], BNs [8], and multi-agent BNs [10]. Thus, the results in this paper may be of some help in developing an automated method for constructing BNs for information retrieval purposes.

References

1. Beeri, C., Fagin, R., and Howard, J.H.: A complete axiomatization for functional and multivalued dependencies in database relations. Proc. of ACM-SIGMOD International Conference on Management of Data (1977) 47-61
2. Dawid, A.P.: Conditional independence in statistical theory. Journal of the Royal Statistical Society **41B** (1979) 1-31
3. Koller, D. and Pfeffer, A. Object-oriented bayesian networks. Proc. of the Thirteenth Conference on Uncertainty in Artificial Intelligence (1997) 302-313
4. Pearl, J.: Probabilistic Reasoning in Intelligent Systems: Networks of Plausible Inference. Morgan Kaufmann Publishers, San Francisco (1988)
5. Silva, I., Ribeiro-Neto, B., Calado, P., Moura, E., and Ziviani, N.: Link-based and content-based evidential information in a belief network model. Proc. of the Twenty-third Annual ACM SIGIR Conference on Research and Development in Information Retrieval (2000) 96-103
6. Studeny, M.: Multiinformation and the problem of characterization of conditional-independence relations. Problems of Control and Information Theory **18**(1) (1989) 3-16
7. Studeny, M.: Conditional independence relations have no finite complete characterization. Proc. of the Eleventh Prague Conference on Information Theory, Statistical Decision Foundation and Random Processes (1990) 377-396
8. Verma, T. and Pearl, J.: An algorithm for deciding if a set of observed independencies has a causal explanation. Proc. of the Eighth Conference on Uncertainty in Artificial Intelligence (1992) 323-330
9. Wong, S.K.M., Butz, C.J., and Wu, D.: On the implication problem for probabilistic conditional independency. IEEE Trans. Syst. Man Cybern. SMC-A **30**(6) (2000) 785-805
10. Wong, S.K.M. and Butz, C.J.: Constructing the dependency structure of a multi-agent probabilistic network. IEEE Trans. Knowl. Data Eng. **13**(3) (2001) (to appear)
11. Wong, S.K.M. and Wang, Z.W.: On axiomatization of probabilistic conditional independence. Proc. of the Tenth Conference on Uncertainty in Artificial Intelligence (1994) 591-597

Dynamic Expert Group Models for Recommender Systems

DaeEun Kim[1] and Sea Woo Kim[2]

[1] Division of Informatics,
University of Edinburgh, 5 Forrest Hill
Edinburgh, EH1 2QL
United Kingdom
daeeun@dai.ed.ac.uk
[2] Manna Information System
Bangbae-dong 915-9, Seocho-gu
Seoul, 137-060, Korea
seawoo@unitel.co.kr

Abstract. Recently many recommender systems have been developed to recommend items in online commerce markets, based on user preferences for a particular user, but they have difficulty in deriving user preferences for users who have not rated many documents. In this paper we use dynamic expert-group models to recommend domain-specific items or documents for unspecified users, while users give feedbacks of relative ratings over the recommended items or documents. In this system, the group members have dynamic authority weights depending on their performance of the ranking evaluations. We have tested two effectiveness measures on rank order to determine if the current top-ranked lists recommended by experts are reliable.

1 Introduction

The development of recommender systems has emerged as an important issue in the Internet application, and have drawn attention in the academic and commercial fields. An example of this application is to recommend new products or items of interest to online customers, using customer preferences.

Recommender systems can be broadly categorized into content-based and collaborative filtering systems [4,6,7,8]. Content-based filtering methods use textual descriptions of the documents or items to be recommended. A user's profile is associated with the content of the documents that the user has already rated. The features of documents are extracted from information retrieval, pattern recognition, or machine learning techniques. Then the content-based system recommends documents that match the user's profile or tendency [2,8]. In contrast, collaborative filtering systems are based on user ratings rather than the features in the documents [1,8,7]. The systems predict the ratings of a user over given documents or items, depending on ratings of other users with tastes similar to the user.

N. Zhong et al. (Eds.): WI 2001, LNAI 2198, pp. 136–140, 2001.
© Springer-Verlag Berlin Heidelberg 2001

Most recommender systems have focused on the recommendations for a particular user with the analysis of user preferences. Such systems require the user to judge many items in order to obtain the user's preferences. In general, many online customers or users are interested in other users' opinions or ratings about items that belong to a certain category, before they become used to searching for items of interest. For instance, customers in E-commerce like to see top-ranked lists of rating scores of many users for items that retailers provide, in order to purchase specific items. However, recommender systems still have the difficulty in providing relevant rating information before they receive a large number of user evaluations.

In this paper, we use a method to evaluate web documents by a representative board of human agents [5]; we call it an *expert* group. This is different from automatic recommender systems with software agents or feature extractions. We suggest dynamic expert groups among users should be automatically created to evaluate domain-specific documents for web page ranking and also the group members have dynamic authority weights depending on their performance of the ranking evaluations. This method is quite effective in recommending web documents or items that many users have not evaluated. A voting board of experts with expertise on a domain category is operated to evaluate the documents or the items.

The method of developing a new ranking technique based on human interactions has been explored in this paper to handle the problems. We run a pool of experts, human agents to evaluate web documents or products and their authorities are dynamically determined by their performance. Users give feedbacks of relative ratings over recommended items. The application of relative ratings, instead of score ratings in the recommender systems, provides convenience for users and leads to using prior probabilities that the expert-recommended documents or items keep their ranks.

2   Method

We define a group of people with high authority and much expertise in a special field as an expert group. For every category there is a list of top ranked documents or products rated by an expert group, which are sorted by score. Authoritative web pages or items are determined by human expert members. The experts directly examine the content of candidate web pages, which are highly referenced among web documents or accessed by many users. The method of employing an expert group is based on the idea that for a given decision task requiring expert knowledge, many experts may be better than one if their individual judgments are properly combined. In our system, experts decide whether a web document should be classified into a recommended document for a given category.

In our system, we use a weighted linear combination of expert votes. A weighted linear sum of expert votings yields the collaborative net-effect ratings of documents. In this paper, we take the adaptive weighted linear combination method, where the individual contributions of members in the expert groups are weighted by their judgment performance. The evaluation of all the experts are summed with weighted linear combinations. The expert rating results will dynamically change depending on each expert's performance.

We define a rating score matrix $X = [\chi_{ij}]$ when the i-th expert rates a web document d_j with a score χ_{ij}. For each web document d_j, the voting score of an expert committee is given as

$$V(d_j) = \sum_{i=1}^{N_e} \frac{w_i}{\sum_{k=1}^{N_e} w_k} \chi_{ij}$$

where N_e is the number of experts for a given category and w_i is the authority weight for the i-th expert member in the expert pool. We suppose w_i should be positive for all time.

The weight w_i is a dynamic factor, and it represents each expert's authority to evaluate documents. The higher authority weight indicates the expert is more influential to make a voting decision. We update weights of experts by feedback of users about a web document d_j, which uses a gradient-descent method [3]. The weight is changed each session by the following dynamic equation :

$$w_i(t+1) = w_i(t) - \eta[\chi_{ij} - V(d_j)]H_\epsilon(V(d_i), V'(d_i)) + \alpha(w_i(t) - w_i(t-1))$$

where η is a learning rate proportional to the number of user ratings per session, α is the momentum constant, and $V'(d_j)$ is a voting score of a user for an expert-voted document d_j. H_ϵ is a feedback function of users based on relative ratings as follows.

$$H_\epsilon(a, b) = \begin{cases} 1 \text{ if } a - b \geq \epsilon \\ -1 \text{ if } a - b \leq -\epsilon \\ 0 \text{ otherwise} \end{cases}$$

where $|V(d_i), V'(d_i)| < \epsilon$ means that a user is satisfied with an expert-voting site d_i. Some experts may accumulate too much penalty on their authority weights by wrong voting scores and be out of the expert group committee when the weight w_k is too small. Instead of score ratings of documents, the rank information can be extracted from users' relative ratings such as higher/lower/fine, depending on their satisfaction of rank orders over experts' recommendations. If we use relative rating methods, it will be easy to decide users' satisfaction levels.

3   Experiments

We simulated the dynamic process of web document ranking and creations of expert groups depending on their performance. The prediction performance of expert groups in reality will remain for future works. The purpose of the simulation test is to confirm that the dynamic expert groups reflect general users' opinions or ratings and has the potential to recommend documents that has not been rated yet.

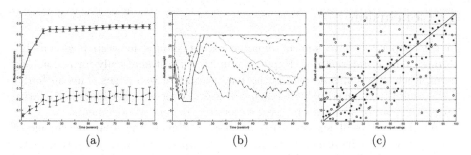

Fig. 1. Simulation results (a) effectiveness performance for a category (solid : Spearmam's correlation, dotdashed : rank order window) (b) weight change (c) an example of distribution of rank orders by expert group ratings and user ratings ('o' : before weight change, '*' : after weight change)

In the simulation, we assumed 20 categories to need expert groups, maximum 10 experts for each expert group, 10000 web documents $d_k, k = 1, .., 10000$ in the movie search engine, and also 500 random users logging into our search engine. We modeled random login patterns of online users as a Poisson process[9]. Each user has an arrival rate, in other words, an access rate and a transaction processing time, thus we define the arrival rate λ_i for a user u_i, for $i = 1, ..., 500$. For a each user u_i, the probability that the user accesses the search engine document within time Δt is $P_i = 1 - e^{-\lambda_i \Delta t}$ where Δt is the basic time unit.

We used two effectiveness measures, Spearman's correlation measure and rank order window measure [3]. Every session we have selected top-100 ranked documents recommended by an expert group for each category and applied the effectiveness measures to top-ranked lists.

Simulation was run 10 times for each category, and one category result is displayed in Fig.1(a). The figure shows the average performance results with 95% confidence intervals. Fig.1(b) shows the transitions of experts' authority weights according to their rating performance. In simulation experiments it happened that some experts had high authority weights for a while and yielded their authority levels to other good experts. Fig.1(c) shows an example of the agreement of rank order between the expert ratings and the user ratings in evaluating documents, while there is no regular pattern of the agreement brefore weight change. After applying adaptive change of authority weights, the rank-order prediction of experts becomes close to the rank order of user ratings.

In our evaluation of experts, we assume that an expert's decision reflects the opinions of most of users and an expert is automatically associated with his/her domain of expertise by measuring performance. However, it is quite different from the real world in many respects. Some true experts with good knowledge may have different opinions and views from general users. The access rate of each user is very irregular in reality. The behavior or access pattern of users will vary from category to category. In some categories, it may be difficult to assemble good experts.

4   Conclusion

In this paper we have shown dynamic expert groups for web page ranking through human interactions. Expert committee is automatically formed among users. Each expert has its own authority to evaluate web pages. This authority is dynamically changed using feedback of users. Users give feedbacks of relative ratings instead of score ratings over expert-recommended documents.

As the user feedback or rating process continues, the dynamic change of authority weights increases weights for good experts and decreases weights for bad experts. It automatically chooses good experts for a given category and thus it improves the effectiveness measures. The system accumulates more user-feedback ratings of recommended documents as time passes, and it can improve the selection of experts. Relative ratings will be useful to apply our expert group models to the real application by providing users with convenience and prior rank orders. However, it may lose the advantages of score ratings which can be extended to collaborative filtering with the analysis of user preferences.

In many application, customers or users are interested in seeing the top ranked documents or products. The recommender system with dynamic expert groups will be a feasible solution to recommend items or documents for unspecified users in the field that automatic recommender systems cannot cover.

References

1. J.S. Breese, D. Heckerman, and C. Kadie. Empirical analysis of predictive algorithms for collaborative filtering. In *Proceedings of the 14th Conference on Uncertainty in Artificial Intelligence*, pages 43–52, 1998.
2. J. Delgado, N. Ishii, and T. Ura. Content-based collaborative information filtering: Actively learning to classify and recommend documents. In *Proceedings of Cooperative Information Agents*, pages 206–215, 1998.
3. D.Kim and S.W. Kim. Dynamic models of expert groups to recommend web documents. In *Proceedings of the 5th European Conference on Research and Advanced Technology for Digital Libraries*, Darmstadt, 2001. Springer.
4. W. Hill, L. Stead, M. Rosenstein, and G. Furnas. Recommending and evaluating choices in a virtual community of use. In *Proceedings of ACM CHI'95*, pages 194–201, 1995.
5. S.W. Kim and C.W. Chung. Web document ranking by differentiated expert group evaluation. In *Proceedings of the 9th International Conference on Human-Computer Interaction*, 2001.
6. P. Resnick, N. Iacovou, M. Sushak, P. Bergstrom, and J. Riedl. Grouplens: an open architecture for collaborative filtering of netnews. In *Proceedings of Computer Supported Cooperative Work Conference*, pages 175–186, 1994.
7. U. Shardanand and P. Maes. Social information filtering: algorithms for automating 'word of mouth'. In *Proceedings of ACM CHI'95*, 1995.
8. I. Soboroff, C. Nicholas, and M. Pazzani, editors. *Proceedings of the SIGIR-99 Workshop on Recommender Systems*. Berkeley,California, 1999.
9. H.M. Taylor and S. Karlin. *An Introduction to Stochastic Modeling*. Academic Press, London, 3rd edition, 1998.

The ABC's of Online Community

Robert McArthur and Peter Bruza

Distributed Systems Technology Centre
Brisbane, Australia
{mcarthur,bruza}@dstc.edu.au

Abstract. Online community is having growing social and commercial impact on the WWW, but what does "community" mean online? Can the level of community be measured? This article articulates an evidential conceptual model of community synthesizing earlier definitions drawn from the literature and creating new core conditions. The four conditions, purpose, commitment, context and infrastructure, we believe are necessary and sufficient for modeling and gauging intra-community "glue", and that without this glue sustainable community cannot manifest.

1 Introduction

Many definitions of online community (OC), virtual, e- or network community have been described. Broadly, publications are in three areas. The first is sociology and is well represented in the work of Barry Wellman [1,2]. Wellman contends that social network analysis, which examines community in terms of the social network of participants rather than in terms of space (neighborhoods), is a better tool for defining and examining computer-supported social networks: "...neighborhood and kinship ties are only a portion of people's overall community networks because cars, planes and phones can maintain relationships over long distances." The strength of these social networks is what determines the nature of community: "Despite the limited social presence of online links, the Net successfully maintains strong, supportive community ties, and it may be increasing the number and diversity of weak ties" [2].

The second area is experiential, reporting the creation and maintaining of internet-centred communities [e.g. 3,4]. Kim [3] states "In terms of their social dynamics, physical and virtual communities are much the same. Both involve developing a web of relationships among people who have something meaningful in common..."

The third area of publication is information technology (IT) articles, such as in the ACM, SIGCHI and CSCW[1] conferences, and books that connect the theory to user's experiences. Researchers from the IT perspective (e.g. [5],[6],[7]) have generally attempted to define OC by identifying salient aspects and underlying principles. For example, Kollock [8] notes "If members of a group will not meet each other in the future, if there is no stability in the names and identities that people adopt, and if there

---

[1] Association for Computer Machinery. Special Interest Group in Computer-Human Interaction, Computer Supported Cooperative Work.

N. Zhong et al. (Eds.): WI 2001, LNAI 2198, pp. 141–147, 2001.
© Springer-Verlag Berlin Heidelberg 2001

is no memory or community record of previous interaction, it will be very difficult to create and maintain a cooperative online community." Kollock [9] also briefly discusses design principles for online communities based on cooperation and writings on both offline & online community.

Preece [10] defines OC: "An online community consists of: *People*, who interact socially as they strive to satisfy their own needs or perform special roles; a shared *purpose*, such as an interest, need, information exchange, or service that provides a reason for the community; *Policies*, in the form of tacit assumptions, rituals, protocols, rules and laws that guide people's interactions; and *Computer systems* to support and mediate social interaction and facilitate a sense of togetherness." Preece believes that "how software is designed affects community development just as the architecture of a house affects those who live in it."

Whittaker *et al.* [11], being the result of a CSCW workshop, lists "key dimensions of community" by defining "'prototypical attributes' so that communities with more such attributes were clearer examples of communities than those that had fewer." Core attributes of a community are: a shared goal, interest, need or activity; repeated, active participation with intense interactions and strong emotional ties between participants; access to shared resources with policies to determine access; reciprocity of information, support and services between members; and lastly a shared context (social conventions, language, protocols).

The above sketch of the literature hopefully convinces the reader that there is little agreement about what OC is and what are the underlying research questions: OC appears to be a complex phenomenon which is difficult to precisely conceptualize and evaluate. However, on the WWW, there is considerable interest about online communities. Part of this interest is commercially driven: nurturing "community" online may create an important foundation for a loyal customer base and marketing channel. Crucial in this regard is the "glue" which keeps users involved in the community. Without this "glue" the OC will feature sporadic and unfocussed visits from users, and hence be of little societal or commercial value. Related to this discussion is the evaluation of "community". For example, given an arbitrary web-based forum that claims to be an OC, can we tell if it is? Is there enough "glue" present to warrant a claim of OC? This paper addresses these issues by providing a conceptual model of OC embodying those aspects that are crucial to fostering community "glue". Moreover, the conceptual model is evidence-based, which promotes its applicability to measurement of the level of community.

2 An Evidential Conceptual Model of Online Community

All chat rooms or Usenet newsgroups are not used in the same manner, even though they may be supported by similar technology. A particular chat room may operate in an open manner: anyone can enter and talk about anything they like. This is akin to going to a party where you may know no one but talk with different people about many topics. Chat rooms may also operate in a thematic manner akin to a mid-morning chat in a workplace's coffee room where the interactions are largely driven by a shared topic or interest. In this setting, how can the community be analysed?

While applying Whittaker *et al*'s definition we have noticed some parts are not clear. For example, what do "*needs*" mean when the very fact the person is involved in the community means they have a need? Also, Preece's definitions include a number of interesting ideas that could dovetail into a combined definition. Most importantly, a definition of online community that is suitable for evaluation and empirical testing is required to test the increasingly unbelievable claims of commercial web sites.

We therefore present the following evidential conceptual model of OC that is based on Preece's and Whittaker's work. The term "evidential" is crucial. With our model we postulate core conditions of OC, and also factors that provide evidence for the existence, or strength, of these conditions. Such a model lends itself more easily to being a "diagnostic" tool of OC. Such a conceptual tool could analyse a particular community or technology and indicate the level of presence of community, as well as being indicative of where more emphasis can be placed to make it function better.

Preece includes *people* and *computer systems* in her definition. We believe that these do not add to a definition that is suitable for evaluation, thus we make a number of assumptions about our online community: 1) People are integral and essential; three or more people may form a community while two or more may form a group; 2) Computer systems, and adequate access to them, are essential; and 3) People have some language in common to be able to use the community. Point 2 does not mean that we are uninterested in the CHI aspects of OC computer systems. It merely states that some such access is a necessary part of an OC.

The core attributes of OC are as follows. We will refer to them as *conditions* for community because we believe that each must be present, in some form, for community to arise. A distinction is drawn between the conditions themselves, which are conceptual, and associated artifacts, which can provide tangible evidence for a condition. We describe example artifacts for each condition.

Purpose

A community cannot arise and be sustained without a *purpose*. This can manifest in different ways. For example, intentional OCs share a common goal like "to stop the uranium mine at Jabiluka". Purpose may also manifest as a shared interest–many online news groups are formed around an interest. The interest may be based around a shared activity such as communal novel writing, or more commonly, the interest may be centred on a certain topic or theme, e.g. Formula 1 motor racing. Whittaker makes a distinction between need and interest, but we do not. We view need as an "extreme" form of interest. For example, someone with bowel cancer may become part of an OC to seek information, and share information and their "burden". Their interest is being driven by a important tangible need.

Artifacts: Goal-based or need-based OCs often have a charter describing the goals, vision and principles of the community. The purpose of the community may be buried in a FAQ with a description of what the community is "about". The purpose of an interest-based community is often implicit: newsgroups based on a topic, or chat rooms based around a theme. The purpose (interest) is clear from the communications (e.g. postings) within the community. It may be possible to extract the underlying topic and associated concepts by concept mapping techniques such as clustering.

Commitment

Commitment alludes to repeated, active, participation committed to the purpose of the community. Observe that repeated, active participation is not sufficient for sustaining community – the participation must be directed towards the purpose of the community. By way of illustration, there may be an individual repeatedly and actively participating in the Formula 1 news group by posting results of Indy car races (a rival form of racing to Formula 1), but this participation is not committed to the news group's goal: sharing of information relevant to Formula 1 racing.

Artifacts: Participation often results in an electronic document of some form, e.g. a posting to a newsgroup, text left on an online bulletin board. Repeated, active participation leaves traces in log-files e.g. as evidence of repeated postings from the same individual to a newsgroup. It is harder to determine whether the participation is committed to the purpose of the community. This involves content analysis of postings, emails and the like and matching the results of this analysis with the purpose of the community. We are unaware of any automatic means to perform the content analysis and associated matching.

Context

Context is a notoriously slippery concept to define clearly. Context, in the OC sense, refers to attributes whose values remain more or less fixed or stable, thereby providing the secure foundations on which the community can be built.
We identify the following forms of context:

- *Implicit knowledge*: refers to items of information that are no longer clarified or disambiguated within the OC as they are assumed to be common knowledge. For example, in the OC surrounding the anti-Jabiluka uranium mine protest, "ERA" refers to: (1) Energy Resources of Australia Limited, (2) a uranium mining company, and (3) this mining company is planning to build and operate a uranium mine at Jabiluka. These three items of information are implicit contextual information. A new member of the OC, or outsider, may not fully understand the communication within the OC without the requisite implicit knowledge.
  Artifacts: Acronyms (local to the OC) and the use of proper names without any associated clarification or definition are evidence of assumed knowledge.

- *Endoxa:*[2] refer to the popular *beliefs* that feed into the purpose of the community. Most members of the community hold such beliefs. The endoxa of a community are stable, changing slowly over time if they change at all. By way of illustration, the members of the Perl programming language community hold the popular belief that "Perl is better than the language C for string processing".
  Artifacts: As endoxa are popular beliefs within the community, they may never be explicitly stated. It may be possible to *infer* some endoxa by analysing communications within the community over a longer time period.

- *Constraints*: Social practices, rules, and policies observed by the majority within the community. For example, the Formula 1 newsgroup has a social convention to place the term "SPOILER" in the title of any posting of race results. Members of the community who do not wish to know the results yet will not have their enjoyment "spoilt" by seeing them beforehand. Some practices may be ritualistic in

---

[2] Endoxa originates from Aristotle–we use it in a similar sense to Gabbay and Woods [12] to mean "popular beliefs", i.e., p is proposition held by almost everyone in the community. Belief in p is considered reasonable, if not desirable, within the context of the community.

nature, though the notion of "ritual" does not seem to have a clear counterpart in an online sense. Rituals are, however, an important aspect of physical communities. *Artifacts:* Constraints are often found in the charter or FAQ of the community.

Infrastructure

This is the physical infrastructure used to support the community, and includes technology, and shared resources such as databases, web pages etc.

We are of the opinion that the above four conditions, purpose, commitment, context and infrastructure, are together necessary and sufficient conditions for intra community "glue" to manifest. Orthogonal to this are aspects of inter-personal "glue" which depend on conditions such as "emotional ties" between members in the community. Inter-personal "glue" is beyond the scope of this article.

Fig. 1 summarizes the above discussion. At one level it represents a conceptual model of OC and what conditions need to be present to allow OC to manifest. At a more specific level, each node can be considered as a probabilistic variable ranging over the appropriate values. By way of illustration, the probabilistic variable CONTEXT could range across the values {*none, shallow, some, comprehensive*} representing various levels of context observed in the OC under scrutiny. Such a topology is one aspect of a belief network. If such a network is enhanced by local probability assessment functions, a probabilistic reasoning mechanism [13] for diagnosing the degree of presence of OC results. The probability assessments can be primed subjectively based on the analysis of artifacts, for example:

Pr(OC=present | PURPOSE=present, COMMITMENT=medium,
                        CONTEXT=comprehensive, INFRASTRUCTURE=partially_present) = 0.6

This formula states that the probability of OC being present is 0.6 given that there has been a purpose identified, there is medium commitment among community members, there is a large amount of context, and community infrastructure has been developed.

In a longer version of this paper we have tested the conceptual model to evaluate an online community at the Australian Broadcasting Corporation.

3 Conclusions and Further Research

Online community is having growing social and commercial impact on the Web, but what does "community" mean online? Can the level of community be measured? This article describes an evidential conceptual model of community based on core community conditions. The four conditions, purpose, commitment, context and infrastructure, we believe are necessary and sufficient for modeling and gauging intra-community "glue". It is our belief that without this glue, sustainable community cannot manifest. In addition we believe it important for ongoing OCs to monitor the level of intra-community "glue" present in order to gauge community "health". The model presented synthesizes earlier definitions of OC drawn from the literature. In addition, it contains some novel aspects. To our knowledge, the notion of community context has never been brought to the foreground as precisely as presented in this paper. Central to context are implicit knowledge and endoxa–the popular beliefs of the community. Both are aspects of the "common knowledge" [12]. We plan to investigate the common knowledge through questions like:"What does the community know?" and "Who knows X in the community?" Answers to such questions will allow expertise management to be formalized. In practice, this will result in tools to support the capture and storage of common knowledge, and allow information needs to be routed more directly to members in the OC with the relevant expertise (knowledge). We applied the model to a study of some OCs at the Australian Broadcasting Corporation. Further studies are planned to better define the condition's artifacts, to decide how to best decide whether an artifact is present, and to develop automatic means, where possible, for the extraction of evidence. This will allow the monitoring of the level of community to be performed more easily and allow efficient data gathering for studying the evolution of a particular community. Some particular questions generated from this study are: do goal-based communities generate more endoxa? Are goal-based communities stronger (more glue) than interest-based? Online community may be a pervasive term, but there is still much to be learnt.

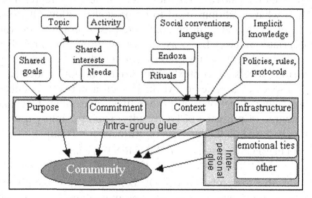

Fig. 1. Conditions for Community

References

1. Wellman, B., Berkowitz, S.D. (Eds): Social Structures: a Network Approach. Cambridge, Cambridge U.P. (1988)
2. Wellman, B., Gulia, M.: Virtual Communities as Communities. In: Smith, M., Kollock, P. (Eds) Communities in Cyberspace. New York, Routledge (1999)
3. Kim, A.J.: Community Building on the Web. Berkeley, Calif., Peachpit Press (2000)
4. Rheingold, H.: The Virtual Community: Homesteading on the Electronic Frontier. New York, Harper-Collins (1994). *An updated version has just been released* (2001).
5. Jones, S.: CyberSociety 2.0: Revisiting Computer-Mediated Communication and Community. Thousand Oaks, Calif., Sage Publications (1998)
6. Smith, M., Kollock, P.: Communities in Cyberspace. New York, Routledge (1999)
7. Sproull, L., Kiesler, S.: Connections: New Ways of Working in the Networked Organization. Cambridge, Mass., MIT Press (1991)
8. Kollock, P.: The Economies of Online Cooperation: Gifts and Public Goods in Cyberspace. In: Smith, M., Kollock, P. (Eds) Communities in Cyberspace. New York, Routledge (1999)
9. Kollock, P.: Design Principles for Online Communities. Paper presented at the Harvard Conference of the Internet and Society, Cambridge MA (1996)

10. Preece,J.:Online Communities:Designing Usability,Supporting Sociability.NY, Wiley (2000)

11. Whittaker, S., Isaacs, E., O'Day, V.: Widening the Net:Workshop Report on the Theory and Practice of Physical and Network Communities. SIGCHI Bulletin,v29,n3,ACM Press (1997)

12. Gabbay, D., Woods, J.: The Reach of Abduction. ESSLLI 2000 Lecture Notes, University of Birmingham (2000)

13. Pearl. J.: Probabilistic reasoning in intelligent systems. Morgan Kaufmann (1988)

Sufficient Conditions for Well-Behaved Adaptive Hypermedia Systems

Hongjing Wu and Paul De Bra

Department of Computing Science
Eindhoven University of Technology
Eindhoven, The Netherlands
{hongjing,debra}@win.tue.nl

Abstract. We focus on well-behaved Adaptive Hypermedia Systems, which means the adaptation engine that executes adaptation rules always terminates and produces predictable (confluent) adaptation results. Unfortunately termination and confluence are undecidable in general. In this paper we discuss sufficient conditions to help authors to write adaptation rules that satisfy termination and confluence.

Keywords: adaptive hypermedia, user modeling, production rules.

1 Introduction

Adaptive Hypermedia Systems (or AHS for short) provide automatically personalized access to hypermedia information sources, most often in the form of Websites. Most AHS provide *adaptive navigation support* and *adaptive content*. The link structure or the presentation of link anchors is different for every user. The actual content on information pages is also different for every user. An overview of systems, methods and techniques for adaptive hypermedia can be found in [B96]. We have developed a reference model for the architecture of adaptive hypermedia applications: the Adaptive Hypermedia Application Model (AHAM) [DHW99REFREF]. AHAM describes AHS at an abstract level, using an architecture consisting of three parts:

- a *domain model* (DM) that describes how the information content of the application is structured (using concepts and concept relationships).
- a fine-grained *user model* (UM) that represents a user's preferences, knowledge, goals, navigation history and other relevant aspects.
- an *adaptation model* (AM) consisting of *adaptation rules*. The rules define the process of generating the adaptive presentation and of updating the user model.

This architecture provides a clear separation of concerns when developing an adaptive hypermedia application.

The implementation part of AHS, called *adaptation engine* (AE), is the software that performs the adaptation (described by rules in AM). *Design issues for a general-purpose adaptation engine* (AE) are discussed in earlier paper REF[WDD01]. We defined a rule language for AHS, AHAM-CA and proposed a static analysis method to decide if for a given DM, UM and AM the AE would always *terminate* and if it would be *confluent* (meaning that the system would generate predictable results). In this paper we discuss how the (sufficient but not necessary) conditions that guarantee *termination* and *confluence* can be relaxed (while remaining sufficient).

N. Zhong et al. (Eds.): WI 2001, LNAI 2198, pp. 148–152, 2001.
© Springer-Verlag Berlin Heidelberg 2001

2 The Adaptation Rule Language

For lack of space we will not give a complete specification of the syntax of our (abstract) rule language, but illustrate it with an example. For details, see [WDD01]. A rule C→A in AHAM consists of a condition (C) and an action (A). While the properties of the language are independent of the syntax that is used, we use an SQL-like syntax for clarity. An example of an AHAM-CA rule is:

> C: **select** C_1.knowledge
>   **where** C_1.knowledge $\geq$ "known"
> A: **update** C_2.ready_to_read := **true**
>   **where** prerequisite(C_1, C_2) **and**
>   **not exists** (**select** C_3
>   **where** prerequisite(C_3, C_2) **and**
> C_3.knowledge < "known")

This is a *generic* rule, containing concept variables C_1, C_2, and C_3. The language also allows for (more or less) *specific* rules that use concepts instead of concept variables. The example rule says that when the knowledge of concept C_1 changes so that it becomes at least "known" then all concepts C_2 for which C_1 was the last prerequisite that was not yet "known" now become "ready_to_read". In this rule language it is all too easy to write rules that may cause infinite loops or unpredictable results. An example of such a rule is:

> C: **select** C_1.attr
>   **where** C_1.attr > 0
> A: **update** C_2.attr := C_2.attr + 1
>   **where** rel(C_1, C_2)

This example also shows that whether or not this rule generates an infinite loop depends on whether the concept relationship "rel" has cycles.

3 Sufficient Conditions for Termination and Confluence in AHS

The AHAM-CA rule language is very powerful, but expressive power always has an impact on system behavior. There is no implicit guarantee that the system is well-behaved. We proposed a static analysis method for termination and confluence [WDD01] for general cases in AHS; the analysis either tells us the rule set is confluent and terminates, or that this can't be determined. REF This section defines some constraints on AHAM-CA rules that guarantee termination and confluence, while at the same time retaining more freedom for the author to write propagation than the sufficient conditions of [WDD01]. We first define some terms and functions that will be used later on.

Definition 1: R_i *may activate* R_j if the execution of action A_i *can* change the database (DM and UM together) from a state in which condition C_j is false to a state in which C_j is true. R_i *may deactivate* R_j if the execution of action A_i *can* change the database from a state in which C_j is true to a state in which C_j is false.

Definition 2: A rule set *terminates* if the rules cannot activate each other indefinitely.

Definition 3: A *rule execution state* S is a pair (d, R_A), where d is a database state (DM and UM) and $R_A \subseteq AM$ is a set of active rules.

Definition 4: A *rule execution sequence* is a sequence σ consisting of a series of rule execution states linked by (executed) rules. A rule execution sequence is *complete* if the last state is (d,∅), i.e., the last state has no active rules. A rule execution sequence is *valid* if it represents a correct execution sequence: only active rules are executed, and pairs of adjacent states properly represent the effect of executing the corresponding rule; for details see [AHW95].

Definition 5: A rule set is *confluent* if, for every initial rule execution state S (produced by an initial database state followed by a set of user modifications), every valid and complete rule execution sequence beginning with S has the same final state.REFREF

Definition 6:
1. Let R: C→A. the function *num* for the number of relationships used in the **where** clause of A (A.**where**) (the exact definition is omitted because of limited space).
2. Let R: C→A
(a) S(R) = the set of attributes which are selected in C
(b) U(R) = the set of attributes to which values are assigned in A
(c) E(R) = the set of attributes used in the right-hand side of assignments in A
(d) A *st-rule* (start rule) is a rule that is triggered by external events or internally generated events. Its action only updates the concept selected by its condition. It describes the change of the values inside the same concept. St-rule represents a set of *st-rules*.
(e) A *pr-rule* (propagation rule) is a rule that propagates the changes of values to different concepts through relationships between these concepts. It would be a sign of bad design if rules propagate changes through means other than concept relationships in AHS. Pr-rule represents a set of *pr-rules*.
(f) Pri(R) is the number to represent the priority of the execution order of rule R.
(g) AM(rel)⊆Pr-rule is the set of rules which propagate their change "through" the relationship type rel.

Now we study constraints that guarantee that the execution of a set of rules terminates and is confluent, and that still give authors a certain expressive power to write rules with propagation. The first few constraints show that a straightforward approach leads to very strict constraints that do not give authors enough freedom.

Constraint 1: $\forall R_i, R_j \in AM$: $S(R_i) \cap U(R_j) = \emptyset$.
This constraint means that rules are not allowed to trigger each other.

Theorem 1: A rule set AM satisfying Constraint 1 terminates.
We omit the (easy) proof. This constraint is very strict as it prohibits propagation. However, it is not yet sufficient to guarantee confluence.

Constraint 2: $\forall R_i, R_j \in AM$:
1. R_i is *independent* from R_j: $(S(R_i) \cup U(R_i) \cup E(R_i)) \cap U(R_j) = \emptyset$.
2. R_i is *self-independent*: $(S(R_i) \cup E(R_i)) \cap U(R_i) = \emptyset$.

This constraint means rules are not allowed to affect (activate or deactivate) each other or themselves and rule execution order won't affect the final result.

Theorem 2: A rule set AM satisfying Constraint 2 terminates and is confluent.
This (easy) proof is also omitted.

While Constraint 1 only guarantees termination, constraint 2 is a sufficient condition for termination *and* confluence. The computational complexity of the algorithm to verify these constraints is $O(N^2 x M^2)$, where N is the number of rules and M is the number of attributes. These constraints are very strict in the sense that it is impossible to describe any propagation (a rule that activates other rules). We define Constraints 3-7 (and 7') to give more expressive freedom to authors.

Constraint 3: AM = St-rule$\cup$Pr-rule, $\forall R_i \in$ St-rule, $\forall R_j \in$ Pr-rule: $Pri(R_i) > Pri(R_j)$.

This is a general constraint for rules to be semantically correct in AHS. It means that the set of rules consists of start rules and propagation rules. This constraint also describes that in each phase of the transition, the start rules execute before the propagation. Priorities help but are not enough to guarantee the termination or confluence.

Constraint 4: The "graph" for every type of concept relationship (except hyperlinks) is acyclic.

Hyperlinks are not used for propagating user-model changes, so they may have cycles. Other relationships are used to propagate the changes between different concepts. It is often not a good design if the relationship type is cyclic, because then the change propagation may never stop. (For instance, cycles in prerequisite relationships do not make sense.) But even with acyclic relationship types, relationships of different types can still interact and cause non-termination that way.

Constraint 5: $\forall rel_1, rel_2 \in$ DM-rel, $rel_1 \neq rel_2$:
$\forall R_i \in$ AM(rel_1), $\forall R_j \in$ AM(rel_2): $U(R_i) \cap S(R_j) = \varnothing$.

This constraint means that rules that use a different type of relationships cannot activate each other.

Theorem 3: A rule set AM terminates if it satisfies Constraints 3-5.
Proof (sketch): A rule set AM consists of a finite number of st-rules and pr-rules. The st-rules won't trigger each other; they are trigged by external and internal events. The st-rules may trigger the pr-rules, and the pr-rules may also trigger pr-rules. The propagation for rules that use a relationship type always terminates because the relationship graph is a DAG. And rules that use a different type of relationships cannot trigger each other, so different DAGs cannot be combined to form a cycle.

Constraint 6: $\forall rel \in$ DM-rel: $\forall R_i, R_j \in$ AM(rel), $R_i \neq R_j$: $U(R_i) \cap U(R_j) = \varnothing$.

This constraint says that every pair of rules containing the same relationship type updates disjoint sets of attributes. In a simple propagation case every attribute is assigned to only once per transition.

Definition 7: $\forall rel_1, rel_2 \in$ DM-rel:
Independent(rel_1, rel_2) holds if $\forall R_i \in$ AM(rel_1), $\forall R_j \in$ AM(rel_2), $R_i \neq R_j$:
  $(S(R_i) \cup U(R_i) \cup E(R_i)) \cap U(R_j) = \varnothing$ **and** $(S(R_j) \cup U(R_j) \cup E(R_j)) \cap U(R_i) = \varnothing$

This definition says that all relationship types are independent; the execution order of rules using different relationship types doesn't matter to the final result.

Constraint 7: $\forall \text{rel}_1, \text{rel}_2 \in \text{DM-rel}, \text{rel}_1 \neq \text{rel}_2, \text{Independent}(\text{rel}_1, \text{rel}_2)$ holds.

Constraint 7': $\forall R \in \text{AM}, R:C \rightarrow A: num(A.\textbf{where}) \leq 1$ **and**

$\forall \text{rel}_1, \text{rel}_2 \in \text{DM-rel}: \quad (\forall R_i \in \text{AM}(\text{rel}_1), \forall R_j \in \text{AM}(\text{rel}_2), \text{rel}_1 \neq \text{rel}_2: \text{Pri}(R_i) > \text{Pri}(R_j))$ **or**
$(\forall R_i \in \text{AM}(\text{rel}_1), \forall R_j \in \text{AM}(\text{rel}_2), \text{rel}_1 \neq \text{rel}_2: \text{Pri}(R_i) < \text{Pri}(R_j))$

This constraint means that each pr-rule has at most one relationship, and the propagation order through all relationship graphs is pre-defined. Constraint 7 needs to calculate many attribute sets, and in most cases we need apply different relationships separately, so it is more natural to just define some execution order for them. We can then use Constraint 7' to replace Constraint 7.

Theorem 4: A rule set AM is confluent if it satisfies Constraint 3-7 (or 7').
Proof (sketch): Constraints 3-5 guarantee AM to terminate, with Constraint 6 AM becomes confluent for the propagation through each relationship graph. Furthermore, with Constraint 7 or Constraint 7' AM becomes confluent for propagation through all relationship graphs.

Constraint 3-7 (or 7') are easy to understand for the author and can be used in most common AHS. Constraint 3 is easy to verify, while Constraint 4 and Constraint 7' rely on the DM alone and are known before analyzing a set of rules. As the number of relationship types is small, the time needed for the algorithm to verify Constraint 3-7 (or 7') is similar to the one to verify Constraint 2.

4 Conclusions

In this paper we proposed some constraints on adaptation rules to obtain sufficient conditions that guarantee termination and confluence for AHS. Checking these constraints has a much lower computational complexity than the static analysis method proposed in [WDD01REF]. Imposing Constraints 3-7 (or 7') still allows an author to write propagating adaptation rules in most common AHS.

References

[AHW95] Aiken, A., Widom, J., Hellerstein, J.M., "Static Analysis Techniques for Predicting the Behavior of Database Production Rules". ACM Transactions on Database Systems, Vol. 20, nr. 1, pp. 3-41, 1995.
[B96] Brusilovsky, P., "Methods and Techniques of Adaptive Hypermedia". User Modeling and User-Adapted Interaction, 6, pp. 87-129, 1996. (Reprinted in Adaptive Hypertext and Hypermedia, Kluwer Academic Publishers, pp. 1-43, 1998.)
[DHW99] De Bra, P., Houben, G.J., Wu, H., "AHAM: A Dexter-based Reference Model for Adaptive Hypermedia". Proceedings of ACM Hypertext'99, Darmstadt, pp. 147-156, 1999.
[WDD01] Wu, H., De Kort, E., De Bra, P., "Design Issues for General Purpose Adaptive Hypermedia Systems". Proceedings of the 12th ACM Conference on Hypertext and Hypermedia, Arhus, Denmark, 2001 (to appear).

Towards Formal Specification of Client-Server Interactions for a Wide Range of Internet Applications

Vadim Doubrovski

IBM Global Services Australia, Level 22, 300 LaTrobe St, Melbourne, 3000, Victoria,
Australia
vdoubrov@au1.ibm.com

Abstract. Traditional way of designing Internet applications involves writing
code for programming the sequence of pages presented to the client and
associated decision-making logic. This makes the interaction flow of an
application unclear and reduces its maintainability. A formal method of
expressing interactions in an Internet application that is based on the notion of
Interaction Machine is proposed. Such formalism can be mapped to interaction
specifications expressed in XML that can be interpreted by an application-
neutral universal controller. Additional advantages of the proposed universal
controller include full synchronization between the client and the server (a well-
known problem for Internet applications), preservation of complete history of
application context that allows for true rollbacks and resumption of long-
suspended applications. The approach can be used for implementing a wide
range of applications including standard HTML-based applications, WML-
based WAP and Business-to-Business XML-based applications.

1 Introduction

Traditional approach to constructing Internet applications includes developing three
main components, namely: presentation, business logic and controlling structures that
govern the overall process of communication between a web client and the
application server. This resembles the Model-View-Controller (MVC) paradigm that
is popular in Smalltalk [1-3] and Java [4]. Presentation (View) is provided by
XHTML, WML or other XML pages that are either static or dynamically generated as
it is the case for Java Server Pages (JSP), Active Server Pages (ASP) and other page
generation techniques. Business logic (Model) is usually implemented as programs,
scripts or components (e.g. DCOM, Java Beans, EJB).

It is a commonly accepted view that clear separation of these two parts from one
another is an essential characteristic of a good application architecture, which among
other things allows for changing the presentation without affecting the business logic
components. At the same time however, there is usually no clear separation between
pure business logic components of an application from those responsible for client-
server interaction and navigation between application's pages that represent the
Controller part of the MVC model.

We propose a formal approach to expressing interaction specifications that
describe the process of information exchange between an Internet client and a server.

N. Zhong et al. (Eds.): WI 2001, LNAI 2198, pp. 153–162, 2001.
© Springer-Verlag Berlin Heidelberg 2001

Such formal specifications act as programs for a finite state machine that forms the core of a universal interaction controller. This approach makes it possible to achieve a clear separation between business logic (Model) and interaction (Controller). We also show that this approach provides a number of additional architectural benefits such as full synchronization between a client and a server and preservation of complete history of application context that allows for true rollbacks and resumption of long-suspended applications.

Section 2 of the paper introduces a formal model for specifying interactions in an Internet application. Section 3 demonstrates how this formal model can be mapped to an XML specification that can be interpreted by a universal interaction controller. Section 4 discusses implementation of the controller and presents the architecture for a typical Internet application that is based on the proposed approach.

2   Formal Model for Describing Interactions

The process of client-server interaction in a typical Internet application consists of a series of elementary interactions whereby each such interaction includes a client's request for information followed by the server's response. Without loss of generality, we can assume that a traditional Internet application that serves HTML pages will be discussed, however, the type of page content is in fact irrelevant to the models described below. All server's responses will be referred to as *pages* regardless of whether they form a stream of HTML for web applications or a stream of WML for WAP applications, or, perhaps, even XML stream for B2B applications that does not represent a page at all in its conventional sense.

Let us consider a system S that can serve pages in response to a client's request. S represents a server executing an application that is dedicated to a single client connection. The terms system and application, therefore, will be used interchangeably when referred to S. We assume that S is a stateful system and its state can be described as a vertex in a multidimensional phase space of it's parameters that will be referred to as *system context*.

An act of information exchange between the system S and the client will be called a *node of interaction* or simply a *node* if it consists of serving a single page as a result of a single client's request. The term *node sequence* will denote zero, one or more nodes following one another in the course of a client-server interaction. When S executes, it enacts certain node sequence, and which nodes are involved in the sequence usually depends on the system context.

We define *application interaction graph (IG)* as a triple

$$IG = (D, T', C) , \tag{1}$$

where D is a set of nodes that can potentially be enacted within the application (these inherently depend on the design); $T': D \times D \mapsto \{0,1\}$ is the transition relation on the set of nodes that assigns 1 to a pair of nodes $d_i, d_j \in D$ iff the node d_i can be followed by the node d_j; $C \subseteq D$ is a set of initial (or entry) nodes. Therefore IG is simply a directed graph with vertices D and edges T'. A node sequence, therefore, represents a realization of a path out of all possible paths within an IG originated from any initial node $c \in C$.

Let's consider a more detailed model of a node. It represents an elementary interaction encompassing the following actions:
- receiving the client's request;
- serving the page that is associated with the node;
- waiting for a client response;
- making transition to the next node within the IG.

In order to formally construct specification of the interaction process not only is it necessary to be able to express possible transitions from one node to another as it is the case with the IG, but also to represent transitions as a function of the current node and the current system context. If we assume without loss of generality that the system context is discrete and finite, then it will be enumerable and can be thought of as an alphabet of system states Σ.

The consequence of this is that the interaction process can now be modeled by a deterministic finite automaton (DFA) [5, 6]. Such an automaton will be referred to as an *Interaction Machine (IM)*. There are however certain semantic differences between a standard DFA and an IM. A DFA is a formalism that determines a set of strings that it accepts, i.e. strings on which it halts in one of the states referred to as accepting states. A more suitable formalism for IM can be based on that for the Moore machine:

$$M = (Q, \Sigma, \Delta, \delta, \lambda, q_0),$$ \hfill (2)

where Q is a finite set of states; Σ is the input alphabet; Δ is the output alphabet; $\delta : Q \times \Sigma \mapsto Q$ is a transition function; $\lambda : Q \mapsto \Delta$ is the output function; $q_0 \in Q$ is the initial state.

The Moore machine formalism can be adopted for specifying an IM in the following way:

$$IM = (D, \Sigma, G, T, \lambda, C),$$ \hfill (3)

where D is a set of nodes; Σ is the alphabet of the system states that represents all vertices in the system's phase space; G is the output alphabet that represents the set of pages that the system can serve; T is the transition function $T(d, a) \mapsto D, d \in D, a \in \Sigma$; $\lambda : D \mapsto G$ is a function that specifies a page $g = \lambda(d)$ served by a node $d \in D$; C is a set of initial nodes.

An interaction machine *IM* (Fig. 1) is said to realize an interaction graph *IG* if *IM* and *IG* have the same set of nodes C, the same set of initial nodes C, and

$$T'(d_i, d_j) \Leftrightarrow (\exists a \in \Sigma)(T(d_i, a) = d_j)$$

There is an important difference in interpretation of the notion of state for IM compared to that for DFA. The set of states for a traditional DFA is represented by nodes D of the IM as the nodes describe the states of interaction. However we use the states of the system S as the alphabet Σ which is the alphabet made of discrete system states from the phase space of the system context. The latter is used as an input alphabet due to the assumption that the system makes the transition decision based on examining its current context. Therefore Σ directly corresponds to the input alphabet of a DFA. Consequently, the IM model includes two different sets of states, namely the IM states D and the system states Σ.

It is clear that for any real system the cardinality of the alphabet Σ will be very large. At the same time for any given node there will be large areas within the system phase space that have the same values of the function T. In other words, there will be relatively small number of possible transitions from any node n within the IG that the IM realizes. These transitions will be determined by relatively small number of parameters from the system context while the other parameters will have no effect on the transition function for the given node n. The fact of whether or not certain transition will be effected is determined by a predicate over such parameters.

Therefore, it is more convenient to consider alphabets Σ_d ($d \in D$) specific for each node d of the IM. Each such alphabet Σ_d can be defined as follows: a state a from the new alphabet is said to have value $a_d^i \in \Sigma_d$ iff a predicate $f_d^i(p_{n1}^i, p_{n2}^i, ..., p_{nk}^i)$ is true, where $p_{n1}^i, p_{n2}^i, ..., p_{nk}^i$ are some parameters from the system context specific for this given predicate and node (Fig. 2).

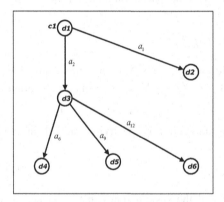

Fig. 1. Example of an Interaction Machine with nodes $d_1 \div d_6$ and edges marked with symbols of the alphabet.

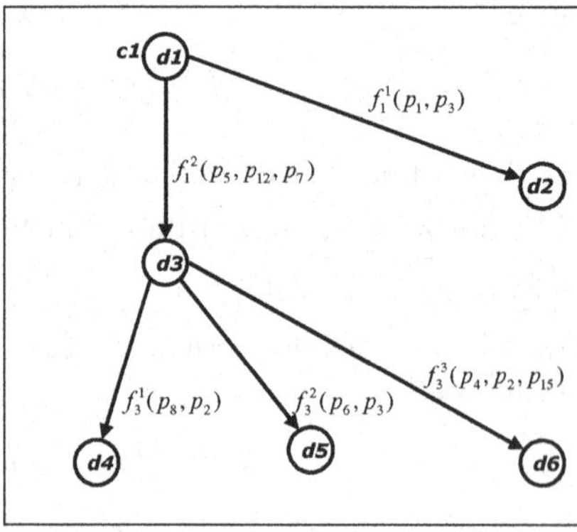

Fig. 2. Example of an Interaction Machine with the alphabet replaced by transition predicates.

Finally an IM can be defined as

$$IM = (D, \bigcup_{d \in D} \Sigma_d, G, T, \lambda, C) , \qquad (4)$$

However now $T(d, a) = T(d, a(d))$ where $a(d) = a_d^i \in \Sigma_d$ iff f_d^i is true.

Therefore, it is assumed that an IM is defined if defined are:
- the set of nodes D;
- the alphabet Σ_d for each node $d \in D$;
- the set of transitions that for each node determines the next target nodes and their corresponding transition predicates f_d^i;
- the set of pages G and a page function $\lambda(d) = g_d \in G$;
- the set of possible initial nodes C.

3   Expressing IM Specifications in XML

The model outlined above can be used as the basis for expressing formal specification for an IM. An abstract machine can then be built to interpret such specifications.

The formal model of the IM can be represented as an object that consists of a series of nodes D. Each node d_i would include a reference to a page $g_i = \lambda(d_i) \in G$ that is to be served upon reaching the node and a navigation object that implements the transition function $T(d_i, a)$, $a \in \Sigma_n$ for the node in question. The transition function is implemented as a number of predicates f_d^i where each predicate is specified together with the corresponding reference to the node to which a transition is made when the predicate evaluates to true.

XML [7] is convenient for expressing the IM model due to its capabilities to represent objects with arbitrary structures in a serialized form of plain text. Wide availability of validating parsers also made the implementation task easier.

Below presented is a largely simplified model of a node Node1 from a sample IM. The comments pertain to the stages of the node's lifecycle.

```
<node id="Node1">
    <!-- This is what is served to the client -->
    <source href="welcome.jsp"/>

    <!--Here a response from the client is awaited -->

    <!--Response received.  Where to go next? -->
    <navigation>
        <go name="param1" value="1" href="#Node2"/>
        <go name="param1" value="2" href="#Node3"/>
        <go name="param2" value="0" href="#Node4"/>
    </navigation>
</node>
```

There is a reference to the page welcome.jsp that will be served at the node (the source tag) and a navigation section that contains three simple predicates (the go tags). Each of them contains a reference to a corresponding target node (the href tag) to which a transition can be made should the predicate evaluate to true (references to nodes Node2, Node3, and Node4 respectively).

A full specification of such IM would consist of a number of nodes connected via node references to form a complete IG. Interpretation of an IM specification starts from one of the initial nodes (the first node by default) and continues until one of the leaf nodes of the IG is reached.

4   Universal Controller for Interpreting IM Specifications

The abstract machine that interprets IM specifications expressed in XML, named XFlow Interaction Controller (XFIC), is implemented as a universal controller in Java using Java Servlet API 2.1. XFIC runs on an application server and replaces servlets that otherwise would need to be written to coordinate session management, page delivery, dispatching client responses and routing the response information to appropriate parts of a user application and to Java Beans that implement application's business logic. IM specifications expressed in XML that XFIC interprets are called *control files* and are stored in the XFIC repository.

4.1   Architecture of Applications Based on XFIC

The use of XFIC for managing interactions addresses the Controller part of the overall application's architecture while the page design corresponds to the Presentation. There also must be present certain application components that implement the Business Logic part. Such components should not be pre-determined and should have dynamic binding due to the interpretive nature of the IM specifications in XML. One should be able to easily build such components and attach them to the application.

Java Beans are used for implementing business logic components because they satisfy all these requirements. Java Beans can implement any necessary business logic, can be separately compiled and have dynamic binding capabilities that XFIC uses through the Java Reflection mechanism. Beans are also used as the way of implementing node predicates in those cases when a predicate is more complex than just a simple comparison. Predicate arguments are passed to a bean by setting certain bean's public attributes and the result of the evaluation is placed in a bean's public attribute too, which can then be inspected by a simple comparison predicate from within the control file. Such mechanism provides full visibility of the public context of the beans from within the control file and therefore facilitates unlimited extensibility of XFIC through the use of beans.

Reflection is used to instantiate beans, pass parameters to and from beans, dynamically invoke methods prescribed by control files and establish a consistent exception handling framework for the whole application. In fact, XFIC completely handles the lifecycle of a bean from its instantiation, to method invocation, to destruction. In order to handle beans in a more manageable manner, XFIC supports three types of beans' lifespan, namely: request, session and application. If a bean has the scope "request", XFIC instantiates it and attaches it to the servlet's request object, which ensures that the bean gets implicitly destroyed when the request object is destroyed. Beans with the scope of "session" are kept alive for the whole duration of a servlet session, however different sessions have their own instances of such beans that they do not share. If a bean is created with the scope of "application" it remains active as long as the servlet engine is running. Instances of such beans can be shared by many concurrent sessions, which facilitates high scalability of applications built with the use of XFIC.

Together the beans that implement business logic and transition predicates are referred to as process beans in the XFIC architecture. Besides process beans an application can include so called view beans that implement dynamic content within JSP.

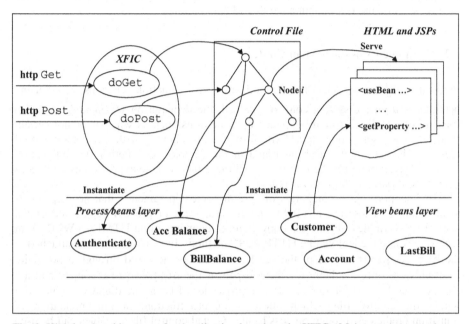

Fig. 3. High level architecture of an application based on the XFIC. Major components shown are the XFIC that is driven by the control file, HTML and JSP pages served by the XFIC during the course of interaction, view beans that JSP use for creating dynamic content and process beans that are invoked from within various nodes to implement predicates and business logic.

The full architecture of any application built with the use of XFIC consists, therefore, of the following major architectural components (Fig. 3):

− XFIC and application's control files that it interprets;
− any pages sourced from any page generation mechanism that is available on the server, including local or remote (through a URL) HTML pages, JSP, CGI scripts, server side includes and any other;
− view beans used for generating dynamic content within JSP;
− process beans that implement complex node predicates and application's business logic.

The task of developing an application based on XFIC consists therefore of the following stages:

- develop an overall scenario of the system interaction based on the use cases and implement the scenario in a control file or a number of control files;
- design and develop static HTML pages and dynamic JSP for the application together with the necessary view beans;
- implement the application's business logic in process beans and embed links to them into appropriate places within the control file.

The process of application design and implementation is now clearly separated into three sufficiently independent areas, each of which requires separate skill set and can be allocated to different teams of developers. This in turn facilitates quicker time to deployment and increases maintainability of applications.

4.2 Components of the System Context

Predicates f_d^i associated with the node transition function are constructed using parameters from the system context. Indeed, the decision on which node should a transition be made to usually depends on conditions such as whether or not certain field has been set within an HTML form on the client, whether a certain record requested by the client has been found in the database or whether the application reaches a given node for the first time. All these facts can be expressed as predicates over various parts of the system context.

XFIC supports three categories of system context parameters that are kept in its symbol table. These are postfields, public properties of process beans, and global control file variables. Postfields correspond to elements of an HTML or WML form received from the client via the HTTP POST method. In fact, any attribute attached to the httpRequest object of the servlet API can be accessed through a postfield. Postfields are only available for the lifespan of the httpRequest object and are discarded at the next interaction. Public properties of beans are directly visible from within the control file, which allows complete freedom in implementation of transition predicates through process beans. Global control file variables can be used for implementing state management and information passing between nodes. A node specification below illustrates the use of the three types of the system context in transition predicates (@ denotes postfields, % - bean properties, and $ - variables):

```
<node id="LoginNode">
   <source href="login.jsp"/>
   <navigation>
     <go name="$loggedIn" value="1" href="#Node2"/>
     <go name="@cancelled" value="1" href="#NoLogin"/>
     <useBean name="person" class="xfic.bean.Person"/>
     <invokeMethod bean="person"
             method="authenticate"/>
     <go name="%person.authenticated" value="true"
             href="#SuccessLogin"/>
     <go href="#FailedLogin"/>
   </navigation>
</node>
```

4.3 Architectural Advantages of the Universal Controller

The described approach provides a number of immediate architectural advantages. Since the server has the ultimate control over the interaction, it becomes possible to keep the complete history of the node sequence. Not only can the history be preserved, but the full system context can be preserved too. This is achieved by serializing the full system context at each node (or on request) and storing it to a persistent storage. Such powerful feature allows XFIC to roll, if required, an application back to any previously saved checkpoint. This ensures that not only does the application presentation appear exactly as it was at the moment of saving the checkpoint but the full context including the states of the process beans and control file variables is also completely restored from the reinstated context snapshot.

The context serialization capability is used in yet another way within XFIC. Apart from facilitating rollbacks it can be used to suspend an application, serialize its full context and store it away to a persistent storage (e.g. a database) in the state of collapse for future use. This becomes possible because of the fact that the current context consists of XFIC's internal tables and an application's process beans that all represent serializable objects and because the context is the full and the only "state aware" part of an application while the other parts are stateless. At a later moment in time (hours, days, years) the application can be reinstated and continue its execution from the point, at which it was suspended. The whole process is completely transparent from the application's and its beans' viewpoint. No special programming effort is required on the part of a bean developer to enable the feature.

Another advantage of the server's control over the interaction process includes the well known problem of synchronizing a web client and a server. The server may serve a page that contains an HTML form and it expects the same form back. At the same time the user may choose to use the browser's history object (e.g. via the "back" button) to go a number of pages back, get a previously visited page, change the information then and re-submit the page. This can desynchronize the client and the server that for many web applications may have a devastating effect. XFIC, on the contrary, if required, can attempt to automatically track the interaction back to the required page and handle the situation correctly.

5 Conclusion

We presented an approach to modeling client-server interactions based on formal specification of the interaction process and on the Interaction Machine formalism, which can be used for a large class of Internet applications. We also discussed the implementation of the abstract machine that processes IM specifications expressed in XML. Advantages of the presented approach include:
- clear and succinct formal specification of the interaction machine instead of having its implementation spread over the application code;
- separation of interaction specification from the presentation (HTML and JSP pages) and encapsulated business logic (process beans), which facilitates truly component based development of Internet applications;

- complete independence of interaction specification from the type of page content which makes the approach equally useful for traditional HTML, WML WAP, and XML-based B2B applications;
- complete control over the interaction process facilitating and enforcing full synchronization between the states of the client and the server;
- the ability to keep track of the complete state of an application including its full system context and the ability to make snapshots at checkpoints or at each node;
- implementation of a true roll-back function to any saved checkpoint with consistent reinstatement of the full system context;
- the ability to suspend a session for unlimited time with full serialization of the complete system context and saving it to a persistent storage. This can be followed by a resumption of the session at a later stage with the complete reinstatement of the system context without loosing application's consistency and integrity;
- tools and systems integration through the ability by a tool to generate XML-based interaction specifications.

Use of the XFIC also substantially decreases time to deployment of a wide range of Internet applications.

Acknowledgements. We would like to acknowledge contribution of Richard Paris, who provided extremely clear, elegant, efficient and reliable implementation of XFIC in Java, Jay Strosnider, conversations with whom were very valuable and stimulating, and Oscar Adinolfi, without whose support the project could not have been implemented.

References

1. Shan, Y.-P.: MoDE: A UIMS for Smalltalk. Proc. OOPSLA '90 (1990) 258-268
2. Adams, S.S.: MetaMethods: The MVC Paradigm. HOOPLA 1(4), (1988)
3. Krasner, G.E., Pope, S.T.: A Cookbok for Using the Model-View-Controller User Interface Paradigm in Smalltalk-80. J. O-O Prog., 1(1988) 26-49
4. Niemeyer, P., Peck, J.: Exploring Java. O'Reilly & Assoc. (1996)
5. Lewis, L.H., Papadimitriou, C.H.: Elements of the Theory of Computation. Prentice-Hall (1998)
6. Hopcroft, J.E., Ullman, J.D.: Introduction to Automata Theory, Languages, and Computation. Addison-Wesley (1979)
7. Extensible Markup Language (XML). W3C Recommendation, 2nd edn, World Wide Web Consortium, (2000); available at http://www.w3.org/TR/2000/REC-xml-20001006

Collecting, Visualizing, and Exchanging Personal Interests and Experiences in Communities

Yasuyuki Sumi and Kenji Mase

ATR Media Integration & Communications Research Laboratories,
Seika-cho, Soraku-gun, Kyoto 619-0288, Japan
sumi@mic.atr.co.jp

Abstract. In this paper, we propose a notion of facilitating encounters and knowledge sharing among people having shared interests and experiences in museums, conferences, etc. In order to show our approach and current status, this paper presents our project to build a communityware system situated in real-world contexts. The aims of the project are to build a tour guidance system personalized according to its user's individual contexts, and to facilitate knowledge communications among communities by matchmaking users having shared interests and providing real and/or virtual places for their meetings. In this paper, we first show PalmGuide, hand-held tour guidance system. After that, we show two Web-based systems to increase the level of "community-awareness". One is Semantic Map, a visual interface for exploring community information, such as exhibits and people (exhibitors and visitors). Another is AgentSalon, a display showing conversations between personal agents according to their users' profiles and interests.

1 Introduction

In this paper, we propose a notion of facilitating encounters and knowledge sharing among people having shared interests and experiences in museums, conferences, etc. In order to show our approach and current status, this paper presents our project to build a communityware system [4] situated in real-world contexts.

In investigating how to create such communityware situated in real-world contexts, we have chosen exhibition-type applications such as museums and open houses at research laboratories. The reason is because these are places where knowledge is accumulated and/or conveyed to people by seeing, touching, and experiencing actual exhibits, and where exhibitors as specialists provide knowledge to visitors with diverse interests and viewpoints.

The aims of the project are to build a guidance system personalized according to its user's individual contexts, and to facilitate knowledge communications among communities by matchmaking users having shared interests and providing real and/or virtual places for their meetings [11].

The followings show our scenario of knowledge communications using our system [12].

N. Zhong et al. (Eds.): WI 2001, LNAI 2198, pp. 163–174, 2001.
© Springer-Verlag Berlin Heidelberg 2001

Tour navigation. Users carry their own PalmGuide, hand-held guidance system, during the tour. PalmGuide manages its owner's profile and visiting records so far and recommends exhibits according to his/her current situation (location and time) and interests. He/she can browse information of the recommended exhibits on PalmGuide.

Exhibit display. The user can obtain a personalized explanation of each exhibit by connecting PalmGuide with exhibit displays located at individual exhibit sites.

Information kiosk. Our information kiosks are connected with servers via a LAN and enable visitors to access accumulated community information. In order to increase the "community-awareness" among people involved in an exhibition, the kiosks provide users with services such as visually showing the relationships between visitors and exhibitors according to their interests and touring histories. The community services on the kiosks are almost identical with off-site services provided via the Internet. However, in the case of the kiosks, we can offer more sophisticated services situated in location and time, e.g., highlighting information related with the front exhibit. Moreover, the kiosks located at the exhibition site have the potential to facilitate real face-to-face meetings between visitors with shared interests.

Off-site services. By using Web-based system, potential visitors can preview exhibit-related information at their home/office beforehand. As will be described later, we provide users with Semantic Map, a tool for visually exploring exhibit-related information. Each user's behavior when using Semantic Map, such as keyword selection, is used to quantify the user's preference, which will then be exploited for the personalization of the guide agent while actual touring at the exhibition site.

Community network. We believe that providing people involved in an exhibition with visualized community networks, by structuring all users' contextual information accumulated in the actual exhibition site, will help new encounters among users sharing interests and community formation. The community network's structure is a graph whose nodes represent visitors, exhibitors, and exhibits and will have connections between people and exhibits according to the degree of attachment to exhibits. Here, by attachment to exhibits, we mean exhibitors being involved in the exhibits and visitors being interested in them, i.e., highly rating them on PalmGuide. Accordingly, the Semantic Map users can discover partners who might be interested in collaborating in the future.

In this paper, we first show PalmGuide. After that, we show two Web-based systems to increase the level of "community-awareness". One is Semantic Map, a visual interface for exploring community information, such as exhibits and people (exhibitors and visitors). Another is AgentSalon, a kiosk located at the exhibition site displaying conversations between personal agents according to their users' profiles and interests.

2   PalmGuide: Personal Tour Assistant

The user of our system carries PalmGuide, a hand-held guidance system, while touring an exhibition. A personal guide agent runs on PalmGuide and provides tour navigation information, such as exhibit recommendation, according to the user's contexts, i.e., personal interests and temporal and spatial situations (Figure 1). The guide agent running on PalmGuide can migrate to and provide personalized guidance on individual exhibit displays or information kiosks that are ubiquitously located in the exhibition site. It keeps its user's personal profile and touring records, which are used for personalizing the presentation of individual exhibits and matchmaking with other users having shared interests and touring records.

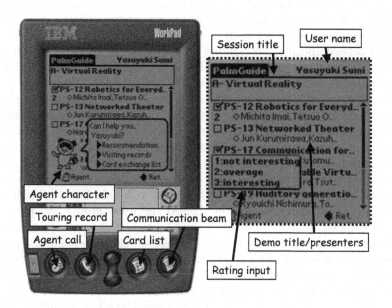

Fig. 1. PalmGuide display.

Connecting PalmGuide with exhibit displays by infrared updates the user's visiting history. This architecture allows us to capture the visiting histories of users without special methods such as employing location detection devices. The updated history of a user renews the personal guidance information, e.g., exhibit recommendations, on PalmGuide.

On PalmGuide, the user can rate individual exhibits that he/she visited so far (Figure 1). The ratings improve the precision of the exhibit recommendations by the guide agents. That is, exhibits sharing keywords with exhibits rated highly by the user are highly recommended, and exhibits sharing keywords with exhibits rated lowly are lowly recommended. The ratings are also used for building community networks. That is, a high rating for a certain exhibit by the user is represented as a link between the user and the exhibit on community networks; this is described next.

3 Semantic Map: Visual Explorer of Community Information

We built Semantic Map (Java applet) as a visual interface for exploring community information accessible via the Internet and on information kiosks located in exhibition sites.

We believe that providing people involved in an exhibition with visualized community networks, by structuring all users' contextual information accumulated in the actual exhibition site, will help new encounters among users sharing interests and community formation. The community network's structure is a graph whose nodes represent visitors, exhibitors, and exhibits and will have connections between people and exhibits according to the degree of attachment to exhibits.[1] Accordingly, the Semantic Map users can discover partners who might be interested in collaborating in the future.

The Semantic Map shown in Figure 2 displays the graphical relationships between exhibits presented in the last open house of the authors' laboratories. The rectangular icons in the graph signify exhibit titles and the oval icons signify keywords or participants (including exhibitors, i.e., researchers, and visitors). The keywords are technical terms characterizing the contents of the exhibits, which were previously extracted from outline texts prepared by exhibitors. This Semantic Map provided the users with graphs, with links between exhibit icons and keyword/participant icons; this helped the users browse the information space of the exhibition.

However, since the number of keyword/participant icons is huge, a graph including all of these keyword/participant icons is unable to provide useful visualization. Therefore, we have adopted a method with only the keyword/participant icons selected by the user being displayed based on his/her interests. As a result, the graph of Semantic Map can be structured based on an individual user's interests. For example, if a user selects the keyword "agent", he/she can view a partial graph formed with only "agent"-related papers. If the user selects other keywords, Semantic Map restructures the graph based on the corresponding viewpoint.

The guide agent keeps the selected keywords/participants as a part of its user's mental context, and uses the data for the personalization of Semantic Map whenever the user accesses information kiosks.

The exhibit icons and participant icons have links with related Web pages, e.g., project pages, personal home pages, and automatically generated touring diaries. Therefore, Semantic Map can be used for a visual interface for exploring information spaces of exhibitions, conferences, etc.

---

[1] Here, by attachment to exhibits, we mean exhibitors being involved in the exhibits and visitors being interested in them, i.e., highly rating them on PalmGuide.

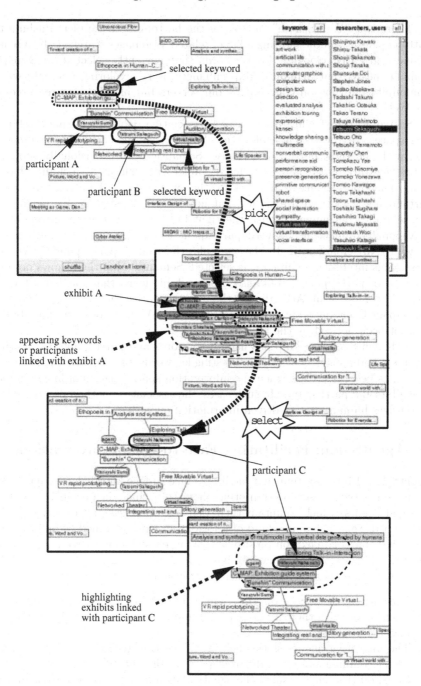

Fig. 2. Visual exploration of community information with Semantic Map.

There is a "Web Search" button on the bottom of the applet. Pushing the button opens a window showing a list of related Web pages searched , by a search engine (currently, Google), for keywords that currently selected on Semantic Map. It means that Semantic Map enhances users' exploring not only within community information collected by our servers but also in open resources on the Web.

Semantic Map facilitates its user's associative exploring of huge information spaces. In the example of Figure 2, when a user clicks the "exhibit A" icon with the right button of a mouse, Semantic Map provisionally shows all of the keyword/participant icons having links with exhibit A, including hidden icons. Therefore, the user can check for the existence of unknown keywords and participants related with exhibits that he/she is interested in. By moving the mouse while continuing to push the right button and releasing on one of the provisionally appearing keyword/participant icons, the user can select a new keyword/participant icon. In the example, the icon of participant C, who expressed his interest in exhibit A, is selected. Semantic Map then shows not only the icon of participant C but also other exhibit icons that participant C expressed his interest in. Accordingly, the user can notice the existence of not only participant C having a shared interest in exhibit A but also other exhibits that had not been noticed by the user yet.

Although Semantic Map has lists of keywords and participants as shown in the figure and its user can select interesting keywords/participants from the lists, these lists become useless when the information space consists of huge numbers of exhibits and participants. In such cases, the associative method presented here encourages human interest-driven information exploring.

4   AgentSalon: Facilitating Face-to-Face Conversations

AgentSalon [13] is a system that facilitates face-to-face knowledge exchange and discussion between users by tempting them to a chat via prompting by their personal agents, which maintain their personal interests and experiences. We prototyped AgentSalon as a kind of information kiosk assumed to be located in a meeting place of an exhibition site, with a large touch panel screen. AgentSalon has a big display for use by two to five users simultaneously.

The following is a scenario of using AgentSalon.

1. Personal guide agents on the PalmGuide of individual users migrate to AgentSalon with their users' personal information and are displayed as animated characters.
2. The migrating agents share their users' visiting records and interests and detect common as well as different parts in this information.
3. Based on the above results, the agents plan and begin conversations in front of the users. By observing the conversations, the users can efficiently and pleasantly exchange information related to an exhibit.
4. Because AgentSalon can access community information such as information on each exhibit and other users' personal information via the network,

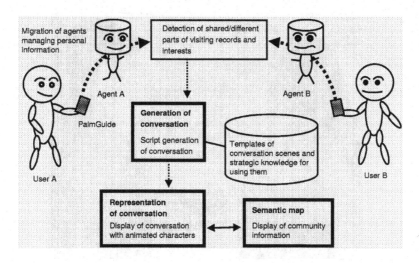

Fig. 3. System architecture of AgentSalon.

users can browse detailed information about exhibits or users referred by the agents.

As Figure 3 illustrates, AgentSalon consists of the following three components.

Generation of conversation. Generates scripts of *interesting* conversation using personal information managed by agents. It is a knowledge-based system having utterance templates and strategic rules to tailor scripts depending on context.

Representation of conversation. According to the generated scripts, this controls and represents utterances and behavior of animated agents by using Microsoft Agent. Stream of conversations, entrance and exit of agents, and simple interaction with users are controlled by using JavaScript.

Semantic map. A visual interface for browsing community information accumulated in the Web server. It shows semantic relationships between exhibits and people involved with them and helps a user to associatively explore large information spaces according to his/her interests.

AgentSalon runs on Microsoft Internet Explorer. Animated agents are displayed on the top of Semantic map using Microsoft Agent. The display is a touch panel, so users can manipulate Semantic map with their fingers and interact with their agents. Figure 4 shows AgentSalon used by two users.

In current implementation, when a certain agent enters the salon, its user's icon appears in Semantic map. At the same time, icons of exhibits that he/she has visited and evaluated as *interesting* appear and are linked with his/her icon. Therefore, it visualizes relationships (overlaps and differences) between touring experiences and the individual interests of users.

The following are example of conversation scenes performed by agents.

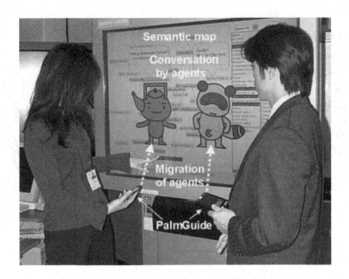

Fig. 4. AgentSalon in use.

Fig. 5. Example scene of AgentSalon (1): Mutual recommendations.

- Suppose that *user A* has visited *exhibits 1, 2, 3* and *4*, and *user B* has visited *exhibits 2, 4, 5* and *6*. In this case, their agents will notice that the users have commonly visited *exhibits 2* and *4*, i.e., they share some interests in exhibits. Therefore, *user A*'s agent recommends *exhibits 1* and *3* to *user B*, and *user B*'s agent recommends *exhibits 5* and *6* to *user A* (See Figure 5).

- When two users' evaluations of a commonly visited exhibit are different (e.g., *user A* is interested in *exhibit 1*, but *user B* is not), their agents prompt a discussion about the exhibit. For example, the agent of *user A* says "*Exhibit 1 was interesting!*", and then the agent of *user B* replies "Really? We didn't like it." By observing the dialog, *user A* and *user B* can know that they have

Fig. 6. Example scene of AgentSalon (2): Stimulating discussion.

Fig. 7. Example scene of AgentSalon (3): Topic offering by salon agent.

differing opinions about a shared experience (i.e., visiting *exhibit 1*), which efficiently leads them into a stimulating discussion (See Figure 6).

– The salon agent has more global view on Web resources than other agents belonging to individual users. When no events (e.g., entry of new agent) happen for a while, the salon agent offers a topic, such as pointing the most popular exhibit among PalmGuide users (See Figure 7).

5   Related Works

Our community network is similar to the social network proposed by [5], which is a network representation of relationships between people and knowledge. There have been other related studies such as a matchmaking agent that searches for people who share similar interests [1], a visualizing tool for helping community formation [2], recommender systems by collaborative filtering (e.g., [10]). These studies are related to ours since they aim at supporting collaborative knowledge communications by quantifying human interests and preferences. The above systems, however, only involve a desktop computing paradigm. Therefore, users have to explicitly input their preferences and queries. Our effort in prototyping a personal guidance system embeds such systems into real-world contexts so that the systems can semiautomatically work according to the contexts of users.

Related to AgentSalon, there have been some works to support knowledge sharing and creation such as systems to help collaborative Web browsing (e.g., Silhouettell [9] and Let's Browse [7]); asynchronous knowledge sharing using alter-ego agents [8,6]; and a helper agent who provides conversation topics to first-meeting users in a virtual meeting space [3]. However, their knowledge resources are commonly static information such as previously prepared knowledge bases. On the other hand, AgentSalon uses personal information constantly accumulated by personal agents on PalmGuides carried by users. Such information is embedded in the real world, therefore, information presented by AgentSalon has potential to instantly influence users' ongoing (touring) behavior and accelerate collaborative knowledge sharing and creation among communities.

The essential jobs of AgentSalon are to detect and represent shared/different parts of the personal information (e.g., interests and touring records) of several users. In terms of this, we have already proposed a method to visualize shared/different parts of several users' individual viewpoints during online discussion [14]. The Semantic map running on AgentSalon plays a similar role. However, efforts to read the shared/different parts from the visualized information spaces and to utilize it for further discussion are fully up to users. AgentSalon automatically reads the shared/different parts of users' knowledge/interests and represents them as *conversational stories*. Therefore, the cost of information conveyance between users decreases, and more casual usage and understanding are encouraged.

6   Conclusion and Future Work

We have shown our attempts to increase of awareness of shared interests and experiences among communities by presenting our ongoing project of a guidance system for exhibition tours. We believe that building a context-aware personal guide agent will facilitate community formation based on shared interests and knowledge exchanges within communities.

Without the connectivity with real-world contexts, knowledge exchange in a digitized world, even one which has rich information, will not be effective. Therefore, accumulating real-world contexts and connecting these with the digitized world, i.e., our investigation's focus, are very important issues.

Finally, the following issues remain to be solved before achieving a communityware system.

- We need to create personal agents that can each capture the context and information of its user from every possible digitized data that daily involves the user, in order to use the current exhibition guidance system as an everyday personal assistant.
- We have to continuously work on finding solutions to social issues such as the authorization and privacy of exchanged information.
- We want a communityware system that allows asynchronous/distributed communications depending on agent mediation. Accordingly, we need a method for the externalization, communication, and presentation of agent knowledge with multi-goal scripts, so that agents can semi-automatically interact with each other on behalf of their users.

Acknowledgments. Extraordinary valuable contributions to this work have been made by Tetsushi Yamamoto and Tadashi Takumi. Keiko Nakao took part in the design and illustration of the agent characters. Finally, we would like to thank Ryohei Nakatsu for his continuous support.

References

1. Leonard N. Foner. Yenta: A multi-agent, referral-based matchmaking system. In *Proceedings of the First International Conference on Autonomous Agents (Agents'97)*, pages 301–307. ACM, 1997.
2. Fumio Hattori, Takeshi Ohguro, Makoto Yokoo, Shigeo Matsubara, and Sen Yoshida. Socialware: Multiagent systems for supporting networked communities. *Communications of the ACM*, 42(3):55–61, 1999.
3. Katherine Isbister, Hideyuki Nakanishi, Toru Ishida, and Cliff Nass. Helper agent: Designing an assistant for human-human interaction in a virtual meeting space. In *Proceedings of CHI 2000*, pages 57–64. ACM, 2000.
4. Toru Ishida. Towards communityware. In *Proceedings of the International Conference and Exhibition on the Practical Application of Intelligent Agents and Multi-Agent Technology (PAAM-97)*, pages 7–21, 1997.
5. Henry Kautz, Bart Selman, and Mehul Shah. The hidden web. *AI Magazine*, 18(2):27–36, 1997.
6. Hidekazu Kubota, Toyoaki Nishida, and Tomoko Koda. Exchanging tacit community knowledge by talking-virtualized-egos. In *Proceedings of Agents 2000*, pages 285–292. ACM, 2000.

7. Henry Lieberman, Neil W. Van Dyke, and Adrian S. Vivacqua. Let's browse: A collaborative browsing agent. *Knowledge-Based Systems*, 12(8):427–431, 1999.
8. Toyoaki Nishida, Takashi Hirata, and Harumi Maeda. CoMeMo-Community: A system for supporting community knowledge evolution. In Toru Ishida, editor, *Community Computing and Support Systems*, volume 1519 of *Lecture Notes in Computer Science*, pages 183–200. Springer, 1998.
9. Masayuki Okamoto, Hideyuki Nakanishi, Toshikazu Nishimura, and Toru Ishida. Silhouettell: Awareness support for real-world encounter. In Toru Ishida, editor, *Community Computing and Support Systems*, volume 1519 of *Lecture Notes in Computer Science*, pages 316–329. Springer, 1998.
10. Upendra Shardanand and Pattie Maes. Social information filtering: Algorithms for automating "word of mouth". In *Proceedings of CHI'95*, pages 210–217. ACM, 1995.
11. Yasuyuki Sumi, Tameyuki Etani, Sidney Fels, Nicolas Simonet, Kaoru Kobayashi, and Kenji Mase. C-MAP: Building a context-aware mobile assistant for exhibition tours. In Toru Ishida, editor, *Community Computing and Support Systems*, volume 1519 of *Lecture Notes in Computer Science*, pages 137–154. Springer, 1998.
12. Yasuyuki Sumi and Kenji Mase. Communityware situated in real-world contexts: Knowledge media augmented by context-aware personal agents. In *Proceedings of the Fifth International Conference and Exhibition on the Practical Application of Intelligent Agents and Multi-Agent Technology (PAAM 2000)*, pages 311–326, 2000.
13. Yasuyuki Sumi and Kenji Mase. AgentSalon: Facilitating face-to-face knowledge exchange through conversations among personal agents. In *Proceedings of Agents 2001*, pages 393–400. ACM, 2001.
14. Yasuyuki Sumi, Kazushi Nishimoto, and Kenji Mase. Personalizing shared information in creative conversations. In *IJCAI-97 Workshop on Social Interaction and Communityware*, pages 31–36, 1997.

Audio Content Description in Sound Databases

Alicja A. Wieczorkowska[1] and Zbigniew W. Raś[2,3]

[1] Polish-Japanese Institute of Information Technology, ul. Koszykowa 86,
02-008 Warsaw, Poland
alicja@pjwstk.waw.pl or awieczor@uncc.edu
[2] University of North Carolina, Computer Science Dept.,
Charlotte, NC 28223, USA
[3] Polish Academy of Sciences, Inst. of Comp. Science, ul. Ordona 2,
01-237 Warsaw, Poland
ras@uncc.edu

Abstract. Sound database indexing requires metadata to represent audio content of the data. If the metadata are not attached to the database by its creator, content information has to be extracted directly from sounds, using descriptors based on sound analysis. In this paper, authors present a number of sound descriptors based on various forms of signal analysis. Telescope Vector trees (TV-trees) and Frame Segment trees (FS-trees) are applied to represent audio content on the basis of the extracted sound descriptors and metadata provided by the database creator (if only available). Such a representation of audio content of the database is used to speed up the search of the audio material in multimedia databases.

1 Introduction

Multimedia databases are developed very extensively nowadays. However, audio databases are still in a stage of conceptive research. The existing commercial products provide only very simple tools for audio data, for instance searching by the name or format [18]. Therefore, there is a great need for research in the domain of audio databases.

Digital sound data are much more difficult to process for the purpose of information extraction than text data. Sound waves can be represented using many formats. In an uncompressed form sound is represented as raw data (i.e. when sampled amplitude is recorded) but in Internet applications sounds are represented in highly compressed formats, such as MPEG-3, RealAudio, QuickTime etc., using various compression methods [12], [17]. Metadata describing these files for the purpose of content-based searching of an audio database can be provided by their creators. For musical files, for instance, such metadata usually include information about the performer, title etc. However, such information is not satisfactory in a more sophisticated search, for example if someone has to query a database for all pieces containing a musical phrase either similar or identical to another phrase. For such a purpose, new features (descriptors) associated with audio signal have to be extracted directly from audio files.

N. Zhong et al. (Eds.): WI 2001, LNAI 2198, pp. 175–183, 2001.
© Springer-Verlag Berlin Heidelberg 2001

2 Audio Content Description in Multimedia Databases

Description of audio content of digitized sound can be based on:
- general metadata (title, artist, year etc.),
- time-domain analysis of sound,
- frequency analysis,
- other analyses.

Such descriptors can be used for classification or recognition purposes (see Fig.1).

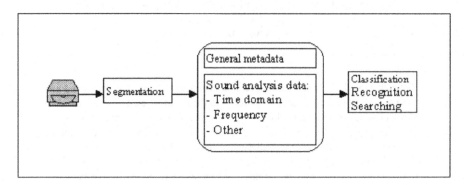

Fig. 1. Description of audio content in multimedia databases

2.1 Metadata

The most readable way to annotate digital sound data is to attach metadata character-izing audio content of the file. The metadata (for example title, duration, names of artists, names of instruments, etc.) can be associated with the whole recording or with its short time segments (scores, text). Most existing audio databases allow metadata-based indexing. Frame Segment tress (FS-trees) can be used for compact representa-tion of audio metadata content [18]. For instance, window segments representing longest segments of an audio signal with respect to some homogeneity predicate can be associated with all nodes of an FS-tree. Search for window segments satisfying some metadata related properties is now simplified to tree search algorithms. Data-bases created in recording studio usually are annotated with metadata appropriate for given recording, but in case of other databases metadata frequently are not available.

2.2 Signal-Based Descriptors

In applications where metadata have not been attached to the file, audio content can be described by means of signal-processing based descriptors. These descriptors can be calculated complementarily for databases already annotated with metadata.

Feature vector created on the basis of sound analysis can be used for classification purposes for any data. This is why it is reasonable to annotate all data with signal-based descriptors, even they are already annotated with some metadata (which may appear insufficient for some purposes).

3 Extraction of Sound Descriptors

Signal-based sound descriptors can be calculated using time analysis, frequency (spectrum) analysis, or time-frequency analysis illustrating evolution of the spectrum in time. There are also special kinds of sound analysis, such as spectral analysis, based on spectral analysis of sound, or linear prediction. Their coefficients can also be used as sound descriptors.

3.1 Time Domain Analysis

The basic way to describe sound signal is to use descriptors derived from time domain of the sound. The most popular time-domain descriptors are [13], [14], [21]:
- density of zero-crossings (number of zero-crossings per frame of N samples),
- density of peaks of time envelope,
- differences between frames.

These descriptors can be applied to any sounds. There are additional descriptors, used in synthesizers, for classifying sounds of musical instruments. These descriptors, characterizing the envelope of the time domain, are as follows:
- attack,
- decay,
- sustain level, and
- release.

They characterize length (or level) or consequents parts of the sound. However, such descriptors cannot be applied to other sounds without preprocessing.

3.2 Spectral Analysis

Frequency domain can be characterized using any frequency analysis method. The most popular one is based on Fourier transform, usually applied in a form of discrete Fourier transform (DFT) or fast Fourier transform (FFT) for short time segments of the length $K=2^k$, where $k \in \{8,...,14\}$. Long Time Average Spectrum (LTAS) can also be calculated, for example for frames 20 seconds or less long [6].

Descriptors that can be applied to any sound data (see [1], [8], [9], [13], [14], [15], [16], [20], [21]) are listed below:
- density of spectral peaks (number of peaks per frame of K samples),
- amplitude of actual DFT peaks,
- order of higher peaks,
- spectral moments of various orders,
- differences between frames.

For sounds of musical instruments, the following descriptors can be applied:
- brightness B of the sound:

$$B = \sum_{n=1}^{N} n \cdot A_n \Big/ \sum_{n=1}^{N} A_n \tag{1}$$

where: A_n – amplitude of nth partial in the spectrum,
N – number of partials available in the spectrum;
- formants, i.e. maxims of the spectral envelope,
- spectral irregularity I:

$$I = \log_{10}\left(\sum_{n=2}^{N-1} \left| 20\log_{10}(A_i) - \frac{20\log_{10}(A_{n+1} + A_n + A_{n-1})}{3} \right| \right) \tag{2}$$

- statistical parameters:
  o   average amplitude and frequency variations,
  o   histograms,
  o   average spectrum (average amplitude level),
  o   standard deviations,
  o   autocorrelation and cross-correlation,
  o   contents of the selected groups of partials in spectrum (low/mid/high partials), for instance described by Tristimulus approach:

$$t_1 = G_1/G, \quad t_2 = G_2^4 \big/ G, \quad t_3 = G_5^N \big/ G \tag{3}$$

where: N – as above,

$$G = G_1 + G_2^4 + G_5^N \tag{4}$$

$$G_i^m = 0.85 \cdot G_{\max} + 0.15 \cdot \sum_{k=1}^{m} G_k \tag{5}$$

or used in a modified form:

$$T_1 = A_1^2 \Big/ \sum_{n=1}^{N} A_n^2, \quad T_2 = \sum_{n=2}^{4} A_n^2 \Big/ \sum_{n=1}^{N} A_n^2, \quad T_3 = \sum_{n=5}^{N} A_n^2 \Big/ \sum_{n=1}^{N} A_n^2 \tag{6}$$

and the others.

Spectral parameters are frequently calculated for the frequency domain divided into bands, sometimes called *critical bands*. Frequency range is often divided into 12 (Fletcher), 24 (Zwicker) or 48 bands. The most popular division is into 24 bands, called *barks*, widely used in sound processing [23]. The division of human auditory range into barks is presented in Tab. 1.

Sound descriptors mentioned in this section can be calculated for spectral bands. Critical bands are also used in MPEG-3 standard of sound compression for perceptual audio coding.

Table 1. Critical bands according to Zwicker

No.	Central frequency [Hz]	Width [Hz]
1	50	100
2	150	100
3	250	100
4	350	100
5	450	110
6	570	120
7	700	140
8	840	150
9	1000	160
10	1170	190
11	1370	210
12	1600	240
13	1850	280
14	2150	320
15	2500	380
16	2900	450
17	3400	550
18	4000	700
19	4800	900
20	5800	1100
21	7000	1300
22	8500	1800
23	10500	2500
24	13500	3500

3.3 Other Analyses

Apart from descriptors mentioned in two previous subsections, there is also a possibility to apply descriptors based on other analyses. Let us mention some of them [3], [7], [10], [21], [22]:
- time-frequency analysis, for example McAulay-Quatieri analysis or wavelet analysis,
- cepstral analysis, where spectral elements are logarithmed,
- linear predictive coding (LPC), used in speech processing,
  and others.

Coefficient obtained in the analyses mentioned above can also be used as a basis to calculate sound descriptors. For instance, wavelet analysis gains popularity recently and is used for description of musical sounds. Even very simple parameterization using wavelets can lead to results comparable with more sophisticated methods [22]. Wavelet analysis does not require pitch calculation, which is usually a basis of most parameterizations, and any errors in pitch calculation may lead to false description that characterizes harmonic relation is sound. This drawback can be avoided using wavelet based sound description.

3.4 Remarks

All the descriptors mentioned in this section have already been used in experiments with automatic classification of musical sounds [2], [4], [11], [19], [21]. Correctness of the classification varies, basically approaching 80% at the instrument level, and exceeding 95% at family. Results are not exactly comparable, since they have been obtained for various datasets (even if based on the same audio CDs), with various divisions of data into classes, various number of classes. Additionally, many classification algorithms have been applied, and various testing procedures. The classification algorithms used range from simple statistic-based methods to sophisticated AI algorithms. The algorithms tested in published experiments include k-nearest neighbor method, Bayesian classifiers, artificial neural networks, decision trees, rough set based classification algorithms, hidden Markov models, support vector machines and so on. Results obtained for neural networks even reached 100% of correctness, but small sizes of datasets (4 classes) do not allow comparison with other methods.

Sound data annotated with signal-based descriptors and originated from different DB have to be exactly synchronized in time for their correct comparison [13].

4 Audio Content Representation Using TV-Trees

Trees similar to telescopic vector trees (TV-trees) can be used for content description representation of audio data in a multimedia database [18].

Each audio signal is divided into N window segments. Each window segment is represented as a vector consisting of K acoustical descriptors such as those listed in previous section. So we have a set of N elements where each element is a K-dimensional vector. We may represent this set as $(K \times N)$-matrix. If needed, we can reduce K to a smaller number using Singular Value Decomposition method [18]. The next step is to introduce the notion of a distance between two vectors (for instance we can take term distance or cosine distance). Now, the set of N vectors can be seen as a set of N points in K-dimensional space. These points have to be divided into disjoint clusters, where in each cluster we should keep points which similar with respect to maximal number of coordinates. These coordinates are called active dimensions.

Let us assume that our plan is to represent the set of N points as a TV-tree of order 2 which means that the construction of only 2 clusters per node is allowed. So, we divide our set of N points into 2 clusters maximizing the total number of active dimensions in both clusters. For each cluster we repeat the same procedure, again trying to maximize the total number of active dimensions in the corresponding subclusters. For instance, if $\{[5, 3, 20, 1, 5], [0, 0, 18, 42, 4], [0, 0, 19, 39, 6], [9, 10, 2, 0, 6]\}$ is the initial cluster, then the following two subclusters will be generated: $\{[0, 0, 18, 42, 4], [0, 0, 19, 39, 6]\}, \{[5, 3, 20, 1, 5], [9, 10, 2, 0, 6]\}$. The initial cluster has only the last dimension active. After split, the first subcluster has 5 dimensions active and second one has the last two dimensions active. We continue this procedure till all subclusters are relatively dense (all points are closed to each other with respect to all dimensions). For instance, in the example above, the first subcluster is dense.

The underlying structure (see figure 2) for this method is a binary tree with nodes storing information about the center (c) of a corresponding cluster, the smallest radius (r) of a sphere containing this cluster, and its list of active dimensions ($d_1, d_2, ..., d_s$).

Assume now that user wants to search an Audio DB for audio signals close (some threshold λ should be given) to an audio signal presented as an incomplete K-dimensional vector α of acoustical descriptors. We search recursively our TV-tree checking at each node if:

- its active dimensions cover the complete dimensions of vector α,
- all complete dimensions of vector α which are active at this node are closed to its center (with respect to λ).

If the first condition is satisfied, we stop the search. Otherwise the search is continued.

If both conditions are satisfied, the cluster assigned to that node is returned and its each point is evaluated (if it meets the threshold λ).

In [21], [22] definitions of instruments in terms of acoustical descriptors have been learned using KDD methods. We believe that these definitions can be used for automatic extraction of hidden metadata associated to an audio file and the same can improve the knowledge about semantics of audio files represented by Frame Segment trees (FS-trees) introduced in [18].

5 Summary

Annotating of multimedia databases is of great interest nowadays. The scope of currently elaborated, by Moving Pictures Experts Group (MPEG), standard MPEG-7 is to provide standard of multimedia content description. However, this standard does not comprise the extraction of descriptors (nor search algorithms). Therefore, there is a need to elaborate extraction of sound descriptors that would be attached to sound files [5].

This paper reviews audio descriptors based on various kinds of sound analysis. They have already been used in experiments performed by researchers all over the world. These descriptors are used to construct TV-trees that allow efficient access to high dimensional data. This representation of an audio database is useful since number of descriptors can be large. However, because of great variety of possible queries in audio databases, large number of sound descriptors is unavoidable.

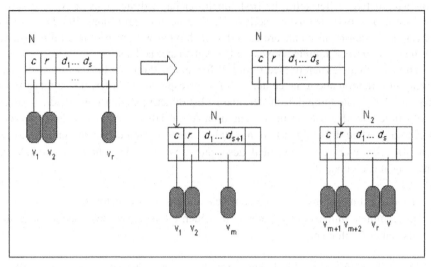

Fig. 2. Insertion into a telescopic vector tree

References

1. Ando S., Yamaguchi K., Statistical Study of Spectral Parameters in Musical Instrument Tones, J. Acoust. Soc. of America, 94, 1, July 1993, 37-45
2. D'Autilia R., Guerra F., Qualitative Aspects of Signal Processing Through Dynamic Neural Networks, in: Representations of Musical Signals (G. De Poli, A. Piccialli, C. Roads, Eds.), MIT Press, Cambridge, Massachusetts, 1991, 447-462
3. Garnett G. E., Music, Signals, and Representations: A Survey, in: Representations of Musical Signals (G. De Poli, A. Piccialli, C. Roads, Eds.), MIT Press, Cambridge, Massachusetts, 1991, 325-369
4. Herrera P., Amatriain X., Batlle E., Serra X., Towards instrument segmentation for music content description: a critical review of instrument classification techniques, International Symposium on Music Information Retrieval ISMIR 2000, Plymouth, MA, October 23-25, 2000
5. ISO/IEC: MPEG-7 Overview (version 3.0), International Organisation For Standardisation, ISO/IEC JTC1/SC29/WG11, Coding of Moving Pictures and Audio, N3445, Geneva, May/June 2000
6. Jansson E. V., Sundberg J., Long-Time-Average-Spectra Applied to Analysis of Music. Part I: Method and General Applications, Acustica, Vol. 34, 1975, 15-19
7. Keele D. B. Jr., Time-Frequency Display of Electro-Acoustic Data Using Cycle-Octave Wavelet Transforms, 99th Audio Engineering Society Convention, New York 1995, preprint 4136
8. Kostek B., Wieczorkowska A., Parametric Representation of Musical Sounds, Archive of Acoustics, 22, 1, Institute of Fundamental Technological Research, Warsaw, Poland, 1997, 3-26
9. Krimphoff J., McAdams S., Winsberg S., Caractérisation du Timbre des Sons Complexes. II. Analyses acoustiques et quantification psychophysique, Journal de Physique IV, Colloque C5, supplement J. de Physique III, 4, 3ème Congrès Français d'Acoustique, I, 1994, 625-628

10. Maher R. C., Evaluation of a Method for Separating Digitized Duet Signals, J. Audio Eng. Soc., Vol. 38, No. 12, 1990, 956-979

11. Martin K. D., Kim Y. E., Musical instrument identification: A pattern-recognition approach, 136th meeting of the Acoustical Society of America, October 13, 1998. Internet: ftp://sound.media.mit.edu/pub/Papers/kdm-asa98.pdf

12. McGloughlin, Multimedia: concepts and practice, Prentice Hall, Upper Saddle River, NJ, 2001

13. Papaodysseus C., Roussopoulos G., Fragoulis D., Panagopoulos Th., and Alexiou C., A New Approach to the Automatic Recognition of Musical Recordings, J. Audio Eng. Soc., Vol. 49, No. 1/2, 2001, 23-35

14. Paraskevas M., Mourjopoulos J., A Statistical Study of the Variability and Features of Audio Signals: Some Preliminary Results, 100th AES Convention, preprint 4256, Copenhagen 1996

15. Pollard H. F., Jansson E. V., A Tristimulus Method for the Specification of Musical Timbre, Acustica, Vol. 51, 1982, 162-171

16. Reuter C., Karl Erich Schumann's Principles of Timbre as a Helpful Tool in Stream Segregation Research, Joint International Conference 1996, College of Europe at Brugge, Belgium, 8-11 September 1996, II Int. Conf. on Cognitive Musicology, 212-219

17. Sharda N. K., Multimedia information networking, Prentice Hall, Upper Saddle River, NJ, 1999

18. Subrahmanian V.S., Multimedia Database Systems, Morgan Kaufmann Publishers, San Francisco, CA, 1998

19. Toiviainen P., Optimizing Self-Organizing Timbre Maps: Two Approaches, Proc. Joint Int. Conf., II Int. Conf. on Cognitive Musicology, 1996, College of Europe at Brugge, Belgium, 8-11 September 1996, 264-271

20. Uematsu H., Ozawa K., Suzuki Y., Sone T., A Consideration on the Timbre of Complex Tones Only Consisting of Higher Harmonics, Proc. 15th Intern. Congress on Acoustics, Trondheim, Norway 1995, 509-512

21. Wieczorkowska A., The recognition efficiency of musical instrument sounds depending on parameterization and type of a classifier (in Polish), Ph.D. Dissertation, Technical University of Gdansk, 1999

22. Wieczorkowska A., Towards Musical Data Classification via Wavelet Analysis, in: Foundations of Intelligent Systems, Proceedings of ISMIS'00, Charlotte, NC, (Z. W. Ras, S. Ohsuga, Eds.), LNCS/LNAI, No. 1932, Springer-Verlag, 2000, 292-300

23. Zwicker E., Zwicker U. T., Audio Engineering and Psychoacoustics: Matching Signals to the Final Receiver, the Human Auditory System, J. Audio Eng. Soc., Vol. 39, No. 3, March 1991, 115-126

Intelligent Interfaces for Distributed Web-Based Product and Service Configuration

L. Ardissono[1], A. Felfernig[2], G. Friedrich[2], D. Jannach[2], R. Schäfer[3],
and M. Zanker[2]

[1] Dipartimento di Informatica, Università di Torino, Italy
liliana@di.unito.it
[2] Computer Science and Manufacturing Research Group, University of Klagenfurt, Austria
{felfernig, friedrich, jannach, zanker}@ifit.uni-klu.ac.at
[3] DFKI, Saarbrücken, Germany
ralph.schaefer@dfki.de

Abstract. This paper emphasizes on the enhancement of web-based selling technology for complex products. The approach of the EC-funded CAWICOMS[1] project is twofold: provision of technologies both for customer-adaptive Web-interfaces for the configuration of mass-customized products as well as for the integration of configuration systems along the supply-chain. Within this paper we first motivate the demand for personalized and adaptive Web-interfaces of product configurators as an efficient means for customer relationship management. In addition, we sketch scenarios where product configuration takes place at several stages in the supply chain and the involved configuration systems have to cooperatively solve a distributed configuration task.

1   Introduction

Web-based product configuration tools enable businesses to market complex customizable products and services by using the new technologies of electronic commerce, whereby customers can tailor the configurable products according to their specific needs and requirements. In a Web-based environment special emphasis must be given to the customer interaction with the sales system, i.e., such a selling system should be personalizable and adapt to heterogeneous customer interests and skills. In addition, the digital economy of the 21st century will be based on flexibly integrated webs of highly specialized solution providers, therefore the joint product configuration of organizationally and geographically distributed providers must be supported. This requires the extension of current configuration technology to include distributed knowledge bases and co-operative problem solving behavior. Based on real-world applica-

---

[1] Customer-Adaptive Web Interface for the Configuration of products and services with Multiple Suppliers. The work takes place with the financial support of the IST Programme of the European Union under contract IST-1999-10688.

N. Zhong et al. (Eds.): WI 2001, LNAI 2198, pp. 184–188, 2001.
© Springer-Verlag Berlin Heidelberg 2001

tion scenarios, the CAWICOMS project is carried out in order to overcome obvious shortcomings of current configuration technology.

For presentation purposes we will shortly sketch these requirements and our approach based on the guiding application scenario *configuration of telephone switching systems:* Telephone switching systems consist of modules plugged into frames, which are mounted on racks. Cables connect the modules and frames, resulting in a network topology imposed on top of the hierarchical physical structure. In addition, several external hardware components and subsystems such as PCs or routers are connected to the switching node. Further the functionality of the system depends on a set of software applications that are installed on the hardware. The whole system can be decomposed into subsystems supplied by different organizational units or independent companies.

2   Adaptive User Interfaces and Personalized Interaction

When commercializing complex customizable products online, there may be various classes of users of the configurator that differ in properties such as skills, needs and knowledge levels. In current Web-based configurators there is typically only one standard interface with a predefined interaction style that cannot be tailored to these different types of users. As an example, adaptive configurator interfaces that tailor the system behavior according to the level of expertise of the user, are able to match these requirements. Experienced users may configure the product at some detailed technical level, whereas a novice user might only enter some high-level features and will have a need for more guidance and extra help during the configuration process.

An adaptive configuration tool will classify the current user with respect to different properties (e.g., expertise or interest in product characteristics such as reliability) and generate an interface that adapts flexibly according to this classification. We address this problem by customising the following aspects of the interaction:

a)   *Adaptation of the configuration process:* It aims at reducing the communication overhead for the customer during the interaction with the configuration system. Therefore, reasoning on the content and the sequence of the set of required interaction steps is necessary.

b)   *Adaptation of the presentation of configuration solutions:* This refers to the selection of the information most relevant to the user and the presentation of this information at a level of technical detail suited to his/her domain expertise.

These adaptation aspects rely on a user model representing the system's beliefs on the user characteristics. The customisation of the configuration process is based on the use of personalisation rules, represented within a rule-based system (ILOG JRules[2]). As the user interface is dynamically generated during the interaction, the level of detail addressed can be adapted to the most recent hypotheses about his/her knowledge and interests. For estimating the user's interests we ascribe *Multi-Attribute-Utility Theory (MAUT)* (see [5]) as evaluation process to the user. According to MAUT, the

---

[2] See ILOG (www.ilog.com) for reference.

configurable artifact can be evaluated as weighted addition of the evaluation with respect to its relevant *value dimensions*. For taking into account the uncertainty occurring in the interpretation of the user's behaviour, we use *Bayesian networks* (BNs) as a probabilistic inference mechanism (see [4]). For each interaction type, e.g., user self-assessment or various kinds of inputs during the configuration process, there is a BN interpreting the user's actions. For estimating the user's knowledgeability the approach of [3] is extended. There are BNs which interpret both actions which indicate that the user knows (resp. does not know) the implications of a parameter for the relevant dimensions, e.g. by selecting or changing a parameter value (resp. by using the help function of the system).

3   Distributed Configuration

The driving application scenarios show that there does not exist a single business entity in the value chain of supplied goods and services that has complete pricing and product knowledge on the whole customer solution. Further this knowledge may only be partially shared among business partners for reasons of privacy and security. Therefore, we have to enable current configuration technology towards co-operative problem solving.

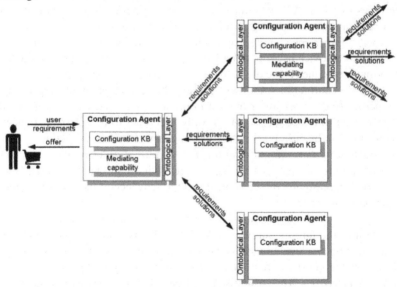

Fig. 1. Architectural sketch

As Figure 1 depicts, in our approach information sources as well as problem-solving agents with local knowledge (*Configuration KB*) are integrated. The value chain typically has a tree structure where each node is represented by a configuration agent that either represents the main vendor or one of the suppliers. Except for the leaves, all nodes of the tree possess *mediating capabilities* that allow them to decompose their configuration problem and assign subtasks to their supplying configuration systems.

In a realistic supply chain setting the involved configuration systems must be seen as legacy systems that have their proprietary knowledge representation mechanisms. Therefore, we employ an *ontological layer* based on a logic theory of configuration described in [1] that enables communication by mapping the specific representations onto more general ontological concepts from the configuration domain. Each configuration agent comprises the local knowledge necessary to customise a specific product or service of the company behind. These products or services that are part of the distributedly configured overall solution may share resources and have defined connection points vs. each other. Agents that have to observe restrictions that reference on not locally configured components need to have a limited view on these parts of the overall configuration solution. This view is provided to it by an agent with mediating capabilities. Further these mediating agents are responsible for taking measures for resolution in case of conflict occurrence. For more detailed information on co-operation mechanisms refer to [2].

4   The CAWICOMS Environment

The outcome of the CAWICOMS project is an integrated environment supporting development, execution, and maintenance of (distributed) Web-based configuration applications. This environment consists of a set of components, which entail a set of improvements concerning the applicability in real world settings.

Knowledge Sharing Support. One of the major aims of CAWICOMS is the integration of heterogeneous configuration environments to support a distributed configuration process. A prerequisite for such a process is knowledge sharing between the engaged configuration systems. CAWICOMS provides a set of standardised XML Schema[3] definitions forming an ontology for distributed configuration. This ontology can be seen as a standard interchange format for configuration knowledge bases, which significantly reduces efforts of knowledge interchange.

Distributed Problem Solving. Beside an effective support for knowledge interchange between configuration environments supported by the knowledge acquisition component, CAWICOMS provides mechanisms for integrating those systems at the execution level. An ontological layer is imposed on each (remote) supplier configuration platform, which maps the generic configuration concepts onto the proprietary representation of the supplier system. Furthermore, a set of protocols implementing distributed problem solving algorithms (e.g., based on Distributed Constraint Satisfaction, see e.g., [6]) is supported that allow co-operative problem solving behaviour.

Integration with existing Platforms. The CAWICOMS environment supports seamless integration into existing e-commerce application platforms. Typical frameworks provide services like product catalogue management, shopping cart, customer man-

---

[3] See the World Wide Web Consortium (www.w3c.org) for reference.

agement, procurement, purchase orders, payment transactions, and pricing. The CAWICOMS architecture relies on these services provided by the underlying layer. By providing a standardised schema for representing complex product structures and by integrating this schema in industrial standard Business Communication Languages (e.g. cXML, see www.cxml.org for reference), CAWICOMS supports the extension of basic framework functionalities with additional support for distributed and personalised configuration.

Improved Knowledge Acquisition. Due to the increasing size and complexity of configuration knowledge bases an effective design and maintenance support for configuration knowledge bases is required. In order to offer a more user-oriented knowledge acquisition process, the configuration knowledge is represented in UML (Unified Modeling Language) – the corresponding constraints are represented in OCL (Object Constraint Language). The major advantage of applying those languages in the configuration context is that they are comprehensible for a large community of potential users and are adopted in established industrial software development processes. As a consequence of the approach of [1] the application of configuration systems is no more restricted to specialists with corresponding knowledge in the area of formal description languages (basic representation languages of the underlying configuration systems).

Standard Components. For the implementation of the CAWICOMS prototype state-of-the-art Internet technologies are applied (Java Server Pages, Enterprise JavaBeans). All components of the prototype are implemented within a three-tier architecture conformant to J2EE (Java 2 Enterprise Edition).

For further information see http://www.cawicoms.org.

5   References

1. Felfernig, A., Friedrich, G. and Jannach, D. (2000). *UML as domain-specific language for the construction of knowledge-based configuration systems.* International Journal of Software Engineering and Knowledge Engineering (IJSEKE), vol. 10 (4), pp. 449-469.
2. Felfernig, A., Friedrich, G., Jannach, D. and Zanker M. (2001). *Towards distributed configuration.* Proc: Joint German/Austrian Conference on Artificial Intelligence, 24th German / 9th Austrian Conference on Artificial Intelligence, KI-2001, Vienna.
3. Jameson, A. (1990). *Knowing What Others Know – Studies in Intuitive Psychometrics.* PhD thesis, University of Amsterdam, Netherlands.
4. Pearl, J. (1988). *Probabilistic Reasoning in Intelligent Systems: Networks of Plausible Inference.* San Mateo, CA. Morgan Kaufmann.
5. Winterfeld, D. von and Edwards, W. (1986). *Decision analysis and behavioral research.* Cambridge, England. Cambridge University Press.
6. Yokoo, M., Durfee, E., Ishida, T. and Kuwabara, K. (1992). *Distributed Constraint Satisfaction for Formalizing Distributed Problem Solving.* 12th IEEE Int. Conference on Distributed Computing Systems, pp. 614-621.

Using Networked Workshop System to Enhance Creative Design

Sunny S.J. Lin[1], Eric Z.-F. Liu[2], M.C. Cheng[2], and S.M. Yuan[2]

[1] Center for Teacher Education, National Chiao Tung University, Hsinchu, Taiwan 31151,
R.O.C.
sunnylin@cc.nctu.edu.tw
[2] Department of Computer and Information Science, National Chiao Tung University,
Hsinchu, Taiwan 31151, R.O.C.
{totem, native, smyuan}@cis.nctu.edu.tw

Abstract. This study examined the usefulness of networked workshop instruction, an instructional method that emphasizes presentation, discussion, evaluation, and knowledge construction. In workshop instruction, web-based peer assessment was used to evaluate students' performance. Twenty-four computer and information science graduate students enrolled in a course "Web and Database Integration" and were assigned to nine teams. Each team was instructed to design a web-based system capable of performing certain functions. Functioning similar to how researchers and scientists would in a workshop, participants orally presented their ideas and web-based peer assessment was conducted to increase critical feedback during a team designs their own product. One creative products and qualitative comments from professors were presented to demonstrate the students' high quality achievement.

1 Introduction

Industry and academia often hold workshops to promote products or technical information. Therefore, this study presents an innovative instructional method, Networked Workshop Instruction (hereinafter referred to as NWI), that coordinates student learning in a manner similar to researchers and scientists attending a workshop. NWI aims to enhance collaborative design through presentation, discussion, evaluation, and knowledge construction.

NWI for graduate level education largely concentrates mainly on presentation in the form of report writing and oral presentation. In the design process, students interact with teachers and among themselves to create novel design concepts. A web-based learning system that supports NWI allows interaction to occur at different times and places. Web-based Peer assessment can also play a role in NWI to increase critical feedback [12, 15] and evaluate design products and oral presentations. Therefore, NWI is structured in parallel to the underlying principles of constructivism and social constructivism [9-11]. Despite the innovation of this instructional method, NWI has

N. Zhong et al. (Eds.): WI 2001, LNAI 2198, pp. 189–194, 2001.
© Springer-Verlag Berlin Heidelberg 2001

received relatively little attention [1, 6, 8, 13], thereby making the effectiveness of this approach a contentious issue. Therefore, this study initially raises the following question: Is Networked Workshop Instruction in a graduate degree an effective strategy to promote creative design through collaborative team?

2 NWI

The NWI instructional method is embedded in the precepts of constructivism and social constructivism [9-11] that advocate the active participation of students during instruction. Notable examples of successfully using workshop instruction can be found undergraduate courses of computer science [13], chemistry [6], mathematics [21], biology [8], and counseling [4]. These studies required students to hand in written reports, such as self-reflection essays as well as records of student-teacher meetings and small group discussions and, then, orally present those findings [1, 4]. Although face-to-face workshop instruction is well documented [4-6, 8, 14], the feasibility of using the Internet to support social interaction or social construction of knowledge has not been explored. To our knowledge, only two studies conducted for computer related courses [3] and for teacher training [13] have applied a instruction strategy similar to the one used herein.

NWI initially requires that students freely form collaborative design teams and, then, each team discusses the preliminary design concepts with the teacher. Each team must report on their design progress in written format in three stages: design concept compilation, system design plan, and system implementation. In addition to design products, the design progress should include the contributions of each member. Thus, a team report must include members' personal observations. During the design process, a team must interact through face to face meetings, on-line chat rooms and e-mail. Finally, the team conducts peer assessment to evaluate the design products in three stages and prepare for the oral presentation.

In addition to a network environment that supports reports, discussions, and mutual peer evaluation, face to face interactions between teachers and fellow students during oral presentations and discussions are encouraged. A balance of the two is necessary because some messages (e.g., emotions of persuasiveness) can be conveyed through non-oral information (e.g., posture, tone of voice, and attire) during face-to-face meetings. Asynchronous interaction can not replace this important social interaction that has an underlying learning process.

NWI revolves around four instructional elements to enhance collaborative design: Presentation, Discussion, Evaluation and knowledge Construction, simplified as PDEC. Those elements are individually described as follows.

1) *Presentation*: Each team is instructed to present their design product in written and oral forms. Students must read design-related information, such as papers and technical reports, as a basis for selecting a design theme, compiling previous works and new concepts, and generating three reports of design progress. Each report must include a record of the group's division of labor, personal observations of each member, and a complete report of group results. This process can hopefully train the student's writing

presentation ability. Most, each team must orally present their finals at the final design stage.

2) *Discussion*: Discussion in NWI consists of asynchronous communication through a web-based learning support system developed for NWI, the exchange of E-mail, and face to face discussions. Such venues of discussion can hopefully facilitate brain storming, reflection, questioning, or even confrontation so that a team can draw up a comprehensive design plan.

3) *Evaluation*: In NWI, although the teacher and students are involved in evaluation, peer assessment is the primary focus. Peer assessment requires that, in addition to grading peer assignments, students must offer suggestions for revision. Students who offer effective suggestions or modifications are awarded additional points towards their overall course grade. Related investigations [2, 7, 15] conferred that the greatest strength of peer assessment lies in its ability to provide students with a greater amount of feedback, i.e., more detailed and more timely, than in a traditional classroom. Peer feedback can then be used to modify the original assignment. Teacher evaluation involves more than merely grading assignment; they must also monitor student collaboration and determine whether all students are fulfilling course requirements. In addition, teachers should be aware of the possibility of mutual grading to boost scores, mutual boycotting to reduce scores, or inappropriate suggestions when revising the assignment.

In our previous instructional experiences, some administrators or departments remain suspicious of mutual student assessment in completely determining grades. Some individuals suspect that peer assessment helps teachers avoid their responsibilities and doubt whether students have adequate specialized knowledge to grade peer assignments. To quell such suspicions, teachers should actively participate in peer assessment if they choose to adopt this approach.

4) *Knowledge Construction*: Constructivism espouses that students can develop their own knowledge only if they actively participate in learning. Therefore, NWI encourages students to interact with each other before designing and evaluate others' assignments after they hand in their own design products. Moreover, NWI facilitates knowledge construction through activities such as brainstorming among teachers and fellow students, asking questions, criticizing, comparing, or exchanging ideas.

3 Procedures of NWI

Research was conducted for the three months, October-December 1999. Details regarding related projects, NWI, peer assessment and teacher grading processes are provided as follows.

Students first collaborated with teacher in identifying Web and Database Integration related design themes of their projects. Some topics were generated from teacher-student discussion, e.g., web-based public bus route guidance system, web-based personalized digital library system, web-site recommendation system, web-based book store, and financial simulation system. Work was divided into three parts: survey work compilation, system design and system implementation reports. Survey work compilation required that students collect related papers, web-sites and practical work. After reading and comparison, these reports we arranged into a web-page report. System design required that the student group plan a system design direction that is innovative or has value based on results from the survey work compilation stage and before the system is finished. They had to explain design requirements, functions, meanings and problems to be overcome. System implementation involved implementing the system design plans to a point at which the system should be operational.

3.1   Two Way Blind Assessment Procedures

The entire peer assessment process is two-way and anonymous. In other words, the assessors and the assessed parties are unaware of each other's identities. Given that the author is revealed once the oral presentation is made, oral presentations did not begin until after three rounds of web-page reports. Previous research [15] has demonstrated that anonymity makes students more willing to make detailed criticisms and comments, thereby making more emotion-free and objective assessments possible. In addition, each assessor must assess all assignments.

Peer assessment for these three tasks requires only one round, similar to a summative evaluation, and different from the formed peer assessment (whereas upon completion of the evaluation, the submitting student must improve his or her assignment before the second round) used in some investigations [7]. The peer assessment criteria have no detailed division; the sole requirement is that global grading and comments are made for the overall assignment. Before peer assessment, students hold discussions to agree on what constitutes good, medium and poor results. Peer assessment scores range from 30-95.

3.2   One Way Blind Assessment Procedures

During the oral presentation, students must directly display the system program on a PC screen, explain the direction of survey work compilation and system design concepts. Students conduct one-way anonymous assessment. Each assessor must assess all oral presentations, and all members of each group must orally present their findings.

Assessment orientation is divided into presentation ability (i.e., the clarity with which a student explains the system design), the completeness of slides and transparencies, and the persuasiveness of the conclusion. Assessor scores range from 0-3; very poor, poor, good and very good. After peer assessment, the teacher makes summary comments and raises problems to stimulate student discussion.

3.3   Teacher Assessment Procedures

The "teachers" in this study were a class professor and teaching assistant. The assistant was carefully selected for his (or her) ability and previous experience with peer assessment. However, to maintain the integrity of this research, the assistant was not involved in data analysis.

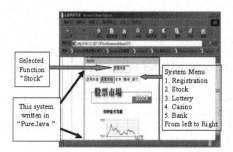

System description: The system was developed using Java RMI/CORBA technology. It is a finance game simulation environment. Users initially deposit money in a bank account and, then, use this account to make stock market investments, place bets or purchase lottery tickets in order to make money.

Fig. 1. Finance Simulation System

4   A Selected Creative Product

Interface design: Attractive and suitable interface, a very high level of art design.

System function: Many functions have not yet been realized (e.g. stock, lottery, casino, and bank).

Applicability: The framework is clearly arranged and can involve many practical economic applications. With further effort, this can become a functionally very powerful system.

Future development: This provides an interesting on-line entertainment feature, with promising commercial value.

5   Conclusions

This study has demonstrated that when the NWI method is applied to a computer and information science course at graduate degree, where the students are capable and highly motivated, the overall performance of students was excellent. Unfortunately this research can not answer some of the deeper questions. For example, when it comes to improving learning results, which of the four key elements in NWI, i.e., presentation, discussion, peer assessment and constructivism, predominate? Such questions require further research and the application of standard empirical methods (e.g., random sampling, experimental design and control groups).

Acknowledgements. The authors would like to thank the National Science Council, Taiwan, R.O.C, under Contract Nos. NSC89-2520-S-009-013 and NSC89-2520-S009-016.

References

1. Arrendondo, D.E., and Rucinski, T.T.: Using the Workshop Approach in University Classes to Develop Student Metacognition. Innovative Higher Education, **18** (1994), 273-288.
2. Bangert-Drowns, R.L., Kulick, C.L.C., Kulick, J.A., and Morgan, M.T.: The instructional effect of feedback in test-like events. Review of Educational Research, **61** (1991), 213-238.
3. Gale, C., Bourne, J.R., Thompson, B.: Creating a workshop on the World Wide Web: The experiences of Internet 101, In ERIC database ED429533, 1997.
4. Goldstein, G.S.: Using a Group Workshop to Encourage Collaborative Learning in an Undergraduate Counseling Course. Teaching of Psychology, **20** (1993), 108-110.
5. Hall, A.G.: A Workshop Approach Using Spreadsheets for the Teaching of Statistics and Probability. Computers and Education, **25** (1995), 5-12.
6. Ingham, A.M., and Gilbert, J.K.: The Workshop-Interview Technique in Higher Education: A Versatile Method for Selection and Monitoring of Science Students. Assessment and Evaluation in Higher Education, **17** (1992), 29-43.
7. Liu, E.Z.F.: Networked peer assessment system: an analysis of student segments. A thesis for the master degree of Computer and Information Science of National Chiao-Tung University, 1999.
8. McKinley, C.J., and Stoll, W.R.: A Method of Improving Student Learning in Physiology: The Small Group Workshop. Advances in Physiology Education, **11** (1994), 16-23.
9. Resnick, M.: Beyond the Centralized Mindset, Proceedings of the International Conference on the Learning Sciences, 1997.
10. Roth, W.M.: From everyday science to science education: how science and technology studies inspired curriculum design and classroom research. Science and Education, **6** (1997), 372-296.
11. Schwartz, D.L., Black, J.B., and Strange, J.: Dyads have a fourfold advantage over individuals inducing abstract rules, Paper presented at the Annual Meeting of the American Educational Research Association, Chicago, 1991.
12. Topping, K.: Peer Assessment Between Students in Colleges and Universities. Review of Educational Research, **68** (1998), 249-276.
13. Veen, W., Lam, I., and Taconis, R.: A virtual workshop as a tool for collaboration: towards a model of telematic learning environments," Computers Educ., **30** (1998), 31-39.
14. Vierheller, T.R.: A workshop on UNIX, Workstations, and Internet Connections. Journal of College Science Teaching, **27** (1997), 39-43.
15. Zhao, Y.: The effects of anonymity on computer-mediated peer review. International Journal of Educational Telecommunications, **4** (1998), 311-345.

Discovering Seeds of New Interest Spread from Premature Pages Cited by Multiple Communities

Naohiro Matsumura[1,3*], Yukio Ohsawa[1,2**], and Mitsuru Ishizuka[3]

[1] TOREST, Japan Science and Technology Corporation
[2] Graduate School of Systems Management, University of Tsukuba, 3-29-1 Otsuka, Bunkyo-ku, Tokyo 112-0012, Japan
[3] Dept. of Electronic Engineering, The University of Tokyo, 7-3-1 Hongo, Bunkyo-ku, Tokyo 113-8656, Japan

Abstract. The World Wide Web is a great source of new topics significant for trend birth and creation. In this paper, we propose a method for discovering topics, which stimulate communities of people into earnest communications on the topics' meaning, and grow into a trend of popular interest. Here, the obtained are web pages which absorb attentions of people from multiple interest-communities. It is shown by a experiments to a small group of people, that topics in such pages can trigger the growth of peoples' interests, beyond the bounds of existing communities.

Keywords: Communities, Interest Spread, Web Links

1 Introduction: Which Topics Grow into Trends?

Some new topics grow into a prevalent concept, if they satisfy the desire of people for information. Simple and sensational imformation comes quickly spread to fit to uncertain minds desiring information [1].

Our aim is to detect topics which can be spread to satisfy a wide range of people. People first become aware of the topic, understand and accept it. Then, the topic grows to be established and will not decay as easily as lies. Topics leading to such a prevalence is worthwhile finding for commercial/personal benefits. In this paper, the problems addressed are:

1) How and what kind of topics grow into a trendy interest ?
2) How can we support the awareness of human community on such topics ?

In section 2, problem 1) will be discussed on for making a strategy for challenging problem 2). In section 3, we point out why previous Web-mining methods could not find such opinions we aim at. In section 4, a new method *Agora on Links*

---

* e-mail:matumura@miv.t.u-tokyo.ac.jp
** e-mail:osawa@gssm.otsuka.tsukuba.ac.jp

N. Zhong et al. (Eds.): WI 2001, LNAI 2198, pp. 195–199, 2001.
© Springer-Verlag Berlin Heidelberg 2001

based on Web links, fitting our goal is presented. The method obtains Web-pages, including topics which are premature but will be accepted as significant for a wide range of communities, beyond the boundary of personal interests. Conclusional remarks are in Section 6.

2   A Mechanism of the Topic Growth into a Trend

For question 1) above, we go after the mechanism of community extensions. We define a community as a group of people sharing some value, as people in the society of artificial intelligence sharing the value admiring the aim to make AI studies, although their interests are not precisely equal. People in different communities do not see each other usually - if they do, we regard them as one community because they already share established values for which to gather.

If multiple communities have an occasion to meet for talking on a newly born opinion or topic, and if a new value appears to be shared there, participants will evaluate each other positively on the value (as the measure to evaluate other people) and find it meaningful to be re-organized into a greater community sharing the new value.

This means that a new encountering of communities, differing in previous interests but sharing a topic, can be a trigger to the innovation of a new strong idea as pointed in [2,3]. Further, the awareness on various relations (difference, similarity, or others) between one's initial belief (constructed in the community one usually belongs to) and new information (which may come from another community) urges the topic to be understood and established in each community.

For example, the robot succor games RoboCup seemed just curious when it appeared first, but matched with latent interests of various research-communities, who gathered and achieved new innovations.

3   The Concept of *Agora on Links*

Following the topic-spread model above, we present a method "Agora on Links" for aiding the discovery of web pages on new topics premature but attracting multiple interest-communities, by visualizing those topics and their links with the interests of already established communities.

Studies have been devoted to extracting communities from hyper-links on the Web ([4]-[8]). The method in [6] obtains *hub* pages, linking to *authority*-pages (linked from many pages as ones obtained by Google [7]) popular to established communities. The method in [8] obtains *cores*, i.e. groups of densely linked authorities and hubs, for finding emerging communities. On the other hand, our aim is to find premature topics possible to be the seeds of communities not emerging yet. This is for grasping significant yet latent trends, hard to find due to the premature prevalence.

At least two obstacles exist for predicting future trends. The first is the extreme rareness of trend-outbreak signs. As pointed in section 2, if a group of communities often see each other, they would have already evolved into a super-community. Prediction methods relying on past frequent patterns [9] or relatively (i.e. not very) rare patterns in rich past data [10,11], are not applicable here. The second is the hidden causes for a trend outbreak i.e., the interest- context of each community and the relationships among communities, hard to be fully considered as features (data attributes) to be used in data analysis/mining. In order to cope with these obstacles, we apply the two principles below, and visualize the signs of a trend for stimulaing user's imagination of hidden causes rather than fully automated prediction.

Principle 1: Popular communities exist, each made of people sharing some popular (authorized/established) value.

Principle 2: If a new topic attracts different-interest popular communities, it will grow into a new trend to grow among those communities.

4   The Method of *Agora on Links*

Corresponding to Principle 1, the set of authority-pages or top pages representing each community, from the output pages from Google are obtained by looking at links to those pages [8]. We regard the page of the highest-rank according to Google, in each community, as the archive-page representing a (popular or emerging in the sense of [8]) community. Selecting a single page for representing one community here is in order to form a comprehensible visualization of the output as shown later in Fig.1.

Then, corresponding to principle 2, pages linked from multiple archive-pages but are not in any community themselves are taken as novel topics attracting multiple communities, called *agora-topic* pages after the name of ancient Egyptian inter-community meetings. The algorithm outline for obtaining Web pages representing agora-topics is as follows.

Step 1: A query representing user's interest domain is entered to a search engine (Google here, obtaining 10^5 to 10^6 pages).

Step 2: Communities, of pages obtained in Step 1, are obtained as in [8] and archive-pages are selected from communities.

Step 3: Pages, not in the communities but linked from multiple archive-pages, are obtained as agora-pages. Having all obtained results by here, archive-pages (black nodes), agora-pages (red nodes) and the links between them are visualized as in Fig.1.

5   Evaluation: Agora Topics Spread in Groups of People

The Evaluation Experiment :

Stage 1. An interest domain is fixed, a group (appropriate number for talking) of people relevant to the domain gathered, and the domain-name is input as a query (e.g. "information retrieval").

Stage 2. The output graph adding real and fake red nodes, as if they all were really obtained as agora-pages, is shown to the subjects. That is, some red nodes, not really obtained, were added with red links to black archive-nodes. Subjects reported individual impressions and exchanged ideas in the group.

We conducted evaluations of the two stages above, for various queries.

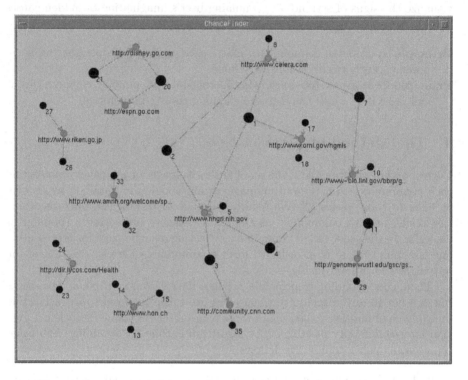

Fig. 1. The output of *Agora on Links*, for domain query "human genome."

For query "human genome," three subjects in Human Genome analysis area were gathered. In stage 2, all Web pages in the black nodes in Fig.1 were said to represent common knowledge in the area backgrounds. On the other hand, subjects said the red (agora) nodes showed pages of growing interests. More concretely, red nodes were said to be the target of interests from various institutes in or relevant to the area, which seldom meet in frequent workshops but are considered to achieve significant discoveries if they exchange knowledge with each other.

For example, in Fig.1, the largest cluster of nodes and links is the group of American human-genome research institutes, looking at growing interest trends, e.g., the venture-company Celera the leading institute NIH in genome research. On the other hand, the left-hand small cluster is Japanese institutes, looking at (linking to) Riken, the most active in the identification of mouse genomes. In fact, these institutes in red are ones who have data sources of human or mouse genomes, and it is useful for researchers in other institutes to look at those data. In other words, Web pages having such data is the agora for researchers.

For all queries including other domains, we had 53 black nodes in total, of which 37 were said to be of established interests in the area. Only 3 black nodes appealed as directions for new decisions for future research. On the other hand, the 12 red nodes included 8 "interesting for thinking of future work" in subjects' individual impressions, with embodied comments about possible decisions they may make. Their discussions lead to their awareness on significant new problems, e.g., "what should the evaluation criteria of a search engine be, for measuring user's real satisfactions?" and "who seeks information retrieval techniques for tasks?" through discussing with looking at red pages.

6   Conclusions

A hypothesis on the growth of a minor topic to be a wide spread interest to the majority of people is given, and an algorithm is shown for detecting such topics from the Web, corresponding to the model. The method was applied to Web links in specific domains, and it was shown the visual output aids in the discovery and the growth of meritorious concepts.

References

1. Allport,G.W and Postman, L., *The Psychology of Rumor*, H.Holt.(1947)
2. Clark,K.B., and Fujimoto,T. *Product Development Performance: Strategy, Organization, and Management in the World Auto Industry*. Boston: Harvard Business School Press. (1990)
3. Koestler, A., *The Act of Creation*, New Yourk: Liveright (1964)
4. Chakrabarti, S. et al, Automatic Resource Compilation by Analyzing Hyperlink structure and Associated Text. In *Proc. of WWW7* (1998)
5. Gibson, D., Kleinberg, J. and Raghavan, P. Inferring Web communities from line topology. In *Proc. of 9th ACM Conference on Hypertext and Hypermedia* (1998)
6. Kleinberg, J. Authoritative sources in a hyperlinked environment, IBM Research Report RJ 10076 (1997)
7. Brin, S. and Page,L. The anatomy of a large scale hypertextual web search engine. In *Proc. of 7th World-Wide Web conference (WWW7)*, (1998)
8. Kumar,S.R., et al, Trawling the Web for Emerging Cyber-communities In Proc. of *WWW8* (1999)
9. Mannila, H, et al, "Disocvering Frequent Episodes in Event Sequences" in *Proc. First Conf. on Knowledge Discovery and Data Mining (KDD95)*, 1995.
10. Weiss, G.M. and Hirsh,H. "Learning to Predict Rare Events in Event Sequences," in *Proc. of KDD-98*, 359-363, 1998.
11. Suzuki, E. and Kodratoff, Discovery of Surprizing Exception Rules Based on Intensity of Implication, in *Principles of Data Mining and Knowledge Discovery*, LNAI 1510, 10–18, Springer, 1998.

Personalized Web Knowledge Management

Koichi Takeda and Hiroshi Nomiyama

Tokyo Research Laboratory, IBM Research
1623-14 Shimotsuruma, Yamato, Kanagawa 242-8502, Japan
TEL: +81-46-215-4569, FAX: +81-46-273-7428
{takeda, nomiyama}@trl.ibm.co.jp
http://www.trl.ibm.com/projects/s7710/dl/index_e.htm

Abstract. In this paper, we propose a novel approach for personalized Web knowledge management by incorporating dynamic (e.g., news articles) and static (e.g., technical papers) Web contents. We can integrate these two types of information by using intelligent crawling and metadata creation and provide a visual interface to personalize and navigate through the tailored information to an individual user.

1 Introduction

The World-Wide Web (WWW) has often been characterized by two extreme aspects of information sources: a gigantic archive of Web pages and the largest broadcasting infrastructure on earth for delivering constantly and asynchronously updated information. Our daily information needs would be often satisfied by a subtle combination of contents of these two types. Although the Web search engines, "push" technology, and big portal Web sites have been commonly used for serving the needs, the gap between the growth of the number of relevant WWW pages and the cognitive limit (complexity of search and the amount of relevant information) of users is getting wider and wider.

This problem has been one of the central issues in the research as well as business community, and tackled intensively for the last few years in such areas as personalization[7], ranking[5, 3], and collaborative filtering[6]. One clear vacancy in the prior work, however, is that each approach is focused on either of the above two aspects of the Web, and effective combination of these two aspects has not been known. In this paper, we propose a novel approach for tailoring the Web information by associating latest information with referential Web pages, and providing a multiple-view interface for a user to personalize and navigate through the relevant information.

2 Site Outlining

As shown in Figure 1, our daily information request would usually include "what's new" (today's headlines, stock information, and so on) and authoritative information (sightseeing, market forecast, research papers, and so on). While the latter type of information could be nicely defined and handled by PageRank[5] and HITS[1] algorithms, the former type of information has been less formulated and studied.

Site outlining[10] was proposed to handle such dynamic Web information. It was based on version control and feature extraction mechanism over the snapshots of Web pages, and *Information visualization*[8, 4], where

N. Zhong et al. (Eds.): WI 2001, LNAI 2198, pp. 200–204, 2001.
© Springer-Verlag Berlin Heidelberg 2001

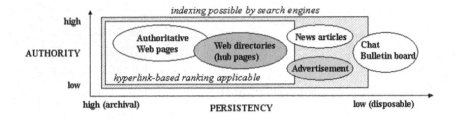

Fig. 1. Categorization of Textual Web Pages

- each snapshot of a Web page can be characterized by metadata including a collection of links (URLs with annotations) and paragraphs (textual blocks),
- "what's new" information is defined as difference between metadata for two consecutive snapshots of a Web page,
- once the objects (links and paragraphs in a Web page) are identified, their persistency is computed based on the duration and a number of snapshots (or the time span) they are included, and
- changes in pieces of Web information can be visualized in terms of numeric, textual, and temporal features. For example, comparing the numbers of updated links in Web pages for the last 24 hours, 24-48 hours, and 48-72 hours can be used to visualize recent active Web pages.

3   Personalized Web Knowledge Management

Site outlining provides two ways for personalizing the Web information sources – site taxonomy and filtering keywords – and several *views* for digesting "what's new" information. Site taxonomy is a hierarchical directory of Web pages which is similar to a collection of "favorite links" in the Web browser. Site outlining regularly crawls and keeps tracking changes of individual Web pages defined in the site taxonomy. Filtering keywords are used to filter links and paragraphs that should carry interesting information to the user.

Digesting of Web information are described below.

3.1   Web Page Activity Ranking

The Web page activity is measured in terms of the following parameters.

- Number of links and paragraphs included in each snapshot
- Number of keywords included in the links and paragraphs
- Lifespan of the links and paragraphs
- Average frequency to update (delete/add) one link
- Average size (in bytes) of paragraphs in the Web pages
- Average size (in bytes) of annotations to the links
- Average and Maximum numbers of links included in a snapshot
- Average and Maximum numbers of new links in a snapshot
- Average and Maximum numbers of deleted links in a snapshot

This type of information can be used to find which Web pages are worth monitoring and how often they need to be visited. In this way, hundreds of Web pages in the user's site taxonomy can be ranked based on their activity measure. It will be also used to classify Web pages into dynamic and archival ones.

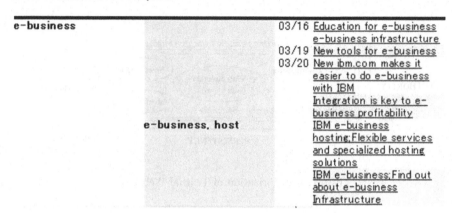

Fig. 2. Hot Topic

3.2   Active Area Guide

Given a site taxonomy (tree) of Web pages, we can use the following statistics to approximate the *activity* of each subtree: Let T be a subtree and W be a set of Web pages that directly belong to the category corresponding to T.

1. The number N_S of Web pages in W which were updated during the given period of time.
2. The number N_A of distinct links which are included in one of the snapshots of the Web pages in W.

N_S can be used to overview the active information sources in the category area, while N_A can be used to overview the amount of new information in the category area.

3.3   Hot Topics

For each subcategory of a site taxonomy, we can compute the frequency of terms appearing in the Web pages under the subcategory. If a term appears much more often for a given period of time than is does in average, the term is considered as a hot topic of the period. Figure 2 shows that in the subcategory "IBM" of IBM-related Web pages, the term "e-business" is recognized as a hot topic of the week (3/13/2001-3/20/2001), and the links (and paragraphs, if any) including the word are arranged along the timeline to form a "thread" of e-business topic. If the frequency alone is used to identify the hot topics, the word "IBM" would always be the hottest topic of the subcategory. The word will not be eliminated by using an ordinary stop word list. The word statistics computed for the subcategory for a reasonable period should be the source of such information.

3.4   Headlines

Similar to the idea of hot topics, we can identify collections of terms jointly appearing in individual links and paragraphs the Web pages under the subcategory. If a collection of terms jointly appears in several links and paragraphs, these links and paragraphs are considered as referring to the same issue. Such an issue would be a candidate of the "headline" news.

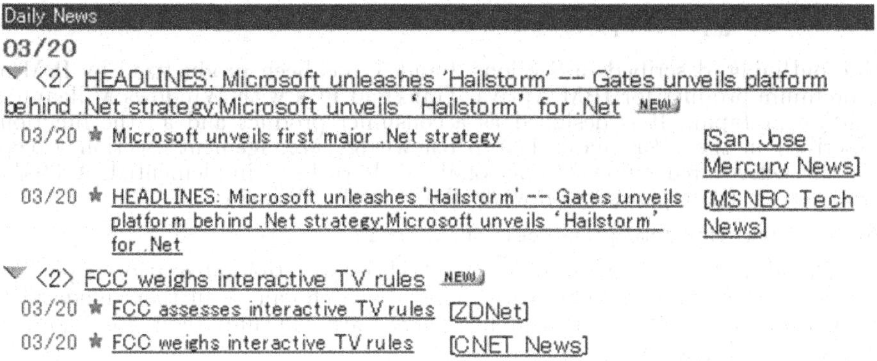

Fig. 3. Headlines of the March 20, 2001 Computer News Web Pages

Figure 3 shows that two headlines are obtained for March 20, 2001. The first one is about a new platform from Microsoft, reported by the San Jose Mercury News and MSNBC Tech News), and the second one is about FCC's assessment on the interactive TV rules, covered by ZDNet and CNET News. Headlines are by default the longest annotations of the links. The first headline includes three terms – Microsoft, .Net, and strategy – shared by its links. The second headline has "FCC" and "interactive TV rules" as common terms.

4   Integration of Dynamic and Persistent Information

As described in the previous section, Site outlining can effectively provide digest information for a personalized collection of interesting Web pages. It now leads us to the goal of personalized Web knowledge management; i.e., integration of dynamic and persistent Web information.

When a set S of new links (paragraph) p is obtained, we can compute related information $rel(p)$ as the following collections of links, paragraphs, and Web pages.

1. Related new links (paragraphs) C_N: those links (paragraphs) that are related to p. By representing each link with a vector of weighted keywords included in the Web page pointed by p, the latent semantic indexing (LSI)[2] can be used to determine the similarity $d(r,p)$ between the Web pages for a link r in S and p, where r is in C_N if $d(r,p)$ is less than a given threshold. If the annotation of links are not very descriptive, we can construct a keyword vector from the contents of Web pages they refer to.
2. Related Web page C_W: each Web page can be regarded as a set, or a *cluster*, of articles and paragraphs it contains. Then the distance between each cluster and p can be computed (e.g. the distance between its centroid and p) and the set of related Web pages can be similarly obtained.
3. Authority/Hub pages C_A: authority/hub pages can be computed based on the HITS algorithm[1] applied to the top k Web pages returned from a search engine and a query consisting of a list of keywords included in p, a list of top k keywords included in C_N, and so on.

These collections of related information form a news package for p and serve as a reliable sources for personalized Web knowledge management. We can then successfully organize and digest latest information with persistent, authoritative information.

5 Prototype Implementation

Site outlining, described in Sections 2 and 3, has been productized by IBM as a premium product for IBM Aptiva/ThinkPad PCs with Windows Millennium Edition in Japan. It is designed as a consumer product and all the functions described in the "Personalized Web Knowledge Management" section, except for the active area guide, for personal use have been implemented. A 30-day trial version (in Japanese) is downloadable at the Web site:

`http://www.ibm.com/jp/pc/personal/msol/.`

The idea of dynamic and persistent Web information integration is pursued by the Tokyo Research Laboratory. This approach can be further enhanced to form a community Web portal site[9], where users can share their site taxonomy and filtering keywords.

6 Concluding Remarks

We have proposed a new approach to make the most of dynamic and persistent Web pages based on information/site outlining techniques. We believe the dynamic aspects of Web information sources can be given more insights to establish more advanced usage of the WWW.

Evaluation of our system is still not very clear. Traditional evaluation of information retrieval systems – precision and recall of relevant information – does not fit our system very well, since the value of dynamic information largely depend on its *freshness* in addition to the traditional *relevance*, and is quite dependent on individual user. A task-oriented evaluation is under consideration, and appears to be interesting if we can reveal the relationship between decision-making and the value of dynamic/persistent Web information.

References

1. S. Chakrabarti and et al. "Automatic Resource Compilation by Analyzing Hyperlink Structure and Associated Text". In *Proc. of 7th International World Wide Web Conference (WWW7)*, 1998.
2. S. Deerwester, S. T. Dumais, G. W. Furnas, T. K. Landauer, and R. Harshman. "Indexing by Latent Semantic Indexing". *Journal of the American Society for Information Science*, 41(6):391–407, Sept. 1990.
3. C. Dwork, R. Kumar, M. Naor, and D. Sivakumar. "Rank Aggregation Methods for the Web". In *Proc. of 10th International World Wide Web Conference (WWW10)*, May 2001.
4. M. Morohashi, K. Takeda, H. Nomiyama, and H. Maruyama. "Information Outlining - Filing the Gap between Visualization and Navigation in Digital Libraries". In *Proc. of Intl. Symp. on Digital Libraries*, pages 151–158, Tsukuba, Japan, Aug. 1995.
5. L. Page, S. Brin, R. Motwani, and T. Winograd. "The PageRank Citation Ranking: Bringing Order to the Web". http://google.stanford.edu/ backrub/pageranksub.ps, 1998.
6. P. Resnik. "Filtering Information on the Internet". *Scientific American*, Mar. 1997.
7. H. Sakagami, T. Kamba, A. Sugiura, and Y. Koseki. "Effective personalization of push-type systems - visualizing information freshness". In *Proc. of 7th International World Wide Web Conference (WWW7)*, 1998.
8. B. Shneiderman. *"Designing the User Interface: Strategies for Effective Human-Computer Interaction" (3rd Edition)*. Addison-Wesley, 1998.
9. S. Staab and et al. "Semantic Community Web Portals". In *Proc. of 9th International World Wide Web Conference (WWW9)*, May 2000.
10. K. Takeda and H. Nomiyama. "Site Outlining". In *Proc. of ACM Digital Libraries '98*, pages 309–310, Pittsburgh, PA., Jun. 1998.

Event and Rule Services for Achieving a Web-Based Knowledge Network[1]

Minsoo Lee[2], Stanley Y.W. Su, and Herman Lam

Database Systems Research and Development Center
University of Florida, Gainesville, Florida
{mslee, su, hlam}@cise.ufl.edu

Abstract. This paper presents the concept of a Web-based knowledge network. A knowledge model is first described and then the overall architectural framework of the knowledge network is discussed. The implemented prototype system allows providers of information resources and/or application system services to publish not only their data resources and/or services on Web pages, but also their knowledge in the form of events, rules, and triggers associated with the contents and operations of these pages. Internet users can access these Web pages, subscribe in a registration process to some published events on a page, and provide values for event filters and customizable rules. The subscribers can also specify additional triggers and rules of their own to be processed on the subscribers' sites. At run-time, when an event is posted by a provider (human or automated application system), event filters are processed, the relevant subscribers are notified, and both the provider and subscribers' triggers and rules are processed on their respective sites. The architectural framework allows both providers and subscribers of information resources and services to contribute their knowledge to the Internet, thus forming a Web-based knowledge network instead of the present data/information network. The knowledge network is constructed by a number of replicable software components, which can be installed at various network sites. They, together with the existing Web servers, form the knowledge Web servers.

1 Introduction

The rapid growth of the World Wide Web has made it possible for numerous data resources on the Internet to be accessed quite easily. Data in the form of text, images, and audio/video files are abundant on the Internet. The Web provides a basic information infrastructure for people and organizations to publish these data and for Web surfers to retrieve the data by using browsers and search engines; however, it does not provide a means for the specification and management of human and organizational "knowledge". Data can be of use for decision-making, but only knowledge can help people and organizations to make the right decisions. Our goal is to make the Internet more intelligent by populating it with human and organizational

[1] Acknowledgement: The research is supported by the National Science Foundation, USA (Grant #EIA-0075284).

[2] Author's current affiliation is Oracle Corporation, 2op10 Oracle Parkway, Redwood Shores, CA 94065, USA. E-mail: Minsoo.Lee@oracle.com.

N. Zhong et al. (Eds.): WI 2001, LNAI 2198, pp. 205–216, 2001.
© Springer-Verlag Berlin Heidelberg 2001

knowledge. To achieve this goal, the Web technology needs to be extended to meet the following requirements. First, there should be a general knowledge model that users can use to specify their knowledge on the Web. Second, there needs to be a mechanism to integrate and embed the knowledge into the existing Web infrastructure. Third, efficient techniques and a flexible way of processing knowledge need to be provided. Here, flexibility means that the processing mechanism should be easily adaptable to modifications made to knowledge specifications. Fourth, an easy way of managing the specified knowledge needs to be provided.

In this work, we introduce a general framework, which extends the current Web model by allowing information providers and software or application system owners to specify their knowledge in terms of objects and their associated events, triggers, and rules, and to publish them using Web-based GUI tools on the Web. Event specification is a mechanism to publicize anything of potential interest to others, such as the states of a database, the activation of an application system, the publication or modification of a Web page, etc. Event notification is a mechanism to inform the users or automated systems that have registered for an event when the event has occurred. Event filtering is a mechanism for processing data conditions specified by users and automated systems to determine if they should be notified on the occurrence of an event. Rules are high-level specifications of data constraints and organizational policies, strategies, and regulations. They capture small granules of logic and control, which otherwise are hard-coded in programs. Their execution may invoke application systems, send emails to users, interact with on-line users, etc. Triggers are specifications to link events to rules or rule structures, and they allow rules to be processed when the corresponding events are posted. The framework described in this paper allows both information providers and users to contribute and share their knowledge over the Internet, thus forming a "knowledge network" to facilitate better information searching, filtering, processing, and dissemination in the Internet. Knowledge specified by objects and their associated events, triggers, and rules are managed and processed by a number of replicable software components, which enhance the existing Web servers to make them the Knowledge Web Servers.

The remainder of this paper is organized as follows. Section 2 provides a survey of related work, including rule systems and event notification architectures. Section 3 presents the knowledge model. Section 4 presents the general architecture of the knowledge network. Section 5 describes the key features of the knowledge network. Section 6 describes some applications of the knowledge network. The summary, conclusion, and future work are given in Section 7.

2   Related Research

The concept of rules was originally introduced in the research areas of artificial intelligence and expert systems [1]. The rules were soon incorporated into databases to create a new category of databases, namely, active databases [2,3]. Event-Condition-Action (ECA) rules have been used in many of these systems. They are composed of three parts: event, condition, and action. The semantics of an ECA rule is, "When an event occurs, check the condition. If the condition is true, then execute the action". The event provides a finer control as to when to evaluate the condition and gives more active capabilities to the database systems. Rules can automatically perform security and integrity constraint checking, alert people of important situations, enforce business policies and regulations, etc.

WebRules [4] is a framework to use rules to integrate servers on the Internet. The WebRules server has a set of built-in events that can notify remote systems, and has a library of system calls that can be used in a rule to connect Web servers. However, it does not include concepts such as event and rule publishing or event filtering. WebLogic [5] also includes a basic form of rules, which are called actions. These actions need to be provided to the WebLogic server at the time when an application is registering for an event. These actions are actually specified with program codes rather than a high-level specification facility.

Several content-based event notification architectures have been recently proposed to provide an abstraction of the communication infrastructure on the Internet. These architectures focus on providing a scalable architecture for event delivery, as well as a mechanism to selectively subscribe to information. Siena [6] proposes a mechanism to maximize the expressiveness of a language to specify filters and patterns while not degrading the scalability. NeoNet [7] provides a rule-based message routing, queueing and formatting system. Gryphon [8] uses an information flow graph, which specifies selective delivery, event transformation and new event generation, to implement a message brokering middleware. Elvin [9] supports full content based routing which does not require a data source to be configured with any information about the recipients. Keryx [10] is a language and platform independent infrastructure to distribute events on the Internet and is based on the publish-subscribe model. JMS [11] provides reliable, asynchronous communication between components in a distributed computing environment. CORBA Notification Service [12] uses an event channel concept and extends the Event Service by providing event filtering and quality of service.

3 Knowledge Model

The knowledge network integrates event service and rule service into the Web environment. A knowledge provider (publisher) can define *events* and *event filter templates* through an event/filter GUI provided by the knowledge network framework. An *event* is the state of an object (i.e., a collection of information encapsulated into an operationally meaningful way) that is deemed important to other objects or users. An event definition includes the event name and also the name and types of the attributes that are carried by the event. An *event filter template* is a simple predicate on event attributes. It defines a class of event notifications by specifying a set of attribute names and types as well as some constraints on their values.

Fig.1 shows the definition of an AirfareSpecialOffer event and an event filter template that specifies the constraints for the attributes of departure city, the destination city, and the preferred airplane ticket price for the *AirfareSpecialOffer* event. A subscriber of the event can specify the filtering values, such as New York, Orlando, and 145, in an event filter template to establish the filter shown in Fig.1.

The knowledge network provides modules that automate the tasks of creating HTML forms used to interact with subscribers. The framework also takes care of the underlying processing of event filtering and event delivery. Therefore, providers and subscribers only need to understand the semantics of an event.

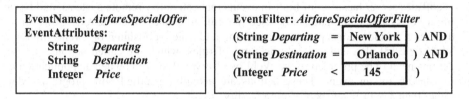

EventName: *AirfareSpecialOffer*
EventAttributes:
  String   *Departing*
  String   *Destination*
  Integer *Price*
	EventFilter: *AirfareSpecialOfferFilter*
	(String *Departing* = [New York]) AND
	(String *Destination* = [Orlando]) AND
	(Integer *Price* < [145])

Fig. 1. Event and Event Filter Example

While the event service supports the integration and linking among different systems on the Internet, rule service provided by the knowledge network helps individual knowledge to be embedded in the Web servers. The rule service is based on our Event-Trigger-Rule (ETR) model [13,14]. The ETR model consists of three elements: event, rule and trigger. Events are already discussed above. A rule is a high-level declarative specification of a granule of executable code that is related to an event or events. A rule is composed of condition, action, and alternative action clauses. Events are associated with rules by trigger specifications. When an event is posted, the rules associated with the event are triggered for processing.

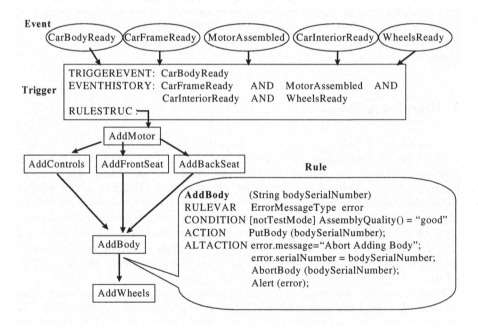

Fig. 2. Example of Events, Triggers, and Rules for modeling car assembly process

Fig. 2 shows an example of using events, triggers, and rules to model the knowledge involved in a Car assembly process. The events notify that the parts required for assembly are ready. The trigger will start processing when the *CarBodyReady* event (TRIGGER EVENT) occurs and tests if all of the parts for assembly are ready via the EVENTHISTORY. If so, the assembly process is allowed to start. The TRIGGEREVENT clause specifies the events that can initiate the evaluation of the EVENTHISTORY part and the execution of the set of rules specified in the RULESTRUC clause. In the TRIGGEREVENT clause, several events can be OR-ed (i.e., connected with a disjunctive operator), which means that the occurrence of any one of the events can initiate the processing of the rules. The EVENTHISTORY allows for checking past event occurrences that form a composite event. Operators such as AND, OR, NOT, sequence(>) are used to specify the EVENTHISTORY. In Fig.2, the simplest case of using AND to test if all of the events have happened is shown. The RULESTRUC clause specifies the set of rules to be executed and also in what order the rules should be executed. Rules can be executed in sequential, parallel, AND synchronized, OR synchronized order. Rules *AddControls*, *AddFrontSeat*, and *AddBackSeat* are executed in parallel, while the rule *AddBody* is AND synchronized, meaning that it must wait until all three preceding rules are finished. The specification of the rule *AddBody* is shown in Fig.2. The Rule *AddBody* performs an operation such as, "If the assembly quality of the interior parts is good, then perform the adding of the Body. Otherwise, stop adding the Body and alert the staff".

When a rule is triggered, the CONDITION clause of the rule is first evaluated. If the condition is true, the statements in the ACTION clause are executed. Otherwise, the statements in the ALTACTION (i.e., alternate action) clause are executed. A rule has an interface that specifies what parameters are used in the rule body (i.e., condition, action and alternative action). The actual values of these parameters are provided by the event at run-time. There are several important syntax clauses within a rule. The RULEVAR clause has the declaration of the variables that are used in the rule body. A customizable rule variable type, which allows the value to be customized based on an individual user's need, is also supported. These variables are place holders for values in the rule and use a separate storage exclusively for storing the users' customized values. The customizable rule variable uses a special lookup mechanism during run-time to instantiate the variable with a different value for different users. The CONDITION clause is specified with a guarded expression. A guarded expression is composed of two parts: a guard part and a condition expression part. The guard part is provided to screen out cases in which the rule must be skipped, such as error situations or invalid data values, etc. In Fig. 2, the *notTestMode* method in the CONDITON clause of the *AddBody* rule is a guard and checks if the assembly is "not operating in test mode". If it is not test mode (i.e., the guard evaluates to true), then the rule executes as described previously. If it is test mode, then the whole rule will be ignored, which is the desired result because only the sequence of assembly operations is being tested. ACTION and ALTACTION clauses are composed of statements to be executed, such as method calls or assignment statements, statements that post events, etc.

The ETR model improves the ECA rule model in several ways, especially in the following three aspects. First, it readily supports distributed environments. It separates the specifications of events from those of rules. By allowing this separation, the events can be defined independently of the rules and vice versa, which is essential for a distributed environment. In the distributed environment, events can be defined at one site and rules can be defined at another site. The remote event can be associated to a local rule by a trigger specification. Second, it has the built-in consideration for performance issues. As an example, the ETR model provides a more efficient mechanism to process composite events. In most ECA rule systems, a composite event is specified by creating a single large expression, which includes all participating events and their relationships. The processing of composite events in ECA rule systems is also initiated when "any" of the participating events in the expression occur. In many real world situations, the occurrence of some, but not all, of the events in a composite event expression should trigger the processing of rules. The ETR model separates the TRIGGER EVENT and EVENT HISTORY to add a finer control on the evaluation of composite events. Third, the ETR model allows more complex structures of rules to be triggered by events. A linear tree or graph *structure* of rules can be given in a trigger specification, and a rule can participate in many rule structures. This kind of rule specification is more general and powerful than a set of *prioritized* rules, which is used in most ECA rule systems.

In the knowledge network, rule service is provided in two forms. The first is provided by the provider in the form of customizable rules that are published. The rules are linked to published events, and the rule execution can be customized by the individual subscribers. This enables subscribers to use remote services provided by the event provider. The second is for subscribers of events to privately define and hook up their rules on the subscriber sites to the subscribed events. This enables subscribers to freely and safely define triggers and rules on their local systems. Complex and secure processing of triggers and rules become possible in this way.

4   Knowledge Network Architecture

The architecture, as shown in Fig. 3, is symmetric. A standard Web server is enhanced with three additional components: a Knowledge Profile Manager, an Event Server, and an Event-Trigger-Rule (ETR) Server. A Web server enhanced with these modules is referred to as a knowledge Web server. The same components are available on both the *provider site* (the publisher of information/service) and *subscriber site* (the client of information/service). However, for the purpose of explaining the architecture, we distinguish the *provider site* from the *subscriber site*.

The *Knowledge Profile Manager* is a component which provides GUI tools to support the build-time activities, such as defining and managing events, filters, triggers, and rules. It includes a persistent storage for storing the meta-data. It is also responsible for translating and transferring the meta-data to the Event Server and the ETR Server. The *ETR Server* is responsible for run-time processing of triggers and rules. The processing of triggers includes the processing of composite events and the scheduling of rule execution. A code-generation approach is used for the processing of rules. Rule specifications are first compiled into Java classes. Using the class loading and reflection capabilities of Java to execute or dynamically change the rules during run-time, the ETR Server combines the flexibility of the interpretative approach and the efficiency of the compiled approach. The design and implementation of the ETR Server is described in detail in [15,14]. The *Event Server* handles registration for subscribing to events, filtering events, and sending event notifications to subscribers and also to the ETR Server to initiate rule processing.

The interactions that take place during publishing, subscription, and notification are shown in Fig. 3. As shown by step ① in Fig. 3, the publisher defines events and filter templates through the GUI provided by the Knowledge Profile Manager, which transforms and transfers this information to the Event Server. Similarly, the publisher can also define and publish (provider-side) rules and triggers, which associate the published event with the published rules. This information is stored in the provider's ETR Server. In step ②, users from subscriber sites can perform registration to subscribe to the published events through the Event Server. During this registration, subscribers can provide filtering values to establish filters and also link the subscribed event to a published rule on the provider site, which is customized with values provided by the subscriber. Furthermore, the users can define (subscriber-side) rules and triggers, which associate the registered events with the rules on their own sites, as shown by step ③. Subsequently, in step ④, when an event instance is generated on the publisher site, the event is filtered by the Event Server to identify the legal subscribers of the event. Additionally, it is locally forwarded to the ETR Server on the publisher site to trigger the execution of the associated rules (e.g., business policy, security policy, etc.) that have been customized by the subscribers during registration. At the same time, the event is sent over the Internet to notify those subscribers of the event whose filters' data conditions are satisfied. Upon receiving the event, the Event Server on a subscriber site may then forward the event to its ETR Server to fire rules, which capture the knowledge of the subscriber.

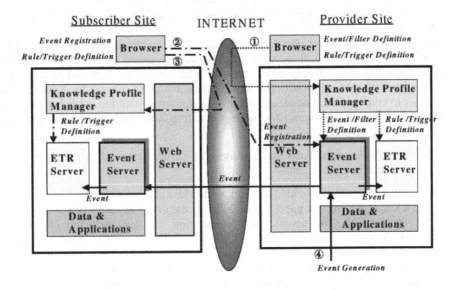

Fig. 3. General Architecture

In the presented framework of the knowledge network, all information resources, application services, as well as the knowledge of providers and subscribers, can be shared by all the Internet users.

5   Key Features of the Knowledge Network

The key features of the knowledge network are: publishing knowledge, event filtering and notification, trigger and rule processing, and knowledge profile management.

5.1   Publishing Knowledge

The knowledge network infrastructure can support the concept of publishing knowledge by providing an easy-to-use tool such as the Knowledge Profile Manager to the providers. Through the Web-based GUI of the Knowledge Profile Manager, the provider can define events, event filter templates, and provider-side rules. The steps involved in publishing events, event filters, and provider-side customizable rules are as follows. First, the provider defines an event by specifying the event name and attribute names and types. Second, one or more attributes of the event are selected. For each of the selected attributes, a filter type can be selected. The attribute type decides the applicable filter types. As an example, an integer attribute type would allow equal, range, greater than, and less than types of filters to be applied; whereas, string attribute types would only allow equal type and single selection type (i.e., the publisher will provide a list of values, and subscribers can only select a single one from the list of values), or multi-selection type (i.e., subscribers can select multiple values from the list of values provided by the publisher). Third, the provider defines customizable rules that have variables whose values can be customized by the subscribers. As a result of these steps, two XML files are automatically created and placed in the Event Server directory by the GUI: an event form specification and rule form specification. All of these steps are easily accomplished through the Web-based GUI. Then, the provider only needs to create a link in a Web page that refers to the URL of the Event Manager with the name of these two XML files as input parameters in order to complete the knowledge publishing. Assuming that the publisher gave the names *event.xml* and *rules.xml* for the two resulting XML files, the link would look something like this:

```
http://www.publishersite/EventServer?eventform=event.xm
l&ruleform=rules.xml
```

Assume that the publisher added this link with a text saying "Click here to subscribe to the XXX event" on his page, where XXX is the event name. When a subscriber clicks on the link, the actual event registration and rule selection forms are automatically generated based on these XML files using a document-driven approach. Therefore, the provider need not perform any coding for the forms nor understand how the underlying knowledge Web server works. When a subscriber clicks on the link, the Event Server interprets the XML files and dynamically creates an HTML form by transforming the event filter template into the visual elements, such as input boxes, drop-down boxes, and multiple radio buttons. Provider-side rules will also display input boxes for the customizable rule variables to allow the subscriber to assign values to them. After the subscriber fills in the form, the information is provided to the Event Server for further processing to install event filters, store rule customizations, and activate triggers for the subscriber.

5.2 Event Filtering and Notification

Several data structures and algorithms have been developed and implemented for matching a large variety of generated events against a large collection of user filters.

We use an inverted index [16] data structure for filters that requires an exact match of the generated event attribute value against the filter values specified by the subscribers. The mapping from an (event attribute, value) pair to the corresponding inverted list of users is implemented as a hash table.

During registration, the user can also specify a range type event filter. For example, assume that the subscriber U1 created a filter for the price range of [100, 200]. When the Airfare Special Offer price is given by a travel agency, we want to determine if the given price falls within the filter range. Using a modified version of 2-3 Trees (or Red-Black Trees) [17] is one way of solving the range search problem. We have also implemented another data structure, Range Table structure [18], which is suitable for range searches. The Range Table structure is in the form of a table. Each entry of the table consists of two elements. The first one is a unique integer number (a minimum or a maximum value that belongs to some range), and the second one is a list of users. The entries in the table are sorted in ascending order. Two consecutive entries of the table store the start value and the end value of an interval. Assume that the integer number in the first entry is N, and the number of the second entry is M. In this case, the corresponding list of users stored in the first entry is the list of users who have registered for the value range [N, M]. Comparing it to the modified 2-3 Tree version, this structure has a better search time complexity. For situations where intensive event generation is present, the search operation will be dominant. By implementing and integrating these two structures into the framework, the publisher may choose the suitable structure that will fit his/her application domain, depending on the frequencies of insert, search, and delete operations.

5.3 Trigger and Rule Processing

On the provider site, a provider can log onto the Knowledge Profile Manager in the provider mode and define provider-side rules that are connected to a published event. Provider-side rules can be private (to the provider) or public (available for use to subscribers). The public provider-side rules become ready for execution when a subscriber selects them at the time of performing the event registration. Provider-side rules enable the subscriber to customize and install some amount of processing logic (i.e., trigger and rules) on the provider site. Automatic processing on the provider site eliminates the need to carry large amounts of data over to the subscriber site, and also allows for common operations to reside on a single provider site, instead of being replicated on multiple subscriber sites.

On the subscriber site, the subscriber can log onto the Knowledge Profile Manager in the subscriber mode to view his/her subscribed events and define subscriber-side rules and triggers, which are linked to the subscribed events. Subscriber-side processing has two big advantages, which enables a real world scenario to be implemented with the Knowledge Network. First, subscriber-side processing relaxes privacy concerns. Subscribers may have valuable information which they do not want to expose, yet the information is required when performing certain operations in rules. Keeping this information in subscriber-side rules eliminates such concerns. Second, the subscriber-side processing of triggers and rules supports the modeling of complex relationships among events subscribed from different publishing sites. For example, a subscribing site which processes bids may need to wait until all of the participating bidding sites have sent in their bids. This status can be checked using our trigger concept on the subscriber site, and once the bids are all received as events, a rule (or rules) will be fired to process the bids.

When an event occurs on the provider site, the event will first be filtered to identify the subscribers and invoke the relevant provider-side rules. Then, the event will be sent to the subscriber sites and invoke the processing of the subscriber-side triggers and rules. Since the processing of triggers and rules is supported on both the provider and subscriber sites, it does not particularly burden any one of the participants in this publish/subscribe model. A specific application of the knowledge network will dictate the amount of provider-side or subscriber-side trigger and rule processing. Efficiency in trigger and rule processing is gained by parallel processing of distributed triggers and rules.

5.4 Knowledge Profiles

Knowledge profiles contain the Meta-information (or definitions) about the events, triggers, and rules. The Knowledge Profile Manager is the component that maintains the knowledge profiles. The Knowledge Profile Manager consists of a Web-based GUI component and a persistent storage component. The Web-based GUI is implemented as an applet and servlet combination. It acts as the front-end and enables the user to easily populate the Web site with knowledge elements. The user has two modes of logging in to the Knowledge Profile Manager: provider mode and subscriber mode. If granted to login with the provider mode, the provider menu will allow access to an event editor, rule editor, and trigger editor. The user can use these tools to publish events, triggers, and rules on the knowledge Web server. The tools also allow the user to update and delete the knowledge elements. If granted to login with the subscriber mode, the subscriber menu will allow access to a viewer for browsing subscribed events, a rule editor and a trigger editor. The user can use these tools to define triggers and rules related to subscribed event definitions imported from remote knowledge Web servers. The user can also update and delete these knowledge elements using the tools. Users can also be granted the authority both as a provider and a subscriber on a knowledge Web server.

6 Applications

The knowledge network is most suitable for applications that require real-time collaboration among multiple parties over the Internet. A good example can be found in e-commerce such as business exchanges which provide meeting places for suppliers and buyers of products. Assume that an auto part business exchange named iExchange manages its registered buyer's preferences and provides daily recommendations to buyers about their items of interest, as well as urgent notifications about discount specials from suppliers. iExchange will first subscribe to the price events and special discount events published by supplier sites. The price events will be filtered to only those items that iExchange is closely monitoring and will be delivered to the knowledge Web server of iExchange. On iExchange's knowledge Web server, iExchange has a rule for each buyer that will automatically generate item recommendation events based on the buyer's preferences. Assuming that iExchange provides buyers with a private Web page on its site, iExchange can allow buyers to subscribe to these item recommendation events by publishing them on the private Web page. iExchange can additionally publish a customizable rule that is tied to the item recommendation event. The rule checks if a specific item appears in the recommendation in a specific price range and then automatically performs a specific action, such as buy 50 items, using the buyer's account information. The item, price range, and action are customizable by the client. In this way, iExchange is acting as a provider to its clients in the knowledge network while synthesizing and reproducing information that it subscribed to.

7 Conclusion

In this paper, we have presented the concept, architecture, features, and an example application of a knowledge network. This work was motivated by the limitations we observed in the existing Internet and Web technologies for supporting the emerging applications, such as e-commerce and enterprise integration. We extended the existing Internet-Web infrastructure by adding event and rule services as a part of the information infrastructure. Events, rules, and triggers, which relate events to the evaluation of event history and the activation of rules, can be used to capture human and enterprise knowledge in the Internet, making the Internet an active knowledge network instead of a passive data network. The event, event filter, event history, and rule processing capabilities of the knowledge network offer very powerful and useful services to enable the timely delivery of relevant data and the activation of operations.

There are some issues that need to be addressed in the future research. First, there are security issues related to event delivery and rule triggering. Since event notifications can initiate the execution of rules which may activate application systems, the potential damages caused by not having the proper security control on event and rule processing can be substantial. Second, in this work, we assume that knowledge providers and consumers of an application domain use the same ontology. That is, the terms used in defining objects and their associated events, triggers, and rules are understood by all users in that application domain. This assumption is not realistic because different users may have different interpretations and understanding of the same terms. These differences need to be resolved by some ontological mappings. One way to practically solve this problem would be to provide an ontology server for specific business domains rather than supporting the entire business domain. Third, rules contributed by different users and/or organizations may have contradictions, cyclic conditions, redundancies, and subsumptions among them. Techniques for validating the distributed knowledge base have to be introduced and applied to detect these problems. Fourth, event notifications can be very time-consuming when a very large number of people and organizations have subscribed to the same events. Techniques for efficient delivery of events and the data associated with the events are needed. The above problems are being investigated at the Database Systems R&D Center at the University of Florida.

References

1. L. Brownston, R. Farrell, and E. Kant. Programming Expert Systems in OPS-5: An Introduction to Rule-Based Programming. Addison-Wesley, Reading, MA (1985).
2. U. Dayal, B.T. Blaustein, A.P. Buchmann, et al. The HiPAC Project: Combining Active Databases and Timing Constraints. In ACM SIGMOD Record, Vol. 17(1), March (1988) 51-70.
3. J. Widom, (ed.). Active Database Systems: Triggers and Rules for Advanced Database Processing. Morgan Kaufmann, San Francisco, California (1996).
4. I. Ben-Shaul and S. Ifergan. WebRule: An Event-based Framework for Active Collaboration among Web Servers. In Computer Networks and ISDN Systems, Vol. 29(8-13), October (1997) 1029-1040.
5. BEA, WebLogic Events, http://www4.weblogic.com/docs/techoverview/ em.html
6 A. Carzaniga, D.S. Rosenblum, and A.L. Wolf. Achieving Expressiveness and Scalability in an Internet-Scale Event Notification Service. In Proc. of the 19th ACM Symposium on Principles of Distributed Computing (PODC2000), Portland, OR, July (2000) 219-227.
7. NEONet, http://www.neonsoft.com/products/NEONet.html
8. G. Banavar, M. Kaplan, K. Shaw, R.E. Strom, D.C. Sturman, and W. Tao. Information Flow Based Event Distribution Middleware. In Proc. of Electronic Commerce and Web-based Applications Workshop at the International Conference on Distributed Computing Systems (ICDCS99), Austin, TX, May 31 - June 4 (1999).
9. D. Arnold, B. Segall, J. Boot, A. Bond, M. Lloyd, and S. Kaplan. Discourse with Disposable Computers: How and Why you will talk to your Tomatoes. In Proc. of USENIX Workshop on Embedded Systems (ES99), Cambridge, MA, March (1999).
10. S. Brandt and A. Kristensen. Web Push as an Internet Notification Service. W3C Workshop on Push Technology. http://keryxsoft.hpl.hp.com/doc/ins.html, Boston, MA, September (1997).
11. Sun Microsystems. Java Message Service API, http://java.sun.com/products/jms/, January 22 (2001).
12. Object Management Group (OMG), CORBA Notification Service, specification version 1.0. June 20 (2000).
13. H. Lam and S.Y.W. Su. Component Interoperability in a Virtual Enterprise Using Events/Triggers/Rules," in Proceedings of OOPSLA '98 Workshop on Objects, Components, and Virtual Enterprise, Vancouver, BC, Canada, Oct. 18-22 (1998) 47-53.
14. M. Lee, S.Y.W. Su, and H. Lam. Event and Rule Services for Achieving a Web-based Knowledge Network. Technical Report, UF CISE TR00-002, University of Florida (2000).
15. M. Lee, S.Y.W. Su, and H. Lam. Parallel Rule Processing in a Distributed Object Environment. In Proc. of the Int'l Conference on Parallel and Distributed Processing Techniques and Applications (PDPTA'99), Las Vegas, NV, June (1999) 410-416.
16. A. Tomasic, H. Garcia-Molina, and K. Shoens. Incremental Updates of Inverted Lists for Text Document Retrieval. In Proc. of the ACM SIGMOD Conference, May (1994) 289-300.
17. E. Horowitz, S. Sahni, and D. Mehta. Fundamentals of Data Structures in C++, W.H. Freeman, NY (1995).
18. M. Grueva. A Framework for Event Registration, Filtering, and Notification over the Internet. Master's Thesis, University of Florida (1999).

Knowledge-Based Validation, Aggregation, and Visualization of Meta-data: Analyzing a Web-Based Information System

Heiner Stuckenschmidt[1] and Frank van Harmelen[2,3]

[1] Center for Computing Technologies, University of Bremen
[2] AIdministrator BV, Amerfoort,
[3] AI Department, Vrije Universiteit Amsterdam

Abstract. As meta-data become of increasing importance to the Web, we will need to start managing such meta-data. We argue that there is a strong need for *meta-data validation and aggregation*. We introduce the Spectacle Workbench for verifying semi-structured information and show how it can be used to validate, aggregate and visualize the meta-data of an existing Information System. We conclude that the possibility to verify and aggregate meta-data is an added value with respect to contents-based access to information.

1 Motivation: Meta-data on the Web

The information society demands large-scale availability of data and information. With the advent of the World Wide Web huge amounts of information is available in principle, however, size and the inherent heterogeneity of the Web makes it difficult to find and access useful information. A suitable information source must be located which contains the data needed for a given task. Once the information source has been found, access to the data therein has to be provided. A common approach to this problem is to provide so-called meta-data, i.e. data about the actual information. This data may cover very different aspects of information: technical data about storage facilities and access methods co-exist with content descriptions and information about intended uses, suitability, and data quality. Concerning the problem of finding and accessing information, the role of meta-data is two-fold: On the side of information providers it serves as a means of organizing, maintaining, and cataloguing data, on the side of the information users meta-data helps to find, access and interpret information. Recently, standards have been proposed that cover different aspects of meta-data, especially the syntax for coding, the model structure, and content of a meta-data model. Some of these standards are:

- Syntactic Standards: HTML, XML, RDF (see http://www.w3c.org)
- Structural Standards: RDF schemas (see http://www.w3.org/TR/rdf-schema/), Topic Maps (see http://topicmaps.org/)
- Content Standards: Dublin Core (see http://dublincore.org/)

N. Zhong et al. (Eds.): WI 2001, LNAI 2198, pp. 217–226, 2001.
© Springer-Verlag Berlin Heidelberg 2001

These standards mentioned provide good guidance to design and encode meta-data for information resources on the World Wide Web. However, there are still some severe problems that are addressed neither by structural nor by content standards. These problems are concerned with the relation between information and meta-data about it. Some of the most important are:

Completeness: In order to provide full access to an information source, it has to be ensured that all the information is annotated with the corresponding meta-data. Otherwise, important or useful parts of an information source may be missed by meta-data driven search methods or cannot be indexed correctly.

Consistency: Meta-data about the contents of available information is only useful if it correctly describes these contents. In fact, meta-data that is not consistent with the actual information is an even bigger problem than missing meta-data, because mechanisms relying on meta-data will produce wrong results without warnings.

Accessibility: In order to be useful, meta-data has to be accessible not only to the information provider but especially to users who want to access it. Therefore, an important question is how a comprehensive description of an information source can be provided and accessed by potential users.

In this paper we describe a system for the validation of semi-structured information that can be used to check the completeness and consistency of meta-data with respect to the information it describes. We apply this approach to an existing information system and show how it can be used to generate and visualize an aggregated meta-data model for a large part of the information system in such a way that accessibility is improved.

2 BUISY: A Web-Based Environmental Information System

The advent of web-based information systems came with an attractive solution to the problem of providing integrated access to environmental information according to the duties and needs of modern environmental protection. Many information systems were set up either on the Internet in order to provide access to environmental information for everybody, or in intranets to support monitoring, assessment and exchange of information within an organization. One of the most recent developments in Germany is BUISY, an environmental information system for the city of Bremen that has been developed by the Center for Computing Technologies of the University of Bremen in cooperation with the public authorities. The development of the system was aimed at providing unified access to the information existing in the different organizational units for internal use as well as for the publication of approved information on the internet.

Meta-data plays an important role in the BUISY system. It controls the access to individual web pages. Each page in the BUISY system holds a set of

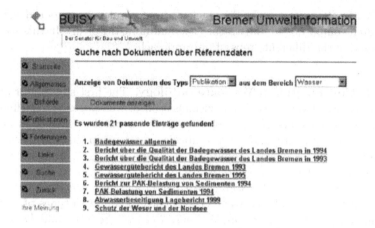

Fig. 1. The Meta-Data Driven Document Search Facility

meta-data annotations reflecting its contents and status [7]. The current version of BUISY supports a set of meta tags annotating information about the data-object's type, author, dates of creation- and expiration, as well as relevant keywords and the topic area of the page. The "Status" meta-tag indicates whether the data-object is part of the Internet or the Intranet section of BUISY.

```
<meta name="Status" content="Freigegeben"/>
<meta name="Typ" content="Publikation"/>
<meta name="Author" content="TJV"/>
<meta name="Date" content="10-04-1999"/>
<meta name="Expires" content="31-12-2010"/>
<meta name="Keywords" content="Wasser, Gew\"{a}sserg\"{u}te, Algen"/>
<meta name="Bereich" content="Wasser"/>
```

At the moment, this meta-data is used to provide an intelligent search facility for publications of the administration concerned with environmental protection. The user selects a document type and a topic area. Based on the input, a list of available publications is generated (see figure 1).

3   Using the Spectacle Workbench

We have developed an approach to solve the problems of completeness, consistency, and accessibility of meta-data identified above. This is done on the basis of rules which must hold for the information found in the Web site, both the actual information and the meta-data (and possibly their relationship) [6]. This means that besides providing web site contents and meta-data, an information provider also defines classification rules (also called: integrity constraints) for this information. An inference engine then applies these integrity constraints to identify the places in the web-site which violate these constraints. This approach has been implemented in the Spectacle content management tool, developed by the Dutch company AIdministrator (www.aidministrator.nl). In this section, we will describe the different steps of our approach.

Step 1. Constructing a Web-site ontology. The first step in our approach to content-based verification and visualisation of web-pages is to define an ontology of the contents of the web-site. Such an ontology identifies classes of objects on our web-site, and defines subclass relationships between these classes. For example, pages can be about water. These can again be subdivided into new subclasses: *Gewässer* (watercourses), *Weser* (a river in Bremen) *Grundwasser* (groundwater) *Abwasser* (wastewater) and *Anlagen* (technical installations). Further, we included some classes corresponding to types of documents that might appear in the system. We chose *Berichte* (reports) and *Verordnungen* (legislations). This leads to a hierarchy of pages that is based on page-contents, such as the example shown in Figure 2.

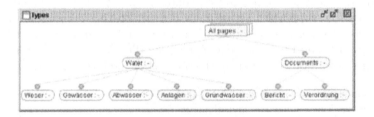

Fig. 2. An Example Classification Tree

A subtle point to emphasize is that the objects in this ontology are *objects in the web-site*, and not objects in the real-world which are described by the web-site. For example, the elements in the class "river-drainage" are not (denotations of) different river-drainage systems in the environment of Bremen, but they are *web-pages* (in this case: web-pages talking about river-drainage systems). As a result, any properties we can validate for these objects are properties of the *pages on the web-site*, as desired for our validation purposes.

Step 2. Defining the classification criteria for the ontology. The first step only defines the classes of our ontology, but does not tell us which instances belong to which class. In the second step, the user defines rules determining which web-pages will be members of which class. In this section, we will briefly illustrate these rules by means of three examples.

Figure 3 specifies that a rule is about "water" if the keyword "wasser" appears in the meta-information of the web-page. The rule succeeds if the following code appears in the web-page:

```
<meta name="Keywords" content="Wasser">
<meta name="Typ" content="Bericht>
```

In the typical case, a page belongs to a class if the rule defined for that class succeeds for the page. However, it is also possible to define classes by negation: a page belongs to a class when the corresponding rule fails on that page. This is indicated by a rectangle in the class-hierarchy (instead of a rounded box). In Figure 9 for example, the class 'missing-attributes' will contain all pages that do NOT contain the attribute NAME in the <META>-tag.

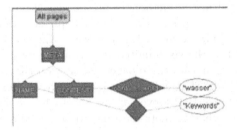

Fig. 3. Example of a Classification Rule Using Meta-Data

Step 3. Classifying individual pages. Whereas the human user of Spectacle performs the previous steps, the next step is automatic. The definition of the hierarchy in step 1 and the rules in step 2 allows an inference engine to automatically classify each page in the class hierarchy. Notice that classes may overlap (a single page may belong to multiple classes). The rule format (adopted from [5]) has been defined in such a way as to provide sufficient expressive power while still making it possible to perform such classification inference on large numbers of pages (many thousands in human-acceptable response time). After these three steps, we have a class hierarchy that is populated with all the pages of a given site.

4   Applying Spectacle to the BUISY System

The ability of the Spectacle system to classify web-pages according to the meta-data contained in every page enables us to use the system to perform the tasks we claimed to be necessary for meta-data management on the internet, i.e. the validation, aggregation and visualization of the meta-data annotations in the BUISY system. At that time the BUISY system contained approximately 1500 pages which are not maintained centrally, but the different topic areas of the systems had been supplemented by different persons after the initial development phase that ended in 1998. Due to this fact, we expected to be faced with incomplete and inconsistent meta-data annotations in the different parts of the system. We performed some validation and some aggregation experiments on this meta-data which are reported in the next sections.

4.1   Validating Meta-data

Checking Meta-Attributes and Values. After we extracted the pages that are actually supposed to contain information, we can start to check the completeness of the annotated meta-information. In our analysis, we focused on the meta-information assigning a page to a certain topic area. In the BUISY system this information is stored in the meta-attribute named "Bereich". So the first task is to check whether all pages which passed the pre-selection contain the meta-attribute "Bereich". The result of this test was rather negative. We found that about one hundred of the six hundred fifty contents pages do not contain the "Bereich" attribute. Another three pages did contain the attribute but without a value. It is very likely that not all pages which were included into the BUISY system are annotated yet. However, using Spectacle, we are able to find these pages and to decide whether meta-data has to be added or not.

Check for Missing Keywords. The validation of the keyword annotations actually existing in the system is the next step of our analysis. In order to judge the quality of the present annotations we defined some keywords covering important aspects of the information found in the system. We chose the keyword according to the classes described in step 1. We used the keywords to compare the keyword annotations with the contents of the page using a full text search on the whole page.

The validation revealed that most pages containing a keyword in the text did not have this keyword in the meta-data annotation. Using Spectacle, we were able to identify these pages and present them to the systems administrator who has to decide if the keyword has to be added.

4.2   Aggregating Meta-data

The validation of meta-data discussed in the previous section is all done on the <META>-tags which are distributed across the 1500 pages of the BUISY system. At construction time, such a distributed organization of the meta-data is rather attractive: each page can be maintained separately, containing its own meta-data. Page-authors can directly update the meta-data annotations when updating a page, and no access to a central meta-data repository is needed. However, when we want to use the meta-data to create content-based navigation maps (as in the next section), or as the basis for a meta-data-based search engine, such a distributed organization of the meta-data is no longer attractive. We would then much rather have fast access to a central meta-data repository instead of having to make remote access to 1500 separate pages when looking for certain meta-data.

Using the validation process described in section 3 we analyzed the Web-site
with respect to membership of pages to different topic areas. The result of this
step is a classification of pages into a number of classes, based on the application
of the classification rules to the <META>-tags in the pages. This yields a populated class-hierarchy of pages. Such a populated class hierarchy can be stored
in a combined RDF and RDF Schema format [2]. The following statements are
taken from the RDF Schema encoding of the Webmaster type hierarchy. The
first three show how of the types "water", "Gewässer" and "Weser" and their
subtype relationship are encoded in standard RDF Schema.

```
<rdfs:Class rdf:ID="water"/>

<rdfs:Class rdf:ID="Gew\"{a}sser">
   <rdfs:subClassOf rdf:resource="#water"/>
</rdfs:Class>

<rdfs:Class rdf:ID="Weser">
   <rdfs:subClassOf rdf:resource="#water"/>
</rdfs:Class>
```

. . .

The following is an example of an RDF encoding of instance information: the
URL mentioned in the "about" attribute is declared to be a member of the class
"water" (and consequently of all its supertypes, by virtue of the RDF Schema
semantics.

```
<rdf:Description
    about="http://www.umwelt.bremen.de/buisy/scripts/buisy.asp?
        doc=Badegewaesserguete+Bremen">
   <rdf:type resource="#Gew\"{a}sser"/>
</rdf:Description> ...
```

These automatically generated annotations constitute an aggregated description of a web site that can be used to get an overview of its contents. The annotations are machine-readable, but they are hard to use by a human web-master.
This is the reason why we not only generate an aggregated meta-data model,
but also provide a condensed visualization on the basis of the aggregated model.
We will discuss this visualization intended for human use in the next section.

4.3 Meta-data Visualization

Spectacle supports the automatic generation of so-called cluster maps about a
web-site. A cluster map visualizes an instantiated hierarchy of pages by grouping
pages from the same class into a cluster. These clusters may overlap if pages
belong to more than one class.

The map generated from the classes described above (figure 4) shows some
interesting features. The first thing that attracts attention is the fact that again

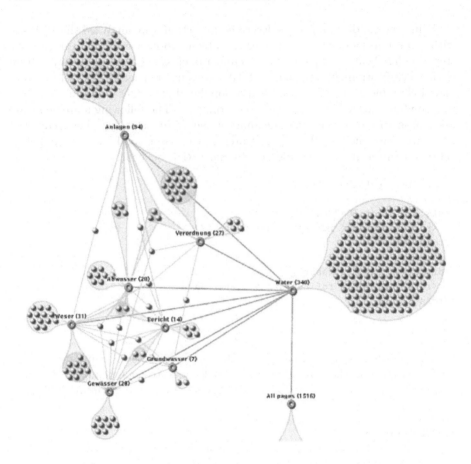

Fig. 4. Cluster Map of the Water Subsystem

most of the pages could not be classified into one of the keyword classes. The better part of the approximately one thousand pages analyzed do not even contain information about the topic area water. This can be explained by the fact that a content map always contains all pages of a web site. However, there are also many pages which contain relevant contents, but do not belong to one of the keyword classes (page cluster at the right-hand side of the page). The interesting part of the content map is its left side where the pages from the different keyword classes and their membership in these classes are displayed. We can clearly identify pages about technical facilities and waste water as well as pages containing information about legislation concerning one or both of these topics.

Automatically constructed figures such as figure 7 are compact enough to display many hundreds of pages in a single small image (the map contains 340 pages). This should be compared with the output from traditional search engines, where a set of more than 300 pages is typically presented as 15 pages with 25 URLS each. The format of figure 4 is much more useable in practice.

5   Discussion

We argued that meta-data plays an important role in information management on the Internet and mentioned existing problems. We identified the need for validation, aggregation and visualization of meta-data and presented a knowledge-based approach to these tasks. We introduced the Spectacle content management system which implements the approach and presented some results in applying it to a web-based environmental information system. Two mayor implications are drawn from our experiments.

Meta-Data Validation is Necessary and Possible. While meta-data standards cover many questions of what kinds of meta-data to use and how to represent it, guaranteeing completeness, consistency and accessibility of meta-data is still a problem in web-age information management. There is a need for methods to check information sources for the existence of meta-data and to relate it to the actual content of the information source.

Our experiments also showed that Spectacle implements a promising approach to meta-data management. It enables us to perform completeness, consistency, and plausibility checks on meta-data. We can locate pages with missing meta-data, compare information contents and meta-data and produce hints towards missing keywords. The graphical interface of the systems supports the inspection of large information systems, the aggregation of meta-data annotations, and the visualization of the aggregated model.

Aggregated Meta-Data is an Added Value. The ability to create an aggregated content model of an information system and store it in RDF format provides opportunities that go far beyond an inspection of existing meta-data. The aggregated model can serve as intelligent interface for an information source. This interface can be used by next generation search engines to get a quick overview of the contents in order to decide whether a detailed search is promising or not. Appropriate inference services like the one reported in [3] can be used to answer queries about the contents of an information source on the basis of the meta-data model.This ability could even be enhanced by using more expressive languages for the representation of aggregated meta-data. A promising language for this purpose is described in [4]. The idea of using aggregated meta-data for answering queries about information is of great interest with respect to the notion of a semantic web promoted by Tim Berners Lee [1] and has to be further investigated in the future.

References

1. Tim Berners-Lee and Mark Fischetti. *Weaving the Web: The Original Design and Ultimate Destiny of the World Wide Web by its Inventor.* Harper, San Francisco, Oktober 1999.
2. Pierre-Antoine Champin. Rdf tutorial. Available at http://www710.univ-lyon1. fr/ champin/rdf-tutorial/, June 2000.

3. Stefan Decker, Dan Brickley, Janne Saarela, and Jürgen Angele. A query and inference service for rdf in proceedings of ql'98 - the query languages workshop. 1998.
4. D. Fensel, I. Horrocks, F. Van Harmelen, S. Decker, M. Erdmann, and M. Klein.
   Oil in a nutshell. In *12th International Conference on Knowledge Engineering and
   Knowledge Management EKAW 2000*, Juan-les-Pins, France, 2000.
5. M.-C. Rousset. Verifying the world wide web: a position statement. In F. van Harmelen and J. van Thienen, editors, *Proceedings of the Fourth European Symposium on
   the Validation and Verification of Knowledge Based Systems (EUROVAV97)*, 1997.
6. Frank van Harmelen and Jos van der Meer. Webmaster: Knowledge-based verification of web-pages. In M. Ali and I. Imam, editors, *Proceedings of the Twelfth
   International Conference on Industrial and Engineering Applications of Artificial
   Intelligence and Expert Systems, (IEA/AEI99)*, LNAI. Springer Verlang, 1999.
7. Thomas Vögele, Heiner Stuckenschmidt, and Ubbo Visser. Buisy - using brokered
   data objects for environmental information systems. In Klaus Tochtermann and
   Wolf-Fritz Riekert, editors, *Hypermedia im Umweltschutz*, Marburg, 2000. Metropo-
   lis Verlang.

Online Handwritten Signature Verification for Electronic Commerce over the Internet

W. Sardha Wijesoma, K.W. Yue, K.L. Chien, and T.K. Chow

School of Electrical and Electronics Engineering,
Nanyang Technological University,
Singapore 639798
eswwijesoma@ntu.edu.sg

Abstract. There is a lot of potential in using on-line handwritten signature verification over the Internet. Banks and Government bodies recognize signatures as a legal means of authentication. Compared with other electronic identification methods such as fingerprints scanning and retinal vascular pattern screening, it is easier for people to migrate from using the popular pen-and-paper signature to one where the handwritten signature is captured and verified electronically. In an era where electronic commerce and online banking are gaining world-wide popularity and huge acceptance among the common masses, there has to be a way of verifying the identity of the potential client in cyberspace. A verification model incorporated with an appropriate algorithm is proposed to facilitate on-line handwritten signature verification for electronic commerce over the Internet. The client/server architecture and the verification algorithm used are presented to demonstrate the feasibility of on-line handwritten signature as an authentication means for e-commerce.

1   Introduction

The handwritten signature is one of the ways to authorize transactions and authenticate the human identity [1]. The other common means include:
   a)   Passwords or Personal Identification Number (PIN)
   b)   Biological characteristics such as fingerprint or retinal vascular pattern
   The passwords or PIN method is most widely used at present. However it is not always easy to remember them. This is especially true in today's context where a person requires multiple passwords to gain access to many secured applications like banking services, office computer networks and other Internet applications.
   The biological characteristic method has a social stigma attached to it [1]. Fingerprints are widely regarded as a means of verification either for the very young or for the illiterate. Furthermore, with its widespread use in the criminal justice system, it is not an attractive means of verification. Retinal vascular pattern recognition is an expensive system to implement given the hardware involved. Above all, most people are skeptical and uncomfortable in giving away their biological characteristics.
   Presently, signatures signed on paper are accepted as a verification means for many uses. For these signatures, there is only a static visual record. Many people are used to

N. Zhong et al. (Eds.): WI 2001, LNAI 2198, pp. 227–236, 2001.
© Springer-Verlag Berlin Heidelberg 2001

such handwritten signatures as a means of acknowledgment. Banks recognize the signature as a legally accepted means of verifying the identity of an individual. This is because a signature is distinctive enough that it is highly unlikely that any two persons would have exactly the same signature except in the event of a forgery [1].

Up till now, signatures are still verified manually by human inspection. This is highly subjective and hence inaccurate. As a result, computer based verification approaches, both off-line (static) and on-line (dynamic), have been developed in the hope of solving this problem. Off-line verification systems determine the genuineness of a signature purely by examining its overall geometric shape captured by a camera or an optical scanner. On the other hand, on-line systems not only capture the actual shape but also pen dynamics (such as time evolution of position coordinates like speed and acceleration) of the signatures. Dynamics-related features are "invisible" by nature because they are not apparent from a visual inspection of a signature copy. Hence on-line systems are preferred.

2   Motivation for an Online Signature Verification System

Since the introduction of online purchases over the Internet, the credit card number inscribed on its plastic surface has been the tool used to validate most e-commerce transactions. Regardless of the identity of the user, the purchase is valid as long as the correct card number is entered. This is astonishing as there is essentially no 'personal' identification required to authorize a transaction besides the possession of a credit card, in which case, can be stolen. The misuse of credit cards is not just limited to online purchases. Shops and restaurants also offer credit card payments. Again, a lost credit card could have been picked up and used for payment. Although in this case, the user is required to sign on the receipts, this is not a full proof method. The user could have obtained and forged the signature sample found on the back of a credit card. The onus is thus on the shop's employee to do a quick verification of the signature visually. This is impractical. Further more, it is often difficult to spot a well-forged signature through the naked eye.

There are valid reasons to advocate on-line handwritten signature verification. Firstly, handwritten signature is the most popular means of authenticating the identity of the user. The common masses are familiar with the use of signature as a way of acknowledgement and verification. Banks and financial institutions recognize the handwritten signature as a legally accepted means of verifying the individual's identity. In the United States, there now exists a law allowing many types of legally binding agreement to be sealed using electronic signatures over the Internet [2]. There is thus much potential in introducing on-line handwritten signature verification over the Internet for e-business. With electronic signature and Net-conveyed records having the same legal standing as a pen-and-paper document, this would marry the old value of consumer protection with the newest technologies so that the full measure of the benefits that e-commerce has to offer could be achieved [3]. Hence there exists great commercial potential in on-line handwritten signature verification. In addition, the online signature is merely a progression from the present popular system of manual pen-and-paper signature verification. With on-line signature verification, the only minor change is to get accustomed to signing on an electronic tablet instead of on a piece of paper and allowing the handwritten signature to be verified objectively by the computer.

3   Architectural Requirements for the Verification System

Two important aspects contribute to a feasible verification system. They are the architectural requirements and the verification methodology. The former is discussed in this section.

For an on-line handwritten signature verification to be feasible over the Internet, the key architectural features that, in our opinion, warrant special attention are security, platform independence and the ability to accommodate multiple verification sessions simultaneously.

Security is a vital part in any monetary transaction. In a signature verification application, security is viewed in two respects viz., to prevent the sensitive signature data from being tampered or eavesdropped and, to prevent the verification system and its database from being corrupted. Both respects are of paramount importance especially when the intentions of the users are unclear with internet connectivity.

Developing an architecture that is platform independent is a prerequisite for any verification system to gain easy acceptance among users. With this feature, the executable program when downloaded from the central server can be executed regardless of the operating system used, be it Windows, Macintosh or LINUX. Also, the verification program can be hosted on any type of servers irrespective of the server operating systems.

Like any application implemented over the internet, there is always the possibility of having multiple clients logging on to an application simultaneously. For signature verification, the architecture must allow multiple signature acquisition sessions to take while maintaining an ordered verification sequence.

4   The Algorithmic Aspects of the Verification System

The algorithm of a signature verification system is what determines the authenticity of a signature instance. Its purview stretches from the extraction of features from a sample of signature instances of a signer; right to the verification stage where a final authenticity measure is given for a particular instance of a test signature. Genuine signatures falsely rejected or forgery signatures falsely accepted contribute to the False Rejection (FR) rate and False Acceptance (FA) rate respectively, both of which are common measures of performance for a signature verification system.

The working of the verification process is as follows: initially a potential user enrolls on the system by providing signature samples or instances. Features are extracted from this set of signature samples. These features statistically encapsulate the characteristics of an individual signer and they constitute the reference feature set. Subsequently, the verification algorithm then compares the features extracted from a test signature instance with its reference features. Depending on some correlation or distance-measure, it determines the likely authenticity of the signature.

On the notion of automating the task of signature verification, two important areas in algorithmic design demand careful attention. One, it is the choice of features used and two, the comparison strategy that is deployed in the hope of selecting only relevant features for comparison.

Each feature provides a measure on a certain aspect of a signature. In general features can be broadly classified as shape-related or timing-related. Shape features describe certain measures of shape of a signature. Time features capture the dynamic information during signing. Within each category, they can be further subdivided into global or local features. Global features are single-valued measures that dictate an entire analysis of a signature specific to a certain aspect. Local features comprises of a series of measurements that spells the specific changes at different segments of the signature.

The verification stage extracts features from the test signature to be verified as its inputs from which the basis for evaluation and comparison is formulated. It is here that several levels of sophistication are developed, all aimed to deal with the very real problems pertaining to the nature of signature verification.

The first aspect native to signature verification is the problem of intra-signer variations. It is because that no two signature instances produced are exactly similar. Verification accuracy is thus very much dependant on how well the signer is consistent when signing from one instance to another. The signer being inconsistent during this enrollment would contribute to a large statistical spread for some features and hence, to some extent dilutes the boundaries for successful discrimination. Thus, it is imperative that the algorithm seeks out consistent and yet unique features that should contribute to the verification outcome. Uniqueness can be a measure of the amount of isolation in a particular person's feature value as compared to the same feature of a general person's handwriting [4].

Second, it is necessary to devise a method in which the relative importance of some features is stressed over others [5]. It is intuitive that no two signers are consistent in every feature aspect. As an example, one signer could be very consistent in reproducing the shape of the signature but lacks timing consistency while the other is consistent in time but lacks shape accuracy. In this case, it is necessary to weight in favor of the consistent features.

Third, we envisage that some features could possibly add an added level of discrimination when evaluated together with other features. Depending on the features used, many such unique relationships can be established. The algorithm has to allow for such a fusion in the hope of foiling skillful forgers. An obvious example is perhaps weighting the importance of time-related features over shape-related features for the reason that signing dynamics is what an illicit forger cannot see from a static instance of a signature. All these aspects are the very native problems encountered in the development of a signature verification system. They are important prerequisites and have to be carefully considered for successfully implementation.

5   Implementation of the Verification Architecture

5.1   Network Architecture

Fig. 1 shows a three-tier client/server model was implemented for signature verification. This architecture is preferred over the two-tier models because it is more secure, has higher scalability and has more ability to handle multiple clients [10]. Using the three-tier model, the verification application can be centrally managed on the server, thus easing system administration.

Browser/Applet

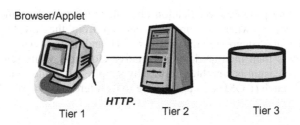

HTTP.

Tier 1   Tier 2   Tier 3

Fig. 1. A three-tier client/server architecture

Java was the chosen language in the implementation. Besides being the Internet programming language for deploying applications on the Internet, Java is object-oriented, distributed, secure, platform independent and multithreaded. All these features satisfy the requirements that were laid out in Sect. 3. In particular, the Java applet and the Java servlet were used for the client and server side respectively. The entire implementation of the three-tier client/server model for the on-line handwritten signature verification was split into two parts: enrolment and verification.

5.1.1   Enrolment Process

In the enrolment process, the user will be presented with an applet, which has a text box for entering the name and a blank area for him/her to sign within. The user will be required to sign several times on the applet using an electronic pen pad. As the user is signing on the applet, the individual x and y coordinates of the signature will be captured by the applet. As the algorithm that is being used (dynamic) requires the timing profile of the signer, the applet will also be capturing the time from the system clock as the user is signing his/her name. When the user is satisfied with his/her enrolment, he/she will submit the data to the server via an Applet-Servlet communication protocol. The servlet on receiving the data performs a query using the Structured Query Language (SQL) to insert the data into the database implemented using Microsoft Access. A message will then be returned to the user acknowledging the success or failure of his/her enrolment.

232   W.S. Wijesoma et al.

5.1.2   Verification Process

In the verification process, the user inputs his login name accompanied with his signature in the applet. These data will then be sent to the servlet. The servlet then searches for a person's representative signatures, or sample instances, in the database based on the login name. The sample instances together with the test signature instance will be compared to determine the test instance's authenticity. This authenticity measure will subsequently be displayed in the applet informing the user if his/her signature is accepted.

5.2   Verification Algorithm

Fig. 2 shows the proposed verification algorithm that was implemented. The input stage on the left is where features are derived from the raw test signature data captured. They are categorized into shape-related and timing-related features. Each of these features is then measured for its relative closeness to its reference instances. This distance measure is weighted further by simple fuzzy rules and its output yields the degree of match (DOM) of a test feature to its references.

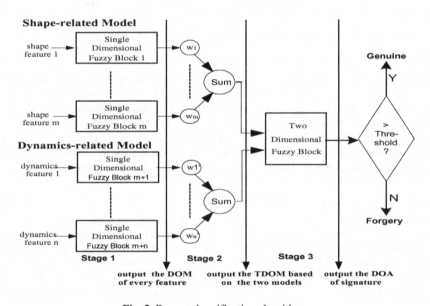

Fig. 2. Proposed verification algorithm

It is evident that no signer is consistent in every aspect when signing. It follows that not every feature should contribute equally in determining the authenticity of a signature. It would be devastating to utilize features that the signer could not repeatedly reproduce with confidence. Also, one would expect if a particular feature is very different from those extracted from the general population of signers, there is a high chance that this feature offers greater discrimination towards forgeries. Thus it is both the consistency and a feature's isolation in the population of signatures that we formulate the basis on which we apportion weights to each feature. This feature selection process was implemented in stage 2. It is formulated as an optimization problem. The object of optimization is to determine the weight of each feature constituting the feature subset for the signer that will maximize a suitably chosen discriminating function. For this kind of problem, genetic algorithms (GAs) can provide for an effective solution [6]. The personalized feature vectors are firstly encoded into chromosomes as shown in Fig. 3. For example, the binary sequence '1111' in each cell represents maximum contribution of a feature while '0000' indicates zero contribution of a feature. Each weight is multiplied with its DOM and aggregated to give the *total degree of match* (TDOM) for the feature domain.

1	2	3	4	5	6	7	8	9	10
1001	0010	0000	0101	0100	1010	1011	0001	0000	0001

Fig. 3. 4-bit coding of shape features onto a chromosome

To evaluate the goodness of a chromosome, verification is carried out on n_1 samples of genuine and n_2 samples of forged signature instances of a person using the set of features as defined by the chromosome. Now the chromosome's fitness is calculated using the following fitness function:

$$ F = (1 - FR) \times \frac{1}{n_1} \sum_{i=1}^{n_1} D1_i + (1 - FA) \times \frac{1}{n_2} \sum_{j=1}^{n_2} (100 - D2_j) \ . \tag{2} $$

$D1_p$ is the TDOM for the ith genuine sample, and $D2_j$ the TDOM for the jth forgery sample. FR is the false rejection rate and FA the false acceptance rate obtained for the total reference and forged signature samples $(n_1 + n_2)$ based on the shape and dynamic feature vectors alone.

It may be noted that the fitness value of a chromosome is based on how well it contributes to the successful verification on two fronts. One is the magnitude of the TDOMs the chromosome gives rise to for both genuine and forgery samples. It is conjectured that larger the TDOM that results for genuine samples and smaller the TDOM for forgery samples, better the chromosome is. The other is that, obviously, smaller the false rejection and acceptance rates (type I and II errors) that result, better the chromosome is. Hence the fitness evaluation function is defined by adding the average of the TDOM for genuine reference samples to the average of (100-TDOM) for forgery samples, each weighted by acceptance rate and rejection rate respectively.

In stage 3, fuzzy logic is used to weight the relative importance of shape and dynamic contributions to determine the overall degree of accuracy (DOA) of the test signature instance. Through fuzzy logic, heuristics concocted by a human expert can be included to model the special characteristics which he observes. Detailed description and results of the genetic algorithm and fuzzy logic based verification algorithm used is given in [4], [9].

6   Results

The database consists of 1230 genuine signatures from 41 persons and 410 forgeries from six forgers. For each signer, there are 30 genuine samples and 10 forgery samples generated by two different forgers. In collecting genuine signature samples the signer was allowed to get accustomed to signing on the tablet using the stylus before providing 30 genuine samples over three separate sessions. The sessions were spaced a few days apart and each time, 10 samples were collected.

As for forgeries only skilled forgeries were taken into account. Each forger was shown all copies of the genuine signature samples of the 41 signers and allowed to forge 10 to 20 of these persons' signatures they thought they could forge. After permitting the forgers to practice as long as necessary, forgery samples were collected for each signature. Cash rewards were used to motivate the forgers. In the resulting database of signatures, the first 10 genuine samples of each signature were used to determine the optimal personalized shape and dynamic feature sets and the other remaining 20 genuine samples plus the 10 forgeries were used for testing.

6.1   Experimental Results

The parameters chosen for the GA algorithm are, tournament size of 3, crossover probability of 0.95, mutation probability of 0.09, and a stop condition of 50 generations or a maximum fitness of 195. Fig. 4 shows the error trade-off curve between FR (False Rejects) rate and FA (False Accepts) rate obtained for different thresholds for the proposed verification system. The lowest average error-rate is 5%.

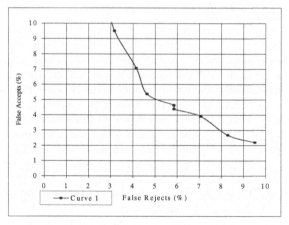

Fig. 4. Error trade-off curves

7   Discussions

With the implementation of the proposed three-tier client-server architecture, an important observation was made on the client side. It was found that different operating systems provide varying acquisition accuracy. In our application, the acquisition accuracy is defined by counting the number of coordinates captured by the applet for a time-accurate executed stroke. Fig. 5 depicts the approximate acquisition rates of the Java applet when executed on two most popular types of operating systems. Their acquisitions rates were plotted on a base 10 logarithmic scale. Ideally, the acquisition rate should be greater than the sampling rate of the digitizing tablet. A typical maximum sampling rate for electronic tablets is 200 Hz. Thus, it can be seen that the two versions of Windows OS have acquisition rates well short of 200Hz.

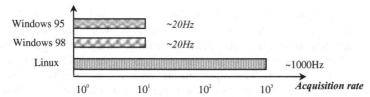

Fig. 5. Acquisition rate of the Java applet tested for different Operating Systems

This important observation directly affects the viability of widespread implementation of the proposed architecture in the marketplace. According to the IDC review report for 1997 [7], in the client operating environment review and forecast, there were 179 million installed Win95/98 operating systems. That is a 60% of the market share if Win95/98 is compared against DOS, Win3.x, NT, Mac and UNIX. In the later report by IDC for the year 1999/2000, Microsoft's Windows NT workstation alone accounted for $US1.6 billion out of the $US6.7 billion growth in the PC/client operating environment. At present, market dominance of existing operating systems seems to hinder the adoption of our model for signature verification over the Internet.

An alternative is to use a different programming language for the architecture construction. However, this is not favored when constructing applications for widespread connectivity. The Java programming language is perhaps the only language that allows for developing platform-independent applications at present. This feature is important in e-business if we are to ensure that a system is able to target as large a market as possible.

Also, it was observed that Java is relatively slow in its execution as compared to other languages. Every time a program is executed, it has to go through the Java Virtual Machine, an interpreter, which then converts the Java byte codes to native codes. This is what makes Java platform independent but at the same time, makes it slower since time is always spent in the conversion to native codes. The Applet is interpreted instead of being executed [8].

However this slight delay is not significant enough to be of a concern. For those critics on the speed issue, there are just-in-time compilers (from Visual Café) to correct this problem.

The selection of a personalized feature vector based on the discriminating ability of the feature vector as a whole is an effective approach to on-line signature verification based on a parametric approach. However, what is primarily lacking in this investigation is a field test of a real-time on-line on-site system based on the signature verification system we discussed. Expert forgers should be hired with the intent to beat the system. Signatures that are falsely accepted have to be carefully examined. The basis for evaluation should be compared to that of a trained person. Bank tellers, for one, fit this description. If bank tellers were unable to discriminate an instance produced by a skilled forger, it would be a bonus if the verification system considers that instance as a forgery. We believe that it is through these extensive tests that the task of verification can be fully automated.

8   Conclusion

Signature being the most common way to authenticate a person's identity is the way for authorizing electronic transactions for e-business. With both shape and pen-dynamics captured on-line, they give better discrimination against forgery. The three-tier client/server architecture provides the connectivity in which signature can be verified over the Internet. The algorithm is designed to specifically select the personalized feature vectors that formulate a person's signature class model. It adds another level of discrimination to successfully foil skillful forgers.

On-line handwritten signature verification thus marry the old value of consumer protection with the newest technologies so that the full measure of the benefits that e-commerce has to offer could be achieved.

References

1. Nalwa, V. S.: Automatic on-line signature verification, Proceedings of the IEEE, Vol. 85, (February 1997) 213-239
2. http://www.cnn.com/2000/ALLPOLITICS/stories/06/03/clinton.e.signatures.02
3. The Straits Times, 19 June 2000
4. Ma Mingming, and Wijesoma, W.S.: Selecting Optimal Personalized Features for On-line Signature Verification using GA, Proc. of IEEE Syst. Man and Cybern., USA (Oct 2000)
5. Ma Mingming, Wijesoma, W.S., and Eric Sung,: An Automatic on-line signature verification system based on three models, Proc. of 2000 Canadian Conf. on Electrical and Computer Engineering, (2000) 890-894
6. D. Goldberg, Genetic Algorithms in Search, Optimization, and Machine Learning. Addison-Wesley, Reading, MA (1989)
7. http://www.idc.com
8. Bob Breedlove, et al.: Web Programming Unleashed, Sams.net Publishing (1996)
9. Wijesoma, W.S. and Ma Mingming: On-line Signature Verification using a Computational Intelligence Approach, 7th Fuzzy Days, Dortmund (2001) (Accepted)
10. Orfali, R., Harkey, D. Edwards, J.: Client/Server Survival Guide, 3rd edn. John Wiley and Sons Inc. (1999)

A Data Model for XML Databases

Vilas Wuwongse[1], Kiyoshi Akama[2],
Chutiporn Anutariya[1], and Ekawit Nantajeewarawat[3]

[1] Computer Science & Information Management Program,
Asian Institute of Technology, Pathumtani 12120, Thailand
{vw, ca}@cs.ait.ac.th
[2] Center for Information and Multimedia Studies, Hokkaido Unversity,
Sapporo 060, Japan
akama@cims.hokudai.ac.jp
[3] Information Technology Program, Sirindhorn International Institute of Technology,
Thammasat University, Pathumtani 12120, Thailand
ekawit@siit.tu.ac.th

Abstract. In the proposed data model for XML databases, an XML element is directly represented as *a ground (variable-free) XML expression*—a generalization of an *XML element* by incorporation of variables for representation of implicit information and enhancement of its expressive power—while a collection of XML documents as a set of ground expressions, each describing an XML element in the documents. Relationships among elements in the collection as well as integrity constraints are formalized as *XML clauses. An XML database*, consisting of: (i) a document collection (or an *extensional database*), (ii) a set of relationships (or an *intensional database*) and (iii) a set of integrity constraints, is therefore modeled as an *XML declarative description* comprising a set of ground XML expressions and XML clauses. Its semantics is a set of ground XML expressions, which are explicitly described by the extensional database or implicitly derived from the intensional database and satisfy all the specified set of constraints.

1 Introduction

An XML document need only be *well-formed*, i.e., its tags be properly nested, but not conform to a particular DTD or Schema. Hence, XML is considered as a variation of *semistructured data*—data which may be varied and are not restricted to any particular schema or structure [1,13]. Management of semistructured data by highly-structured modeling techniques, such as relational and object-oriented models, not only results in a very complicated logical schema, but also requires much effort and frequent schema modifications. Consequently, development of an appropriate and efficient data model for XML documents has become an active research area with major current models based on *graphs* [1,8,10,13], *functional programming* [12], *hedge automaton* (aka. *forest automaton*) [15] and *Description Logic* [11]. However, these models alone do not have sufficient mechanisms to represent and manipulate all important characteristics and functionalities of XML

N. Zhong et al. (Eds.): WI 2001, LNAI 2198, pp. 237–246, 2001.
© Springer-Verlag Berlin Heidelberg 2001

data, such as provision of supports for DTD validation, integrity constraints and query processing as well as possession of well-defined semantics and efficient reasoning mechanism. Their extensions and integration of additional formalisms, which may complicate the models and make their understanding difficult, are required to overcome this limitation. For example, by application of *first-order logic theory*, the graph model in [10] has incorporated a facility for expression of and reasoning with *path and type constraints*.

By employment of *Declarative Description* theory [2,3] , this paper develops *XML Declarative Description (XDD)* theory [6,16], serving as a *data model for XML databases*, with an attempt to provide, in its single formalism, a simple yet expressive mechanism to succinctly and uniformly represent both explicit and implicit information, rules, relationships and structural/integrity constraints.

An *XDD description* is a set of ordinary XML elements, extended XML elements with variables, called *XML expressions*, and their constraints and relationships represented in terms of *XML clauses*. Its meaning does not yield only all the explicit information, represented by ordinary XML elements, but also includes all the implicit information described by the XML expressions with variables and the XML clauses in the description. Moreover, the data model allows DTDs and queries to be represented in terms of XDD descriptions, and also provides mechansims to verify a document validity [6,7] and to evaluate the queries [5,6,7].

Sect. 2 defines XML expressions, Sect. 3 develops a data model for XML databases, Sect. 4 formalizes XML databases, Sect. 5 reviews current, related works and compares them with the proposed one, and Sect. 6 draws conclusions.

2   XML Elements and XML Expressions

Ordinary XML elements are ground or variable-free. In order to express implicit information and enhance their expressive power, their definition will be formally extended by incorporation of variables, and then called *XML expressions*.

Let $\sum_X$ be an *XML expression alphabet* comprising the symbols in the seven sets defined in Table 1. An *XML expression* on $\sum_X$ takes one of the forms:

1. *evar*,
2. $<t \ \ a_1 = v_1 \ldots a_m = v_m \ \ pvar_1 \ldots pvar_k />$,
3. $<t \ \ a_1 = v_1 \ldots a_m = v_m \ \ pvar_1 \ldots pvar_k > v_{m+1} </t>$,
4. $<t \ \ a_1 = v_1 \ldots a_m = v_m \ \ pvar_1 \ldots pvar_k > e_1 \ldots e_n </t>$,
5. $<ivar> e_1 \ldots e_n </ivar>$,

where   - $evar \in V_E$,   - $k, m, n \geq 0$,   - $t, a_i \in (N \cup V_N)$,   - $pvar \in V_P$,
        - $v_i \in (C^* \cup V_S)$, - $ivar \in V_I$,   - e_i are XML expressions on $\sum_X$.

The order of the attribute-value pairs $a_1 = v_1 \ldots a_m = v_m$ and the order of the *P*-variables $pvar_1 \ldots pvar_k$ are immaterial, while the order of the expressions $e_1 \ldots e_n$ is important. XML expressions with and without variable will be referred to as *non-ground XML expressions* and *ground XML expressions* (or XML

Table 1. The alphabet $\sum_X$.

Sets	Set Elements	Conditions	Specialization into
C	*Characters*	'\$' $\notin C$	-
N	*Names* (either *element types* or *attribute names*)	Not beginning with "\$N:"	-
V_N	*Name-variables (N-variables)*	Beginning with "\$N:"	Names in N
V_S	*String-variables (S-variables)*	Beginning with "\$S:"	Strings in C^*
V_P	*Attribute-value-pair-variables (P-variables)*	Beginning with "\$P:"	Sequences of attribute-value pairs
V_E	*XML-expression-variables (E-variables)*	Beginning with "\$E:"	Sequences of XML expressions
V_I	*Intermediate-expression-variables (I-variables)*	Beginning with "\$I:"	Parts of XML expressions

elements), respectively. An expression of the second, the third or the fourth form is referred to as a *t-expression*, while that of the fifth form as an *ivar-expression*. A ground *t*-expression will also be called a *t*-element. An *I*-variable is employed to represent an XML expression when its structure or nesting pattern is not fully known. For example, the expression $<ivar> e_1 \ldots e_n </ivar>$, where e_i are expressions, represents a set of XML expressions which contain the sub-expression sequence $e_1 \ldots e_n$ to an arbitrary depth.

As an example of ground XML expressions, consider the element a of Fig. 1. Obviously, mappings between ordinary XML elements and ground XML expressions are straightforward. The expressions a' and a'' of Fig. 1 represent examples of non-ground XML expressions on $\sum_X$, which employ various types of variables for the representation of groups or classes of XML elements with some common structures, attributes or subelements. It will be seen in Fig. 1 that both a' and a'' can be specialized into the element a.

3   XDD: A Data Model for XML Databases

Based on an *XML specialization generation system*, to be defined in Definition 1, an *XML specialization system* and *XML declarative descriptions*, which serve as a data model for XML documents, will be formulated.

Definition 1. Let $\Delta_X = \langle \mathcal{A}_X, \mathcal{G}_X, \mathcal{C}_X, \nu_X \rangle$ be an *XML specialization generation system*, where

- $\mathcal{A}_X$ is the set of all XML expressions on $\sum_X$,
- $\mathcal{G}_X$ is the subset of $\mathcal{A}_X$ comprising all ground XML expressions on $\sum_X$,
- $\mathcal{C}_X$ is the set of all *basic specializations*, which is the union of the sets:
  - Variable Renaming: $(V_N \times V_N) \cup (V_S \times V_S) \cup (V_P \times V_P) \cup (V_E \times V_E) \cup (V_I \times V_I)$
  - Variable Expansion: $(V_P \times (V_N \times V_S \times V_P)) \cup (V_E \times (V_E \times V_E))$
  - Variable Removal: $(V_P \times V_E \times V_I) \cup \{\varepsilon\}$, where ε denotes the null symbol

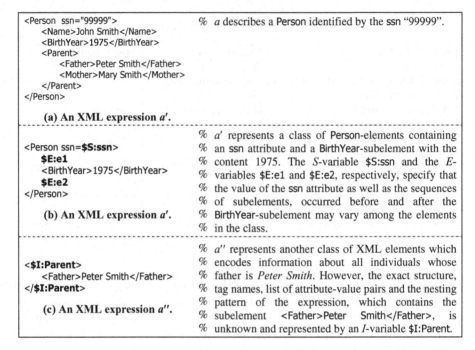

Fig. 1. XML expression examples.

- Variable Instantiation: $(V_N \times N) \cup (V_S \times C^*) \cup (V_E \times \mathcal{A}_X) \cup (V_I \times (V_N \times V_P \times V_E \times V_E \times V_I))$
- $\nu_X : \mathcal{C}_X \rightarrow partial\_map(\mathcal{A}_X)$ is the *basic specialization operator*, which determines, for each basic specialization c in $\mathcal{C}_X$, the change of an XML expression in $\mathcal{A}_X$ caused by c and is defined in Table 2.   □

Fig. 2 shows that successive applications of the given basic specializations c_1, c_2 and c_3 to the expression a' of Fig. 1, by the operator ν_X, yield the element a.

Definition 2. Based on Δ_X, let $\Gamma_X = \langle \mathcal{A}_X, \mathcal{G}_X, \mathcal{S}_X, \mu_X \rangle$ be an *XML specialization system*, where

- $\mathcal{S}_X = \mathcal{C}_X^*$ is the set of all sequences of zero or more basic specializations in $\mathcal{C}_X$ and their elements are called *specializations*, and
- $\mu_X : \mathcal{S}_X \rightarrow partial\_map(\mathcal{A}_X)$ is the *specialization operator*, which determines, for each specialization s in $\mathcal{S}_X$, the change of an XML expression in $\mathcal{A}_X$ caused by s and is defined in terms of the basic specialization operator ν_X such that: For each $a \in \mathcal{A}_X$,
  - $\mu_X(\lambda)(a) = a$, where λ denotes the null sequence,
  - $\mu_X(c \cdot s)(a) = \mu_X(s)(\nu_X(c)(a))$, where $c \in \mathcal{C}_X$ and $s \in \mathcal{S}_X$.   □

Example 1. With reference to Fig. 2, let $\theta = (c_1 c_2 c_3) \in \mathcal{S}_X$. By the definition of the operator μ_X, it follows that θ can specialize the expression a' into a, i.e., $a =$

Table 2. The basic specialization operator ν_X.

Type	Basic Specialization	Given $a \in \mathcal{A}_X, \nu_x(c)(a)$ is Obtained from a by
1. Renaming	$c = (v, u) \in (V_N \times V_N) \cup (V_S \times V_S) \cup$ $(V_P \times V_P) \cup (V_E \times V_E) \cup (V_I \times V_I)$	Replacement of all occurrences of v in a by u.
2. Expansion • *P-variable*	$c = (v_P, (u_N, u_S, v'_P))$ $\in (V_P \times (V_N \times V_S \times V_P))$	Simultaneous replacement of all occurrences of v_P in a by the sequence of the pair $u_N = u_S$ and the *P*-variable v'_P.
• *E-variable*	$c = (v, (v_1, v_2)) \in V_E \times (V_E \times V_E)$	Simultaneous replacement of each occurrence of v in a by the sequence $v_1 v_2$.
3. Removal • *P-, E-variable*	$c = (v, \varepsilon) \in (V_P \cup V_E) \times \varepsilon$, where ε denotes the null symbol	Removal of each occurrence of v in a.
• *I-variable*	$c = (v, \varepsilon) \in V_I \times \varepsilon$, where ε denotes the null symbol	Removal of each occurrence of $<v>$ and of $</v>$ in a.
4. Instantiation • *N-variable*	$c = (v, n) \in V_N \times N$	Simultaneous replacement of each occurrence of v in a by n
• *S-, E-variable*	$c = (v, u) \in (V_S \times C^*) \cup (V_E \times \mathcal{A}_X)$	Simultaneous replacement of each occurrence of v in a by u.
• *N-variable*	$c = (v_I, (u_N, u_P, u_E, w_E, v'_I))$ $\in V_I \times (V_N \times V_P \times V_E \times V_E \times V_I)$	Simultaneous replacement of each occurrence of the v_I-expression $<v_I> e_1 \ldots e_n </v_I>$ in a by the v_N-expression $<u_N\ u_P>$ $u_E <v'_I> e_1 \ldots e_n </v'_I> w_E$ $</u_N>$.

$\mu_X(\theta)(a')$ or by shorthand notation $a = a'\theta$. Similarly, the $I:Parent-expression a'' of Fig. 1 can be specialized into the element a by some specialization in $\mathcal{S}_X$. Due to page limitation, such a specialization will not be given. □

Based on the XML specialization system Γ_X, XML declarative descriptions and other related concepts can now be defined.

Let a set $\mathcal{K}$ comprise *constraint predicates*. A constraint on Γ_X is a formula $q(a_1, \ldots, a_n)$, where q is a constraint predicate in $\mathcal{K}$ and a_i an XML expression in $\mathcal{A}_X$. Given a ground constraint $q(g_1, \ldots, g_n), g_i \in \mathcal{G}_X$, its truth and falsity are assumed to be predetermined. Denote the set of all true ground constraints by *Tcon*. A specialization θ is applicable to a constraint $q(a_1, \ldots, a_n)$ if θ is applicable to $a_1, \ldots, a_n$. The result of $q(a_1, \ldots, a_n)\theta$ is the constraint $q(a_1\theta, \ldots, a_n\theta)$. The notion of constraints introduced here is useful for defining restrictions on XML expressions in $\mathcal{A}_X$.

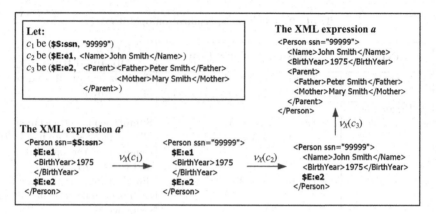

Fig. 2. Successive applications of $\nu_X(c_1), \nu_X(c_2), \nu_X(c_3)$ to the expression a' of Fig. 1.

Definition 3. An *XML clause* on Γ_X is a formula of the form:

$$H \leftarrow B_1, \ldots, B_n \tag{1}$$

where $n \geq 0$, H is an XML expression in $\mathcal{A}_X$ and B_i an XML expression in $\mathcal{A}_X$ or a constraint on Γ_X. H is called the *head* and $(B_1, \ldots, B_n)$ the *body* of the clause. An *XML declarative description* or simply an *XDD description* on Γ_X is a (possibly infinite) set of XML clauses on Γ_X. $\qquad\square$

Let C be an XML clause $(H \leftarrow B_1, \ldots, B_n)$. If $n = 0$, C is called a *unit clause*, if $n \geq 0$, a *non-unit clause*. When it is clear from the context, a unit clause $(H \leftarrow)$ is simply written as H. The head of C is denoted by $head(C)$ and the set of all XML expressions and constraints in the body of C by $object(C)$ and $con(C)$, respectively. Let $body(C) = object(C) \cup con(C)$. A clause C' is an instance of C iff there is a specialization $\theta \in \mathcal{S}_X$ such that θ is applicable to $H, B_1, \ldots, B_n$ and $C' = C\theta = (H\theta \leftarrow B_1\theta, \ldots, B_n\theta)$. A clause C is a *ground clause* iff C comprises only ground XML expressions and ground constraints.

Associated with an XDD description P on Γ_X is the mapping T_P on $2^{\mathcal{G}_X}$:

$$T_P(X) = \{head(C\theta) \mid C \in P,\ \theta \in \mathcal{S}_X,\ C\theta \text{ is a ground clause},$$
$$object(C\theta) \subset X,\ con(C\theta) \subset Tcon\} \tag{2}$$

Definition 4. Let P be an XDD description on Γ_X. Based on T_P, the declarative semantics of P, denoted by $\mathcal{M}(P)$, is defined by

$$\mathcal{M}(P) = \bigcup_{n=1}^{\infty} T_P^n(\emptyset) \tag{3}$$

where $T_P^1(\emptyset) = T_P(\emptyset)$ and $T_P^n(\emptyset) = T_P(T_P^{n-1}(\emptyset))$ for each $n > 1$. $\qquad\square$

4   Modeling XML Databases

In XDD data model, an ordinary XML element is represented directly by a ground XML expression in $\mathcal{G}_X$. A class of XML elements, which share certain similar components and structures, can also be represented by an XML expression with variables in $\mathcal{A}_X$, as illustrated in Fig. 1.

An XML document, comprising a sequence of n XML elements, is formalized as an XDD description, consisting of n ground XML unit clauses, each of which describes its corresponding XML element in the document.

An extensional XML database, comprising m documents $D_1, \ldots, D_m$, is then represented as an XDD description $XDB_E = P_1 \cup \ldots \cup P_m$, where for $1 \leq i \leq m$, P_i is an XDD description, representing the document D_i and comprising only unit clauses.

A set of integrity constraints on an XML database is modeled as an XDD description XDB_C comprising a set of XML non-unit clauses, each of which describes a particular constraint on the database.

An intensional XML database is formalized as an XDD description XDB_I comprising a set of XML non-unit clauses, each of which describes a rule or a relationship among XML elements.

An XML database, consisting of the three parts: an extensional database XDB_E, a set of integrity constraints XDB_C and an intensional database XDB_I, is modeled as an XDD description $XDB = XDB_E \cup XDB_C \cup XDB_I$.

The semantics of XDB, $\mathcal{M}(XDB)$, yields all the directly represented XML elements in the extensional database XDB_E, i.e., those expressed by unit clauses, together with all the derived ones, which are inferred from the specified intensional database XDB_I and satisfy all the restrictions defined by XDB_C.

Example 2. Fig. 3 gives an example of modeling an XML database as an XDD description $XDB = XDB_E \cup XDB_C \cup XDB_I$, where

- $XDB_E = C_{elm1}, \ldots, C_{elm4}$ represents an extensional database,
- $XDB_C = C_{ref}$ models a set of integrity constraints, which restricts a referential integrity constraint on the state attribute of the Person-element, i.e., the state attribute must refer to the id of a State-element, and
- $XDB_I = C_{anc1}, \ldots, C_{anc4}$ formalizes an intensional database, which describes human knowledge about ancestor relationships.

The database's meaning, $\mathcal{M}(XDB)$, is a set of XML elements including those elements in the extensional database, i.e., the elements $C_{elm1} - C_{elm4}$, together with those which are deducible from the database and satisfy the constraints, such as

```
<Ancestor ancestor="11111" descendent="55555" />
<Ancestor ancestor="55555" descendent="99999" />
<Ancestor ancestor="11111" descendent="99999" />
```

Thus, it is readily seen that although such information is not explicitly specified in the database, it can be uncovered through the clauses $C_{anc1}, \ldots, C_{anc4}$.   □

C_{elm1}: `<Person ssn="99999" state="NY" gender="Male">`
       `<Name>John Smith</Name>`
       `<BirthYear>1975</BirthYear>`
       `<Parent mother="55555" />`
    `</Person>`

C_{elm2}: `<Person ssn="55555" state="NY" gender="Female">`
       `<Name>Mary Smith</Name>`
       `<BirthYear>1950</BirthYear>`
       `<Parent father="11111" />`
    `</Person>`

C_{elm3}: `<Person ssn="11111" state="NY" gender="Male">`
       `<Name>Tom Black</Name>`
       `<BirthYear>1920</BirthYear>`
    `</Person>`

C_{elm4}: `<State id="NY">`
       `<Name>New York</Name>`
    `</State>`

% C_{elm1}-C_{elm4} describe
% contents of the database,
% which contains three
% Person-elements and a
% State-element, assuming
% that the ssn attribute of the
% Person element is of the
% type ID, while the father
% and mother attributes of
% the Parent-element and the
% state attribute of the
% Person-element are of the
% type IDREF.

(a) XML extensional database $XDB_E = \{C_{elm1}, ..., C_{elm4}\}$.

C_{ref}: `<ValidPerson ssn=`**`$S:ssn`**` state=`**`$S:state $P:attr`**`>`
    `$E:PersonData`
  `</ValidPerson>`
    ← `<Person ssn=`**`$S:ssn`**` state=`**`$S:state $P:attr`**`>`
      `$E:PersonData`
    `</Person>`,
     `<State id=`**`$S:state`**`>`
      `$E:StateData`
     `</State>`.

% C_{ref} restricts that a Person-
% element is valid if the
% value of its state-attribute
% matches the id of some
% particular state-element.

(b) A set of integrity constraints $XDB_C = \{C_{ref}\}$.

C_{anc1}: `<Ancestor ancestor=`**`$S:X`**` descendent=`**`$S:Y`**`/>`
   ← `<ValidPerson ssn=`**`$S:Y $P:PersonAttr`**`>`
     `$E:PersonData`
     `<Parent father=`**`$S:X $P:ParentAttr`**`/>`
   `</ValidPerson>`.

C_{anc2}: `<Ancestor ancestor=`**`$S:X`**` descendent=`**`$S:Y`**`/>`
   ← `<ValidPerson ssn=`**`$S:Y $P:PersonAttr`**`>`
     `$E:PersonData`
     `<Parent mother=`**`$S:X $P:ParentAttr`**`/>`
   `</ValidPerson>`.

% C_{anc1} and C_{anc2} define that
% if X is the father or the
% mother of Y, then X is also
% an ancestor of Y.

C_{anc3}: `<Ancestor ancestor=`**`$S:X`**` descendent=`**`$S:Z`**`/>`
   ← `<Ancestor ancestor=`**`$S:Y`**` descendent=`**`$S:Z`**`/>`,
     `<ValidPerson ssn=`**`$S:Y $P:PersonAttr`**`>`
      `$E:PersonData`
      `<Parent father=`**`$S:X $P:ParentAttr`**`/>`
     `</ValidPerson>`.

C_{anc4}: `<Ancestor ancestor=`**`$S:X`**` descendent=`**`$S:Z`**`/>`
   ← `<Ancestor ancestor=`**`$S:Y`**` descendent=`**`$S:Z`**`/>`,
     `<ValidPerson ssn=`**`$S:Y $P:PersonAttr`**`>`
      `$E:PersonData`
      `<Parent mother=`**`$S:X $P:ParentAttr`**`/>`
     `</ValidPerson>`.

% C_{anc3} and C_{anc4} recursively
% specify that if X is the
% father or the mother of Y
% and Y is an ancestor of Z,
% then X is also an ancestor
% of Z.

(c) XML intensional database $XDB_I = \{C_{anc1}, ..., C_{anc4}\}$.

Fig. 3. XML database $XDB = XDB_E \cup XDB_C \cup XDB_I$.

5   Related Works

In the *graph-based model* [1,8,10,13], a collection of XML documents is represented as a directed, edge-labeled graph. However, the model alone does not facilitate means for representation and restriction of constraints and DTDs.

The *functional programming approach* [12] can model XML documents as well as formalize various kinds of query operations, such as navigation, nesting, grouping and joining. However, similar to the graph model, it lacks a mechanism for restriction of integrity and structural constraints on XML documents.

In *hedge automaton approach* [15], a document is represented as a hedge and a set of documents conforming to a DTD as a *regular hedge language*. It employs a *hedge automaton* to verify the document validity with respect to a DTD. However, other kinds of constraints are not expressible.

Based on *Description Logic (DL)*, [11] develops a formalism for representing and reasoning about DTDs. A query is formulated as a DTD and its answer is the set of documents conforming to such a DTD. However, this mechanism is insufficient because many important query operations, e.g., extraction, selection and joining, cannot be represented in terms of DTDs.

Compared with other models, XDD provides a more direct and succinct insight into the computation of and reasoning with XML data. It naturally combines the XML syntax and its semantics, in order to provide effective means for modeling XML data and their interrelationships. It has sufficient expressive power to represent human knowledge and to infer information implicit in XML data. Note also that XDD is not a logic programming language. In contrast to logic programming languages and Datalog [14], declarative semantics of an XDD description can be defined without introduction of such complex notions as interpretations, models and logical consequences.

6   Conclusions

XDD—an expressive, declarative XML data model—has been developed. It is founded on a theoretical basis upon which representation and computation of as well as reasoning with XML data can be carried out in a uniform and succinct manner. Integration of XDD with an appropriate computational paradigm, e.g., *Equivalent Transformation (ET)* [3], allows efficient manipulation and transformation of XML documents, query evaluation and validation of documents against given DTDs. In order to help demonstrate and evaluate the effectiveness of the XDD data model, *XDD System*—a Web-based XML engine, available at http://kr.cs.ait.ac.th/xdd—has been implemented under the ET paradigm.

The XDD facilities for direct representation and reasoning about both the semantic and syntactic aspects of XML data allow users to precisely formulate queries and obtain query results, which may be implicit in the database, thus resulting in a substantial improvement in the precision of a retrieval. In addition, with the abilities to model XML DTDs and to validate the document conformance [7], XDD readily supplies sufficient means for query optimization, which exploits knowledge on the DTDs. This is a part of an ongoing research. Moreover, [16] shows that XDD can be applied to model the *Semantic Web* [9].

Acknowledgement. This work was supported in part by Thailand Research Fund.

References

1. Abiteboul, S, Buneman, P., Suciu, D.: Data on the Web: From Relations to Semistructured Data and XML. Morgan Kaufmann Publishers, CA (2000)
2. Akama, K.: Declarative Semantics of Logic Programs on Parameterized Representation Systems. Advances in Software Science and Technology, Vol. 5. (1993) 45–63
3. Akama, K., Shimitsu, T., Miyamoto, E.: Solving Problems by Equivalent Transformation of Declarative Programs. J. Japanese Society of Artificial Intelligence, Vol. 13 No.6 (1998) 944–952 (in Japanese)
4. Akama, K., Anutariya, C., Wuwongse, V., Nantajeewarawat, E.: A Foundation for XML Databases: Query Formulation and Evaluation. Technical Report, Computer Science and Information Management Program, Asian Institute of Technology, Thailand (1999)
5. Anutariya, C., Wuwongse, V., Nantajeewarawat, E., Akama, K.: Towards Computation with RDF Elements. Proc. Int. Symposium on Digital Library 1999 (ISDL'99), Tsukuba, Japan, (1999) 112–119
6. Anutariya, C., Wuwongse, V., Nantajeewarawat, E., Akama, K.: Towards a Foundation for XML Databases. Proc. 1st Int. Conference on Electronic Commerce and Web Technologies (EC-Web 2000), London, UK. Lecture Notes in Computer Science, Vol. 1875. Springer-Verlag, Berlin Heidelberg New York (2000) 324–333
7. Anutariya, C., Wuwongse, V., Akama, K., Nantajeewarawat, E.: A Foundation for XML Databases: DTD Modeling. Technical Report, Computer Science and Information Management Program, Asian Institute of Technology, Thailand (1999)
8. Beech, D., Malhotra, A., Rys, M.: A Formal Data Model and Algebra for XML. W3C XML Query Working Group Note, September 1999 (1999)
9. Berners-Lee, T. Weaving the Web. Harpur, San Francisco (1999)
10. Buneman, P., Fan, W., Weinstein, S.: Interaction between Path and Type Constraints. Proc. ACM Symposium on Principles of Database Systems, PODS (1999)
11. Calvanese, D., De Giacomo G., Lenzerini, M.: Representing and Reasoning on XML Documents: A Description Logic Approach. J. Logic and Computation, Vol. 9, No. 3 (1999) 295–318
12. Fernández, M., Siméon, J., Suciu, D., Wadler, P.: A Data Model and Algebra for XML Query. Draft Manuscript (1999)
13. Goldman, R., McHugh, J., Widom, J.: From Semistructured Data to XML: Migrating the Lore Data Model and Query Language. Proc. 2nd Int. Workshop on the Web and Databases (WebDB '99), Philadelphia, Pennsylvania (1999)
14. Liu, M.: Deductive Database Languages: Problems and Solutions. ACM Computing Surveys, Vol. 31, No. 1 (1999)
15. Murata, M.: DTD Transformation by Patterns and Contextual Conditions. Proc. SGML/XML '97 Conference (1997)
16. Wuwongse, W., Anutariya, C., Akama, K., Nantajeewarawat, E.: XML Declarative Description (XDD): A Language for the Semantic Web. IEEE Intelligent Systems (to appear)

Conference Information Management System: Towards a Personal Assistant System

Tsunenori Mine[1], Makoto Amamiya[1], and Teruko Mitamura[2]

[1] Kyushu University, 6-1 Kasugakouen, Kasuga 816-8580, JAPAN,
mine@is.kyushu-u.ac.jp,
http://www-al.is.kyushu-u.ac.jp/ mine
[2] Carnegie Mellon University, 5000 Forbes Avenue, Pittsburgh, PA 15213, USA
teruko@cs.cmu.edu,
http://www.cs.cmu.edu/ teruko

Abstract. We are aiming to develop a personal assistant system which handles its user's files stored in his/her computers and his/her interesting information that can be accessed on the Web. The system categorizes the files and Web pages gathered and extracts information specified by him/her and stores it into a structured database for use as the knowledge of its dialogue module. This paper presents a prototype of the system that handles information about conferences of interest to the user. The system extracts conference names, submission deadlines, dates, URIs and locations from e-mail messages the user has received, and web pages gathered by both crawling and meta-search. Extracted information is stored into a database so that the user can interactively search conference information via a user interface with natural language queries.

1 Introduction

After the concept of the WWW was first proposed in 1989, the number of Web pages grew to exceed 800 million pages by Feb, 1999[1]. They provide manifold services and are one of the most important resources accessed easily in the world. Among their useful services, the Internet search engines are playing the important role to find the information users want. Although they try to provide useful and relevant search results to their users, they still return a lot of non-relevant results because of the lack of information to convey user's intention, part of which coming from the isolation between search and evaluation process[5]. Therefore, it is important to make use of user's responses as feedback to his/her own search process. In addition to retrieving relevant web pages, extracting and storing frequently accessed information in the database is useful for reducing the search time, and enabling the information to be used as new knowledge for both human and agents.

In this paper, we present a prototype of our personal assistant system which handles the information about conferences of interest. It consists of the following modules: Information Retrieval & Web page gathering(**IRWG**), Information Filtering(**IF**), Information Extraction(**IE**), DataBase Manager(**DBM**), and User

N. Zhong et al. (Eds.): WI 2001, LNAI 2198, pp. 247–253, 2001.
© Springer-Verlag Berlin Heidelberg 2001

Interface(**UI**) that analyzes user's natural language query and learns user's preference and interests. The **IE** module extracts conference names, deadlines, dates, URIs, and locations from e-mail messages the user received and web pages gathered by both crawling and meta-search. Extracted information is stored into a database so that the user can search it interactively via the **UI** with a natural language query.

2   Conference Information Management System

2.1   Overview of Our Prototype System

The left side of figure 1 shows the overview of a prototype system. **IRWG** performs meta-search and polling of some interesting sites that are often visited by a user, and the sites included in the conference announcement messages the user received by e-mail. It traverses the relevant pages linked from those sites as a base-point. **IF** divides the relevant information and non-relevant information to the user with SVM^{light}[2]. **IE** extracts a set of named entities specified at each category. The extraction rules consist of pattern matching rules and detection rules. The pattern matching rules are hand-coded as regular expressions and select the candidates for named entities. The detection rules are constructed from the N-gram statistics of negative data, which are results extracted and detected incorrectly. The detection rules score each candidate named entity to be extracted and detect its boundary words. The detection rules are learned with negative feedback data. **DBM** stores the set of information extracted by the **IE** module into a structured database and retrieves information specified by the user's query from the database. In the interactive mode, **DBM** accepts only the information confirmed by a user. **UI** is the interface between a user and other modules. **UI** analyzes the user's natural language query and transforms it into an S expression format. **UI** talks to other modules using a sentence in S expression format. The right side of figure 1 shows the data flow between modules in the case where a user performs a Web search when s/he isn't satisfied with the answer returned from the **DBM**. **UI** learns user's preference related to concepts specified for each category. In the case of the conference category, these are topics, conference names, locations, dates and so on. Such preference cues are recorded in the user profile(**UP**). The **UP** is shared by not only **UI** but also **IRWG** so that it searches Web pages about conferences that the user likes, provided that it is maintained only by the **UI**. In the current system, **UI** is implemented with Java except for morphological analyzer, and other modules are written in perl. The rest of this section focuses on the **UI** and **IE** module.

2.2   User Interface(UI)

The **UI** is one of the most important parts of this system. **UI** performs some simple natural language processing: morphological analysis, word expansion with a dictionary and pattern matching with rules predefined for each category. **UI**

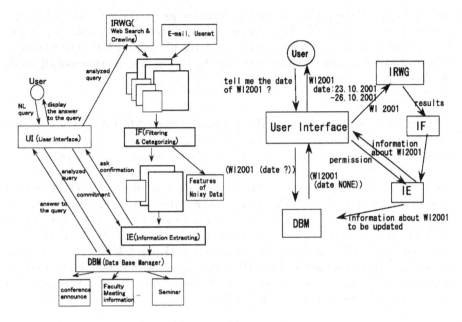

Fig. 1. The overview of the system and the data flow between modules in the Web searching process

transforms an analyzed query into an S expression format, which has the following format: **(category (attribute value) .. (attribute value))**

When a query asks the value of an attribute, its value slot is replaced with a question mark **?**. If a query asks the name of a category or attribute X, X has a mark **:?**. If a query asks whether or not the value X is correct, X has a mark **:OK?** and is expressed as X**:OK?**. The following shows examples that transform natural language queries into S expressions.

Where is the location of the conference ? → (conference (location ?))
When is the conference held ? → (conference (date ?))
What is the topic of the conference ? → (conference (topic ?))
What are the conferences whose topic includes NLP ? → (conference:? (topic NLP))
Is the location of the conference Maebashi ? → (WI2001 (location Maebashi:OK?))

User Profile(UP): UP consists of 3 fields: category, attribute, and example. The category 'conference' includes 9 attributes: conference name, topic, location, date, URI, deadline, speaker, organizer and organization. The example field of topic attribute includes a set of ('words', value) pairs such as: (Information Retrieval,10) (Information Extraction,10) (Natural Language Processing,18) (Machine Translation,12). Those examples of 'words' are extracted from user's queries and manually input by the user. The value of 'words' is the number of occurrences that the 'words' have appeared in queries. Those examples are used to rank the results in reply to a user's query. The relevance value of a retrieved document is calculated by summing all weights of 'words', which are included in both the document and in the example field of **UP**. The weight of 'words' is calculated by dividing their value by the total of the values of all words in the example filed of the attribute.

Interactions between User and UI, and between Modules: The resulting replies to a user's query first comes from **DBM** via **UI**. When s/he is not satisfied with them, s/he can ask **UI** to perform re-searching of relative pages on the Web. In that case, **UI** passes his/her query to **IRWG**. After searching Web pages relevant to the query, **IRWG** sends the results to **IF**. **IF** filters and categorizes them, and sends the results to **IE**. After extracting named entities specified in the category of the results, **IE** sends them to **UI** so that **UI** will get the user's permission to store the results in the database. If s/he is satisfied with the results from **IE**, s/he gives the permission to **IE** via **UI**. After receiving the permission, **IE** sends them to **DBM**(See the right side of figure 1). In case s/he is not satisfied with the results extracted by **IE**, s/he can ask **UI** to show the pages filtered by **IF** or retrieved by **IRWG**.

Displaying Results Returned from DBM: The **UI** module displays the information with two formats: calendar format and simple string format. The calendar format is used for listing up many results retrieved from the database, and the string format is for returning a simple answer. For example, when **DBM** extracts all information about conferences held in 1999 and 2000 in order to reply the query (conference (date *.*.1999) (date *.*.2000)), which are transformed from a natural language query such as *Show conferences to be held in 1999 and 2000*, **UI** shows the results with a calendar format (see figure 2).

2.3   Extraction Module

The extraction rules for matching named entities, such as conference names, are hand-coded with perl's regular expressions. The detection rules for named entities are constructed from the N-gram statistics of negative data. The number of extraction rules for conference names is currently 29. Before applying extraction rules, the extraction module searches for areas that are candidates for a named entity. That search is performed with heuristic rules constructed from 50 conference announcement articles. The extraction procedure for named entities is performed as follows:

1. apply pattern matching rules that consist of regular expressions.
2. apply detection rules that consist of the difference between positive and negative N-gram data. Positive data are constructed from the labeled data of conference name and negative data are results returned incorrectly.
3. rank the detected candidates.

Fig. 2. An example displayed with a calendar format

Preliminary Experiments of Conference Name Extraction. To evaluate the current extraction performance with pattern matching rules, we first used web page data including the keywords 'CALL for Paper' or 'CFP'. The number of raw data pages is 482. After manually checking the data, the number of conference announcements is 141. Among them, the extraction module extracted and detected 85 conference names correctly or partly correctly(60.3%). This result was gotten without any heuristic rules to account for the structure of HTML tags. Next, we used 250 conference announcement e-mail articles to show the effectness of detection rules. Detection rules were constructed from the experimental results without detection rule.

	correct	partly correct	wrong	correctness(w. partly correct)
No detection rule	123	106	21	49.2 % (91.6 %)
detection rule	144	75	31	57.6 % (87.6 %)

These results indicate that 1) we need to add rules that handle the HTML tag structure to get a higher extraction rate for Web pages, 2) detection rules constructed from negative data are effective to detect boundaries of conference names, but also cause more errors. We need to investigate the relationships between positive data and negative data to improve detection rules.

3   Related Works

The related works are user adaptive information retrieval, information extraction, information filtering and recommendation system.

The DeadLiner[6] is a specialized search engine that handles conference announcement. It monitors specified web pages, news groups and E-mail articles widely distributed on the Internet. The DeadLiner has been been constructed for academic researchers, while we aim to construct our system as a personal assistant system that helps the user search, recommend and digest the information the user wants. WebKB(e.g. [4]) project has been trying to construct machine readable knowledge bases from the WWW. It is really challenging research. However, the WebKB system only focuses on building knowledge bases specified by users without any interaction between the users and the system, although the knowledge should be interactively updated. A lot of user adaptive search engines have been proposed (e.g. [8],[3],[7],[5]). They infer users' preference and interests from their retrieval history and browsing behaviors to search the next web page to be recommended with making use of them. Most of the systems unfortunately only focus on retrieval and not the extraction of named entities the users find interesting. In order to realize a personal assistant system, it is indispensable to integrate retrieval and extraction via an interactive interface.

4   Conclusion

In this paper, we presented a conference information management system that learns a user's interests and preferences from his/her queries via a **UI** module. The system has also the function of managing conference announcement messages distributed by e-mail to the user and gathered from web pages the user wants. The system extracts conference name, topic, location, paper submission deadline, URL and date, and stores them into a structured database. If the extraction is performed in the interactive retrieving process between the user and **IRWG** module, the extracted results are passed to the user to get his/her confirmation before passing them to **DBM**. We are currently working to realize practical extraction performance on conference names, to merge more than one page that indicates the same conference announcement, and to handle different formats like Web page and e-mail articles. The latter challenge is not easy but crucial to realize a useful personal assistant system. After that, we plan to extend our system so that it handles other announcement types such as local meetings, seminars and lectures. In the future, this system will be extended to be a more robust question and answering system for conference information management.

References

1. S. Lawrence and C. L. Giles. Accessibility of Information on the Web, Nature, 400(6740), pp. 107–109, 1999.

2. T. Joachims. SVM^{light} version 3.50 `http://ais.gmd.de/\ {}thorsten/svm_light/` 2000.

3. M. Balabanovic. An adaptive web page recommendation service. In W. Lewis Johnson and B. Hayes-Roth, editors, *Proceedings of the First International Conference on Autonomous Agents (Agents'97)*, pp. 378–385, 1997.

4. M. Craven, D. DiPasquo, D. Freitag, A. McCallum, T. Mitchell, K. Nigan, and S. Slattery. Learning to construct knowledge bases from the world wide web. *Artificial Intelligence*, 118(1–2):69–113, 2000.

5. T. Helmy, T. Mine, and M. Amamiya. Adaptive exploiting user profile and interpretation policy for searching and browsing the web on kodama system. In *Proceedings of the 2nd International Workshop on Natural Language and Information Systems(NLIS 2000)*, pp. 120–124, 2000.

6. A. Kruger, C. L. Giles, F. Coetzee, E. Glover, G. Flake, S. Lawrence, and C. Omlin. DEADLINER: Building a new niche search engine. In *Ninth International Conference on Information and Knowledge Management, CIKM 2000*, pp. 272–281, 2000.

7. H. Lieberman. Letizia: An agent that assists web browsing. In Chris S. Mellish, editor, *Proceedings of the Fourteenth International Joint Conference on Artificial Intelligence*, pp. 924–929. 1995.

8. M. Pazzani, J. Muramatsu, and D. Billsus. Syskill & webert: Identifying interesting web sites. In *Proc. of 13th National Conference on Artificial Intelligence(AAAI-96)*, 1996.

Automatic Intelligence Gathering from the Web: A Case Study in Container Traffic

José Perdigao, Anjula Garg, Thomas Barbas, Stefan Scheer,
Giuseppe Mastrangelo*, and Giovanna Rubino*

European Commission, Joint Research Centre, TP 361, I-21020 Ispra(VA), Italy
*ORIGIN Italia Spa, Milano, Italy
{Jose.Perdigao,Anjula.Garg,Thomas.Barbas,
Stefan.Scheer}@jrc.it

Abstract. The Internet provides one of the largest public repositories of data available to all with a networked computer. The amount of data available is so large, and so easily available that it opens up a wonderful possibility to extract the data, normalise it for the problem at hand, and package it for output to users who may not have the time or technical capacity to directly make full use of the information sources on the web. This paper describes a project where large amounts of data for the movement of containers were turned into a consolidated database that could assist members of the anti-fraud community investigating customs or other fraud relating to the transport of goods using containers. The main emphasis was placed on how these vast amounts of data could be harnessed systematically and disseminated over the Internet to those interested.

1 Introduction

The Internet has opened a channel of access to an interwoven labyrinth of information over an almost ubiquitous platform - the *World Wide Web*. Graphical web browsers have enabled all types of users to access and share information with one another. Beyond the initial thrill, most mature users do not just surf the web aimlessly, but rather use it as a *source of information* [5]. This is also the case for people working in the wider area of intelligence gathering. Investigators and analysts search for new information on the web to augment or validate other information at their disposal, such as tips from informants, various evidence from investigation cases or information obtained from commercial (for-a-fee) databases.

The application of the work of this paper is in the area of operational and intelligence activities by anti-fraud authorities at the European Union and the national member state level. For most of these agencies, automatic intelligence gathering from the web is seen increasingly as an important component of their operational and strategic intelligence development strategies to augment other information that they obtain from paid commercial databases.

The objectives of the project we describe in this paper were to investigate *the complete cycle* from acquisition of data for movement of containers from the web, all the way to dissemination of the findings, going through a number of stages in between. The *discovery* process generated a set of web targets, which were in turn

N. Zhong et al. (Eds.): WI 2001, LNAI 2198, pp. 254–261, 2001.
© Springer-Verlag Berlin Heidelberg 2001

continuously probed. The primary business objective of achieving new capacity in container traffic monitoring was the main guide for the *discovery* of content. Data extracted from these targets was achieved by the *acquisition* process. The acquisition and the *structuring* processes were then used for filtering, validating and transforming the content into a normalised form, and finally, the *dissemination* phase was used to package the contents and deliver it to authorized users of the system[5].

2 The Problem of Container Tracking

Container tracking is an issue of general importance because companies are putting more demand on accurate monitoring, to make better business decisions. The tracking data for containers can be used not only to track the position of a container (thus offering also a service to customers), but also to identify areas where costs can be reduced, for example, the costs of transporting back empty containers that pile up in remote ports [7].

We look at it from the point of view of a controller or anti-fraud analyst for whom container tracking is a very important issue for the carriers and other related economic operators. This is because containers from various carriers are involved in cases of fraud. It is also one major part of the larger problem of multi-modal transport tracking where providing historical information for container movement can provide major help.

3 Approaches for Container Tracking

In the following sections we briefly survey various approaches for container tracking. At present, container tracking can take different forms, these make use of:

1. Leased lines and direct-dial communication between computers
2. Low-orbitting satellites
3. Mobile telecommunications
4. Radio tagging and
5. The Internet

Until recently, most companies used *leased lines* for data communication [8]. However, for reasons of cost, more and more companies are moving over to the Internet. *Low-orbitting satellite tracking* system require that a container must have a special unit fixed on the side of the container. Satellite tracking systems only return the coordinate positions of a container at a pre-set time interval and do not provide other information about whether the container is stationery, or on a railway sliding, or resting in a terminal. The further growth of infrastructure-based systems (both container-based and port-based) or the increasing connectivity of IT systems could eventually make satellite tracking obsolete.

Mobile telecommunications, currently only cover a very small percentage of the world's land surface, although the coverage is growing.

Radio tagging of containers is another possible way of tracking containers, but this system needs a worldwide infrastructure of readers to communicate with tags, and none of the companies seem interested in investing the large amount of money required for setting up the infrastructure.

Finally, container tracking via the *Internet* presents the problems that not all container companies are ready to offer services over the Internet, and that the tracking data offered is quite diverse from one company to another. In order to use the information on the Internet, one needs to keep track of the ever changing web sites that offer information for container tracking. Also because these web sites only offer recent container tracking information, a method needs to be devised to preserve historic data.

4   Use of Commercial Databases for Container Tracking

Anti-fraud or control organisations in the European Union have long had a need for collecting and analysing data relating to the movements of ships and containers, to either solve cases or to detect and prevent fraud, or protect payment or even customs duties collection systems. Based on interviews with some investigators, analysts and search intermediaries accessing commercial databases, the relevant information they often search for includes:

1. Company information: owners, directors, addresses, telephone numbers, links to other companies etc.
2. Information concerning ships: routes followed, owners etc.
3. Information concerning containers: route tracking, owners etc.

For this type of information these agencies currently use commercial databases such as Lloyds[9], PIERS (*P*ort *I*mport *E*xport *R*eporting *S*ervice) [15], Tradebytes [13], Dun & Bradstreet [3] or Worldbase [17]. These commercial systems can for example be used to expand or validate information from shipping documents that investigators have in their case files. One of the problems with commercial databases like the ones mentioned here is that they are often not up-to-date, in that there is always a latent period between these commercial database companies receiving information and their making it available to their customers. Most often the information found is not sufficient, but constitutes nonetheless an important lead for other searches. In addition the cost of using these information services tends to be quite high. These databases do not offer any information regarding containers, and the work described here complements the information provided by them.

5   The Solution and the Resulting Software

This section provides information about how we *identified* web sites, *extracted* the relevant information, *populated* the database, and finally developed the user interface to *exploit* the consolidated data.

5.1   Identification of Web Sites

For this first task we needed to identify and classify all important web sites that could give us useful information for containers and their movements.

Based on the initial limited list of web sites and container numbers given to us by investigators who handle cases of fraud for containers, we used Copernic2000[1] to make several searches with keywords related to containers. The searches produced a large number of web sites and we had to in fact limit the search by ascertaining which sites were carrier sites and provided on-line tracking systems. Thus from a first list of approximately 100 web sites, we narrowed down the list to about 10 container carrier web sites which offered on-line tracking.

5.2   Extraction of Information for Containers

By gathering information, we mean collecting retrieved information from the predetermined set of web sites. In this project we mainly worked with dynamic pages, which means that these were constructed automatically as a result of a query placed on the web site. Fig. 1 gives an overall view of the architecture we used for extracting information for container movements from the web.

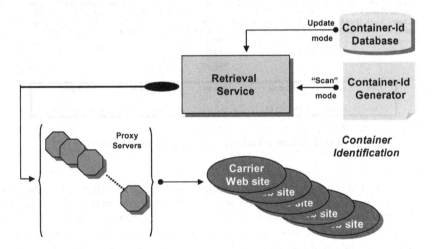

Fig. 1. Architecture for Gathering Information from the Web

The system primarily consists of a *Retrieval Service*. The *Retrieval Service* is the software responsible for retrieving information from various web sites and updating of the database. In order to use the *Retrieval Service*, it is necessary to know the unique number of the container being tracked in advance. This number can be obtained in two ways: one is from past experience of case investigations or observations, provided the number can be disclosed, and the other is through the generation of a random list of container numbers based on the standard naming scheme for containers given in [1].

5.3 Populating the Database

The objective for this step was to extract the relevant information for containers from an HTML file and transform it into a convenient Java object, using a software package W4F [16].

In order to download information from the selected web sites, it was necessary first to select the information items to retain (for downloading to the database and further processing) and those to discard. Each web site has a different structure (see Fig. 2 for an example), it was therefore necessary to study their structures to implement programs that could extract the necessary information.

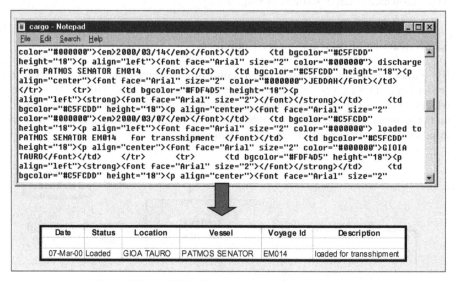

Fig. 2. A Raw HTML file from which data was extracted

We created two database tables for each carrier. In the table *<Carrier>ContainerHistory* (where *Carrier* is the carrier company) all data related to each container is saved, whereas in the *<Carrier>Containers* one finds the log of queries for specific containers. The frequency of the visit to a web site and consequent updating of our database differs from site to site depending on how often the information is updated at their web site. Once the frequency of update of a web site has been determined, we set up our retrieval system in such a way that all information available is extracted and that no interim information is lost. The information retrieved was placed in the database according to the data model created for the purpose.

We decided to use Oracle DBMS to store all data downloaded from the web for two different reasons. Firstly, we needed a database that could handle large amounts of data and provide good performance. Secondly, we wanted to use the database in two different ways, one to allow users to use WebDB to directly extract data in bulk, and the other to create a special interface to the database to allow occasional users to extract data without having to learn specific SQL commands.

We also chose JDBC (see section on The Tools Used and Lessons Learnt), to have the possibility to change the database application software without having to change the underlying software for the interface.

5.4 Exploitation via the Resulting Software

With the methodology described in the previous sections, we produced a simplified, but very powerful tool to obtain data for the movement of containers. A sample of the output is given in Fig 3. This is the result of querying the database for all information relating to a specified container.

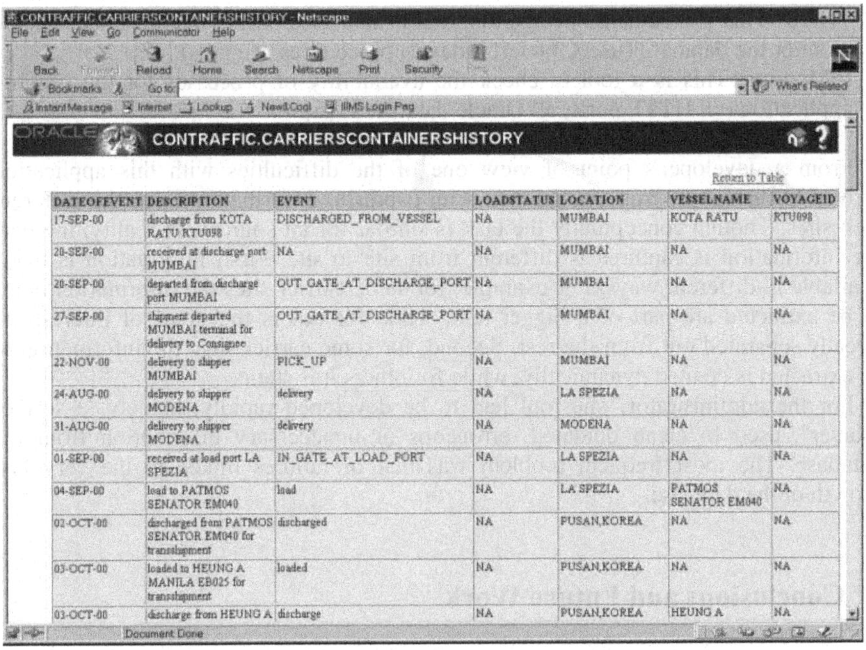
CONTRAFFIC.CARRIERSCONTAINERSHISTORY

Return to Table

DATEOFEVENT	DESCRIPTION	EVENT	LOADSTATUS	LOCATION	VESSELNAME	VOYAGEID
17-SEP-00	discharge from KOTA RATU RTU098	DISCHARGED_FROM_VESSEL	NA	MUMBAI	KOTA RATU	RTU098
20-SEP-00	received at discharge port MUMBAI	NA	NA	MUMBAI	NA	NA
20-SEP-00	departed from discharge port MUMBAI	OUT_GATE_AT_DISCHARGE_PORT	NA	MUMBAI	NA	NA
27-SEP-00	shipment departed MUMBAI terminal for delivery to Consignee	OUT_GATE_AT_DISCHARGE_PORT	NA	MUMBAI	NA	NA
22-NOV-00	delivery to shipper MUMBAI	PICK_UP	NA	MUMBAI	NA	NA
24-AUG-00	delivery to shipper MODENA	delivery	NA	LA SPEZIA	NA	NA
31-AUG-00	delivery to shipper MODENA	delivery	NA	MODENA	NA	NA
01-SEP-00	received at load port LA SPEZIA	IN_GATE_AT_LOAD_PORT	NA	LA SPEZIA	NA	NA
04-SEP-00	load to PATMOS SENATOR EM040	load	NA	LA SPEZIA	PATMOS SENATOR EM040	NA
02-OCT-00	discharged from PATMOS SENATOR EM040 for transshipment	discharged	NA	PUSAN,KOREA	NA	NA
03-OCT-00	loaded to HEUNG A MANILA EB025 for transshipment	loaded	NA	PUSAN,KOREA	NA	NA
03-OCT-00	discharge from HEUNG A	discharge	NA	PUSAN,KOREA	HEUNG A	NA

Fig. 3. Results Of Accessing the Database for Information for a Specific Carrier

The data can be sorted directly in Oracle at the time it is extracted from the database or, it can be imported into other software to do further analysis (visualizing networks of entities, advanced statistical analysis etc.).

6 The Tools Used and Lessons Learnt

This project is very interesting in terms of the variety of tools and languages used to obtain data from the web and making it available to users. We give here a list of the tools used, with a short description of what each tool provides for the project.

1. W4F: W4F[12] is a toolkit for the generation of wrappers for Web sources. The wrappers are generated as Java classes which we further developed to extract data and populate the database.
2. Oracle8.0 with its web interface WebDB [13]
3. Java: This is Sun's software for creating and safely running software programs in both stand-alone and networked environments [9].
4. JDBC: JDBC is a set of classes and interfaces written in Java to allow other Java programs to send SQL statements to a relational database management system [11].
5. VisualAge: This is a development environment used to create Java classes. It is used to synchronize the work of developers working remotely on the same directory structure.
6. TOAD: This is a database design tool that is also used during maintenance tasks to monitor the database (users, tables, indexes, procedures, triggers) [12].
7. IPMonitor: This is a tool to check the availability of processes for the specific application (all HTTP ports, all Oracle databases) [6].

From a developer's point of view one of the difficulties with this application proved to be the programs concerned with capturing information from the different web sites. Though conceptually the task is similar for all sources, in reality, the way the information is captured is different from site to site. First, information is made available in different ways. For example, for some carrier sites the information items to be extracted are part of a bigger text, while for others the items of interest are already separated out from the rest. Second, for some carrier sites the information to be extracted is created dynamically, while for others it is static.

For the administrator, one tool had to be developed rapidly, namely, a sort of "parser", used to clean outdated, erroneous or unnecessary information from the database. The most frequent problem was that of failures linked to the very fast growth of the database.

7 Conclusions and Future Work

The work described in this paper addresses only one part of the bigger problem of information about container traffic. Our effort concentrated on what can be done with open source information from the web. The result is a database that allows historical searches about the itineraries of a good part of legally registered containers and a common interface from which to access different carrier web sites for real-time queries.

Since it is not feasible to provide a system that encompasses all aspects of container information (such as internet services of container shipping lines, container rail services, containers lessors' services, ports and terminals information services, container depots etc.), we would like to concentrate future work to address a list of around 20 container companies, and, in parallel, look also at leased containers. Leased containers in fact pose a greater challenge for two reasons. Firstly, there are only few web sites at present that offer information about leased containers, but which nonetheless account for a bit less than half of all movements. Secondly, getting information from leased container companies requires an additional loop in the data extraction process which is that we first need to query the leasing company to know which carrier has leased the container from them; after that the carrier web site needs to be queried for that specific container, which is not a trivial task.

The project has generated a lot of interest from specialist anti-fraud and customs intelligence agencies, and we expect to get support from various member states of the European Union for the continuation of the work described here.

In addition, we think that our approach is of value to many monitoring tasks that need to be based on open source information. It is likely that such projects will need to use similar tools and that their developers will face similar difficulties.

References

1. Containers BIC-CODE: Official Register of Internationally Protected ISO Alpha Codes for Identification of Container Owners, Bureau International Des Containers, (1999)
2. Copernic: www.copernic.com
3. Dun & Bradstreet: http://www.dnb.com/
4. Garg, A.: Automatic Intelligence Gathering from the Web: Exploratory Analysis, European Commission Joint Research Centre, Technical Note I.00.137, December 2000
5. Hackathorn, R.: Web Farming for the Data Warehouse, Exploiting Business Intelligence and Knowledge Management, (1999)
6. IPMonitor: http://www.mediahouse.com/
7. Jefferey, K.: Recent Developments in Container Tracking technology, February (1999)
8. Jefferey, K.: Container Shipping and the Internet, April (1999)
9. Lloyds: http://www.lloyds.com/
10. Java: http://developer.java.sun.com/
11. JDBC: http://java.sun.com/products/jdbc/
12. TOAD: http://www.toadsoft.com/
13. Tradebytes: http://www.tradebytes.com/
14. Oracle: www.oracle.com
15. Piers (Port Import Export Reporting Service):
    http://www.piers.com/default_OLD.asp
16. W4F: World Wide Web Wrapper factory http://db.cis.upenn.edu/W4F/
17. Worldbase: http://www.dbeuro.com/Worldbase/index.htm

The Work Concept RBAC Model for the Access Control of the Distributed Web Server Environment

Won Bo Shim[1] and Seog Park[2]

[1] Dept. Computer Science, Sogang University,
121-742, Seoul, Korea
cool96@chch.ac.kr

[2] Dept. Computer Science, Sogang University,
121-742, Seoul, Korea
spark@dblab.sogang.ac.kr

Abstract. Role Based Access Control method, the most suitable access control concept available today in a distributed web server system within a domain, will be applied in this paper to suggest a solution to the situation of being asked to follow the verification process from each server when accessing multiple web servers while working on the task. Work concept that is higher, more abstract, and more inclusive concept than Role will be imported to the existing RBAC so that the user could select Work instead of Role when doing one's work which then leads to the way to complete the work more efficiently using the right provided by each server based on the selected Work.

1 Introduction

When implementing the access control for the resources in the information system, the horizontal concept of the Role is needed to solve some problems as well as the vertical concept.

For example, the user who is in the Restructuring Task Force team in a company does the restructuring work for the company.

Varieties of company's resources are needed to complete this task.

Assumption could be made that the company's resources are distributed and managed by different servers based on their tasks within the information system, and these resources in the server are protected by access control method 'RBAC'.

Sometimes, multiple roles from multiple servers are combined to form a complex right to provide the user a mean to help to complete his task without invading the existing integrity of the vertical structure. 'Work' is the term used in this paper to indicate this concept.

By using the Work concept, flexibility to the RBAC operation which has the vertical Role structure only is added by allowing the user have the horizontal right of the Role in a distributed web environment, and the user can be controlled in accessing the web servers based on the rights of the Role assigned to each server. As a result, the user

N. Zhong et al. (Eds.): WI 2001, LNAI 2198, pp. 262–266, 2001.
© Springer-Verlag Berlin Heidelberg 2001

can access multiple web servers transparently as if accessing one web server without obtaining each certification from each web server.

2   The Roles of the Multiple Web Servers in the Same Domain

For example, when the user needs to access web documents which are distributed throughout multiple web servers to complete his task, he may try to access the web document in site A first, then the site A will check whether he has already been certified. If the user has not been certified before he can obtain the certification by providing his ID and password, and upon the successful completion of the certification process, he can continue to work on his task in site A.[5],[6]

While working on a task in site A, it may be necessary for the user to access site B to complete his task when the user tries to access the document in site B.

At that time, site B will request the user to follow another certification process, and the user can only continue his work in site B upon another successful completion of certification process by providing his ID and password.

In reality, many web documents are hyper-linked throughout multiple servers as well as within the server, and accessibility of each document is controlled based on each web server's security policy. The user will find it difficult to complete his task smoothly due to many requests of unnecessary additional certification processes in this environment. In order to allow the user to access multiple web servers transparently without following unnecessary certification processes, the Work concept is imported in this paper. When the user selects a Work upon the successful completion of the certification process, he can obtain all the rights of the roles of each web server that are mapped to this Work.

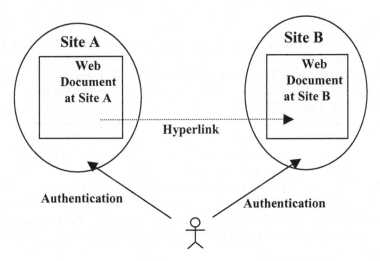

Fig. 1. Access to the web servers controlled by RBAC

3 Introduction of Work Concept

3.1 The Abstract of Work Concept and the Work Concept RBAC Model

Fig. 2. describes the Work concept in general and shows how the user can proceed the user's task when multiple web servers exist in the same domain and each web server has its own role role structure.

The RBAC built in site A has different structure from the RBAC built in site B.

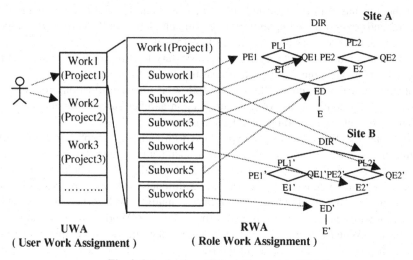

Fig. 2. Introduction of Work Concept to RBAC

Work is divided into multiple Subworks, and each Subwork is linked to the roles in site A and site B.

For example, Subwork1 has PE1 role in site A, and PL2' role in site B.

On the contrary, Subwork2 has QE1 role in site A, and QE2' role in site B.

These Subworks belong to Work1.

If the user is assigned to the Work1 at this time, he can proceed his work with PE1 right in site A, and PL2' right in site B.

We can assume that a user is assigned two works in his company called Project1 and Project2, and Project1 is divided into 6 Subworks.

Each Subwork is then mapped to each different role in each server.

If the user selects Project1 which is one of the Work assigned to him, then this user can access the web servers with the rights of the roles mapped in site A and site B, and these sites are being accessed through the Subworks which belong to the Project1.

3.2 Definition of RBAC Using Work Concept

We can define the Work Concept RBAC Model formally as follows.

1) U : Users, W : Works, SW : Subworks,
   ST : Sites, R : Roles, P : Permissions, S : Sessions
2) $RH \subseteq R \times R$: Role Hierarchy
3) $SW \subseteq W$: Work consists of Subworks.
4) $SW \subseteq ST \times R$: Subwork consists of roles in sites.
5) $UA \subseteq U \times SW$: Subwork is assigned to the user.
6) $PA \subseteq P \times R$: Permissions are assigned to each roles.
7) subworkroles function : $SW \rightarrow R$
   $subworkroles(sw_i) \subseteq \{r \mid (st_i,r) \in SW\}$: Function which gets roles to be assigned
   to Subwork sw_i in site i.
8) user function : $S \rightarrow U$, Function which gets the user involving in session s_i.
9) Subworks function : $S \rightarrow SW$, Function which gets the Subworks involving in
   session s_i by the user, $subworks(s_i) \subseteq \{sw \mid (user(s_i),sw) \in UA\}$
10) sessionroles function : $S \rightarrow R$,
   $roles(s_i) \subseteq \{r \mid (\exists r' \geq r)[sw' \in subworks(s_i) \wedge (user(s_i),sw') \in UA \wedge r' \in (subworkroles(sw'))]$

4   Implementing RBAC Concept Model for the Multiple Web Server Access Control in the Same Domain

When the user accesses the web document in multi server, the user will be asked to certify himself, and upon the successful completion of the certification process, the works assigned to the user will be shown.

Then the user selects one of the works to perform among multiple works assigned to him. Let's suppose that the user selects a Work called Project1.

As shown in Fig. 3., when a work is selected, the subworks of the corresponding Work, Project1, will be displayed on the screen.

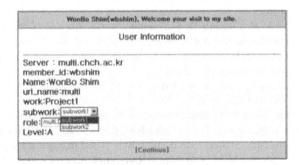

Fig. 3. Subworks of the selected work

Because these subworks are mapped to the roles in each server, the user can now have the necessary roles' access rights for each server needed to complete his task.

The information about the corresponding user's role and access control will be delivered in cookie format by the Role Server.

5 Conclusion

Efficient Access control is needed in a distributed web environment as having many users and many web servers. In order to reduce the number of errors occurred in user management and in network resources management and also to reduce the management fee, extended RBAC model that is the result of the Work concept imported to the most suitable access control - Role Based Access Control - was introduced and defined.

Using this extended RBAC model, the user is now able to access multiple web servers to complete his task without the unnecessary certification process in a distributed web server environment.

Additionally, with simple implementation, we showed the Work Concept RBAC Model guarantees the transparency and efficiency when a user processes his task in the multiple web server environments.

Acknowledgements. This work was supported by grant No.2000-1-303-001-3 from Basic Research Program of the Korea Science and Engineering Foundation.

References

1. D. Ferraio, J. Cugini and R. Kuhn, : Role-based Access Control(RBAC): Features and motivations, Proc. of 11th Annual Computer Security Application Conference (1995)
2. Ravi Sandhu and Joon S. Park : Secure Cookies on the Web, IEEE Internet Computing, July-August (2000)
3. J. F. Barkely, A. V. Cincotta, D. F. Ferraiolo, S. Gavrilla and D. R. Kuhn : Role Based Access Control For the World Wide Web, 20th NCSC (1997)
4. R. Sandhu, E. Coyne, H. Feinstein, and C. Younman : Role-Based Access Control Models, IEEE Computer Magazine Vol. 29 (1996)
5. Won Bo Shim, Seog Park : Using RBAC for the Fine Granularity Access Control of the Distributed Web Documents, ICT (2001)
6. Won Bo Shim, Seog Park : Implementing Web Access Control System for the Multiple Web Servers in the Same Domain Using RBAC Concept, ICPADS (2001)
7. E. C. Lupu and M.S. Sloman : Reconciling Role Based management and Role Based Access Control , Second ACM Wrokshop on Role-Based Access Control (1997)

A New Conceptual Graph Generated Algorithm for Semi-structured Databases

Kam Fai Wong[1], Yat Fan Su[1], Dongqing Yang[2], and Shiwei Tang[2]

[1] Department of Systems Engineering and Engineering Management
The Chinese University of Hong Kong
{kfwong,yfsu}@se.cuhk.edu.hk
[2] National Laboratory on Machine Perception
Peking University, Beijing 100871, China
{dqyang,swtang}@pku.edu.cn

Abstract. As the World Wide Web grows dramatically in recent years, there is increasing interest in semi-structured data on the web. Semi-structured data are usually represented in graph format, many graph schemas have then been proposed to extract schemas from those data graphs. Conceptual graphs, which use incremental conceptual clustering method to extract schemas, have initially been proposed in 2000. In this paper, we revise the original algorithm to generate a conceptual graph by proposing some new operators in the construction process. The results have shown that with the revised algorithm, the quality of the conceptual graphs has been improved for query optimization.

1. Introduction

As the World Wide Web becomes more popular, semi-structured data on the web has become an important research topic. Semi-structured data are usually represented in graph format, such as Object Exchange Model (OEM) [1]. In traditional database, schemas play an important role in query optimization. Similarly, accurate and approximate graph schemas have been proposed to extract schematic information from semi-structured data, e.g., [2, 3, 4, 5]. Accurate graph schemas usually produce large schema graphs, sometimes even much larger than the original data graphs, e.g., [2]. In contrast, approximate graph schemas usually produce small schema graphs, e.g., [3, 4, 5]. Conceptual graph proposed in [5] is an approximate graph schema, its size is generally very small compared with the original data graph, and it does not require any pre determined parameter, which is usually required by other approximate graph schemas, e.g., [3, 4]. In this paper, we introduce two more operators, namely *merge()* and *split()* to the conceptual generation algorithm. Experiments have shown that with the revised algorithm, conceptual graphs can achieve better in query optimization. The rest of the paper is organized as follows. In Section 2, we give and explain the revised algorithm. In Section 3, the result of querying without conceptual graphs, with the old algorithm and revised algorithm are compared. In Section 4, conclusions are given.

N. Zhong et al. (Eds.): WI 2001, LNAI 2198, pp. 267–271, 2001.
© Springer-Verlag Berlin Heidelberg 2001

2. Conceptual Graphs and the Revised Algorithm

Conceptual graphs use incremental clustering method to cluster objects. Instead of setting pre-determined parameters, such as the number of clusters allowed, conceptual graphs introduce a utility function. The function will be evaluated on all possible clusters each time a new node (vertex) is clustered. The cluster resulting in best utility function value becomes the home of the new node. The utility function is constructed based on the outgoing edges and incoming edges of the clustered nodes, with the heuristics to group nodes with similar outgoing edges and incoming edges into the same cluster. The constructions of the utility function are the same in the old and revised algorithm.

2.1 The Original Algorithm

In [5], the original algorithm used to generate a conceptual graph basically has two operators: assign nodes to a new cluster (hereafter referred to as *create()*) and assign nodes to an existing cluster (i.e., *accommodate()*). Each time a new node is assigned, the *create()* operator creates a new cluster to temporarily accommodate the new node. If the resulting utility function value is the best, the new cluster survives. The *accommodate()* operator simply assigns a node to an existing cluster in the schema graph.

2.2 The Revised Algorithm

The incremental clustering techniques proposed in [6] provide the basis for our revised algorithm. In the revised algorithm, in addition to the *create()* and *accommodate()* operators, we include two other operators: *merge()* and *split()*. Given two clusters, *merge()* creates a new cluster and makes the two clusters the children of the new one. Conversely, given a cluster with a set of children, *split()* deletes the parent cluster and promote its children up one level. *merge()* only operates on the two best children of a cluster in terms of utility function value when assigning a node of a data graph. While *split()* only takes place on the best child of a parent cluster.

3. Evaluation of the Revised Algorithm

In the evaluation, synthetic data graphs are used. The parameters used in [5] to generate synthetic data graphs are adopted. Regular path expressions are used in query evaluation.

3.1 Experimental Setup

In the evaluation, a set of synthetic data graphs are generated, the sizes of the graphs range from 2,500 nodes to 40,000 nodes. For each data graph, 100 random regular path expressions are constructed according to the label paths on the graph. The regular path expressions are divided into two groups. One group consists of expressions with the closure operator ("*") and the other expressions without. The first group is design-ed for those queries with a large or very large target set (hereafter we refer it as large queries), the second group is designed for queries with small target set (hereafter kno-wn as small queries). We define small queries and large queries as:

- Small queries: queries usually retrieve only a small set of nodes from a data gra-ph, e.g.,

$$select\ a.b.c.d.e.(f/g).h$$

- Large queries: queries result in several tens or several hundreds of nodes to be re-trieved from a data graph, e.g.,

$$select\ a.*.b.*.c.d$$

Conceptual graphs with original and revised algorithms are both generated for each data graph. For each generation algorithm, conceptual graphs with depth first and bre-adth first traversal orders over the nodes of the data graphs are both generated, their sizes are then compared.

For each data graph, small queries and large queries are posted. Query costs of query without conceptual graphs, query with conceptual graphs generated by the ori-ginal algorithm (refer to as the original conceptual graph thereafter) and query with conceptual graphs generated by the revised algorithm (refer to as the new conceptual graph) are recorded and compared.

Query cost is measured in terms of the number of nodes being traversed to find the required answer. For query without schema graphs, time to find the answer is equal to the number of nodes directly traversed over the data graph. For query with schema graphs, it equal to the sum of the following items:

- the number of nodes traversed over the schema graph to rewrite the original query Q into Q^s;
- the number of the nodes traversed over the original data graph to find the target set of the rewritten query Q^s.

3.2 Experimental Results

Fig. 1 compares the query costs over small queries between query without schema graphs (represented with Series 1), query with new conceptual graphs (represented with Series 2) and query with original conceptual graphs (represent as Series 3). It is important to state that each value on the y-axis represents the average query cost over the 50 regular path expressions chosen as small queries for each specific data graph. Values on x-axis represent the sizes of the data graphs (i.e., number of nodes in the graph). From the figure, we see that Series 1 and Series 2 nearly overlap, this implies that for small queries, query with new conceptual graphs has the same cost with query without schema graphs. Series 3 is a little bit higher over Series 1 and Series 2, imply-ing that for small queries, query with original conceptual graphs costs more than que-ry without conceptual graphs, but the surplus is small.

Fig. 2 compares the query costs over large queries between the same candidates, i.e., query without schema graphs (represented with Series 1), query with new con-ceptual graphs (represented with Series 2) and query with original conceptual graphs (represent as Series 3). Each value on the y-axis represents the average query cost over the 50 regular path expressions chosen as large queries for each specific data graph. Values on x-axis again represent the sizes of the data graphs. From the figure, we see that Series 3 lies below Series 1 a little, this implies that for large queries, query with original conceptual graphs has less cost than query without schema graphs, but the margin is small. Series 2 performs best. This implies that for large queries, query with revised conceptual graphs can help save cost reasonably.

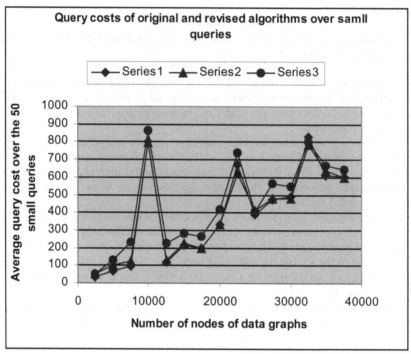

Fig. 1. Query costs of the original and revised algorithms over small queries

4. Conclusions

In this paper, we introduce the *merge()* and *split()* operators in the revised conceptual graph generation algorithm. Operators merge() and split() have the effect of guarding skewed data in the generation of a conceptual graph. Experiments have shown that quality of the resulting schema graphs was improved in query optimization for both small queries and large queries.

Acknowledgements. This work is partially supported by the National Key Basic Research Special Foundation under the grant G1999032705.

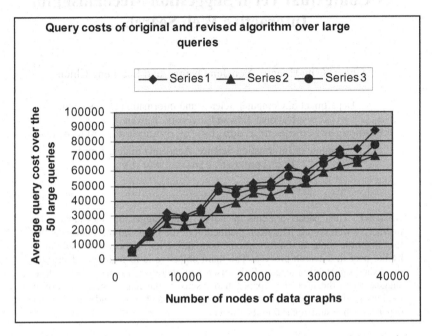

Fig. 2. Query costs of the original and revised algorithms over large queries

References

1. Y. Papakonstantinou, H. Garcia, and J. Widom. Object exchange across heterogeneous information sources. In *Proceedings of International Conference on Data Engineering, 1995*
2. R. Goldman and J. Widom. Dataguides: Enabling query formulation and optimization in semi-structured database. In *Proceedings of the 23rd International Conference on Very Large Data Base, 1997*
3. S. Nestorov, S. Abiteboul, and R. Motwani. Extracting schema from semi-structured data. In *Proceedings of the ACM SIGMOD International Conference on Management of data, 1998*
4. S. Nestorov, S. Abiteboul, and R. Motwani. Inferring structure in semistructured data. In *Proceedings of Workshop on Management of Semistructured data, 1997*
5. Qiu Yue Wang, Jeffrey Xu Yu, Kam-Fai Wong, "Approximate Graph Schema Extraction for Semi-Structured Data". In *Proceedings of the 7th International Conference on Extending Database Technology, 2000*
6. D. Fisher. Knowledge acquisition via incremental conceptual clustering. In J. Shavlik and T. Dietterich, editors, *Readings in Machine Learning*. Morgan Kaufmann Publishers,1990.

A Contextual Term Suggestion Mechanism for Interactive Web Search

Chien-Kang Huang[1], Yen-Jen Oyang[1], and Lee-Feng Chien[2]

[1]Department of Computer Science and Information Engineering,
National Taiwan University, Taiwan.
ckhuang@mars.csie.ntu.edu.tw, yjoyang@csie.ntu.edu.tw,
[2]Institute of Information Science, Academia Sinica, Taiwan.
lfchien@iis.sinica.edu.tw

Abstract. This paper presents a novel term suggestion mechanism for interactive web search. The main distinction of the proposed mechanism is that it exploits the contextual information among the series of query terms submitted by the user in a search process. The main objective is to facilitate identifying the exact information need of the user and therefore to make better term suggestion to the user. This paper also discusses the main issues concerning implementation of the proposed term suggestion mechanism and reports some experimental results regarding its effects.

1   Introduction

Identifying users' information need is always one of the most fundamental and challenging issues in the development of Web search engines. What makes this issue challenging is that most Web users give only short queries. Recent analyses of search engine logs revealed that the average length of Web queries is about 2.3 words [6,12]. Aimed at tackling the short query nature in the Web environment, incorporating some kind of term suggestion mechanisms [4] has become a common practice in search engine design [1,5,8].

One conventional approach to making term suggestions is to extract relevant keyterms from the retrieved documents [2,7,14]. The relevance between the original query term and the keyterms in the retrieved documents is computed based on their positions or occurrences in documents. Measures such as mutual information and x^2-test are commonly employed in computing the relevance. An alternative approach in making term suggestion is based on how query terms are relevant in a collected log of user queries [3,6,10,11]. Similarity measures such as co-occurrence in query sessions[1] and common URL destination[3] have been proposed for clustering the query terms.

Nevertheless, when responding to a new query request, all the existing term suggestion mechanisms discussed above fail to exploit the contextual information

---

[1] A query session contains a series of query transactions submitted by a user for a certain information need. It will be formally defined in section 3.

N. Zhong et al. (Eds.): WI 2001, LNAI 2198, pp. 272–281, 2001.
© Springer-Verlag Berlin Heidelberg 2001

embedded in the query session that the current query request belong to. In other words, when making term suggestions, all the existing mechanisms look at only the terms submitted in the current query request and do not take into account the query terms submitted by the same user in prior requests. The significance of the contextual information is well illustrated in the example in Fig. 1. The query terms in these three query sessions were submitted by three different users with different information needs but all three sessions contain the term "Taiwan University Hospital". By looking at the entire sessions, one can easily figure out that the first user was looking for a hospital with a high-quality department of Obstetrics and Gynecology, and the second user wanted to find some medical journals, and the third user wanted to find a hospital in the southern part of Taipei. However, no one can figure out the real needs of the users if only given the term "Taiwan University Hospital".

Session	Query Terms
Session 1	1. Obstetrics and Gynecology Department 2. Women and Children Hospital 3. <u>Taiwan University Hospital</u>
Session 2	1. <u>Taiwan University Hospital</u> 2. Medical College of Taiwan University 3. Taiwan University Medical Library 4. Journal 5. Medial Journal
Session 3	1. Cathay General Hospital 2. WanFang Hospital 3. <u>Taiwan University Hospital</u> 4. Tri-Service General Hospital

Fig. 1. Examples of contextual information in query sessions.

Also, the current term suggestion mechanisms only reply the suggested terms in a list without organizing these suggested terms according to the different search interests. For example, if all the queries in the Fig. 1 are suggested terms of "Taiwan University Hospital", a user who submits the "Taiwan University Hospital" will get a long list without any organization and find most terms are not related to his/her search interests. However, if the suggested terms are organized by different search concepts, user will be able to quickly find terms that are related to his search interest. Thus, the contextual information in different sessions can be used to find the different search concepts for each query terms.

Based on the observations discussed above, we therefore propose in this paper a novel term suggestion mechanism which can provide organized term suggestions, and can effectively exploits the contextual information in the query session that the search engine is currently responding to. In the following part of this paper, section 2 presents an overview of the proposed term suggestion mechanism. Sections 3, 4, and 5 discuss three main issues concerning implementation of the proposed mechanism, respectively. Section 6 reports the results from the experiments conducted to analyze the effectiveness of the proposed mechanism. Finally, concluding remarks are given in section 7.

2   Overview of the Proposed Term Suggestion Mechanism

Fig. 2 depicts the basic operations of the proposed term suggestion mechanism. The kernel term suggestion module operates based on a term relevance analysis conducted in advance on a collected log of users queries. The query log that contains the query transactions submitted to search engines is first partitioned into a number of query sessions and relevance among the query terms in the log is computed based on how these query terms are clustered in query sessions. The result from the term relevance analysis is then exploited by the term suggestion module on-the-fly. When a user submits a new query term q_k after having submitted a series of query terms q_1, q_2, ..., q_{k-1} previously, the term suggestion module will suggest terms that are not only relevant to the currently submitted term q_k but also the previously submitted terms q_1, q_2, ..., q_{k-1}.

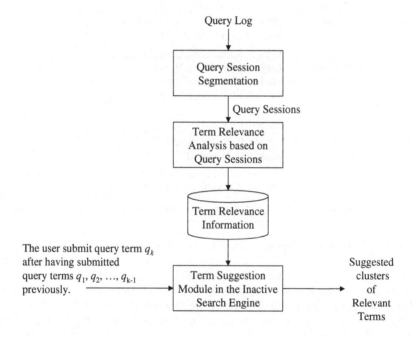

Fig. 2. The basic operations of the proposed term suggestion mechanism.

To develop an interactive search engine that incorporates the proposed term suggestion mechanism, the following three issues must be addressed.

1. How to partition the query log into query sessions accurately. In other words, how to determine the boundary of each query session.
2. How to measure the relevance between each pair of query terms in the log.
3. How to exploit term relevance in making term suggestion on-the-fly.

These three issues will be elaborated in the next three sections, respectively.

3   Query Session Segmentation

The user behavior study conducted by Silverstein et al. revealed that queries for a single information need come clustered in time[12]. Based on this observation, we therefore use a time threshold as delimiter to segment query sessions. For each query transaction T, we examine the following three pieces of information from the query log:

1. t: timestamp at which the query transaction was submitted.
2. id: the IP address of the machine at which the query transaction was submitted.
3. q: the URL string in the query transaction.

We then define a query session as follows:

A query session S is a sequence of query transactions $(T_1, T_2,...,T_n)$ with
  1. $id_1 = id_2 = ... = id_n$;
  2. $t_{i+1} - t_i$ < *time threshold, for all* $1 \leq i \leq n-1$, *where time threshold is a parameter to be set;*
  3. *no other query transactions can join S to form a larger query session.*

Given the definition above, we still need to determine the time threshold value to use. In order to select a reasonable threshold value, we conducted some analysis on a query log. This query log was collected on a proxy server in National Taiwan University, which services 52 organizations including 20 universities and colleges in Northern Taiwan. Table 1 shows the statistics of the log.

Table 1. The statistics of the query log used for analysis.

Time span of the log	126 days (2000/4/26 ~ 2000/9/5)
No. of clients	21,421
No. of query transactions	2,369,282
No. of distinct query transaction	218,362

Fig. 3 shows how the number of segmented query sessions that contain two or more query transactions varies with different time threshold value. We are interested in query sessions containing two or more query transactions because the following term relevance analysis is based on these query sessions. Since the curve in Fig. 3 saturates around 300 seconds, we therefore select 5 minutes as the time threshold. It is interesting that the same 5-minute time threshold was also used by Silverstein et al[12]. Table 2 shows the number of query sessions containing more than one query transactions out of the total number of query sessions, if the 5-minute time threshold is applied. It is also interesting to learn that the percentage is very close to that reported by Silverstein et al.

4   Measure of Term Relevance

With query sessions segmented, the next step is to perform relevance analysis among query terms. The relevance analysis proposed in this paper is based on a term co-occurrence matrix defined as follows.

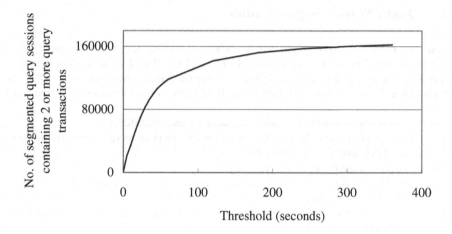

Fig. 3. How the number of segmented query sessions that contain two or more query terms varies with different time threshold values.

Table 2. The number of query sessions containing two or more query transactions versus the total number of query sessions under the 5-minute time threshold.

	No. of sessions	Percentage
1 query transaction per session	455,454	74%
> 1 query transactions per session	160,180	26%
Total	615,634	100%

Definition: *The co-occurrence matrix C of the distinct query terms in a query log, denoted by $q_1, q_2,...,q_n$, is an n by n matrix with $C_{i,j}$ = the number of query sessions containing both query terms q_i and q_j.*

Three similarity estimation functions are applied in our relevant analysis – Jaccard coefficient, dependence coefficient and cosine coefficient, which are defined as follows[9].

$$\text{Jaccard}(q_u, q_v) = \frac{C_{u,v}}{C_{u,u} + C_{v,v} - C_{u,v}} \tag{1}$$

$$\text{Dependence}(q_u, q_v) = \frac{C_{u,v}}{\min(C_{u,u}, C_{v,v})} \tag{2}$$

$$\cos(q_u, q_v) = \frac{\sum_{\forall q_j \in Q}(C_{u,j} \cdot C_{v,j})}{\sqrt{\sum_{\forall q_j \in Q} C_{u,j}^2} \cdot \sqrt{\sum_{\forall q_j \in Q} C_{v,j}^2}} \tag{3}$$

The relevance of each pair of query terms is then computed using the co-occurrence matrix. Fig. 4 shows the algorithm for computing the term relevance. One may note that the algorithm does not apply a uniform formula to all the cases. The reason behind adopting this practice is due to some empirical experiences.

```
function compute_relevant_term_set(qᵤ, Q, C, R)
{ Input:
      qᵤ: the query term of concern
      Q: the set of all query terms in the log
      C: the co-occurrence matrix
  Output:
      R: relevant term set
  R = ∅
  For every qᵥ in Q {
      if ( C_{u,v} ≥ √(C_{u,u}) )

        R = R ∪ {qᵥ}
      else if ( ⁴√(C_{u,u}) ≤ C_{u,v} ≤ √(C_{u,u}) )

        if (C_{u,u} >> C_{v,v} or C_{u,u} << C_{v,v})
            if (Dependence(qᵤ, qᵥ) > threshold₁)
            then R = R ∪ {qᵥ}
        else
            if (Jaccard(qᵤ, qᵥ) > threshold₂)
            then R = R ∪ {qᵥ}
        else if ( C_{u,v} ≤ ⁴√(C_{u,u}) ) {

        If (cos(qᵤ, qᵥ) > threshold₃)
        then R = R ∪ {qᵥ}
  }
  return R;
}
```

Fig. 4. The algorithm for computing the relevant term set.

5   Exploiting Contextual Information in Making Term Suggestion

Once the relevance between each pair of query terms in a query log has been computed in advance, the interactive search engine has all background information to start operating. This is an empirical term suggestion algorithm based on the term relevance computed in last section. As mentioned earlier, the major distinction of the proposed term suggestion mechanism is that it exploits the contextual information embedded in the query sessions that is currently being handled.

First we organize the suggested terms with the following *term organization process.*

1. *Collect all relevant terms.* Apply the algorithm in Fig. 4 to collect all relevant terms from query sessions. Assume that q_u is the concerning query, R is the set of all relevant terms of q_u, and q_v is one of the relevant terms. Continuing step 2 and 3 below for each q_v in R.

2. *Extract highly co-related terms*. If Jaccard(q_u, q_v) > threshold$_4$, then q_v is labeled as "highly co-related" term of q_u, and remove it from the term set R.

3. *Extract highly dependent terms*. If $C_{u,v}/C_{v,v}$ > threshold$_5$, then q_v is labeled as "highly dependent" term of q_u, and remove it from the term set R.

4. *Clustering remaining relevant terms*. In this step, we will organize the relevant terms remaining in set R according to different search concepts. To divide the relevant terms into different clusters, a clustering approach is applied. We take the cosine coefficient between each pair of q_u's relevant terms as the similarity value, and apply the single link hierarchical clustering algorithm [13]. The clustering procedure will stop, if the similarity between any two clusters is smaller than threshold$_6$.

The above term organization process will produce three types of relevant terms, i.e., highly co-related, highly dependent, and others that are clustered. In our experience, the highly co-related terms are often synonyms of the query terms. The highly dependent terms are infrequent terms, but more specific in expression. As for the terms grouped in the same clusters are most with similar requests.

Then *the term suggestion process* can be performed. Basically, the process re-ranks and filters the relevant terms of the current query term q_k by estimating scalar-cluster-based relevance between each pair of the relevant terms and previous query terms q_1, q_2,...,q_{k-1} . The terms the process will suggest are not only relevant to q_k but also relevant to some of the previous query terms. The procedure of the term suggestion process is described as follows.

1. Assume that q_k is the current query term submitted by user, q_1, q_2,...,q_{k-1} are the previous query terms. S is the set of all clusters of relevant terms of q_k, which is generated with the above procedure, and q_r is a relevant term appearing in S.

2. For each q_r in S, calculate the contextual cosine coefficient. The contextual cosine coefficient is defined as equation (4) in which the cosine coefficients are defined similar to equation (3).

$$\text{contextual\_cos}(q_r, q_1, q_2, \cdots, q_{k-1})$$
$$= \cos(q_r, q_{k-1}) + \alpha \cos(q_r, q_{k-2}) + \cdots + \alpha^{k-1} \cos(q_r, q_1) \quad (4)$$

If the contextual_cos(q_r, q_1, ..., q_{k-1}) < threshold$_7$, q_r is removed from the corresponding cluster in S. If the corresponding cluster doesn't contain any more relevant terms, the cluster will be removed from S.

3. Re-rank the relevant terms in each cluster according to their contextual cosine coefficients.

4. Re-rank all the clusters in S, according to the average contextual cosine coefficients of each cluster. Assume that CL is a cluster in S. The average contextual cosine coefficient is defined as equation (5).

$$\text{avg\_contextual\_cos}(CL, q_1, q_2, \cdots, q_k) = \frac{1}{|CL|} \sum_{q_r \in CL} \text{contextual\_cos}(q_r, q_1, q_2, \cdots, q_k) \quad (5)$$

In the above procedure, step 3 and 4 are performed for re-ranking the order of the suggested terms and the clusters of the terms. All the highly co-related terms, highly dependent terms and the final S will be sorted according to their relevance and suggested to the user who submits the query. In the next section, we will discuss the effectiveness of this empirical algorithm.

6 Experimental Results

In order to study the effectiveness of the proposed term suggestion mechanism, we conducted some experiments. The log used for relevance analysis and term suggestion is the same as query log used in session segmentation experiment. Some statistics of the query log were already listed in Table 1 and Table 2. In Table 3, we illustrate the obtained different term suggestion results for a same query term in different sessions. The first row presents an example that shows the clusters of relevant terms suggested by the proposed mechanism when given only one query term "NTU" (an abbreviation of National Taiwan University), and the following rows show how the suggested terms affected by different previous queries "library" and "hospital". It is noted that all of the illustrated queries and suggested terms are all translated in English from Chinese.

Table 3. The terms suggested by the proposed mechanism when given some query terms with high frequency in our proxy server log.

Query Sessions	Term Suggestion

1.NTU	Suggested Dependent Terms for "NTU"
	 NTU Hompage, Taiwan University
	Suggested Clusters of Relevant Terms for "NTU"
	1. Library, NTU Library, National Library, Journal
	2. Language Training and Testing Center,
	     NTNU Language Tranining Center
	3. NTU Computer Center, NTU EE
	4. NTU Hospital, NTU Medial College, Library of NTU Medical
	     College, Medical Journal, NTU Medical Department
	5. University, Campus
	6. NCKU, YMU, NCCU, TKU, FJU, SCU
	7. NTU BBS, Palm BBS
	8. Entrance Examination, Admission Announcement

1.library 2.NTU	Suggested Dependent Terms for "NTU" NTU Hompage, Taiwan University Suggested Clusters of Relevant Terms for "NTU" 1. NTU Library, National Library, Journal 2. Medical Journal 3. Language Training and Testing Center
1.hospital 2.NTU	Suggested Dependent Terms for "NTU" NTU Hompage, Taiwan University Suggested Clusters of Relevant Terms for "NTU" 1. NTU Hospital, NTU Medial College, NTU Medical Department, Library of NTU Medical College, Medical Journal

The illustrated example is not an extreme case. In our experiments, many high frequency queries can obtain appropriate suggestions. A quantitative experiment was also conducted to evaluate how effective the proposed mechanism can reduce the number of query requests that the user needs to issue to get the desired information. In the experiment, each query session in our log is fed into the proposed mechanism. If one of the terms suggested by the proposed mechanism at one step of the query session appears at a later step of the query session, it is said that the proposed mechanism makes a successful term suggestion. Table 4 shows the statistics of the experiment results from analyzing 160,180 query sessions. The statistics reveals that the proposed mechanism makes successful term suggestions to 20.4% of the query sessions and can reduce the average number of transactions that the user needs to submit in one session from 2.75 to 2.3.

Table 4. The statistics of the experiment results.

Total No. of query sessions containing 2 or more query transactions	No. of sessions with successful term suggestions	Avg. No. of suggested terms for each query transaction	Avg. No. of transactions in a query session	Avg. No. of query transactions that the successful term suggestions reduce
160,180	32,665 (20.4%)	15.87	2.75	0.45

7   Concluding Remarks and Future Research Issues

Identifying users' information need is always one of the most fundamental and challenging issues in the development of Web search engines. What makes this issue challenging is that most Web users give only short queries. This short queries problem leads to the development of term suggestion mechanisms. This paper presents a novel term suggestion mechanism that exploits the contextual information among the series of query terms submitted by the user in a search process. The contextual information exploited helps the search engine identifying the exact need of the user.

Though the experimental results look promising, further study is needed on the following three issues that concern implementation of the proposed term suggestion mechanism:

1. how to partition the query log into query sessions so that each query session really corresponds to the query terms submitted by a user in a single information need.
2. how to measure the relevance between each pair of query terms in the log.
3. how to exploit term relevance in making term suggestion on-the-fly.

Regarding the first issue, this paper just uses a time threshold to delimit the boundary of a query session. A better effect may result if the term relevance computed in the next stage is fed back to the session segmentation stage. For the second and third issues, the practices adopted in this paper are based on empirical experiences. Therefore, it is of interest to conduct more experiments to learn the effects of alternative strategies, including different clustering algorithms and similarity measurements.

References

1.   AltaVista Inc. http://www.altavista.com

2. P.G. Anick and S. Tipirneni, "The paraphrase search assistant: Terminology feedback for iterative information seeking" in Proceedings of 22nd International ACM SIGIR Conference on Research and Development in Information Retrieval (SIGIR-99), pages 153-159, 1999.
3. D. Beeferman and A. Berger, "Agglomerative clustering of a search engine query log" in Proceeding of International ACM SIGKDD Conference on Knowledge (KDD-00), pages, 2000.
4. N.J. Belkin, "Helping people find what they don't know" in Communication of ACM (CACM), Vo.43, No8, pg 58-61,Aug 2000.
5. Hotbot Inc. http://www.hotbot.com
6. B.J. Jansen, A. Spink, J. Bateman, and T. Saracevic, "Real life information retrieval: A study of user queries on the web" SIGIR FORUM, 32(1), 1998.
7. S. Jones and M.S. Staveley, "Phrasier: a system for Interactive Document Retrieval Using Keyphrases" in Proceedings of 22nd International ACM SIGIR Conference on Research and Development in Information Retrieval (SIGIR-99), pages 160-167, 1999.
8. Lycos Inc. http://www.lycos.com
9. C. C. Manning, H. Schutze, Foundations of Statistical Natural Language Processing: 8. Lexical Acquisition, Cambridge, MA: MIT Press.
10. R. Nordlie, "User revealment – a comparison of initial queries and ensuing question development in online searching and in human reference interaction" in Proceedings of 22th International ACM SIGIR Conference on Research and Development in Information Retrieval (SIGIR-99), pages 11-18, 1999
11. N.C.M. Ross and D. Wolfram, "End user searching on the Internet: an analysis of term pair topics submitted to the excite search engine" in Journal of the American Society of Information Science, Vol.51, pp.949-958, 2000
12. C. Silverstein, M. Henzinger, H. Marais, and M. Morics, "Analysis of a very large AltaVista query log," Technical Report 1998-014, Digital Systems Research Center, 1998.
13. van Riemsdijk, Henk, and E. Williams, Information Retrieval, Cambridge, MA: MIT Press. 1979
14. J. Xu and W.B. Croft, "Query expansion using local and global document analysis" in Proceedings of 19th International ACM SIGIR Conference on Research and Development in Information Retrieval (SIGIR-96), pages 4-11, 1996

3DGML: A 3-Dimensional Graphic Information Retrieval System

Jong Ha Hwang, Keung Hae Lee, and Soochan Hwang

Department of Computer Engineering, Hankuk Aviation University, 412-791, Korea
{hwangjh, khlee, schwang}@mail.hau.ac.kr

Abstract. This paper presents a web-based information retrieval system for 3-D graphic data. We describe a 3-D database system and its web-based user interface supporting semantics of 3-D objects. Our system offers a content-based retrieval for 3-D scenes that few graphic database systems are capable of. The user can pose a visual query involving 3-D shapes and spatial relations on the web interface. The data model underlying the retrieval system models 3-D scenes using domain objects and their spatial relations. An XML-based data modeling language called 3DGML has been designed to support the data model. It offers an object-oriented 3-D image modeling mechanism that separates low level implementation details of 3-D objects from their semantic roles in a 3-D scene. We discuss the retrieval system and the data modeling technique in detail. We believe our work is one of the earliest efforts to take advantage of XML for 3-D graphics.

1 Introduction

The explosive growth in the number of web-based applications has made the support of multimedia data in web-based information systems a hot research topic. Graphic data is probably one of the most frequently used data types in today's web applications. The significance of 3-dimensional (3-D) graphic information has been demonstrated in many areas such as e-commerce, web-based learning, virtual reality, geographic information system, and games [1,2,3]. 3-D graphic database systems play an important role in many applications.

As more image and graphic data are used in applications, the methods that support content-based retrievals of 3-D graphic information are desired. Most current 3-D graphic systems focus on visualizing 3-D images. They usually model a 3-D graphic image using lines and polygons with information on their placements in the space. One problem with this approach is that it is difficult to store semantics of 3-D objects in a scene. The lack of such information makes it difficult to retrieve or manipulate a particular domain object separately from others.

We have developed a 3-D graphic data model that supports a content-based retrieval for 3-D scenes. This paper presents the data model and a web-based information retrieval system based on it. The 3-D graphic data model, called 3DGML(3-

N. Zhong et al. (Eds.): WI 2001, LNAI 2198, pp. 282–291, 2001.
© Springer-Verlag Berlin Heidelberg 2001

Dimensional Graphical Markup language), allows the semantics of 3-D objects to be incorporated into a 3-D scene. This support of semantic information allows for a content-based retrieval of scenes. Scenes are modeled as compositions of 3-D graphic objects. A set of primitive 3-D objects is used as building blocks for modeling 3-D scenes instead of lines and polygons. Larger 3-D objects are defined through a composition of other objects.

In our database system, the user can search scenes using shapes, descriptions and spatial relations of 3-D objects they contain. A query on the shape of an object enables a scene to be retrieved based on a particular shape it contains. A query on a spatial relation allows scenes to be searched based on relative placements of objects in the space. Finally, a query can use textual descriptions of objects and scenes.

The 3-D graphic retrieval system presented in this paper was implemented using XML. 3DGML is an XML vocabulary defined using an XML DTD(Document Type Definition). The choice of XML as the description mechanism of our data model makes the database system suited to web-based information systems. 3-D images are modeled as XML documents, which are validated before being stored in the database. The user can pose content-based queries using a web browser. A query result is presented to the user through the web browser.

The remainder of this paper is organized as follows. The next chapter discusses previous research related to our work. Chapter 3 describes 3DGML and modeling 3-D images with it. Chapter 4 presents the information retrieval system for 3-D graphic information that we developed. Chapter 5 concludes the paper.

2   Related Works

Most current works on graphic database systems are centered on the processing of 2-dimensional graphic data such as images and maps [4,5,6,7]. Research on 3-D graphics has mainly concerned about the visualization of data to provide the user with a 3-D feel [2,3,8]. Existing graphic systems traditionally rely on low-level geometrical objects such as points, lines, and polygons in representing 3-D data. These systems treat a 3-D object as a collection of lines and polygons rather than a unit of manipulation. It prevents them from supporting content-based retrievals or manipulations of 3-D objects. Only recently, MPEG standard committees have started working on the issues of modeling 3-D images [9,10]. MPEG-4 SNHC(Synthetic, Natural, and Hybrid Coding) aims to develop techniques for representing synthetic images with natural objects efficiently. 3-D objects are represented by 3-D meshes(surfaces), norm vectors, and their features such as color, texture, etc. However, modeling 3-D objects as semantic units is not addressed by MPEG.

There have been some efforts to model the spatial relations of objects for 3-D scenes. Xiong and Wang described a technique supporting similarity search for a chemical application [11]. They represent a 3-D object using points in the Euclidean Space. An object is a 3-D graph consisting of one or more substructures of connected subgraphs. Similarity of two objects is determined by comparing their substructures and edges. Gudivada and Jung proposed an algorithm for retrieving images of relevance based on similarity to user queries [12]. In their image representation scheme, an image is converted to a symbolic/iconic image with human assistance. The symbolic/iconic image is obtained from each domain object by associating a name or an icon with it. The location of a domain object is represented by its centroid coordinate. This method also determines the spatial relation of objects using the connectivity of graphs.

While the works discussed above considered geometrical similarity, they did not discuss modeling the semantics of 3-D objects. Their views still remain graph-oriented. In order to address the problems discussed above a new data model is needed that treats 3-D objects as first class objects in modeling. The new data model should represent 3-D data using semantic units rather than primitive geometrical objects.

XML has been widely used for describing complex data types. The openness and the extensibility via the Data Type Definition mechanism make XML an excellent vehicle for defining new languages with a relatively small effort [13]. Several domain specific languages have already been designed with XML before. Examples of such languages are SVG(Scalable Vector Graphics), CML(Chemical Markup Language), MathML(Mathematical Markup Language), and MusicML [14,15]. As their names suggest it, these languages commonly bring the capability to markup and browse complex data types to the user in their targeted application domains. While the use of XML is growing in other areas, we have not found systems that model 3-D scenes with XML. We view that 3-D graphic data modeling can also benefit from XML. Our work is probably one of the earliest efforts to take advantage of XML in 3-D graphics.

3   Modeling 3-D Graphic Data in 3DGML

3.1   Data Model

We first present the data model used in our system. The model supports an object-oriented 3-D data modeling. It models 3-D scenes using domain objects and their spatial semantics. A 3-D scene is an image consisting of one or more 3-D objects which are meaningful in a domain. Fig. 1 shows the inheritance hierarchy that is used for modeling 3-D scenes in our system.

A 3-D scene is modeled using three types of components: 3-D objects contained in the scene, spatial relations on the objects, and descriptors. A simple 3-D object is modeled using basic objects. A *basic object* is a system-defined 3-D graphic object. Examples of basic objects are cube, sphere, and cylinder. An object of an arbitrary shape that is difficult to model with basic objects only, such as pyramid, triangular prism, etc, is defined using one or more polygons. Such an object is called a *user-defined object*. Each polygon of a user-defined object may have associated properties as with basic objects. A complex 3-D object is modeled as a composition of basic objects, user-defined objects, and other complex objects.

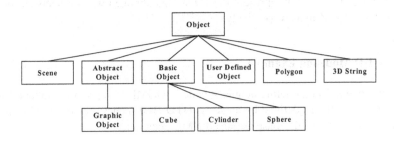

Fig. 1. Hierarchy diagrams

Every 3-D object within a scene exists in the form of a *Gobject* (*Graphic object*). A Gobject is defined by extending an abstract object. An *abstract object* is a skeletal object that is used as a prototype of other objects. It is a template that does not physically exist in a scene. It specifies the shape of a 3-D object and partially describes its appearance. For example, an abstract object may define structure, color, and texture for its child objects. Hence, the modeling of a scene typically involves defining abstract objects first. In many cases, abstract objects represent semantic units such as building, street, etc that are germane to an application domain.

The definition of an abstract object consists of descriptive meta-information called descriptor, compound objects, and a 3-D string that defines spatial relation on the objects. A compound object may be comprised of one or more of basic objects, user-defined objects, or other compound objects. A compound object uses other objects that are defined elsewhere by referring to their id's. The color and texture information relating to the appearance of an object may be associated with lower level components such as basic objects and user-defined objects. The location of an object belonging to an abstract object denotes its relative position within the abstract object.

Every 3-D object embedded in a scene is a Gobject. To create a Gobject, an abstract object needs to be specialized by adding further information required to render its clone in a specific scene context. The information on the location, rotation, and scaling in the context of a particular scene needs to be specified in addition to what the abstract object has already defined. Separating the structure information of an object from its physical rendering for a scene and the use of prototype based object instantiation simplify the process of creating new 3-D objects. Objects of a kind can easily be modeled without creating many superfluous classes.

We developed the notion of *3-D string* to encode the spatial relation of 3-D objects contained in a scene or nested in another object. A 3-D string can express the concepts such as A is located to the left of B (left-right relation), A is above B (top-bottom relation), and A is closer than B(front-back relation). The representation of a 3-D string is derived from the 1D string technique [16]. A 1D string is an encoding of the order of the positions of objects in the linear space. A 1D string is defined in terms of the objects participating in a spatial relation and a set of ordering symbols that denote spatial orders of objects in the space. The ordering symbols used for 1D strings are

"<" and "=" which means closer and equal, respectively. A 3-D string is a 3-tuple (u, v, w), where u, v, and w represent the 1D strings obtained when objects are projected to the X, Y, and Z-axis, respectively.

3.2   A 3-D Modeling Example

We designed a data modeling language called 3DGML to support the model discussed in Section 3.1. It was defined by an XML DTD. 3-D scenes are described using XML tags and stored in the database as parsed XML documents.

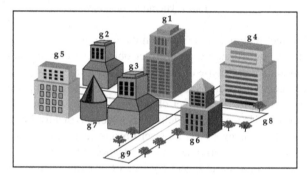

Fig. 2. The 3-D scene of "Street A"

We now show an example 3DGML document that models a 3-D scene. Fig. 2 shows a scene called "Street A" that will be used in our discussion below. It is a 3-D scene of buildings and streets in a city. Fig. 3 is a stripped version of a document that models the scene in 3DGML.

The model in Fig. 3 defines the scene "Street A". It contains two major blocks: the *Definition* block that defines abstract objects a1 through a6 and the *Content* block that defines the actual contents of the scene. We discuss the *Content* block first.

The *Content* block contains the definitions of Gobjects g1 through g9 which model the objects labeled in Fig. 3, correspondingly. A Gobject may be defined by using an abstract object as its prototype, in which case its features should be modified as needed. A Gobject may also be defined using other Gobjects. Object g2 is an example of a Gobject defined using a4, an abstract object, as its prototype. It is a concrete extension of a4, which is specifically placed at the position (-4, 0, 0) in the scale of (2 2 0). That is, its width and height are twice as long as what a4 defines.

Object g7 shows an example of a compound object. It is defined in terms of two cylinders, namely, g71 and g72, which are also defined as Gobjects. g71 is a cylinder whose bottom circle has 1 as its radius(*b_radius*). The radius of its top circle(*t_radius*) is 0, which means that it is a cone. g72 is a cylinder with the radius of size 1.5. The spatial relation between the two objects, encoded in the *Td_string* of g7, states that g71 is located above g72.

```
<?xml version="1.0" encoding="EUC-KR"?>
<!DOCTYPE TDGML SYSTEM "3dgml.dtd">
<Scene>
<Descriptor name="Image Name" value="Street A" type="string"/>
<Definition>
    <! .... The definitions of abstract objects a1 through a6 -->
</Definition>
<Content>
    <! ....The definitions of Td_string for this content -->
    <Gobject oid="g1" ref_id="a3">
        ....
    </Gobject>
    <Gobject oid="g2" ref_id="a4">
        <Descriptor name="BuildingType" value="Office" type="string"/>
        <Descriptor name="Rent" value="100000" type="string"/>
        <Transform location="-4 0 0" scaling="2 2 0" />
    </Gobject>
    <! ....The definitions of Gobjects g3 through g6 -->
    <Gobject oid="g7">
        <Descriptor name="BuildingType" value="Church" type="string"/>
        <Td_string u="g71=g72" v="g72<g71" w="g71=g72"/>
        <Transform location="-2 0 4"/>
            <Gobject oid="g71" basic_type="cylinder" >
                <Transform location="0 1 0"/>
                <Size t_radius="0" b_radius="1" height="0.5"/>
            </Gobject>
            <Gobject oid="g72" basic_type="cylinder">
                <Transform location="0 0 0"/>
                <Size t_radius="1.5" b_radius="1.5" height="1"/>
            </Gobject>
    </Gobject>
    <! ....The definitions of Street Gobject g8 and g9 using a6 -->
</Content>
</Scene>
```

Fig. 3. The definition of the scene in Fig. 2

We now narrow our discussion to the modeling of building g2 in the Fig. 3 for the most part. This building will also be used in the example retrieval to be discussed in the next section. The 3DGML model shown in Fig. 3 defines building g2 in a two-step process. It first defines an abstract object, a4, which resembles the shape of the target object, g2. It then defines g2 as a Gobject by declaring a4 to be its prototype and specifying additional information needed to create a concrete graphic object to be inserted in the scene. We show its definition in Fig. 4.

According to the definition of the abstract object a4, it consists of three basic objects (*Bobject*), namely, b4, b5, and b6 and a compound object c5. The objects b4, b5, and b6 are of the cube type. c5 is a component that represents the middle portion of the building. The definition of a4 contains one descriptor, which describes it as a building. The *Td_string* element of a4 defines the spatial relation for the objects con-

```
<Aobject oid="a4">
  <Descriptor name="ObjectType" value="Building2" type="string"/>
  <Td_string u="b4=c5=b5=b6" v="b4<c5<b5<b6" w="b4=c5=b5=b6"/>
  <Bobject oid="b4" type="cube">
    <Transform location="0 0 0" scaling="1 1.5 1"/>
    <Appearance color="0 0 1"/>
  </Bobject >
  <Component oid="c5" ref_id="a2">
    <Transform location="0 1 0"/>
    <Appearance color="0 0 1"/>
  </Component>
  <! ....The definitions of cube b5 and b6 -->
</Aobject >
```

Fig. 4. The definition of abstract object a4

tained in it. It specifies the spatial relation of b4, b5, b6, and c5. The u value of the 3-D string specifies the ordering of the four objects with respect to the X-axis as "b4 < c5 < b6 < b7." They are on the same locations along the other two axes.

The type of a basic object being used is defined by the *type* value given to its *oid*. The size and the actual shape of a basic object are defined by its other elements such as *Transform*, *Appearance*, and *Size*. The information defined by the basic object still is not specific enough to be used in a scene as it barely defines the information needed by a4. This example defines the relative location and scaling factors within a4 and the default color for the basic objects contained in it. These values may need to be modified or complemented with further information to fit it in a specific scene.

4   A 3-D Information Retrieval System

The current prototype system has been implemented and runs with IIS(Internet Information Server) of Microsoft on the Windows NT platform. We now describe retrievals of 3-D scene that are supported by the system. The XML parser was implemented in ASP using DOM API [17]. Parsed XML documents are stored in the MS-SQL server. The current implementation provides a scene editor that we developed to help create valid 3DGML documents.

A couple of sample queries on the 3-D database system are now described. Fig. 5 shows the screens displayed by the retrieval system. The query screen shown in Fig. 5(a) is the user interface with which the user enters queries. The user specifies search conditions using descriptions or the shape of an object to be found. The search condition on the descriptors specified in this example looks for the scenes that contain an "office" object of which monthly rent is less than 100,000.

When a query is based on a shape, the user may browse existing abstract objects using the 3-D scene editor provided by the system. The query processing is based on a simple comparison of oid's of abstract objects. If the desired shape does not exist in the system yet, the user may first define a new abstract object and then use it in the

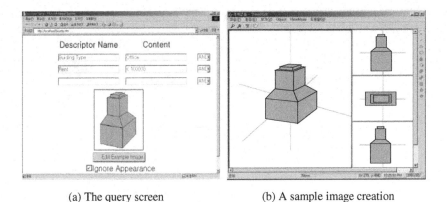

(a) The query screen   (b) A sample image creation

Fig. 5. A sample query

search. The comparisons made during a search are based on the structure of the object to be found. The component objects comprising a search object and their spatial relation must match those of a scene to find. For example, the number and types of B-objects, the structures of Component objects, and Td_string's are compared. The current implementation does not consider the transform and appearance information for matching.

Fig. 5(b) shows the process of creating a search object on the 3-D image editor. The descriptor information and the definition of the object are converted to an XML document using the 3DGML DTD. A parsed form of the document is stored in the database and used for search. The system will find the scenes containing the building specified in Fig. 5(a).

Fig. 6 shows a retrieval session where the query includes a spatial relation on objects in addition to the shapes of objects. The user first specifies the objects and the spatial relation required of them on the query screen. The system searches the database for 3-D scenes containing the objects and satisfying the specified spatial relation. Fig. 6(a) specifies that the search should find scenes containing three objects, two of which represent buildings and face each other across the other object, street. The scenes shown in Fig. 6(b) are returned as the result of the query.

The spatial relation of the objects contained in a search object is defined by the three components of a 3-D string: u, v, and w. The fields near the bottom of Fig. 6(a) specify which of the three components are used. The above example uses u and w, but not v. The OR connective applied to the values of the two components specifies that the spatial relation condition be satisfied with respect to any of two axes X and Z. If "building < street < building" is true with respect to either the X-axis or the Z-axis, it satisfies the specified spatial condition (actual comparison is based on the shapes of objects, not their names). The heights of the buildings or the street are not considered in comparing objects. Only the left-right and front-back relations are meant to be significant in this example.

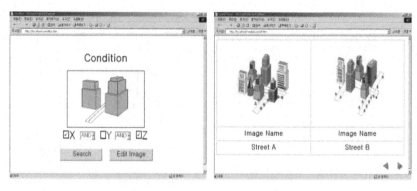

    (a) A query screen   (b) The result screen

Fig. 6. An example of spatial relation query session

5 Conclusion

Few database systems support content-based retrievals of 3-D graphic information. We presented a web-based database system that offers a content-based retrieval of 3-D scenes. One of the significant features that our system introduced is its support of semantic modeling for 3-D scenes. 3-D objects are modeled using semantic units rather than the primitive geometrical objects such as lines and polygons that are typically found in other graphic systems. An XML-based data modeling language called 3DGML was described in detail. It separates the implementation details of a 3-D object from its semantic usage and supports modeling scenes in an object-oriented way. The concept of 3-D string that we came up with allows the system to formally express spatial relations for 3-D objects in a scene. A content-based retrieval of 3-D objects on our system was described using several examples. Search may be based on 3-D shapes and spatial relations.

While XML has become a popular research topic in many application domains, few XML applications are known to support 3-D graphic data. Our study demonstrates that XML can make an excellent description tool for 3-D graphics. We expect that the 3-D information retrieval systems described in the paper will be useful for many graphics applications that require 3-D semantics. For future work, we are planning on providing the support of similarity query based on shapes of objects. We also consider that representing spatial relations according to a specific viewpoint is another important issue to be investigated in the future.

Acknowledgements. This work was partly supported by grant No. 98-0102-06-01-3 from the Basic Research Program of the Korea Science & Engineering Foundation and Internet Information Retrieval Regional Research Center.

References

[1]   R. G. Menendez and J. E. Bernard, "Flight Simulation in Synthetic Environments," IEEE Proceedings of the Digital Avionics Systems Conferences, vol. 1, 2000.

[2]   S. Jie, "Visualizing 3-D Geographical Data with VRML," IEEE Proceedings of the International on Computer Graphics, pp.108-110, 1998.

[3]   F. M. Weinhaus and V. Devarajan, "Texture Mapping 3D Models of Real-World Scenes," ACM Computing Survey, vol. 29, no. 4, pp. 325-368, 1997.

[4]   A. D. Bimbo, *Visual Information Retrieval*, Morgan Kaufmann, 1999.

[5]   D. Yining, B, S. Manjunath, C. Kenney, M. S. Moore, and S. Hyundoo, "An Efficient Color Representation for image Retrieval," IEEE Transactions on Image Processing, vol. 10, no. 1, pp. 140-147, 2001.

[6]   R. Brunelli and O. Mich, "Image Retrieval by Example," IEEE Transactions on Multimedia, vol. 2, no. 3, pp. 164-171, 2000.

[7]   K. W. Hung and M. A. Yong, "A Content-based Image Retrieval System Integration Color, Shape and Spatial Analysis," IEEE Proceedings of the International Conference on Systems, Man, and Cybernetics, vol. 2, pp. 1484-1488, 2000.

[8]   S. Hwang, S. Cho, T. Wang, and P. C.-Y. Sheu, "A Fast 3-D Visualization Methodology Using Characteristic Views of Objects," International Journal of Software Engineering and Knowledge Engineering, vol. 8, no. 1, 1998.

[9]   Q. Huang, A. Puri, and Z. Liu, "Multimedia Search and Retrieval: New Concepts, System Implementation, and Application," IEEE Transactions on Circuits and System for Video Technology, vol. 10, no. 5, pp. 679-692, 2000.

[10] J. Hunter, "MPEG-7 Behind the Scenes", D-Lib Magazine, vol. 5, no. 9, 1999.

[11] W. Xiong and J. T. L. Wang, "Fast Similarity Search in Database of 3D Objects," IEEE International Conference on Tools with Artificial Intelligence, pp.16-23, 1998.

[12] V. N. Gudivada and G. S. Jung, "Spatial Knowledge Representation and Retrieval in 3-D Image Database," IEEE Proceedings of the International Conference on Multimedia Computing and Systems, pp. 90-97, 1995.

[13] T. Bray, J. Paoli and C. M. Sperberg-McQueen, Extensible Markup Language (XML) 1.0, http://www.w3.org/TR/1998/REC-xml-19980210, 1998.

[14] W3 Consortium, Extensible Markup Language(XML) Activity, XML Activity, http://www.w3.org/XML/Activity.html, 1998.

[15] W3 Consortium, Scalable Vector Graphics (SVG) 1.0 Specification, http://www.w3.org/TR/2000/CR-SVG-20001102/, 2000

[16] S. K. Chang, Q. Y. Shi, and C. W. Yan, "Iconic Indexing by 2-D Strings," IEEE Transactions on Pattern Analysis and Machine Intelligence, vol. 9, no. 3, 1987.

[17] W3C Consortium, Document Object Model (DOM), http://www.w3.org/DOM/, 1998.

An Evolutionary Approach to Automatic Web Page Categorization and Updating

Vincenzo Loia and Paolo Luongo

Dipartimento di Matematica ed Informatica,
Università di Salerno,
84081 Baronissi (Salerno), Italy
{loia,pluongo}@unisa.it

Abstract. Catalogues play an important role in most of the current Web search engines. The catalogues, which organize documents into hierarchical collections, are maintained manually increasing difficulty and costs due to the incessant growing of the WWW. This problem has stimulated many researches to work on automatic categorization of Web documents. In reality, most of these approaches work well either on special types of documents or on restricted set of documents. This paper presents an evolutionary approach useful to construct automatically the catalogue as well as to perform the classification of a Web document. This functionality relies on a genetic-based fuzzy clustering methodology that applies the clustering on the context of the document, as opposite to content-based clustering that works on the complete document information.

1 Introduction

The World Wide Web (WWW or Web) is a cheap and powerful environment for sharing information among specialized communities. The unexpected widespread use of the WWW, the presence of heterogeneous data sources, the absence of recognized organization models, make difficult, in many cases frustanting, the task of Internet searching. One solution to this problem is to categorize the Web documents according to their topics. This explains why popular engines (Altavista, Netscape and Lycos) changed themselves from crawler-based into a Yahoo!-like directories of web sites. Just to give an example of the difficulty of this task, Yahoo! maintains the largest directory list composed of 1.2 million of terms thanks to the support of thousands of human editors.

Many researches have been involved in the study of automatic categorization. Good results have been reported in case of categorization of specific documents, such as newspapers [7] and patent documents [11]. Infoseek experimented neural network technology, other approaches have used clusters generated in a dynamic mode [13] [8].

N. Zhong et al. (Eds.): WI 2001, LNAI 2198, pp. 292–302, 2001.
© Springer-Verlag Berlin Heidelberg 2001

The impressive evolution of the Web makes difficult the management of consistent category directories. This drawback has an immediate effect in a lost of precision reported by the most popular Web search engines (they return only a fraction of the URLs of interest to user [14], have a small coverage of available data [10], suffer of instability in output for same queries submissions [15].

This work presents a clustering-based Web document categorization that faces with positive results, the two fundamental problems of Web clustering: the high dimensionality of the feature space and the knowledge of the entire document. The first problem is tackled with an evolutionary approach. The genetic computation assures stability and efficiency also in presence of a large amount of data. About the second issue we perform a clustering based on the analysis of the context rather than the content of the document. Context-based clustering strongly reduces the size of the Web document to process, without grave fall of performances.

2   A Contextual View of a Web Page

Let us consider a link in a Web page: in general we note the existence of sufficient information spent to describe the referenced page. Thus this information may be used to categorize a document. The process starts with an initial list of URLs, and, for each URL, retrieves the web document, analyzing the structure of the document expressed in terms of its HTML tags. For each meaningful tag, contextual data are extracted. For example, when the <A> tag is found containing an URL, an URL Context Path (URL: C_1: C_2:...: C_n) is defined, containing the list of the context strings C_i so far associated to the URL. For example, let us consider the following fragment of an HTML page from Altavista:

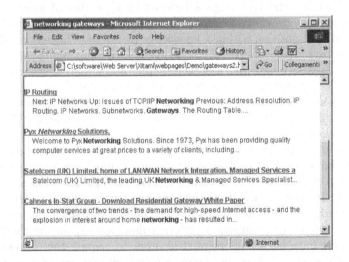

Fig. 1. Example of contexts in a Web page.

The following context paths are created:

1. "http://www.dc.turkuamk.fi/LDP/LDP/nag/node27.html"
   "IP Routing"
   > "Next: IP Networks Up: Issues of TCP/IP Networking Previous: Address Resolution. IP Routing. IP Networks. Subnetworks. Gateways. The Routing Table...."
   > "Networking Gateways"

2. "http://pyx.net/":
   "Pyx Networking Solutions. "
   > "Welcome to Pyx Networking Solutions. Since 1973, Pyx has been providing quality computer services at great prices to a variety of clients, including..."
   > "Networking Gateways"

3. "http://www.satelcom.co.uk/":
   "Satelcom (UK) Limited, home of LAN/WAN Network Integration, Managed Services a "
   > "Satelcom (UK) Limited, the leading UK Networking & Managed Services Specialist..."
   > "Networking Gateways"

4. "http://www.instat.com/catalog/downloads/resgateway.asp":
   "Cahners In-Stat Group - Download Residential Gateway White Paper "
   > "The convergence of two trends - the demand for high-speed Internet access - and the explosion in interest around home networking - has resulted in..."
   > "Networking Gateways"

Any URL is analyzed through a breadth-first visiting: first the complete page is analyzed, then for each external link a new visiting is triggerred on the corresponding host. Next step regards the clustering process that exploits the Context Paths database and the categories-based catalogue in order to evaluate the membership value of each URL to a set of categories.

3   Architecture

Usually a Web search engine exploits two basic technologies for document retrieval: - *indexing* the Web page is indexed by a number of words or phrases representing an abbreviated version of the page itself; - *directories* the page is represented by a position within a knowledge hierarchy. This section shows how our system enables to classify a Web document with a precision comparable with a directory approach and with a dimensionality and updating speed comparable with an indexing technique. Our system returns a database of the most meaningful categories that characterize a Web area (a set of URLs) under analysis. This task is done thanks to an evolutionary process that updates the previous, existing catalogue.

At instant t_0 we assume the availability of an initial catalogue, used as a kind of training set. The evolved catalogue, containing new category entries, is then used to classify the Web documents. The system is based on a client-server architecture in order to distribute the computational agents charged to load the document from the Web and to classify the document itself.

The evolution layer consists of different modules: (1) on the client-side the *SpiderAgents* have been implemented in order to acquire the context paths of the Web documents, (2) on the server-side the software agents *Genetic Engine* have been realized in order to collect the context paths and to transform them into genotypes. This enables to produce, through the genetic-based process, the catalogue, and (3) the agents *Clusterizer* has been designed to classify the Web documents.

Here follows a short discussion about the basic technologies employed for the automatic categorization.

Spidering: the goal of the spidering process is to perform a parsing of the document in order to extract the information concerning the context paths;

Classification: we use a model of *context fuzzy clustering*, based on syntax analysis (part of speech) and semantic analysis (WordNet [18]) of the information derived from the context paths;

Evolution of the category catalogue: the context fuzzy clustering is embedded into a genetic framework able to produce automatically an updating procedure on the catalogue.

The system is written in Java 2 [16], the distributed computation is managed using **Remote Method Invocation** (**RMI**) technology supported by the SUN platform **JDK**.

4   Clustering Methodology

Let **T** be the set of the noun phrases. $\forall x \in T$ we define $\widetilde{x}$ as the *fuzzy set* "noun phrases *similar to* **x**", formally:

$$\widetilde{\mathbf{x}} = \{(t, \mu_x(t)) \mid \forall t \in T\}$$

with $\mu_x : T \to [0,1]$ as membership function.

The function is defined in order to give higher values for the noun phrase that generalizes the original term of the category. The function takes into account the synonyms for each simple term contained into the noun phrase of the category, rejecting the terms that are not synonyms or related terms. Any synonym of the simple term has a weight: the weights are higher for hypernym synonyms (generalization terms) and lower for hyponym synonyms (specialization terms), hence the clustering method brings up generalization with respect to each document matched. The membership value of a noun phrase, derived from a combination of simple terms, is given as an average of the synonyms weights.

Given **P(T)** as the power set of T, let us define the following similarity measure:

Let $x = (t_1, \dots, t_n) \in P(T)$ and $t_i \in T \; \forall i = 1..n$
$\qquad y = (h_1, \dots, h_p) \in P(T)$ and $h_j \in T \; \forall j = 1..p$

$$\mathbf{S_K}(\mathbf{x}, \mathbf{y}) = \sum_{j=1}^{p} \sum_{i=1}^{n} (\mu_{t_i}(h_j))^K \qquad \text{(shortly } x \oplus_k y) \qquad (1)$$

where **K** is the *similarity factor* of the measure.

Given a couple $(x, y) \in P(T)^2$ we define **G**: $P(T) \times P(T) \to [\,0,\,1]$ as the *coverage* of y on x:

$$\mathbf{G(x, y)} = \frac{|\{h_j|\ h_j \in y\ and\ \exists\ t_i \in x\ \ni'\ \mu_{t_i}(h_j) > 0\}|}{|x|} \qquad \text{(shortly } x \sqcap y)$$

$$\text{(2)}$$

Each category (or sub-category), defined by its noun phrases, is viewed as a cluster $\mathbf{C_j} \in \mathbf{P(T)}$. Objects of the cluster are URLs extracted from the Web documents: each URL has an associated **Context Path** as *feature vector*, represented by $\mathbf{CP_i} \in P(T)$ (for the ith context path).

In order to evaluate the membership grade μ_{ij} of the $\mathbf{CP_i}$ on cluster $\mathbf{C_j}$, a *familiarity grade* $\mathbf{A_{ij}}$ is defined; this parameter is the weight returned by the matching between context path and category, computed as the similarity measure on $\mathbf{P(T)}$ between $\mathbf{C_j}$ and $\mathbf{CP_i}$.

Up now the clusters are statically defined (their noun phrases are fixed). The dynamical behavior is provided by the genetic exploration (as defined in the next paragraph) and by a *specialization grade* **s** for each cluster, that allows us to vary the cluster dimension. The specialization grade exploits the *similarity factor* $\mathbf{K}$ that enables to modify the incidence of each similarity grade for the single terms. The next formula defines the familiarity grade using the specialization grade s_j for cluster C_j.

Familiarity Grade:

$$A_{ij} = \frac{C_j \oplus_{s_j} CP_i}{noun\ phrases\ matched\ by\ CP_i\ on\ C_j} \qquad \text{(3)}$$

$A_{ij} \in [0,\ 1]$

Membership Grade:

$$\mu_{ij} = A_{ij} \cdot (C_j \sqcap CP_i)\ \ \mu_{ij} \in [0,\ 1] \qquad \text{(4)}$$

Our clustering method exploits the concept of the *overlapping* flexibility; it allows objects to belong to all clusters.

Overlapping Property:

$$\sum_{j=1}^{|C|} \mu_{ij} \geq 0 \qquad \text{(5)}$$

Finally, the clustering method maximizes the following *Index of Quality* $J(C)$, for which an *Influence Grade* **m** is introduced in order to reduce the impact of lower μ_{ij} values. At the increasing of **m** more relevant will be the weight of the clusters characterized by a higher specialization (membership grade).

Index of Quality:

$$J(C) = \sum_{j=1}^{C}(J_j) \qquad \text{(6)}$$

$$
J_j = \begin{cases} (\sum_{i=1}^{N} \mu_{ij})^m & \text{no subcategory in } C_j \\ ((\sum_{i=1}^{N} \mu_{ij} + 1) \cdot \sum_{c}^{subcategs\ C_j} J_c)^m & \text{otherwise} \end{cases} \tag{7}
$$

with $m \in [1,\infty)$ and J_j as Index of Quality for the jth category.

Index of Quality is skilled to specialize the categories, in order to contrast the generalization spur arising from the computation of matching weights.

5   Genetic Framework

1. **Representation of genomes** – the genome is defined through a tree-based structure, namely *Category Forest*, introduced as a hierarchical model of the thematic categories. Each category is represented by a *Category Tree*. A Category Tree is identified by a *Root Category* representing a main topic. Starting from a Root Category we find the subcategory nodes (specialization of a topic) which, in their turn, may be parents of more specific topics as shown in the Figure 2.

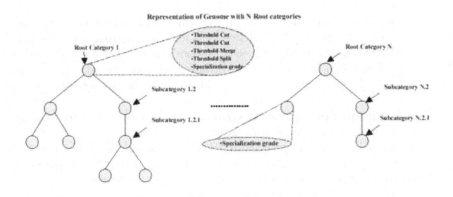

Fig. 2. Representation of Genomes.

Each root node is supported by three threshold values useful to handle the specialization grade of the thematic category.

The subcategories can be defined **fixed** in the parent category, by means of a marker; this is useful to do not move the subcategory into other parent categories as effect of the mutation operator.

2. **Definition of the fitness function** - Two different evaluations are introduced. The first, named *Clustering Fitness*, is computed by the clustering methodology in terms of Index of Quality. The second factor is the *Quality of*

Distribution (QoD), measuring the quality of distribution of the document into thematic categories. This value is computed by averaging the membership grades of the document, for each category or subcategory.

- **Clustering Fitness (Index of Quality)**, see the formulas (6) and (7)
- **Quality of Distribution (QoD):**

$$QoD = \frac{\sum(QoD_{category})}{\#root\ categories}$$

$$QoD_{category} = \frac{\widehat{\mu} + \sum(QoD_{category}\ of\ the\ subcategories)}{\#subcategories+1}$$

where $\widehat{\mu}$ is the average of membership values of the document into the category (root category or subcategory).

- **Fitness function of the individual:**

$$Fitness = QoD * ClusteringFitness$$

3. **Definition of the Crossover operator** – The crossover point is chosen randomly taking into account the root categories that can not be broken by crossover.
4. **Definition of mutation operators** – The following mutation operators are defined:
   - **Mutation Cutting** – Choose randomly both a root category and a subcategory into it: the subcategory is removed together with its subtree.
   - **Mutation Merging** – Choose randomly a root category and extract randomly two "sister" subcategories (nodes with the same parent category). The operator merges the root nodes of the two selected subcategories.
   - **Mutation Specialization Grade**– Choose randomly a root category and modify its specialization grade.
   - **Mutation Exchange Parent (Swap)** – Choose randomly a root category and extract randomly two subcategories with different parent categories. Hence, the operator swaps the parent categories.
   - **Mutation Change Parent** – Choose randomly both a root category and a subcategory. Hence, the operator moves the subtree in another parent category randomly.

6   Testing

In order to verify the efficiency of our clustering methodology we take as target the Open Directory Project(ODP) [9] a well known (public domain) project of human categorization of Web documents. We use the synonyms and related terms, computed in advance for each category of the catalogue, using WordNet [18].

Our experiment has been conducted on the following subset of the categories catalogue of ODP :

Science	Health	Arts	Bookmarks
Business	Test	Home	Sports
Private	World	Computers	Regional
Reference	Shopping	Games	News
Society	Recreation		

The URLs, with their short description, are collected in an HTML document in order to extract the corresponding Context Paths.

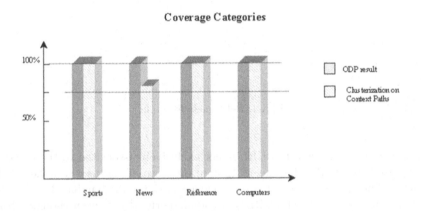

Fig. 3. Coverage Categories.

Figure 3 reports the behavior of our approach compared with ODP. We obtained automatically the same "human" categorization for the categories Sports, Reference and Computer.

As shown in the figure, the "News" category is not totally covered. This happens because into this category there are URLs not completely described. Below we give an example of context paths of some URLs (contained into ODP database) that our clustering is not able to associate to the right "News" category.

"http://www.bcity.com/bollettino:"
　"International Bulletin"
　　"International politics. Italian, French and (some) English."

"http://www.pressdigest.org/":
　"Pressdigest"
　　"International and Multilingual press digest."

The reason of this drawback is due to the WordNet database: the term "news" is not related to "bulletin" and "digest" as synonyms.

In order to highlight the role of fuzziness, Figure 4 shows the membership value of the URL http://attention.hypermart.net associated to the category "News".

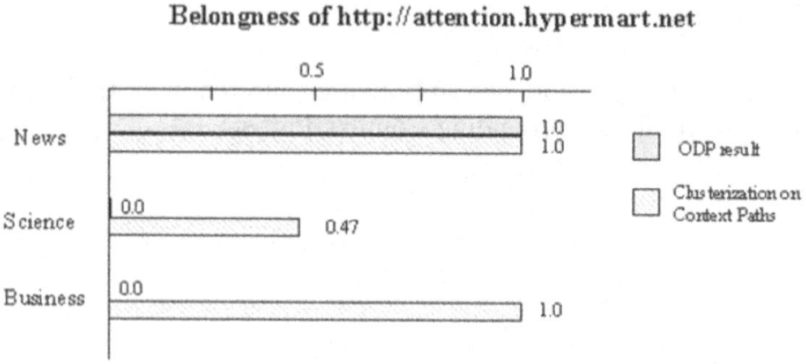

Fig. 4. Belongness example.

As noted in Figure 4, the URL is not exclusively associated to the category (as opposite of ODP): this means that in our case, if the user searches URLs about technology into the category "Science" , the search engine shall be able to return a reference to the URL attention.hypermart.net, even though with a membership value lower than the News category.

7   Related Works

The role of cluster, as useful strategy to improve Web search engine behaviors, has reported an increasing interest in these recent years. A well explored issue is to cluster the results of a Web search to better formulate the query. In [4] the query refinement, obtained also thanks to the user's feedback, guarantees a customization of a search space that better fits the user's need. In [2] it is proved how a graph partitioning based clustering technique, without the constraint to specify pre-specified ad-hoc distance functions, can effectively discover Web document similarities and associations. A linear time algorithm which creates clusters on the analysis of phrases shared between Web documents is discussed in [17]. A machine learning approach has been used in [12] and [6] for efficient topic-directed spidering and relevant topic extraction. A fuzzy matching for information retrieval searching is discussed in [5].

About the use of contextual information, the ARC system [3] automatically compiles a list of authoritative Web resources on a topic. [1] is the first concrete effort of a context-based categorization even though the methodology does not support fuzzy partitioning and the search of the better partitioning could suffer of the usual drawbacks concerning traditional clustering algorithms.

Conclusions

In this paper, we present a methodology able to cluster web document into thematic categories. The clustering algorithm is based on a fuzzy clustering method that searches the best categories catalogue for web document categorization. The categorization is performed by context, this means that the clustering is guided by the context surrounding a link in an HTML document in order to extract useful information for categorizing the document it refer to. This approach enables to be media independent, hence to perform the same strategy also for images, audio and video. As key issue of our clustering methodology we use an evolutionary approach inheriting the benefits of a genetic-level explorations. The positive benchmarks reported by comparing our results with a public-domain, significant category-based catalogue stimulates further development of our research.

References

1. Attardi, G., Di Marco S., and Salvi, D. (1998). Categorisation by Context. *Journal of Universal Compouter Science*, 4:719-736.
2. Boley, D., Gini., M., Gross, R., Hang, E-H., Hasting, K., Karypis, G., Kumar, V., Mobasher, B., and Moore, J. (1999). Partioning-based clustering for Web document categorization *Decision Support System*, 27 (1999) 329-341.
3. Chakrabarti, S., Dom, B., Gibson, D., Kleinberg, J., Rahavan, P., and Rajagopalan, S.(1998). Automatic resource list compilation by analyzing hyperlink structure and associated text. *Seventh International World Wide Web Conference*, 1998.
4. Chang, C-H., and Hsu, C-C. (1997). Customizable Multi-Engine Search tool with Clustering. *Sixth International World Wide Web Conference*, April 7-11, 1997 Santa Clara, California, USA.
5. Cohen, W. (1998). A web-based information system that reasons with structured collections of text. *Agents'98*, 1998.
6. Craven, M., DiPasquo, D., Freitag, D., McCallum, A., Mitchell, T., Nigam, K., and Slattery, S. (1998). Learning to extract symbolic knowledge from the World Wide Web. *AAAI-98*, 1998.
7. Hayes, J., and Weinstein, S. P. (1990). CONSTRUE-TIS: A system for content-based indexing of a database of news stories. *Second Annual Conference on Innovative Applications of Artificial Intelligence*, 1-5.
8. Iwayama, M. (1995). Cluster-based text categorization : a comparison of category search strategies. *SIGIR-95*, pp. 273-280.
9. Open Directory Project. URL: http://dmoz.org/about.html
10. Lawrence, S. and Giles, C. L. (1999). *Nature*, 400:107-109. *Sixteenth International Joint Conference on Artificial Intelligence (IJCAI-99)*.
11. Mase, H., Tsuji, H., Kinukawa, H., Hosoya, Y., Koutani, K., and Kiyota, K. (1996). Experimental simulation for automatic patent categorization. *Advances in Production Management Systems*, 377-382.
12. McCallum, A., Nigam, K., Rennie, J., and Seymore, K. (1999). A Machine Learning Approach to Building Domain-Specific Search Engine. *Sixteenth International Joint Conference on Artificial Intelligence (IJCAI-99)*.
13. Sahami, M., Yusufali, S., and Baldoando, M. Q., W. (1998) SONIA: A service for organizing networked information autonomously. *Third ACM Conference on Digital Libraries*.

14. Selberg, E. (1999) *Towards Comprehensive Web Search*. PhD thesis, University of Washington.
15. Selberg,E and Etzioni, O. (2000). On the Instability of Web Search Engine. *RIAO 2000*.
16. JDK Java 2 Sun. http://java.sun.com
17. Zamir, O., and Etzioni, O. (1988). Web Document Clustering: A Feasibility Demonstration. *SIGIR'98*, Melbourne, Australia, ACM Press.
18. A Lexical Database for English. URL: http://www.cogsci.princeton.edu/ wn/

Automatic Web-Page Classification by Using Machine Learning Methods

Makoto Tsukada*, Takashi Washio, and Hiroshi Motoda

Institute of Scientific and Industrial Research,
Osaka University
Mihogaoka, Ibaraki, Osaka 567-0047, JAPAN
{tsukada,washio,motoda}@sanken.osaka-u.ac.jp

Abstract. This paper describes automatic Web-page classification by using machine learning methods. Recently, the importance of portal site services is increasing including the search engine function on World Wide Web. Especially, the portal site such as Yahoo! service, which hierarchically classifies Web-pages into many categories, is becoming popular. However, the classification of Web-page into each category relies on man power, which costs much time and care. To alleviate this problem, we propose techniques to generate attributes by using co-occurrence analysis and to classify Web-page automatically based on machine learning. We apply these techniques to Web-pages on Yahoo! JAPAN and construct decision trees, which determine appropriate category for each Web-page. The performance of this proposed method is evaluated in terms of error rate, recall, and precision. The experimental evaluation demonstrates that this method provides acceptable accuracy with the classification of Web-page into top level categories on Yahoo! JAPAN.

1 Introduction

At present, the number of Web-pages on World Wide Web is increasing significantly. The task to find Web-pages, which present information satisfying our requirements by traversing hyperlinks, is difficult. Therefore, we use search engines frequently on the portal site. There are two kinds of search engines. i.e., directory-style search engines such as Yahoo! JAPAN[1] and ISIZE[2], and robot-style ones such as goo[3], excite[4] and altavista[5]. The latter displays the lists of Web-pages, which contain input keywords without checking themes characterizing respective Web-pages. For this reason these search engines are likely to provide misdirected Web-pages. On the other hand, in directory-style search engines, Web-pages stored in a database are classified with hierarchical categories compatible with their themes in order. This enables us to obtain Web-pages including information that meets our purpose by not only following input keywords but also traversing hyperlinks classifying Web-pages into categories in systematic order.

---

* Currently in CRM/BI Consulting and Services, Business Innovation Services, IBM Japan.

N. Zhong et al. (Eds.): WI 2001, LNAI 2198, pp. 303–313, 2001.
© Springer-Verlag Berlin Heidelberg 2001

However, directory-style search engines at present require that man power classify a large number of Web-pages into each appropriate category according to their contents. Therefore, this task costs much time and care. This indicates that the task to classify an ever increasing number of Web-pages becomes increasingly difficult. For example, Yahoo! JAPAN, a typical directory-style search engine, receives tremendous amount of requests to enter Web-pages into the database daily. It then occasionally takes several weeks to determine an appropriate category for each theme of Web-page, and confirms this entry in the database. We deem that automatic Web-page classification affords much easier construction of the database, and contributes to reductions in costs and man power successfully.

In the past, a considerable number of studies has been made on text classification of newspaper articles, based on k-nearest neighbor, support vector machine and so on[7][8][9][10][11][12]. In addition, many comparative studies of these methods have so far been made[7][8][9]. However, no studies in the above aim to classify Web-pages and to apply supervised learning in terms of the classification based on man power. In addition, although there is some research of supervised learning for Web-page classification in Yahoo! U.S.A.[6][13], only a few attempts at this kind of research have been made. Furthermore, no one has ever tried to classify Web-page in Japanese search engines automatically by supervised learning. Under these circumstances, our study aims at developing a technique by which to classify Web-page automatically by supervised machine learning using a man-made class attribute. In addition, we develop a method for attribute generation by using co-occurrence analysis. We then apply these techniques to classify Web-pages into top-level categories included in the index of Yahoo! JAPAN. By constructing decision trees, we evaluate them in terms of three criteria, i.e., error rate, recall and precision.

This paper is organized as follows. Our developed technique is explained in section 2. We apply these methods to classification of Web-pages in Yahoo! JAPAN and assess the accuracy of decision trees in section 3. Finally the paper ends with the concluding remarks in section 4.

2 The Proposed Methods

2.1 Extraction of Nouns from Web-Pages

In the directory-style search engine, a great deal of Web-pages classified and registered in the database are interconnected with hyperlinks and make a hierarchical tree structure to improve usability. A node in this structure indicates a category whose name accords with themes represented by Web-pages in it. As Fig. 1 illustrates, Yahoo! JAPAN has some subcategories such as *"Gambling"* below the parent category of *"Recreation and Sports"*. Furthermore, there can be hyperlinks from one category to some other categories or to top-level categories. Therefore a Web-page may be classified into multiple categories simultaneously.

We focus on the top-level page of Yahoo! JAPAN [13] and assign distinct class labels to some top-categories on this page. Web-pages corresponding to

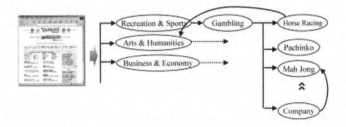

Fig. 1. The structure of hyperlinks in Yahoo! JAPAN.

each class are downloaded separately as Fig. 2 illustrates,

$$class_c \leftrightarrow \{Page_1^c, \ldots, Page_i^c, \ldots\},$$

where $Page_i^c$ indicates i-th Web-page labeled $class_c$.

We then delete all of tags such as <A HREF > and <IMG > from documents of Web-pages described by Hyper Text Markup Language and extract all nouns by morphological analysis. Morphological analysis is a technique to divide a sentence into parts of speech such as nouns, pronouns, relative pronouns, adjectives and adverbs. We suppose that some nouns in the sentence are typical to the theme of Web-page among others. For this reason we extract some nouns from documents of Web-pages. We refer to each noun as an *item* and form a *transaction page_i^c* which consists of some items $word_{ij}^c$ as follows.

$$Page_i^c =< word_{i1}^c, \ldots, word_{ij}^c, \ldots >,$$

where $word_{ij}^c$ indicates the j-th item extracted from $Page_i^c$. In addition, we integrate them into a set of transactions for each class label.

Though the system of Japanese morphological analysis can easily separate nouns from adjectives and adverbs, its problem is that it extracts not only the stems of nouns but also the desinences obscuring the meaning of nouns. These items do not imply distinct meanings from the stems of nouns. Therefore we eliminate these desinences from all transactions. Additionally, insignificant nouns such as *"thing"*, *"something"*, *"which"* and *"who"* that appear in many

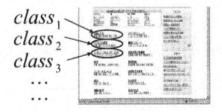

Fig. 2. Download of Web-pages according to the categories in the top page.

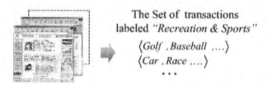

Fig. 3. The set of transactions each consisting of some items

sentences may not represent the theme of Web-pages. We select these kinds of pronouns and relative pronouns as objectively as possible, and add these pronouns to a *stoplist*. Moreover, the technical terms specialized in WWW's field are considered to be insensitive to the theme of an Web-page. For example, *"hyperlink"*, *"tag"*, *"page"*, *"form"* and *"frame"* are exceptionally popular in WWW's field and used frequently regardless of the Web page class. Even if some of these terms are strongly associated with the theme of Web-pages in a domain, these words do not provide effective information for the classification as they are involved in many other pages. We also add these WWW specific terms to the stoplist. Finally we eliminate items in the stoplist from all transactions, and construct refined transactions $Page_i^c$.

2.2 Generation of Attributes

We generate attributes to design tabular data from Web-pages by applying *basket analysis* typical of association analysis and well-known in the field of data mining. Basket analysis targets a set of transactions consisting of a set of items. A function of basket analysis is to derive itemsets having *support* greater than a user specified threshold. The support of an itemset I means how frequently I appears, and it is defined as the ratio of the number of transactions including the itemset to the total number of transactions. Itemsets having support greater than its threshold *"minimum support"* are called *"frequent itemsets"*, and the basket analysis generates all frequent itemsets. It is known that Apriori algorithm[15] efficiently extracts all frequent itemsets from the massive transaction data.

We apply the basket analysis and make frequent itemsets extracted from Web-pages as the attributes, which reflect the features of Web-pages for each class label. This is based on the simple assumption that the set of nouns characterizing the Web-pages occurs very frequently. We specify a minimum support value in advance. An example is presented in Fig. 4. Next, we merge frequent itemsets for respective classes into a set of attributes as follows.

$$\{ \underbrace{Itemset_1^1, Itemset_2^1}_{frequent\ itemset\ :\ class_1} ,\dots, \quad \underbrace{Itemset_l^c,\dots}_{frequent\ itemsets\ :\ class_c} \quad ,\dots\},$$

where $Itemset_l^c$ indicates the l-th-*frequent Itemset* extracted from the sets of transactions labeled $class_c$. These attributes are numbered as

$Attribute_1, Attribute_2,$
$\ldots, Attribute_l, \ldots$ in a sequential order. Then, the sub-data D_c composed of transactions labeled $class_c$ is constructed as depicted in Table 1 where every $flag_{mn}^c$ is represented as

$$flag_{mn}^c = \begin{cases} 1 : \forall Itemset_n^c \subset page_m^c \\ 0 : \text{the others} \end{cases}$$

This serves to predict the class of new examples by verifying whether specific nouns exist in the document of the Web-page or not. We repeat this procedure across all classes, and integrate D_c of every class into a whole data $Data = \cup_{i=1}^C D_i$ where C is the number of classes.

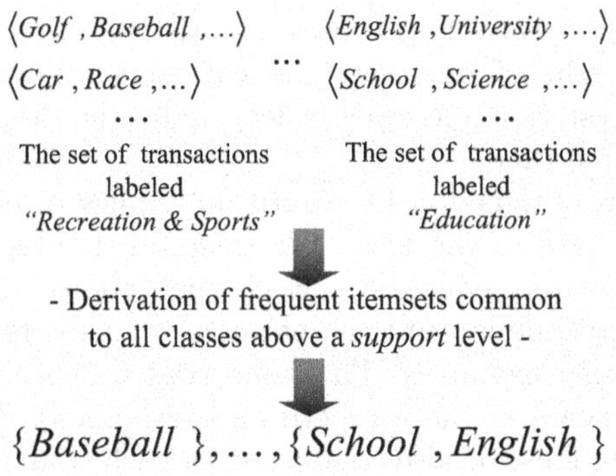

$\langle Golf, Baseball, \ldots \rangle$ $\langle English, University, \ldots \rangle$

$\langle Car, Race, \ldots \rangle$ $\cdots$ $\langle School, Science, \ldots \rangle$

$\cdots$ $\cdots$

The set of transactions   The set of transactions
labeled   labeled
"Recreation & Sports"   "Education"

- Derivation of frequent itemsets common
to all classes above a *support* level -

$\{Baseball\}, \ldots, \{School, English\}$

Fig. 4. Derivation of frequent itemsets common to all classes above a *support* level

Table 1. A sub-data set D_c for $class_c$

	$Attribute_1$ ... $Attribute_n$ ...	class
$Page_1^c$	$flag_{11}^c$	... $class_c$
...	... ...	... $class_c$
$Page_m^c$	... ... $flag_{mn}^c$	... $class_c$
...	... ...	... $class_c$

2.3   Binary Class Data

We divide *Data* into a set of local data $Data_c$, each having examples of binary classes: positive examples of $class_c$ and its negative examples. The main reason is that a major supervised learning method can not classify each instance into multiple classes at once, though some documents may belong to multiple categories.

2.4   Application of Decision Tree Learning

Once $Data_c$ is obtained for each class, a decision tree learning technique C4.5[14] is applied for the classification of Web-pages. The main reason why we chose the decision tree method for the Web-page categorization is the comprehensibility of the induced decision rule. If we apply the other classification methods such as K-nearest neighbors and neural network, the conditions for the classification is not explicitly shown, and the check of the validity of the classification may not be easy for the analysts of the portal site. Decision tree algorithms create a tree data structure that can be used to classify new instances. Each node of a decision tree contains a test, and the result is used to decide the branch to follow from that node for each new instance. A decision tree is inferred by growing it from the root downward and greedily selecting the next best attribute for each new branch added to the tree. C4.5[14] uses a statistical criterion called *gain ratio* to evaluate the "goodness" of a test. The leaf nodes contain class labels instead of tests. When a test example reach a leaf node, the decision tree classifies it using the label stored there.

After the tree is obtained, C4.5 algorithm applies *n-fold cross-validation* to evaluate the error rate of the tree. This method divides all examples into n subsets of approximately equal size. Each time one of the n subsets is used as a set of testing examples and the other $n - 1$ subsets are put together to form a set of training examples. The same trial is repeated n times, and the averaged performance over the n repetition is evaluated. Strictly speaking, the attribute generation must be also conducted for each trial. However, because the basket analysis is a time consuming process, it is done only once over the entire data in this study. This approximation would not affect the evaluation result significantly since the frequency of the frequent itemsets may not change very much across datasets, each with size of $(n - 1)/n$ of the total, used for n-fold cross validation.

3   Experimental Evaluation

3.1   Experimental Settings

We performed the experiments on the classification of Web-pages on 5 domains of 14 top-categories in Yahoo! JAPAN: "*Arts & Humanities*", "*Business & Eco-nomy*", "*Education*", "*Government*" and "*Health*". We randomly downloaded 200 Web-pages per category. Because some pages belong to multiple categories, the total number of the Web-pages becomes less than 1000. But, we further added some pages by downloading from randomly selected categories among them to achieve the number of 1000 pages in the data.

Next, the HTML tag removal and the morphological analysis are applied to the data of each Web-page. The morphological analysis is done by using the system "*chasen*"[16] developed at Nara Institute of Science and Technology, and its set of noun keywords $Page_i^c$ is derived. We generated meaningful attributes based on the 1000 $Page_i^c$ data by applying basket analysis under three support levels, 10%, 20% and 30%, and obtained three data sets of *Data*: Sup10, Sup20 and Sup30 respectively. Finally we constructed a decision tree for sub-data D_c of Sup10, Sup20 and Sup30 by C4.5[14] which is the most representative tool of decision tree learning.

3.2 Performance Measures

The performance of the induced classifier is evaluated in terms of *Error rate*, *Recall*, and *Precision*. First, we define *Error rate* as follows.

$$Error\ rate = \frac{the\ number\ of\ all\ testing\ examples\ classified\ erroneously}{the\ number\ of\ all\ testing\ examples}$$

Error rate denotes the rate of both positive and negative testing example classified erroneously by a decision tree. The lower rate represents the higher accuracy of the decision tree.

In addition, we define *Recall* and *Precision* used in the evaluation of a information retrieval system frequently.

$$Recall = \frac{the\ number\ of\ testing\ examples\ classified\ correctly\ as\ positive}{the\ number\ of\ positive\ testing\ examples}$$

$$Precision = \frac{the\ number\ of\ testing\ examples\ classified\ correctly\ as\ positive}{the\ number\ of\ testing\ examples\ classified\ as\ positive}$$

The less the leak of classification from positive examples is, the larger *Recall* is, and the smaller the classification error of positive examples is, the larger *Precision* is. Both *Recall* and *Precision* are the indicators taking only positive examples into consideration. Therefore they qualify themselves for the reasonable evaluation of how correctly the decision trees can provide testing examples with the positive decision of the class labels. The mean value of each measure over the 4 times validations is used for the evaluation in the experiment of 4-fold cross-validation.

3.3 Results

Table 2 shows the results of the evaluation: means of *Error rate*, *Recall*, and *Precision* for the decision trees. The first column shows the data set labels. The second and the third columns of the upper half show the number of attributes generated and the minimum support level. Table 2 indicates that the values of *Precision* are higher than those of *Recall* for each category. Generally speaking, the values of *Recall* and *Precision* have a trade off relation by their definitions. Table 2 shows that *Precision* is much better than *Recall* in the trade off for the higher minimum support values. The values of *Error rate* almost lies between 8% and 16%. The results also show a tendency that the values of *Error rate* are lower for the lower support values. In case of lower minimum support, the decision tree can have better accuracy, i.e., lower *Error rate* and higher *Recall*, because it is induced from larger number of attributes, i.e., more information on the given data. On the other hand, the decision tree uses only a limited number of significant attributes under higher minimum support, and this effect increases the value of *Precision*, because the Web-pages characterized by the significant attributes are selected for each class.

Table 2. Performance of decision trees classifying examples(%).

data	attribute	minsup (%)	"Arts & Humanities"			"Business & Economy"		
			Error rate	Recall	Precision	Error rate	Recall	Precision
Sup10	823	10	12.6	50.5	79.2	14.3	56.5	67.6
Sup20	78	20	13.3	44.0	80.8	15.0	45.5	69.6
Sup30	19	30	13.9	32.0	95.3	13.6	45.5	77.4

data	"Education"			"Government"			"Health"		
	Error rate	Recall	Precision	Error rate	Recall	Precision	Error rate	Recall	Precision
Sup10	8.30	69.0	86.7	13.8	45.5	76.1	8.90	65.0	87.2
Sup20	10.9	65.2	77.5	14.2	38.5	80.4	16.1	46.6	64.7
Sup30	10.4	57.5	86.6	14.5	32.5	86.7	15.3	29.3	83.0

Table 3. Instances of the attributes(in case of Sup20).

Arts & Humanities	Business & Economy	Education	Government	Health
illustration	enterprise	success	society	research
renewal	business	classroom	politics	life
image	guide	school	policy	age
reproduction	month	learning	election	environment
without-notice	information	education	opinion	medical
{without-notice,	{month,	{learning,	activity	health
reproduction}	information}	education }		
c	...	...	...	...

Table 3 shows some concrete instances of the attributes derived from the transactions of Web-pages. Notation {A,B..} in Table 3 represents an attribute which is a frequent itemset consisting of multiple nouns. It is clear that specific nouns tend to appear in the Web-pages that belong to a specific class. Moreover, some specific combinations of nouns characterize the Web-pages of each class. Thus, the application of attribute generation based on basket analysis has a contribution to provide some information for the inductive classification.

We present a concrete decision tree under the conditions of data: Sup20 and class: *Arts & Humanities*. ''Arts & Humanities'' labeled on the leaf means that the conclusion is classified as "*Arts & Humanities*", otherwise the conclusion is classified as not "*Arts & Humanities*". The decision tree contains some decision nodes conditioned by the combinations of multiple nouns. This clarifies that the attributes consisting of multiple nouns have some contribution to the classification.

```
illustration = 1: ''Arts & Humanities''
illustration = 0:
```

```
|    guide = 1: non-''Arts & Humanities''
|    guide = 0:
|    |    {without-notice,reproduction} = 0: non-''Arts & Humanities''
|    |    {without-notice,reproduction} = 1:
|    |    |    contents = 1: non-''Arts & Humanities''
|    |    |    contents = 0:
|    |    |    |    {month,information} = 1: non-''Arts & Humanities''
|    |    |    |    {month,information} = 0:
|    |    |    |    |    election = 0: ''Arts & Humanities''
|    |    |    |    |    election = 1: non-''Arts & Humanities''
```

A simple rule derived from this decision tree by tracing a branch is

```
illustration = 1 -> ''Arts & Humanities''.
```

When a certain Web-page contains the noun "illustration", we can recognize that this Web-page belongs to the category of *Arts & Humanities* from this rule.

```
illustration = 0
guide = 0
{without-notice,reproduction} = 0
-> non-''Arts & Humanities''
```

This rule is for the other class. When a certain Web-page doesn't contain the nouns "illustration", "guide" and the combination of "without-notice" and "reproduction" at all, this Web-page is concluded not to belong to the category of "*Arts & Humanities*".

4   Discussion

In the research of text categorization, methods of attribute generation have been focused, and the high dimensional feature vector consisting of the attributes has been used to represent each text. However, this causes the sparse distribution of the text in the high dimensional feature space, and prevents efficient and accurate text categorization. Thus, many researchers in text categorization has attached importance to the aggressive dimensionality reduction of the feature space, and developed techniques to remove or lump comparatively uninformative features. One of the representative approach of dimensional reduction is the use of thesaurus. In this field, respective words, which occur in documents, are assigned to features respectively. We also tried a method to use Japanese thesaurus to lump the variety of the words appearing in the texts for the purpose of comparison with the technique based on basket analysis. We applied this method of attribute generation to the same data as described in 3.1, and evaluated the results under same conditions. In consequence, the method generating attributes by thesaurus couldn't afford higher performance.

According to the result of Table 2, the minimum support level in the basket analysis is a parameter to change *Error rate* and the trade off between *Recall* and *Precision* resulted in the classification. Thus, the basket analysis used in the attribute generation provides a measure to tune these performances in addition to the generation of attributes. The minimum support level can be set depending on the objective of the Web-page classification. If the objective is to classify the Web-pages in a given data set, the minimum support should be set at a low value, since the high accuracy of the classification is needed in this objective. On the other hand, if the objective is to collect some Web-pages of a class from massive Web-page data, the minimum support should be set at a high value, because the high *Precision* of the classification is obtained, i.e., only the high purity of the classified Web-pages is obtained. Since the value of *Precision* can be very high for a high minimum support level, the proposed approach can provide an efficient measure to collect Web-pages of an objective class.

The proposed approach also provides a set of informative rules to classify the Web-pages. These rules can be referred to pick up some relevant conditions to manually classify the Web-pages for the directory-style search engines such as Yahoo! JAPAN. This is an advantage of our approach, which uses rule-based inductive classification.

5   Conclusion

Though a few studies worked on the Web-page classification for the directory-style search engines, none of them have reported the detailed performance of their approaches[6][13]. In contrast, we developed techniques including attribute generation and classification to classify Web-pages without using man power, and evaluated the detailed performance of the techniques. In summary, the proposed technique can be used for the automated collection of Web-pages of an objective class from massive data.

Some issues remain for our future work. One is the evaluation of the classification of Web-pages in various categories, because the evaluation has been made only for the top level category classification of Yahoo! JAPAN. We also intend to develop an approach for hierarchical classifications along the hierarchy of the directory-style search engines.

References

1. Yahoo! Japan < http : //www.yahoo.co.jp/ >.
2. ISIZE < http : //www.isize.com/ >.
3. goo < http : //www.goo.ne.jp/ >.
4. excite < http : //www.excite.co.jp/ >.
5. altavista < http : //www.altavista.com/ >.
6. Yahoo! U.S.A < http : //www.yahoo.com/ >.
7. Yang, Y. and Liu, X., A re-examination of text categorization methods.
8. Yang, Y., An Evaluation of Statistical Approaches to Text Categorization. April 10, 1997.
9. Yang, Y. and Pederson, J. O., A Comparative Study on Feature Selection in Text Categorization.

10. Iwayama, M. and Tokunaga, T., Hierarchical Bayesian Clustering for Automatic Text Classification. 14th International Joint Conference on Artificial Intelligence(IJCAI'95), pp.1322-1327, Montreal, 1995.
11. Iwayama, M. and Tokunaga, T., Cluster-Based Text Categorization: A Comparison of Category Search Strategies. 18th Annual International ACM SIGIR Conference on Research and Development in Information Retrieval (SIGIR'95), pp.273-280,Seattle, 1995.
12. Joachims, T., Text Categorization with Support Vector Machines:Learning with Many Relevant Features.
13. Mladenić, D., Turning Yahoo into Automatic Web-Page Classifier. 13th European Conference on Artificial Intelligence Young Researcher Paper(1998).
14. Quinlan, J. R., *C4.5: Programs for Machine Learning*, Morgan Kaufmann, 1993.
15. Agrwal, R. and Srikant, R., First algorithms for mining association rules, In *Proceedings of the 20th VLDB Conference*, pp.487-499, 1994.
16. chasen $< http : //chasen.aist - nara.ac.jp/index.html.en >$.

A Theory and Approach to Improving Relevance Ranking in Web Retrieval

Z.W. Wang and R.B. Maguire

Department of Computer Science, University of Regina
Regina, Saskatchewan, Canada S4S 0A2
{zhiwei/rbm}@cs.uregina.ca

1 Introduction

1.1 The Necessity for Similarity-Based Matching

The development of the World Wide Web (WWW) makes a huge amount of information available on-line, and the amount of information continues to increase. As of March 2001 the Google search engine searches 1,346,966,000 Web pages. Many search systems have been developed to manage this massive collection of information. Investigation shows that the primary method used by these systems is classification. Unfortunately, classification has an intrinsic restriction. Consider this example. Recently, we sent a query that consists of the word "computer" to Google, and Google found 33,220,000 relevant Web pages. This number far exceeds anything that people can possibly begin to read. This problem is *intrinsic* to classification, which means it cannot be avoided. The problem is explained by the Pigeonhole Principle (i.e. Dirichlet's Box Principle) [10]. Suppose we can classify Web pages using all the English words in a dictionary. Given a particular keyword, let us calculate on average how many Web pages will be classified as relevant. Let $totalKeywords$ be the number of all keywords in a vocabulary list. Let $averageKeywords$ be the average number of keywords that a Web document may have. Let the number of all Web pages be n. Let the number of relevant Web pages be $numberRelevant$. Then we have:

$$numberRelevant \approx \frac{n \times averageKeywords}{totalKeywords}.$$

If $n = 1346966000$, $averageKeywords = 100$, and $totalKeywords = 10000$, then $numberRelevant$ is 13469660.

To address this problem, many search engines employ *relevance ranking*. When presenting the search results, such search engines assign a number to each document to indicate its degree of relevance. This number usually is calculated based on the *hits* (occurrences) of the keywords in the document. The Web pages then are sorted in descending order of relevance. This approach actually is a very simple form of similarity-based matching which has been intensively studied in the vector space model used in the field of information retrieval [2,8, 16].

N. Zhong et al. (Eds.): WI 2001, LNAI 2198, pp. 314–323, 2001.
© Springer-Verlag Berlin Heidelberg 2001

This a good direction to follow in order to solve this problem. Unfortunately, problems arise in introducing true similarity-based matching because, as we will show, the theory and methodologies are not sufficient in the conventional model. In this paper, we will present a new model and approach to dealing with the problem. This new method has a sound theoretical basis and offers guidelines for designing new types of Web search systems.

1.2   Deficiencies of the Traditional Vector Space Model

Very briefly, the main idea of similarity-based matching in the vector space model can be stated as follows: Documents (i.e. Web pages) and queries are indexed and represented as vectors in a Euclidean space. A similarity/dissimilarity function is chosen to determine the similarity (i.e. degree of relevance) of each document to the query. The documents then are sorted according to the value of the similarity function. The result presented to the user is a list of documents in descending order of similarity.

This approach is intuitively appealing, but our observation shows that there are at least the following problems with the conventional vector space model:

(1) Precise interpretation and definition of similarity/dissimilarity functions, as well as their formal properties, are not fully studied. Typically, a similarity/dissimilarity function is justified based on intuitive arguments or geometric properties [12]. Consequently, as we will show in Example 1, some similarity/dissimilarity functions show abnormal features that are contradictory to common sense.

(2) The conventional vector space model has not been able to justify a suitable and universally applicable similarity/dissimilarity function. Many different similarity/dissimilarity functions have been proposed and studied. However, there are no general criteria to determine in which situations a particular similarity/dissimilarity should be used.

(3) Euclidean distance is a simple and natural way to measure the closeness of two vectors. If the ranking result using a similarity/dissimilarity function is the same as using the distance function, then there is no need for the similarity/dissimilarity function. If the results are different, one should be able to justify not using the Euclidean distance.

Let us consider an example to support our argument in point 1.

Example 1 *Assume that a system uses the popular pseudo-cosine function to determine the similarity between vectors:*

$$scos(\mathbf{q}, \mathbf{d}) = \frac{\sum_{i=1}^{n} q_i d_i}{\sum_{i=1}^{n} q_i \sum_{i=1}^{n} d_i}. \tag{1}$$

Let $D = \{\mathbf{d_1}, \mathbf{d_2}, \mathbf{d_3}, \mathbf{d_4}\}$, where $\mathbf{d_1} = (100, 0, 0)$, $\mathbf{d_2} = (0, 100, 0)$, $\mathbf{d_3} = (0, 0, 100)$, $\mathbf{d_4} = (30, 34, 36)$. Suppose that a user does not want articles too focused on a single topic and prefers $\mathbf{d_4}$ the most. Naturally enough, he/she *specifies a query close to d_4, that is $q = \{30, 34, 36\}$. Calculation shows: $scos(q, d_1) = 0.3$, $scos(q, d_2) = 0.34$, $scos(q, d_3) = 0.36$, $scos(q, d_4) = 0.3352$. The ranking is $d_3 \succ d_2 \succ d_4 \succ d_1$, where d_4 is the second last one preferred.*

This example shows, using the pseudo-cosine measure, a document is not found to be the most similar to itself. Common sense suggests that an item should be the most similar to itself.

2 Improving Relevance Ranking Using an Advanced Similarity-Matching Mechanism

2.1 Theoretical Background

In the paper "A Non-Euclidean Model for Web Retrieval" [14], we analyzed the deficiencies in the conventional vector space model and proposed a Riemann space model that addresses these problems. A more detailed and thorough study can be found in [13]. This subsection will only briefly introduce the main idea of relevant topics in an intuitive manner.

The foundation of the Riemann space model is built on axioms that are consistent with our intuition. For example, our intuition suggests that a similarity should have at least the following properties:

(1) Any item should be among those items found to be the most similar to itself.
(2) If a is similar to b to some degree, then b should be similar to a to the same degree.
(3) If a and c are similar to b, then a and c should bear some degree of similarity to each other.

In light of these three requirements, the Riemann space model defines a dissimilarity as follows:

Definition 1 *Let $D \subset \Re^n$. A dissimilarity function $d()$ is a non-negative function from $D \times D$ to $\Re$,*

$$d : D \times D \to \Re, \qquad (a, b) \mapsto d(a, b)$$

satisfying the following axioms: for all $a, b, c \in D$,

$$(1)\ d(a, a) = 0.$$
$$(2)\ d(a, b) = d(b, a).$$
$$(3)\ d(a, b) + d(b, c) \geq d(a, c).$$

Note that the notion of dissimilarity is very similar to the well established mathematical notion *metric* [3,4].

The Riemann space model believes that dissimilarity is an *intrinsic* property of Web space, because it is determined by the contents of the documents. If for all possible pairs of documents, the dissimilarities between them are proportionate to the Euclidean distances, then the similarity function can be replaced by the Euclidean distance, and the Web space can be modeled as a Euclidean space. Otherwise, a non-Euclidean curved space (i.e. Riemann space) will work better.

Example 2 *Consider 5 documents (points):* d_1, d_2, d_3, d_4, d_5 *in a 2-dimensional space. Let* $\|d_i, d_j\|$ *represent the dissimilarity between* d_i *and* d_j *measured by a certain formula. Assume that:* $\|d_1, d_2\| = \|d_2, d_3\| = \|d_3, d_4\| = \|d_4, d_1\| = a$. *We can arrange* d_1, d_2, d_3 *and* d_4 *in a Euclidean plane so that the four points are the vertices of a parallelogram. In this case, the Euclidean distance is consistent with the dissimilarity measure.*

However, let us further assume that: $\|d_1, d_5\| = \|d_2, d_5\| = \|d_3, d_5\| = \|d_4, d_5\| = a$. *Euclidean plane geometry tells us that, in this case, there is no way to arrange all these 5 points in a plane so that the Euclidean distance is consistent with the dissimilarity measure.*

On the other hand, if we place these 5 points on the surface of a sphere, with d_5 *at the north pole and the other 4 points evenly distributed along the equator, the length of the great circle arc between the points is a measure that is consistent with the dissimilarity measure.*

The great circles are the *geodesics* on a sphere. They correspond to straight lines in a Euclidean space. Example 2 shows that the dissimilarity may not be consistent with Euclidean distance, but can be consistent with the geodesic distance on a curved surface.

In the conventional vector space model, Web space is thought of as a flat space. The curvature is zero everywhere and hence the *topography* is a flat plane. A similarity/dissimilarity function is thought to be applied on the whole space. If the ranking results of two different similarity/dissimilarity functions are different, it is an indication of inconsistency. There exist many similarity/dissimilarity functions and not all of them are consistent with each other [6,9]. This inconsistency cannot be explained in the vector space model. As a result, there exists a long standing open problem, that is, how to find a set of criteria to determine under what conditions a particular similarity/dissimilarity function should be used.

However, the same phenomenon can be explained in the Riemann space model. In the Riemann space model, Web space is curved. Just like there are mountains, canyons, and plains on the Earth, the *topography* at different regions in Web space is different. If a similarity/dissimilarity function fits in one region, there is no guarantee that it fits in other regions. In this explanation, we need as many similarity/dissimilarity functions as the number of different types of topography in Web space. This also explains why there is always motivation to invent new similarity/dissimilarity functions. We need a function for each type of topography.

From this point of view, the diversity of similarity/dissimilarity functions is not an indication of disagreement, but support for the notion that Web space is curved. These similarity/dissimilarity functions are not in conflict with each other; instead, they cooperate with each other.

2.2   Localization

Riemann space can explain previously unexplained phenomena, but a more practical question is, how to apply it in Web retrieval to improve the performance of relevance ranking.

In the Riemann space model, Web space is a curved space, and the dissimilarity is the geodesic distance. The geodesic distance provides a good mental image for the notion of *dissimilarity*, but it is difficult to implement. The calculation of true geodesic distance involves integration on a differentiable manifold. This is too complicated to be of practical use. We will not exert efforts in this direction.

Instead, we will take a more pragmatic approach. Web space is a curved space. Intuitively, it is like a surface. The shape of the surface may be very complicated; however, a portion of the surface is homeomorphic to a portion of a Euclidean space (a flat space), and it can be simulated by a portion of this *flat* space. This flat space is the *tangent space*.

Given a query, it corresponds to specifying a point $\mathbf{q}$ in the Web space. In the vector space model, the similarities of *all* documents to the query should be calculated in order to rank the documents. For a small collection of documents, this method is fine. But for a large collection of documents such as found in the Web space, this practice is unnecessary and wasteful.

In the Riemann space model, we divide the retrieval procedure into different stages. In the first stage, we formulate a query and consider it as a point in the Web space. In the second stage, we use a less computationally expensive retrieval method, i.e. classification, to filter out any obviously irrelevant Web pages, and localize the ranking candidates to a small collection, i.e. a neighborhood of the query. In the third stage, we use a more advanced, and hence more computationally expensive method, to rank the documents in the neighborhood. Since the method is more advanced, the ranking is expected to be more accurate. Since this expensive ranking is performed only in a neighborhood, the overall computational cost is reduced.

2.3   Associated Basis

The next task is to construct this more advanced ranking method in a neighborhood. To this end, we will use a linear function. Theoretically, this linear function should be able to simulate any complicated similarity function, and provide the same ranking result in the neighborhood. To do this, we need to build a curvilinear coordinate system in every tangent space according to the *associated basis*. Given a point $\mathbf{q}$ in a Riemann space, its associated basis can be roughly thought as a set of n independent vectors, where n is the number of dimensions of the (curved) space. The angles between each pair of vectors are not necessarily right angles. More importantly, these angles change when $\mathbf{q}$ changes to another place. For the sake of simplicity, we omit the strict mathematical definition for an associated basis which can be found in [13]. In the following paragraphs, we will use analogies to explain why a simple linear function can be used to simulate a complicated similarity function, and what an associated basis looks like.

First we explain why a linear function can simulate a complicated similarity function. Let us consider a 2-dimensional curved space. It can be thought of as a surface in $\Re^3$. Given a point $\mathbf{q}$, a similarity function is supposed to be able to approximate the geodesic distances of other points to $\mathbf{q}$. A linear function in the tangent space (i.e. tangent plane, in this 2 dimensional case) can only calculate the straight line distances of the corresponding points in the tangent plane to $\mathbf{q}$. However, if we use the *curvilinear coordinate system* [1,7] defined by the associated basis, and limit the calculation inside a neighborhood of $\mathbf{q}$, the geodesic distance will be a monotonic function of the straight line distance. As far as ranking is concerned, the result is the same. This is somewhat like the fact that a surface can be approximated by a polyhedron. The difference is that a polyhedron has only a finite number of facets, but in our approach, for a neighborhood of each point $\mathbf{q}$, the neighborhood corresponds with a portion in T_q, the tangent plane of $\mathbf{q}$.

Next we explain associated bases. Consider a neighborhood of $\mathbf{q}$. It is a part of the surface and can be viewed as a homeomorphism of a region in a plane. A homeomorphism is a one-to-one correspondence between the points of two geometric figures that is continuous in both directions. Intuitively, one can consider the region in the plane to be made of rubber which can be deformed to the shape of the neighborhood. If you have a grid in the plane in which two sets of lines are at right angle, after deformation, the angles may not be right angles. If, for each point in the plane region, there is a set of two vectors which are along the directions of the two sets of grid lines before the deformation, these vectors form orthogonal bases. After deformation, the angles between these pair of vectors are not necessarily right angles. Moreover, at different points, the angles may vary. These pairs of vectors assign every point in the neighborhood an associated basis. The associated basis at $\mathbf{q}$ defines a curvilinear coordinate system in the tangent plane. The angles between vectors in the associated basis of $\mathbf{q}$ are associated with the shape of the surface at $\mathbf{q}$. In the case of Web space, the shape in a neighborhood of a point decides the geodesics, which in turn decide how similarity is calculated.

In Subsection 2.5, we will show how to use associated basis to calculate the dissimilarity.

2.4 Curvilinear Coordinate System

The curvilinear system is a fundamental mathematical concept. However, since it is not used as often as the orthonormal coordinate system, people may not be familiar with it. In this subsection, we review some relevant basic concepts and show how to calculate the inner product of two vectors using a curvilinear coordinate system.

A fundamental operation in a vector space is the *inner product*. A basis $T = \{\mathbf{t_1}, \mathbf{t_2}, \dots, \mathbf{t_n}\}$ is *orthonormal* if $\mathbf{t_i} \cdot \mathbf{t_j} = \delta_{i,j}$, where $\mathbf{t_i} \cdot \mathbf{t_j}$ is the inner product of $\mathbf{t_i}$ and $\mathbf{t_j}$ and $\delta_{i,j}$ is the Kronecker Delta defined as:

$$\delta_{i,j} = \begin{cases} 1 \text{ if } i = j \\ 0 \text{ otherwise} \end{cases}.$$

In the conventional vector space model, it is assumed that the keywords form an orthonormal basis. In this case, the relationships between two keywords are *dyadic*, which means having only two choices. If two keywords are *synonyms*, they are combined into one keyword and treated as identical, i.e., $t_i \cdot t_i = 1$. If two keywords cannot be thought as synonyms, they are thought to be totally unrelated, i.e., $t_i \cdot t_i = 0$. There is little evidence to support these assumptions.

In a curvilinear coordinate system, the angles between each pair of axes are not necessarily right angles. Let $T = \{t_1, t_2, \ldots, t_n\}$ represent the vectors in the associated basis. Define an array $g = \{g_{i,j}\}_{i,j=1,\ldots,n}$ as below:

$$g = \begin{pmatrix} t_1 \cdot t_1 & t_1 \cdot t_2 & \ldots & t_1 \cdot t_n \\ t_2 \cdot t_1 & t_2 \cdot t_2 & \ldots & t_2 \cdot t_n \\ \ldots & \ldots & \ldots \ldots \\ t_n \cdot t_1 & t_n \cdot t_2 & \ldots & t_n \cdot t_n \end{pmatrix}.$$

If $g_{i,j} = \delta_{i,j}$, then T forms an orthonormal coordinate system. Otherwise T forms a *curvilinear coordinate system*. If we assume that the keywords form a curvilinear system, then we do not need to require that the relationship between two keywords is either identical or totally unrelated. This is more natural than the orthonormal view.

2.5   Associated Bases and Keywords

In the Riemann space model, we assume that the keywords form associated bases. We will show that this is an important improvement. In this assumption, we do not require the relationship between a pair of keywords to be the same for every collection of documents. This provides a theoretical basis for Formula 2.

We mentioned that the angles between each pair of vectors in an associated basis are not necessarily right angles and these angles change when query q changes to another place. Semantically, this means that, if the topic being discussed changes, the relationships between keywords may change. This assumption is reasonable. For example, given two keywords "father" and "mother," if the discussion is about "parents' duties," the two words should be considered as closely related. However, if the topic discussed is "women rights," most likely they are unrelated.

Our next task is to define the relationship between keywords. Like many other researchers [5,11,15], we will make use of the statistical information about distributions of keywords in documents.

Let $D = \{d_1, d_2, \ldots, d_m\}$ be a subset of Web documents. Each document $d_i, i = 1, 2, \ldots, m$, is represented as

$$d_i = (w_{i,1}, w_{i,2}, \ldots, w_{i,n}),$$

where $w_{i,j}$ is the weight of keyword t_j in document d_i. The weights may be determined by the frequency of a keyword in a document, the occurrence of a keyword in a document, or any other formula. Generally, weight $w_{i,j}$ indicates the degree of relevance between keyword t_j and document d_i.

Consider the $(m \times n)$ matrix

$$w = \begin{pmatrix} w_{1,1} & w_{1,2} & \cdots & w_{1,n} \\ w_{2,1} & w_{2,2} & \cdots & w_{2,n} \\ \cdots & \cdots & \cdots\cdots \\ w_{m,1} & w_{m,2} & \cdots & w_{m,n} \end{pmatrix}.$$

Each column of matrix w consists of the weights of the corresponding keywords in all the documents in D.

A simple way to define the inner product between keywords is:

$$\mathbf{t_i} \cdot \mathbf{t_j} = \sum_{k=1}^{m} w_{i,k} w_{j,k}. \tag{2}$$

It is easy to verify that this formula satisfies the definition of inner product. It is obvious that the value of the inner product may change if the set of documents changes. This complies with the fact that they form associated bases. Note that this is only a primitive formula. Further improvement may possible. As long as the formula satisfies the definition of inner product, all our arguments hold.

An important issue is that without the concept of associated basis, Formula 2 cannot be justified. When dealing with a small collection of documents, one might put all the documents in D, without bothering with all the details we discuss here. Actually, this approximates the document space as a Euclidean space. But when dealing with a large collection of documents, such as Web space, difficulties arise. If all of the documents are used, computation is not possible. If a sample set of documents is used, it is impossible to know which sample to choose, because different samples give different results. However, by introducing the concept of associated basis, these problems do not exist. To the contrary, this phenomenon can be viewed as direct supporting evidence of associated basis, and indirect evidence that the Web space can be more accurately modeled as a curved space.

A possible criticism may be that, for some document set $D = \{\mathbf{d_1}, \mathbf{d_2}, \ldots, \mathbf{d_m}\}$, the set of keywords $T = \{\mathbf{t_1}, \mathbf{t_2}, \ldots, \mathbf{t_n}\}$ may not be linearly independent. For instance, this happens when $m < n$. To solve this, we may require that D contain n linearly independent vectors (i.e. documents). This requirement seems reasonable, in that to infer something, one must have a minimum requirement of available information.

After $\mathbf{t_i} \cdot \mathbf{t_j}$ is defined for $i = 1, \ldots, n; j = 1, \ldots, n$, we can define the inner product of any pair of documents. Let $\mathbf{d_i}, \mathbf{d_j}$ be two document vectors:

$$\mathbf{d_i} = (w_{i,1}, w_{i,2}, \ldots, w_{i,n}),$$

$$\mathbf{d_j} = (w_{j,1}, w_{j,2}, \ldots, w_{j,n}).$$

Then $\mathbf{d_i}$ and $\mathbf{d_j}$ can be expressed as linear combinations of vectors in T:

$$\mathbf{d_i} = w_{i,1}\mathbf{t_1} + w_{i,2}\mathbf{t_2} + \ldots + w_{i,n}\mathbf{t_n},$$

$$\mathbf{d_j} = w_{j,1}\mathbf{t_1} + w_{j,2}\mathbf{t_2} + \ldots + w_{i,n}\mathbf{t_n}.$$

The inner product of $\mathbf{d_i}$ and $\mathbf{d_j}$ is:

$$\mathbf{d_i} \cdot \mathbf{d_j} = (w_{i,1}\mathbf{t_1} + w_{i,2}\mathbf{t_2} + \ldots + w_{i,n}\mathbf{t_n}) \cdot (\mathbf{d_j} = w_{j,1}\mathbf{t_1} + w_{j,2}\mathbf{t_2} + \ldots + w_{i,n}\mathbf{t_n})$$

$$= \sum_{k,l=1}^{n} w_{i,k}w_{j,l}\mathbf{t_k} \cdot \mathbf{t_l}.$$

From $\mathbf{t_k} \cdot \mathbf{t_l} = g_{k,l}$, we have:

$$\mathbf{d_i} \cdot \mathbf{d_j} = \sum_{k,l=1}^{n} g_{k,l}w_{i,k}w_{j,l}. \qquad (3)$$

Note that when T is an orthonormal system equation (3) will be written as:

$$\mathbf{d_i} \cdot \mathbf{d_j} = \sum_{k=1}^{n} w_{i,k}w_{j,k}. \qquad (4)$$

This is the ordinary formula used in Euclidean space.

When the inner product is defined, the distance between the query $\mathbf{q} = (q_1, q_2, \ldots, q_n)$ and a document $\mathbf{d} = (d_1, d_2, \ldots, d_n)$ is:

$$dist(\mathbf{q}, \mathbf{d}) = \sqrt{\sum_{i,j=1}^{n} g_{i,j}(q_i - d_i)(q_j - d_j)}, \qquad (5)$$

As we explained, in a neighborhood of query $\mathbf{q}$, ranking according to this distance produces the same result as with the *true* dissimilarity function.

3   Conclusion

In our implementation of an experimental system, we found many important and interesting issues such as how to cluster keywords to reduce the cost of computation. These issues are the focus of continuing research. The main contributions of this paper are as follows: First, we justified the application of similarity-based matching in Web retrieval. This way, the methodology used in traditional information systems can be transplanted into Web retrieval, and a more advanced ranking can be used in connection with the classification method in Web search systems. Secondly, we introduced the associated basis. The relationships between keywords are considered. This is more reasonable than the conventional vector space model. Thirdly, our approach is dynamic, which means we also consider the set of documents in which we are interested.

The theory and methodology introduced in the paper provide a sound theoretical basis and practical guidelines for designing new types of Web search systems.

References

1. G. Arfken. Curvilinear coordinates. In 3rd, editor, *Mathematical Methods for Physicists*, pages 86–90. Academic Press, Orlando, FL, 1985. §2.1.
2. P. Bollmann and S.K.M. Wong. Adaptive linear information retrieval models. In *Proceedings of the ACM SIGIR Conference on Research and Development in Information Retrieval*, pages 157–163, 1987.
3. Robert T. Craig. *Modern Principles of Mathematics*. Prentice-Hall, Inc./ Englewood Cliffs, N.J., 1969.
4. A. Gray. *Modern Differential Geometry of Curves and Surfaces with Mathematica*, chapter Metrics on Surfaces. CRC Press, Boca Raton, FL, 2nd edition, 1997.
5. M. E. Maron and J. L. Kuhns. On relevance, probabilistic indexing and informatiin retrieval. *Journal of the Association for Computing Machinery*, 7:216–244, 1960.
6. M. J. McGill, M. Koll, and T. Noreault. An evaluation of factors affecting document ranking by information retrieval systems. School of Information Studies, Syracuse University, Syracuse, New York 13210, 1979.
7. P. M. Morse and H. Feshbach. *Methods of Theoretical Physics, Part I*, chapter Curvilinear Coordinates, pages 21–31. McGraw-Hill, New York, 1953.
8. G. Salton and M. J. McGill. *Introduction to Modern Information Retrieval*. McGraw-Hill, New York, 1983.
9. H.J. Schneider, P. Bollmann, F. Jochum, E. Konrad, U. Reiner, and V. Weissmann. Leistungsbewertung von information retrieval verfahren (live). Projektbericht, Technische Universitat, Berlin, 1986.
10. D. Shanks. *Solved and Unsolved Problems in Number Theory*, page 161. Chelsea, New York, 4th edition, 1993.
11. H. F. Stiles. The association factor in information retrieval. *Journal of the ACM*, 8:271–279, 1961.
12. Z. W. Wang. An analysis on vector space model based on computational geometry. Master's thesis, Department of Computer Science, University of Regina, 1993.
13. Z. W. Wang. Riemann space model and similarity-based web retrieval. Ph.D. thesis, Department of Computer Science, University of Regina, 2001.
14. Z. W. Wang, R.B. Maguire, and Y. Y. Yao. A non-Euclidean model for web retrieval. In *The First International Conference on Web-Age Information Management (WAIM'2000)*, Shanghai, 2000. Accepted.
15. S. K. M. Wong, W. Ziarko, Raghavan, and P. C. N. Wong. On modeling of information retrieval concepts in vector spaces. *ACM Transactions on Database Systems*, 12(2):229–321, 1987.
16. Y. Y. Yao. measuring retrieval performance based on user preference of documents. *Journel of the American Society for Information Science*, 46(2):133–145, 1995.

A Fast Image-Gathering System on the World-Wide Web Using a PC Cluster

Keiji Yanai, Masaya Shindo, and Kohei Noshita

Department of Computer Science, The University of Electro-Communications
1-5-1 Chofugaoka, Chofu-shi, Tokyo 182-8585, JAPAN
{yanai,shindo-m,noshita}@igo.cs.uec.ac.jp

Abstract. Thanks to the recent explosive progress of WWW (World-Wide Web), we can easily access a large number of images from WWW. There are, however, no established methods to make use of WWW as a large image database. In this paper, we describe an automatic image-gathering system from WWW, in which we use both keywords and image features. By exploiting some existing keyword-based search engines and selecting images by their image features, our system obtains, with high accuracy, images that are strongly related to query keywords. This system has been implemented on a parallel PC cluster, which enables us to gather more than one hundred images from WWW in about one minute.

1 Introduction

Thanks to the recent explosive progress of WWW (World-Wide Web), we can easily access a large number of images from WWW. Hence, we can regard WWW as a huge image database. However, most of those images on WWW are not classified with appropriate keywords.

We can use commercial search engines for searching WWW for HTML documents by giving them related keywords. In a similar way, we can also use some image-search engines for searching WWW for images related to keywords. Most of image-search engines, however, search for images by using only keywords in HTML documents including images, without analyzing the contents of those images. As a result, they tend to return images that are not appropriate images to the given keywords.

As a method of image-searching, content-based image retrieval (CBIR) has been investigated [1,2]. The conventional keyword-based image search methods require appropriate keywords, attached to all images in a database, which have to be made by hand in advance, whereas CBIR does not require such keywords. In CBIR, some types of similarity between images are computed using image features extracted from images. Thus, we can search for images similar to query images.

For constructing an image-search system on WWW based not only on keywords but also on the contents of images, in this paper, we propose an automatic image-gathering system on WWW, into which we have integrated a keyword-based search method and a CBIR method. In our system, a user gives query

N. Zhong et al. (Eds.): WI 2001, LNAI 2198, pp. 324–334, 2001.
© Springer-Verlag Berlin Heidelberg 2001

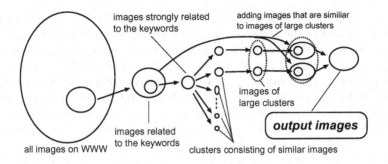

images strongly related to the keywords

adding images that are similiar to images of large clusters

images of large clusters

output images

all images on WWW

images related to the keywords

clusters consisting of similar images

Fig. 1. Processing flow of image-gathering.

keywords to the system at the beginning of a search, and obtains output images related to the keywords. We have implemented the system on a PC cluster as a parallel system for achieving fast image-gathering, which enables us to gather more than one hundred images from WWW in about one minute. In this paper, we describe our method of gathering images from WWW, an implementation of the system and results of experiments.

2   Our Method of Image-Gathering

The final goal of our image-gathering system is to gather images on WWW related to the query keywords given by a user as input. Note that our system is not called an image "search" system but an image "gathering" system, since our system has the following properties: (1) it does not search for images over the whole WWW directly, (2) it does not make a database in advance, and (3) it makes use of search results obtained by commercial keyword-based text-search engines.

Figure 1 shows the processing flow. Since an image on WWW is usually embedded in an HTML document that explains it, the system exploits some existing commercial keyword-based WWW search engines, and it gathers URLs (Universal Resource Locator) of HTML documents related to query keywords. In the next step, using those gathered URLs, the system fetches HTML documents from WWW, analyzes them, and evaluates the extent of relation between the keywords and images embedded in HTML documents. If it is judged that images are related to keywords, the image files are fetched from WWW. According to the extent of relation to the keywords, we divide fetched images into two groups: images in group A having stronger relation to the keywords, and others in group B. For all gathered images, image features are computed.

In CBIR, a user has to provide query images to the system, because it searches for images based on the similarity of image features between query images and images in an image database. In our system, instead of providing query images, a user only needs to provide query keywords to the system. Then, we select images strongly related to the keywords as group A images, remove noise images from them, and regard them as query images only by examining keywords. Removing noise images is carried out by eliminating images which belong to relatively small clusters in the result of image-feature-based clustering for group A images. Images which are not eliminated are regarded as appropriate images to the query keywords, and we store them as output images. Our preference of larger clusters to smaller ones is based on the following heuristic observation: an image that has many similar images is usually more suitable to an image represented by keywords than one that has only a few similar images. Next, we select images that are similar to the query images from group B in the same way as CBIR, and add them to output images.

Some WWW image search systems such as WebSeer[3], WebSEEk[4] and Image Rover[5] have been reported so far, which can be regarded as an integration of keyword-based search and content-based image retrieval. These systems search for images based on the query keywords, and then a user selects query images from search results. After this selection by the user, the systems search for images that are similar to the query images based on image features. These three systems carry out their search in an interactive manner. Our system is different from those in that our system only needs one-time input of query keywords. Our system is able to gather a large number of various images related to the keywords, since it is unnecessary for a user to indicate query images during the processing, and the whole processing is executed automatically. The three systems quoted above require gathering images over WWW in advance and making large indices of images on WWW. In contrast to those systems, due to exploiting existing keyword-based search engines, our system does not require making a large index in advance.

3   Collection and Selection

The image-gathering process in our system consists of a collection part and a selection part.

3.1   Collection Part

In the collection part, by means of some commercial keyword-based WWW search engines, the system obtains URLs, and then, by using those URLs, it gathers images from WWW. The algorithm is as follows:

1. A user provides the system with query keywords.
2. The system sends queries to commercial keyword-based search engines, and obtains URLs of HTML documents related to the keywords.
3. The system fetches HTML documents indicated by the URLs from WWW.
4. The system analyzes HTML documents, and extracts URLs of images embedded in the HTML documents with image-embedding-tags ("IMG SRC" and

"A HREF"). For each of those images, the system calculates a score which represents the intensity of relation between the image and the query keywords. The score is calculated by checking the following conditions:

Condition 1: Each time one of the following conditions is satisfied, 3 points are added to the score.
- In case the image is embedded by "SRC IMG" tag, "ALT" field of "SRC IMG" includes the keywords.
- In case the image is linked by "A HREF" tag directly, words between "A HREF" and "/A" include the keywords.
- The name of the image file includes the keywords.

Condition 2: Each time one of the following conditions is satisfied, 1 point is added to the score.
- "TITLE" tag includes the keywords.
- "H1, ..,H6" tags include the keywords, if these tags are located just before the image-embedding-tag.
- "TD" tag including the image-embedding-tag includes the keywords.
- Ten words just before the image-embedding-tag or ten words after it include the keywords.

If the final score of an image is higher than 3, the image is classified into group A. If it is higher than 1, the image is classified into group B. The system fetches only image-files whose image belongs to either group A or B. If the size of a fetched image-file is larger than a certain predetermined size, the image is sent to the selection part.

5. In case the HTML document does not include image-embedding-tags at all, the system fetches and analyzes other HTML documents linked from it in the same manner described above, provided that it includes a link tag ("A HREF") which indicates URL of HTML documents on the same web site.

3.2   Selection Part

In the selection part, the system selects appropriate images for the query keywords out of images which are collected in the collection part. The selection is based on the image features as described below.

1. In the first step, for each of the collected images, the system makes a color histogram as image features [6]. Rather than making a color histogram directly for the RGB color space, we make it for the Lu^*v^* color space into which the RGB color space is converted. The reason for this is that the Lu^*v^* color space is known to represent the human color sense better than the RGB color space [7]. We quantize the Lu^*v^* color space into 216 (6 for each axis) bins, and make a color distribution histogram for each image. In the current implementation, we use these simple image features, although we can use other sophisticated image features proposed in many CBIR researches.

2. For each pair of images in group A, the distance which represents the degree of dissimilarity between the two images is calculated based on their image features. In the calculation of the distance, we do not adopt the Euclid distance but the distance which considers the proximity in the color space [8].

3. Based on the distance between images, images in group A are clustered by the cluster analysis method. Since we intend to make clusters so that images in the same one are similar to each other, we adopt the farthest neighbor method (FN): we define the distance between clusters as the largest distance between two images belonging to mutually different clusters. In the beginning, each cluster has only one image. For each pair of clusters, if the distance between them is smaller than a certain threshold, they are merged into the same cluster. The system repeats merging clusters, until all distances between clusters are more than the threshold.
4. The system throws away small clusters which have fewer images than a certain threshold value. It stores all images in the remaining clusters as output images.
5. The system selects images in group B if they have a small distance from images in the remaining clusters of group A, and adds them to output images.

4   Implementation

In our system, unlike the conventional image search systems for WWW, we do not make any index of images in advance, and we gather images from WWW on demand.

Because of this, the image-gathering process takes much longer time than that of the conventional systems. In order to speed up the whole process, we implement our system on a PC cluster, by which we achieve not only parallel processing within the collection part but also concurrent processing of the collection and selection parts.

Parallel processing within the collection part means that the system generates many collection processes on multiple PCs, and they gather images from WWW in parallel.

Concurrent processing of the collection and selection parts means that, before all the constituent processes of the collection part terminate, some processes in the selection part start. In the collection part, the process terminates when a collection process has collected all HTML documents and image files indicated by URLs. This implies that the load of the system gradually decreases, since the number of active collection processes decreases as time progresses. When the system starts access to HTML documents of all URLs obtained from text-based search engines, without waiting for the completion of fetching all the images, we can start to extract image features from images which have been already fetched and also compute distances between images in group A (Figure 2).

The system consists of a master PC and some slave PCs as shown in Figure 3. The master PC issues search requests to keyword-based WWW search engines, manages URLs of HTML documents related to the keywords returned from the search engines, and select images from group A and B sent from slave PCs based on their images features.

Each slave PC has one management process(MP), some image collection processes(ICP) and one image analysis process(IAP).

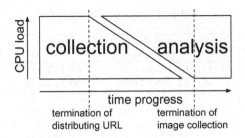

Fig. 2. Concurrent processing of the collection part and the analysis part.

An MP receives URLs from the master PC, and distributes them to ICPs in the same slave PC. Each ICP fetches HTML documents indicated by URLs handed by the MP, extracts URLs of image files, and evaluates the intensity of relation between images and query keywords. It fetches highly evaluated images from WWW, and transfers them to an IAP in the same slave PC.

An IAP receives images from ICPs, and extracts image features from the images. Every time it receives a new image in group A, it computes distance between the new one and ones received before. In addition, for computing distances between images in different slave PCs, the system chooses a particular slave PC all of whose ICPs have been done before any other slave PC, and makes this PC receive all the images features from other slave PCs. This slave PC is called the

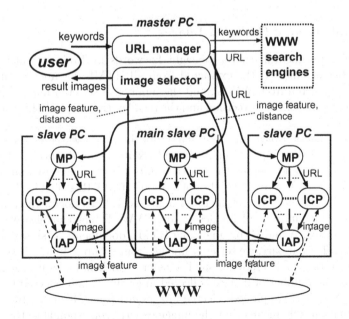

Fig. 3. Parallel image-gathering system.

Table 1. Experimental results.

query keywords	num. of URLs	images in group A		images in group B		total (A+B)	
		collected	selected	collected	selected	collected	selected
lion	1363 (10)	72 (84)	**62 (93,95)**	216 (26)	**66 (42,49)**	288 (41,86)	**128 (67,73)**
apple	1418 (24)	97 (86)	**76 (95,87)**	237 (50)	**99 (72,60)**	334 (61,58)	**175 (82,71)**
baby	1746 (39)	85 (48)	**73 (53,95)**	528 (74)	**272 (83,58)**	613 (70,64)	**345 (77,62)**
desk	1280 (37)	76 (90)	**72 (92,97)**	212 (50)	**84 (71,56)**	288 (61,37)	**156 (81,72)**
keyboard	1521 (18)	39 (95)	**38 (95,97)**	167 (60)	**58 (73,43)**	206 (66,49)	**96 (82,57)**
tiger	1871 (6)	57 (71)	**51 (75,95)**	178 (33)	**71 (42,50)**	235 (42,96)	**122 (56,69)**
Nomo†	951 (5)	38 (95)	**34 (97,92)**	28 (25)	**14 (36,72)**	66 (65,100)	**48 (79,88)**
Mt.Fuji	3165 (28)	541 (71)	**317 (91,75)**	837 (42)	**158 (66,30)**	1378 (53,84)	**475 (82,53)**

†. name of a major league baseball player.

main slave PC. The IAP in the main slave PC computes all distances between images which have been gathered by different slaves. After all ICPs terminate,

PC. No images themselves are sent to the master PC so as to reduce the data volume to be sent.

5   Experimental Results

We have implemented the system on a Linux-based PC cluster, which consists of one master PC and eight slave PCs. Their CPUs are Intel Celeron 400Mhz, 450Mhz or 500Mhz, and their memory size is 256MB.

5.1   Evaluation of Gathered Images

We show experimental results for eight keywords in Table 1, which describes the number of image URLs extracted from all HTML documents, the number of images collected from WWW, and the number of selected images. Numerical values in () represent the precision and the recall of the image URLs, the collected or selected images.

In the collection part, we used five major Japanese search engines, Goo, Infoseek Japan, Lycos Japan, Ocn Navi, and Excite Japan to obtain URLs related to the keywords, and merged the search results of five engines by omitting duplications. For each keyword, we obtained about 2000 URLs of HTML documents in about ten seconds. We fetched and analyzed HTML documents, and we obtained several hundreds of images from WWW. Fetched images were divided into two groups, A and B, by analyzing HTML documents as shown in Table 1.

In the selection part, we selected images from group A by the image-feature-based clustering and removing small clusters which have fewer images than 5 percent of the number of images collected in group A, and selected images from group B by CBIR. We judged selected images either as OK or NG by the subjective evaluation. OK means that the image exactly corresponds to the keywords, and NG means that it does not. In Table 1 we describe the precision, which is defined to be $N_{OK}/(N_{OK} + N_{NG})$, and the recall, which is defined to be $N_{OK_{sel}}/N_{OK_{col}}$, where N_{OK}, N_{NG}, $N_{OK_{sel}}$, and $N_{OK_{col}}$ are the number of OK images, the number of NG images, the number of OK images in selected images, and the number of OK images in collected images, respectively. The recall only for the collected images is defined to be $N_{OK_{col}}/N_{OK_{URL}}$, where $N_{OK_{URL}}$ is the number of OK images in image URLs extracted from all HTML documents, and it is relatively high for most of the keywords. For the five keywords in the table, both the precision and the recall of images selected from group A are over 87%. This shows that most of high-scored images at the keyword-based evaluation are correct. The precision of images selected from group B is between 36% and 83%. It is superior to the precision of images collected as group B in all experiments.

As the final output of each experiment, we obtained output images the number of which was about half of the number of collected images, and the precision is improved much compared to the precision of collected images, which are collected by only evaluation of the keywords. Especially, for targets whose color is essential to discriminate their images, for example, "apple" and "lion", we obtained better improvement. Both the precision and the recall of most of output images are about 70%, which implies that our method is effective for image-gathering from WWW.

Since Mt.Fuji is the most popular mountain in Japan, there are many images of Mt.Fuji in Japanese web sites. There are relatively fewer images of "Nomo" than images related to other keywords, since "Nomo" is a person's name. However, because most of "Nomo" images are fetched from sports news web sites and appropriate keywords are always attached to their ALT tags, their recall becomes very high.

5.2   Comparison of Execution Time

In Table 2, we compare the execution time in terms of the execution type. It shows the execution time in case of the sequential execution of the collection part and the analysis part, and as well as in case of the concurrent execution of them with zero slave PCs and six slave PCs. Note that zero slave PCs means that one PC plays both roles of a master PC and a slave PC at the same time. In this experiment, we used "lion" as a query keyword and carried out image-gathering using 1145 URLs fetched from search engines.

In the parallel execution with zero slave PCs, the speed-up is 1.11 times compared to the sequential execution with zero slave PCs. The more the number of slave PCs increases, the greater speed-up is obtained. In the experiment with six slave PCs, the minimum execution time is 65 seconds, and the speed-up is 3.63 times compared to the sequential execution time with zero slave PCs. This shows that the parallel implementation on a PC cluster is effective.

Figure 4 shows the execution time, where the number of slave PCs varies from one to eight. As the number of slave PCs increases, the execution time has become shorter.

In order to evaluate the variation of the execution time according to the number of slave PCs, we define time overhead TO [9] that represents an overhead

Table 2. Comparison of the processing times in the sequential execution and in the concurrent execution.

the number of slaves	execution form	execution time (seconds) (collection/analysis)	speed-up
0	sequential	236(192/44)	——
0	concurrent	213	1.11
6	sequential	107(63/44)	2.21
6	concurrent	65	3.63

of the execution time in the experiment compared to the ideal execution time T_{ideal} by n slave PCs. It is defined as follows:

$$TO = \frac{T_n}{T_{ideal}} - 1 \qquad (1)$$

where T_n is the execution time by n slave PCs. If all PCs have the same CPU speed, T_{ideal} is T_1/n. Since the CPU speed of PCs used in this experiments are different, we define T_{ideal} as the harmonic mean of the execution time T_1^k on the k-th PC as follows:

$$T_{ideal} = \frac{1}{\dfrac{1}{T_1^1} + \dfrac{1}{T_1^2} + \cdots + \dfrac{1}{T_1^n}} \qquad (2)$$

Figure 5 shows the time overhead TO, where the number of slave PCs varies from one to eight. TO is increasing nearly in proportion to the number of PCs. Many ICPs tend to be idle during the processing of the collection part, since the number of URLs assigned for each image collection process(ICP) decreases as the number of PCs increases.

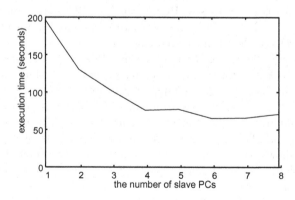

Fig. 4. Execution time according to the number of slave PCs.

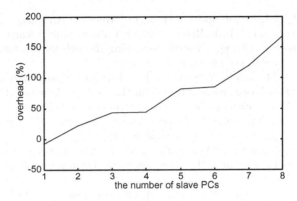

Fig. 5. Time overhead.

In this experiment, the fastest execution was achieved by six slave PCs. Even if we add more slave PCs, practically no more speed-up will be achieved, and the time overhead will further increase. This is due to the increase of idle processes, the increase of communication, and the limitation of bandwidth of communication lines to the Internet.

6   Conclusions

In this paper, we described design, implementation, and experiments of a fast automatic image-gathering system from WWW. We have achieved the high precision and recall that are about 70% without any knowledge about target images by means of both the keyword-based selection and the image-feature-based selection. The only input we have to supply to the system is a list of query keywords. Furthermore, we have achieved fast image-gathering from WWW by implementing the system as a parallel system on a PC cluster.

In the current implementation, we use only a color histogram as an image feature for image-selecting. For future work, we plan to exploit textures and edges as image features and integrate word histograms of HTML documents with image features. Some parameters for thresholds used in the system are given by hand at present, we plan to decide them by learning.

Acknowledgments. A part of this work was supported by a grant from the Okawa Foundation for Information and Telecommunications.

References

1. V.N. Gudivada and V.V. Raghavan, "Content-based image retrieval-systems," *IEEE Computer*, vol. 28, no. 9, pp. 18–22, 1995.
2. A. D. Bimbo, *Visual Information Retrieval*, Morgan Kaufmann, 1999.

3. C. Framkel, M.J. Swain, and V. Athitsos, "Webseer: An image search engine for the world wide web," Tech. Rep. TR-96-14, University of Chicago, 1996.
4. J. Smith and S.F. Chang, "Visually searching the web for content," *IEEE Multimedia*, vol. 4, no. 3, pp. 12–20, 1997.
5. S. Sclaroff, M. LaCascia, S. Sethi, and L. Taycher, "Unifying textual and visual cues for content-based image retrieval on the world wide web," *Computer Vision and Image Understanding*, vol. 75, no. 1/2, pp. 86–98, 1999.
6. M.J. Swain and D.H. Ballard, "Color indexing," *International Journal of Computer Vision*, vol. 7, no. 1, pp. 11–32, November 1991.
7. U. Gargi and R. Kasturi, "An evaluation of color histogram based methods in video indexing," in *International Workshop on Image Databases and Multimedia Search*, 1996, pp. 75–82.
8. J. Hafner, H.S. Sawhney, W. Equitz, M. Flickner, and W. Niblack, "Efficient color histogram indexing for quadratic form distance functions," *IEEE Trans. on Pattern Analysis and Machine Intelligence*, vol. 17, no. 7, pp. 729–736, 1995.
9. T. A. Marsland and F. Popowich, "Parallel game-tree search," *IEEE Trans. on Pattern Analysis and Machine Intelligence*, vol. 7, no. 4, pp. 442–452, 1985.

MELISSA: Mobile Electronic LSA Internet Server Search Agent

Hal D. Brian and Max H. Garzon

The University of Memphis, Memphis, Tennessee, USA
{hbrian, mgarzon}@memphis.edu

Abstract. Searching the World Wide Web for desired information is becoming increasingly challenging with the growing number of web servers and pages. Commonly used search engines often return broken links, out-of-date information, and unrelated pages. This project presents an alternative to these search engines by describing an architecture for a mobile autonomous search agent. MELISSA searches Internet web servers on the user's behalf and reports results back to the user in real-time that are up-to-date and free of broken links. In addition, MELISSA suppresses most unrelated pages by applying Latent Semantic Analysis (LSA), a statistical method for extracting and representing meaning in text corpora. An experiment comparing MELISSA to the AltaVista Internet search engine reveals significant improvements in search engine performance.

1 Introduction

Internet search engines play a vital role in the Internet and electronic commerce. Eight-five percent of Internet users use indexed search engines to find information, locate and buy goods, and research purchase decisions [6]. However, these search engines are not comprehensive or always current and fail to index sites equally. Search engine coverage has decreased substantially in the past two years with no engine indexing more than about sixteen percent of the publicly indexable web [6]. Results are also frequently out-of-date due to the time required to index all new or modified pages. Lawrence and Giles compares the current state of search engines to "a phone book which is updated irregularly, is biased toward listing more popular information, and has most of the pages ripped out." [6] Although indexed search engines offer speedy results, they often force users to sift through thousands of web pages to find those that are truly relevant. On average, half the information retrieved will be irrelevant, and as little as twenty percent of the available relevant information is retrieved [6]. For these reasons, indexed search engines provide poor search results which hampers information retrieval.

Mobile search agents[1] offer a solution to this problem. Assuming the universal adoption of agent technology, mobile search agents could search the Internet in real-

---

[1] "Mobile agents" are programs capable of being transferred to remote hosts in order to carry out different tasks on behalf of their users. [4]

N. Zhong et al. (Eds.): WI 2001, LNAI 2198, pp. 335–339, 2001.
© Springer-Verlag Berlin Heidelberg 2001

time to provide the most current information, eliminating broken links and including pages that are overlooked by current indexed search engines. Until now, real-time searches have not been feasible using conventional means due to the time required to scan all web pages. Mobile search agents, however, can be simultaneously dispatched to many web servers shortening the time to receive search results. This approach promises to eliminate the shortfalls of indexed search engines by guaranteeing a comprehensive, up-to-date, and unbiased search. This project will show that mobile search agents can improve Internet search results over current indexed search engines. The IBM Aglets Workbench supplies the search agent architecture and environment, and a statistical technique called Latent Semantic Analysis is incorporated into the search agent to improve search results.

2 Methods

2.1 Java-Based Mobile Search Agent Architecture

MELISSA, Mobile Electronic LSA Internet Server Search Agent, was developed using IBM's Aglet Software Development Kit (ASDK 1.0.3) to demonstrate the usefulness of mobile software agents for information retrieval. IBM defines an aglet as a "mobile Java object that visits aglet-enabled hosts in a computer network. It is autonomous, since it runs in its own thread of execution after arriving at a host, and reactive, because of its ability to respond to incoming messages." [3] The distinct advantage of its mobility is the aglet's ability to interact with the desired service or database on the same host [5]. In this project, the aglets are able to search for relevant web pages on the host web server with minimal network traffic.

The Java Aglet Application Programming Interface (J-AAPI) enables aglets to operate effectively in a secure environment [3]. This is because a built-in security mechanism protects aglets and aglet-enabled hosts from hostile agents while allowing trusted aglets to operate freely. Java's features of "write-once, run-anywhere" operation, multi-platform support, object serialization, persistence, and class-loading mechanisms are all shared by aglets [8]. This makes the Aglet Software Development Kit the ideal tool for developing mobile agents for electronic commerce. Thus, J-AAPI provides the necessary environment for mobile agents to interact safely on the Internet.

MELISSA is modeled after the aglet master-slave architecture [7]. Using this model, the master aglet containing the user interface first obtains the search text and a correlation threshold from the user. Next, MELISSA dispatches its aglet slaves to each web server to independently search for relevant web pages. Each slave aglet then gathers text from the available web pages for statistical analysis. Finally, a list of web pages that correlate above the given threshold are returned to the master aglet for display. The Aglet Transfer Protocol (ATP) handles the transportation of slaves and the messaging between master and slaves [4]. Using this agent architecture, MELISSA is capable of compiling a list of web pages correlating to the user's search text in real-time.

2.2 Latent Semantic Analysis

To enhance MELISSA's search results, Latent Semantic Analysis (LSA) is incorporated into the slave agent. LSA is defined as a "method for extracting and representing the contextual-usage meaning of words by statistical computations applied to a large corpus of text." [1] In this case, LSA extracts the meaning of the words in the user's search text and compares it to the meaning extracted from each web page. The basic idea is that the "totality of information about all the word contexts in which a given word does and does not appear provides a set of mutual constraints that largely determines the similarity of meaning of words and set of words to each other." [1] LSA is based on singular value decomposition (SVD), a mathematical matrix decomposition technique which induces representations of the meaning of words from the analysis of text. None of its knowledge comes directly from perceptual information about the physical world. Nevertheless, LSA performs a "powerful and, by the human-comparison standard, correct induction of knowledge" [1]. MELISSA utilizes this highly effective method to determine correlating web pages.

LSA has been shown to closely mimic human judgment of word meaning similarity in a variety of ways. The most notable example involves the Test of English as a Foreign Language (TOEFL). LSA scored as well as average test-takers on the synonym portion after training on about 2,000 pages of English text [2]. In another example of its ability to extract knowledge from text, LSA achieved a passing score on a multiple-choice exam after training on an introductory psychology textbook [2]. These cases are strong evidence that LSA can simulate the intelligence required to distinguish relevant web pages.

Performing the LSA technique involves a series of sequential steps. LSA first represents the search text and web page content as a matrix in which each row stands for a unique word and each column stands for a different web page. Each cell contains the frequency of the corresponding word in the respective web page. LSA applies singular value decomposition to the rectangular matrix in which it is decomposed into the product of three other matrices. "One component matrix describes the original row entities as vectors of derived orthogonal factor values, another describes the original column entities in the same way, and the third is a diagonal matrix containing scaling values such that when the three components are matrix-multiplied, the original matrix is reconstructed." [1] A reduction in the dimensionality of the reconstructed matrix to just two dimensions produces the desired inductive effect. Finally, the correlations are found using Pearson's r.

$$r = \frac{N\sum XY - \sum X \sum Y}{\sqrt{[N\sum X^2 - (\sum X)^2][N\sum Y^2 - (\sum Y)^2]}}$$

3   Experiments and Results

In order to quantify the improvement of information retrieval by mobile agents, a preliminary evaluation of MELISSA's performance was conducted. Search results were compiled using the AltaVista search engine, chosen as an adequate representative of current indexed search engines due to its claim to have the fastest search service available (0.4 - 0.5 seconds average response time), most comprehensive index (140 million page index), and most up-to-date content (refreshed every 28 days). These results were compared to those of MELISSA searching the same sample.

The evaluation proceeded as follows. First, five subjects were searched using AltaVista to produce a representative sample of current Internet search engine performance (100 ordered web pages each case). A designation of hit or miss was assigned to each web page based on subject relevance. This selection was made in an unbiased manner with a hit meaning that the page contained subject-specific information. Pages that merely referred to the subject, contained only links, or were unrelated were counted as misses. The AltaVista sample was then searched by MELISSA creating another ordered list of web pages for each case. Finally, a statistical analysis was conducted on web page hit order, hit percentage, and hit/miss ratio for both AltaVista and MELISSA search results. Hit order pertains to the location of hits in the list, hit percentage is the ratio of hits to total correlating pages based on a user-defined correlation threshold, and hit/miss ratio indicates the density of hits in the results list.

Five test cases were run using the following inputs to the AltaVista search engine: "neural networks," "software agents," "artificial intelligence," "data security," and "web page design." Of the first one hundred matches, the number of hits for each of these cases was 12, 27, 33, 10, and 18, respectively. MELISSA searched the same one hundred pages and returned the following number of matches: 28, 59, 70, 39, and 66 with hits of 11, 23, 31, 9, and 17, respectively.

4   Discussion

A complete assessment of MELISSA's performance can be divided into two comparisons: indexed versus real-time searches and word-match versus LSA correlations. The first comparison involves evaluating response time. The second comparison tests the accuracy of the search results. This project focuses on the second comparison, since it is clear that indexed searches have a significant advantage in response time (0.5 seconds for AltaVista versus 10+ seconds average response time for MELISSA). The objective of this evaluation is to show that the improvement in search results could compensate for the increase in response time.

The experiments revealed an improvement in the location of hits and an increase in hit percentage and hit/miss ratio using MELISSA versus AltaVista. The average increase in hit order was 35%, the average increase in hit percentage was 96%, and the average increase in hit/miss ratio was 147%. These five cases illustrate a trend of increased performance of MELISSA over AltaVista.

This initial evaluation of MELISSA's search results demonstrates the power of Latent Semantic Analysis. In all three categories – hit order, hit percentage, and hit/miss ratio – MELISSA performed better that AltaVista. This improvement can be attributed in large part to the fact that LSA suppresses many of the unrelated pages that AltaVista matches. In some cases, eliminating broken links boosts MELISSA's score. In all, MELISSA represents a measurable improvement over current word-match methods.

Further assessment is needed to fully examine all aspects of MELISSA's capabilities. Future work will include exploration of several variations of mobile agents for information retrieval and an in-depth study of MELISSA's search results versus those of indexed search engines. Although this project presents only preliminary findings, these results are very promising and are an indication that mobile agents can serve an important role in the future of the Internet.

5 Conclusion

Mobile search agents are a viable alternative to current indexed search engines. MELISSA provides real-time searches, eliminating broken links and out-of-date information and suppressing most unrelated pages. Using Latent Semantic Analysis, MELISSA returns web pages that are highly correlated to the user's input by extracting the meanings of web pages. The overhead associated with the agent environment and the increased response time are compensated by the advantages of real-time searches. This preliminary performance evaluation suggests that World Wide Web searches can be improved using this mobile search agent model.

References

1. Landauer, T., Foltz, P., Laham, D.: Introduction to Latent Semantic Analysis. In: Discourse Processes, Vol. 25. (1998) 259-284
2. Landauer, T., Dumais, S.: A Solution to Plato's Problem: The Latent Semantic Analysis Theory of the Acquisition, Induction, and Representation of Knowledge. In: Psychological Review, Vol. 104. (1997) 211-240
3. Lange, D.: Java Aglet Application Programming Interface (J-AAPI) White Paper – Draft 2. IBM Tokyo Research Laboratory (1997)
4. Lange, D.: Agent Transfer Protocol – ATP/0.1. IBM Tokyo Research Laboratory (1997)
5. Lange, D., Oshima, M.: Programming and Deploying Java Mobile Agents with Aglets. Addison-Wesley (1998)
6. Lawrence, S., Giles, L.: Accessibility and Distribution of Information on the Web. In: Nature, Vol. 400. (1999) 107-109
7. Oshima, M., Karjoth G.: Aglets Specification 1.1 Draft. IBM Tokyo Research Laboratory (1997)
8. Wong, D., Paciorek, N., Moore, D.: Java-based Mobile Agents. In: Communications of the ACM (1999)

Construction of a Fuzzy Multilingual Thesaurus and Its Application to Cross-Lingual Text Retrieval

Rowena Chau and Chung-Hsing Yeh

School of Business Systems,
Faculty of Information Technology,
Monash University, Clayton, Victoria 3800, Australia
{Rowena.Chau, ChungHsing.Yeh}@infotech.monash.edu.au

Abstract. Cross-lingual text retrieval (CLTR) is a problem of vocabulary mismatch. To allow multilingual term matching, a multilingual thesaurus is used. However, a multilingual thesaurus encoded with exact translation equivalent only is insufficient for effective CLTR since relevant documents are often indexed by cross-lingual related term. In this paper, a novel approach for automatically constructing a multilingual thesaurus based on fuzzy set theory is proposed. By introducing a degree of relatedness between multilingual terms using the concept of membership degree, partial match of cross-lingual related terms is facilitated.

1 Introduction

With the rapid growth of multilingual information over the Internet, cross-lingual text retrieval has become an important issue whenever web-based information management is concerned. Cross-lingual text retrieval (CLTR) refers to the selection of text in one language based on query in another [3]. Basically, it is a problem of vocabulary mismatch. To solve this problem, a multilingual thesaurus is generally used to suggest corresponding translation equivalents for expanding a query in order to accommodate the vocabulary difference between languages. However, a multilingual thesaurus encoding exact translation equivalents only is insufficient for CLTR. Language is culture bound. Translation equivalents do not always available in a foreign language while co-existing cross-lingual counterparts often varies slightly in meaning. Such intrinsic vagueness of meanings in natural languages implies that reliance on exact match of semantically equivalent terms across languages for CLTR is impractical. Potentially relevant documents are often indexed by semantically similar terms which are partially equivalent. To be effective, a multilingual thesaurus for CLTR should facilitate partial match against cross-lingual related terms. Otherwise, relevant documents indexed by semantically similar terms will be missed out.

In this paper, a novel approach for automatically constructing a multilingual thesaurus based on fuzzy set theory is proposed. By introducing a degree of semantic relatedness between multilingual terms using the concept of membership degree, partial match of terms across languages is made possible. With the support of this

N. Zhong et al. (Eds.): WI 2001, LNAI 2198, pp. 340–345, 2001.
© Springer-Verlag Berlin Heidelberg 2001

fuzzy multilingual thesaurus, recall of CLTR can be reasonably improved as more relevant documents are retrieved. In what follows, Section 2 presents the theoretical background as well as the mathematical model for the construction of a fuzzy multilingual thesaurus. In Section 3, application of the fuzzy multilingual thesaurus in CLTR is discussed. Finally, a conclusive remark is included in Section 4.

2   Construction of a Fuzzy Multilingual Thesaurus

A multilingual thesaurus can be defined as an information structure consisting of sets of terms in multiple languages and a specification of their cross-lingual semantic relations. In this paper, a similar information structure called a fuzzy multilingual thesaurus is constructed. For automatically constructing a multilingual thesaurus, a parallel corpus is employed as the information source of cross-lingual semantic knowledge. By analyzing the corpus statistics of term occurrences, concepts relevant to a term's meaning, together with their corresponding degrees of relevance, are extracted. Considering each term's meaning as an integration of its constituent concepts, the lexical meaning of each term is then represented as a fuzzy set of concepts with relevance degrees of all its constituent concepts as membership values. Based on the similarity of meanings, a degree of cross-lingual semantic relatedness is computed. To get a thesaurus-like information structure that will allow partial matching, a fuzzy relation representing the semantic relation of cross-lingual-related-terms is established. Thereby, a fuzzy multilingual thesaurus relating terms across languages with their degrees of semantic relatedness, ranging from *0* to *1*, is constructed.

2.1   Theoretical Background

Application of fuzzy logic in constructing fuzzy thesaurus for monolingual information retrieval [1,2,4] has been widely discussed over the past three decades and has been accepted as a more realistic approach for semantic knowledge representation. By extending its application to a multilingual environment, it is believed that cross-lingual semantic knowledge may also be effectively represented in a similar way.

To model a fuzzy multilingual thesaurus, the cross-lingual knowledge is viewed as a collection of facts represented by a set of propositions like this:

"Term a is cross-lingual-related-to term b"

To formalize such linguistic relation in fuzzy logic, the concept of a binary fuzzy relation [5] provides the best conceptual framework. Briefly, binary fuzzy relations are fuzzy subsets in the Cartesian Product $X \times Y$, which maps each element in $X \times Y$ to a membership grade between 0 and 1. In other words, let X and Y be two universe of discourse, a binary fuzzy relation R in $X \times Y$ is defined as:

$$R = \left\{ ((x,y), \mu_R(x,y)) \mid (x,y) \in X \times Y, \mu_R(x,y) \in [0,1] \right\} \tag{1}$$

where $\mu_R(x, y): X \times Y \to [0,1]$ is the membership function which gives the degree of membership of the ordered pair *(x,y)* in *R*. That is, this degree of membership indicates the degree to which *x* is related to *y* with respect to *R*.

With the preliminary structure of a binary fuzzy relation, the concept of a fuzzy multi-lingual thesaurus is now defined.

Let *A*, *B* be two sets of terms. Then a fuzzy multilingual thesaurus denoted by *FT* is a binary fuzzy relation defined on *A* ×*B* such that:

$$FT = \left\{ ((a,b), \mu_{FT}(a,b)) \mid (a,b) \in A \times B, \mu_{FT}(a,b) \in [0,1] \right\} \qquad (2)$$

where $\mu_{FT}(a,b): A \times B \to [0,1]$ is the membership function which gives the degree of cross-lingual relatedness indicating the extent to which "*a*" is semantically related to "*b*" across languages.

Through the fuzzy multilingual thesaurus, any single term is now associated to a set of cross-lingual related terms ranked in the order of "closeness". This ranking is crucial since it help to preserve the uncertainty of semantic imprecision by quantifying it as grades and thus allowing such uncertainty to be further exploit for discovering new evidence in some process of approximate reasoning. For instance, based on the degree of cross-lingual relatedness between an index term and a query, the degree of satisfaction of a document in response to an information request can be approximately inferred.

2.2   Mathematical Model of a Fuzzy Multilingual Thesaurus

Given a parallel corpus *D* in two languages, L_A and L_B, we have:

$$D = \{d_k\} \qquad (3)$$

where $d_{k \in \{1,2,...z\}}$ is a parallel document containing identical text in both L_A and L_B versions.

Two sets of terms, *A* and *B*, are extracted from the parallel corpus *D*.

$$A = \{a_i\} \quad \text{where } a_{i \in \{1,2,...x\}} \text{ is a term of } L_A \qquad (4)$$

$$B = \{b_j\} \quad \text{where } b_{j \in \{1,2,...y\}} \text{ is a term of } L_B \qquad (5)$$

For the establishment of semantic relation to be encoded in the thesaurus, meaning of terms has to be determined. In our approach, each document of the parallel corpus is viewed as a specific concept and each term contained in the document is considered constituting to the totality of the concept represented by the document as a whole. Accordingly, degree of relevance between a term and a concept is revealed by the term's relative frequency within a document. Based on the statistics of relative frequencies, lexical meaning of every term is then represented as a fuzzy set of its constituent concepts with the degrees of relevance between term and concepts as membership values.

For $a_i \in A$, its lexical meaning is represented by:

$$a_i = \sum_{d_k \in D} \mu_{a_i}(d_k)/d_k \tag{6}$$

where

$$\mu_{a_i}(d_k) = \frac{Frequency\ of\ a_i\ in\ d_k\ written\ in\ L_A}{Length\ of\ d_k\ written\ in\ L_A} \tag{7}$$

For $b_j \in B$, its lexical meaning is represented by:

$$b_j = \sum_{d_k \in D} \mu_{b_j}(d_k)/d_k \tag{8}$$

where

$$\mu_{b_j}(d_k) = \frac{Frequency\ of\ b_j\ in\ d_k\ written\ in\ L_B}{Length\ of\ d_k\ written\ in\ L_B} \tag{9}$$

A fuzzy multilingual thesaurus FT_{AB} involving two languages, L_A and L_B, modeling the semantic relation of cross-lingual-related-terms is expressed as a fuzzy relation $FT(A,B)$ as follows:

$$FT(A,B) = \begin{bmatrix} \mu_{FT}(a_1,b_1) & \mu_{FT}(a_1,b_2) & \mu_{FT}(a_1,b_3) & \cdots & \mu_{FT}(a_1,b_y) \\ \mu_{FT}(a_2,b_1) & \mu_{FT}(a_2,b_2) & \mu_{FT}(a_2,b_3) & \cdots & \mu_{FT}(a_1,b_y) \\ \mu_{FT}(a_3,b_1) & \mu_{FT}(a_3,b_2) & \mu_{FT}(a_3,b_3) & \cdots & \mu_{FT}(a_3,b_y) \\ \cdot & \cdot & \cdot & \cdots & \cdot \\ \cdot & \cdot & \cdot & \cdots & \cdot \\ \cdot & \cdot & \cdot & \cdots & \cdot \\ \mu_{FT}(a_x,b_1) & \mu_{FT}(a_x,b_2) & \mu_{FT}(a_x,b_3) & \cdots & \mu_{FT}(a_x,b_y) \end{bmatrix} \tag{10}$$

where

$$\mu_{FT}(a_i,b_j) = \frac{|\mu(a_i) \cap \mu(b_j)|}{|\mu(a_i) \cup \mu(b_j)|} = \frac{\sum_{d_k \in D} min(\mu_{a_i}(d_k), \mu_{b_j}(d_k))}{\sum_{d_k \in D} max(\mu_{a_i}(d_k), \mu_{b_j}(d_k))} \tag{11}$$

is defined as the degree of cross-lingual semantic relatedness between two terms, a_i and b_j, based on the similarity of their meanings. If $\mu_{FT}(a_i,b_j)=1$, then a_i and b_j are translation equivalents of each other

3   Cross-Lingual Text Retrieval Based on a Fuzzy Multilingual Thesaurus

By its nature, CLTR is an inference from knowledge whose meaning is not sharply defined. Conventional approach such as classical logic which requires high standards of precision for exact reasoning is thus ineffective because of its inability to grip with the fuzziness involved. On the other hand, fuzzy logic, through the use of approximate reasoning, allows the standards of precision to be adjusted to fit the imprecision of the information involved.

Fuzzy reasoning is an inference procedure that uses fuzzy logic to deduce conclusion from a set of fuzzy IF-THEN rules by combining evidence through the compositional rule of inference [6,7]. Briefly, a fuzzy IF-THEN rule is a fuzzy conditional proposition assuming the form:

"IF x is A, THEN y is B."

where "x is A" and "y is B" are fuzzy proposition and A and B are linguistic values defined by fuzzy sets on universe of discourse X and Y, respectively. By the composition rule of inference, individual conclusion inferred from IF-THEN rules is aggregated to compose an overall conclusion.

Based on the mechanism of fuzzy reasoning, a CLTR system is represented by defining fuzzy IF-THEN rules and converting them into corresponding fuzzy relations as follows:

	Propositions		*Fuzzy relations*
IF	q contains $t \in L_Q$	$\Rightarrow$	$NEED(q, L_Q)$
AND	$t \in L_Q$ is related to $t' \in L_D$	$\Rightarrow$	$FT(L_Q, L_D)$
AND	$t' \in L_D$ is an index term of $d \in D$	$\Rightarrow$	$IND(L_D, D)$
THEN	$d \in D$ is relevant to q	$\Rightarrow$	$REL(q, D)$

Here, $NEED(q, L_Q)$ is a fuzzy query representation function relating a query q and its query terms with weights representing the degree of importance of each query term with respect to that particular query written in L_Q.

$FT(L_Q, L_D)$ is a fuzzy multilingual thesaurus as defined by equation (10). It relates pairs of potential index term and query term to a degree of cross-lingual relatedness based on their semantic "closeness".

$IND(L_D, D)$ is an indexing function relating a document $d \in D$ and its index term to a degree of "aboutness". In other words, it can be considered as a fuzzy indexing function by which documents are described by index terms with term weights.

Finally, $REL(q, D)$ is fuzzy matching function which assigns to each document $d \in D$ a degree of relevance, within the range of 0 and 1, with respect to a particular query q.

In this case, based on the compositional rule of inference, $REL(q, D)$ can be inferred by applying the composition operator to the fuzzy relations representing their premises. Moreover, it is observed that REL can be compiled by composing the fuzzy relations as follows:

$$REL = NEED \circ FT \circ IND \tag{12}$$

where

$$\mu_{REL}(q,d) = \mu_{NEED \circ FT \circ IND}(q,d) \tag{13}$$
$$= \max_{(t,t') \in FT} \left[\mu_{NEED}(q,t) \wedge \mu_{FT}(t,t') \wedge \mu_{IND}(t',d) \right]$$

is the membership function which gives the degree of membership of (q,d) in *REL* indicating the extent to which document d is relevant to query q.

To sum up, given a query from the user, based on the degree of relatedness between multilingual terms as encoded in the fuzzy multilingual thesaurus, a degree of relevance between the document and the query, ranging from *0* to *1*, is computed by means of a matching function. Finally, a ranked list of documents, together with their corresponding degrees of relevance will be returned to the user for examination.

4   Conclusion

A multilingual thesaurus specifying lexical relation between pairs of multilingual terms is an important source of semantic evidence for CLTR. However, to make a multilingual thesaurus work effectively for CLTR, the intrinsic vagueness of meaning in natural languages must be well addressed. Otherwise, closely related documents will be missed out. The fuzzy multilingual thesaurus proposed in this paper thus has applied the fuzzy set theory to introduce a degree of cross-lingual semantic relatedness into the lexical relations among multilingual terms. As a result, partial match between multilingual terms is made possible. Closely related documents containing no translation equivalents of the query terms but only semantically similar cross-lingual related terms will then be retrieved. Therefore, with the support of this fuzzy multilingual thesaurus, recall of CLTR will improve.

References

1. Larsen, H.L. and Yager, R.R.: The use of fuzzy relational thesauri for classificatory problem solving in information retrieval and expert systems. IEEE Trans. Systems, Man and Cybernetics 23 (1993) 31-41
2. Miyamoto, S., Miyake, T. and Nakayama, K.: Generation of a pseudothesaurus for information retrieval based on cooccurences and fuzzy set operations. IEEE Trans. Systems, Man and Cybernetics. 13 (1983) 62-70
3. Oard, D. W. and Dorr, B. J., A survey of multilingual text retrieval. Technical Report. UMIACS-TR-96-19, University of Maryland, Institute for Advanced Computer Studies. (1996)
4. Radecki, T.: Mathematical model of information retrieval system based on the concept of fuzzy thesaurus. Information Processing and Management. 12 (1976) 313-318
5. Zadeh, L.A.: Similarity relations and fuzzy orderings. Information Sciences 3 (1971) 177-206
6. Zadeh, L. A., Outline of a new approach to the analysis of complex systems and decision process. *IEEE Trans. Systems, Man and Cybernetics*. 3 (1973) 28-44
7. Zadeh, L. A., The role of fuzzy logic in the management of uncertainty in expert systems. Fuzzy Sets and Systems. 11 (1983) 199-227

Declustering Web Content Indices for Parallel Information Retrieval [1]

Yoojin Chung [1], Hyuk-Chul Kwon [2], Sang-Hwa Chung [2], and Kwang Ryel Ryu [2]

[1] Research Institute of Computer, Information & Communication,
Pusan National University, Pusan, 609-735, South Korea
chungyj@pusan.ac.kr
[2] School of Electrical and Computer Engineering,
Pusan National University, Pusan, 609-735, South Korea
{hckwon,shchung,krryu}@hyowon.pusan.ac.kr

Abstract. We consider an information retrieval (IR) system on a low-cost high-performance PC cluster environment. The IR system replicates the Web pages locally, it is indexed by the inverted-index file (IIF), and the vector space model is used as ranking strategy. In the IR system, the inverted-index file (IIF) is partitioned into pieces using the lexical and the greedy declustering methods. The lexical method assigns each of the terms in the IIF lexicographically to each of the processing nodes in turn and the greedy one is based on the probability of co-occurrence of an arbitrary pair of terms in the IIF and distributed to the cluster nodes to be stored on each node's hard disk. For each incoming user's query with multiple terms, terms are sent to the corresponding nodes that contain the relevant pieces of the IIF to be evaluated in parallel. We study how query performance is affected by two declustering methods with various-sized IIF. According to the experiments, the greedy method shows about 3.7% enhancement overall when compared with the lexical method.

1 Introduction

In general, Web search engines replicate the Web pages locally, index them, and do keyword based searching in this local collection. In what follows, we use the words *documents* and *Web pages* interchangeably. In this paper, a PC cluster interconnected by a high-speed network card is suggested as a platform for fast IR service. For efficient query processing, specialized indexing techniques have to be used with large document collections. In this work, documents are indexed using inverted files [2]. Since there are several machines in the PC cluster, it is reasonable to distribute the index among them. In this work, the global inverted-index file (IIF) is partitioned into

---

[1] This paper was supported in part by the Korea Science and Engineering Foundation under contact NO. 2000-2-30300-002-3.

N. Zhong et al. (Eds.): WI 2001, LNAI 2198, pp. 346–350, 2001.
© Springer-Verlag Berlin Heidelberg 2001

pieces using the lexical and the greedy declustering methods. The approach used in [3] is similar to ours.

This paper is organized as follows. In Section 2, we present our PC cluster system and we detail the declustering methods. In Section 3, our experiments and results follow. Finally, we conclude with final remarks.

2 Parallel IR System

The overall working mechanism of the parallel IR system model can be explained as follows. We define an entry node as a node that accepts a user query and distributes query terms to processing nodes based on the declustering information described in subsection 2.2. Each processing node consults the partitioned IIF using the list of query terms delivered from the entry node, and collects the necessary document list for each term from the local hard disk. Once all the necessary document lists are collected, they are transmitted to the entry node. The entry node collects the document lists from the participating processing nodes, performs required IR operations and ranks the selected documents according to their scores. Finally the sorted document list is sent back to the user as an IR result.

2.1 Network Architecture

The environment for our parallel IR system is a PC cluster interconnected by a high-speed network card, which is a cost-effective platform for fast IR service. Figure 1 shows the environment where our parallel IR system is implemented, which is an 8-node SCI-based PC cluster system.

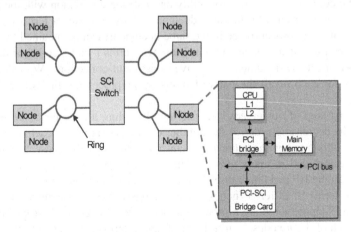

Fig. 1. SCI-based 8 node PC cluster system

2.2 Two Declustering Methods

For the efficient parallelization of the system, it is important to find out the most time consuming part in executing the IR system. Using the sequential IR system developed previously [1], we analyze the system's execution time, and find that the most time consuming part is disk access that takes approximately 45 % of total query execution time.

Thus, it is necessary to parallelize disk access. This can be done by partitioning the IIF into pieces and distributing the pieces to the processing nodes in a PC cluster. Our parallel IR system consists of multiple processing nodes and one of which is an entry node. In our system, documents in the collection are not distributed to multiple processing nodes but all of them are stored in an entry node. But it is desirable to have the IIF appropriately declustered to the local hard disks of the processing nodes because our IR system processes user's query in parallel on a PC cluster.

We can achieve maximum parallelism if the declustering is done in such a way that the disk I/O and the subsequent ranking processes are distributed as evenly as possible to all the processing nodes. We use two declustering methods. The first one is a *lexical declustering* method that just assigns each of the terms (together with its list of document id and weight pairs) in the IIF lexicographically to each of the processing nodes in turn, repeatedly until all the terms are assigned. The second one is a *greedy declustering* method that performs better than the lexical method. Our greedy declustering method tries to put together in the same node those terms that have low probability of simultaneous occurrence in the same query. If the terms in a query all happen to be stored in the same node, the disk I/O cannot be done in parallel and also the ranking processes cannot readily be processed in parallel. For an arbitrary pair of terms in the IIF, how can we predict the probability of their co-occurrence in the same query? We conjecture that this probability has a strong correlation with the probability of their co-occurrence in the same documents. Given a pair of terms t_i and t_j, the probability of their co-occurrence in the same documents can be obtained by the value that is the number of documents in which the two terms t_i and t_j co-occur divided by the number of all the documents in a given document collection. We calculate this probability for each of all the pairs of terms by preprocessing the whole document collection.

In the first step of our greedy declustering algorithm, all the terms in the IIF are sorted in the decreasing order of the number of documents where each term appears. The higher this number the more important the term is in the sense that it is quite likely to be included in many queries. This type of terms also have a longer list of documents in the IIF and thus causes heavier disk I/O. Therefore, it is advantageous to store these terms in different nodes whenever possible for the enhancement of I/O parallelism. Suppose there are n processing nodes. We assign the first n of the sorted terms to each of the n nodes in turn. Each of next n terms is assigned to the node that contains the lowest summation of probability of co-occurrence of the term in the IIF and every term in the node. This process repeats until all the terms in the IIF are assigned. When the size of the document collection is large and thus the co-occurrence probability data is available only for those terms that are significant, the remaining terms are declustered by the lexical method mentioned previously.

3 Experiments

3.1 Comparison of the Greedy and the Lexical Declustering Methods

The greedy declustering method is compared with the lexical method on a test set consisting of 500 queries each containing 24 terms. The 8-node PC cluster is used for the experiment. To generate the test queries we lexically sampled 500 documents from a document collection. From each document, the most important 24 terms are selected to make a query. The importance of a term in a document is judged by the vector space model. Therefore, a term in a document is considered important if its frequency in that document is high enough but at the same time it does not appear in too many other documents.

Table 1. Comparison of the lexical and the greedy declustering methods(unit: sec)

	Lexical declustering	Greedy declustering	Enhancement Ratio (%)
Average query processing time	1.174	1.130	3.7
Average disk access and local IR operation time	0.794	0.749	5.7

Table 1 shows the experimental results comparing the lexical and the greedy declustering methods using those 500 queries on our 500,000-Korean-document collection. The greedy method shows about 3.7% enhancement overall when compared with the lexical method. Since the two methods show differences only during the disk access and the local IR operations performed at the processing nodes, the time spent for those operations is measured separately. In this measurement, the greedy method shows about 5.7% enhancement, which is more significant than the overall enhancement.

3.2 Effect of the Greedy Declustering Method with Various-Sized IIF

In this subsection, the performance of the parallel IR system is analyzed with the number of documents increased up to 500,000. The 8-node PC cluster and the greedy declustering method are used for the experiment. The size of IIF proportionally increases as the number of documents increases. For example, the size of IIF is 300 Mbytes for 100,000 documents, and 1.5 Gbytes for 500,000 documents.

The experimental result is presented in Figure 2. It takes 0.265 seconds to process a single query with the 100,000 document IIF, while it takes 0.477 seconds with the 200,000 document IIF and 1.130 seconds with the 500,000 document IIF. As the IIF size increases, the document list for each query term becomes longer, and the time spent for IR operations increases considerably. As a result, the IR operation eventually takes more time than the disk access, and becomes the major bottleneck.

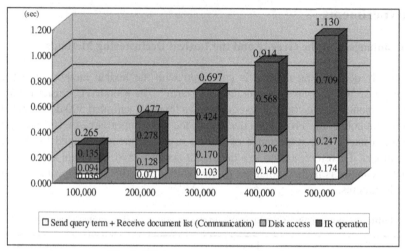

Fig. 2. IIF size vs. query processing time

4   Conclusions

In this paper, we studied the effect of the lexical and the greedy declustering methods for a parallel IR system based on a low-cost high-performance PC cluster system. The data sets used in our experiments consist of newspaper documents. In the near future, we intend to do experiments with various data sets having different characteristics and to evaluate the behavior of our parallel IR system in the presence of very short queries as those found in the Web, which modified by relevance feedback usually have many terms.

References

1. Park, S.H., Kwon, H.C.: An Improved Relevance Feedback for Korean Information Retrieval System. Proceedings of the 16th IASTED International Conference on Applied Informatics, IASTED/ACTA Press, Garmisch-Partenkirchen, Germany (1998) 65-68
2. Frakes, W., Baeza-Yates, R.: Information retrieval – data structures & algorithms. Prentice-Hall (1992)
3. Cormack, G.V., Clarke, C.L.A., Palmer, C.R., Kisman, D.I.E.: Fast Automatic Passage Ranking (MultiText Experiment for TREC-8). The proceedings of the Eighth Text Retrieval Conference (TREC-8), Gaithersburg, Maryland (1999) 735-741

Indexing a Web Site to Highlight Its Content

E. Desmontils and C. Jacquin

IRIN, Université de Nantes
2, Rue de la Houssinière, BP 92208
F-44322 Nantes Cedex 3, France
{desmontils,jacquin}@irin.univ-nantes.fr

Abstract. This article presents a new approach in order to index a Web site. It uses ontologies and natural language techniques for information retrieval on the Internet. The main goal is to build a structured index of the Web site. This structure is given by a terminology oriented ontology of a domain which is chosen a priori according to the content of the Web site. The indexing process uses improved natural language technics.

1 Introduction

In information retrieval processes, the major problem is to determine the specific content of documents. To highlight a Web site content according to a knowledge, we propose a semi-automatic process, which provides a content based index of a Web site using natural language techniques. In contrast with classical indexing tools, our process is not based on keywords but rather on the concepts they represent. In this paper, we first present the general indexing process and the characteristics of used ontologies (section 2). Then, we indicate how the index is build (section 3).

2 Overview of the Indexing Process

The main goal is to build a structured index of Web pages according to an ontology. This ontology provides the index structure. Our indexing process can be divided into five steps:

1. For each page, a flat index is built. Each term of this index is associated with its weighted frequency. This coefficient depends on each HTML marker that describes each term occurrence.
2. A thesaurus allows this process to select candidate concepts that can be labeled by a term of the previous index. In our implementation, we use the Wordnet thesaurus ([1]).
3. Each candidate concept of a page is studied to determine its representativeness of this page content. This evaluation is based on its weighted frequency and on the relations with the other concepts. It makes it possible to choose the best sense (concept) of a term in relation to the context.

N. Zhong et al. (Eds.): WI 2001, LNAI 2198, pp. 351–355, 2001.
© Springer-Verlag Berlin Heidelberg 2001

4. Among these candidate concepts, a filter is produced via the ontology and the representativeness of the concepts. Namely, a selected concept is a candidate concept that belongs to the ontology and has an high representativeness of the page content (the representativeness exceeds a threshold of sensitivity). Next, the pages which contain such a selected concept are assigned to this concept into the ontology.

One of the key elements of this process is the type of ontology used. Many definitions of ontology are available in related works. The definition that we use is the following: "*an ontology provides the common vocabulary of a specific domain and defines, more or less formally, terms meaning and some of their relationships*" [2]

The concepts of an ontology are usually represented by a single linguistic term (a label). However, in our context, this term can be at the same time ambiguous (it represents several concepts) and not always unique (synonyms). As a result, for texts written in natural language, it is necessary to determine the whole set of the synonyms (candidate labels) to define a concept in a single way. Therefore, in our context, an ontology is a set of concepts, each one represented by a term (a label) and a set of synonyms of this term, and a set of relationships connecting these concepts (the specific/generic relationship, the composition relationship...) Currently, the only relationship we take into account is the "isa" relationship. We call this type of ontology a *terminology oriented ontology*. Note that our ontologies do not reflect all the aspects inherent in formal ontologies [2].

The index is build as a XML file on the outside of Web pages. This choice differs from related works especially from work on annotation of Web page like KA2 ([3]), SHOE ([4]). In all the cases, the goal is to use semantic information to improve the information retrieval. However, in these approaches, annotations are included throughout the HTML code using meta-markers. The designer of the pages progressively indicates handled knowledge where it appears. The problem is that any modification or new generation of the pages requires to remake entirely or partly the annotations. Nevertheless, the precision of this process is extremely fine. Moreover, the methods based on annotation are completely manual. Therefore, they are very time expensive and can be carried out only by specialists.

On the contrary, our process is semi-automatic. It enables the user to have a global view on the Web site. It also makes it possible to index a Web site without being the owner of these pages. We do not regard it as a completely automatic process. Adjustments should be carried out by the user. The counterpart of this automatisation is, obviously, a worse precision of the process.

The next section details two significant elements of the process: the determination of the candidate concepts and of their representativeness.

3   Index Building

The well-formed term extraction starts by (1) removing HTML markers from Web pages, (2) dividing the text into independent sentences, and (3) lemmatizing words included in the page. Next, Web pages are annotated with part of speech tags using the Brill tagger ([5]). As a result, each word in a page is annotated with its corresponding grammatical category (noun, adjective...). Finally, the surface structure of sentences is analyzed using term patterns to provide well-formed terms (Noun, Noun+Noun, Adjective+Noun...). For each selected term, we calculate its weighted frequency. This frequency takes into account the frequency of the term and especially the HTML markers which are linked with each of its occurrences. We can notice that the frequency is not a main criterion. Indeed, we work with pages which are of rather restricted size compared to large corpora used in NLP (Natural Language processing). In a Web page containing n different terms, for a given term T_i (with i in 1..n), the weighted frequency $F(T_i)$ is determined as the sum of the p_i weights of HTML markers associated with the p_i term occurences. The result is then normalized. This calculus is shown in formula (1) where $M_{i,j}$ corresponds to the HTML marker weight associated with the jth occurrence of the term T_i. For example, the marker "TITLE" gives a considerable importance to the term ($M_{i,j} = 10$) whereas the marker "B" (for bold) has a quite less influence ($M_{i,j} = 2$). Table 1[1] column 2 shows some results extracted from an experiment on a Web page[2].

$$F(T_i) = \frac{\sum_{j=1}^{p_i}(M_{i,j})}{max_{k=1..n}(\sum_{j=1}^{p_k}(M_{k,j}))} \tag{1}$$

The well-formed terms are different forms representing a particular concept (for example "chair", "professorship"...). In order to determine not only the set of terms included in a page but also the set of concepts in a page, a thesaurus is used. Our experiments use the WordNet thesaurus ([1]). The process to generate candidate concepts is quite simple: from extracted terms, all candidate concepts (all senses) are generated using the thesaurus. A sense is represented by a list of synonym (this list is unique for a given concept). Then, for each candidate concept, the representativeness is calculated according to the weighted frequency and the cumulative similarity of the concept with the other concepts in the page. This last one is based on the similarity between two concepts.

Many measures of similarity are defined in related works. For [6], the information shared by two concepts is indicated in an "isa" taxonomy by the most specific concept that subsumes them. The semantic similarity of two concepts in a taxonomy is the distance between the nodes corresponding to the items which are compared (edge-counting). The shorter the path from one node to another is, the more similar they are. Given multiple paths, one takes the length of the shortest one. A widely acknowledged problem ([7]) with this approach is that it relies on the notion that links in the taxonomy represent uniform distances (but it is most of the time false). [7] describes an alternative way to evaluate semantic similarity in a taxonomy based on the notion of information content. All links in a taxonomy are weighted by an estimated probability (concept occurrences in

---

[1] In this table, terms of the page are in bold font
[2] http://www.cs.washington.edu/news/

corpora), which measures the information content of a concept. The main idea is: the more concepts share information, the more similar they are. The information shared by two concepts is indicated by the information content of the concepts that subsumes them in the taxonomy.

In our context, we use the similarity between two concepts defined by [8], which propose a similarity measure related to the edge distances. It takes into account the most specific subsumer of the two concepts, characterizing their commonalities, while normalizing in a way that accounts for their differences. Our measure performs a little worse than the Resnik's measure ([7]) but better than the traditional edge-counting measure.

Their measure is shown in formula 2 where c is the most specific subsumer of c_1 and c_2, $depth(c)$ is the edge number from c to the taxonomy root, and $depth_c(c_i)$ with i in $\{1, 2\}$ is the edge number from c_i to the taxonomy root through c. The cumulative similarity measure associated with a concept in a page, noted $\widehat{sim}(c)$, is the sum of all the similarity measures calculated between it and all the other concepts included in the studied page.

$$sim(c_1, c_2) = \frac{2 * depth(c)}{depth_c(c_1) + depth_c(c_2)} \qquad (2)$$

Finally, we determine a representativeness coefficient which determines the representativeness of a concept in a document. The coefficient is a linear combination of the weighted frequency and of the cumulative similarity of a concept (formula 3). In this formula, a specific concept is unified with the corresponding synset (set of synonyms) in WordNet. This coefficient is the major one to qualify answers to a request. The empirical values for α and β are respectively 2 and 1.

$$representativeness(synset_i(T_k)) = \frac{\alpha * F(T_k) + \beta * \widehat{sim}(synset_i(T_k))}{\alpha + \beta} \qquad (3)$$

Column 3 of table 1 shows the effect of the representativeness on the concepts order. Concepts are sorted according to their representativeness. Some of them are higher in the column 3 of table 1 than in the column 2 of table 1 (for instance, news#1 or information#1). This is a good result for a page related to news. If we analyse the result in more details, the concepts: news#4 and news#2 have a representativeness equal to 0.47. This is not very different from the degree of news#1 which is equal to 0.5. The explanation is that Wordnet includes too much fine-grained sense distinctions. In fact, in the thesaurus, the three previous concepts all have the same subsumers. Then, an automatic process cannot distinguish these three concepts.

4   Conclusion

Our process shows advantages compared to the traditional indexing methods and even to the methods using manual Web site annotation. The biggest advantage

Table 1. Examples of extracted concepts after the calculus of the representativeness degree.

Concept	Weighted frequency	Representativeness
uw#0	1.0	1.0
award#2, accolade#1, honor#1 ...	0.20	0.7
computer#1, ...	0.41	0.68
information#1, info#1	0.1	0.59
article#3, clause#2	0.30	0.51
news#1, intelligence#4 ...	0.12	0.5
subject#1, topic#1, theme#1	0.01	0.49
university#3	0.37	0.42
seattle#1	0.30	0.31
computer science#1	0.18	0.26
science#2, scientific discipline#1	0.26	0.23
university of washington#0	0.16	0.16

is that selected pages contain not only the keywords (or synonyms) but also the required concepts. Presently, other Web sites on american universities are indexed in order to compare their results to those of the Washington university. In order to improve the indexing results, we may also improve the coverage degree of the ontology on our studied domain. We study also other relationships than the generic/specific relationship in order to improve the process of concepts extraction (the composition relationship).

References

1. G. A. Miller. Wordnet: an online lexical database. *Int. Journal of Lexicography*, 3(4):235–312, 1990.
2. A. Gomez-Perez. Développements récents en matière de conception, de maintenance et d'utilisation des ontologies. In revue terminologies nouvelles, editor, *TIA*, pages 9–20, Nantes, France, 1999.
3. D. Fensel, S. Decker, M. Erdmann, and R. Studer. Ontobroker: Or how to enable intelligent access to the WWW. In *KAW*, Banff, Canada, 1998.
4. S. Luke, L. Spector, and D. Rager. Ontology-based knowledge discovery on the world-wide-web. In *the workshop on internet-based information system, AAAI'96*, Portland, Oregon, 1996.
5. E. Brill. Transformation-based error-driven learning and natural language processing: a case study in part-of-speech tagging. *Computational linguistics*, 21, 1995.
6. J. H. Lee, M. H. Kim, and Y. J. Lee. information retrieval based on conceptual distance in IS-A hierarchies. *journal of documentation*, 49(2):188–207, 1993.
7. P. Resnik. Semantic similarity in a taxonomy: an information based measure and its application to problems of ambiguity in natural language. *Journal of artificial intelligence research*, 11, 1999.
8. Z. Wu and M. Palmer. Verb semantics and lexical selection. In *the 32nd annual meeting of the association for computational linguistics*, Las Cruces, New Mexico, 1994.

Using Implicit Relevance Feedback in a Web Search Assistant

Maria Fasli and Udo Kruschwitz

Department of Computer Science, University of Essex,
Wivenhoe Park, Colchester,
CO4 3SQ, United Kingdom
{mfasli|udo}@essex.ac.uk

Abstract. The explosive growth of information on the World Wide Web demands effective intelligent search and filtering methods. Consequently, techniques have been developed that extract conceptual information from documents to build domain models automatically. The model we build is a taxonomy of conceptual terms that is used in a search assistant to help the user navigate to the right set of required documents. We monitor the dialogue steps performed by users to get feedback about the quality of choices proposed by the system and to adjust the model without manual intervention. Thus, we employ *implicit relevance feedback* to improve the domain model. Unlike in traditional relevance feedback and collaborative filtering tasks we do not need explicitly expressed user opinions. Moreover, we aim at improving the domain model as a whole rather than trying to build individual user profiles.

1 Introduction

In recent years there has been an explosive growth of the sheer volume of information available on the World Wide Web. This information is free and fairly unstructured. Search engines employing standard information retrieval techniques can help to get to some particular piece of information quickly. However, a common phenomenon is that users find it difficult to express their actual information need as a query. Smaller domains like local Web sites face the same problems. For example, a query frequently found in the log files of our sample domain, the University of Essex Web site, is *"languages"*. Someone submitting this request might have a clear idea about what sort of documents should be retrieved by the search engine, e.g. information about the *Modern Languages Unit* (which is the best match *Google*[1] could find in our domain). But there are far more than 1,000 documents which contain the query term despite the fact that the domain consists of less than 30,000 indexable pages. Other top ranked documents retrieved by *Google* contain information about *natural, controlled,* and *Pidgin languages.* In addition to that, there is a large number of documents related to various types of computer languages like *java.*

---

[1] http://www.google.com

N. Zhong et al. (Eds.): WI 2001, LNAI 2198, pp. 356–360, 2001.
© Springer-Verlag Berlin Heidelberg 2001

One way to help the user getting to the best matching documents is to apply some automatically acquired representation of the actual data sources (a "domain model"), something that is feasible for limited domains. We build such a domain model by exploiting markup found in the documents. The result is a set of hierarchies of related terms. These relations are used to initiate simple dialogue steps by displaying candidate terms for query refinement alongside the most highly ranked documents retrieved for a user query. The user's choice to pick a query refinement term proposed by the dialogue system or to select some option considered relevant can be interpreted as *implicit* relevance feedback. We suggest to learn from a user in order to help the next user with a similar request as in collaborative filtering. But, unlike in classical collaborative filtering we do not distinguish a number of user groups. We basically have one large group of users, those who submit queries to the search engine of the particular site. Thus, we aim at improving the domain model of that site rather than user profiles.

2   Related Work

Relevance feedback is a method used to enhance information retrieval results [8,2]. A user initially submits a query, and the system returns a small number of documents. The user then indicates which of the returned documents are relevant to the query. However, judging the relevance of documents may become time consuming and users would prefer another solution. By observing the users' actions rather than expecting explicit user feedback on results we introduce the idea of implicit relevance feedback. Actions the user performs, in our case dialogue steps, are judged to be relevant, everything else is judged as irrelevant.

Our solution can be seen as a particular application of collaborative filtering. Collaborative filtering is based on identifying the opinions and preferences of similar users in order to predict the preferences and to recommend items to others. These techniques are used in a variety of recommender systems ranging from recommending news (e.g. GroupLens [7]) to recommending movies (e.g. Video Recommender [4]). The Community Search Assistant as described in [3] is a software agent which can be used to augment any kind of search engine. The agent works in parallel with the search engine itself and builds a graph of related queries which can be included in addition to the engine's results. The user can then traverse the graph of related queries in an ordered way. Determining relatedness of documents depends on the documents returned by the various queries and not on the terms used for the queries themselves. Furthermore, the use of the search assistant agent enables a form of collaborative search by allowing the users to draw on the knowledge base of queries submitted by others.

Internet search engines have also started incorporating simple collaborative filtering techniques in order to improve search. Such efforts include the popularity engine built by DirectHit[2] which operates using a simple voting mechanism. The popularity engine works by simply tracking the queries input by users and the

---

[2] `http://www.directhit.com`

links that the users follow. Users vote by following a link and therefore the result of a search in such a search engine will return the most popular results for that query.

3   Improving the Domain Model

The search system we apply relies on a sophisticated indexing process that extracts a taxonomy of related concepts from the raw documents. The indexing process distinguishes whether an index term extracted from a document is conceptual information by evaluating the number and nature of various markup environments it is found in. Co-occurrence of different conceptual index terms in the same document defines a notion of *related concepts*. This was explained in detail in [6]. This taxonomy is mainly used in a query refinement task, i.e. if the user query returns a large number of matching documents. In that case the dialogue component determines a set of conceptual terms related to the query. Those terms are selected based on their ability to describe only a subset of documents defined by the original user query. The user is asked to choose one. To use the introductory example, a query for *"languages"* would trigger the dialogue system to offer the following conceptual terms as possible constraints: *second_language, language_department, idl, linguistic, spanish, java* etc.

The strategy applied to determine good discriminating terms (like *java* in the above example) is to check all concepts related to any of the input terms. This is computationally fairly cheap since there are far fewer concepts than keywords, and much of the calculation can be performed offline [5]. Then the three important factors to select a term as a good discriminator or not are: (1) the number of related concepts, (2) the frequency of each of those concepts, and (3) the weights of each of the *related concept* relations.

The frequency of a concept is initially determined by the number of documents for which it was selected as a conceptual index term as opposed to just a normal keyword index. In addition to that, for every concept in the taxonomy the weights associated with each of its identified *related concepts* are equal and sum up to 1. These weights change, if: (1) a concept is offered and selected by the user (increase), or (2) a concept is offered and not selected (decrease).

This will only change weights of relations already in place. The result is that the good parts of the taxonomy will gain importance, the rest will be less and less relevant. But that does not allow the creation of new links overlooked in the automatic construction of the model. We are currently experimenting with that. For example a user decides not to choose any of the offered terms, but inputs *"query languages"*. This will implicitly introduce a new pair of related concepts which may become more important over time. Since we keep track of the dialogue history, we only increase weights associated with the links between any new input and the most recent input. That ensures that we do not run into computational explosion.

The document ranking function we implemented is basically using the vector space model. In addition to that, different weights are given to index terms found in particular markup contexts (e.g. keywords in titles are more important than in free text). This is not new. Search engines like *Google* use similar ranking functions [1]. However, our function goes beyond that in a number of ways. First of all, conceptual terms which were extracted during indexing are of higher weight than other terms. Moreover, every term has a weight which increases with the relative frequency of this term in the pool of all queries submitted to the search system so far. Finally, every concept term has a weight increasing with the frequency of this term being selected in a dialogue step within the collection of all options offered by the system so far. None of the weights in the ranking function has a particularly strong impact on the overall weight of a document.

Finally, a word about the heterogenous nature of our methods which allow explicit relevance feedback. If documents are displayed they come with a box next to them, where a user can judge a document to be relevant or not. Since we keep track of the dialogue history we can again adjust the weights accordingly. This is not implemented yet, but fits into the framework since it is just another parameter in the equation.

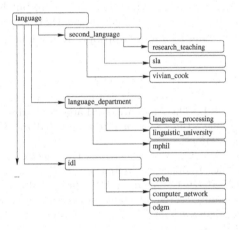

Fig. 1. Partial concept tree for example query "languages"

4   Example

In the example we reduce words to their base forms but apply no stemming. We use the introductory query (*"languages"*). For the calculation of index terms related to the query term we apply some fairly strict thresholds, i.e. frequent terms are not considered by the system. This is the reason why the compound term *english_language* does not seem to be related to *language*. Our experience shows that better discriminating terms can be found by applying stricter thresholds. Figure 1 displays part of the originally constructed hierarchy for the conceptual term *language*. Only the three most relevant related concept terms are presented on the top two levels. It must be interpreted as follows: the system determined the most important concepts that would constrain the original query in order to get to a smaller set of relevant documents. If the user decides to choose *second_language*, then the new query to be evaluated against the database would contain *languages* as well as *second_language* as query terms. Again a large number of matching documents exists for this new query and one option would be to select a new term offered by the search system, e.g. *sla* (which stands for 'second language acquisition'). Alternatively, the user could ignore the proposed options completely and enter some input like *"english"* to continue. The order in which the terms are presented to the user represent their relative importance in respect to the current query applied to the domain model.

Following a trial period the example structure in Figure 1 has changed significantly. Apparently, users querying our system for *"languages"* were mainly interested in the linguistic sense of the query term. The relation between *language* and *idl* ('interface definition language') has disappeared from the list of most relevant related concepts. The fact that *efl* ('English as a foreign language') has become the most relevant potential refinement term for the *"languages"* query, does not reflect a new relation between the terms *language* and *efl* but an increased importance of a relation, which existed before but had initially a much lower weight assigned to it. These changes reflect that only observing real users' behaviour can help getting to a more appropriate domain model.

References

1. BRIN, S., AND PAGE, L. The Anatomy of a Large-Scale Hypertextual Web Search Engine. In *Proceedings of the Seventh International World Wide Web Conference (WWW7)* (Brisbane, 1998).
2. BUCKLEY, C., SALTON, G., AND ALLAN, J. The effect of adding relevance information in a relevance feedback environment. In *Proceedings of the 17th Annual International ACM SIGIR Conference* (1994), pp. 292–301.
3. GLANCE, N. Community Search Assistant. In *Proceedings of the AAAI-2000 Workshop on Artificial Intelligence for Web Search* (Austin, TX, 2000), Technical Report WS-00-01, AAAI Press.
4. HILL, W., STEAD, L., ROSENSTEIN, M., AND FURNAS, G. Recommending and evaluating choices in a virtual community of use. In *Proceedings of CHI'95* (New York, 1995), ACM.
5. KRUSCHWITZ, U. A Rapidly Acquired Domain Model Derived from Markup Structure. In *ESSLLI Workshop on Semantic Knowledge Acquisition and Categorisation* (Helsinki, 2001). To appear.
6. KRUSCHWITZ, U. Exploiting Structure for Intelligent Web Search. In *Proceedings of the 34th Hawaii International Conference on System Sciences (HICSS)* (Maui, Hawaii, 2001), IEEE.
7. RESNICK, P., IACOVOU, N., SUCHAK, M., BERGSTROM, P., AND RIEDL, J. GroupLens: An Open Architecture for Collaborative Filtering of Netnews. In *Proceedings of ACM CSCW'94* (1994), pp. 175–186.
8. VAN RIJSBERGEN, C. J. *Information Retrieval.* Butterworths, 1979.

The Development and Evaluation of an Integrated Imagery Access Engine

Toru Fukumoto and Kanji Akahori

Department of Human System Science Graduate School of Decision Science and
Technology
Tokyo Institute of Technology
2-12-1 Ookayama, Meguro-ku, Tokyo, JAPAN
Tel/Fax: +81-3-5734-3233
fukumoto@ak.cradle.titech.ac.jp

Abstract. Nowadays a lot of engines are proposed but they based on only one point of view; keyword or feature. In this paper, we integrate an engine using both a metadata type and a feature type database. It was built on the Web and all the components are free software. It deals with keywords and allows the result to be grouped by the feature of the contents. We then evaluated it using ten evaluaters, so the grouping method was highly evaluated.

1 Introduction

Over the years large amounts of computer-aided images have been stored in the Internet, owing to widely available digital recording devices, such as digital cameras, scanners, and economical large size storage. For the effective management of those digital images, image albums and filing systems have become the subject of much study, and have developed remarkably. In addition, the Internet is expanding so rapidly that the effective methods of retrieving images from databases has become more and more important.

There are three kinds of image database: the feature type(cited as [1] and [2]), the sensitive type(cited as [3]), and the metadata type(cited as [4]). Each type of these retrieval systems has its merits and demerits, as Table 1 shows. Only one type is not used for any retrieval. So we need to combine and integrate several types. For this reason, we developed an integrated image retrieval database system that combined the feature type and the metadata type and evaluated it using ten people.

In Section 2 the design aim of our system is discussed, in Section 3 the content of the system is introduced. In Section 4 the system, which we introduced in Section 3, is evaluated by testees. In Section 5 our conclusion is presented and the future work is discussed.

N. Zhong et al. (Eds.): WI 2001, LNAI 2198, pp. 361–366, 2001.
© Springer-Verlag Berlin Heidelberg 2001

2   The Design of an Integrated Image Retrieval System

The problems we faced were two. Firstly, how to combine and integrate two engines; the feature type and the metadata type. Secondly, from the view of the retriever, what data he or she puts into the database system; text, or image.

First, there is the important issue of how to integrate the two engines, the metadata type and the feature type. One method is that the results of the two types are simply mixed as they are, some weight to one or other type. These two results have different characters so this method is non-sense. In [9], the query is the keywords and their extraction to a composite hierarchy of domain specific knowledge. This way is domain specific and lacks generality. We decided from these viewpoints that the main item is the metadata type and the sub item is the feature type, so that the user inputs keywords, and the result of the keyword search is grouped by a feature type search.

Second, with regard to how a retriever inputs the search keys, numerous attempts have been made; sketches, keywords, images, and so on. Using a sketch is hard to express a retriever's wants. And a retriever does not always have images to put in. And from the view of interoperability for other retrieval systems, this system is inputted with keywords. First, it searches for images using a metadata type system based on keywords which the retriever specifies, thus getting the first results of this search. Second, it searches using a feature type system based on the pervious results and gets the second results of this search. Finally it combines the two results and shows the retriever the combined results.

We chose the two type engines as follows, from the view of simplicity.

As a metadata type, this system uses keywords in the metadata because they are the basic component of the metadata.

As a feature type, this system used 'retrieval based on areas' [8] because of the simplest comparison method of all systems, and became it does not use RGB color space. Using this method, 8x8 points horizontally and vertically are extracted from images in the database and input image, and the system compares them. The color space is HSI.

In [8] the retrieval score is defined between the source image and the images in the database as follows.

Now, the source image is P, and the image from the database is Q.

$Pxy = (phxy, psxy, pixy)$ meaning each point of a source image in HSI color space. $(1 \leq x,y \leq 8)$

$Qxy = (dhxy, dsxy, dixy)$ meaning each point of an image in the database in HSI color space. $(1 \leq x,y \leq 8)$

Distance of each point

$$Dxy(P,Q) = \sqrt[3]{phxy \times qhxy + psxy \times qsxy + pixy \times qxy}$$

Score

$$S(P,Q) = \sum_{1 \ x,y \ 8} Dxy(P,Q)$$

For an inputted image, this system calculated the score S with all images in the database. The higher this score was, the more similar the two images are. For example, two images Q and R are in the database and P is an inputted image. If $S(P,Q) > S(P,R)$, then the similarity between P and Q is more than between P and R.

3 The Content of the Integrated Image Retrieval System

3.1 System Components

We shall explain the system in detail. On the client side, this system shows a web page made dynamically with PHP3. On the server side, the operating system is Red Hat Linux 6.2, this system is written with C, the web-server is Apache, and the database system is PostgreSQL6.5, so all parts of this system are free software. Server part consists of keyword search engine, feature search engine, grouping part, and input-output part. The keyword engine of this system is a commonly used type, and and/or/not operation is usable. It includes a plain thesaurus, which as mentioned later, makes derivative words from input keywords also searchable.

The action of this system is as follows. It deals with JPEG files, and images are stored in the image database. The keywords with images are in the keyword database. The feature of images is in the feature database. First, on the client side, the user inputs keywords through the web. On the server side, the input-output part receives them and passes them into the keyword search engine. Second, this engine searches for an image-ID with keywords in the keyword database, and lets the results, which are a set of image-IDs, pass into the feature search engine. Third, this engine searches for the image-ID with the set in the feature database, and lets the results pass into the grouping part. Fourth, this part groups them by similarity. Finally the input-output part sends this grouped result to the client and shows them.

3.2 Grouping Method

In this system the result images of the search are grouped by feature.
1. Let $Sk = (a1,a2,\dots,an)$ be the result of the keyword search engine.
2. And each element of Sk, one of which is ai, inputted the feature search engine. The result of one element, ai, is $Ssi = (b1,b2,\dots,bm)$.
3. Compare Sk and Ssi to see whether $ax \in Sk$ and $by \in Ssi$ respectively for $ax = by$ $(1 \leq x \leq n,\ x \neq i,\ 1 \leq y \leq m)$ exists.
4. If it exists, $aj = by$ make a group $Sr = (ai,aj)$. If aj is already included in another group $Sra=(aj,ak,\dots)$, ai is added to $Sra = (ai,aj,ak,\dots)$. If it does not exist, make a group $Sr = (ai)$, of which the only element is ai.

We show this algorithm with a following example. First, $Sk = (1001,1013,1030, 1050,1102)$ is the result of the keyword search engine. Next, one element of Sk, $a1 = 1001$ is picked up and inputting to the feature search engine, and the result is Ss1 $=(1005,1012,1030,1060,1110)$. Image ID 1030 is included both Sk and Ss1, so this system makes a group $Sr = (1001,1030)$. In the same way, one element of Sk, $a3 = 1030$ is picked up and puts into the feature search engine. The result is $Ss3 = (1001, 1102,1072,1130,1111)$. Image ID 1102 is included in both Sk and Ss3, and Image ID 1030 is already included in Sr, so Image ID 1102 is added to the group $Sr = (1001, 1030,1102)$.

How does this system decide the order of a result and show images to the user? Among the groups, firstly, we define a group score, which is the highest score the image is in the group. Second, it compares group scores. The higher the groups score is, the prior they show. In each group, the higher score an image is, the prior it shows.

In Figure 1, there are two groups, Sr1 = (1105,1203,1106) and Sr2 = (1171,1101, 1113). And the score is as show in this figure. The Sr1 groups score is 78.5 at image 1105, and the Sr2 is 76.3 at image 1171. So the images in Sr1 are given priority to those in Sr2. So image 1203 is given priority to Image 1113 even if the score of image 1203 is 55.2 and smaller than that of image 1113, 60.2, which is the smallest in Sr2.

3.3 User Interface

The user inputs keywords into the edit box, chooses the number he or she wants to get from at the list box and pushes the retrieve button. Then the system starts to retrieve images. The result page of the retrieval shows in turn a white image, a red ones, a green one, and so on grouped at the server side. It shows how to divide with colors, but gives no coloring around the images so that the images can be easily viewed. On the right side of each image there is a radio button. If the user chooses one of them and pushes the retrieve button, then this system searches by the feature type. So he or she can get the images that are a little different.

4 The Evaluation of This System

We evaluated the above-mentioned system using evaluators.

We arranged for ten people (all adults). First of all, we stored one hundred images in the database and for each images we attached keywords. The content includes sight, animals, texture and so on. We included pictures of various image types. And it included a plain thesaurus, which we made with a dictionary and which included keywords attached to the images and derivative words from them. Next, we prepared two systems one of which was the integrated image retrieval system, called System A; the other of which takes the grouping method away from System A, called System B. We divided evaluators into two groups, Group A and Group B. Then we picked up five images from the database and show ten evaluators, one at a time. Then we let those in group A retrieve the images using System A, and in Group B, using System B. Fourthly, we let those in Group A retrieve the images using System B and let those in Group B, using System A. In the interval of each retrieval cache of browser was cleared so that it would take the same cost and time to send and show images. Finally, we inquired about the operation and the design of this system from the ten evaluators. In the following section we discuss the results of the evaluation.

  • Time to retrieve

In table 2 the results of the time to retrieve are shown. The retrieval using at System A is either faster than that of System B or the same at significant difference of 1% or 5% level and Group A is no significant difference from Group B. With images especially effective in color, as texture, System A is much faster. But as to the mountain and sunset image, which consist of the same color, System A is same as System B. As lots of images of the result belong to only one group, System A would be equivalent to System B. As the inquiry below mentions, "the sunset image was hard to find". In short, when there are a lot of images which consist of the same color in the database, the result page of retrieval of System A is the same as System B. We need to subdivide to control the threshold under this set of situation.

  • Operation and Design

Table 3 shows the answer at five points for the system which is easy to operate and which is good in its design. System A is better than System B at 5% risk. As to those points, the Inquiry shows the results in detail.

· Inquiry

Seven evaluators said that it was easy to retrieve for classified images. This is about user interface. And four insisted that they kept and saved images as classified or wanted to classify their own images. This is about the method of saving. We inquired about this additionally and they mentioned that they use digital camera actively and had difficulty in arranging images. But the "hard to find of being sunset images", or "difficult to find as only mountain images" indicates that it may be a case hard to retrieve owing to the target image.

From the time to retrieve and inquiry, this system, grouping by a feature type search engine is for the most part effective, except in the case that a lot of images in a database have both the same keywords and the same colors.

5 Conclusion

In this paper, we discussed how to develop an integrated image retrieval database system that combined the feature type and the metadata type of searches and evaluated it using ten people. The effectiveness of integration for search by a metadata type search engine and grouping by feature type search engine is shown, except in the case that a lot of images in a database have both the same keywords and the same colors. Because of this situation, future work will be controlling the number of the results of classification.

In the future, we hope that multimedia retrieval with metadata will be much easier for all people.

Table 1. Merits and Demerits of Database Types

Database Type	Input Method	Search Method	Suitable	Unsuitable
Feature Sensitive	Image	Color, Shape	Color, Texture	Object
Metadata	Text	Text	Object	Color, Texture

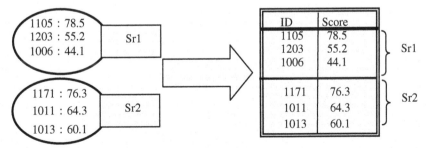

Fig. 1. Ordering Method

Table 2. Average Time to Retrieve (Sec.)   **Table 3.** Operation and Design

Images	System A	System B	
Business	4.3	7.4	**
Texture	5.2	7.3	**
Texture	6.1	6.9	*
Blue Sky	8.0	7.9	
Sunset	7.0	7.5	

	A	B	
Easy to Retrieve	4.4	3.6	*
Easy to Search Result	4.6	3.6	*
Good Design	4.4	3.6	*
Total	4.4	3.4	*

**p<0.01 *p<0.5

References

[1] Kazuhiko KUSHIMA, Hiroki AKAMA, Seiichi KONYA, Masashi YAMAMURO,: Content based Image Retrieval Techniques based on Image Features, Trans. IPS. Japan Vol.40 No.SIG3 (TOD1), (1999) 171-184.

[2] M.Flickner et.al., : Query by Image and Video Content: The QBIC System, IEEE Computer, Vol.28 No.9 (1995) 23-32.

[3] Haruo KIMOTO,: An Image Retrieval System Using Impressional Words and the Evaluation of the System, Trans. IPS. Japan Vol.40 No.3 (1999) 886-898.

[4] Yasushi KIYOKI, Yoshifumi KANEKO, Takashi KITAGAWA,: A Semantic Search Method and Its Learning Mechanism for Image Databases Based on a Mathematical Model of Meaning, Trans. IEICE Japan D- II Vol.J79-D- II No.4, (1996) 509-519.

[5] Toru FUKUMOTO : The Keyword Attachment Reference for the Integration of Image Retrieval, Conference Proceedings of the 1999 Conference of Japan Society for Educational Technology, 169-170.

[6] Toru FUKUMOTO, Kanji AKAHORI, : The Criteria and Evaluation of Metadata/ Keywords in Image Retrieval" Proceedings of the International Conference on Computers in Education 2000, 542-546.

[7] Hiroaki OOBA, Yukihiro ITOH, Hiromasa NAKATANI, : Image Retrieval by Natural Language, JSAI SIG-HICGT-9202-4, (1992) 25-34.

[8] Haruhiko NISHIYAMA, Yutaka MATSUSHITA, : An Image Retrieval System Considering Image Composition, The Trans. of IPS Japan, Vol.37 No.1 (1996) 101-109.

[9] Chabane DJERABA, Marinette BOUET, Henri BRIAND, Ali KHENCHAF, : Visual and Textual Content Based Indexing and Retrieval, International Journal of Digital Library, (2000)2:269-287.

Conceptual Information Extraction with Link-Based Search

Kyung-Joong Kim and Sung-Bae Cho

Department of Computer Science, Yonsei University,
134 Shinchon-dong, Sudaemoon-ku, Seoul 120-749, Korea
uribyul@candy.yonsei.ac.kr sbcho@csai.yonsei.ac.kr

Abstract. Link-based search provides a new vehicle to find relevant web documents on the WWW. Recently, there is quite a bit of optimism that the use of link information can improve search quality as in Google. Usually, text-based search engine returns web sites which have simply the best frequency of user query, so that the result might be different from user's expectation. However, hypertextual search engine finds the most authoritative site. Proposed search engine consists of crawling, storing of link structure, ranking, and personalization processes. User profile encodes different relevances among concepts for each user. For conceptual information extraction from link-based search engine, fuzzy concept network is adopted. Fuzzy concept network can be personalized using the profile information and used to conduct fuzzy information retrieval for each user. By combining personal fuzzy information retrieval and link-based search, proposed search agent provides high-quality information on the WWW about user query. To show the effectiveness of the proposed search engine, a subjective test for five persons is conducted and the result is summarized. The result for five persons shows the usefulness of the proposed system and possibility for personalized conceptual information extraction.

1 Introduction

Search engine is one of the important services of web, and search engines such as Yahoo, Lycos and Altavista are mainly used. Recently, Google and Clever Search are considered as a promising next-generation search engine, which have a common feature of using link structure. While the computation of web document's importance and ordering of search result are based on link structure, link information distills valuable documents that cannot be found using text information. Search result must be the most reliable site that people expect. Google solves the problem of slow speed by computing the importance of web documents before searching takes place [1]. Clever Search distills a large search topic on the WWW down to a size that makes sense to a human user. It identifies authoritative and hub sources about user query [2]. While authoritative and hub sources are calculated using link information, authoritative sources are the most reliable web site about specific topics and hub sources are documents that link to many authoritative sources [3].

N. Zhong et al. (Eds.): WI 2001, LNAI 2198, pp. 367–372, 2001.
© Springer-Verlag Berlin Heidelberg 2001

This paper proposes a system that searches web documents based on link information and fuzzy concept network. We can expect more quality results because it searches using link structure, and more personalized results because it utilizes the fuzzy concept network for more satisfaction to user. Fuzzy concept network calculates the relevance among concepts using fuzzy logic and represents the knowledge of user [4,5]. The construction of fuzzy concept network is based on user profile. Search engine selects the web sites appropriate for user by processing fuzzy document retrieval using fuzzy concept network as user knowledge. Fuzzy concept network and fuzzy document retrieval system can be used for effective personalization method.

The rest of this paper is organized as follows. In Section 2, we propose architecture of personal web search engine using link structure and fuzzy concept network. In Section 3, we show search results and personalization process. Conclusions are discussed in Section 4.

2   Conceptual Link-Based Search

Fig. 1 shows the architecture of personal web search engine using hyperlink structure and fuzzy concept network. Search engine consists of crawling, storing of link structure, ranking, and personalization processes. It uses only link information to find relevant web pages, so that Store Server stores the link structure of web for efficient searching. Crawler extracts link information from crawled web pages and then sends URL and link information to Store Server. As user submits a query, search engine executes a ranking algorithm, which constructs base set using text-based search engine and finds authoritative and hub sources. Fuzzy document retrieval system based on fuzzy concept network is responsible for personalization process. A fuzzy concept network is generated for each user by the information on user profile. Using the fuzzy concept network generated, fuzzy document retrieval system finds the best documents for user.

2.1   Ranking

1.   If i is a document in base set, authoritative weight of i is a_i and hub weight of i is h_i. a_i and h_i are initialized to 1.

2. a_i and h_i are updated by following formula.

$$a_i = \sum h_j \quad (j \text{ links to } i) \tag{1}$$

$$h_i = \sum a_j \quad (j \text{ is linked by } i) \tag{2}$$

3.   Normalize weight of authoritative and hub so that the sum of squares is 1.
4.   Until authoritative and hub weights converge, repeat 2 and 3.

From converged weights of authoritative and hub, best authoritative and hub sources are decided.

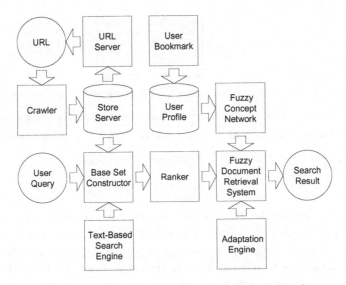

Fig. 1. System overview of the proposed web search engine

2.2 Personalization Process

Lucarella proposed fuzzy concept network for information retrieval [6]. A fuzzy concept network includes nodes and directed links. Each node represents a concept or a document. $C = \{C_1, C_2, \cdots, C_n\}$ represents a set of concepts. If $C_i \xrightarrow{\mu} C_j$, then it indicates that the degree of relevance from concept C_i to C_j is μ. If $C_i \xrightarrow{\mu} d_j$, then it indicates that the degree of relevance of document d_j with respect to concept C_i is μ. $C_i \xrightarrow{\mu} C_j$ is represented with $f(C_i, C_j) = \mu$. Using fuzzy logic, if $f(C_i, C_j) = \alpha$ and $f(C_j, C_k) = \beta$ then $f(C_i, C_k) = \min(\alpha, \beta)$. $C_i \xrightarrow{\mu} d_j$ is represented with $g(C_i, d_j) = \mu$. A document d_j has a different relevance to concepts. A document d_j can be expressed as a fuzzy subset of concepts.

$$d_j = \{(C_i, g(C_i, d_j)) \mid C_i \in C\} \tag{3}$$

If there are many routes from C_i to C_j, $f(C_i, C_j)$ is decided with the maximum value.

For each document $h \in H$, on the basis of the binary indexing relation I, the document descriptor I_h of h is a fuzzy subset of C defined as follows.

$$D = \begin{bmatrix} d_{11} & d_{12} & \cdots & d_{1n} \\ d_{21} & d_{22} & \cdots & d_{2n} \\ \vdots & \vdots & \cdots & \vdots \\ d_{m1} & d_{m2} & \cdots & d_{mn} \end{bmatrix} \tag{4}$$

$$d_{ij} = I_{h_i}(C_j) ,\ 1 \le i \le m ,\ 1 \le j \le n$$

$C = \{c_1, c_2, \cdots, c_n\}$ is a set of concepts. A fuzzy concept matrix K is a matrix where $K_{ij} \in [0,1]$. The (i, j) element of K represents the degree of relevance from concept c_i to concept c_j. $K^2 = K \otimes K$ is the multiplication of the concept matrix.

$$K^2{}_{ij} = \bigvee_{l=1}^{n} (K_{il} \wedge K_{lj}) ,\ 1 \le i, j \le n \tag{5}$$

$\vee$ and $\wedge$ represent the max operation and the min operation, respectively. Then, there exists an integer $\rho \le n-1$, such that $K^\rho = K^{\rho+1} = K^{\rho+2} = \ldots$. Let $K^* = K^\rho$. K^* is called the transitive closure of the concept matrix K. Missed information of fuzzy concept network can be inferred from the transitive closure of itself. The relevance degree of each document, with respect to a specific concept, can be improved by computing the multiplication of the document descriptor matrix D and the transitive closure of the concept matrix K as follows.

$$D^* = D \otimes K^* \tag{6}$$

D^* is called the expanded document descriptor matrix.

3 Experimental Results

Proposed system selects the five authoritative results as a source of personalization. It makes a document descriptor of these documents. The ranking of these five documents is reordered with respect to user's interest, which is recorded in a user profile. User profile is constructed from the information of user's bookmark. Crawling URL's in the bookmark, HTML documents are extracted from web. Relevance between two keywords are computed by the value of cooccurrence in the documents crawled. If the cooccurrence number of two keywords is the maximum, relevance value is 1.0. Otherwise, the relevance between two keywords is the proportion of cooccurrence to the maximum. User profile contains 10 concepts as follows: "Book," "Computer," "Java," "Internet," "Corba," "Network," "Software," "Unix," "Family," and "Newspaper." User profile contains 20 degrees of relevance between 10 concepts. A fuzzy concept network for a user is generated based on 20 degrees of relevance in the user profile. Unrecorded information can be inferred from the transitive closure of the fuzzy concept network. Expanded document descriptor results from multiplication of the document descriptor and user's fuzzy concept network. The sum of the degree of relevances with respect to concepts decides new ranking of the documents.

In this experiment, five users evaluate five authoritative documents about "Java." Each user evaluates five documents. Table 1 and 2 show the search result of a query of "Java." It selects "java.sun.com" as the best authoritative site about "Java." Table 3 shows the personalized results of search engine about "Java" for five users. Shade box shows if personalized rank is equivalent to that ranked by user.

Table 1. Search result of java (authoritative result) and comparison with Google

Authoritative result		Google	
1.	java.sun.com	1.	java.sun.com
2.	www.javalobby.org	2.	java.sun.com/docs/books/tutorial/
3.	javaboutique.internet.com	3.	softwaredev.earthweb.com/java
4.	java.about.com/compute/java/mbody.htm	4.	javaboutique.internet.com/
5.	www.javaworld.com	5.	www.sun.com/java/

Table 2. Search result of java (hub result)

Hub result	
1.	industry.java.sun.com/products
2.	java.sun.com/industry
3.	java.sun.com/casestudies
4.	industry.java.sun.com/javanews/developer
5.	industry.java.sun.com/jug

Table 3. Personalized search result (Shade box shows that personalized rank is equal to user-checking's.)

User 1	User 2	User 3	User 4	User 5
2	1	2	1	2
1	2	1	3	1
3	3	3	2	3
4	4	5	5	4
5	5	4	4	5

4 Conclusions

To find relevant web documents for a user, the proposed search engine uses link structure and fuzzy concept network. Search engine finds authoritative and hub sources for a user query using link structure. For efficient searching, link structure is stored in advance. Fuzzy document retrieval system personalizes link-based search results with respect to user's interest. User's knowledge is represented using fuzzy concept network. Search engine finds relevant documents in which user is interested and reorders them according to user's interest. Using user's feedback about search results, it is possible to change the value of fuzzy concept network. This adaptation procedure helps to get better results to fit user's preference.

References

1. Brin, S., Page, L.: The anatomy of a large-scale hypertextual web search engine. The Seventh International WWW Conference. (1998)
2. The Clever Search, http://www.almaden.ibm.com/cs/k53/clever.html.
3. Kleinberg, J.: Authoritative sources in a hyperlinked environment. IBM Research Report RJ 10076. (1997)
4. Chen, S. -M., Horng, Y.-J.: Fuzzy query processing for document retrieval based on extended fuzzy concept networks. IEEE Transactions on Systems, Man, and Cybernetics, vol. 29, no. 1. (1999) 96-104
5. Chang, C.-S., Chen, A. L. P.: Supporting conceptual and neighborhood queries on the world wide web. IEEE Transactions on Systems, Man, and Cybernetics, vol. 28, no. 2. (1998) 300-308
6. Lucarella, D., Morara, R.: FIRST: Fuzzy information retrieval system. Journal of Information Science, vol. 17, no, 2. (1991) 81-91

World Wide Web – A Multilingual Language Resource

Fang Li[1], Huanye Sheng[1], and Wilhelm Weisweber[2]

[1] Dept.of Computer Science & Engineering, Shanghai Jiao Tong University,
200030 Shanghai, China
{Fli, hysheng}@mail.sjtu.edu.cn
[2] Dept. of Computer Science, Technical University of Berlin
Franklinstr.28/29, D-10587 Berlin, Germany
ww@cs.tu-berlin.de

Abstract. This paper argues that the World Wide Web could be regarded not only as an information resource but also as a dynamic, multilingual, least controlled, easy to access and untagged language corpus. In order to support this idea, we realized a method, which is able to extract bilingual lexicons from parallel WWW pages by two-stage alignment. Language pairs of German, English and Chinese have been selected but the realization is independent of any natural language, domain or markup.

1 Introduction

It is well known that the Internet hosts a huge amount of information. It has been regarded as the largest and the least controlled medium with incredible growth day by day. Most pieces of textual information on the World Wide Web (WWW) is expressed in one or more natural language. These huge amount of Web documents form an unlimited, multilingual corpus.

In the field of natural language processing corpus preparation is a non-trivial task. It is one of the most labor intensive work. Moreover some corpora created by individual institutes and language centers are tailored to some individual tasks, based on some specific theory. These corpora have different tag sets, different format, are difficult to share or to be reused for other tasks. On the contrary the Internet is an international medium shared by many people everywhere in the world. Natural language processing can benefit from the WWW as a multilingual language corpus, in four different aspects:

1. *Standardization*: Documents on the Internet are formatted with the help of standardized markup languages such as HTML, XML and so on. Therefore the documents on the Internet have the same basic format. For example, XML-based encoding for a corpus is possible (see [1], [2]). Any other tag format used for tagging a corpus can be transferred into a XML-based which allows a maximum of portability and theory-independence. On the other hand existing tools for information

N. Zhong et al. (Eds.): WI 2001, LNAI 2198, pp. 373–378, 2001.
© Springer-Verlag Berlin Heidelberg 2001

processing such as information extraction and information retrieval can be applied to natural language processing. Thus it is easier to realize standardization on the Internet

2. *Dynamic maintenance*: The Internet is well known for its rapid changes and growth. Many individuals or institutions dynamically maintain their Web sites which can reflect changes of time, technologies, economics, socials or politics. Along with these changes, languages also change. New words, composite words and all kinds of jargon can be found on the Internet.

3. *Unlimited size*: Corpora are normally confined by their size. Linguistic rules may not be derived from these size-limited corpora. Using statistical methods on the corpus are always faced with "sparse data", when there is insufficient data to train one's model accurately. In the today's "the more data, the better" world, the Internet is suitable to be a corpus with a huge capacity.

4. *Multilingual corpus*: Many kinds of natural languages can be found on the WWW, although the majority of documents are still written in English. Research works on multilingual or even some ethnic languages can be based on the Internet.

Considering these advantages and the features of the Internet we regard the Internet as a multilingual corpus and developed a method to extract bilingual lexicons from this corpus. In the following we explain the method we use and some conclusions are discussed.

2   Bilingual Lexicon Extraction

Bilingual lexicon extraction is based on Web pages which are translations of each other. They are called parallel pages (see [3], [4]). There are many types of Web pages: main pages, content pages and reference pages. Normally information on main pages is very informative and concise because they serve as an index to content pages or other Web sites. We choose main pages as our research object, because many main pages have parallel pages in another language.

In order to extract bilingual lexicons from those parallel pages, we need to solve two problems:
1. Identify words or phrases from the text
2. Find their translations on the parallel pages
The traditional way to identify words or phrases is morphological and syntactic analysis, i.e. tokenization or chunking. We use a different way to do this task. According to the observations on main pages our algorithm consists of two steps.

2.1   The First Step of the Algorithm

• Use tag information to segment a string of tokens.

- Make an alignment on these tokens extracted from the parallel pages based on tag similarity and bilingual lexicons found before.

All documents on the Web are organized by human beings. Tags are put before a complete component of a language such as a paragraph, a sentence, a phrase, a subject, a verb or so. We can fully rely on these tags to segment while extracting pure text from a markup file. Then the bitext extracted from parallel pages is aligned. The alignment uses a dynamic algorithm which is based on a maximum similarity on tag and lexical information between parallel pages. Suppose S_i is the i-th text fragment of a page, T_j is the j-th text fragment of the parallel page, TS_i is a tag before S_i, while TT_j is a tag before T_j. We define the similarity as the following:

$$Sim(S_i, T_j) = Tag\_Sim(TS_i, TT_j) + Word\_Pairs(S_i, T_j) \qquad (1)$$

Tag_Sim(TS, TT) (see formula 2) reflects the similarity between TS_i and TT_j and LCS means the longest common subsequence.

$$Tag\_Sim(TS_i, TT_j) = 2*LCS(TS_i, TT_j) / (Length(TS_i) + Length(TT_j)) \qquad (2)$$

In formula 3 *Word_Pairs(S, T)* reflects the possibility of translating S_i into T_j based on bilingual lexicons constructed before. *WC(S)* and *WC(T)* mean the number of words in S_i and T_j, respectively. *Number_Of_Word_Pairs(Si T)* is the number of translation pairs between *Si* and T_j found in the dictionary which is created from scratch and updated after each run.

$$Word\_Pairs(S_i, T_j) = 2* Number\_Of\_Word\_Pairs(S_i, T_j) / (WC(S_i) + \qquad (3)$$
$$WC(T_j))$$

For the alignment, six situations are considered (see [5]): one-to-one, one-to-zero, zero-to-one, one-to-two, two-to-one and two-to-two. After the first alignment we get the results which are word-to-word, phrase-to-phrase, fragment-to-fragment and sentence-to-sentence.

2.2   The Second Step of the Algorithm

- Use a language-specific stop-list to segment further.
- Make an alignment according to the length.

A stop-list is used to further segment on those fragment-to-fragment, sentence-to-sentence alignments. There are two advantages to segment a string of tokens and to filter stop words. Stop words are usually meaningless. It is not necessary to make an alignment on these stop words. After segmentation we apply again an alignment algorithm which is based only on the length of both. It is more likely that long words are translated into long words and short words are translated into short ones.

After two times of alignment we get bilingual lexicons. These translations are verified by human beings and stored into the dictionary as a source of bilingual lexicons used in the next run. The main features of our system are:

1. *Language independence*: There is no language specific processing. Every natural language, no matter it is a western language or non-alphabetic language, is regarded as a string of tokens. We rely on the structural information in a markup file.
2. *Incremental extraction*: The result (bilingual lexicons) can be fed back as a resource for alignment during each run. This can improve the alignment result and saves the labour for creating a seed dictionary at the beginning.

3 Evaluation and Analysis of the Results

The algorithm has been evaluated with German and English Web pages. Based on the result extracted from 60 pairs of Web pages: 30 pairs of different university Web sites and 30 pairs of randomly collected pages from different domains using search engines. The precision for the first step of alignment is 85.14%.

Suppose the result of the first step is correct we check the precision of the second step of alignment. The precision is 85.38%. Recall has not been considered because Internet can be regarded as a huge corpus.

The method is implemented in Java and is independent of any markup, natural language and domain. The coverage of the dictionary and the similarity degree between parallel pages influence the alignment precision and also the precision of the acquisition of translation pairs. When the extraction is performed on domain-oriented Web pages the precision will be higher than the result described above. The computation time grows linear to the size of the dictionary. Domain extraction can keep the dictionary at a reasonable size.

We compared the resulting German-English dictionary which is extracted from the Internet with a commercial German-English dictionary (Langenscheidts Taschenwörterbuch Englisch containing more than 80000 entries) and with an electronic German-English dictionary (about 3.6 MB with more than 114000 entries). Only 37.68% of the entries of our result extracted from the Internet can be found in the commercial dictionary and 34.08% can be found in the online dictionary. The other 62.32% of the entries cannot be found in the commercial dictionary and 65.92% cannot be found in the electronic dictionary. Analysing these translation lexicons extracted from the Internet we made some observations:

- many proper names of people, companies, place and goods occur, such as *Albert Einstein, SAP, Bodensee, Neuschwanstein* etc.

- many complex words (composites) occur, for example, *Barockkirchen, Basisinstallationen, Benutzerberatung* etc. Using composites is a specific feature of the German language.
- some newly created words occur especially in the area of information and communication technology, such as *webmaster, webteam, infocenter, kernel-hacking* etc.
- many context translations occur such as *Ausländer* translating into *international students of the university, Fahrpläne* translating into *bus and train timetable, nach oben* translating into *back to top* in a Web page.

Such online extracted translation pairs really reflect the usage of words, their morphological forms, their collocations and different senses. It is a simple and easy way to catch up with the rapid development of terminology on the WWW and to make a broad coverage of translations.

4 Conclusion

In this paper a method to automatically extract bilingual lexicons from the Internet has been proposed. Using this method the extraction of lexicons instead of bilingual dictionaries is also possible. Many phrases can be collected online. Either bilingual dictionaries or monolingual lexicons can be acquired from the Internet. Internet is the biggest multilingual language corpus in the world.

However, the Internet as a language corpus has some difficulties concerning processing. There are many writing errors such as no blank between two words in western languages, colloquia terms are used, for example *laufende Projekte* (ongoing projects), *nach oben* (to above), *Chinamade* etc. Different character sets exist. For Chinese there are at least two encodings: GB2312 and Big5. Many Web pages use dynamic Java or frames and the system cannot extract text directly from these pages. However it can still extract the text after the URL address for the frame has been identified. More and more companies and some Web sites have different style and different content pages in different languages instead of parallel pages.

Although such problems exist in the processing, our method has shown the possibility and perspective to consider the Internet as a dynamic, multi-lingual language corpus in the future.

References

1. Die, N., Bonhomme, P., Romary, L.: XCES: An XML-based Encoding Standard for Linguistic Corpora. Proceedings of the Second International Conference on Language Resources and Evaluation, Athens, Greece, (2000) 121-126
2. Mengel, A., Lezius, W.: An XML-based Representation Format for Syntactically Annotated corpora. Proceedings of the Second International Conference on Language Resources and Evaluation, Athens, Greece, (2000) 825-830

3. Resnik, P.: Parallel Strands: A Preliminary Investigation into Mining Web for bilingual Text, in: Farwell, D., Gerber, L., Hovy, E. (ed.): Machine Translation and the Information Soup: Third Conference of the Association for Machine Translation in the Americas (AMTA-98), Langhorne, PA, Lecture Notes in Artificial Intelligence 1529, Springer, October, 1998

4. Li, F., Sheng, HY., Weisweber, W.: Extracting and aligning Bilingual Text from Internet Resources. Proceedings 5th Natural Language Processing Pacific Rim Symposium Beijing, China, Nov. 5-7 (1999) 1-5

5. Gale, W., Church, K.W.: A Program for Aligning Sentences in Bilingual Corpora. Computational Linguistics Vol. 19 (1993) 75-102

Query by History Tree Manipulation

Takashi Sakairi and Hiroshi Nomiyama

IBM Research, Tokyo Research Laboratory,
1623-14, Shimotsuruma, Yamato-shi, Kanagawa-ken 242-8502, Japan
{sakairi, nomiyama}@jp.ibm.com

Abstract. This paper describes a novel technique for refinement of
search queries: query by history tree manipulation (QBHTM). QBHTM
visualizes query histories by means of trees, and allows users to retrieve
information by manipulating the trees. The Boolean AND operator is
represented by the parent-child relation of nodes in the tree. QBHTM
enables users to see the summary of the queries, and to compare them.
This advantage is important for understanding characteristics of collections of documents.

1 Introduction

A wide variety of people use information retrieval systems to get desired information from digital libraries or the World Wide Web; however, it is not always
easy, since the number of documents is huge, and people vary in information
technology skill. Novice users have problems with formulating a query [7].

Typically, a user modifies the search queries iteratively until the user finds a
satisfactory result. If the number of the result is too large, the user searches for
another query within the current result. If the number of the result is too small,
the user returns to one of the previous results.

In this paper, we propose a novel user interface technique for refinement of
search queries: query by history tree manipulation (QBHTM). QBHTM visualizes a query history by means of a tree, and allows users to retrieve information
by manipulating the tree.

2 Query by History Tree Manipulation

2.1 Hub-and-Spoke Strategy

Researchers have observed Web page navigation patterns [3,6,12]. They found
that Web users navigate Web pages using a hub-and-spoke strategy. Users navigate from the hub page, and repeatedly go forward to spokes and back to the
hub. We hypothesized that the hub-and-spoke strategy would also be beneficial
for understanding characteristics of collections of Web sites and Web pages. First
users roughly retrieve a document collection to be analyzed, then repeatedly narrow down from the collection. Such sequences of queries can be treated as a tree.

N. Zhong et al. (Eds.): WI 2001, LNAI 2198, pp. 379–383, 2001.
© Springer-Verlag Berlin Heidelberg 2001

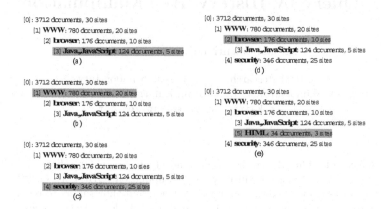

Fig. 1. Examples of queries using history tree manipulation.

If the complete group of queries is visualized by means of a tree structure, it is easy for users to compare groups of queries.

We propose a novel technique for refinement of search queries: query by history tree manipulation (QBHTM). QBHTM represents the history of search operations by following a tree: the root node indicates a set of documents to be retrieved, and each node except the root node has a search query and indicates a result document set retrieved from within the document set of the parent node. QBHTM is suitable for the hub-and-spoke strategy.

Users can do the following operations on a history tree:

Change the current node. Users can change the current node by clicking a node. The new current node is highlighted. The current node is used for displaying the results and the metadata describing the distribution of the retrieved documents.

Add a node. Users can add a new search query as a child node of the current node by adding a new restrictive criteria. The added node then becomes the current node.

The Boolean AND operator is represented by the parent-child relation of the nodes, since the new query is performed within the document set of the parent node. The Boolean OR operator can be specified within a single node.

Fig. 1 shows examples of queries using QBHTM. Each node displays the serial number of a query, the search query, and a summary of the retrieved results. To conserve space, the tree structure is shown as indented lines. Fig. 1 (a) shows a query history when a user searches three queries sequentially. The first operation searches for documents that contain the word "WWW" within the whole document set. The second operation searches for documents that contain the word "browser" within the results of the first query. The third operation searches for documents that contain at least one of the words "Java" or "JavaScript" within the results of the second query. If the user wants to search for documents that contain the word "security" within the results of the first query, first the user clicks the "WWW" node as shown in Fig. 1 (b), then the user adds the "security" node as shown in Fig. 1 (c). If the user wants to search for documents that contain the "HTML" within the result of the second query, first the user clicks the "browser" node as shown in Fig. 1 (d), then the user adds the "HTML" node as shown in Fig. 1 (e).

QBHTM enables users to do basic operations easily. Users can change the current node by clicking the node, and refine queries by adding nodes. QBHTM also enables users to see the summary of the queries, and to compare them. This advantage is important for understanding characteristics of collections of documents.

2.2   Query History Reuse

As is done in programming by example systems such as Chimera [9], QBHTM enables users to reuse the query history by the following operations.

Cut/copy/paste. Users can edit the structure of the query history by cut, copy, and paste operations to reuse parts of the query history.
Save/load. Users can save the complete query history, and can load it later to reuse the history.

Tree structure editing functions are useful for comparing multiple collections of documents. Users can easily perform the same queries to another document collection by copying parts of the query history.

3   Prototype

We designed and implemented the QBHTM as a prototype of an information retrieval system. The system is based on our site outlining technology [11]. The system collects Web pages periodically, and allows users to analyze characteristics of collections of Web sites and Web pages. Fig. 2 shows an example screen from the prototype system. The bottom area is used for displaying the search query history tree.

4   Related Work

Filter/Flow [13] and VQuery [8] provide graphical user interfaces for Boolean queries. Filter/Flow uses the metaphor of water flowing through a filter, and VQuery uses Venn-like diagrams. QBHTM is different from these techniques in that it focuses on the query histories. Although QBHTM is not suitable for complex Boolean queries, it provides interactive search query refinement in a simple way: by changing the current node and by adding new nodes. Therefore it should be easier for casual users to get the desired information.

CS^3[10] provides a graphical interface for defining and refining rule-based tree for concept-based retrieval. If good rules are defined, users can obtain desired

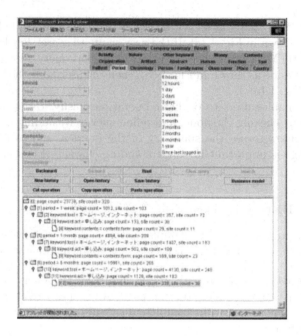

Fig. 2. An example screen from the prototype system.

information by using concept-based retrieval. However, defining rules are not easy for casual users.

Since it is natural to represent an operation history as a tree, the basic technique can also be applied to many systems other than information retrieval systems such as Web browsers. MosaicG [2], and NetWeb [4] display the navigation history of the Web pages by means of a tree structure. Although the systems are relates to QBHTM, a combination of the Web browsers and search engines cannot substitute QBHTM. The Web browsers display the navigation history so it is difficult for users to see the summary of queries, on the other had QBHTM displays the summary of queries.

The Northern Light search site[1] and Grouper [14] cluster search results automatically into a tree hierarchy of categories. QBHTM comes from the opposite perspective, visualizing a search query history as a tree. In automatic clustering systems, even if users specifies same query, the users see different hierarchies for different result sets, so it is difficult for the users to compare the result sets. In QBHTM, the users can see same structure of the trees for difficult result sets, so it is easy for the users to compare the result sets.

Online Public Access Catalogues (OPACs) [1,5] maintain a history of queries. Users can perform query operations on the result collections from previous queries. However, OPACs are systems for retrieving specific documents, while

---

[1] http://www.northernlight.com/

ours is designed not only for retrieving specific documents but also for understanding characteristics of collections of Web sites and Web pages.

5   Conclusion

We have introduced a novel information retrieval user interface technique, QB-HTM. QBHTM visualizes query histories by means of trees. Users can refine the search queries interactively by changing the current node and by adding new nodes. QBHTM help users to understand characteristics of the collection of document by displaying the summary of queries. In addition, users can reuse parts of the query history by editing the tree, and can reuse the entire query history by saving and loading it.

References

1. Agosti, M. and Masotti, M.: Design of an OPAC Database to Permit Different Subject Searching Accesses in a Multi-Disciplines Universities Library Catalogue Database. In Proc. of ACM SIGIR'92 (June 1992), pp. 245–255.
2. Ayers, E. Z. and Stasko J. T.: Using Graphic History in Browsing the World Wide Web. In Proc. of 4th Int. World Wide Web Conf. (December 1995).
3. Catledge, L. D. and Pitkow, J. E.: Characterizing Browsing Strategies in the World-Wide Web. In Proc. of 3rd Int. World Wide Web Conf. (April 1995).
4. Cockburn, A. and Jones, S.: Which Way Now? Analysing and Easing Inadequacies in WWW Navigation. Int. Journal of Human Computer Studies, Vol. 45, No. 1 (July 1996), pp. 105–129.
5. Fox, E. A. and France, R. K.: Development of a Modern OPAC: From REVTOLC to MARIAN. In Proc. of ACM SIGIR'93 (June 1993), pp. 248–259.
6. Greenberg, S. and Cockburn, S.: Getting Back to Back: Alternate Behaviors for a Web Browser's Back Button. In Proc. of 5th Ann. Human Factors and the Web Conf. (June 1999).
7. Hölscher, C. and Strube, G.: Web Search Behavior of Internet Experts and Newbies. In Proc. of 9th Int. World Wide Web Conf. (May 2000).
8. Jones, S.: Graphical Query Specification and Dynamic Result Previews for a Digital Library. In Proc. of ACM UIST'98 (November 1998), pp. 143–151.
9. Kurlander, D. and Feiner, S.: A History-Based Macro by Example System. In Proc. of ACM UIST'92 (November 1992), pp. 99–106.
10. Lu, F., Johnsten, T., Raghavan, V., and Traylor, D.: Enhancing Internet Search Engines to Achieve Concept-based Retrieval. In Proc. of InForum'99 (May 1999).
11. Takeda, K. and Nomiyama, H.: Site Outlining. In Proceedings of ACM DL'98 (June 1998), pp. 309–310.
12. Tauscher, L. and Greenberg, S.: How People Revisit Web Pages: Empirical Findings and Implications for the Design of History Systems. Int. Journal of Human-Computer Studies, Vol. 47, No. 1 (July 1997), pp. 97–137.
13. Young, D. and Shneiderman, B.: A Graphical Filter/Flow Representation of Boolean Queries: A Prototype Implementation and Evaluation. Journal of the American Society for Information Science, Vol. 44, No. 6 (July 1993), pp. 327–339.
14. Zamir, O. and Etzioni, O.: Grouper: A Dynamic Clustering Interface to Web Search Results. In Proc. of 8th Int. World Wide Web Conf. (May 1999).

Web-Based Information Retrieval Using Agent and Ontology

Kwang Mong Sim[1] and Pui Tak Wong[2]

[1] Department of Information Engineering,
Chinese University of Hong Kong, Shatin, NT, Hong Kong.
kmsim@ie.cuhk.edu.hk
[2] Information Service Department,
Hong Kong International Container Terminals, Hong Kong.

Abstract. With notoriously large and ever-increasing number of websites, users face the challenge of searching, filtering and monitoring ever-changing information of astronomical magnitude. This research has engineered a society of agents for: (1) locating desirable number of URLs, (2) browsing multiple websites simultaneously and (3) monitoring changes in websites. Since WWW is being used across many cultures, text documents may use different terms for the same concept. By using ontological relations of words, (i) a query processing agent (**QPA**) assists users in selecting desired number of URLs and (ii) information filtering agents (**IFAs**) are used to retrieve information. Additionally, information monitoring agents are used to constantly monitor and report changes in websites. Experimental results demonstrated that the **QPA** can find appropriate number of URLs and **IFAs** are successful in filtering relevant information in many instances.

1 Introduction

Although the WWW provides ample resources of information, finding relevant information can often be difficult even with powerful search engines. Even though there are many extant search engines, they are primarily being used to locate (initial) information sources (e.g. URL links for users' queries). While conventional search engines assist users in locating information sources, the tasks of retrieving the required information from the list of prescribed URL links and monitoring changes in these information sources rest heavily on the users. Hence, even if users may know where to retrieve desirable information they have to (1) actually visit the website(s) (2) repeatedly and regularly visit the websites to retrieve up-to-date information. While (1) is time consuming, (2) may cause unnecessary Internet traffic. To address all the issues listed above, this research has designed and engineered a society of *query processing agent (QPA), information filtering agents (IFAs)* and *information monitoring agents* that automate the tasks of retrieving information in the WWW. Section 2 explicates how a QPA locates information sources for user queries using an *ontology* [1]. The agents that perform the tasks of browsing websites, filtering relevant information using ontology and monitoring changes are expounded in sections 3 and 4 respectively. Results from the experiments performed to evaluate the QPA and IFAs are presented in section 5. Section 6 concludes this paper by summarizing the contributions of this research.

N. Zhong et al. (Eds.): WI 2001, LNAI 2198, pp. 384–388, 2001.
© Springer-Verlag Berlin Heidelberg 2001

2   Query Processing Agent

To address the problem of the ever-increasing information sources over the WWW, a QPA was developed to help users locate relevant URLs. Using ontological relations the QPA assists users locate desirable numbers of URLs by pruning the number of sources through specialization or by broadening the search using generalized terms or synonyms. The QPA processes queries in two stages. In the first stage, the QPA locates URLs by executing conventional search engines. In the second stage, a number of relevant information sources are selected based on the desirable number of URLs specified by a user. If the number of URLs found falls beyond the range, the QPA will (1) remove any *stop words* [2] from the query before (2) executing the a *select information sources* (SIS) function [3]. SIS makes use of ontological relations such as *synonym, hyponym* (specialization) and *hypernym* (generalization) among keywords in the query and words in WORDNET [4]. It generates a set of words that is synonymous to keywords in the original query. These are words that are closest in meaning to the original query (the rationale is to use alternatives that best preserve the meaning intended in the original query). For each synonym generated, there are three possible cases:

1. The result returns a number of ULRs within the range specified by a user.
2. If the number of ULRs from the first stage > upper bound specified by a user, the concept in the query is specialized. SIS attempts to find a set of hyponyms provided by WORDNET. Each hyponym is used to generate an alternate query that may return a number of URLs within the range.
3. If the number of information sources < lower bound, SIS attempts to find a set of hypernyms using WORDNET. As in (2), each hypernym is used to generate an alternate query that may return a number of URLs within the range.

3   Information Filtering Agents

To relieve users from having to browse many websites to retrieve information, several information filtering agents (IFAs) are used to visit multiple websites concurrently. While agents in Amalthaea and FAB employed keyword vectors and user interests to extract information, IFAs are designed to recognize ontological relations of words. Searching in IFAs are guided by information filters that scan for keywords that are (i) exact match, (ii) synonyms, (iii) hyponyms and (iv) hypernyms. The are several possible outcomes when an IFA browses a website:

1.   The URL can be connected and exact or related keywords in the query can be found in the website
2.   The URL can be connected but keywords cannot be found and
     •   Alternate link(s) can be found by traversing links on the original URL
     •   No alternate link can be found
3.   The URL cannot be connected at all.

If a URL can be connected, the page pointed to by the URL will be retrieved. Words from the web page will be extracted and HTML tags are removed forming a series of strings S that will be stored in an IFA's local database for reuse during the evaluation phase. All stop words are removed from S. The content of the web page can be validated by scanning for exact match of keywords in the query against the list of words in S. If exact keywords cannot be found, the IFA will search for (1) synonyms, (2) hyponyms and (3) hypernyms in S using the respective filters. Each filter attempts to find a series of keywords $\{k_1, k_2, ...k_n\}$ in S. The relevance of a website is determined by the number of keywords in $\{k_1, k_2, ...k_n\}$ that can be found in S. If S contains m keywords in $\{k_1, k_2, ...k_n\}$ which has a cardinality of n, then the relevance of the website is m/n multiplied by a factor 1.0, 0.9, 0.7 and 0.6 respectively for the exact-match, synonym, hyponym and hypernym filters. For instance, if all the keywords from the original query can be found in S, the URL link receives the highest relevance score of 1.0 and evaluation stops. While it is more apparent that a synonym is closest in meaning to an original keyword, a hyponym generates a higher score than a hypernym because a specialized term is *more likely* to fall within the scope of a user's interest than a generalized term (eg. users looking for information on birds is *more likely* to be interested in robins than animals). Furthermore, a user may specify a threshold for the IFA to determine the relevance of a website.

If the relevance of a URL is determined to be below the specified threshold, it seems likely that the content of the web page has been changed since the search engine last indexed the page. Although its content is changed, the web site that contains the page is unlikely to change its main theme entirely. Hence, it seems that there is a very high chance that other interesting pages can be found within the website and the IFA is programmed to traverse the website looking for alternate URL links that may be relevant to the original query. The heuristic that the IFA uses to navigate alternate URL links is also based on the ontological relations of words. Before the IFA starts to navigate the alternative URLs, all the URL links within the website are gathered and ranked according to their relevance computed as follows. A (hyper-)link in a web page is usually associate with some texts that provide some descriptions about the URL. An IFA ranks a URL link using the exact, synonym, hyponym and hypernym information filters to guide its navigation. If the descriptions in a URL contain exact words in the original query, it will be visited first followed by links containing synonyms, hyponyms and hypernyms of the original query. Additionally, an IFA may also explore a frame set. In this research, a frame set is treated as a collection of web pages (or frames) but in general it may contain presentation information such as layouts. The IFA recursively explores and traverse each frame in a frame set.

4   Information Monitoring Agents

If it is determined that a website contains relevant information, users may use IMAs to frequently monitor changes in the websites. An IMA monitors changes in a website based on the specification given by the user. Users have the options of instructing IMAs to monitor changes in: (i) a particular page, (ii) areas within a page that are emphasized, for instance, texts that are underlined, in italic, or in bold and (iii) a specified location within a page. The changes in a web page, in specific cells, in areas of a page that are underlined, in bold or in italic can be detected by computing the check sum using *CRC32*. An example on monitoring changes in specific cells of a table within a web page, is given in Fig. 1. Each page in a website is divided into *cells*. Each cell can be of numeric or string types. This option of detecting changes in a cell is particularly useful when users only wish to be informed of updated information of a specific item of some on-line information (eg. NASDAQ index or US$-JPY exchange rate). In Fig. 1, the IMA monitors the contents of a numeric cell that is located in row 2, column 2 of a table in a financial website. The IMA checks the contents of the cell (eg., Hang Seng Index) every 5 seconds as specified by the user. Since the content fluctuated > 5% (from 17110 to 19010) as specified by the user, the IMA reported the changes.

5   Experimentation and Evaluation

2 sets of experiments were carried out to evaluate the (1) effectiveness of the QPA in locating desired numbers of URLs and (2) IFAs in filtering relevant information.

Experiment 1: Queries in this experiment were selected from www.metaspy.com. Although 30 queries were tested, a total of about 200 alternate queries was generated by replacing keywords with hypernyms, hyponyms and synonyms. While space limitations preclude listing the alternate queries here, details are reported in [5]. For all queries, the QPA was able to generate alternate queries that return desired number of URLs. The success rates of locating ±10%, ±20%, and ±40% from the *baseline* (the default number of URLs found using a conventional search engine) were also recorded. The average success rate for locating the number of URLs with the above deviations was 70.5%. The results show that through the use of ontological relations of keywords the QPA can locate desired numbers of URLs in many instances.

Experiment 2: This experiment, carried out in 2 parts, measured the relevance of the URLs explored by the IFAs by searching for keywords in a query. In the first part, using only exact word filter, the IFAs searched for keywords that exactly matched those in a query. In the second part, all other filters were used. For both parts, although only 20 user queries were used, a total of 276 URLs were explored by the IFAs [5]. The relevance of the URLs determined using exact word filters and using ontological relations of words were recorded. For 6 out of the 20 queries, the average relevance increased when all filters were used. This was because the IFAs were able to detect related keywords that would have been ignored if only exact word filters were used. The results demonstrated that by establishing ontological relations among words, the IFAs is more likely to filter relevant information appropriate for a query.

6 Conclusion

The paper has presented a society of agents that bolsters web-based information retrieval. Through the use of IFAs and IMAs, users are relieved of the tasks of browsing, filtering and monitoring information. Multiple websites appropriate for a query can be visited and monitored in parallel by several IFAs and IMAs.

Experimental results demonstrated that in many situations, when ontological relations among words are considered, (1) the QPA is more likely to locate desirable numbers of URLs and (2) the IFAs are more likely to filter relevant information.

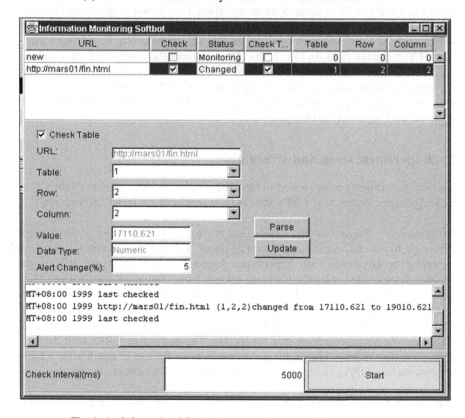

Fig. 1. An Information Monitoring Agent Detecting Changes in a table

Reference

1. N. Fridman and C. Hafner. The State of the Art in Ontology Design. AI Magazine, Fall 1997, pp 53-74.
2. David St-Onge. *Detecting and Correcting Malapropisms with Lexical Chains*. March 1995.
3. K. M. Sim and P.T. Wong. Engineering Information Discovery and Monitoring Systems Along the Dimensions of Agency and Ontology. In Proceedings of the 1st Asia-Pacific Conference on Intelligent Agent Technology, 1999, pp 332-336.
4. G.A. Miller. WORDNET: An On-line Lexical Database. International Journal of Lexicography 3-4, pp 235-312.
5. P.T. Wong. An Agent-based Approach for Information Filtering over the Internet. MSc Thesis, Dept. of Comp., HK Poly. Univ., HK., 2000.

Content-Based Sound Retrieval for Web Application

Chunru Wan, Mingchun Liu, and Lipo Wang

School of Electrical and Electronic Engineering
Nanyang Technological University
Block S2, Nanyang Avenue, Singapore 639798
{ecrwan, P147508078, elpwang}@ntu.edu.sg

Abstract. It is both challenging and desirable to be able to retrieve sound files relevant to users' interests by searching the Internet. Unlike the traditional way of using keywords as input to search for web pages with relevant texts, query example can be used as input to search for similar sound files. In this paper, content-based technology has been applied to automatically retrieve sounds similar to the query-example. Features from time, frequency and coefficients domains are firstly extracted from each sound file. Next, Euclidean distances between the vectors of query and sample audios are measured. An ascending distance list is given as retrieval results. Experiments have been conducted on a sound database with 414 files from 16 classes. Further, we propose to classify the query audio into three classes, speech, music and other sound, with much fewer features and then search relevant files only in that subspace. This way, the retrieval performance could be further increased with the saving of computing time as well. Simulations show that our method leads to better results compared to the Soundfisher software in terms of both retrieval quality and completeness.

1 Introduction

Few search engines allow users to search the Internet with sounds as query inputs. However, users could benefit from the ability to direct access to these medias, which contain rich information but couldn't be precisely described by words.

Content-based retrieval thus has emerged from the wide spread of web applications. In the recent years, some researchers have applied this technology in audio retrieval. A general audio classification and retrieval system is built by Wold, et al, with a demo program online [1]. A nearest feature line method is proposed by Stan for the same kind of task [2]. In [3], a system for query a music database by humming is described along with a scheme for representing the melodic information in a song as relative pitch changes. Other techniques involved in audio retrieval such as structured representation of audio support for browsing, active search algorithm for quickly detect and locate known sounds, are described in [4] and [5] respectively.

In this paper, we retrieve similar sound files using Eclidean distance measurement between query and sample feature vectors. The rest of paper is organized

N. Zhong et al. (Eds.): WI 2001, LNAI 2198, pp. 389–393, 2001.
© Springer-Verlag Berlin Heidelberg 2001

as follows. Feature extraction and normalization along with the database are discussed in section 2. The audio retrieval and its performance have been discussed in section 3. To further increase the performance and ease for browsing, the first hierarchy of audio directory can be automatically generated by k-nearest neighbor (k-NN) classifier, which is described in section 4. Finally, conclusions and discussions are included in section 5.

2   Feature Extraction

Feature extraction is the first step towards content-based retrieval. Here, we extracted features from time, frequency and coefficient domains and combine them to form a feature vector for each audio file in the database.

2.1   The Database

There are 414 sound files all together in the database, which forms 16 classes. All files are in 'au' format with sample rate of 8000Hz. The file length ranges from 0.25 second to less than ten seconds. A brief description of the database is given in Table 1.

Table 1. Structure of the database

Class name	File number	Class name	File number
1. Speech	53	Violin-pizzicato	40
Female	36	3. Sound	62
Male	17	Animal	9
2.Music	299	Bell	7
Trombone	13	Crowds	4
Cello	47	Laughter	7
Oboe	32	Machines	11
Percussion	102	Telephone	17
Tubular-bell	20	Water	7
Violin-bowed	45	Total	414

2.2   Feature Extraction

Since the audio files are short clips, segmentation is omitted. Each audio file is directly divided into frames of 256 samples, with 50% overlapping at the two adjacent frames. Silence reduction is done before the feature extraction. If the energy of an individual frame is below a predefined threshold, the whole frame is ignored.

After silence reduction, the audio frames are hamming-windowed and 48 features are extracted for each frame. Means and standard deviations of the frame-based features are computed as the final features for each file. The 48

Table 2. Structure of 48 extracted features

1. Time domain (9 features)	Mean and standard deviation of volume root mean square, zero-crossing ratio and frame energy. Volume dynamic ratio, silence ratio and total energy.
2.Frequency domain (26 features)	Mean and standard deviation of frequency centroid, bandwidth, four sub-band energy ratios, pitch, salience of pitch, first two formants, the amplitude at individual formants and spectrogram.
3.Coefficientdomain (13 features)	Mean of first 13 orders of MFCCs (Mel-Frequency Cepstral Coefficients).

features can be sorted into temporal, frequency and coefficients domains, as shown in Table 2.

After feature extraction, we normilize the feature values accross the whole database. Normalization can ensure that contributions of all audio feature elements are adequately represented. The magnitudes of the feature element values are more uniform after normalization and this will prevent particular feature from dominating the whole feature vector.

3   Audio Retrieval

The advent of world wide web has importance of information retrieval. It has increased the need for automated information retrieval for multimedia database in recent years. Here, we access and retrieve audio by its extracted feature vector. When a user inputs a query audio file and requests for finding relevant files to the query, both the query and each document in the database are represented as feature vectors. A measure of the similarity between the two vectors is computed, and then a list of files based on the similarity are fed back to the user for listening and browsing. The user may also refine the query to get more audio material relevant to his or her interest by relevant feedback.

To measure the performance of the contented based retrieval system, the precision and recall are used [6], as defined by

$$\text{Precision} = \frac{\text{relevant files retrieved}}{\text{total files retrieved}}, \tag{1}$$

$$\text{Recall} = \frac{\text{relevant files retrieved}}{\text{total files relevant}}. \tag{2}$$

The precision provides an indication of the quality of the answer set, while the recall considers the number of relevant documents retrieved. In an ideal situation, precision is always 1 at any recall point. In the experiment, we assume that the files in the same class are relevant; otherwise, they are non-relevant. Hence, the performance can be measured automatically without hearing the sound.

To test the performance of audio retrieval, the leave-one-out experiment is conducted. Each file is selected from the database as query and searched from the rest of files. Most often, users only browse the files ranked in the top list.

For this concern, top ten retrieved files for three queries from speech, music, and sound respectively are listed at the left column under each query in Table 3. The results are compared with soundfisher^{TM} software beta version 4, from Musclefish LLC [1] at the right column. Their precision and recall are also given in the table where only the top ten records are considered.

Table 3. Result of audio retrieval (compared with SoundFisher from Musclefish LLC)

Query	Female		Percussion		Laughter	
No.1	Female	Female	Percussion	Percussion	Laughter	Laughter
No.2	Female	Water	Percussion	Violinbowed	Laughter	Animal
No.3	Female	Female	Percussion	Telephone	Animal	Machines
No.4	Female	Male	Percussion	Oboe	Water	Percussion
No.5	Male	Male	Percussion	Telephone	Animal	Machines
No.6	Female	Percussion	Trombone	Cello	Animal	Laughter
No.7	Water	Female	Violinbowed	Percussion	Percussion	Crowd
No.8	Male	Female	Violinbowed	Animal	Percussion	Crowd
No.9	Male	Percussion	Violinbowed	Violinpizz	Laughter	Percussion
No.10	Male	Male	Percussion	Oboe	Laughter	Bell
Precision	0.5	0.4	0.6	0.2	0.4	0.2
Recall	0.14	0.11	0.06	0.02	0.67	0.33

4   Hierarchical Searching

For almost every existing text web search engine, there is a directory through which one can browse from a broader area to a more specific area. These directories are often built and maintained manually. We can automatically establish such a hierarchy for audio retrieval. For example, we can firstly classify audio files into three major classes: speech, music, and other sound. This is treated as the first level hierarchy.

A k-nearest neighbor (k-NN, k=2) classifier is used to classify the audio into the above three major classes. When all the 48 features are used, the accuracy is 96.6% of the testing set. After dropping one 'worst' feature, the accuracy increases. This may be caused by too high feature dimension for the given training patterns. We continue to drop 'worst' feature at a time, the classification accuracy varies up and down slightly along with the feature dimension. When the feature dimension reduced to 9, 100% accuracy can be achieved. If we further drop features, the performance will drop monotonically down to 83% with only one feature selected. Based on this observation, we chose the remained 9 features for classifying audio into the first hierarchy. After the classification, we then use more features to retrieve the files in a specific class in stead of the whole database. Thus, the precision and recall rates will be improved with less computation time.

5   Conclusions and Discussions

In this paper, content-based audio retrieval is conducted based on the features extracted from time, frequency and coefficient domains. The Euclidean distance measurement is used to search sound files relevant to the query example. Further, an audio hierarchy is built by k-NN classifier using a small set of features from the whole feature vector. Thus query audio can be firstly classified into speech, music, or sound, and then retrieve files only in the subspace. Consequently, precision and recall rates could be improved with the saving of computing time as well. Simulations show that our method leads to better results compared to the Soudfisher software in terms of both retrieval quality and completeness.

For a real system, in case of long files, we can segment them into smaller segments and do classification individually. The recognized classes can be taken as terms, which is the key element in text retrieval. With obtained terms, some text retrieval strategies can be applied to audio retrieval and searching by using both keywords and query example. How to extract key clips for long audio file and deal with database growing dynamically are other challenging fields for audio browsing. Future content-based audio retrieval system must also provide access to conceptual semantics not just low level features.

References

1. Wold, E., Blum, T., Keislar, D., et. al.: Content-based classification, search, and retrieval of audio. IEEE Multimedia, (1996) 27–36,
2. Li, S. Z.: Content-Based Classification and Retrieval of Audio Using the Nearest Feature Line Method. IEEE Transactions on Speech and Audio Processing, Vol. 8, No. 5, (2000) 619–625
3. Ghias, A., Logan, J., Chamberlin, D., Smith, B.C.: Query by humming: musical information retrieval in an audio database. Proceedings of the third ACM international conference on Multimedia, (1995) 231–236
4. Melih. K., Gonzalez, R.: Audio retrieval using perceptually based structures. Proceedings of IEEE International Conference on Multimedia Computing and Systems, (1998) 338–347
5. Smith, G., Murase, H., Kashino, K.: Quick audio retrieval using active search. Proceedings of IEEE International Conference on Acoustics, Speech and Signal Processing, vol 6, (1998) 3777–3780
6. Grossman, D.A., Frieder, O.: Information Retrieval: Algorithms and Heuristics. Kluwer Academic Publishers (1998)

Collaborative Filtering Using Principal Component Analysis and Fuzzy Clustering

Katsuhiro Honda[1], Nobukazu Sugiura[1],
Hidetomo Ichihashi[1], and Shoichi Araki[2]

[1] Graduate School of Engineering, Osaka Prefecture University,
1-1 Gakuen-cho, Sakai, Osaka, Japan
honda@ie.osakafu-u.ac.jp
http://www.ie.osakafu-u.ac.jp/ honda/
[2] Advanced Technology Research Laboratories,
Matsushita Electric Industrial Co.,Ltd.,
3-4 Hikaridai, Seika-cho, Souraku-gun, Kyoto, Japan

Abstract. Automated collaborative filtering is a popular technique for reducing information overload. In this paper, we propose a new approach for the collaborative filtering using local principal components. The new method is based on a simultaneous approach to principal component analysis and fuzzy clustering with an incomplete data set including missing values. In the simultaneous approach, we extract local principal components by using lower rank approximation of the data matrix. The missing values are predicted using the approximation of the data matrix. In numerical experiment, we apply the proposed technique to the recommendation system of background designs of stationery for word processor.

1 Introduction

Automated collaborative filtering is a popular technique for reducing information overload and has seen considerable successes in many area [1], [2], [3]. The prevalent algorithms used in the collaborative filtering are neighborhood-based methods. In the neighborhood-based methods, the subset of appropriate users is chosen based on their similarity to an active user and the weighted aggregate of their ratings is used to generate predictions for the active user. GroupLens [1], [2] first introduced an automated collaborative filtering system using a neighborhood-based algorithm and provided personalized predictions for Usenet news articles. The original GroupLens system used Pearson correlations to weight user similarity and estimate the rating by computing the weighted average of deviations from the neighbor's mean. From these points of view, the collaborative filtering can be represented as the problem of predicting missing values in a data matrix.

Missing values have frequently been encountered in data analysis in real applications. There are many approaches to handle data sets including missing values. Several methods that extract principal components without elimination

N. Zhong et al. (Eds.): WI 2001, LNAI 2198, pp. 394–402, 2001.
© Springer-Verlag Berlin Heidelberg 2001

or imputation of data have been proposed [4] [5] [6]. Shibayama [5] proposed a PCA(Principal Component Analysis)-like method to capture the structure of incomplete multivariate data without any imputations and statistical assumptions. The method is derived using the lower rank approximation of a data matrix including missing values, which accomplishes the minimization of the least square criterion.

In this paper, we propose a new approach for the collaborative filtering in which we estimate missing values using local principal components. The new method is based on the simultaneous application of PCA and fuzzy clustering, which is a technique for partitioning an incomplete data set including missing values into several fuzzy clusters by using local principal components. The simultaneous approaches [7] [8] to the multivariate data analysis and fuzzy clustering have been proposed since Fuzzy c-Varieties (FCV) clustering was first proposed by Bezdek et al. [9] [10], which can be regarded as a simultaneous approach to PCA and fuzzy clustering. FCV clustering partitions a data set into several linear clusters formed as linear varieties and thus we can extract local principal component vectors as the basis vectors of the prototypical linear varieties. Though it is difficult to describe the characteristics of a large-scale database by only one statistical model, we often obtain a practical knowledge from local model in each cluster. The least square criterion is the same as that of the objective function of FCV when no missing value is involved, hence our novel technique is an extension of FCV into incomplete data sets. By the proposed clustering, missing values in the data matrix are estimated using the local principal components. The advantage of the method is the low memory requirements. Once we obtain the local linear models, we can predict the missing values from a few simple linear models, while we need to retain all elements of the correlation matrix in the general neighborhood-based methods.

In numerical experiment, we apply the proposed technique to the recommendation system of background designs of stationery for word processor and compare the performance of the technique with that of the original GroupLens algorithm and a non-personalized prediction method.

2 Extraction of Local Principal Components and Estimation of Missing Values

Neighborhood-based methods are the most prevalent algorithms used in the collaborative filtering. In the neighborhood-based methods, the subset of appropriate users is chosen based on their similarity to an active user and the weighted aggregate of their ratings is used to generate predictions for the active user. Therefore, the collaborative filtering can be a task of predicting missing values in some user-item matrix. In this section, we introduce a technique for the extraction of local principal components and use them for the estimation of missing values.

2.1   Fuzzy c-Varieties Clustering and Local Principal Component Analysis with Least Square Criterion

The simultaneous approaches [7] [8] to the multivariate data analysis and fuzzy clustering have been proposed since Fuzzy c-Varieties (FCV) clustering was proposed by Bezdek *et al.* [9] [10], which can be regarded as a simultaneous approach to Principal Component Analysis (PCA) and fuzzy clustering. Because FCV partitions data using linear varieties as the prototypes of the clusters, we can also extract local principal component vectors as the basis of the prototypical linear varieties. Though it is difficult to describe the characteristics of a large-scale database by only one statistical model, we sometimes are able to obtain a practical knowledge from the local model in each cluster.

Let $X = (x_{ij})$ denotes a $(n \times m)$ data matrix consisting of m dimensional observation of n samples. The goal of the simultaneous approach of PCA and fuzzy clustering is to partition the data set by using local principal component vectors that represent local linear structures. FCV is a clustering method that partitions a data set into C linear clusters. The objective function of FCV with entropy regularization [11] consists of distances from data points to p dimensional prototypical linear varieties spanned by $\boldsymbol{a}_{cj}$'s as follows:

$$\min L_{fcv} = \sum_{c=1}^{C} \sum_{i=1}^{n} u_{ci} \Big\{ (\boldsymbol{x}_i - \boldsymbol{b}_c)^{\mathrm{T}} (\boldsymbol{x}_i - \boldsymbol{b}_c)$$

$$- \sum_{j=1}^{p} \boldsymbol{a}_{cj}^{\mathrm{T}} R_{ci} \boldsymbol{a}_{cj} \Big\} + \lambda \sum_{c=1}^{C} \sum_{i=1}^{n} u_{ci} \log u_{ci}, \tag{1}$$

$$R_{ci} = (\boldsymbol{x}_k - \boldsymbol{b}_c)(\boldsymbol{x}_i - \boldsymbol{b}_c)^{\mathrm{T}}, \tag{2}$$

where u_{ci} denotes the membership degree of the data point $\boldsymbol{x}_i$ to the cth cluster and $\boldsymbol{b}_c = (b_{c1}, \cdots, b_{cm})$ is the center of the cth cluster. The entropy term of Eq.(1) is for fuzzification. The larger λ is, the fuzzier the membership assignments are. Because we derive $\boldsymbol{a}_{cj}$'s as the eigenvectors of the fuzzy scatter matrix, $\boldsymbol{a}_{cj}$'s can be regarded as local principal component vectors.

In this paper, we extract the local principal components by using least square criterion [4] [5]. We define the least square criterion for local principal component analysis using membership u_{ci} and entropy regularization as

$$\varphi = \sum_{c=1}^{C} \mathrm{tr} \Big\{ (X - Y_c)^{\mathrm{T}} U_c (X - Y_c) \Big\} + \lambda \sum_{c=1}^{C} \sum_{i=1}^{n} u_{ci} \log u_{ci}, \tag{3}$$

where $U_c = \mathrm{diag}(u_{c1}, \cdots, u_{cn})$. $Y_c = (y_{cij})$ denotes the lower rank approximation of the data matrix X in cth cluster,

$$Y_c = F_c A_c^{\mathrm{T}} + 1_n \boldsymbol{b}_c^{\mathrm{T}}, \tag{4}$$

where $F_c = (\boldsymbol{f}_{c1}, \cdots, \boldsymbol{f}_{cn})^{\mathrm{T}}$ is the $(n \times p)$ score matrix and $A_c = (\boldsymbol{a}_{c1}, \cdots, \boldsymbol{a}_{cp})$ is the $(m \times p)$ principal component matrix. The problem is to determine F_c, A_c and $\boldsymbol{b}_c$ so that the least square criterion is minimized.

From the necessary condition $\partial \varphi / \partial b_c = \mathbf{0}$ for the optimality of the objective function φ, we have

$$b_c = (\mathbf{1}_n^{\mathrm{T}} U_c \mathbf{1}_n)^{-1} X^{\mathrm{T}} U_c \mathbf{1}_n, \tag{5}$$

and Eq.(3) can be transformed into

$$\varphi = \sum_{c=1}^{C} \Big\{ \mathrm{tr}(X_c^{\mathrm{T}} U_c X_c) - 2\mathrm{tr}(X_c^{\mathrm{T}} U_c F_c A_c^{\mathrm{T}}) $$

$$+ \mathrm{tr}(A_c F_c^{\mathrm{T}} U_c F_c A_c^{\mathrm{T}}) \Big\} + \lambda \sum_{c=1}^{C} \sum_{i=1}^{n} u_{ci} \log u_{ci}, \tag{6}$$

where $X_c = X - \mathbf{1}_n b_c^{\mathrm{T}}$. From $\partial \varphi / \partial F_c = O$,

$$F_c A_c^{\mathrm{T}} A_c = X_c A_c. \tag{7}$$

Under the condition that $A_c^{\mathrm{T}} A_c = I_p$, we have $F_c = X_c A_c$ and the objective function is transformed as follows:

$$\varphi = \sum_{c=1}^{C} \Big\{ \mathrm{tr}(X_c^{\mathrm{T}} U_c X_c) - \mathrm{tr}(A_c^{\mathrm{T}} X_c^{\mathrm{T}} U_c X_c A_c) \Big\} $$

$$+ \lambda \sum_{c=1}^{C} \sum_{i=1}^{n} u_{ci} \log u_{ci} $$

$$= L_{fcv}. \tag{8}$$

Therefore it can be said that Eq.(3) is equivalent to the objective function of FCV and the minimization problem is solved by computing the p largest singular values of the fuzzy scatter matrix and their associated vectors, when the data matrix doesn't include a missing value.

2.2 Local Principal Components of Data with Missing Values

Unfortunately there is no general method to deal with missing values in fuzzy clustering. Miyamoto et $al.$ [12] proposed an approach that can handle missing values in Fuzzy c-Means (FCM) [10]. FCM is a fuzzy clustering method that partitions a data set into several spherical clusters. Ignoring the missing values, the objective function of FCM is written as follows:

$$\psi = \sum_{c=1}^{C} \sum_{i=1}^{n} u_{ci} \sum_{j=1}^{m} d_{ij}(x_{ij} - b_{cj})^2 + \lambda \sum_{c=1}^{C} \sum_{i=1}^{n} u_{ci} \log u_{ci}, \tag{9}$$

where d_{ij} is defined by

$$d_{ij} = \begin{cases} 1 & ; x_{ij} \text{ is observed.} \\ 0 & ; x_{ij} \text{ is missing.} \end{cases}$$

and the entropy term is added for fuzzification. This strategy is useful only for spherical clustering.

In this subsection, we enhance the method to partition an incomplete data set including missing values into several linear fuzzy clusters using least square criterion. To handle the missing values, we minimize only the deviations between x_{ij}'s and y_{cij}'s where x_{ij}'s are observed, and y_{cij}'s corresponding to missing values are determined incidentally.

The objective function to be minimized is defined by the convex combination of Eqs.(3), (9) and the entropy term as follows:

$$L = \alpha\varphi + (1-\alpha)\psi + \beta \sum_{c=1}^{C} \sum_{i=1}^{n} u_{ci} \log u_{ci}$$

$$= \sum_{c=1}^{C} \sum_{i=1}^{n} u_{ci} \sum_{j=1}^{m} d_{ij} \left\{ \alpha(x_{ij} - \sum_{k=1}^{p} f_{cik} a_{cjk} - b_{cj})^2 + (1-\alpha)(x_{ij} - b_{cj})^2 \right\}$$

$$+ \beta \sum_{c=1}^{C} \sum_{i=1}^{n} u_{ci} \log u_{ci}, \tag{10}$$

where α is a constant which defines the tradeoff between FCM and local principal component analysis. When α is 0, Eq.(10) is equivalent to Eq.(9).

To obtain a unique solution, the objective function is minimized under the constrains that

$$F_c^{\mathrm{T}} U_c F_c = I_p \quad ; c = 1, \cdots, C, \tag{11}$$

$$F_c^{\mathrm{T}} 1_n = O \quad ; c = 1, \cdots, C, \tag{12}$$

$$\sum_{c=1}^{C} u_{ci} = 1 \quad ; i = 1, \cdots, n, \tag{13}$$

and $A_c^{\mathrm{T}} A_c$ is orthogonal.

To derive the optimal A_c and b_c, we rewrite Eq.(10) as follows:

$$L = \sum_{c=1}^{C} \sum_{j=1}^{m} \left\{ \alpha(x_j - F_c a_{cj} - 1_n b_{cj})^{\mathrm{T}} U_c D_j (x_j - F_c a_{cj} - 1_n b_{cj}) \right.$$

$$\left. + (1-\alpha)(x_j - 1_n b_{cj})^{\mathrm{T}} U_c D_j (x_j - 1_n b_{cj}) \right\} + \beta \sum_{c=1}^{C} \sum_{i=1}^{n} u_{ci} \log u_{ci}, \tag{14}$$

where

$$X = (x_1, \cdots, x_j, \cdots, x_m),$$

$$D_j = \mathrm{diag}(d_{1j}, \cdots, d_{nj}).$$

From $\partial L / \partial a_{cj} = 0$ and $\partial L / \partial b_{cj} = 0$, we have

$$a_{cj} = (F_c^{\mathrm{T}} U_c D_j F_c)^{-1} F_c^{\mathrm{T}} U_c D_j (x_j - 1_n b_{cj}), \tag{15}$$

$$b_{cj} = (1_n^{\mathrm{T}} U_c D_j 1_n)^{-1} 1_n^{\mathrm{T}} U_c D_j (x_j - \alpha F_c a_{cj}). \tag{16}$$

In the same way, we can derive the optimal F_c and u_{ci}. Eq.(10) is equivalent to

$$L = \sum_{c=1}^{C} \sum_{i=1}^{n} u_{ci} \Big\{ \alpha(\boldsymbol{x}_i - A_c \boldsymbol{f}_{ci} - \boldsymbol{b}_c)^{\mathrm{T}} D_i (\boldsymbol{x}_i - A_c \boldsymbol{f}_{ci} - \boldsymbol{b}_c)$$

$$+ (1 - \alpha)(\boldsymbol{x}_i - \boldsymbol{b}_c)^{\mathrm{T}} D_i (\boldsymbol{x}_i - \boldsymbol{b}_c) \Big\} + \beta \sum_{c=1}^{C} \sum_{i=1}^{n} u_{ci} \log u_{ci}, \qquad (17)$$

and $\partial L / \partial \boldsymbol{f}_{ci} = \boldsymbol{0}$ and $\partial L / \partial u_{ci} = 0$ yields

$$\boldsymbol{f}_{ci} = (A_c^{\mathrm{T}} D_i A_c)^{-1} A_c^{\mathrm{T}} D_i (\boldsymbol{x}_i - \boldsymbol{b}_c), \qquad (18)$$

$$u_{ci} = \exp \Big\{ -\Big(\alpha(\boldsymbol{x}_i - A_c \boldsymbol{f}_{ci} - \boldsymbol{b}_c)^{\mathrm{T}} D_i (\boldsymbol{x}_i - A_c \boldsymbol{f}_{ci} - \boldsymbol{b}_c)$$

$$+ (1 - \alpha)(\boldsymbol{x}_i - \boldsymbol{b}_c)^{\mathrm{T}} D_i (\boldsymbol{x}_i - \boldsymbol{b}_c) \Big) / \beta - 1 \Big\}, \qquad (19)$$

where

$$X = (\boldsymbol{x}_1, \cdots, \boldsymbol{x}_i, \cdots, \boldsymbol{x}_n)^{\mathrm{T}},$$
$$D_i = \mathrm{diag}(d_{i1}, \cdots, d_{im}).$$

The proposed algorithm can be written as follows.

Step1 Initialize $U_c, A_c, \boldsymbol{b}_c, F_c$ randomly in each cluster and normalize them so that they satisfy the constraints Eqs.(11)-(13) and $A_c^{\mathrm{T}} A_c$ is orthogonal.

Step2 Update A_c's using Eq.(15) and transform them so that each $A_c^{\mathrm{T}} A_c$ is orthogonal.

Step3 Update F_c's using Eq.(18) and normalize them so that they satisfy the constraints Eqs.(11) and (12).

Step4 Update $\boldsymbol{b}_c$'s using Eq.(16).

Step5 Update U_c's using Eq.(19) and normalize them so that Eq.(13) holds.

Step6 If

$$\max_{i,c} | u_{ci}^{NEW} - u_{ci}^{OLD} | < \epsilon,$$

then stop. Otherwise, return to Step3.

2.3   Estimation of Missing Values Using Local Principal Components

We propose a technique for estimating missing values using the lower rank approximations of the data matrix derived in local principal component analysis. Because the lower rank matrix Y_c derived in each cluster includes no missing values, we can estimate the missing values in the data matrix X by replacing them with the corresponding elements of Y_c. It means that we estimate the missing values on the assumption that the data points including missing values are on the linear varieties spanned by local principal component vectors. The procedure entails two steps.

1. Select the cluster c in which the active user i has largest membership u_{ic}.
2. Predict the missing value x_{ij} from the corresponding element y_{cij}.

The clustering part and the lower rank approximation part correspond to the selection of neighbors and the prediction using selected neighbors' ratings in the neighborhood-based methods respectively. Therefore, it can be said that the novel technique is one of the neighborhood-based methods where the selection of neighbors and the prediction of missing values are applied simultaneously.

Once we estimate the local linear models, we can predict the ratings of new active users. The memberships and the principal component scores of the new active users are estimated by Eqs.(19), (18) and we can predict y_{cij} using Eq.(20).

$$y_{cij} = \sum_{k=1}^{p} f_{cik} a_{cjk} + b_{cj} \tag{20}$$

3   Experimental Results

We implemented the novel technique presented in the previous section for the collaborative filtering and tested them with "kansei" data set that is the set of psychological evaluation data composed of 285 instances in which each user evaluated 8 different images used as background designs of stationery for word processor. Fig. 1 shows the 8 background designs. Each user evaluated the images

Fig. 1. 8 background designs

on a scale from 1 to 7 based on the semantic differential (SD) method as shown in Fig.2.

modern  traditional

Fig. 2. Seven-point Rating Scale

Each user withheld ratings for 2 items randomly and the predicted ratings were computed for those 2 items using local principal components derived by the proposed clustering method. The tradeoff parameter α and the weighting parameter of fuzziness β were set to 0.8 and 0.5 respectively, and the users were partitioned into two clusters. In addition, we also predicted the ratings using original GroupLens [1] and a non-personalized prediction method [13]. In the non-personalized prediction method, we computed the ratings using deviation-from-mean average over all users. Table 1 compares the result of them.

Table 1. Comparison of Results

Algorithm	MAE	ROC
Non-personalized Method	0.963	0.479
Original GroupLens	1.055	0.513
Proposed Method	1.066	0.591

For assessing the accuracy of the three prediction methods, we used not only the mean absolute error (MAE), but also the receiver operating characteristic (ROC) sensitivity. ROC sensitivity is a measure of the diagnostic power of a filtering system [13]. The sensitivity refers to the probability of a randomly selected good item being accepted by the filter. The greater the value is, the richer the performance becomes. The maximum value is one. In this paper, the items whose ratings are larger than 5 or smaller than 3 are regarded as good items. Although the proposed method had largest MAE, it provides the best performance according to ROC sensitivity. It indicates that the proposed method possesses the ability to recommend good items to active users.

4   Conclusions

In this paper, we proposed a new approach to the collaborative filtering. The new method is based on a simultaneous application of PCA and fuzzy clustering and is a kind of neighborhood-based methods. For the prediction of the ratings, users are partitioned into several linear clusters. It can be said that the clustering part is responsible for the selection of the neighborhood. The larger the cluster number is, the fewer the neighbors are.

Our future work is to determine the ability of the proposed method by using some other benchmarks.

References

1. Resnick, P., Iacovou, N., Suchak, M., Bergstrom, P., Riedl, J.: Grouplens: An Open Architecture for Collaborative Filtering of Netnews. Proc. of ACM Conference on Computer-Supported Cooperative Work (1994) 175–186
2. Konstan, J. A., Miller, B. N., Maltz, D., Herlocker, J. L., Gardon, L. R., Riedl, J.: Grouplens: Applying Collaborative Filtering to Usenet News. Communications of the ACM, Vol.40, No.3 (1997) 77–87
3. Shardanand, U., Maes, P.: Social Information Filtering: Algorithms for Automating "Word of Mouth". Proc. of ACM Conference on Human Factors in Computing Systems (1995) 210–217
4. Wiberg, T.: Computation of Principal Components when Data are Missing. Proc. of 2nd Symposium on computational Statistics (1976) 229–236
5. Shibayama, T.: A PCA-Like Method for Multivariate Data with Missing Values. Japanese Journal of Educational Psychology, Vol.40 (1992) 257–265 (in Japanese)
6. Shum, H., Ikeuchi, K., Reddy,R.: Principal Component Analysis with Missing Data and its Application to Polyhedral Object Modeling. IEEE Transactions on Pattern Analysis and Machine Intelligence, Vol. 17, No. 9 (1995) 854–867
7. Yamakawa, A., Honda, K., Ichihashi, H., Miyoshi, T.: Simultaneous Approach to Fuzzy Cluster, Principal Component and Multiple Regression Analysis. Proc. of International Conference on Neural Networks (1999)
8. Oh, C.-H., Komatsu, H., Honda, K., Ichihashi, H.: Fuzzy Clustering Algorithm Extracting Principal Components Independent of Subsidiary Variables. Proc. of International Conference on Neural Networks (2000)
9. Bezdek, J. C., Coray, C., Gunderson, R., Watson, J.: Detection and Characterization of Cluster Substructure 2. Fuzzy c-Varieties and Convex Combinations Thereof. SIAM J. Appl. Math., Vol.40, No.2 (1981) 358–372
10. Bezdek, J. C.: Pattern Recognition with Fuzzy Objective Function Algorithms. Plenum Press, New York (1981)
11. Miyamoto, S., Mukaidono, M.:Fuzzy c-Means as a Regularization and Maximum Entropy Approach. Proc. of 7th International Fuzzy Systems Association World Congress, Vol.2 (1997) 86–92
12. Miyamoto, S., Takata, O., Umayahara, K.: Handling Missing Values in Fuzzy c-Means. Proc. of 3rd Asian Fuzzy Systems Symposium (1998) 139–142
13. Herlocker, J. L., Konstan, J. A., Borchers, A. Riedl, J.: An Algorithmic Framework for Performing Collaborative Filtering. Proc. of Conference on Research and Development in Information Retrieval (1999)

iJADE IWShopper: A New Age of Intelligent Mobile Web Shopping System Based on Fuzzy-Neuro Agent Technology

Raymond S. T. Lee

Department of Computing, Hong Kong Polytechnic University
Hung Hom, Hong Kong
csstlee@comp.polyu.edu.hk

Abstract. Owing to the increasing number of mobile e-commerce applications using WAP technology, intelligent agent-based systems becoming a new trend of development in the new millennium. Traditional web-based agent systems suffer various degrees of deficiency in terms of the provision of 'intelligent' software interfaces and light-weighted coding to be implemented in WAP devices. In this paper, we propose a comprehensive and intelligent-agent platform known as *i*JADE (*i*ntelligent **J**ava **A**gent **D**evelopment **E**nvironment) for the development of smart (via the implementation of 'Conscious Layer'), compact and highly mobile agent applications. From the implementation point of view, we introduce the *i*JADE IWShopper - an intelligent mobile web shopping system using fuzzy-neuro agent technology - the integration of WAP and Java Servlets technology with our *i*JADE APIs. Promising results in terms of agent mobility, fuzzy-neural shopping efficiency and effectiveness are obtained.

1 Introduction

The exponential growth of the Internet industry in recent years brings new chances for business, especially in the field of e-commerce. Various e-commerce systems, ranging from C2C (Consumer-to-Consumer) e-commerce such as e-auction, to inter-organizational B2B (Business-to-Business) e-business for the international e-marketplace [2][9], have been operated in cyberspace. Agent technology, with its automatic delegation of tasks, autonomous and highly mobile characteristics in the Web environment, is starting to play an important role of e-commerce in the new millennium.

However, contemporary agent systems such as IBM Aglets [1] and ObjectSpace Voyager [10] focus on the mobility and multi-agent communications. The 'core' functions of intelligent agents (IA) - the AI (Artificial Intelligent) counterpart with intelligent capabilities including machine learning, intelligent pattern recognition and classification functions - are difficult to implement. In a typical e-shopping scenario, most of the time we are handling 'inexact' product selection criteria. For instance, in choosing a pair of shoes, we may base our choice on factors such as the 'degree of fitness' instead of the exact size, or 'preferred patterns' instead of the exact pattern match. In these cases, we are dealing with different degrees of 'fuzziness', which can

N. Zhong et al. (Eds.): WI 2001, LNAI 2198, pp. 403–412, 2001.
© Springer-Verlag Berlin Heidelberg 2001

be efficiently handled by AI technologies such as fuzzy systems. With the integration of machine learning technique such as neural networks, an 'intelligent' product selection and advisory system can be constructed [7].

Another major shortcoming of contemporary agent-based systems is that, for the Internet user who would like to invoke mobile agents, a dedicated agent operating system such as the Tahiti server for IBM Aglets [1] has to been installed in the client machine (e.g. your office PC) and the back-end server (e.g. the cyberstore). However, in a mobile e-commerce system such as Internet shopping via WAP phone (namely 'm-shopping' stands for mobile-shopping), due to the limitation in memory capability and communication speed in contemporary WAP phone technology, it is infeasible and impractical to install these agent operating systems into the WAP phones, let alone to the manipulations of multi-agents in such environments.

In this paper, we propose a comprehensive and truly intelligent agent-based framework, known as *i*JADE (pronounced as 'IJ') - intelligent Java Agent Development Environment. To compensate for the deficiency of contemporary agent software platforms such as IBM Aglets and ObjectSpace Voyager Agents, which mainly focus on multi-agent mobility and communication, *i*JADE provides an ingenious layer called the 'Conscious (Intelligent) Layer' which implements various AI functionalities into multi-agent applications. From the implementation point of view, we will demonstrate one of the most important applications of *i*JADE in the mobile e-commerce environment: *i*JADE IWShopper. With the integration of Java Servlet technology in the 'Technology Layer' of *i*JADE model, *i*JADE IWShopper provides an innovative intelligent agent-based solution in MEB (Mobile Electronic Business) with the integration of four different technologies: 1) WAP technology for mobile e-commerce (in the *i*JADE 'Support Layer'), 2) mobile agent technology based on Aglets (in the *i*JADE 'Technology Layer'), 3) Java servlets for servlet-side agent dispatch in WAP servers, and 4) AI capability in the 'Conscious Layer' using fuzzy-neural networks as the AI backbone - an extension of the previous research on fuzzy agent-based shopping using FShopper technology [4].

2 *i*JADE Model – Intelligent Agent-Based Web Development Platform

2.1 *i*JADE Framework: The ACTS Model

In this paper, we propose a fully integrated intelligent agent model called *i*JADE (pronounced 'IJ') for intelligent Web mining and other intelligent agent-based e-commerce applications. The system framework is shown in Fig. 1.

Unlike contemporary agent systems and APIs such as IBM Aglets [1] and ObjectSpace Voyager [10], which focus on the multi-agent communication and autonomous operations, the aim of *i*JADE is to provide comprehensive 'intelligent' agent-based APIs and applications for future e-commerce and Web mining applications.

Fig. 1 depicts the two levels of abstraction in the *i*JADE system: a) the *i*JADE system level - ACTS model, and b) the *i*JADE data level - DNA model. The ACTS model consists of 1) Application Layer, 2) Conscious (Intelligent) Layer, 3)

Technology Layer, and 4) Supporting Layer. The DNA model is composed of 1) Data Layer, 2) Neural Network Layer, and 3) Application Layer.

Compared with contemporary agent systems which provide minimal and elementary data management schemes, the *i*JADE DNA model provides a comprehensive data manipulation framework based on network neural technology. The 'Data Layer' corresponds to the raw data and input 'stimulates' (such as the facial images captured from the Web camera and the product information in the cyberstore) from the environment. The 'Neural Network Layer' provides the 'clustering' of different types of neural networks for the purposes of 'organization', 'interpretation', 'analysis' and 'forecasting' operations based on the inputs from the 'Data Layer', which are used by *i*JADE applications in the 'Application Layer'.

Another innovative feature of the *i*JADE system is the ACTS model, which provides a comprehensive layering architecture for the implementation of intelligent agent systems, explained in the next sections.

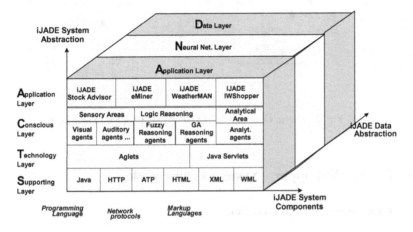

Fig. 1. System Architecture of *i*JADE (v1.2) model

2.2 Application Layer Including IWShopper

This is the uppermost layer that consisting of different intelligent agent-based systems, which are based on the intelligent agent components provided by the 'Conscious Layer' and the data 'knowledge fields' provided by the DNA model.

Concurrent applications (*i*JADE v1.0) implemented in this layer include:

- *i*JADE Stock Advisor, an intelligent agent-based stock prediction system using time series neuro-oscillatory prediction technique [6].
- *i*JADE eMiner, the intelligent Web-mining agent system on e-shopping [3]. It consists of the implementation of 1) FAgent, an automatic authentication system based on human face recognition [5], and 2) FShopper, a fuzzy agent-based Internet shopping agent [4].
- *i*JADE WeatherMAN, an intelligent weather forecasting agent which is the extension of previous research on multi-station weather forecasting using fuzzy neural networks [8].

- *i*JADE IWShopper, an integrated intelligent fuzzy shopping agent with WAP technology for intelligent mobile shopping, as proposed in this paper.

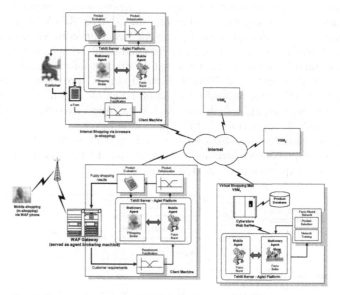

Fig. 2. System Overview of *i*JADE IWShopper for m-shopping

3 *i*JADE IWShopper – System Framework

3.1 IWShopper: System Overview

As an extension to the previous work on Fuzzy Shopper (FShopper) [4], a fuzzy shopping agent for Internet shopping, *i*JADE IWShopper provides an integrated intelligent agent-based solution for m-shopping via a WAP device. Based on the *i*JADE model discussed in section 4, *i*JADE IWShopper integrates the following technologies to develop the application: 1) Mobile agent technology based on Aglets for the agent framework (the 'Technology Layer' of the *i*JADE model), 2) Java Servlets technology for the manipulation of the server-side operations in the brokering machine (the 'Technology Layer' of the *i*JADE model), and 3) FShopper - intelligent fuzzy-neural based shopping operations (the 'Conscious Layer' of the *i*JADE model).

Fig. 2 depicts the overall system framework of *i*JADE IWShopper on m-shopping (mobile shopping via WAP phone) using *i*JADE technology in different cyberstores. Actually, Fig. 2 demonstrates two situations of 'intelligent agent shopping': 1) Fuzzy Internet shopping via a Web browser, and 2) Fuzzy WAP shopping (IWShopper) using a WAP phone as the WAP device. In other words, any agent-based cyberstores can be operated in this framework provided that their agent servers conform to MASIF (Mobile Agent System Interoperability Facility) standards. More importantly, under this infrastructure, both Web-based e-shopping and MEB m-shopping can operate simultaneously!

The system framework of the IWShopper consists of the following modules:

1. Customer requirement definition (CRD)
2. Requirement fuzzification scheme (RFS)
3. Fuzzy agents negotiation scheme (FANS)
4. Fuzzy product selection scheme (FPSS)
5. Product defuzzification scheme (PDS)
6. Product evaluation scheme (PES)

In this *i*JADE agents brokering center, there are two types of *i*JADE agents: 1) FShopping Broker - A stationary agent that acts as a buyer broker on behalf of the customer. This autonomous *i*JADE agent contains all necessary information and analytical techniques (provided by the 'Conscious Layer' of the model), such as the requirement for fuzzification and defuzzication, product evaluation techniques, etc; 2) Fuzzy Buyer - A mobile *i*JADE agent that acts as a virtual buyer in the virtual marketplace. It corresponds to all agent communication, interaction and negotiation operations.

After the customer has input all his/her product requirements (e.g. color, size, style, fitness) into the WAP phone, WShopping Broker (in the brokering center) will convert all these fuzzy requirements into fuzzy variables by using the "embedded" knowledge (i.e. the membership functions) with its knowledge base. Of course, WShopping Broker will also be responsible for the form data validation jobs as well. Sample fuzzy membership functions for selected attributes for shoes, including color and degree of fitness, are shown in Fig. 3.

$$Color\,(color) = \{red, yellow, blue\}$$

$$color = \left\{ \begin{array}{l} Light, Normal, Deep\,|\,\forall \mu_{color}(Light), \\ \mu_{color}(Normal), \mu_{color}(Deep) \in [0,1] \end{array} \right\}$$

$$\mu_{color}(Light) = \begin{cases} 1 & if\ 0 \leq x \leq 64 \\ \dfrac{96-x}{32} & if\ 64 \leq x \leq 96 \\ 0 & otherwise \end{cases}$$

$$\mu_{color}(Normal) = \begin{cases} \dfrac{x-64}{32} & if\ 64 \leq x \leq 96 \\ 1 & if\ 96 \leq x \leq 160 \\ \dfrac{192-x}{32} & if\ 160 \leq x \leq 192 \\ 0 & otherwise \end{cases}$$

$$\mu_{color}(Deep) = \begin{cases} 1 & if\ x \geq 192 \\ \dfrac{x-160}{32} & if\ 160 \leq x \leq 192 \\ 0 & otherwise \end{cases}$$

$$Fitness = \left\{ \begin{array}{l} Loose, Fit, Tight\,|\,\forall \mu_{fitness}(Loose), \\ \mu_{fitness}(Fit), \mu_{fitness}(Tight) \in [0,1] \end{array} \right\}$$

$$\mu_{fitness}(Loose) = \begin{cases} 1 & if\ 0 \leq x \leq 3 \\ 4-x & if\ 3 \leq x \leq 4 \\ 0 & otherwise \end{cases}$$

$$\mu_{fitness}(Fit) = \begin{cases} x-3 & if\ 3 \leq x \leq 4 \\ 1 & if\ 4 \leq x \leq 7 \\ 8-x & if\ 7 \leq x \leq 8 \\ 0 & otherwise \end{cases}$$

$$\mu_{fitness}(Tight) = \begin{cases} 1 & if\ x \geq 8 \\ x-7 & if\ 7 \leq x \leq 8 \\ 0 & otherwise \end{cases}$$

Fig. 3. Sample Membership Functions for Color and Degree of Fitness

Once Fuzzy Seller collects all the customer fuzzy requirements, it will perform the product selection based on a fuzzy neural network (provided by the *i*JADE DNA data model). Actually, the fuzzy neural network is an integration of fuzzy technology and Feedforward Backpropagation neural network (FFBP), provided by the *i*JADE Conscious Layer. A schematic diagram of the network framework is depicted in Fig. 4.

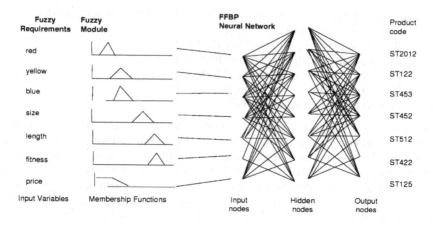

Fig. 4. Fuzzy-neural Network for Product Selection

Fig. 4 illustrates the FPSS using fuzzy-neural network for product selection (e.g. a pair of shoes). The fuzzy neural network consists of two parts: the fuzzy module and the FeedForward BackPropropagation (FFBP) neural network module. The fuzzy module provides the network with a bundle of fuzzy variables as input nodes. In the example, the fuzzy variables consist of color components (i.e. red, yellow and blue), size, length, degree of fitness and price.

4   Experimental Results

4.1   Introduction

From the implementation point of view, m-shopping in cyberstores is performed for simulation purposes. For the product database, over 200 items under eight categories were used to construct the e-catalog. These categories were: T-shirt, shirt, shoes, trousers, skirt, sweater, tablecloth, napkins. We deliberately chose softgood items instead of hardgoods such as books or music (as commonly found in most e-shopping agent systems), so that it would allow more room for fuzzy user requirement definition and product selection.

For neural network training, all the e-Catalog items were 'pre-trained' in the sense that we had pre-defined the attribute descriptions for all these items to be 'fed' into the fuzzy neural network for product training (for each category). Totally, eight different neural networks were constructed according to each different category of product.

From the experimental point of view, two sets of tests were conducted: the Round Trip Time (RTT) test and the Product Selection (PS) test. The RTT test aims at an evaluation of the "efficiency" of the IWShopper in the sense that it will calculate the whole round trip time of the iJADE agents, instead of calculating the difference between the arrival and departure time to/from any particular server. The RTT test will calculate all the 'component' time fragments starting from the collection of the user requirement from the WAP phone, fuzzification, to the product selection and evaluation steps in the brokering center (WAP gateway) and various cyberstores, so that a total picture of the performance efficiency can be deduced. Comparison with fuzzy e-shopper (FShopper [4]) will be conducted.

In the Product Selection (PS) test, since there was no definite answer to whether a product would 'fit' the taste of the customer or not, a sample group of 40 candidates were used to judge the 'effectiveness' of the IWShopper. Details was illustrated in the following sections.

4.2 Round Trip Time (RTT) Test

In this test, two *i*JADE Servers were used: the T1server and the T2server. The T1server was situated within the same LAN of the client machine while T2server in a remote site (within the campus).
Results of the mean RTT after 100 trials for each server are shown in Table 1.
As shown in Table 1, the total RTT is dominated by the Fuzzy Product Selection Scheme (FPSS), but the time spent is still within an acceptable timeframe: 5 to 7 seconds. Besides, the difference of RTT between the server situated in the same LAN and the remote site was not significant except in the FANS, whereas Fuzzy Buyer needs to take a slightly longer 'trip' than the other. Of course, in reality, it depends heavily on the network traffic.

Table 1. Mean RTT summary after 100 trials

Time (msec.)	IWShopper (m-shopping)		FShopper (e-shopping)	
	T1server	T2sever	T1server	T2sever
Server location	Same LAN as client	Remote site	Same LAN as client	Remote site
A. In WAP phone & WAP gateway (IWShopper) / Client browser (FShopper)				
CRD	-		-	
RFS	25	73	310	305
B. In Cyberstore (both IWShopper & FShopper)				
FANS	225	1304	320	2015
FPSS	3120	3311	4260	4133
A. In WAP phone & WAP gateway (IWShopper) / Client browser (FShopper)				
PDS	310	335	320	330
PES	53	102	251	223
TOTAL RTT	3733	5125	5461	7006

Compared with e-shopping using the FShopper [4], m-shopping using the IWShopper provides a more efficient result, mainly due to two reasons: 1) In the IWShopper scenario, all the cyberstores and WAP gateways are configured with the *i*JADE agent framework, better management of fuzzy shopping operations is provided, and more importantly the fuzzy agents are 'lightweighted' since all the related fuzzy evaluation APIs are implicitly provided by the *i*JADE framework. 2) As the major task of the WAP device is the collection of customer requirements and display of selection results, all the invoking, dispatching and manipulation of fuzzy agents (which was originally done in the client machine) is now switched to the brokering center, as reflected by the short processing time in the RFS and PES processes.

4.3 Product Selection (PS) Test

Unlike the RTT test, in which objective figures can be easily obtained, the PS test results rely heavily on user preference. In order to get a more objective result, a sample group of 40 candidates was invited for system evaluation. In the test, each candidate would "buy" one product from each category according to his/her own requirements. For evaluation, they would browse around the e-catalog to choose a list of the 'best five choices' (L) which 'fit his/her taste'. In comparison with the 'top five' recommended product items (i) given by the fuzzy shopper, the 'Fitness Value (FV)" is calculated as follows:

$$FV = \frac{\sum_{n=1}^{5} n \times i}{15} \quad where \ i = \begin{cases} 1 & if \ i \in L \\ 0 & otherwise \end{cases}$$

In the calculation, scores of 5 to 1 were given to 'correct matches' of the candidate's first to fifth 'best five' choices with the fuzzy shopper's suggestion. For example, if out of the five "best choices" selected by the customer, products of rank no. 1, 2, 3 and 5 appear in the fuzzy shopper recommended list, the fitness value will be 73%, which is the sum of 1, 2, 3 and 5 divided by 15.

In this experiment, four different product selection schemes are adopted:
1) Simple product selection (using product description matching - traditional technique)
2) Product selection based on FFBP neural network training
3) Product selection based on fuzzy product description - no network training is involved
4) IWShopper - product selection based on fuzzy-neural training

The corresponding Fitness Values (FV) and the degree of improvement (against the 'traditional' technique) under the eight different product categories are shown in Table 2.

In view of the IWShopper PS result, it is not difficult to predict that the performance of the Fuzzy Shopper is highly dependent on the "variability" (or "fuzziness") of the merchandise. The higher the fuzziness (which means more variety), the lower the score. As shown in Table 2, skirts and shoes are typical examples in which skirts scores 65% and shoes scores 89%. Nevertheless, the average score is still over 81%. Note that these figures are only for illustration purposes, as human justification and product variety in actual scenarios do vary case by case.

Comparing different product selection techniques, IWShopper outperforms the FShopper by over 40%; compared with the 'traditional technique', a promising improvement of 48% is attained.

Another interesting phenomenon is found in comparing the PS of the 'Pure FFBP training' and the 'Pure Fuzzy PS'. Overall, although the former outperforms the later by 5%, the 'Pure Fuzzy PS' technique produces 'exceptionally good' results in certain product categories such as shirt, skirts and sweater, which are all 'fuzzy' products in which the fuzzification technique might help in fuzzy product selection.

Table 2. Fitness value for the eight different product categories under different product selection schemes

Product category	Fitness Value FV% (% Improvement)			
	Simple product search	Pure FFBP Training	Pure Fuzzy product search	IWShopper (Fuzzy-neural)
T-shirt	48	58 (+21)	54 (+13)	81 (+69)
Shirt	41	48 (+17)	53 (+29)	78 (+90)
Shoes	56	68 (+21)	58 (+4)	89 (+59)
Trousers	52	63 (+21)	56 (+8)	88 (+69)
Skirts	32	38 (+19)	45 (+41)	65 (+103)
Sweater	45	53 (+18)	55 (+22)	81 (+80)
Tablecoth	57	67 (+18)	61 (+7)	85 (+49)
Napkins	53	64 (+21)	58 (+9)	86 (+62)
Average score	48.0%	57.4% (+20%)	55.0% (+15%)	81.6% (+70%)

5 Conclusion

In this paper, we proposed an integrated 'intelligent agent' model, namely *i*JADE, for the development of intelligent multi-agent based applications. From the implementation point of view, we have developed the *i*JADE IWShopper - an intelligent shopping agent for mobile shopping (via a WAP device) on the Internet.

More importantly, IWShopper demonstrates how different technologies (including mobile agent technology for mobile agent framework construction, Java Servlet technology for server-side programming, WAP technology for mobile computing and AI for 'intelligent' machine learning, classification and selection) can be successfully integrated into the *i*JADE model to develop a truly 'smart' agent for MEB (Mobile E-Business). Hopefully it can offer new insight not only into AI technologies, but also into how these technologies can be effectively applied to contemporary e-commerce and m-business.

Acknowledgment. The authors are grateful to the partial supports of the Departmental Grants for *i*JADE WShopper Project 4.61.09.Z028 from the Hong Kong Polytechnic University.

References

1. Aglets. URL: http://www.trl.ibm.co.jp/aglets/.
2. Chan Henry, Lee Raymond, Dillon T. S. and Chang E. (Eds.): E-Commerce: Fundamentals and Applications. John Wiley & Sons Ltd., forthcoming (2001).
3. Lee R. S. T. and Liu J. N. K.: *i*JADE eMiner - A Web-based Mining Agent based on Intelligent Java Agent Development Environment (*i*JADE) on Internet Shopping. To appear in the Fifth Int'l Conference on Knowledge Discovery and Data Mining (PAKDD'2001). Lecture Notes in Artificial Intelligence series, Springer-Verlag (2001).
4. Lee R. S. T. and Liu J. N. K.: Fuzzy Shopper - A fuzzy network based shopping agent in E-commerce environment. In Proc. of the International ICSC Symposium on Multi-Agents and Mobile Agents in virtual organizations and E-commerce (MAMA'2000), December 11-13, Wollongong, Australia (2000).
5. Lee R. S. T. and Liu J. N. K.: FAgent - An Innovative E-Shopping Authentication Scheme using Invariant Intelligent Face Recognition Agent. In Proc. of International Conference in Electronic Commerce (ICEC'2000), Seoul, Korea (2000) 47-53.
6. Lee R. S. T. and Liu J. N. K.: Tropical Cyclone Identification and Tracking System using Integrated Neural Oscillatory Elastic Graph Matching and Hybrid RBF Network Track Mining Techniques. IEEE Transaction on Neural Network, 11(3) (2000) 680-689.
7. Lee, R. S. T. and Liu J. N. K.: Teaching and Learning the A. I. Modeling. In Innovative Teaching Tools: Knowledge-Based Paradigms (Studies in Fuzziness and Soft Computing 36), L. C. Jain (eds), Physica-Verlag, Springer (2000) 31-86.
8. Liu J. N. K. and Lee R. S. T.: Rainfall Forecasting from Multiple Point Source Using Neural Networks. In Proceedings of IEEE International Conference on Systems, Man, and Cybernetics (SMC'99), Vol. II, Tokyo, Japan (1999) 429-434.
9. Turban E., Lee J., King D. and Chung D. (Eds.): Electronic Commerce: A Managerial Perspective. Prentice Hall, (2000).
10. Odyssey URL: http://www.genmagic.com/.

Wireless Agent Guidance of Remote Mobile Robots: Rough Integral Approach to Sensor Signal Analysis

J.F. Peters[1], S. Ramanna[1], A. Skowron[2], and M. Borkowski[1]

[1] Computer Engineering, Univ. of Manitoba, Winnipeg, MB R3T 5V6 Canada
{jfpeters,ramanna,maciey}@ee.umanitoba.ca
[2] Institute of Mathematics, Warsaw Univ., Banacha 2, 02-097 Warsaw, Poland
skowron@mimuw.edu.pl

Abstract. A rough integral multiple sensor fusion model for wireless agent guidance of remote mobile robots is presented in this paper. A rough measure of sensor signal values provides a basis for a discrete form of rough integral that offers a means of aggregating sensor values and to estimate by means of a sensor signal how close robot is to a target region of space. By way of illustration, the actions of a collection of robots are controlled by a wireless system that connects a web agent (called a Guide Agent or GA) written in Java and pairs of Radio Packet Controller (RPCs) modules (one attached to a workstation and a second RPC on board a robot). The web GA analyzes robot sensors signals, communicates robot movement commands and assists other web agents in updating some parts of a web page that implements a real-time robot traffic control system. This web page displays the current configuration of a society of mobile robots (stopping, direction of movement, avoiding, wandering, mapping, and planning). Only a brief description of the web GA is given in this paper.

1 Introduction

Considerable work has already been carried out in the study of various forms of agents in the context of rough sets (e.g., [12]-[15]), rough mereology (e.g., [1]-[2]), approximate reasoning by agents (e.g., [3]-[5]), and sensor fusion (e.g., [6]-[9]). An agent is an independent process capable of responding to stimuli from its environment and communicating with other agents in its society. In this paper, the focus is on the design of a form of web agent called a Guide Agent (GA). The web GA described in this paper receives and analyzes robot sensors signals, communicates robot movement commands (usually originating from a human robot traffic controller) and assists other agents in updating some parts of a web page that implements a real-time robot traffic control system. The web page displays the current configuration of a society of mobile robots (stopping, direction of movement, avoiding, wandering, mapping, and planning). The contribution

N. Zhong et al. (Eds.): WI 2001, LNAI 2198, pp. 413–422, 2001.
© Springer-Verlag Berlin Heidelberg 2001

of this paper is the modeling of web agents that classify sensor signals using rough integration to measure the effectiveness of a navigation plan to achieve an objective. This paper is structured as follows. The basic concepts underlying sensor signal analysis by a web-based guide agent are briefly presented, namely, set approximation and rough membership functions (Section 2), rough measures (Section 3) and discrete rough integrals (Section 4). Multi-sensor fusion, identification of relevant sensors, a model of a web guide agent, and an example of a web-based wireless system for guiding the actions of mobile robots are presented in Section 5.

2   Basic Concepts of Rough Sets

Rough set theory offers a systematic approach to set approximation [13]. To begin, let $S = (U, A)$ be an information system where U is a non-empty, finite set of objects and A is a non-empty, finite set of attributes, where $a : U \to V_a$ for every $a \in A$. For each $B \subseteq A$, let there is associated an equivalence relation $Ind_A(B)$ such that

$$Ind_A(B) = \{(x, x') \in U^2 \mid \forall a \in B.a(x) = a(x')\}$$

If $(x, x') \in Ind_A(B)$, we say that objects x and x' are indiscernible from each other relative to attributes from B. The notation $[x]_B$ denotes equivalence classes of $Ind_A(B)$. Further, partition $U/Ind_A(B)$ denotes the family of all equivalence classes of relation $Ind_A(B)$ on U. For $X \subseteq U$, the set X can be approximated only from information contained in B by constructing a B-lower and B-upper approximation denoted by $\underline{B}X$ and $\overline{B}X$ respectively, where $\underline{B}X = \{x \mid [x]_B \subseteq X\}$ and $\overline{B}X = \{x \mid [x]_B \cap X \neq \emptyset\}$.

Definition 1. *Let $S = (U, A)$ be an information system. Further, let $\wp(U)$ denote the powerset of U, $B \subseteq A$, $u \in U$ and let $[u]_B$ be an equivalence class of an object $u \in U$ of $Ind_A(B)$. The set function*

$$\mu_u^B : \wp(U) \to [0, 1], \text{where } \mu_u^B(X) = \frac{|X \cap [u]_B|}{|[u]_B|} \quad \text{for any } X \in \wp(U)$$

is called a rough membership function.

A rough membership function provides a classification measure inasmuch as it tests the degree of overlap between the set X in $\wp(U)$ and equivalence class $[u]_B$. The form of rough membership function in Def. 1 is slightly different from the classical definition where the argument of the rough membership function is an object x and the set X is fixed [14].

3   Rough Measures

Let $S = (U, A)$ be an information system, $X \subseteq U$, $B \subseteq A$, and let $Ind_A(B)$ be the indiscernibility relation on U. The tuple $(X, \wp(X), U/Ind_A(B))$, where $\wp(X)$ denotes the family of subsets of X and $U/Ind_A(B)$ denotes a set of all equivalence classes determined by $Ind_A(B)$ on U, is called an *indiscernibility space* over X and B. Let $u \in U$. A non-negative and additive set function $\rho_u : \wp(X) \rightarrow [0, \infty)$ defined by $\rho_u(Y) = \rho'(Y \cap [u]_B)$ for $Y \in \wp(X)$, where $\rho' : \wp(X) \rightarrow [0, \infty)$ is called a *rough measure* relative to $U/Ind_A(B)$ and u on the indiscernibility space $(X, \wp(X), U/Ind_A(B))$. The tuple $(X, \wp(X), U/Ind_A(B), \{\rho_u\}_{u \in U})$ is a *rough measure space* over X and B.

Example 1 (Sample Non-Negative Set Function). The rough membership function $\mu_u^B : \wp(X) \rightarrow [0, 1]$ is a non-negative and additive set function.

Proposition 1. [19] $(X, \wp(X), U/Ind_A(B), \mu_u^B)$ is a rough measure space over X and B.

Other rough measures based on upper {lower} approximations are possible but consideration of these other measures is outside the scope of this paper.

4   Discrete Rough Integral

Rough integrals were introduced in [15], and elaborated in [19]. In what follows, let $X = \{x_1, \ldots, x_n\}$ be a finite, non-empty set with n elements. The elements of X are indexed from 1 to n. The notation $X_{(i)}$ denotes the set $\{x_{(i)}, x_{(i+1)}, \ldots, x_{(n)}\}$ where $i \geq 1$ and $n = card(X)$. The subscript (i) is called a permutation index because the indices on elements of $X_{(i)}$ are chosen after a reordering of the elements of X. This reordering is "induced" by an external mechanism. Next, we use a functional defined by Choquet in 1953 in capacity theory [16] to define a discrete rough integral.

Definition 2. *Let ρ be a rough measure on X where the elements of X are denoted by $x_1, \ldots, x_n$. A particular form of a discrete rough integral of $f : X \rightarrow \Re^+$ with respect to the rough measure ρ is defined by*

$$\int f \, d\rho = \sum_{i=1}^{n} (f(x_{(i)}) - f(x_{(i-1)}))\rho(X_{(i)})$$

where $\bullet_{(i)}$ specifies that indices have been permuted so that $0 \leq f(x_{(i)}) \leq \ldots \leq f(x_{(n)})$, $X_{(i)} := \{x_{(i)}, \ldots, x_{(n)}\}$, and $f(x_{(0)}) = 0$.

This definition of a discrete rough integral is a variation of the definition given in Pawlak et al. [19] and a formulation of the Choquet integral by Grabisch [17]. It should be observed that in general the Choquet integral has the effect of "averaging" the values of a measurable function. This averaging closely resembles the well-known Ordered Weighted Average (OWA) operator [18].

Proposition 2 (Pawlak et al. [19]). *Let* $0 < s \leq r$. *If* $a(x) \in [s, r]$ *for all* $x \in X_a$, *then* $\int a \, d\mu_u^e \in (0, r]$ *where* $u \in U$.

5 Multi-sensor Fusion

Consider, next, the case where there is interest in discovering which sensor is more relevant among a set of sensors. The term relevance in this context denotes the "closeness" of a set of experimental sensor values relative to a set of a pre-calibrated, target sensor values that are considered important in a classification effort. The identification of relevant sensors provides a form of sensor fusion. The term sensor fusion generally refers to some process of combining sensor readings [11]. Further, assume that each of the sensors have the same model with essentially the same accuracy. At this stage, we will ignore the issue of the accuracy of a sensor, and trust that each sensor in a set of sensors produces output with low error.

5.1 Relevant Sensors

Assume that a denotes a proximity sensor that responds to stimuli (energy from a reflecting surface) with distance measurements. Let $\{a\} = B \subseteq A$ where $a : U \to [0, 0.5]$ where each sample sensor value $a(x)$ is rounded to two decimal places. Let $(Y, U - Y)$ be a partition defined by an expert and let $[u]_e$ denote a set in this partition containing u for a selected $u \in U$. We further assume the elements of $[u]_e$ are selected relative to an interval $(u - \varepsilon, u + \varepsilon)$ for a selected $\varepsilon \geq 0$. We assume a decision system (X_a, a, e) is given for any considered sensor a such that $X_a \subseteq U$, $a : X_a \to \Re^+$ and e is an expert decision restricted to X_a defining a partition $(Y \cap X_a, (U - Y) \cap X_a)$ of X_a. Moreover, we assume that $X_a \cap [u]_e \neq \emptyset$. The set $[u]_e$ is used to classify sensors and is given the name "classifier". By way of illustration, we give the following two tables.

Let $u = 0.425$ and $\varepsilon = 0.2$, and obtain $[0.425]_e$ with values in the interval $[a(0.225), a(0.625)] = [0.2, 0.6]$. The aim is to fuse the sample values in each signal using a rough integral, and evaluate the rough integral value relative to $[u]_e$. From Table 1(a) compute $\int a \, d\mu_u^e = 0.1$ and $\int a \, d\mu_u^e = 0.239$ from Table 1(b). The first integral value lies outside the target interval $[0.2, 0.6]$ and the second integral value falls inside $[0.2, 0.6]$. Let $\bar{u}$ denote the average value in the

Table 1. (a)   **Table 1. (b)**

$X\backslash\{a,e\}$	a	e
$x_1 = 0.203$	0.2	0
$x_2 = 0.454$	0.45	1
$x_3 = 0.453$	0.45	1
$x_4 = 0.106$	0.11	0
$x_5 = 0.104$	0.10	0

$X\backslash\{a,e\}$	a	e
$x_2 = 0.454$	0.45	1
$x_9 = 0.455$	0.46	1
$x_{10} = 0.401$	0.4	1
$x_{11} = 0.407$	0.41	1
$x_{12} = 0.429$	0.43	1

classifier $[u]_e$, and let $\delta \in [0,1]$. Then, for example, the selection R of the most relevant sensors in a set of sensors is found using

$$R = \left\{ a_i \in B : \left| \int a_i \, \mu_u^e - a(\bar{u}) \right| \le \delta \right\}$$

In effect, the integral $\int a_i \, d\mu_u^e$ serves as a filter inasmuch as it "filters" out all sensors with integral values not close enough to $a(\bar{u})$.

5.2 Guide Agent

A web-based guide agent (GA) is a web-based independent process that interacts with external devices via the internet and radio packet interfaces.

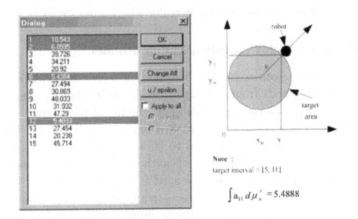

Fig. 1. Tracking Mobile Robot

The form of GA described in this article engages in sensor signal analysis and communicates navigation commands that direct an external device (e.g., a mobile robot) to navigate inside a specified region of space. The GA also provides input to other agents responsible for updating and maintaining a web page used to monitor the changing configuration of a system of commanded devices (e.g., motors on robots). Sample output in the form of a group of 15 range sensor readings from a sensor named a_{11} onboard an external device is shown in Fig. 1. Let a_{11} be the name of a robot ranging sensor (e.g., let a_{11} be an ultrasonic sensor that computes the distance L_0 travelled by an emitted sound wave that reflects back from an object where $L_0 = (vt\cos\theta)/2$) [10]. For simplicity, we assume that the velocity v of a sound wave in a medium is fixed, and θ (the angle of separation between transmitter and receiver in relation to a detected object) is also fixed. Then $[u]_e$ is a finite set of sample durations $\{u, t_1, t_2, \ldots\}$ considered representative of ideal timings by an expert. Sample output from a moving robot that monitors groups of 15 sensor readings at a time is shown in Fig. 1. In this case, the agent learns that the robot is maintaining an average distance of 5 cm from the center of a circle with radius 12 cm. At some point, the agent diverged from the center a distance of 39 cm (reading 3), then, after adjusting its position three times (readings 4 and 5), it slips back into the desired circle. Ideally, the integral value should equal $a_{11}(\bar{u})$ when the robot is navigating correctly.

5.3 Basic Guide Agent Algorithm

A guide agent begins with a universe of objects reflecting possible sensor values, a set of sensors, classifier set $[u]_e$, signal value threshold u, boundary value δ, and time limit t. A sensor signal measures the distance between a robot and a reflecting medium such as a wall in corridor where a mobile robot is navigating.

5.4 Example: Web-Controlled Mobile Robots

A pair of mobile robots exchanging information with a web GA (sensor signals from robot, commands from web agent) is shown in Fig. 2(a) and 2(b). Each robot is equipped with compass (module at the top of the "tower" of each robot in Fig. 2(a)), 6 ranging sensors, and Radiometrix Radio Packet Controller or RPC [20]. A RPC can send {receive} to {from} another RPC. It communicates at 40 Kbits/s over 433.92 MHz channels in the UHF band. Each robot RPC (Fig. 2(a)) communicates with a companion RPC (Fig. 2(b)) plugged into a Dallas Semiconductor TINI board that connects to an I/O port on a computer [21]. The TINI board has its own computer programmable in Java and makes it possible to web-enable remote electrical devices connected to ports on the TINI board. In this article, an ideal view of each robot is given where each robot is equipped with 6 ranging sensors to measure distances between the robot and the approximate center of a bounded region. We also assume that the bounded region is approximately circular. A GA monitors the direction of travel and relative position of a particular robot. It is also assumed that boundaries periodically move. Each robot has its own web GA and 6 ranging sensors. Each sensor provides

Guide Agent Algorithm

```
Input:        U, A, [u]_e, δ, t;       // universe, sensors, classifier, bound, ms delay
Constraint:   |∫ a dρ − a(ū)| ≤ δ      // sensor signal within an acceptable range
Output:       R                         // measured response to selected sensor
while (true) {
  delay(t); sample = integrate(read(sensorSignal));
  switch (sample) {
    (|sample − a(ū)| ≤ δ):{
      turnLeft; moveForward; stop;           // begin zigzag movement
      sample = integrate(read(a));
      switch (sample) {
        (|sample − a(ū)| ≤ δ):
          turnRight; moveForward; stop;    // zigzag
        (|sample − a(ū)| > δ): stop; u = calibrate(sample, u);
      } // switch
    (|sample − a(ū)| > δ): stop; u = calibrate(sample, u);
  } // switch
} // while (End Algorithm)
end Algorithm
```

distance measurements making it possible to estimate of the relative position of the robot.

Fig. 2. (a) Web Guided Robot   **Fig. 2. (b)** Radio Control Pack Modules

Assume that each sensor has a detection range from 0.1 cm to 30 cm and that sensor readings are made continuously and stored in a queue. Let $a_i, a_i(t)$ be the ith sensor and i^{th} sensor reading at time t, respectively. Sensor queues are analyzed for each collection of 10 readings. Assume we are interested in sensor readings in the range 30 cm ± 6cm where 30 is the approximate center of a circular "ambling" region for a robot whose mission is to explore its bounded environment. A summary of the integral values for two separate experiments with sensor signal samples gathered over time is given in the control chart in Fig. 3, where the Upper {Lower} Control Limits 30.87{6.03} have been chosen arbitrarily. Since the average integral value is inside the target interval, the web GA continues using the same circular region in guiding robot actions. If one of the boundaries were to move (e.g., a door opens) and the robot is able to move beyond the boundary of the circular region, the web GA would calibrate u (we assume u is a parameter such as duration in the model for an ultrasonic sensor) to facilitate new exploration by the robot.

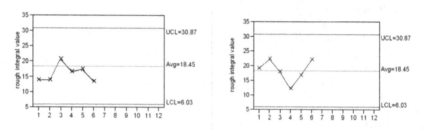

Fig. 3. Sample Navigation Control Charts for Rough Integral Values

Remark. Suppose we are interested in estimating for a considered period of time if an agent moving around in a circular region with obstacles such as walls. The meaning of this can be estimated by an expert looking at the plot in Fig. 3 relative to the requirement stipulated by $[u]_e$. We can imagine a decision table with sample sensor signals (not single sample signal values but a set of sample signal values) where a decision to view a signal as acceptable is approximated by $\int a \, d\rho$, which is deemed "close enough" to $a(\bar{u})$ for sensor a. That is, the integral value tends to reflect (approximate) an expert decision about the appropriateness of robot movements relative to the target region. That is, the integral computes the aggregative effect reflected by sensor values relative to the "walking region". The set $[u]_e$ provides a basis for classifying sensor signals.

6   Conclusion

This article presents an application of a discrete form of rough integral in the design of a web guide agent that guides the actions of a mobile robot. This integral computes an ordered weighted average and provides a means of sensor fusion. The rough integral is superior to other known forms of weighted averaging because it is computed relative to a classification requirement reflected in $[u]_e$. Further, the set $[u]_e$ makes it possible to classify sensor signals inasmuch as it prescribes "ideal" parameter values for a ranging sensor in a required region of space considered safe for the movements of the robot being controlled by a navigation agent. In a sense, $[u]_e$ provides a schema that mediates between the sensors and planner for a web agent responsible for guiding the movements of a remote mobile robot. In this context, the term *schema* denotes a mediating representation. Hence, $[u]_e$ is also called a classification schema, a fundamental feature in the intelligence of an agent. In a complete web-based robot control system, a collection of robots would be controlled remotely (e.g., a web page accessed in control centers in Tokyo and other cities in Japan could be used to monitor and control a collection of robots designed to inspect railway tracks).

Acknowledgment. The research of Sheela Ramanna and James Peters has been supported by the Natural Sciences and Engineering Research Council of Canada (NSERC) research grant 194376 and research grant 185986, respectively. The research of Maciej Borkowski has been supported by a grant from Manitoba Hydro. The research of Andrzej Skowron has been supported by grant 8 T11C 025 19 from the State Committee for Scientific Research (KBN) and from a grant from the Wallenberg Foundation.

References

1. L. Polkowski, A. Skowron, Rough mereology: A new paradigm for approximate reasoning, Int. Journal of Approximate Reasoning 15/4 (1996) pp. 333-365.
2. L. Polkowski, A. Skowron, Rough mereological foundations for design, analysis, and control in distributed systems, Information Sciences: An Int. Journal 104/1-2 (1998) 129-156.
3. A. Skowron, J. Stepaniuk, J.F. Peters, Approximation of information granule sets. In: Ziarko W. Yao Y., Proc. of the 2nd Int. Conf. on Rough Sets and Current Trends in Computing (RSCTC'00), 16-19 Oct. 2000, Banff, Canada, 33-40.
4. A. Skowron, Approximate reasoning by agents in distributed environments. In: Proc. Int. Conf. on Intelligent Agent Technology (IAT'01) [to appear].
5. A. Skowron, Toward intellligent systems: Calculi of information granules. In: Proc. Int. Workshop on Rough Set Theory and Granular Computing (RSTGC'01), Bull. of Int. Rough Set Society 5(1/2), Matsue, Shimane, Japan, 20-21 May 2001, 9-30.
6. J.F. Peters et al., Sensor fusion: A rough granular approach. In: Proc. of Int. Fuzzy Systems Association World Congress (IFSA'01), Vancouver, July 2001 [to appear].
7. J.F. Peters et al., Sensor fusion: A rough Petri net model. In: Proc. of Int. Fuzzy Systems Association World Congress (IFSA'01), Vancouver, July 2001 [to appear].
8. J.F.Peters, L.Han, S.Ramanna, Rough neural computing in signal analysis, Computational Intelligence, vol. 1, no. 3, 2001, 493-513.
9. J.F. Peters et al., Sensor, filter, and fusion models with rough Petri nets, Fundamenta Informatica 34, 2001, 1-19.
10. J. Fraden, Handbook of Modern Sensors: Physics, Design, and Applications (Springer-Verlag, Berlin, 1996).
11. R.R. Brooks, S.S. Iyengar, Multi-Sensor Fusion, Upper Saddle River, NJ: Prentice-Hall PTR, 1998.
12. Z. Pawlak, Rough sets, Int. J. of Computer and Information Sciences, Vol. 11, 1982, 341-356.
13. Z. Pawlak, Rough Sets: Theoretical Aspects of Reasoning About Data (Kluwer Academic Publishers, Boston, MA, 1991).
14. Z. Pawlak, A. Skowron, Rough membership functions. In: R. Yager, M. Fedrizzi, J. Kacprzyk (Eds.), Advances in the Dempster-Shafer Theory of Evidence (John-Wiley & Sons, NY, 1994) 251-271.

15. Z. Pawlak, On rough derivatives, rough integrals, and rough differential equations, ICS Research Report 41/95, Institute of Computer Science, Nowowiejska 15/19, 00-665 Warsaw, Poland (1995).
16. G. Choquet, Theory of capacities, Annales de l'Institut Fourier 5 (1953) 131-295.
17. M. Grabisch, Alternative expressions of the discrete Choquet integral. In: Proc. 7th IFSA World Congress, Prague (25-29 June 1997) 472-477.
18. R.Yager, On ordered weighted averaging aggregation operators in multi-criteria decision making, IEEE Trans. on System, Man and Cybernetics 18 (1988) 183-190.
19. Z. Pawlak, J.F. Peters, A. Skowron, Z. Surai, S. Ramanna, M. Borkowski, Rough measures: Theory and application. In: Proc. Rough Set Theory and Granular Computing (RSTGR'2001) Japan (2001) [to appear].
20. Radiometrix: http://www.radiometrix.co.uk
21. TINI: http://www.ibutton.com/TINI/index.html

Ontology-Based Information Gathering Agents

Yi-Jia Chen[1] and Von-Wun Soo[2]

[1] Advanced Technology Center, Computer and Communication Research Lab, Industrial
Technology Research Institute, Bldg. 51, 195-11 Sec. 4, Chung Hsing Rd., Chutung, Hsinchu,
Taiwan, 310, R.O.C.
jchen@itri.org.tw
[2] Department of Computer Science, National Tsing Hua University, 101 Kuang Fu Rd.,
Sec. 2, HsingChu, Taiwan, 300, R.O.C.
soo@cs.nthu.edu.tw

Abstract. A well-known problem of World Wide Web (WWW) is that it contains ultra-large amount of information that often makes it difficult for users to find out their desired information. We propose and implement architecture of ontology-based information gathering agents. The ontology is represented by object-oriented approach with procedural attachments. The information gathering agents could carry out the search by wrapping the search engines of various kinds as their search methods and perform planning and integration of the partial information gathering results. The users also can represent their queries in terms of the shared domain ontology to reduce their conceptual gaps with agents. It shows how information gathering agents could utilize domain knowledge and integrate information gathered from disparate information resources and provide much more coherent results for the users.

1 Introduction

World Wide Web (WWW) can be regarded as a huge distributed digital library that contains rich information. But it is hard for users to retrieve desired information from it without a powerful information gathering tool. So many search engines are designed for gathering information in the WWW. But they all have some drawbacks [1]. The search engines can't provide the result with high precision. The domain ontology may help the content matching and thus increase the precision of information gathering. "An ontology is a formal, explicit specification of a shared conceptualization [2] ". There are many researches about ontologies, ex: CYC [3] and WordNet [4]. Structured content representations coupled with linguistic ontologies like WordNet can support content-based retrieval [5]. Recently XML schema and XML/RDF are also a similar effort toward the goal to overcome the difficult information gathering problems for the web, for example: Semantic Web [6].

In this paper we design architecture of ontology based information gathering agent. The agent could utilize the domain ontology to extract and integrate the information form disparate search engines and web pages.

N. Zhong et al. (Eds.): WI 2001, LNAI 2198, pp. 423–427, 2001.
© Springer-Verlag Berlin Heidelberg 2001

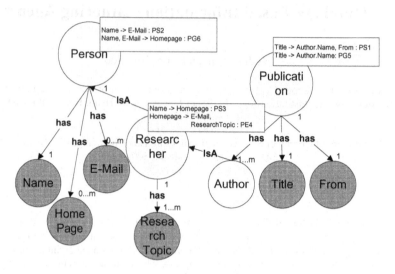

Fig. 1. The ontology of "Publication".

2   Representation of Domain Ontology and Queries

We use the traditional object-oriented language to represent the ontologies. The basic element of the ontology is a "class". A class is an abstract description or a conceptualization. There are two relations in the ontologies: "IsA" and "Has". "IsA" shows the subset and inheritance relation between two classes. "Has" shows the "part-whole" relation. Because the ontology is the domain knowledge that the agents use to gather information in the WWW, it should also contain some "procedure attachments" to guide the agent's gathering process. The procedure attachment's format is: *<input>* → *<output>* : *<procedure>*. The procedure attachment means that: given the <procedure> with the <input>, it should return the <output>. The <procedure> uses three kinds of web resources to complete its mission: *general search engines, special search engines* and normal web documents. The difference between general search engines and special search engines will be discussed in section 3.2. These three kinds of procedures provide different reliabilities about correctness of information. In general, the reliability order among them is: *web documents > special search engines > general search engines.* If the procedure's name starts with "PG", it uses general search engines to gather information. If the procedure's name starts with "PS", it uses special search engines. If the procedure's name starts with "PE", it extracts information from normal documents.

Fig. 1 shows our ontology representation of "Publication". It will be the main example through this paper. In Fig. 1, the shaded classes are "ground classes" and the others are "abstract classes". There are real values in the ground classes, but not in the abstract classes. After the user learns the ontology descriptions of "Publication", he can use it to represent his query about "Publication". The user can generate an object (instance) of the ontology, fill in known values in the known fields, and set the other interested fields as unknown. Since there are some unknown values in the new object, we call it as a "partial object" of the "Publication". If there is no unknown value in an object, we call it as a "complete object".

Assume we are going to search class A's object, and we use A's procedure attachments to search, it is a *self search*. If we use the procedure attachments of A's parents to search A's object, it is a *parent search*. With the ontology's "IsA" relations, we can take a better searching strategy. With the hierarchical searching strategy, the agent can pursue higher precision with the self-search first. But it also can get higher recall with parent search, if the result of self-search is not enough.

3   Agent Architecture and Operations

We formulate the information gathering process as a cycle of 4 basic operations in the agent architecture: *planning, search, information extraction* and *information integration*. The agents are dispatched by the *agent center*, and they will send their gathering results back to the agent center.

3.1   Planning

There may be many procedure attachments in every class. So the planning operation is going to look for a proper procedure attachment as the agent's next step. We use a dynamic and greedy searching method to look for the best procedure of the next step. The agents would send their result back to the agent center. Our greedy method would pursue the procedure attachments that have higher precision. There are three criteria to prioritize the procedure attachments:

1. Self-search or parent search: In general, the self-search would have a higher precision than the parent search.
2. The types of procedure attachments: There are three types of procedure attachments: PE, PS and PG. The comparison of precision among them would be: PE > PS > PG.
3. The number of the input and output of the procedure attachment: If the information source that needs to be inputted with more values, it would return more specific answers. The agent also prefers the information source that can output more data.

We use a utility function as a heuristic for choosing the next operation. The utility function and example is described in more detail in [7].

3.2   Search

The searching operations use existing search engines to help looking for information in the WWW. There are two kinds of search engines: general search engines and special search engines. The general search engines are such as: AltaVista, Excite, Hotbot… and so on. These search engines often get thousands of documents that contain users' query terms, but more than often the users could not find exactly what they need. The special domain search engines are indexed and customized for particular purposes. For example: BigYellow (www.bigyellow.com). These special domain search engines could provide more reliable result. So we design the agent to use special domain search engines first. If the user couldn't get satisfying results, then it would try to use the general search engines.

3.3   Information Extraction

After the searching process, the agent may get some web documents. In the process of information extraction, the agent extracts further information among these related documents, and some unknown values of the original partial object may be instantiated with extracted values. Two kinds of documents would be sent to the operation: unstructured documents and semi-structured documents. In this operation, the agent uses the specialized wrapper to extract information from the semi-structured documents or yellow pages, and use a specific parser to parse the unstructured documents.

3.4   Information Integration

There are two kinds of information integration in the system: the "ground integration" and the "abstract integration".

The agent would carry with a partial object and then choosing a proper procedure from its procedure attachments. Several candidate answers would be found after the extracting procedure. These possible values may have the same meanings but are not in the same surface forms. So the ground integration would use some domain specific heuristic to integrate these values. Because this operation integrates values, which are different but are the same meaning, for an individual object, we call this kind of operation as "the ground integration".

There are too many information sources in the WWW, their stored data sets are not identical. The agent can't guarantee that query the same thing in different information sources can be easily integrated. We should specify some abstract integration rules to solve this problem. Examples of abstract integration rules are shown as: *"Publication: Publication.Title"*. It means that if two objects of "Publication" have the same "Publication.Title" then their component objects can be integrated together. The abstract integration would integrate information from different sources and those sources also may use different representation to indicate the same thing, so the abstract integration also needs the ability of ground integration.

3.5   The Agent Center

The agent center receives the query, a partial object, from the user. And then sends out an agent with the partial object to gather information in the WWW. There is an *operation stack* and a *result queue* in the agent center. If the agent has generated new partial objects, it would send them back to the agent center. The agent center would try to integrate the back objects with those objects in the operation stack and result queue by abstract integration operations. And any integratable object would be integrated. After abstract integrating, if the back objects were still partial objects, they would be pushed into the operation stack. Any object that becomes complete object would be putted into the result queue. Then the agent center would pop up the partial object from the operation stack, and send another agent with the partial object to gather information. The whole process wouldn't stop until the operation stack is empty, and the complete objects in the result queue would be the answers to the user.

4   Conclusion

In this paper, we use domain ontology to represent the agent's world knowledge and use this ontology to integrate the information resources in the WWW. The users can represent their queries in terms of the ontology to mitigate their gaps with agents. The agents utilize the domain ontology and corresponding support (procedure attachments, parsers, wrappers and integration rules) to gathering information about users' queries in the WWW. If the system designer provides other domain ontology and corresponding support, the agent should work fine under the same ontology-based information gathering agent architecture.

Acknowledgments. This work was financially supported by the National Science Council, Taiwan, Republic of China, under the grant No. NSC 89-2213-E-007–066 and also by Program for Promoting Academic Excellence of Universities under grant number 89-E-FA04-1-4. This paper is also a partial result of Project 3XS1B11 conducted by ITRI under sponsorship of the Ministry of Economic Affairs, R.O.C.

Reference

1.   Patrick Lambrix, Nahid Shahmehri and Niclas Wahllöf: A Default Extension to Description Logics for Use in an Intelligent Search Engine. Proceeding of IEEE System Sciences. (1998)
2.   Rudi Studer, V. Richard Benjamins and Dieter Fensel.:   Knowledge Engineering: Principles and models. Data & knowledge Engineering. Vol. 25. (1998) 161-197
3.   D.B. Lenat.:   CYC: A Large-Scale Investment in Knowledge Infrastructure. Communication of ACM. Vol. 38, No. 11. (1995)
4.   Miller, G.A.: WordNet: a lexical database for English.   Communications of the ACM. Vol. 38, No.11. (1995) 39–41
5.   Nicola Guarino, Claudio Masolo, Guido Vetere.: OntoSeek: Content-Based Access to the Web. IEEE Intelligent Systems. Vol. 14. Issue 3. (1999)
6.   Semantic Web. http://www.semanticweb.org.
7.   Yi-Jia Chen.:   Ontology-based Information Gathering Agents.   Master Thesis, National Tsing Hua University. (1999)

An Effective Conversational Agent with User Modeling Based on Bayesian Network

Seung-Ik Lee, Chul Sung, and Sung-Bae Cho

Computer Science Department, Yonsei University, 134 Shinchon-dong, Sudaemoon-ku, Seoul
120-749, Korea
{cypher, sungc}@candy.yonsei.ac.kr, sbcho@csai.yonsei.ac.kr

Abstract. Conversational agents interact with users using natural language interface. Especially in Internet space, their role has been recently highlighted as
a virtual representative of a web site. However, most of them use simple pattern
matching techniques without considering user's goal. In this paper, we propose a
conversational agent that utilizes user model constructed on Bayesian network for
the responses consistent with user's goal. The agent is applied to the active guide
of a website, which shows that the user modeling based on Bayesian network helps
to respond to user's queries appropriately with the their goals.

1 Introduction

Most Internet sites provide a simple keyword-based search engine, which is difficult to
give right information because they do not consider user's goals. As an alternative for
the dumb interfaces of web sites, conversational agents are recently being developed because they have conversations with users by processing natural language. However, most
conversational agents, e.g., Eliza [1] and ALICE(Artificial Linguistic Internet Computer
Entity, http://www.alicebot.org), have the shortcomings of not being able to take into
accounts user's intentions because of their simple sequential pattern matching based on
keywords.

One of the techniques for modeling user's intentions or goals is to use Bayesian
network. It is an intuitive and parsimonious representation of probability distributions
and effective in diagnosing user's needs and thus provides useful enhancements to legacy
software applications when embedded within them. Pynadath [2] used probabilistic
models for making inferences about the goals of car drivers in navigation. Albrecht [3]
applied Bayesian models in action prediction in a multi-user computer game. Horvitz [4]
worked to build models for inference and decision-making under uncertainty about user's
goals at each level of the task hierarchy with Bayesian networks.

In this paper, we propose a conversational agent that can have more intelligent conversations by inferring diverse user goals through user modeling based on Bayesian
network and apply it to the guide of a website to show the usefulness.

2 Conversational Agent

Fig. 1 shows the overall structure of the conversational agent. After preprocessing user's
queries to correct typos and supplant synonyms, *Goal Inference* module infers user's

N. Zhong et al. (Eds.): WI 2001, LNAI 2198, pp. 428–432, 2001.
© Springer-Verlag Berlin Heidelberg 2001

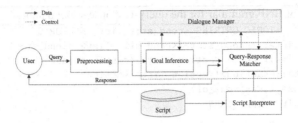

Fig. 1. The architecture of a conversational agent

goals. When this module cannot infer user's goals because of insufficient information, the Dialogue Manager requests the user to give more information. Once the goal is inferred, the agent presents an appropriate answer by searching the knowledge base or script. This requires the *Goal Inference* to play an important role in finding the appropriate answer by reasoning goals during the mixed-initiative interactions with the user [7].

2.1   User Model Based on Bayesian Network

Fig. 2 shows the user model for the introduction of a web site with Bayesian network. Evidence variables of a node are represented as parent nodes. Each evidence variable represents a set of keywords. For example, the evidence variable 'place' represents keywords like 'position' and 'location'. We construct a user model for the introduction of a specific site with Bayesian network. When the information from a query is insufficient

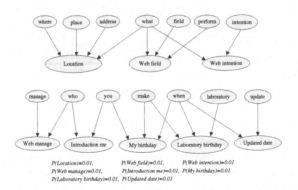

Fig. 2. Bayesian network architecture for modeling user goals

for the transition from the current goal to a more detailed one, the agent requests more information to the user.

List 1 A part of BNF grammar for the query-response script database

```
<topic_decl>::=TOPIC QSTRING <cond_stmt_list> ENDTOPIC
<cond_stmt_list>::=<cond_stmt>|<cond_stmt_list> <cond_stmt>
<cond_stmt>::=<if_cond> <action_list> <continuation>
<action_list>::=<action>|<action_list> <action>
<action>::=<say>|<say_one_of>
<if_cond>::=IF <expr> THEN
```

2.2   Knowledge Representation and Matching

Knowledges for the matching of queries to responses are described in a database called script and a part of the script grammar is illustrated in List 1 using BNF notation. It is composed of a list of query (or condition) and response pairs. Topic is the primary component that represents a query-response pair in the grammar.

Scripts are interpreted and loaded into memory by script interpreter when the agent start running. The condition part in each topic is transformed into a Boolean expression and the keywords listed in the condition part are transformed into a regular expression as in Fig. 3.

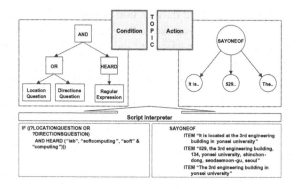

Fig. 3. Internal representation of a part of the script

the condition part of each topic is compared with the goal information, the query, and the keyword list extracted during the goal inference. This process returns the scores of all the topics as a result. Different types of matching components, like goals, keywords, or Boolean operators, are assigned different scores depending on their types. When all the topics are assigned scores, the highest topic is presented to the user as a response to his query.

3   Simulation Results

The conversational agent has been applied to the introduction of a website to show the usability and possibility. Although it is necessary to assign initial probabilities from the analysis of the corpus in case of serious real-world problems, they are given such that they represent the frequencies of the occurrence of the evidence variables in goals because it is sufficient for this tiny model in demonstrating the possibility of the modeling method. Following is an actual conversation with a user.

```
User  : What is your address?
Agent: Which place out of Yonsei univ., Engineering
       building, Professor room, or Laboratory do you want?
User  : Laboratory.
Agent: It is located at the 3rd engineering building in
       Yonsei university.
User  : Tell me where Yonsei university is.
Agent: Yonsei university is 134 Shinchon-dong, Sudaemun-ku,
       Seoul 120-749, Korea.
```

When a user asks the agent "What is your address?," the agent searches synonyms to be replaced with their representative words. In this case, no words are replaced. Then the agent compares some words of the query with the variables of the Bayesian network. As this query contains 'what' and 'address', which are evidences of 'Location', 'Web field', and 'Web intention', their probabilities are looked up from the predefined conditional probability tables as in Fig. 4 (a). Since the probability of 'Location' is over the threshold

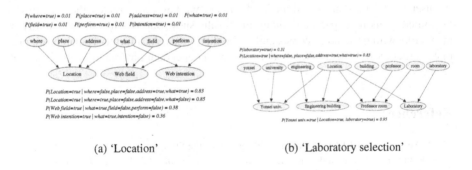

(a) 'Location'   (b) 'Laboratory selection'

Fig. 4. Goal searching procedures

probability 0.8 and greater than the other goals, the agent infers that the user's goal is 'Location'. At this moment, the agent needs more information which of the four detailed goals the user actually wants to know as in fig. 4 (b). The agent asks the user "Which place out of Yonsei univ., Engineering building, Professor room, or Laboratory?" The answer, "Laboratory," makes the 'Laboratory' variable true and thus the agent infers that user goal is 'Laboratory'. With this inferred user goal, the script is searched producing the response "It is located at the 3rd building in Yonsei university."

When the user asks the agent "Tell me where Yonsei university is," the agent takes the 'where' word which is an evidence variable of the Bayesian network.

Fig. 5. Inferring detailed user goals

$P(Location|where)$ is 0.85 as shown in Fig. 4 (a), because 'Location' is condition-ally independent given 'where'. After inferring the user's goal, the agent gathers more information for the next sub goal. The agent takes 'yonsei' and 'university' words in the query and infers 'Yonsei univ.' with the words as in fig. 5. After inferring 'Yonsei univ.', the agent finally answers to the user "Yonsei university is 134 Shinchon-dong, Sudaemun-ku, Seoul 120-749, Korea."

4   Conclusion

In this paper, we have described a conversational agent that can give responses more consistent with user's goals in a specific domain. A Bayesian network is used to construct the user model in a specific domain. Although we have constructed the user model of limited goals in a specific domain, the results show that this has the possibility of interacting with users more consistently with their goals. As a further research, we plan to construct more general user models that are independent on domains with Bayesian network.

References

1. J. Weizenbaun: ELIZA - a Computer Program for the Study of Natural Language Communi-cation between Man and Machine. *Communications of the ACM 9(1).* (1965) 36–45
2. D. Pynadath and M. Wellman: Accounting for Context in Plan Recognition with Application to Traffic Monitoring. *Proc. of the Eleventh Conf. on Uncertainty in Artificial Intelligence.* (1995) 472–481
3. D. Albrecht *et al*: Towards a Bayesian Model for Keyhole Plan Recognition in Large Domains. *Proc. of the Sixth Int. Conf. on User Modeling.* (1997) 365–376.
4. E. Horvitz and T. Paek: A Computational Architecture for Conversation. *Proc. of the Seventh Int. Conf. on User Modeling.* (1999) 201–210
5. F.V. Jensen: An Introduction to Bayesian Networks, *Springer-Verlag.* (1996)
6. N. Friedman *et al*: Using Bayesian Networks to Analyze Expression Data. *Proc. of the Fourth Annual Int. Conf. on Computational Molecular Biology.* (2000) 127–135
7. J.F. Allen: Mixed-Initiative Interaction. *IEEE Intelligent Systems 5* (1999) 14–16

Information Fusion for Intelligent Agent-Based Information Gathering

Yuefeng Li

School of Computing Science and Software Engineering
Queensland University of Technology, Brisbane, QLD 4001, Australia
y2.li@qut.edu.au

Abstract. This paper discusses the problem of information fusion for agent-based information gathering systems. The framework of information gathering in multi-agent environments is presented firstly, and then a cooperative fusion algorithm is presented for unstructured documents. The performance is also made by the traditional methods precision and recall, and it shows that the fusion algorithm is efficient.

1 Introduction

The astonishing growth of the World Wide Web is providing vast amount of information for use. This information can help us in many ways, such as investment, education, entertainment, etc, if we can gather the relevant information from the Web. However, it is difficult for humans to gather right information from the Web because information is vast, uncertain, changing, and distributed.

The notion of information gathering (IG) has been proposed to address this challenge [5]. The ideal goal of IG is to obtain only the information that users need (no more and no less). There are two related research fields for IG. They are information retrieval (IR) and agent-based information systems. For IG, the existent IR models can support the construction of powerful search engines working on queries over well organized collections. Most tasks of information retrieval nowadays, however, include uncertain information. In addition, information is becoming highly distributed in which collections and services are constantly changing. This encourages people to apply intelligent agent-based techniques to design new generation information systems.

The problem of information fusion (integration) has attracted significant attention in artificial intelligence (AI) community and in the database systems community [7]. After the set of collections has been selected for a broker, a key problem for the broker is to fuse the return information from the different collections. This problem in database systems community is described as the "query optimization", or called "collection fusion" [11] [3]. In AI community, the researchers discuss this problem related to "structured data (solutions) synthesis" in multi-agent environments [6]. In this paper we discuss the problem of fusion in multi-agent environments. We will presents a cooperative fusion algorithm for unstructured text documents to extend the functionality of "structured data (solutions) synthesis".

N. Zhong et al. (Eds.): WI 2001, LNAI 2198, pp. 433–437, 2001.
© Springer-Verlag Berlin Heidelberg 2001

2   Agent-Based IG

The goal of *fusion* in Distributed IR [11] is "to combine the retrieval results from multiple, independent collections into a single result such that the effectiveness of the combination approximates the effectiveness of searching the entire set of documents as a single collection". This definition implies that the broker knows all databases (collections) in question, and assumes collections are independent. For a Web-based information system that aims at covering all uncertain and constantly changing information sources that can be reached via the WWW, this assumption is not realistic. For this reason, we now consider the case of multi-agent environments, in where each agent knows some collections (probably overlap), and the broker agent uses the techniques of cooperation to solve problems. We call this kind of system the agent-based IG system.

The following process describes a strategy for agent-based IG:
(1) Send the user information need to each agent$\in \Theta$;
(2) while not(t) // t is the time point of fusion
        Get new retrieved documents;
(3) /* Here we use Θ_t to represent the set of cooperated agents
      * which have sent back the retrieved documents at time t.*/
      Fuse the retrieved documents sent by Θ_t;
(4) Assign the relevant documents to the user;

In the above process, there is a waiting time for the broker agent to get the retrieved documents. This period will be decided by the time of fusion, which is given by the user or the system. During this period, the cooperated agents would typically send back the retrieved documents to answer the user information need. Failure would occur when a particular agent was unavailable (e.g, network failure), or where results could not be obtained. At the time of fusion, the broker agent will evaluate the retrieved documents by using its knowledge about the cooperated agents, and resort the retrieved documents. Lastly, it will return the relevant documents to the user.

3   Cooperative Fusion Algorithm

The difficult problem arises in collection fusion for the case where databases may be used by more than one agent [3]. For example, we may have the case databases D_1, D_2, and D_3 are served by agent B, databases D_2, D_3, and D_4 are served by agent C. The return documents retrieved by agent B could belong to D_1, D_2, and D_3; and the return documents retrieved by C belong to D_2, and D_4. The problem for the broker agent A is to evaluate all of the return documents (sometimes called retrieved documents).

A clue for solving this problem is given by Fuhr [3]. The broker agent A can ask agent B to revise its retrieved documents in case D_2 as well as D_3 are ignored. After that the problem will become the case where different agents access disjoint sets of databases. To use this approach, we have to give a negotiation method to select agents which are willing to revise their retrieved documents. The process of negotiation will take more time. Another drawback is that this approach cannot use multiple opinions for the same question (one kind of cooperation in multi-agent environments).

Considering many agents (rather than 3) which may have different efficiencies in information retrieval, the problem looks so complex, and the evaluation for this problem is not easy. The following algorithm, however provides a cooperative approach for this problem:

(1) for $i=1$ to n // initial the relevant array
$$R(d_i) = 0;$$
(2) for each $\theta \in \Theta_t$ // support evaluation
for each $d \in \Gamma_t(\theta)$
$$R(d) = R(d) + Precision_\theta(\mid \Gamma_t(\theta) \mid);$$
(3) for $j=1$ to m //potential support evaluation
for each $\theta \in \Theta_t$
if $(C_j^t$ is not served by $\theta)$
for each $d \in \mathcal{D}_{t_j}$
$$R(d) = R(d) + Precision_\theta(\mid \mathcal{D}_t \mid);$$
(4) Resort $\mathcal{D}_t$ based on multi-keys;

In this algorithm, the inputs are the set of cooperating agents at time t (Θ_t), the set of retrieved documents at time t $(\mathcal{D}_t = \bigcup_{i=1,\dots,m} \mathcal{D}_{t_i}, \mid \mathcal{D}_t \mid = n)$, and the associated collections $C_1^t, C_2^t, \dots, C_m^t$, where, $\mathcal{D}_{t_i} \subset C_i^t$. We expect the outputs are the relevant degree function R, and the sequence of the retrieved documents.

In this algorithm, a multi-key in step 4 for a document d consists of two keys. The first key is $R(d)$, the second key is $\sum_{\theta \in \Theta_t} weight_\theta(d)$, where $weight_\theta(d)$ is the normalization of d's weight that agent θ provides, it can be computed as follows

$$weight_\theta(d_i) = \frac{1}{\sum_{j=1,\dots,\mid \Gamma_t(\theta) \mid} w_j} w_i,$$

if agent θ provides a set of retrieved documents $\{d_1, \dots, d_{\mid \Gamma_t(\theta) \mid}\}$ with the corresponding weights $\{w_1, \dots, w_{\mid \Gamma_t(\theta) \mid}\}$. The retrieved documents will be divided into some classes firstly based on the first key, in which every document has the same R. In each class the documents then are ordered by the second key.

4   Performance of Fusion Algorithm

The resource for this trial is "http://employment.news.com.au/". From this resource we down-loaded 653 jobs as a collection, which are classified as "Programmer" (by using the inner search engine) at time Tuesday December 14 11:25:01 EST 1999 (see [9]). The information need is described as " What job information is available for programmers, in which programming with Java, C++, and Oracle under Unix is preferred"?

The broker agent (BROKER) sends this user information need to three agents: PIRM-based agent, RSBM-based agent, and SDSM-based agent. At fusion time, each agent provides a set of retrieved documents, in which each document has a collection name, document name and weight (similar value).

The PIRM-based agent uses the probabilistic IR model (see [9]). It provides 130 documents to reply the broker's request. The RSBM-based agent uses the rough set based IF model (see [9]). It first classifies the new documents into some categories, then selects the relevant documents from the categories based on the user information need. It provides 38 documents to reply this request. The last set of retrieved documents comes from SDSM-based agent [8]. This agent uses Dempster-Shafer index model to describe the user information need. It returns 122 documents to reply the broker's request.

The broker, however, does not have any idea about which agents are better. So it assumes that every agent has the same trustworthiness (that means a same precision curve). By using the cooperative fusion algorithm the broker agent divides the retrieved documents into 3 classes, the first class has 38 documents with the support from every agent (3 agents); the second class has 84 documents with the support from 2 agents, the third class has 8 documents with the support from one agent.

By resorting the retrieved documents, the broker agent can select the top part documents to answer its users based on how many documents users want. The result of the experiment on precision and recall are displayed in Fig. 1, where the document cutoff is 15.

To compare with PIRM-based agent and SDSM-based agent, BROKER can get a very high precision. To compare with RSBM-based agent, BROKER can re-pick up the 3 relevant documents that were filtered out by RSBM-based agent. In summary, this experiment shows that the fusion result is better than any single agent. The effectiveness of the combination in this cooperative approach is enhanced rather than only approximated to the effectiveness of searching the entire set of documents as a single collection by any agent (the goal of collection fusion in Distributed IR).

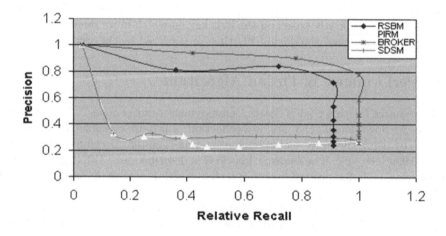

Fig. 1. Fusion Precision/Recall

5   Conclusion

With respect to collection fusion, the problem was first identified in the paper [11]. This approach is to approximate the relevant document distribution over the collections by learning them from the results of past queries. Another approach [1] uses an inference network to rank not only documents at the provider sites. The collection fusion problem can also be solved by either using globally valid document frequencies (if the same cosine-based ranking method is used at each site) or by re-ranking selected (retrieved) documents at the broker site [10].

Metacrawler [2] and Savvy Search [4] are agents that operates at a higher abstraction level by utilizing existing search engines. In contrast to other agent-based systems, BIG [6] performs information fusion. That is, BIG retrieves documents, extracts attributes from the documents, converting unstructured text to structured data, and then integrates the data. Different from this kind of fusion, in this paper we talk about the information fusion in case of unstructured text rather than structured information (data).

In summary, an cooperative fusion algorithm is presented in this paper. It extends the capability of the traditional collection fusion in Distributed IR. By using the technique of cooperation between agents, this algorithm provides an approach for the problem of information fusion on the Web.

References

[1]   J. P. Callan, Z. Lu and W. B. Croft, Searching distributed collections with inference networks, *in Proceedings of SIGIR'95*, 1995, 21-29.

[2]   O. Etzioni, Results from using the metacrawler, *in Proceedings of 4th WWW Conference*, F. Varela and P. Bourgine (Eds.), MIT Press, Cambridge, MA, 1995.

[3]   N. Fuhr, A decision-theoretic approach to database selection in networked IR, *ACM Transactions on Information Systems*, 1999, **17(3)**: 229-249.

[4]   A.E. Howe and D. Dreilinger, Savvy Search :a metasearch engine that learns which search engines to query; *AI Magazine*,1997, **18(2)**: 19-25.

[5]   N. R. Jennings, K. Sycara and M. Wooldridge, A Roadmap of agent research and development, *Autonomous Agents and Multi-Agent Systems*, 1998, **1(1)**: 7-38.

[6]   V. Lesser et al., BIG: an agent for resource-bounded information gathering and decision making, *Artificial Intelligence*, 2000, **118**: 197-244.

[7]   A. Y. Levy and D. S. Weld, Intelligent Internet systems, *Artificial Intelligence*, 2000, **118**: 1-14.

[8]   Y.Li, Modeling intelligent agents for Web-based information gathering, *PhD Thesis*, Deakin University, 2000.

[9]   Y. Li, C. Zhang, and J. R. Swan, An information filtering model on the Web and its application in JobAgent, *Knowledge-based Systems*, 2000, **13(5)**: 285-296.

[10] W. Meng, K.Liu, C. Yu, X. Wang, Y. Chang, and N. Rishe, Determining text databases to search in the Internet, *in Proceedings of 24th VLDB Conference*, 1998. Extended version.

[11] E. M. Voorhees, N. K. Gupta, and B. Johnson-Laird, The collection fusion problem, *in Proceedings of TREC-3*, 1995, 95-104.

An Adaptive Recommendation System with a Coordinator Agent[1]

Myungeun Lim[1] and Juntae Kim[2]

[1]Electronics and Telecommunications Research Institute, Daejon, Korea
melim@etri.re.kr
[2]Department of Computer Engineering, Dongguk University, Seoul, Korea
jkim@dgu.ac.kr

Abstract. This paper presents a recommendation system with a *coordinator agent* that is adaptive to its environment. Recommendation systems that suggest items to users are gaining popularity in the field of electronic commerce. Various methods such as collaborative, content-based, and demographic recommendation have been used to analyze and predict the preference of users. According to the characteristic of the application domain, the performance of each method varies. In the proposed system, we introduce a coordinator agent that adaptively changes the weights of each recommendation method to provide combined recommendation appropriate for the given environment.

1 Introduction

The rapid growth of the electronic commerce has led to the development of personalized recommendation systems. A recommendation system analyzes the personal preference of each user and identifies a set of items that will be of interest to a specific user. Recommendation systems are already being used in many web sites to recommend various items including books, movies, music, news articles, etc. By adopting a recommendation system, one might expect to increase sales by providing the right information to the right user.

There have been various approaches for recommendation systems. Collaborative recommendation systems analyze similarities between users based on their preference data, such as purchase history, and predict a user's preference on certain item based on the similar user's preference on that item [4][8][12]. Because the collaborative method does not require any information on the contents of items, it is more appropriate to recommend items like music or movies, for which the contents are difficult to analyze. Various modifications have also been proposed to improve the performance [5][7]. Content-based recommendation systems analyze the textual information about preferred items, and recommend new items by finding items with similar information [1][11]. Since the content-based method is appropriate when there is rich content information, it has been applied to recommend news articles or web pages. There are also systems that use content-based method and collaborative

---

[1] This research has been supported by Korea Science and Engineering Foundation under contract No. 1999-30300-005-2.

N. Zhong et al. (Eds.): WI 2001, LNAI 2198, pp. 438–442, 2001.
© Springer-Verlag Berlin Heidelberg 2001

method together [2][3]. Demographic recommendation systems are similar to collaborative recommendation systems, but they analyze similarities between users based on their demographic data, such as age, gender, or profession [9]. The distances between users are computed by using that information, and a user's preference on certain item is predicted by using the neighbor's preferences.

All these recommendation methods have their own advantages and disadvantages, and their performance varies according to the characteristic of the application domain to which they are applied. Choosing the most appropriate method is difficult task. Furthermore, the performance of each method may change as the data are accumulated. For example, when there is not enough rating information, the demographic recommendation may outperform other methods, but as more data are accumulated, the collaborative recommendation may show the best performance.

In this paper, we present a recommendation system with a *coordinator agent* that is adaptive to its environment. The system consists of three different recommendation agents and a coordinator agent. The coordinator agent merges the recommended items lists from the three agents and combines them to the final recommendation list. Then the coordinator agent gets feedback on the recommended items and adjusts the weights of the three agents. If one agent's recommended items get better feedback, it increases the weights of that agent. As a result, the system becomes adaptive to the application domain since the item recommended by more appropriate agent gets higher prediction value next time.

2   The Recommendation System with Coordinator Agent

Our recommendation system consists of a content-based agent, a demographic agent, a collaborative agent, and a *coordinator agent*. Figure 1 shows the overall structure of the proposed recommendation system.

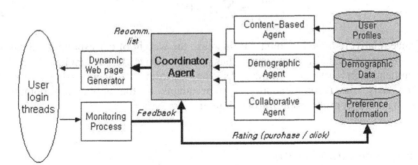

Fig. 1. The structure of the recommendation system with a coordinator agent

The content-based agent makes recommendation by using the textual information describing items. Given a user's preferred item, it analyzes the item description and build a profile consists of keywords extracted from the description. When a recommendation request is given for a user, it extracts the profile of the user and computes similarities between the profile and the descriptions of other items. The profile and the item description are represented as keyword vectors, and cosine similarity between those vectors becomes the prediction value of the item. The demographic agent utilizes the demographic information of each user that is represented as a feature vector. The agent first finds neighbors of the user by computing the distance between feature vectors. Then the prediction value of each item is computed as a weighted average of the ratings of the neighbors. The collaborative agent makes recommendation by using the preference information of similar users. It first computes similarities between users by using Pearson correlation between the ratings of the users. The Pearson correlation represents how the preferences of users are related by comparing each user's relative ratings. Once the correlation is computed, the prediction of preference of a user for an item is computed as the weighted average of the ratings of the highly correlated users.

To automatically adapt to the domain characteristic, the coordinator agent is introduced. The coordinator agent gathers the recommendation lists from each agent, and computes the weighted average of each item's score, then selects top N items for final recommendation. The key idea for the coordinator agent is that the weights for each agent change adaptively according to the characteristic of the application on which the recommendation system runs. Each recommended item is temporarily stored with tags indicating which agent it comes from. The coordinator agent keeps track of the feedback from users, such as click or purchase, on the recommended items, and stores them as hit counts. As more items are recommended and get feedback, the hit count is accumulated for each agent, and the coordinator continuously adjusts the weights by using the accumulated hit count. If the hit count of agent a is H_a, then the weight W^a for agent a is adjusted as equation 1, and the final prediction value of item i for user u is computed as equation 2.

$$W^a = \frac{H_a}{\sum_a H_a} \tag{1}$$

$$P_{u,i}^{TOTAL} = \sum_a P_{u,i}^a \cdot W^a \tag{2}$$

Since relatively large hit count will increase the weight of corresponding agent, the item recommended by that agent has more chance to be included in final recommendation list next time. As the coordinator agent adjusts weights continuously, the recommendation system adapts to the application domain by selecting an appropriate agent for that domain.

3   Experimental Results

The dataset used for the experiment is selected from the EachMovie dataset [10]. The EachMovie dataset has rating information on 1,628 movies by 72,916 users during 18 months period since 1996. Users rated various numbers of movies by the number of stars 0 to 5. In this experiment, we convert the rating values to Boolean since in practical environment such explicit rating scores cannot be obtained easily. Other than the rating information, it contains the movie title, genre, users age, and gender. First we select 2000 users with more than 100 positive rated items. For each selected user the data are divided into 10 sets, each has 10 items, and used as training sets.

We start with 1 training set (10 items). After each agent recommends 10 items, the coordinator agent selects top-10 items among them. These items are compared to the next training set of size 10. If a recommended item is matched to an item in the next training set then it is recognized as a positive feedback, and the weight of the agent that actually recommended the item is increased as described in section 2 by counting total number of hits. Then we increase the size of the training set by including the second training set. Now the training set has 20 items, and by using it we get the new recommendation, and so on.

Table 1. The % increase of average hit ratio as the training set size increases

Mode	Training set size								
	10	20	30	40	50	60	70	80	90
No coordinator	0.0	2.7	6.0	6.7	8.0	8.7	9.3	10.7	13.3
Coordinator	0.0	10.7	29.3	34.7	36.7	43.3	52.0	56.7	66.7

Table 2. The change of weights for each agent as the training set size increases

Agent	Training set size								
	10	20	30	40	50	60	70	80	90
Content-based	0.17	0.14	0.14	0.14	0.13	0.13	0.12	0.11	0.11
Collaborative	0.37	0.40	0.44	0.47	0.50	0.52	0.53	0.56	0.57
Demographic	0.47	0.46	0.42	0.39	0.37	0.35	0.35	0.33	0.32

The performance of the recommendation is measured as the *Hit Ratio* (% of matches among recommended items). The hit ratio represents how many of the recommended items are actually preferred items. As the number of feedback on the recommended items increases, the performance of overall recommendation should increase as the coordinator agent gives more weight to the agent that gets more positive feedback. As Table 1 shows, the average hit ratio of the recommendation with coordinator agent increased 67% from initial hit ratio 0.15, while the average hit ratio without the coordinator increased only 13%, as the training set size increased to 90.

Table 2 shows the change of weights for each agent. For this data set, the collaborative recommendation gets more positive feedback in average, and the weight of the collaborative agent increases to 0.57 while the weight of the content-based agent drops to 0.11. This is because the EachMovie dataset does not have enough information for the demographic agent and the content-based agent. The demographic agent finds neighbors based on age and gender only. The content-based agent gets keywords from the movie titles only, so it always recommends movies that have the words found in the preferred titles. However, the weight of the demographic agent is highest in early stage because there is not enough information for the collaborative agent yet.

4   Conclusions

In this paper, an adaptive recommendation system has been presented. The system consists of three different recommendation agents and a coordinator agent. The coordinator agent adjusts the weights for each agent based on the feedback, and combines recommendations from the three agents according to the weights. As a result, the system becomes adaptive to the application domain, and the performance of recommendation increases as more data are accumulated.

The proposed recommendation system was applied to the EachMovie dataset. The result of experiment showed that, as the number of feedback increases, the hit ratio of the recommendation with coordinator agent increases more rapidly. For an application where the characteristic of the domain is unclear, the adaptive behavior of the proposed recommendation system would be helpful. The system can also be used to automatically switch between different recommendation methods during the transient period, until it collects enough information for an appropriate agent.

References

1. Armstrong R., Freitag D., Joahims T., and Mitchell T., WebWatcher: A learning apprentice for the World Wide Web, *Proceedings of the 12th National Conference on Artificial Intelligence*, 1995.
2. Balabanovic M. and Shoham Y., Fab: Content-based, collaborative recommendation, *Communications of the ACM,* 40(3), 1997.
3. Basu C., Hirsh H., and Cohen W., Recommendation as classification: Using social and content-based information in recommendation, *Proceedings of the 15th National Conference on Artificial Intelligence*, 1998.
4. Billsus, D. and Pazzani, M., Learning collaborative information filters, *Proceedings of the International Conference on Machine Learning*, 1998.
5. Breese J., Heckerman D. and Kadie C., Empirical analysis of predictive algorithms for collaborative filtering, *Proceedings of the 14th Conference of Uncertainty in Artificial Intelligence*, 1998.
6. Good N., Schafer J., Konstan J., Borchers A., Sarwar B., Herlocker J. and Riedl J., Combining collaborative filtering with personal agents for better recommendations, *Proceedings of the 16th National Conference on Artificial Intelligence*, 1999.
7. Herlocker J., Konstan J., Borchers A., and Riedl J., An algorithmic framework for performing collaborative filtering, *Proceedings of the 22nd Conference on Research and Development in Information Retrieval*, 1999.
8. Konstan J., Miller B., Maltz D., Herlocker J., Gordon L., and Riedl J., GroupLens: Applying collaborative filtering to Usenet news, *Communications of the ACM*, 40 (3), 1997.
9. Krulwich B., Lifestyle Finder: Intelligent user profiling using large-scale demographic data, *Artificial Intelligence Magazine,* 18(2), 1997.
10. McJones P., EachMovie collaborative filtering data set, DEC Systems Research Center, http://www.research.digital.com/SRC/eachmovie/, 1997.
11. Pazzani M., Muramatsu J. and Billsus D., Syskill & Webert: Identifying interesting web sites, *Proceedings of the 13th National Conference on Artificial Intelligence*, 1996.
12. Shardanand U. and Maes P., Social information filtering: Algorithms for automating 'word of mouth', *Proceedings of the Conference of Human Factors in Computing Systems*, 1995.

Interactive Web Page Filtering with Relational Learning

Masayuki Okabe* and Seiji Yamada

CISS, IGSSE, Tokyo Institute of Technology
4259 Nagatuta-Cho, Midori-ku, Yokohama 226-8502, JAPAN
{okabe, yamada}@ymd.dis.titech.ac.jp

Abstract. This paper describes a system for collecting Web pages that
are relevant to a particular topic through an interactive approach. Indicated some relevant pages by a user, this system automatically constructs
a set of rules to find new relevant pages. The purpose of the system is to
reduce users' browsing cost by filtering non-relevant pages automatically.
Such an approach can be useful when users do not know how to describe
their requirements to search engines. We describe the representation and
the learning algorithm, and also show the experiments comparing its
performance with a search engine.

1 Introduction

Search engines are indispensable tools to access useful information which might
exist somewhere on the Internet. While they have been getting higher capability
to meet various information needs and large amounts of transactions, they are
still insufficient in the ability to support the users who need to collect a certain
number of Web pages relevant to their purpose. Based on a query(usually composed of a few words[1]) inputted by a user, search engines return a "hit list"
in which so many Web pages are presented in a certain order. However it does
not often reflect the user's intent, and thus the user would waste much time and
energy on judging the Web pages. To resolve this problem and to provide efficient retrieval process, we propose a system which mediates between users and
search engines in order to select only relevant Web pages out of hit list through
the interactive process called "relevance feedback"[5]. Given some Web pages
marked with their relevancy(relevant or non-relevant) by a user, this system
generates a set of rules, called *decision rules*, each of which is a logical rule to
decide whether the user should look a Web page or not. The system constructs
decision rules from the combination of keywords, relational operators and tags
with a learning algorithm which is superior to learn structural patterns. We have
developed this basic framework in document retrieval[3] and found our approach
was promising. In this paper, we applied this method to the intelligent interface
which coordinates the hit lists of search engines in order for individual user to
find their wanted information easily.

---

* Japan Science and Technology Corporation

N. Zhong et al. (Eds.): WI 2001, LNAI 2198, pp. 443–447, 2001.
© Springer-Verlag Berlin Heidelberg 2001

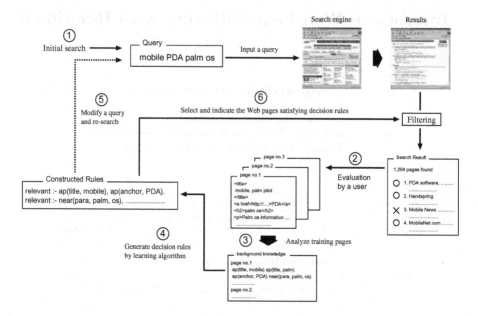

Fig. 1. Interactive Web search

In the remainder of the paper, we describe the interactive process, decision rules, and the experiments.

2   Interactive Web Search with Relevance Feedback

Figure 1 shows the interactive Web search process we propose. This process consists of six steps, each of which corresponds to the number in Figure 1. In step 1 a user starts to search by inputting a query to the system, and then receives the hit list. In step 2 the user evaluates and marks the relevancy(relevant or non-relevant) of its upper (more or less)10 pages in order to teach the system what kind of pages are needed. In step 3 the system makes an analysis of the marked pages by extracting extended keywords and literals which are used to construct decision rules. Based on the literals and a learning algorithm, in step 4 the system generates decision rules to distinguish relevant pages and non-relevant ones. We give the detailed description of decision rules in the next section. Step 5 is prepared for the case that the user noticed the initially or previously inputted query was not proper or sufficient and thinks it's better to do re-search. This step is not always done, thus it is indicated by dashed line. Step 6 is the revision procedure in which the system selects(re-selects) relevant pages based on the newly constructed decision rules to provide the user with the better results. These procedures follow the general relevance feedback process, and the steps from 2 to 6 repeat until the user would collect enough relevant pages.

3   Decision Rules

3.1   Rule Representation

The bodies of decision rules consist of the following literals standing for relations between terms and tags.

- $ap(region\_type, word)$: This literal is true *iff* a word *word* appears within a region of *region_type* in a Web page.
- $near(region\_type, word1, word2)$: This literal is true *iff* both of words w_i and w_j appear within a sequence of 10 words somewhere in a region of *region_type* of a Web page. The ordering of the two words is not considered.

We can easily consider that the importance of words significantly depends on tags of HTML. For example, the words within <TITLE> seem to have significant meaning because they indicate the theme of the Web page. Hence we use the *region_type* to restrict a tag with which words are surrounded. We prepare the *region_type* in the followings.

- *title* : The region surrounded with title tags <TITLE>.
- *anchor* : The region surrounded with anchor tags <A>.
- *head* : The region surrounded with heading tags <H1~4>.
- *para* : The region surrounded with paragraph tags <P>.

3.2   Learning Algorithm

Figure 2 shows the learning algorithm for decision rules. Under the separate-and-conquer strategy[2] this algorithm repeats mainking a new single rule until each of E^+ is covered by some rules. A single rule starts with empty body, and repeats adding a literal until it does not cover any of E^-. The literal is selected from a condition candidate set C, all of which are the possible combinations among *region_types* and keywords in K as its arguments. The criteria for selecting a literal which should be added to the body is based on *information gain*[4]. Using information gain, this algorithm searches a good combination greedily and efficiently. However it sometimes selects a bad literal and stops before completion. In such a case, if a current rule has some literals in its body, the rule restarts from an empty body and resumes adding a literal from C except for the literal l_1 which was firstly added in the previous cycle. If the body of a current rule has no literal, a new keyword is added to K and C is updated. The added keyword is selected from terms in positive training pages E^+.

4   Experiments and Results

In order to answer the question of how many relevant pages we can find more with the proposed system in the condition of looking over a certain pages, we conducted two retrieval experiments. The one is a retrieval *not using* our system(*retrieval1*). In this retrieval, we judged 50 pages from the top of the hit list

---

Input: E^+ : a set of positive training pages, E^- : a set of negative training pages
  C : a condition candidate set, K : a set of extended keywords
Output: R : a set of decision rules.
Variables: $rule$: a decision rule, S : a set of exception literals, l_1 : an exception literal
Initialize: $K \leftarrow$ a set of words in a query. R, S, $l_1 \leftarrow empty.$ $rule \leftarrow relevant:-.$
Repeat
1:   · Investigate the number p of positive training pages satisfying the $rule$
     and the number n of negative training pages satisfying the $rule$.
2:   **if** $n = 0$ **then**
3:     · Add $rule$ to R.
4:     · Remove a positive training page satisfying the $rule$ from E^+.
5:     **if** E^+ is empty **then Finish**
6:     **else** Initialize $rule$, S, l_1.
7:   **else**
8:     · For all literals in $C \cap \overline{S}$, compute the information gain G.
9:     **if** No literal with $G > 0$ **then**
10:      **if** the body of the $rule$ is empty **then**
11:        · Add a keyword to K.
12:        · Update C.
13:      **else**
14:        · Initialize S and $rule$.
15:        · Add l_1 to S, and initialize l_1.
16:      **else**
17:· Select l_{max} having the maximum G.
18:      **if** the body of the $rule$ is empty. **then** $l_1 := l_{max}$
19:        · Add l_{max} to $rule$ and S.

Fig. 2. Learning Algorithm

returned by a search engine. The other is a retrieval *using* our system(*retrieval2*). In this retrieval, we made feedbacks every after we judged 10 pages according to the procedure described in Section 2(excluding the pages which are already judged and decision rules don't satisfy). We made total four feedbacks. In both retrieval, we judged total 50 pages from the same hit list. We used the Google as a test WWW search engine, which is recognized as one of the most powerful search engines. For test questions, we used 20 *topics*(No. 401~420) provided by the small web track in TREC-8(see http://trec.nist.gov). This test collection is often used for evaluating the performance of retrieval systems in Information Retrieval community. We picked up a few words for the initial query to the search engine. Relevance judgment for each page is conducted by the same searcher according to the account written in each topic.

Figure 3 shows the relation between judged pages and relevant pages found in the judged pages. The number of relevant pages is average value per 20 topics. About first 10 pages, there is no difference because two methods judge the same pages. The difference of found relevant pages increases after the first feedback. As a result, retrieval2 got about 5 relevant pages more than retrieval1 after the fourth feedback was done. However the number of found relevant pages differs in every topics. Figure 4 shows the differences of the topics after the fourth feedback. Let A be the number of relevant pages in retrieval1 and B be the one in retrieval2, the difference D is calculated by $D = B - A$. The effect gradually

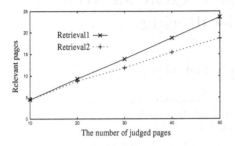

Fig. 3. The average number of relevant pages

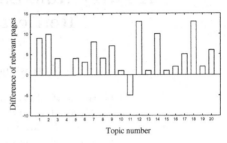

Fig. 4. Difference after the fourth feedback (total 50 pages judged)

increases as the feedback repeats. In figure 4, we can see the effect clearly. Our system produces good results for most of the topics.

5   Conclusion

We described a system which enhances the effectiveness of the WWW Search Engines by using relevance feedback and relational learning. The main function of our system is the application of decision rules which is constructed by relational learning technique. We presented its representation and learning algorithm. Then we evaluated their effectiveness through retrieval experiments. The results showed that our system enables us to find more relevant pages though the effect differs in every questions. Our system needs quick response and moderate machine power. Thus it should be a user side application because search engines cannot afford to attach such a function. One of the future problem is to reduce the cost which users need to judge pages. We plan to apply clustering methods for this problem.

References

1. Baeza-Yates, R. and Ribeiro-Neto, B.: Modern Information Retrieval: Addison-Wesley, Wokingham, UK, (1999)
2. Furnkranz, J.: Separate-and-Conquer Rule Learning, *Artificial Intelligence Review*, Vol.13, No.1 (1999)
3. M. Okabe and S. Yamada: Interactive Document Retrieval with Relational Learning, *Proc. of the 16th ACM Symposium on Applied Computing*, pp.27-31 (2001)
4. Quinlan, J.R., and Cameron-Jones, R.M.: Induction of Logic Programs: FOIL and Related Systems, *New Generation Computing*, Vol.13, Nos.3,4, pp.287-312 (1995)
5. Salton, G. and Buckley, C.: Improving Retrieval Performance by Relevance Feedback, *Journal of the American Society for Information Science*, Vol.41, No.4, pp.288-297 (1990)

A Fuzzy Rule-Based Agent for Web Retrieval-Filtering

S. Vrettos and A. Stafylopatis

Department of Electrical and Computer Engineering
National Technical University of Athens
157 73 Zographou, Athens, Greece
vrettos@cslab.ntua.gr, andreas@cs.ntua.gr

Abstract. This work proposes an intelligent agent for information retrieval and information filtering in the context of e-learning. The agent is composed of five modules: the Indexing module, the User Profile module, the Information Retrieval module, the Information Filtering module, and the Interface module. The Information Retrieval and Information Filtering modules are based on the same Fuzzy Inference System which incorporates user profile knowledge.

Keywords: Approximate Retrieval, Information Filtering, Web-Based Learning Systems, Learning User Profiles.

1 Introduction

An intelligent agent for information retrieval-filtering is presented, which is focused on providing support to students registered to courses published on the Web. We consider all courses available to the student to compose the educational "environment" that the user shares with the agent. This "environment" is indexed by the Indexing module using the *Vector Space Model (VSM)* and *Latent Semantic Indexing (LSI)*. The user is able to retrieve web pages (educational material) either by browsing the contents of a course or by formulating queries to the course material using the agent's Interface module. User's interests (profile) are determined by the Profile module using the content of the educational material that the user selected in the past. Profile information is used in conjunction with VSM and LSI to retrieve pages from course material and to filter the results returned by the meta-search engine of the agent. Retrieval and filtering is performed by a *Sugeno Fuzzy Inference System (FIS)* which is used instead of the traditional Rocchio's algorithm for relevance feedback.

2 Information Retrieval and Filtering

When the case is the retrieval of textual objects, like text documents or HTML pages, these objects are usually represented as vectors in the *vector space language model* [1]. A document collection of d documents and t terms is represented

N. Zhong et al. (Eds.): WI 2001, LNAI 2198, pp. 448–453, 2001.
© Springer-Verlag Berlin Heidelberg 2001

as a $t \times d$ term-by-document matrix A. An element a_{ij} of the matrix is either zero if the i-term of the collection does not appear in the j-document, or equals the frequency of occurance of the i-term in the j-document.

A query is represented as a vector q in the same vector space. A document is retrieved when it contains one or more terms of this query vector. The retrieved documents are then sorted according to the cosine similarity measure between the document and the query vector:

$$\cos \theta_j = \frac{\alpha_j^\top q}{||\alpha_j||_2 ||q||_2} \tag{1}$$

for $j = 1, \ldots, d$. This traditional Information Retrieval (IR)approach using single terms to index documents is suffering from synonymy (a meaning may be expressed by more than one terms) and polysemy (a term may have many different meanings). *Latent Semantic Indexing* applies truncated *Singular Value Decomposition (SVD)* to the term-document matrix to estimate conceptual rather than term indices [4]. Terms that occur frequently together accross the document collection are associated, meaning that a query could retrieve a document even if it contains none of the query terms.

The effectiveness of an IR system is evaluated by the metrics of *precision* and *recall* [4]. A very popular method for improving performance in IR systems is *relevance feedback*, which is based on query reformulation according to the relevant documents that a system retrieves. This feedback is usually taken into account by increasing the weight given to terms occuring in relevant documents, while decreasing the weight of terms occuring in non-relevant documents. Rocchio's algorithm [5] is one of the most effective and widely applied algorithms for relevance feedback. The user specifies which documents from the returned list are relevant (irrelevant) to his/her query. Relevant and irrelevant documents are used to form a new query vector:

$$q_n = \alpha q_o + \beta \frac{1}{R} \sum_{Rel} d - \gamma \frac{1}{I} \sum_{Ir} d \tag{2}$$

where R is the number of relevant documents, I is the number of irrelevant documents and α, β, γ are parameters.

Relevance feedback is also used in the context of Information Filtering (IF). The user specifies which documents are relevant to his/her broad interests or not and the profile vector is calculated using the formula:

$$p_l = \beta \frac{1}{I} \sum_{Int} d - \gamma \frac{1}{NI} \sum_{Ni} d \tag{3}$$

where I is the number of interesting documents, NI is the number of non-interesting documents and β, γ are parameters. This profile vector is used to categorize incoming information as interesting or not to the user. Another popular representation of user's profile is to describe it as a set of documents (Case-Based) that the user has judged to be relevant or not to his/her interests. If an incoming document is close to a relevant document, it is likely to be interesting to the user.

3   Fuzzy Inference System for Relevance Feedback

Fuzzy set theory has been used in the field of information retrieval through fuzzy retrieval models [2], [3]. In this work, fuzzy reasoning is used as a mechanism for relevance feedback in the traditional vector space model. A zero-order Sugeno type fuzzy inference system with two inputs, one output and nine rules has been implemented. The first input is called "Relevance to Query (RQ)" and is equal to the cosine measure between the query vector q and the document vector d. The second input is called "Relevance to Profile (RP)" and represents the cosine measure between the document vector d and the profile. We make use of the document (Case-Based) representation of the user profile, so the RP is equal to the largest cosine measure between the the document vector d and the documents in the profile set. The single output is called "Suggestion (SUG)" and represents the value (strength) by which a document or web page is suggested to the user. The 9-rules used in the fuzzy model are given in Table 1.

Table 1. The rule base of the FIS for relevance feedback

If RQ is HIGH and RP is HIGH then SUG is HIGH
If RQ is HIGH and RP is NORMAL then SUG is NORMAL-HIGH
If RQ is HIGH and RP is LOW then SUG is NORMAL
If RQ is NORMAL and RP is HIGH then SUG is NORMAL-HIGH
If RQ is NORMAL and RP is NORMAL then SUG is NORMAL
If RQ is NORMAL and RP is LOW then SUG is LOW-NORMAL
If RQ is LOW and RP is HIGH then SUG is NORMAL
If RQ is LOW and RP is NORMAL then SUG is LOW-NORMAL
If RQ is LOW and RP is LOW then SUG is LOW

The FIS was created using the MATLAB fuzzy toolbox. Gaussian membership functions having width $\sigma = 0.2$ have been used for both inputs in the antecedent part of the rules. Fuzzy singletons in the consequent part are located at values 0.1, 0.3, 0.5, 0.7 and 0.9 for LOW up to HIGH. The AND operator is min, aggregation method is max, implication method is min and defuzzification is weighted average.

The fuzzy inference approach was tested against Rocchio's algorithm using the Cranfield corpus (http://www.cs.utk.edu/ lsi/) which includes 1398 documents, 225 queries and an average of 8.2 relevant documents per query. The weighting scheme was TF-IDF (Term Frequency - Inverse Document Frequency). The reference model was the upper-bound model in which the top-n relevant documents of the retrieved set are fed back to the system as relevance. In the case of Rocchio's algorithm, the initial query was replaced by the centroid of the relevant documents [5]. In our experiment, we retrieve a set of 100 documents and precision is interpolated at each recall level from 0.0 to 1.0 with step size 0.1. The mean presicion of all queries over all recall levels is calculated for document feedback n=1 up to n=20 and the results are plotted in Fig. 1. We can see that, with the exception of the first feedback (n=1), Rocchio's algoritm outperforms the FIS – in mean values – up to the mean number of relevant documents per query (n=8), while the FIS has better performance than Rocchio's algorithm as more documents are fed to the system.

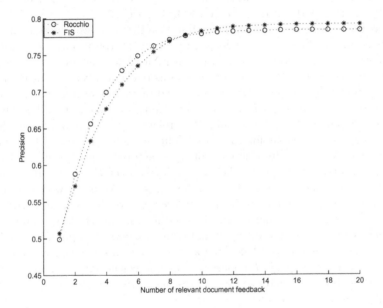

Fig. 1. Mean Precision over the number of retrieved documents.

The adoption of the FIS approach is justified, as it exhibits quite satisfactory performance and is an extensible method that can combine many features of documents (web pages) and user preferences. Furthermore, it can easily be used to re-rank the results of a search engine according to the user's profile. On the other hand, this form of relevance feedback needs more evaluation and in larger text corpus.

4   The Agent Architecture

The agent is composed of the indexing module which is responsible for the pre-processing of the educational material and the creation of the LSI vector space, the profile module that creates the profiles for each user, the information retrieval module to retrieve educational material from the courses, the information filtering module to filter web pages brought from the outside world by the meta-engine, and the interface module between the user and the agent. The agent has been implemented using Perl, HTML and Common Gateway Interface (CGI) and was applied to two courses, regarding computers and robotics respectively, published using the WebCt platform (the Modulates Project).

Indexing Module. Each course contains educational material (mainly in the HTML pages) that include text, images and video. The indexing module removes HTML tabs and commonly used English words like "a", "with", etc, and forms the term-by-document matrix A which is weighted using TF-IDF. Finally, SVD is performed to create the LSI space.

Profile Module. Based on the assumption that queries represent short-term interests and profiles represent long-term interests, the profile set is composed as follows. The *short-term profile* used for information retrieval is created using search profile elements that the user judges as relevant, irrelevant or unknown to his/her query. So the profile set is composed of the set of relevant pages (Rel), the set of irrelevant pages Ir and the set of unknown pages Un. The *long-term profile* is dynamically updated using the preferences and the queries of the user. Every page has a weight for each user. This weight is increased by a factor α every time the user visits this page or by a factor β when the user selects this page as an answer to a query. The same weight is decreased down to a limit by a factor γ every time the user selects a different page. All pages with weight above the threshold t_i are characterized as interesting, while the pages with weight between t_i and t_{in} are characterized as indifferent and the pages under t_{in} are characterized as non-interesting. Finally, an *integrated profile* is created based on the pages that the user has rated as relevant to his/her query. Suppose that d is such a page. If page d is closer, using the cosine measure, to a document d' that has been characterized as interesting in the long-term profile, then the document d' is also included in the Rel set.

Interface module. The kind of profile that will be used for information retrieval and filtering is determined by the selection between two modes. The user selects either the "working on a project" or the "no specific goal" mode to declare his/her general intention. The interaction between the user and the interface is based on a "query cycle" which is composed of a query in the course material and/or transfer of this query to the web.

Information Retrieval module. The user rates whether a page of the returned list is of high, normal or low relevance to his/her query. These selections are stored and used to form the short-term profile. When the user wants to have an optimized query he/she selects the *relevance* button from the process query panel. If the "working on a project" mode is active then the short-term profile is used as such. If the "no specific goal" mode is active then the integrated profile is used instead. For each page in the course material, the two variables (RQ) and (RP) are computed and the ranking is defined by the output (SUG) of the FIS.

Information Filtering module. When the user wants to find information in the web relevant to his/her query in the course material, he/she selects the *Ask Google* button in the process query panel. The query is expanded adding a small number (one or two) of the most closely related terms in the cources using Latent Semantic Analysis. The new query is transferred to the Google search machine and a number of web "snippets" are stored in a temporary file. These short textual descriptions are passed through a stop-list for the removal of common words and the remaining term vectors form the "snippet" vectors. Depending on whether the "working on a project" or "no specific goal" mode is active, the short-term or the integrated profile is used in the FIS. The cosine measure between the "snippets" vectors and the profile defines the RP input to the FIS. On the other hand, the RQ input is created by normalizing the ranking of the search machine to the interval [0,1] (1: first page in the rank - 0: last page). For every "snippet" vector, a suggestion (SUG) is computed by the FIS and a new rank of the "snippets" is created. Ideally, we should use all the terms of a page, but fetching and processing the actual pages is a costly and slow solution that practically limits filtering to a small portion of the retrieved set.

5   Conclusions and Future Work

We have presented an information retrieval-filtering agent aiming at helping students in an e-learning environment which is composed of courses published on the web. User profiles created by the agent, along with the user's queries, are processed by the Fuzzy Inference System, for the retrieval of the course educational material and for the filtering of web pages coming from the meta-search engine of the agent. Future work includes further evaluation of the FIS for relevance feedback and the addition of a browsing module to help students in web navigation [6].

References

1. M.W. Berry, Z. Drmac, and E.R. Jessup. Matrices, vector spaces and information retrieval. *SIAM Review*, 41(2):335–362, November 1999.
2. S.M. Chen and J.Y. Wang. Document retrieval using knowledge-based fuzzy information retrieval techniques. *IEEE Transactions on Systems, Man and Cybernetics*, 25:793–802, 1995.
3. V. Cross. Fuzzy information retrieval. *Journal of Intelligent Information Systems*, 3:29–56, 1994.
4. S. Deerwester, S.T. Dumais, G.W. Furnas, T.K. Landauer, and R. Harshman. Indexing by latent semantic analysis. *Journal of the American Society for Information Science*, 41(6):391–407, 1990.
5. S.T. Dumais. Enhancing performance in latent semantic indexing retrieval. *Technical Memorandum TM-ARH-017527*, September 1990.
6. D. Mladenic. Text-learning and related intelligent agents. *IEEE Expert special issue on Applications of Intelligent Information Retrieval*, July-August 1999.

Implementation Issues and Paradigms of Visual KDD Systems

Jianchao Han and Nick Cercone

Department of Computer Science, University of Waterloo
Waterloo, Ontario, N2L 3G1, Canada
{j2han, ncercone}@uwaterloo.ca

Abstract. We proposed an interactive visualization model for knowledge discovery and data mining, with which four visual KDD systems for different targets have been implemented. The implementation issues are considered and three implementation paradigms, including *image-based* approach, *algorithm-embedded* approach, and *interaction-driven* approach, are presented and discussed. The issues and paradigms presented in this paper can also be used in the design of Web mining and Web agenda.

1 Introduction

Existing approaches for knowledge discovery can be characterized into *algorithm-based approach* and *visualization-based approach* [3,8]. For algorithm-based knowledge discovery, once the algorithms used in the process are determined and executed, the user can hardly participate in the discovery process. If the results are not satisfactory, what the user can do is to adjust the input parameters and rerun the algorithms. Unfortunately, it is often difficult for the user to understand and interpret the outputs and include his/her perception and domain knowledge into the system on-demand. On the other hand, visualization-based approaches provide users with straightforward outputs and can interact with users. However, most visualization systems concentrate on the original data visualization and/or the final results visualization but lack the ability to visualize the entire process of knowledge discovery. Another limitation is that the patterns without natural structures, like various kind of rules, are difficult to present in visual forms.

We proposed an abstract model, RuleViz, for interactive knowledge discovery [7,8], which combines the algorithm-based and visualization-based approaches. The RuleViz model consists of five components, including original data preparation and visualization, data reduction, data preprocessing, pattern learning, and pattern visualization. The RuleViz model provides us with a methodology of designing interactive knowledge discovery system from Web and large data resources, such as discovering the navigational behavior of Web users as well as Web usage Patterns [10].

This paper is organized as follows. We simply review the RuleViz model in Section 2 and consider some general implementation issues independent on

N. Zhong et al. (Eds.): WI 2001, LNAI 2198, pp. 454–463, 2001.
© Springer-Verlag Berlin Heidelberg 2001

applications in Section 3. Then we discuss the implementation paradigms of the RuleViz model in Section 4. The comparison of these implementations will be presented in Section 5. Finally, Section 6 is the concluding remark.

2   The RuleViz Model

Much discussion about the KDD process and its main ingredients are present in the literature [3]. The KDD process relies on a human-system interaction. It is impossible to envision a fully automated process of knowledge discovery because this process requires that the system possess all domain knowledge and be capable of recognizing the intentions of the user. Hence, effective human-machine interaction plays an important role in the KDD process. Various visualization tools can be used to advantage the interaction and help incorporate the user's intentions and navigate through the enormous search spaces interactively.

In order to construct such interactive systems, we suggest an interactive visualization model, RuleViz, which addresses the following aspects [8]: 1) combining algorithm-based and visualization-based approaches for data mining to take their advantages and avoid their disadvantages; 2) visualizing the entire process of knowledge discovery; 3) including the user's perception to guide the KDD process and navigate search for various tasks, such as Web navigation; 4) investigating human-machine interactions for the machine to accept the user's intentions and perceptions; and 5) developing new visual forms for presenting intermediate results and various kinds of final patterns.

According to the KDD process, the RuleViz model consists of five components. For more detailed discussion of the RuleViz model, see [7,8].

Original Data Preparation and Visualization

This component is to specify the data source and data form and present the original data in visual forms such that the user can view the data from different angles as well as get insight into the data (features and tuples) distribution and interesting data areas that are virtually impossible to get from looking at tables of output or simple summary statistics. How the original data is visualized depends on the patterns that are to be discovered.

Data Reduction

Data reduction is to reduce the redundant or insignificant data, or select a small portion to represent the entire set due to time complexity and/or main memory capacity. Large data sets can be reduced and cleaned vertically and horizontally. Usually, data reduction can be performed either by executing algorithms for tuple reduction and feature selection or by using visualization techniques and interaction tools [6].

Data Preprocess

This component is actually a sequence of operations that convert the original data to the target format for the discovery algorithms. The RuleViz model considers the following aspects of data preprocess: *data transformation, feature extraction, missing attribute values handling,* and *numerical attribute discretization.* All these aspects can be accomplished based on efficient algorithms. The numerical attributes can also be performed using visualization techniques and interaction tools. For example, the frequency histogram of continuous attributes can be used to show the values distribution and determine the number of intervals as well as cut-points [8].

Pattern Discovery

This component searches for patterns of interest in a particular representation form. Pattern discovery can be either *algorithm-based* or *visualization-based*. The algorithm-based pattern discovery approach stresses the logic and/or statistics reasoning and attempts to find the patterns behind the data mathematically, while the visualization-based approach is to directly use the images that visualize the preprocessed data [5] or interactively construct the patterns under the user's supervision [1,9].

Pattern Visualization

This component is to visualize the patterns achieved in pattern discovery. For the user's convenience, this component usually provides a collection of visualization routines which can be adapted to different patterns.

3   Implementation Issues

The RuleViz model provides us with a guideline of designing an interactive visualization system for knowledge discovery. To implement the RuleViz model, however, many decisions need to be made and some details should be refined, because there exist many methods for each component, and different methods have different features and can adapt to different tasks. In this section, we summarize and discuss these issues for implementing interactive visualization systems.

3.1   Choosing Visualization Spaces

In general, the visualization of data is based on the display screen which is currently a two-dimensional device. The visual structures may be 1D, 2D, 3D and 3D+time [2]. One-dimensional visual structures are simple but have week representation power, and are typically used as part of larger visual structures. The popular debate is about 2D versus 3D presentations [11], though 3D+time and other higher dimensional visual structures exist. 2D presentations are consistent with the display screen and 2D pictures are not only processed faster on computers but also are familiar and straightforward to the user, as well as easy to interact. 3D presentations are more realistic, powerful to represent human perception, and provide much more space for presenting data.

We suggest that 2D visualization be preferred for the raw data, data reduction and preprocess, while both 2D and 3D visualizations be appropriate for the pattern visualization. The reason is that the visualization of the raw data, data reduction and data preprocessing contains a lot of interactions, and it is usually difficult for the user to specify the interesting features, data areas, and cut-points in 3D pictures due to fewer 3D control widgets. For the final results, however, no more interactivity is needed and the more realistic pictures are preferred.

3.2   Choosing Visualization Techniques

Different visualization techniques have different features and can be used for
different data sets and tasks. The nature and characteristics of a data set can be
revealed by many visual forms, while a visualization technique can be adapted
for various purposes. Moreover, different visualization techniques can be used in
different components in the RuleViz model, but they must be consistent such
that the user can easily understand and conveniently react with the intermediate
results between different components [8,7].

There are three decisions to be made for choosing visualization techniques for
different components: *choosing original data visualization techniques* to focus on
the reveal of the data value and attribute distributions, attribute correlations,
interesting data areas, etc.; *choosing knowledge visualization techniques* to reveal
the natural structures or characteristics; and *choosing visualization techniques
for data reduction and data preprocess* like algorithm-based parameter input
interfaces and visualization-based control widgets.

3.3   Choosing Implementation Paradigms

A KDD process consists of many algorithms including reduction algorithms,
handling missing values, discretizing continuous attributes, mining (learning)
algorithms, and so forth. All approaches can be algorithm-based as well as
visualization-based. For the algorithm-based approach, only the results are displayed [6], while for the visualization-based approaches, the algorithm process
should be visualized. Different approaches can be used in different components,
and in the same components different approaches can also be explored. We propose three implementation paradigms which will be discussed next section.

3.4   Traversability and Navigability

For very large amount of data, it is impossible to accommodate all data items
in the relatively small screen. Therefore, the traversal and navigation among
the data are important. Usually, the efficient view traversibility and strong nav-
igability are required [4]. By *view traversal* we mean the iterative process of
viewing, selecting something seen, and moving to it, to form a path through the
logical data structure which can be characterized by a logical structure graph
and used to organize the data items. Each data item is represented as a node in
the logical structure. The efficient view traversability requires the small number
of out-going links of nodes and short paths between pairs of nodes. On the other
hand, the *view navigation* considers the problems like how to find the shortest
path between pairs of nodes and how to get to the target.

3.5   Human-Machine Interactions

Interaction between the user and machine plays the essential role. An important
decision is how to allocate the functions between the user and the machine as

well as how to communicate between them. Tweedie divides the interactivity in the visualization tools into two categories [12], *direct manipulation* and *indirect manipulation*. The most existing visualization tools exploit direct manipulations in which the physical behavior in the real world is replicated literally. The indirect manipulation, however, can add more "magical" functionality that does not rely on direct physical metaphors.

In addition, response time and processing cost also need considered because they affect the system performance. Well-established interface for a visualization system should take less processing time and response fast.

3.6 Windowing Strategies

In order to clearly display all parts of the data set and concentrate on the specific objects when demand, many visualization tools provide more than one windows and many panels in a window. More windows can provide more spaces for the data but may distract the user. Few windows accommodate less data and cause distortion but attract the user's attention and present correlations better. Several strategies can be considered, such as *Zoom, Overview+Detail,* and *Focus+Context* [2].

3.7 Understanding Human Perception

Finally, the implementation of the RuleViz model is highly dependent on the properties of human perception. Therefore, human perception must be studied carefully, including color perception, shape perception, cluster perception, scale perception, etc. Understanding human perception is difficult because different users may have different perceptions for the same picture.

4   Implementation Paradigms

To implement the RuleViz model, we propose three implementation paradigms which can be identified as follows: *image-based approach*; *algorithm-embedded approach*; and *interaction-driven approach*. In this section, we briefly discuss these three implementation paradigms.

4.1   Image-Based Paradigm

Image-based paradigm has the following characteristics:

- The original data are mapped to an image by using a specific visualization technique to reflect the data distribution and attribute value distribution.
- The user can interactively choose areas from the image in which s/he is interested by using interaction control widgets to clean and reduce the data if necessary. The cleaned data are revisualized and a new image is obtained. This can be repeated until the user is satisfied with the obtained image.

- The obtained image may need preprocessed for discovering patterns. For example, the continuous attributes are discretized in terms of the data value distribution reflected in the image.
- The preprocessed image is explored to find patterns by using specific image-process algorithms.
- Finally, the discovered patterns are represented as images and presented on the display window.

4.2   Algorithm-Embedded Paradigm

The characteristics of this implementation paradigm are as follows:

- Each component in the system is implemented based on embedded one or more algorithms;
- The input parameters for each algorithm are controlled by the user, newly added or prespecified; and the input data are usually the outputs of previous components.
- The outputs of each algorithm are presented to the user in some predefined visual forms;
- The user can perceive the visual outputs, choose to repeat some algorithm or related algorithms by adjusting parameters to see the effects of parameters, and decide what parameters are the best or satisfactory.

4.3   Interaction-Driven Paradigm

By *interaction-driven* we mean that the knowledge discovery process is completely driven by interactions between the user and machine, and the user decides how each step is performed. This implementation paradigm is also called *user-supervised* [1] and has the following features:

- The relevant data identification, data preprocess, and the pattern recognition capabilities of the human beings can be explored to increase the effectiveness of pattern learning.
- The user specifies the task, focuses on the search, and evaluates the intermediate results of the process. Therefore, the domain knowledge can be easily integrated into the systems.
- The user has a deep understanding of the resulting patterns because the discovery process is guided by the user. Hence, the user highly trusts into the results.
- The data preprocess is not an independent component, and usually is done on demand. Thus the preprocessing cost is often reduced. For example, the continuous attributes are discretized only when they are used to split decision tree nodes, while the attributes that are never chosen at any nodes will not be discretized. Moreover, the same continuous attribute may have different splits in different decision tree nodes. In contrast, most algorithm-based systems discretize continuous attributes before the mining algorithms begin [5], and can not be changed during the algorithm execution.

- The user can *undo* and *redo* tasks in any steps at will until the result is satisfying.
- Compared to naive Bayes classification or other subject probability based approaches, this approach is totally subjective, fully depending on the user.

In addition, a combination of above three implementation paradigms is also possible. In a hybrid implementation paradigm, different components of the Rule-Viz model can be implemented in different ways. For example, the data reduction can be done in the image-based method by using control widgets, while the data can be preprocessed in the algorithm-embedded way; the interaction-driven approach can be integrated with algorithms such as feature ranking, split attribute evaluation, etc. in decision tree construction to aid the user to decide which attribute is the best for split in a specific decision tree node in the case that it is difficult to directly observe the attribute values distribution.

5   Implementation Systems and Comparison

We have implemented four interactive knowledge discovery systems for different tasks using different implementation paradigms. Table 1 lists these four systems, their tasks, and implementation paradigms. To compare, we also list the techniques developed for each component in these four systems in Table 2, 3, and 4, respectively.

Table 1. Four implementation systems: AViz, CViz, CVizT, and DTViz

System	Pattern to be learned	Implementation paradigm
AViz	Numerical association rules	Image-based
CViz	Classification rules	Algorithm-embedded
CVizT	Classification rules	Interaction-driven
DTViz	Decision trees	Interaction-driven

The AViz system [5] is used to visualize the discovery process of association rules. AViz first maps tuples from the original data sets to three-dimensional tuples in terms of two conditional continuous attributes and one continuous or categorical attribute specified by the user, and then plots the tuples on the visualization window. The obtained image is repeatedly processed by the user to get the interesting data area. The final data distribution image is discretized according to *bin-packing based equal-depth* method, and a grid is acquired. Each cell in the grid is rendered with the color that is calculated on the basis of *support* and *confidence* of the cell. Finally, the optimized rectangles with the highest *gain* is found according to the colors of cells contained in the rectangles. Three kinds of images are exploited in the AViz system. The first kind is obtained by plotting projected tuples in the data visualization component, data reduction component, and data preprocess component. The second kind is generated by rendering cells in the grid produced through attribute discretization, where the cell colors reflect the cell *support* and cell *confidence*. These two kinds of images are two-dimensional. The third kind of image is three-dimensional and rotating continuously, which are generated by rendering the gain optimized rectangles and leaving other cells unrendered.

The CViz system [6] is used to visualize the entire process of classification rules induction. CViz first divides the display window into parallel coordinates and then draws the tuples from the original data sets as polylines across the parallel coordinates by executing a transformation and scale algorithm. The original data can be reduced by randomly sampling with the condition that a certain number (a specified threshold) of tuples must be contained in each class although the visualization-based tuple selection is also available, and/or by selecting significant features based on the RELIEF algorithm that is embedded in CViz. The missing attribute values in the reduced data set, if any, can be estimated as the most frequent values of the same attribute with respect to the same class labels, which is performed by the embedded *missing values handling* algorithm, while the continuous attributes can be discretized by running the embedded EDA-DB discretization algorithm based on entropy of intervals [6]. The preprocessed data are input as parameters to the learning algorithm ELEM2 [6] that induces a set of classification rules by performing a general-to-specific search in a hypothesis space. Finally, the resulting classification rules are visualized as *strips* across the related parallel coordinates by an embedded *rule visualization* algorithm.

Table 2. Visualization Techniques Used in AViz, CViz, CVizT, and DTViz

System	Data visualization techniques	Knowledge visualization techniques
AViz	2D Plots	3D Rotation Planes
CViz	Parallel Coordinates	Parallel Coordinates-based Rule Strips
CVizT	Table Lens	Table Lens-based Rule Lens
DTViz	Parallel Segments	Tree Structure

Table 3. Data Reduction Techniques Used in AViz, CViz, CVizT, and DTViz

	Feature Selection	Tuple Selection
AViz	Dialog window	Interactive rubber band
CViz	Embedded Algorithm RELIEF	Random sampling
CVizT	Interactive deletion	Random sampling
DTViz	Interactive deletion	Random sampling

Table 4. Data Preprocess and Learning Techniques Used in the Four Systems

	Attribute Discretization	Missing Values Handling	Learning Techniques
AViz	Image-based	Remove	Image-based
CViz	Entropy-based algorithm (EDA-DB)	Most frequent value	Induction algorithm (ELEM2)
CVizT	Interactive Table-Lens	Remove	Interactive Table-Lens
DTViz	Pixel-oriented interaction	Remove	Pixel-oriented interaction

The CVizT [8] and DTViz [9] systems provide another paradigm for implementing the RuleViz model. In the implementation of CVizT, the raw data are visualized in the Table Lens with each attribute value of a tuple being drawn as a color line in the corresponding column. The user can interactively remove uninteresting attributes and/or aggregate several correlated attributes into one. The continuous attributes are discretized on demand to construct the condition part of classification rules, and the discovered rules occupy the display space in which the tuples covered by the rules were drawn. The main characteristic of this implementation is the full interaction between the user and machine.

Similarly, the DTViz system is also fully interactive. The data visualization window is used to interactively visualize the raw data and decision tree node data, select features, and discretize continuous attributes, while the decision tree visualization window is used to interactively grow and prune the decision trees according to the current tree structure and node evaluation.

Another important characteristic of CVizT and DTViz is that three components, including data preprocess, pattern learning, and pattern visualization are combined together to form an iterative process. In the CVizT system, a classification rule is generated in each iteration, while in the DTViz system, a decision tree node is split in each iteration.

6   Concluding Remark

In this paper, we introduced our interactive model for knowledge discovery which combines the algorithm-based approach and the visualization-based approach. We also discussed the implementations issues of this model, and proposed three paradigms of the model implementation. Four interactive systems have been implemented for different tasks using different implementation paradigms. During the implementation of these systems, new algorithms and methods for different components and steps of the KDD process have been developed. Experiments were performed on these four systems using the artificial data set, census data, and the UCI repository data sets, which will be reported in the future paper. Our experimental results demonstrate that the RuleViz model can provide a methodology for developing interactive KDD systems and the systems developed according to the RuleViz model take advantage of both algorithm-based and visualization-based approaches.

Our future work will be focusing on using this methodology to develop interactive Web mining visualization systems. Business Web sites usually contains a wide range of topics to provide information for users who have different interests and goals. Visually selecting related Web sites and contents as well as visitors will be very important. Related visitors and personalization and Web navigation can be used to mine the Web usage patterns and Web classifications. No general rules can be followed in this process. The expertise palys an essential role in some specified cases where domain knowledge and expert experience can be utilized by using the RuleViz model.

Acknowledgments. The authors are members of the Institute for Robotics and Intelligent Systems (IRIS) and wish to acknowledge the support of the Networks of Centers of Excellence Program of the Government of Canada, the Natural Sciences and Engineering Research Council, and the participation of PRECARN Associates Inc. We also wish to thank Glaxo Wellcome Corp. of Mississagua, Canada for their financial contribution.

References

1. M. Ankerst, M. Ester, and H. P. Kriegel, Towards an Effective Cooperation of the User and the Computer for Classification, *Proc. of KDD-2000*, pp.179-188, 2000.
2. S. K. Card, J. D. Mackinlay and B. Shneiderman, Readings in Information Visualization: Using Vision to Think, *Morgan Kaufmann Publishrs*, Inc. 1999.
3. U. M. Fayyad, G. Piatetsky-Shapiro, P. Smyth, and R. Uthurusamy, Advances in Knowledge Discovery and Data Mining, *AAAI Press / The MIT Press*, 1996.
4. G. W. Furnas, Effective View Navigation, *Proc. of CHI, ACM Conference on Human Factors in Computing Systems*, pp. 367-374, 1997.
5. J. Han and N. Cercone, AViz: A Visualization System for Discovering Numerical Association Rules, *Proc. of the 4th Pacific-Asia Conference on Knowledge Discovery in Databases*, pp. 269-280, Kyoto, Japan, April 2000.
6. J. Han, A. An, and N. Cercone, CViz: A Visualization System for Rule Induction, *Proc. of the 13th Biennial Conference of the Canadian Society for Computational Studies of Intelligence*, pp. 214-226, Montreal, Canada, May 2000.
7. J. Han and N. Cercone, Visualizing the Process of Knowledge Discovery, *Journal of Electronic Imaging*, SPIE 9(4), pp. 404-420, 2000.
8. J. Han and N. Cercone, RuleViz: A Model for Visualizing Knowledge Discovery Process, *Proc. of KDD-2000*, pp.223-242, Boston, USA, August 2000.
9. J. Han and N. Cercone, Interactive Construction of Decision Trees, *Proc. of PAKDD-2001*, pp.575-580, Hong Kong, April, 2001.
10. J. Srivastava, R. Cooley, M. Deshpande, and P.-N. Tan, Web Usage Mining: Discovery and Application of Usage Patterns from Web Data, *SIGKDD Explorations*, 1, 2000.
11. E. R. Tufte, Visual Explanations: Images and Quantities, Evidence and Narrative, *Cheshire, CT: Graphics Press*, 1997.
12. L. Tweedie, Characterizing Interactive Externalizations, *Proc. of CHI'97, ACM Conf. on Human Factors in Computing Systems*, pp. 375-382, 1997.

Re-engineering Approach to Build Domain Ontologies

Ahmad Kayed and Robert M. Colomb

Computer Science and Electric Engineering, University of Queensland, Brisbane QLD
4072, Australia {kayed,colomb}@csee.uq.edu.au

Abstract. Building ontology is changing from being an art to be a science. There are many attempts to re-engineer the process of building ontology [4], to categorize the applications that use ontology for better understanding [23], to study the common features of well-known existing ontologies [18], to provide environment and tools for ontology development [5], and to provide theoretical foundations for ontology [10]. In our experience of building ontological-base tendering system [15], we face the problem of building ontology. From these efforts and from our experience we demonstrate how to build ontologies for tendering process domain using conceptual graphs. Instead of reinventing the wheel, we reverse engineer EDI structures to build abstract ontology for tendering structures. Also, we use data-mining techniques to build abstract domain ontology from existing on-line catalogs.

1 Introduction

In our attempt [14], [15], [13] to automate the tendering process using the Internet we have faced many problems. One of them is the ontology. In a closed environment, all parties can sit and define what their terms mean. In small communities, the ontological problems hide and very small standardization efforts can solve them. In an open environment like the Internet ontology is not a trivial problem. In the tendering domain solving ontological problems will solve problems like price comparison, information overload, heterogeneity, matching, etc [15].

Using natural language to model the tendering makes any process associated with tendering automation extremely difficult. We implemented our ontologies using Conceptual Graphs (CGs). CGs are method of knowledge representation developed by Sowa [20] based on Charles Peirce's Existential Graphs and semantic networks of artificial intelligence [21]. According to Sowa [20], CGs have a direct mapping to and from natural language and a graphic notation designed for human readability. Conceptual graphs have all the expressive power of logic but more intuitive and readable. Many popular graphic notations and structures ranging from type hierarchies to entity-relationship or state transition diagrams

N. Zhong et al. (Eds.): WI 2001, LNAI 2198, pp. 464–472, 2001.
© Springer-Verlag Berlin Heidelberg 2001

can be viewed as special cases of CGs [24]. CGs are semantically equivalent graphic representation for first order logic.

Building ontology is changing from being an art to be a science. We start to see actual attempts to create a methodology for ontology building. The first attempts were focusing on how should ontology be [7] [9]. [4] provide engineering methodology for ontology building. To cope with these methodologies, in section 2 we summarize ontology building methodologies around ontology life cycle of [4]. In section 3 we express our experience in using existing tools to build domain ontology for tendering domain. Section 4 shows how we build the abstract structures ontology. Section 5 concludes the paper.

2   Ontology Building Process

There are many attempts to define a methodology for ontology construction. Examples are [6] [5] [22]. Ontology building life cycle moves forward through the following states: specification, conceptualization, formalization, integration, implementation, and maintenance [4] [5]. Although there are many differences among these methods, there are many common things. In the following we will summarize ontology building methodologies around these steps.

Specification. This step is important and will direct other activities. In this step, a plan of main tasks should be defined. Many questions should be answered. Example are: How much time and resources do you need? What are your scope and purposes, why ontology being built, the type of uses and end-users. The answers of these questions should be written in the requirement specification documents [5]. [3] [8] define this step by creating motivating scenarios. These scenarios identify the intuitively possible applications and solutions for ontology. They use informal competency questions to define ontology's purposes.

Conceptualization. This includes extracting terms and categorizing them in a conceptual model. This step is fundamental. [6] use knowledge elicitation techniques to extract terms. They use different resources to collect these terms. Examples are: Experts, books, handbooks, tables, other ontologies, text analysis, interviews, etc.

Formalization. This step varies from domain to anther. [23] define four levels of ontology formalization:

- Highly-informal: Expressed loosely in natural language.
- Structured-informal: Expressed in a restricted and structured form of natural language.
- Semi-formal: Expressed in an artificial formally defined language.
- Rigorously-formal: Meticulously defined terms with formal semantics, theorems and proofs of such properties as soundness and completeness.

Implementation. Ontology implementation means determining the technology which will be used to implement the ontology, integrate the new ontology with existing ones and ontology maintenance. Ontology implementation should provide systemic tools that meet ontology purposes. User should be able to browse, search, and evaluate ontology.

Ontology is not just a collection of words: ontology consists of logical relations, axioms and concepts taxonomy. Many researchers build their ontologies using different types of logic. In general First Order Logic (FOL) is used to implement ontology. Examples are Knowledge Interchange Format (KIF), Knowledge Query and Manipulation Language (KQML), Description Logic (DL) like LOOM, CLASSIC, BACK, etc. In some cases, higher and enhanced logic may be used such as conceptual graphs (CG), lexical conceptual Graphs (LCG), Description graphs (DG), context logic, Prolog, etc.

3   Extracting Common Concepts from E-catalogs

A common ontology is important to build sharable catalogs. Moreover, using ontology, facilitator (software agent) can translate from one catalog to another. The idea of using shared ontology to build (describe) e-catalogs is a working research problem. CommerceNet [2] are building a pilot virtual catalogs using common ontology. To do so, they first create ontology for each company (e.g., IBM, HP), then create the catalogs for each company. The reverse process of this still valid i.e. building ontology from existing catalogs. Integrating different catalogs can be done by creating a common ontology to describe the contents of these catalogs.

Building a new ontology from scratch is not a simple task. In our application (tendering) we have built two types of ontology: one for structures called Abstract Structures Ontology (ASO) and the other for domain concepts called Abstract Domain Ontology (ADO). For example, if a buyer wants to call for a tender, (s)he uses a structure from ASO and uses ADO to fill this structure [15].

In the concept acquisition process, we need to reuse existing resources to build our ontology. If we agree that ontology is an explicit specification of conceptualization [7], we also need to agree that this knowledge is implicit in many applications. This knowledge may be abstracted from existing resources. In our attempts to build ontologies for an on-line tendering system [13], we have discovered that many existing resources contain this knowledge. We conducted experiment to extract concepts from exiting catalogs. In the following we will summarize our steps to build ADO:

- Collect e-catalogs
- Extract top concepts
- Refine the results
- Categorize the concept
- Define the relations between concepts
- Build the ontological hierarchy
- Formalize the concepts

We collected nineteen catalogs for the item PC from the Web from different sites (e.g. Compaq, Dell) and converted them to text format. Another group, headed by Smith [1] who is working on text-mining software, run their algorithm [19] on this data to extract concepts for PC. The result was interesting. The following are the top concepts with their weighted-order, which are very much related to the concept PC.

keyboard 4195 [MB-SDRAM] 4195 monitor 3662 color 3662 sound 3638 drive 3569 card 3149 speakers 2854 cache 2755 [KB] 2755mouse 2388 [CD-ROM] 1867 stereo 1560 [V.] 1524 [WINDOWS] 1475 modem 1412 [GB-ULTRA-DMA-HDD] 1182 included 1104 [PCI] 1025 [MB] 1025 [MB-VRAM] 969 kbps 807[WIN] 806 [MMX] 792 software 777 graphics 723 player 720 [USB] 715 [GB-HDD] 698 video 637 ports 616 [INTEL-PENTIUM-II-MHZ] 608 [3D] 595 multimedia 572 account 567 pad 567 [US-ROBOTICS] 567 system 495 scroll 492 hours 481 [MHZ] 479 fax 456 expandable 448 [VRAM] 437 shared 437 bus 395 [MPEG-1] 365 upgradable 330 [AGP] 319 [INTEL-CELERON-MHZ] 278 board 236 [GB] 165.

To refine the results, we combined some words to form concepts. Examples are: "Color monitor", "Sound drive card", "Video player", etc. We used relation between words to combine them, i.e. if the distance between some words is less than a threshold, then we can potentially combine them and check for evidence to relate these combined words with the main concept. From the data, it is clear that the word "color" and "monitor" are close to each other. We have found evidence (in the text) that the concept "color monitor" has a "good" relation with the concept "PC". Combining the words (color monitor) as one concept is better than separating them to two concepts (i.e. color, monitor).

We noticed that some concepts are really good concepts to be added to the ontology (e.g., Software, Processor, Warranty, etc.). But other concepts are just instances. We categorized these concepts into groups. For example, "CELERON" and "PENTIUM" are instances of "Processor", "VRAM" and "Cache" are instances of "Memory", "GB" and "MB" are Type-of memory-units, and so on.

We used CG to implement this ontology. We defined basic relations to define classes in this ontology. Examples of basic relations are Synonyms, Is-a, Kind-Of, Collection-Of, Part-Of, Instance-Of, Has-Property, Has-Feature, Instance-Of, Role-of, Left Positive-Ass-With, Negative-Ass-With, etc.

We implemented the previous e-catalogs in CG using concepts from ADO. Figure 1 is an example. We have found that some concepts are not defined explicitly in the ontology but they are sub-type of concepts in ADO. Examples are: IDE is sub-type of HDD (Hard Disk Derive), CPU-Fan is part-of CPU, CPU is a synonym of processor, etc.

The level of abstraction is important issue in ontology building. High level of abstraction is useless, at the same time, a low level of abstraction will not generate a good ontology. Losing low-level concepts is not a drawback in the

---

[1] *http : //www.csee.uq.edu.au/ ∼ aes/*

world of ontology. Since the purpose is to cover most (not all) the space of concept world. Rules for the level of abstraction are needed to generate a "good" ontology [16]. The full details of our experiment is accessible via URL [2].

$[Class : PC]-$
     $\leftarrow (Type - Of) \leftarrow [Class : Computer]$
     $\leftarrow (Properties) \leftarrow [Name : "IBM"]$
     $\leftarrow (Collection - Of) \leftarrow [Class : CPU]-$
         $\leftarrow (Properties) \leftarrow [Speed : "166"] \leftarrow (Unit) \leftarrow [Speed - Unit : MHz]$
         $\leftarrow (Properties) \leftarrow [CPU - Brand : "Intel"]$
         $\leftarrow (Properties) \leftarrow [CPU - Type : "Pentium"]$
     $\leftarrow (Collection - Of) \leftarrow [Class : RAM]$
         $\leftarrow (Properties) \leftarrow [RAM - Size : "16"] \leftarrow (Unit) \leftarrow [Memory - Unit : MB]$
     $\leftarrow (Collection - Of) \leftarrow [Class : HDD]$
         $\leftarrow (Properties) \leftarrow [HDD - Size : "2.1"] \leftarrow (Unit) \leftarrow [Memory - Unit : MB]$
         $\leftarrow (Type - Of) \leftarrow [HDD : "IDE"]$
     $\leftarrow (Collection - Of) \leftarrow [Class : Modem]$
     $\leftarrow (Collection - Of) \leftarrow [Class : CD - ROM]$
     $\leftarrow (Collection - Of) \leftarrow [Class : SoundDriveCard]$
   etc.

Fig 1. Example of catalog implementation using CG and ADO concepts

4   Abstract Structure Ontology

We built our ASO from basic ontological elements. We called these elements signatures. In CGs, signature is a graph, which fixes the arity of a relation and shows the greatest concept types this relation type can link. A signature of a relation type enforces minimal coherence in knowledge representation.

Ontology stores abstract knowledge to be reused in different system that use the same abstract knowledge. We built some primitives that are needed to build a bid or a tender. These primitives with other components will form ASO.

In tendering domain, different standards were used to build tendering structures [13]. A well-known one is the EDIFACT. In the following we will describe how we build ASO.

---

[2] $http : //www.csee.uq.edu.au/ \sim kayed/ProCat1/PC\_Catalogs/index.html.$

Building EDIFACT messages. EDI is the well-known standard protocol for inter-business transactions. EDI has two standard protocols: private (ANSI X12) and public (UN EDIFACT ISO 9735) [11]. EDI transfers structured data by agreed message standard between computer applications. EDI has been extensively and successfully implemented, and is growing in popularity. Others like [17] [25] [11] describe EDI as inflexible, insufficient, ambiguous, closed, expensive, slow, and supports only one-to-many relationships. In tendering domain, EDIFACT 850 (EDIFACT Purchase Order Message) has been used frequently to facilitate on-line tendering. We have used EDIFACT 850 to build CG tendering structures.

Converting EDI to CG. To illustrate how we have used these structures to build ontology, we will demonstrate only one example, that is tender invitation structure. The tender invitation structure (TIS), see figure 2, is to inform the tenderers of the scope of the procurement. The tender invitation provides basic information on the procurement and guidance to the tenderers on the participation. We derived the component of TIS from UN EDIFACT ISO 9735 request for quote message [1].

We have defined TIS as a nested CG, containing information about the scope of the procurement, the address and conditions of contracting entity, nature of contract, duration/completion of contract, eligibility, award criteria, rules on participation, and objects specifications.

Formally TIS is defined using the type function of CG as follows:

$Type \quad TIS(x) \quad is$

$[TenderingConceptualStructures(TCS) : *x]-$
$(ATTR) \leftarrow [ContractingEntity]-$
$\quad (ATTR) \leftarrow [Address]$
$\quad (ATTR) \leftarrow [Name]$
$(ATTR) \leftarrow [ContractingDuration]$
$(ATTR) \leftarrow [Eligibility]$
$(ATTR) \leftarrow [AwardCriteria]$
$(ATTR) \leftarrow [ParticipationRules]$
$(ATTR) \leftarrow [Services])-$
$\quad (ATTR) \leftarrow [Identification]$
$\quad (ATTR) \leftarrow [Description]$
$\quad (ATTR) \leftarrow [Quantity]$
$\quad (Measure) \leftarrow [Unit]$
$\quad (RelevantDate) \leftarrow [ProductionDate]$
$\quad (RelevantDate) \leftarrow [Expirydate]$
...etc.

Fig 2. Part of tender invitation structure (**TIS**).

Building Signatures: As we said earlier, signature is a graph relation relates two or more concepts. For example, the following graph:

$$[ContractingEntity(CE)] \leftarrow (ATTR) \leftarrow [CE\_Attributes]$$

is a signature for the relation (ATTR).

We should note that ontological signature concepts are the maximal concepts i.e. signature concepts subsume all data signature concepts. Also we should note that a relation might take one or more signature. We have built an algorithm to extract these signatures. The following are signatures for the TIS in figure 2:

$S1 : [TIS] \leftarrow (ATTR) \leftarrow [TISAttributes]$

$S2 : [CE] \leftarrow (ATTR) \leftarrow [CEAttributes]$

$S3 : [Service] \leftarrow (ATTR) \leftarrow [ServiceAttributes].$

Readers are encouraged to visit [12] for more details.

5   Conclusions

In the tendering process domain, ontology is needed to solve many heterogeneity problems [14]. Buyers/sellers in a specific domain can use a common ontology to describe their needs/offers. Using formal structures has advantages over the standardized approach (e.g. EDIFACT messages). The EDI approach needs a pre-agreement about everything, but here we just need to agree about the common ontology. The ontology contains abstract concepts that will form the primitives to construct a tender or a bid. This is more flexible and can be stored in knowledge base. Ontology will make it easy to build tools to transfer from a friendly user interface (like the Web) to a logical structure (knowledge base).

The contribution of this paper can be summarized as merging existing methodologies of building ontologies with our own experiment of building ontologies in the tendering domain. Also we deployed the CG literature and text-mining techniques to build ontologies for e-commerce applications. We reused existing resources (like EDI, e-catalogs, etc.) to build ontologies for the electronic tendering domain.

Acknowledgment. The authors acknowledge the school of CSEE at the University of Queensland for financial support for this project. We acknowledge Andrew Smith for his help in extracting the ADO concepts using his text-mining tools.

References

1. Peder Blomberg and Sren Lennartsson. *Technical assistance in Electronic Tendering Devlopment – FINAL REPORT Technical assistance in electronic procurement to EDI - EEG 12 Sub-group 1.*
   http://simaptest.infeurope.lu/EN/pub/src/main6.htm, June 1997.
2. CommerceNet. *White Paper: CommerceNet Smart Catalog Pilot Status Update.* URL: $http://www.commerce.net/research/reports/white\_papers/smart.html$, 1996.

3. Fadel, Fadi G., M. Fox, and M. Gruninger. A generic enterprise resource ontology. In *Proceedings of the Third Workshop on Enabling Technologies- Infrastructures for Collaborative Enterprises , West Virginia University*, 1994.

4. M. Fernandez, A. Gomez-Perez, and N. Juristo. *Methodology: From Ontological Art Towards Ontological Engineering*. Workshop on Ontological Engineering. ECAI'96 PP 41-51, 1996.

5. M. Fernandez, A. Gomez-Perez, and J. Sierra. Building a chemical ontology using methodology and the ontology design environment. *IEEE Intelligent Systems*, 14,1:37–46, 1999.

6. A. Gomez-Perez and D. Rojas-Amaya. Ontological reengineering for reuse. *Lecture Notes in Computer Science*, 1621:139–149, 1999.

7. Thomas R. Gruber. Toward principles for the design of ontologies used for knowledge sharing. *International Journal of Human-Computer Studies*, 43(5,6):907–928, 1995.

8. M. Gruninger and M. Fox. The role of competency questions in enterprise engineering. In *Proceedings of the IFIP WG5.7 Workshop on Benchmarking - Theory and Practice, Trondheim, Norway*, Jan 94.

9. N. Guarino. Formal ontology and information systems. In *Proc. of the 1st International Conference, Trento, Italy*, 6-8 June 1998.

10. N. Guarino and R. Poli. Editorial: The role of formal ontology in the information technology. *International Journal of Human-Computer Studies*, 43(5,6):623–624, 1995.

11. Ravi Kalakota and Andrew B. Whinston. *Frontiers of Electronic Commerce*. Addison-Wesley Publishing Company, Inc., 1996.

12. Ahmad Kayed. *Home Page. http : //www.csee.uq.edu.au/ ∼ kayed/*, 2001.

13. Ahmad Kayed and Bob Colomb. *Book Chapter: Business to Business Electronic Commerce: The Electronic Tendering*. In Internet Commerce and Software Agents: Cases, Technologies and Opportunities, Edited by Syed M Rahman and Robert J Bignall, IDEA GROUP PUBLISHING Hershey (USA), 2001.

14. Ahmad Kayed and Robert M. Colomb. Infrastructure for electronic tendering interoperability. In *The Australian Workshop on AI in Electronic Commerce, conjunction with the Australian Joint Conference on Artificial Intelligence (AI'99) Sydney, Australia, ISBN 0643065520*, pages 87–102, Dec. 1999.

15. Ahmad Kayed and Robert M. Colomb. Conceptual structures for tendering ontology. In *The Second Workshop on AI in Electronic Commerce (AIEC 2000), conjunction with the Sixth Pacific Rim International Conference on Artificial Intelligence (PRICAI 2000), ISBN 0643066268*, pages 71–82, Aug. 2000.

16. Ahmad Kayed and Robert M. Colomb. Ontological and conceptual structures for tendering automation. In *the Eleventh Australasian Conference on Information Systems (ACIS2000), BRISBANE, AUSTRALIA, ISBN 1 86435 512 3*, 6-8 December 2000.

17. Steven O. Kimbrough and SCott A. Moore. On Automated Message Processing in Electronic Commerce and Work Supprot Systems: Speech Act Theory and Expressive Felicity. *ACM-TOIS*, 15,4:321–367, October 1997.

18. N.Fridman Noy and C.D. Hafner. The state of the art in ontology design. *AI Magazine*, Fall:53–74, 1997.

19. Andrew Smith. Machine learning of well-defined thesaurus concepts. In *The Text and Web Mining Workshop, conjunction with the Sixth Pacific Rim International Conference on Artificial Intelligence (PRICAI 2000)*, Aug. 2000.

20. J. F. Sowa. *Conceptual Structures: Information Processing in Minds and Machines*. Addison-Wesley, Reading, Mass., 1984.

21. J. F. Sowa. Syntax, semantics, and pragmatics of contexts. *Lecture Notes in Computer Science*, 954:1–15, 1995.

22. Mike Uschold. Building ontologies: Towards a unified methodology. In *16th Annual Conf. of the British Computer Society Specialist Group on Expert Systems*, Cambridge, UK, 1996.

23. Mike Uschold and Robert Jasper. A framework for understanding and classifying ontology applications. In V. Benjamins, B. Chasdrasekaran anf A. Gomez-Perez, N. Guarino, and M. Uschold, editors, *Proceedings of the IJCAI-99 workshop on ontologies and Problem-Solving Methods (KRR5)*, volume 18, pages 1–11, Stockholm, Sweden, Aug. 2 1999. CEUR-WS.

24. Eileen C. Way. Conceptual graphs: Past, present, and future. In William M. Tepfenhart, Judith P. Dick, and John F. Sowa, editors, *Proceedings of the 2nd International Conference on Conceptual Structures : Current Practices*, volume 835 of *LNAI*, pages 11–30, Berlin, August 1994. Springer.

25. Hung Wing. *Ph.D. Thesis: Managing Complex, Open, Web-Deployable Trade Objects*. Dep. of Computer Science and Electrical Engineering, University of Queensland-Australia, 1998.

Discovery of Emerging Topics between Communities on WWW

Naohiro Matsumura[1,3], Yukio Ohsawa[2,3], and Mitsuru Ishizuka[1]

[1] Graduate School of Engineering, University of Tokyo,
7-3-1 Hongo, Bunkyo-ku, Tokyo, 113–8656 Japan
{matumura, ishizuka}@miv.t.u-tokyo.ac.jp
[2] Graduate School of Systems Management, University of Tsukuba,
3-29-1 Otsuka, Bunkyo-ku, Tokyo, 112–0012 Japan
osawa@gssm.otsuka.tsukuba.ac.jp
[3] TOREST, Japan Science and Technology Corporation,
2-2-11 Tsutsujigaoka, Miyagino-ku, Sendai, Miyagi, 983–0852 Japan

Abstract. In the real world, discovering new topics covering profitable items and ideas (e.g., mobile phone, global warming, human genome project, etc) is important and interesting. However, since we cannot completely encode the world surrounding us, it's difficult to detect such topics and their mechanisms in advance. In order to support the detection, we show a method for revealing the structure of WWW by using the KeyGraph algorithm. Empirical results are reported.

1 Introduction

In our daily lives, a new topic sometimes become suddenly popular. The topic might seem insignificant at first sight, however, it turns out to match potential needs of us. *The Tipping Point* [1] describes this kind of phenomenon where a 'little' thing can make a big difference in the future. For example, how does a novel written by an unknown author become a bestseller? Why did the crime-rate drop so dramatically in New York City? Malcolm Gladwell answers to these questions as follows [1]:

> ... ideas and behavior and message and products sometimes behave just like outbreaks of infectious disease. They are social epidemics. The Tipping Point is an examination of the social epidemics that surround us.

The infectious disease usually spreads through the virus. Whereas, we cannot detect the social epidemics(new topics) and their mechanisms in advance since we cannot completely decode the world surrounding us. Detection of a *Tipping Point*, in face of this obstacle, could be a big chance for our various activities because competitors are not aware of such new topics. We here interpret 'topics' in the broad sense that cover new items, problems, ideas, and so on. Here we introduce some recent examples of new significant topics:

N. Zhong et al. (Eds.): WI 2001, LNAI 2198, pp. 473–482, 2001.
© Springer-Verlag Berlin Heidelberg 2001

Mobile Phone: Considering the appearance of mobile phones, there were essentially two factors. First, mobile phones conquered the inconvenience of beepers that people had to find a public phone when a beeper rang. Second, mobile phones were equipped with the functions of the Internet and E-mail services. Due to the synergy effects of these factors satisfying our needs, mobile phones began to get popular.

Global Warming: The awareness of global warming realized the collaboration of automobile and ecological preservation communities, and consequently brought about hybrid automobiles which have minimal exhaust emissions for preserving the earth ecology.

Human Genome Project: Many researchers in the field of artificial intelligence, biology, and medical science are collaborating on the human genome project to analyze the human genome and to reveal its effects. As we expect the conquest of fatal illnesses, the human genome project is in the limelight.

These topics were born when new collaborations of existing interests satisfy our potential needs or demands. Although the hidden factors might be 'submerged' in human mind, we believe that a few signs can be mined from a database on human behaviors reflecting human mind. For this purpose, the web is an attractive information source for its size and sensitivity to trends. The web consists of an abundance of communities [2,3], each corresponding to a cluster of web pages sharing common interest. Since a community means a chunk of shared interest, it is considered that a web page supported(or linked) from some communities satisfies their interests, and shows the movement direction of the widen human world, considering the synergy effects mentioned above. From this point of view, we are expecting the structure of WWW might be a key to understand the real world. In this paper, we show a method for revealing the structure of WWW by using KeyGraph algorithm [13] to inspect that WWW reflects the real world, and that the revealed structure of WWW supports our detection of new significant topics.

The rest of this paper is organized as follows. In Section 2, we describe our approach for understanding the real world through WWW, and an experiment is shown in Section 3. The results are discussed on in Section 4, and finally we conclude this paper in Section 5.

2   Understanding Human Society on WWW Structure

We try to understand the movement of the human society through the structure of WWW which is composed of communities and their relations. In this section, we first introduce previous studies for the discovery of communities, and the discovery of their relations. Then, we introduce KeyGraph algorithm [13] and our approach for applying KeyGraph to WWW.

2.1   The Discovery of Communities

Broder et al.[2] reported on an algorithm of clustering web pages based on the similarities of contents. The merit of this approach is to be able to apply not only to hyper-text(e.g., web pages) but also plain-text. However, indexing web pages accurately is difficult because the contents of web pages are not always concentrated on certain themes. In contrast to the content-based approach, links in web pages can be reliable information because they reflect human judgement[5]. Kumar et al.[3] defined a community on the web as a dense directed bipartite subgraph, and actually discovered over 100,000 communities. His idea was innovative because he was the first who formulated a community mathematically in our knowledge. The bipartite graph, however, comes to include pages of different interests, if it is expanded to a wide area at the Web. As another use of links, Kleinberg [4] and Brin and Page [5] used the link structures for ranking web pages. Their main idea was based on mutual reinforcing, i.e., the more a web page is referred, the more authoritative the web page becomes, and the more authoritative a web page becomes, the higher the web page ranks. The highly ranked web pages tend to be the representative web pages of communities. This method is useful for finding reliable pages, but is not suitable for our aim because we prefer premature significant pages to authorized ones. Compared with these methods, we aim at communities each having a shared interest.

2.2   The Discovery of Relations

Matsumura et al.[7] tried to find new combinations of different communities sharing common topics to discover promising new topics on the web. His idea was based on the co-citation concept originated in the bibliometrics [6]. However, the community was different from our aim in this paper in the point that he regarded each of the web pages obtained by Google[1] as a community. On the other hand, Kautz et al.[8] made REFERRAL WEB, a social network graph designed to find an expert who is both reliable and likely to respond to the user. Also, Leonard [9] described a matchmaker system named Yenta for finding people with similar interests and introduce them to each other. Both systems reveal the potential relations between individuals. Our aim is also to discover potential and interesting relations among the communities on WWW.

From Subsec. 2.1 and 2.2, we need a new method for discovering such latent relations among communities, each having an interest shared by Web pages in the community. For this purpose, the next section introduce KeyGraph.

2.3   KeyGraph Algorithm

KeyGraph [13] is originally an algorithm for extracting assertions based on co-occurrence graph of terms from textual data. The strategy of KeyGraph comes from considering that a document is constructed like a building for expressing new ideas based on traditional concepts as follows:

> This building has *foundations* (statements for preparing basic concepts), walls, doors and windows(ornamentation). But, after all, the *roofs*(main

---

[1] Google is a search engine to which Brin and Page's algorithm [5] is applied. Google is available at http://www.google.com/.

ideas in the document), without which the building's inhabitants cannot be protected against rains or sunshine, are the most important. These roofs are supported by *columns*. Simply put, KeyGraph finds the roofs.

The processes of KeyGraph are composed of four phases.

0) Document preparation: Prior to processing a document D, *stop words* [10] which have little meaning are discarded from D, words in D are stemmed [11], and phrases in D are identified [12]. Hereafter, a *term* means a word or a phrase in processed D.

1) Extracting foundations: Graph G for document D is made of nodes representing terms, and links representing the *co-occurrence* (term-pairs which frequently occur in same sentences throughout D). Nodes and links in G are defined as follow:

- **Nodes.** Nodes in G represent high-frequency terms in D because terms might appear frequently for expressing typical basic concept in the domain. High frequency terms are the set of terms above the 30th highest frequency(we denote this set by HF).
- **Links.** Nodes in HF are linked if the association between the corresponding terms is strong. The association of terms w_i and w_j in D are defined as

$$assoc(w_i, w_j) = \sum_{s \in D} \min(|w_i|_s, |w_j|_s), \tag{1}$$

where $|x|_s$ denotes the count of x in sentence s. Pairs of high-frequency terms in HF are sorted by *assoc* and the pair above the (*number of nodes in G*) - 1 th tightest association are represented in G by links between nodes.

2) Extracting columns: The probability of term w to appear is defined as $key(w)$, and the $key(w)$ is defined by

$$key(w) = 1 - \prod_{g \subset G} \left(1 - \frac{\sum_{s \in D} |w|_s |g - w|_s}{\sum_{s \in D} \sum_{w \in s} |w|_s |g - w|_s}\right). \tag{2}$$

Sorting terms in D by *keys* produces a list of terms ranked by their association with cluster, and the 12 top *key* terms are taken for *high key terms*.

3) Extracting roofs: The strength of column between a *high key term* w_i and a high frequency term $w_j \subset HF$ is expressed as

$$column(w_i, w_j) = \sum_{s \subset D} \min(|w_i|_s, |w_j|_s). \tag{3}$$

Columns touching w_i are sorted by $column(w_i, w_j)$, for each *high key term* w_i. Columns with the highest *column* values connecting term w_i to two or more clusters are selected to create new links in G.

Finally, nodes in G are sorted by the sum of *column* of touching columns. Terms represented by nodes of higher values of these sums than a certain threshold are extracted as the keywords for document D.

2.4 Our Approach

By focusing on the analogy between a document and other textual data, Key-Graph can be applied to a variety of topics. For example, KeyGraph has been adopted to

- find areas with the highest risks of near-future earthquakes from data of observed past earthquakes [14],
- get timely files from visualized structure of our working history [15],
- construct planning to guide concept understanding in WWW [16],
- make tools for shifting human context into disasters [17],
- discover potential motivations and fountains of chances [18].

In a document D, high-frequency terms are used for expressing typical basic concept, and term-pairs which frequently occur in the same sentences mean strong association throughout D (see Subsect. 2.3).

In this paper, we extend the use of KeyGraph to another kind of data, i.e., Web-page set (corresponding to D, document in Subsec. 2.3) including Web-pages (each corresponding to a sentence in Subsec. 2.3) having URL-links, each corresponding to words in Subsec. 2.3. That is, high-frequency links (which are the URLs pointing to other web pages) in a collection W of web pages show popular web pages, and link-pairs which frequently occur in the same web pages show strong relations in W [6]. Our fundamental hypothesis here is that the occurrence of a document and a collection of web pages have common causal structures, and our strategy for applying KeyGraph is based on this analogy.

Let us be more formal. A web page(which URL is u) is translated to a sentence as

$$u\ u_1\ u_2\ u_3\ \cdots\ u_i\cdots u_n. \tag{4}$$

Where $u_i(i = 1, 2, 3, \ldots, n)$ are the URLs contained in the web page. A document is formed by combining sentence, shown in eq. (4), for each web page of a collection. By this translation, we can obtain the document reflecting the link structure of WWW.

In order to understand the real world through the document, we have to piece out the situation between asserted keywords(*roofs*) and the basic concepts(*foundations*). In the metaphor of KeyGraph, the context structure expressed by links(*columns*) connecting assertions with basic concepts. We expect that a graphical output of KeyGraph helps us in understanding potential interests and the underlying relation between them, and loads us to the understanding of the structure of the interests of people in the real human society.

3 An Example of Experiment

In this section, we report on our experiment where we applied KeyGraph to two sets of collections C_A and C_B, each of which contains 500 popular web pages obtained by Google for the input query 'human genome', to follow the changes of the communities with time. The difference between the collections is the date: C_A is obtained on November 26, 2000, and C_B is on March 11, 2001.

After C_A and C_B were translated into two documents as described in Subsect. 2.4, for each document KeyGraph output URLs as *roof*(asserted) keywords. The URLs for C_A and C_B are shown in Table 1 and Table 2, and the graphical outputs are in Fig. 1 and in Fig. 2 respectively. Comparing Table 1 with Table 2, we can recognize the movement among them. For example,

```
http://www.ncbi.nlm.nih.gov
http://www.nhgri.nih.gov
http://www.sanger.ac.ul
```

appear in both the Tables. These are the most authorized research institutes in the area of human genomics. On the other hand,

```
http://www.tigr.org
http://www.celera.com
```

appear only in Table 2. These are newly growing research organizations in the area. This movement reflects events/situations of the real world in the topic of human genome, and means that KeyGraph could detect the major changes in the society. However, we cannot see why these changes occurred, from these tables.

Next, let us pay attention to the Fig. 1 and Fig. 2 to piece out the movement. In the figures, the single-circle and double-circle nodes show *fundation* and *roof* pages respectively, and links among nodes show *columns*. Comparing both the figures, we can imagine two situations as follows.

- http://www.ncbi.nlm.nih.gov,   http://www.nhgri.nih.gov,
  http://www.
  tigr.org, http://www.sanger.ac.ul, etc. are densely connected to each other. That is, these web pages are considered to be well established web pages in the topic of human genome.
- The situation around Celera Genomics(http://www.celera.com) changes dramatically from Fig. 1 to Fig. 2. Therefore, it can be assumed that something big event might have occured between November 26, 2000 and March 11, 2001. From this, we can clearly understand how much(and whose) acceptance Celera won from various established communities.

These are natural interpretations of the URLs and figures, with imagination based on common sense. In the next section, we discuss these interpretations by looking back the real events/situations.

4   Discussions

In the field of human genome, revolutionary events were occured in 2000 and 2001. In the White House on June 26, 2000, J. Craig Venter, president and

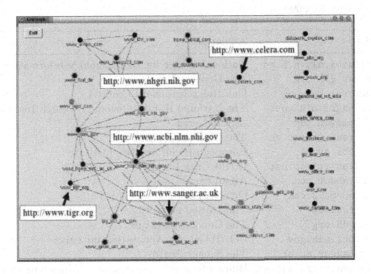

Fig. 1. A graphical output of KeyGraph for the input query 'human genome'(November 26, 2000). We can recognize a big cluster, which are composed of http://www.ncbi.nlm.nih.gov, http://www.nhgri.nih.gov, http://www.tigr.org, http://sanger.ac.ul, etc. Note that http://www.celera.com is isolated from the big cluster, although the company had a worldwide fame.

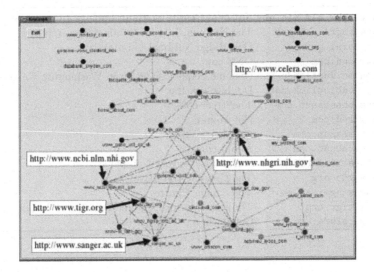

Fig. 2. A graphical output of KeyGraph for the same query(March 11, 2001). The major web pages of the clusters is almost the same as above cluster in Fig. 1. However, http://www.celera.com began to be supported by the clusters.

Table 1. An output list of KeyGraph for a collection of web pages on 'human genome'(Nov. 26, 2000).

URL	Affiliation
www.ncbi.nlm.nih.gov	National Center for Biotechnology Information
gdbwww.gdb.org	The Genome Database
www.ornl.gov	Oak Ridge National Laboratory
www.nhgri.nih.gov	The National Human Genome Research Institute
www.amazon.com	Amazom.com
www.gene.ucl.ac.uk	The Galton Laboratory
www.ebi.ac.uk	European Bioinformatics Institute
ad.doubleclick.net	DoubleClick Inc.
home.about.com	About.com
www.omega23.com	Omega23.com
www.fool.de	The Motley Fool
www.gdb.org	The Genome Database
lpg.nci.nih.gov	CGAP Genetic Annotation Initiative
www.sanger.ac.uk	The Sanger Centre
www.genetics.utah.edu	Human Genetics Department in University of Utah

Table 2. An output list of KeyGraph for a collection of web pages on 'human genome'(Mar. 11, 2001).

URL	Affiliation
www.ncbi.nlm.nih.gov	National Center for Biotechnology Information
www.nhgri.nih.gov	The National Human Genome Research Institute
www.ornl.gov	Oak Ridge National Laboratory
www.cnn.com	CNN.com
genome.wustl.edu	Genome Sequence Center in Washington University
ad.doubleclick.net	DoubleClick Inc.
www.thestreet.com	TheStreet.com
r.wired.com	Not Found
www.amazon.com	Amazom.com
home.about.com	About.com
onhealth.webmd.com	OnHealth Network Company
www.gdb.org	The Genome Database
www.sanger.ac.uk	The Sanger Centre
www.tigr.org	The Institute for Genomic Research
www.celera.com	Celera.com

chief scientific officer of Celera Genomics corporation(http://www.celera.com), Francis S. Collins, Director of the National Human Genome Research Institute (sponsored by the U.S. National Institutes of Health) (http://nhgri.nih.gov) were celebrated by U.S. President Bill Clinton and British Prime Minister Tony

Blair for the achievements of the human genome analysis. Celera Genomics and the U.S. Human Genome Project has been entered into a keen competition for leadership. Celera Genomics is an ambitious venture corporation, which began to sequence the human genome on September 8, 1999 by using the whole genome shotgun technique. On the other hand, the U.S. Human Genome Project is an international scientific effort to map and sequence the 3 billion genetic codes, involving more than 1000 scientists from five countries (China, France, Japan, the U.K., and the U.S.A.). Both two rivals independently accomplished the analysis of most of the human genome at almost the same time, and their papers were appeared in *Science* [20] and *Nature* [19] respectively in February 2001. With the complete sequencing of the human genome, pharmaceutical companies will create new medicine for patients of all ages. Since Celera Genomics goes release the sequences of the human genome, Fig. 2 might show the sign of the genesis of post-genome era.

Considering these real events/situations, the changes of the structures shown by Fig. 1 and Fig. 2 (e.g., Celera Genomics grew to be widely supported) are considered to reflect the real society.

5   Conclusions

In this paper, we introduced a method for aiding human awareness on significant novel, i.e., emerging topics. Here, the algorithm of KeyGraph is extended to be a method for the analysis and visualization of cocitations between Web pages. Communities, each having members (Web pages, their authors/readers) with common interests are obtained as graph-based clusters, and an emerging topic is detected as a Web page relevant to multiple communities. Experiments, an example of which is presented in this paper, show that the aimed effect of our method is realized.

The co-occcurrence of links in WWW often suffers from problems specific to WWW[21]. In the future work, we plan to improve KeyGraph algorithm to fit the link structure of WWW.

References

1. Malcolm Gladwell: THE TIPPING POINT: How Little Things Can Make a Big Difference. Little Brown & Company, 2000.
2. Andrei. Z. Broder, Steven. C. Glassman, and Mark. S. Manasse: Syntactic Clustering of the Web. Proceedings of the 6th World Wide Web Conference, 1997.
3. Ravi Kumar, Prabhakar Raghavan, Sridhar Rajagopalan, and Andrew Tomkins: Trawling the web for emerging cyber-communities. Proceedings of the 8th World Wide Web Conference, 1999.
4. Jon M. Kleinberg: Authoritative Sources in a Hyperlinked Environment. Journal of the ACM, Vol. 46, No. 5, pp. 604–632, 1999.
5. Sergey Brin and Lawrence Page: The Anatomy of a Large-Scale Hypertextual Web Search Engine. Proceedings of 7th World Wide Web Conference, 1998.

6. H. D. White and K. W. McCain: Bibliometrics. Annual Review of Information Science and Technology, Vol. 24, pp. 119–186, Elsevier, 1989.

7. Naohiro Matsumura, Yukio Ohsawa, and Mitsuru Ishizuka: Discovering Promising New Topics on the Web. Proceedings of the 4th International Conference on Knowledge-Based Intelligent Engineering Systems & Allied Technologies, pp. 804–807, 2000.

8. Henry Kautz, Bart Selman, and Mehul Shah: The Hidden Web. AI magazine, Vol. 18, No. 2, pp. 27–36, 1997.

9. Leonard N. Foner: Yenta: A Multi-Agent, Referral-Based Matchmaking System. Proceedings of the 1st International Conference on Autonomous Agents, pp. 301–307, 1997.

10. G. Salton and M. J. McGill: Introduction to Modern Information Retrieval, McGraw-Hill, 1983.

11. M. F. Porter: An Algorithm for Suffix Stripping, Automated Library and Information Systems, Vol. 14, No. 3, pp. 130–137, 1980.

12. J. Cohen: Highlights: Language- and Document- Automatic Indexing Terms for Abstracting, Journal of Amerimcan Society for Information Science, Vol. 46, pp. 162–174, 1995.

13. Yukio Ohsawa, Nels E. Benson and Masahiko Yachida: KeyGraph: Automatic Indexing by Co-occurrence Graph Based on Building Construction Metaphor. Proceedings of the Advances in Digital Libraries Conference, pp. 12–18, 1998.

14. Yukio Ohsawa, Masahiko Yachida: Discover Risky Active Faults by Indexingan Earthquake Sequence. Proceedings of the International Conference on Discovery Science, pp. 208–219, 1999.

15. Yukio Ohsawa: Get Timely Files from Visualized Structure of Your Working History, Proceedings of the 3rd International Conference on Knowledge-Based Intelligent Engineering Systems & Allied Technologies, 1999.

16. Seiji Yamada, Yukio Osawa: Navigation Planning to Guide Concept Understanding in the World Wide Web, Proceedings of Autonomous Agents, pp. 114–115, 2000.

17. Yumiko Nara and Yukio Ohsawa: Tools for Shifting Human Context into Disasters, Chance Discovery and Management session, Proceedings of the 4th International Conference on Knowledge-Based Intelligent Engineering Systems & Allied Technologies, 2000.

18. Yukio Ohsawa, Hisashi Fukuda: Potential Motivations and Fountains of Chances, Chance Discovery from Data session, Proc. International Conference on Industrial Electronics, Control and Instrumentation, 2000.

19. International Human Genome Sequencing Consortium: Initial sequencing and analysis of the human genome, Nature 409, pp. 860–921, 2001

20. J. Craig Venter, et al.: The Sequence of the Human Genome, Science 291: pp. 1304–1351, 2001.

21. Krishna Bharat, Monika R. Henzinger: Improved Algorithms for Topic Distillation in a Hyperlinked Environment, Proceedings of the 21st ACM SIGIR Conference on Research and Development in Information Retrieval, pp. 104–111, 1998.

Mining Web Logs to Improve Web Caching and Prefetching

Qiang Yang, Henry Haining Zhang, Ian T.Y. Li, and Ye Lu

School of Computing Science
Simon Fraser University
Burnaby, BC, Canada V5A 1S6
(qyang, hzhangb, tlie, yel)@cs.sfu.ca

Abstract. Caching and prefetching are well known strategies for improving the performance of Internet systems. The heart of a caching system is its page replacement policy, which selects the pages to be replaced in a proxy cache when a request arrives. By the same token, the essence of a prefetching algorithm lies in its ability to accurately predict future request. In this paper, we present a method for caching variable-sized web objects using an n-gram based prediction of future web requests. Our method aims at mining a prediction model from the web logs for document access patterns and using the model to extend the well-known GDSF caching policy. In addition, we present a new method to integrate this caching algorithm with a prediction-based prefetching algorithm. We empirically show that the system performance is greatly improved using the integrated approach.

Keywords: Web log mining, web caching and prefetching

1 Introduction

As the World Wide Web rapidly grows, researchers and industry practitioners have designed various effective caching algorithms to contain improve the Web's quality of service. The idea behind web caching is to maintain a highly efficient but small set of retrieved results in a system cache, such that the system performance can be notably improved since common user queries can be directly answered by objects in the cache.

Lying in the heart of caching algorithms is the so-called ``page replacement policy'', which specifies conditions under which a new page will replace an existing one. Many replacement policies have been proposed over the years, including the LRU-K algorithm [OOW93], which rejects the Least-Recently-Used objects in most recent K accesses, the GD-size policy [CI97] which considers access costs and varying page sizes, and an enhancement of the GD-size algorithm known as GDSF [ALCJ99] which incorporates the frequency information. The basic idea behind most of these caching algorithms is to rank objects based on their access trend by considering factors such as size, frequency and cost. The pages that are "young", relative to its last access, are ranked higher while pages that are "old" are ranked lower. Researchers have also looked at prefetching popular documents in order to improve system performance [CFKL95, MC98, CY97, Duc99].

N. Zhong et al. (Eds.): WI 2001, LNAI 2198, pp. 483–492, 2001.
© Springer-Verlag Berlin Heidelberg 2001

In the Internet environment, the paging needs usually ranges over an extended period of time, and the fetching of a web page can be a long process. For example, a group of users querying a travel web site about potential travel plans will likely pose requests over a period of several days. Once the request is completed, the reference rate will gradually die out as the users' interest in this page is reduced. When this happens, it is important for a web server or a proxy server to notice the change in this trend, so as to better prepare for the caching of objects that are more likely to be accessed often in the near future.

The key observation we made is that it is possible to learn a predictive model using the vast amount of browsing log data and use it to enhance our caching policy. The past log data provides training for the predictive model, which can be used for predicting web objects that are likely to be accessed by users based on current access sequences. Those objects in the cache that are predicted to occur will be given a higher priority when computing a ranking of the cached objects. As a result, objects that are retained in the cache are more likely to be used again. In addition, although prediction can play a role of retaining objects in the cache when they are about to be replaced, thus having a significant impact in increasing caching performance, many predicted objects fall outside the cache. Therefore, to fully exploit the power of prediction we introduce an integrated caching and prefetching algorithm. In this approach, we use prediction for both object retention and prefetching. The contribution of our work is twofold. First, we introduce a predictive caching algorithm which utilizes a trained prediction model from past log data to further enhanced the well-known GDSF caching policy. Second, we propose a new method to integrate the predictive caching algorithm with an n-gram based prefetching algorithm to more efficiently exploit the predictive power of the n-gram based prediction approach.

The organization of the paper is as follows. In the next section, we review the work in caching and present our motivation. In Section 3 we introduce the formal prediction model for n-gram based prediction, and present the experimental results using the proposed model in predictive caching. In Section 4, we integrate prefetching into the caching model, and conclude in Section 5.

2   Background

Caching is a mature technique that has been widely applied in many computer science areas. Among those areas, Operating Systems and Databases are two most important ones. Currently, the World Wide Web is becoming another popular application area of caching. Below, we briefly review caching in these areas.

The widespread LRU (Least-Recently-Used) algorithm is a good approximation to the optimal page replacement algorithms by considering the age as well as the reference frequency of a page. It is based on the assumption that pages which have been heavily used in the past will probably be used again in the near future, and pages which have not been used recently will probably remain unused for a long time. Consequently, in the LRU algorithm, the page that has not been used for the longest period of time is replaced. This algorithm is chosen as the page replacement policy by almost all commercial systems.

   The LRU-K algorithm is motivated by knowing that the popular LRU algorithm is not always appropriate for the database environment (for more details, see [CD85]). The key observation is that LRU keeps only the time of last reference to each page when making page replacement decision. Thus, the LRU algorithm cannot well distinguish between frequently referenced pages and infrequently referenced pages due to the limited information it is based on. The basic idea of LRU-K is to consider the time of the last K references to a page and uses such information to make page-replacement decision. To quote the original description in [OOW93] :

> The page to be dropped (i.e., selected as a replacement victim) is the one whose Backward K-distance, is the maximum of all pages in buffer.

   The increasing usage of the World Wide Web has led to a great deal of traffic on the Internet, which in turn results in the degradation of network performance. Therefore, it is desirable that the traffic is reduced or smoothed by caching the popular web objects. With this goal, web caching, noted for variable-sized objects, has become an active research area and gained a lot of attention [AWY99,Mar96,Gla94].
   Caching can be done at various levels in the network. It can lie on the side of a web server, a caching proxy, or a client. Caching proxies are a special kind of servers that are responsible for locating a cached copy of an object that is required. Web servers and caching proxies are higher-level caches, while client caches are at lower levels. Web caching is different from traditional caching in several ways. An important difference is that the size of web objects is not uniform, and the transfer time costs are not unique either. For the purpose of maximizing the hit ratio or byte-hit ratio, it is better for a caching replacement policy to take factors such as size and network cost into account.
   One of the most successful algorithms is the GD-size algorithm introduced by Pei and Irani [CI97]. When a new object arrives, GD-size increases the ranking of a new object i by the cost of the removed object. Let S_i be the size of the new object i, C_i be the cost of object i, and K_i, the key value, be the rank of object i. Furthermore, let L be an inflation factor for a newly admitted object, where L is updated as the key value of the most recently removed object. Then, if i is in the cache, then the key value of object i is

$$K_i = L + C_i / S_i \tag{1}$$

   Otherwise, if i is new and not yet in the cache, then

$$L = \min_j K_j \tag{2}$$

where j denotes objects in the cache. Then the object l with $K_l=L$ is ejected, and object i is inserted in the cache with K_i set according to Equation 1.

   As an enhancement of the GD-size algorithm, Arlitt et. al [ALCJ99] introduced the frequency factor F_i which counts of number of references so far. With this new factor, the key value can be computed as

$$K_i = L + F_i * C_i / S_i \tag{3}$$

Both algorithms perform very well across a number of domains, as shown in a number of empirical tests [ALCJ99,CI97].

Another performance improvement strategy is to *prefetch* documents that are highly likely to occur. Prefetching can be done on either the server side, client side or the proxy-server side [CFKL95] discussed an integrated model of prefetching and caching in a file system.   [MC98] discussed an approach called top-ten for prefetching, by prefetching the top-ten popular documents. In [CY97] Chinen and Yamaguchi prefetch the referenced pages from hyperlinks embedded in the current object. [Duc99] improved this idea by also considering the frequency of accesses of the hyperlinks.   Later in the paper in Section 5, we discuss an integrated model by combining prediction, caching and prefetching in a unified framework, and demonstrate that the resulting system outperforms caching alone.

3   Learning N-gram Models from Web Server Logs

Given a web-server browsing log L, it is possible to train a path-based model for predicting future URL's based on a sequence of current URL accesses. This can be done on a per-user basis, or on a per-server basis. The former requires that the user-session be recognized and broken down nicely through a filtering system, and the latter takes the simplistic view that the accesses on a server is a single long thread. We now describe how to build this model using a single sequence L using the latter view. An example of the log file is shown in Figure 1.

up lherc upl com--[01/Aug/1995 00 08 52-0400] "GET
/shuttle/resources/orbiters/endeavour-logo gif HTTP/1 0" 200 5052

prn9 j51 com--[01/Aug/1995 00 08 52-0400] "GET/images/xyz html HTTP/1 0" 200 669

139 230 35 135--[01/Aug/1995 00 08 52-0400] "GET/images/NASA-logosmall gif HTTP/1 0" 200 786

Fig. 1. NASA log file example

We build an n-gram prediction model based on the object-occurrence frequency. Each sub-string of length n is an n-gram. These sub-strings serve as the indices of a hash table T that contains the model. During its operation, the algorithm scans through all sub-strings exactly once, recording occurrence frequencies of documents' requests of the next m clicks after the sub-string in all sessions. The maximum occurred request (conditional probability greater than *theta*, where *theta* is a threshold set at 0.6 in our experiments) is used as the prediction of next m steps for the sub-string. In this case we say that the n-gram prediction has a window-size m. The algorithm for building a path-based model on sub-strings is described below.

We observe that many of the objects are accessed only once or twice, and a few objects are accessed a great many times. Using this well-known fact (also known as the *Zipf* distribution), we can filter out a large portion of the raw log file and obtain a compressed prediction model. In our filtering step, we removed all URL's that are accessed 10 times or less among all user requests.

As an example, consider a sequence of URL's in the server log: {A,B,C,A, B,C,A,F} Then a two-gram model will learn on the two-grams shown in Table 1, along with the predicted URL's and their conditional probabilities.

Table 1. A learned example of n-gram model

2-Gram	Prediction
A, B	{ < C, 100% > }
B, C	{ < A, 100% > }
C, A	{ < B, 50% >, < F, 50% > }

Applying n-gram prediction models has a long tradition in network systems research. Su et. al. [SYLZ00] compared *n*-gram prediction models under different sized *n*, and presented a cascading algorithm for making the prediction. Silverstein et al [SHMM98] provided a detailed statistical analysis of web log data, pointing out the distribution of access patterns on web pages. [KL96,JP99,SKS98] studied path-based prediction models for networked systems.   In our work, we need to adapt the prediction

Normally, there simultaneously exist a number of sessions on a web server. Based on their access sequences, our prediction model can predict future requests for each particular session. Different sessions will give different predictions to future objects. Since our prediction of an object comes with a probability of its arrival, we can combine these predictions to calculate the future occurrence frequency of an object. Let O_i denote a web object on the server, S_j be a session on a web server, $P_{i,j}$ be the probability predicted by a session S_j for object O_i. If $P_{i,j}=0$, it indicates that object O_i is not predicted by session S_j. Let W_i be the future frequency of requests to object O_i. If we assume all the sessions on a web server are independent to each other, we can obtain Equations 4 and 5.

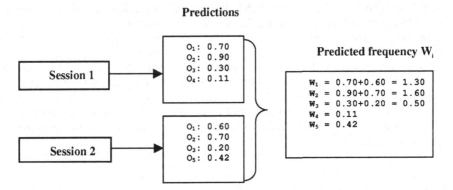

Fig. 2. Prediction to frequency weight calculation

To illustrate Equation 4, we map three sessions in Figure 2. Each of these sessions yields a set of predictions to web objects. Since sessions are assumed independent to each other, we use Equation 4 to compute their weights W_i. For example, object O_1 is predicted by two sessions with a probability of 0.70 and 0.60, respectively. From

$$W_i = \sum_j P_{i,j} \tag{4}$$

Equation 4, W_1 = 1.3. This means that, probabilistically, object O_1 1.3 times in the near future.

Once the access frequency $W(p)$ of a page p is predicted, we incorporate the $W(p)$:

$$K(p)=L+(W(p) + F(p))*C(p)/S(p) \tag{5}$$

In this formula, we add $W(p)$ and $F(p)$ together in Equation 5 as a combined frequency term. This implies that the key value of a page p is determined not only by its past occurrence frequency, but also affected by its future frequency. The more likely it occurs in the future, the greater the key value will be. The rationale behind our extension is that we look ahead some time in the request stream and adjust the replacement policy.

We have conducted a series of experimental comparisons with two data logs that we are able to obtain. In the experiments, the EPA (United States Environmental Protection Agency) data contains a day's worth of all HTTP requests to the EPA WWW server located at Research Triangle Park, NC. The NASA data is from NASA Kennedy Space Center WWW server in Florida containing 17 days' worth of requests. Before experiments, we removed un-cacheable URLs from the access logs. A URL is considered un-cacheable when it contains dynamically generated content such as CGI scripts. We also filtered out requests with unsuccessful HTTP response code.

The results illustrating both hit rates and byte-hit rates are shown in Figure 3. The algorithms under comparison are n-gram, GDSF, GD-Size, LFUDA (least-frequently-used with dynamic aging), and the LRU method [ALCJ99]. Overall, the n-gram algorithm outperforms the other algorithms using all of the selected cache sizes. It is obvious from the figures that the performance gain is substantially larger when the n-gram algorithm is applied on the NASA dataset. This observation can be explained by considering the difference between the two datasets. The EPA dataset is the web log data collected over a period of 24 hours. We have used the first 12 hours of data for training and the remaining data for evaluation. The users' access pattern may vary dramatically between the two time periods and thus decreasing the prediction accuracy. By comparison, 6 days of the NASA log data are used for training while the remaining 7 days of data are used for evaluation. The users' access patterns are much more stable over this extended period of time, making the training data much more representative of the actual access patterns. This no doubt aids tremendously in prediction accuracy.

4   Integrated Caching and Prefetching

So far we have shown that predictive caching improves system performance in terms of hit rate and byte hit rate. These two metrics implicitly reflect reduction of network latency. In this section, we investigate an integrated caching and prefetching model to further reduce the network latency perceived by users. The motivation lies in two aspects. Firstly, from Figure 3, we can see both the hit rate and byte hit rate are growing in a log-like fashion as a function of the cache size. Our results consist with those of other researchers [CI97, RV98, AFJ98, ACDFJ99]. This suggests that hit rate or byte-hit rate does not increase as much as the cache size does, especially when cache size is large. This fact naturally leads to our thought to separate part of the cache memory (e.g. 10% of its size) for prefetching. By this means, we can trade the minor hit rate loss in caching with the greater reduction of network latency in prefetching. Secondly, almost all prefetching methods require a prediction model. Since we have already embodied an n-gram model into predictive caching, this model can also serve prefetching. Therefore, a uniform prediction model is the heart of our integrated approach.

In our approach, the original cache memory is partitioned into two parts: cache-buffer and prefetch-buffer. A prefetching agent keeps pre-loading the prefetch-buffer with documents predicted to have the highest weight W. The prefetching stops when the prefetch-buffer is full. The original caching system behaves as before on the reduced cache-buffer except it also checks a hit in the prefetch-buffer. If a hit occurs in the prefetch-buffer, the requested object will be moved into the cache-buffer according to original replacement algorithm. Of course, one potential drawback of prefetching is that the network load may be increased. Therefore, there is a need to balance the decrease in network latency and the increase in network traffic. We next describe two experiments that show that our integrated predictive-caching and prefetching model does not suffer much from the drawback.

In our prefetching experiments, we again used the EPA and NASA web logs to study the prefetching impact on caching. For fair comparison, the cache memory in cache-alone system equals the total size of cache-buffer and prefetch-buffer in the integrated system. We assume that the pre-buffer has a size of 20% of the cache memory. Two metrics are used to gauge the network latency and increased network traffic:

Fractional Latency: The ratio between the observed latency with a caching system and the observed latency without a caching system.

Fractional Network Traffic: The ratio between the number of bytes that are transmitted from web servers to the proxy and the total number of bytes requested.

As can be seen from Figure 4 and 5, prefetching does reduce network latency in all cache sizes. On EPA data, when cache size is 1% (approximately 3.1MB), fractional latency has been reduced from 25.6% to 19.7%. On NASA data, when cache size is 0.001%(~ 240KB), fractional latency has been reduced from 56.4% to 50.9. However, as can be seen from Figure 4 and 5, we pay a price for the network traffic, whereby the prefetching algorithm incurs an increase in network load. For example, in NASA dataset, the fractional network traffic increases 6% when cache size is 0.01%. It is therefore important to strike for a balance the improvement in hit rates and the network traffic. From our result, prefetching strategy better performs in a larger cache size while relatively less additional network traffic is incurred.

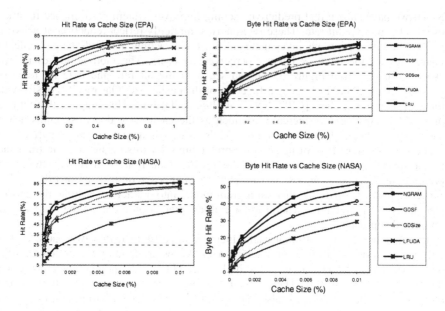

Fig. 3. Hit and byte hit rates results using EPA and NASA logs.

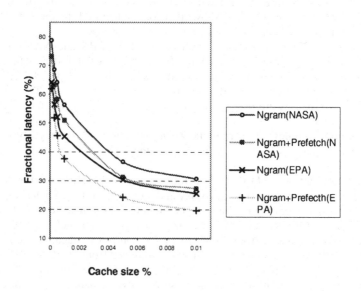

Fig. 4. Fractional Latency Comparison

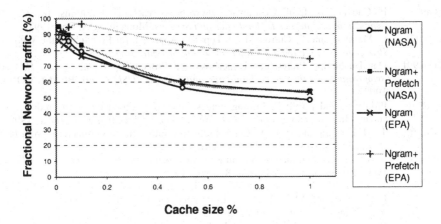

Fig. 5. Fractional Network Traffic

5   Conclusions and Future Work

In this paper, we applied association rules minded from web logs to improve the well-known GDSF algorithm. By integrating path-based prediction caching and prefetching, it is possible to dramatically improve both the hit rate and byte hit rate while reducing the network latency. In the future, we would like to extend our approach by taking into account other statistical features such as the data transmission rates that can be observed over the Internet.

Acknowledgement. We thank Michael Zhang for interesting discussions. This work is supported by Canadian NSERC and IRIS research grants. We also thank Zhong Su and HJ Zhang at Microsoft Research China for early collaboration on n-gram based prediction.

References

[ALCJ99]   M. Arlitt, R. Friedrich L. Cherkasova, J. Dilley, and T. Jin. Evaluating content management techniques for web proxy caches. In *HP Technical report*, Palo Alto, Apr. 1999.

[AWY99]   C. Aggarwal, J. L. Wolf, and P. S. Yu. Caching on the World Wide Web. In *IEEE Transactions on Knowledge and Data Engineering*, volume 11, pages 94-107, 1999.

[CFKL95]   Pei Cao, Edward W. Felten, Anna R. Karlin and Kai Li. A Study of integrated Prefetching and Caching Strategies. In *Proceedings of the ACM SIGMETRICS Conference on Measurement and Modeling of Computer Systems*, May 1995.

[CD85]   H. T. Chou and D. J. DeWitt. An evaluation of buffer management strategies for relational database systems. In *Proceedings of the Eleventh International Conference on Very Large Databases*, pages 127-141, August 1985.

[CI97]   P. Cao and S. Irani. Cost-aware www proxy caching algorithms. In *USENIX Symposium on Internet Technologies and Systems*, Monterey, CA, Dec. 1997.

[CY97]   E. Markatos and C. Chironaki. A Top Ten Approach for Prefetching the Web. In *Proceedings of the INET'98 Internet Global Summit*. July 1998

[Duc99]   Dan Duchamp. Prefetching Hyperlinks. In *Proceedings of the Second USENIX Symposium on Internet Technologies and Systems (USITS '99)*, Bouder, CO Oct 1999.

[JP99]   Pitkow J. and Pirolli P. Mining longest repeating subsequences to predict www surfing. In *Proceedings of the 1999 USENIX Annual Technical Conference*, 1999.

[KL96]   T. M. Kroeger and D. D. E. Long. Predicting future file-system actions from prior events. In *USENIX 96*, San Diego, Calif., Jan. 1996.

[Mar96]   E. Markatos. Main memory caching of web documents. In *Computer networks and ISDN Systems*, volume 28, pages 893-905, 1996.

[MC98]   K. Chinen and S. Yamaguchi. An Interactive Prefetching Proxy Server for Improvement of WWW Latency. In *Proceedings of the Seventh Annual Conference of the Internet Society (INEt'97)*, Kuala Lumpur, June 1997.

[OOW93]   E. J. O'Neil, P. E. O'Neil, and G. Weikum. The LRU-K page replacement algorithm for database disk buffering. In *Proceedings of the 1993 ACM SIGMOD International Conference on Management of Data*, pages 297-306, May 1993.

[SKS98]   S. Schechter, M. Krishnan, and M.D. Smith. Using path profiles to predict http requests. In *Proceedings of the Seventh International World Wide Web Conference Brisbane, Australia.*, 1998.

[SYLZ00]   Zhong Su, Qiang Yang, Ye Lu, and HongJiang Zhang. Whatnext: A prediction system for web requests using n-gram sequence models. In *Proceedings of the First International Conference on Web Information Systems and Engineering Conference*, pages 200-207, Hong Kong, June 2000.

[SYZ00]   Zhong Su, Qiang Yang, and HongJiang Zhang. A prediction system for multimedia pre-fetching on the internet. In *ACM Muldimedia Conference 2000*. ACM, October 2000.

Mining Crawled Data and Visualizing Discovered Knowledge

V. Dubois, M. Quafafou, and B. Habegger

IRIN, 2 rue de la houssinière 44072 NANTES Cedex 03, FRANCE
{dubois, quafafou, habegger}@irin.univ-nantes.fr

Abstract. This paper presents a challenging project which aims to extend the current features of search and browsing engines. Different methods are integrated to meet the following requirements : (1) Integration of incremental and focused dynamic crawling with meta-search; (2) Free the user from sifting through the long list of documents returned by the search engines; (3) Extract comprehensive patterns and useful knowledge from the documents; (4) Visual-based support to browse dynamic document collections. Finally, a new paradigm is proposed combining the mining and the visualization methods used for search and exploration.

1 Introduction

Search of information from the web becomes more and more complex and there are many factors biasing the success of such information seeking processes [1]. In some situations keywords are not sufficient to express the desired information needs. An iterative process is often necessary to discover a useful piece of information. We think that the third search engine generation will be certainly "smart integrated engines that enrich data web crawling and searching features with a collection of interactive, visual, mining and more generally intelligent functions to make both the search and exploration processes more dynamic, fruitful, understandable and collaborative". This paper contributes to achieve this "dream" by integrating different components to meet the following requirements : (1) integration of incremental and focused dynamic crawling with meta-search, (2) free the user from sifting through the long list of documents returned by the search engines, (3) extract comprehensive patterns and useful knowledge from the documents, (4) visual-based support to browse dynamic document collections.

Section 2 is dedicated to the dynamic aspects of searching and crawling. Section 3 describes the foundations of our web mining method which is based on probabilistic networks and functional dependencies. An incremental graph visualization method with a dynamic structure is given is section 4. Both mining and visualization methods are closely related as the result of each one is used to refine the results of the other. Section 5 presents experimental results and shows the interest of our approach considering the "mad cow" query. Finally section 6 is a conclusion that presents the current state of our work and underlines the main future developments.

N. Zhong et al. (Eds.): WI 2001, LNAI 2198, pp. 493–497, 2001.
© Springer-Verlag Berlin Heidelberg 2001

2   Dynamic Search and Crawling

A query is generally reduced to a single or a small set of words and each URL in the returned list is referred to as a hit. In order to return such list in a reasonable time, search engines generally use a local index and/or local collection of web pages. Such indexes and collections are built by using a crawler to automatically create its index and collect web pages that are stored in huge databases. However, this approach faces different problems essentially related to the huge size of the web [8] and the storage of its complete image. The rate at which pages change is a second crucial problem to deal with. Predictive web changing models [7] are at the basis of the major strategies for re-indexing the expected modified pages. The web is updated by millions of users in an uncontrolled way. Important existing pages may be deleted and links to authority pages may be broken which increases the users frustration during web browsing.

The objective of dynamic searching and crawling is to resolve these problems. The difference of dynamic searching when compared to static searching is that it does not limit its results to those found in an outdated index but explores the web in its current state. Dynamic searching is limited by the efficiency cost, essentially the number of irrelevant downloaded pages, of a crawler that retrieves and analyzes pages on the fly. This type of crawling is often referred to as focused crawling in that it is guided by a given query or topic of interest. Building such efficient crawlers is a challenge for dynamic web exploration [2].

A crawling process can basically be split into two main subparts : (1) downloading a page and (2) extracting the links of a page. These two components communicate together by respectively sending to the other the newly downloaded pages and the last extracted links. In this scheme the crawling strategy can be defined in terms of filters placed before and after each of these parts.

The work presented in this paper only makes use of two types of filters which are sufficient to evaluate the idea we put front. The first, a contextual filter, uses the nearness of a link to prune links related to servers which previously gave bad links The second, a content filter, uses statistical methods to calculate a representative document vector and rejects any document whose vector doesn't contain one of the keywords. Of course, only the main words are selected according to both document-dependent and document collection-dependent measures according to term importance as used in automatic text analysis [6].

Putting together static and dynamic searching avoids the static and incomplete information stored in the databases of search engines while still having a set of a priori relevant documents to initiate the dynamic crawling. The usefulness of this hybrid approach is detailed in [5]. In this case the seed URLs used to start crawling are the result of a static search : the list of URLs returned by a query on a given subject to a classic search engine.

3   Dependencies and Graph

A graph is a natural and universal structure giving an abstract representation of knowledge. From a semantic point of view, we want to represent the influence between words in a graph. As a starting point, we turned towards functional dependencies. Functional dependency is a key concept in database community. A functional dependency, noted $A \rightarrow b$ *holds* in a relation whenever the set A of attribute values allows to determine the value of the attribute b. We use functionnal dependencies as a starting point to define a crude dependence graph $G(r)$

$$(a \rightarrow b) \in G(r) \Leftrightarrow (\exists A, a \in A, A \rightarrow b \text{ holds in } r \text{ and is minimal})$$

It is possible to refine this by using approximative dependency instead of classical one. But approximative dependency property is a boolean property : it either holds or doesn't. So, we improve this definition by scoring potential dependencies. Interresting local scores are found in the bayesian networks community. We use such scores to evaluate approximative dependencies : if A would be a good set of parents for b in a bayesian network, we consider that A carries important information on b, i.e. b depends on A. In the case where $A = \{a\}$, MML (Minimum Message Length) score is equivalent to mutual entropy measure. This way, MML score may be considered as a generalisation of the mutual entropy.

Let $s(A, b)$ be the MML score associated to node b and parent set A. This score depends on the data. We define the *overall dependence* (*ov*) between two nodes a and b by $ov(a \rightarrow b) = \max_{a \in A \subset \Omega - \{b\}} s(A, b)$.

We define the *dependence graph* as the graph G such that :

$$a \rightarrow b \in G \Leftrightarrow (ov(a, b) > 0) \wedge |\{ A \subset \Omega - \{b\} | s(A, b) > ov(a, b) \}| \leq n$$

The set of parents A of a given node b is the union of the at most n best parent sets $P_i(b)$ according to s. Note that if $\forall A \subset \Omega - \{b\}, s(A, b) \leq 0$, then b has no parents (no one is good enough as parent). Using a maximum number of parent sets prevents having a graph with too many links, and provides an easy way to control the number of edges. It takes advantage of the score, and it is not possible when using only classical (exact or approximative) dependencies.

Textual data can be easily converted to a data table using words as attributes. Instead of using exact MML scores, we perform an approximation, taking advantage of the binary nature of attributes. The most useful property of this approximation is computational. It is based on the principle that conditional information quantity $L(b|A)$ may be evaluated by counting the minimum error any predictor would commit if given the values of A and guessing the values of b. This error is in turn evaluted statistically by data instance comparisons. For an extensive demonstration of this approximation properties, see [9].

Our MML-based local score is the following : $S(A, b) = L(b|A) - 2^{|A|}$, where $L(b|A)$ is the mean encoding length for the value of b for one instance, given the values of the instance on A. It is approximated by $L(b|A) \simeq -\log(e(b|A))$, where $e(b|A)$ is the least expected error probability on b given A. e is in turn approximated by $e(b|A) \simeq \frac{1}{2} - \frac{\sqrt{2.p(b_= | A_=) - 1}}{2}$, with $X_=$ as the event that two random instances share the same value on attribute X. This last approximation requires a full page of calculus, wich is part of [9]. If the dependency is exact ($e = 0$), the given formuluas are all exact. The higher $e(b|A)$ grows, the less accurate is our approximation. Hopefully, our goal is to find the best dependencies.

4   Incremental Graph Visualization

The first challenge encountered for automatically displaying a graph is the high number of nodes and links. Automaticaly displaying graph is a computationnaly hard problem. Only a 2D visualization is considered, so, a bounded visualization space is easily mapped to the screen. The added constraints are mainly related to the visualization aspects : 1) Space : the graph spreads across all the available visualization space; 2) Edge length : the distribution of edge lengths has a low variance after a sufficient number of iterations; 3) Edge number : a minimum number of edges crossing each other.

In our approach words that are closely related appear in the same area of the map when the other words are moved away. This approach overlaps some proprieties of maps produced by Kohonen's self-organizing algorithm (SOM). The interest of this kind of neural network has been shown for interactive exploration of document collections [3]. WEBSOM is a major system developed to organize automatically full-text document collections using the SOM algorithm. In addition, empirical studies compare maps generated by firstly the SOM algorithm and then by human subjects considering the same set of documents. Lin's conclusions [4] during this study clearly shows the interest of maps for searching and browsing : (1) to assist users to spot an area of the display, (2) to help users to memorize the display structure and (3) to support user decisions. To display a static graph, SOM may be use by the following way : the input space is the visualization space, and the output space is the word space (given a point, the network return the nearest word in this space).

In addition to the previous displayed constraints, we need to handle dynamic aspects. First, data may arise at any time. Second, we have to display the graph quite often. The solution we chose is to rely on an iterative process that in turn uses the word positions as an heuristic to find best parents, and then uses the graph to find better word positions in the 2D visualization space. The main advantage is that already learned positions are used as an heuristic to compute the new network topology whenever data changes.

5   Experimental Results

An important task is the Global Multi-level structure exploration. We consider here around 440 documents the crawled and analyzed. All the information contained is analyzed and a probabilistic network is learned structuring the information contained in all crawled documents. As we have said before, the dynamic modification of this structure is guided by two criteria. The first one is the search for the graph optimizing a scoring function, whereas the second is related to its visualization. The graph with the best appearance is kept. Multi-level explorations can be achieved by our proposed system. In fact the user may explore the global structure of the whole graph or only focus his attention on a local part of the structure represented by a connected component. In an example where we have set the query to "mad cow" and selected the words "cow", "cows" and "hormones", only connected components containing at least one word from the selected ones are drawn. It involves other words like "British", "organs", "danger", "contamination". This information and the structure can play an important role in querying reformulation and textual data analysis.

6 Conclusion

We have presented in this paper a dynamic search and exploration system helping to find useful information and to understand events and phenomena. We propose here an integrated environment coupling different dedicated methods as dynamic search, mining and visualization. A first prototype was developed using both C++ and Java. We have to further develop both theoretical and practical aspects of this work. Currently, we are improving the synchronization between our different processes especially the ones related to the crawling task. More sophisticated applications have been developed.

References

1. David Hawking, Nick Craswell, Donna Harman, Results and Challenges in Web Search Evaluation, www8, Toronto, 1999.
2. Junghoo Cho, Hector Garcia-Molina "The Evolution of the Web and Implications for an incremental Crawler." In Proceedings of 26th International Conference on Very Large Databases (VLDB), September 2000.
3. T. Kohonen, Self-Organizing Maps, Springer series in information sciences.
4. Lin, X. (1995). Searching and Browsing on Map Displays Proceedings of ASIS'95 (Chicago, October, 1995) pp. 13-18.
5. I. Ben-Schaul, M. Herscovici, M. Jacovi, Y. S. Maarek, D. Pelleg, M. Shtalhaim, V. Soroka and S. Ur, Adding support for Dynamic and Focused Search with Fetuccino, WWW8, Toronto 1999.
6. G. Salton, C. S. Yang and C. T. Yu, A theory of term importance in automatic text analysis, Journal of the American Society for Information Science, vol. 26 (1), 1975, pp. 33-44.
7. Brian E. Brewington and George Cybenko, How dynamic is the web? in WWW9 conference 2000.
8. Andrei Broder, Ravi Kumar, Farzin Maghoul, Prabhakar Raghavan, Sridhar Rajagopalan, Raymie Stata, Andrew Tomkins, Janet Wiener, Graph structure in the web, WWW9 conference 2000.
9. V. Dubois and M. Quafafou, Discovering Graph Structures in high Dimensional Spaces. In Data Mining II (Proceedings of Data Mining 2000, Cambridge)

Categorizing Visitors Dynamically by Fast and Robust Clustering of Access Logs

Vladimir Estivill-Castro and Jianhua Yang

Department of Computer Science & Software Engineering,
The University of Newcastle, Callaghan, NSW 2308, Australia.

Abstract. Clustering plays a central role in segmenting markets. The identification of categories of visitors to a Web-site is very useful towards improved Web applications. However, the large volume involved in mining visitation paths, demands efficient clustering algorithms that are also resistant to noise and outliers. Also, dissimilarity between visitation paths involves sophisticated evaluation and results in large dimension of attribute-vectors. We present a randomized, iterative algorithm (a la Expectation Maximization or k-means) but based on discrete medoids. We prove that our algorithm converges and that has subquadratic complexity. We compare to the implementation of the fastest version of matrix-based clustering for visitor paths and show that our algorithm outperforms dramatically matrix-based methods.

1 Introduction

Capturing useful information from Web visitors is an important task for Website design and evaluation [19,22,24,28]. There has been an increased demand for understanding behavior of Web users due to the expansion of the Web and the increased number of Web-based applications [20,27]. Tracking users is essential to provide the elements for answering the most crucial questions for most organizations adapting to the Web [23]: Does the Web really work? In other words, does the Web attract visitors? and if so, do those visitors turn into customers? So Web-site owners discover more knowledge by data mining techniques, and implement them for Web-site analysis settings [19]. With basic statistical methods, we can summarize the raw information from users into various useful categories, such as the number of hits by domain, by file path, by day, by hour. Web Usage Mining [24] is a methodology for the extraction of knowledge from Web visitation data. Most work has concentrated on association rule extraction [2,17, and their references] and some success has been achieved in clustering towards Web personalization [12] and with categorical sequences [13]. Clustering is a central process inside data mining, it is a task of identifying groups in a data set by some natural criteria of similarity. It is typically used to categorize the market. The literature contains several examples in which clustering is illustrated in commercial applications that fundamentally aims at understanding what are the types of customers of an organization. Thus, clustering is to play a central role in grouping the visitors of a Web-site, and towards identifying whether the site is being

N. Zhong et al. (Eds.): WI 2001, LNAI 2198, pp. 498–507, 2001.
© Springer-Verlag Berlin Heidelberg 2001

used as expected, optimize the performance of a Web server, or discover which products are being purchased by which visitors. Based on different criteria, Web users are expected to be clustered and useful knowledge can be extracted from user access history. A common criteria is interests among Web users, and finding similar interests can be performed by clustering users navigation paths. If a site is well organized, there would be strong correlation among users interests and their navigation paths.

Many applications can then benefit from the knowledge obtained [3,10,20,22, 27]. For example, after user-clustering shows similar information needs, dynamic hypertext links among Web pages could be suggested for users in the same cluster. Another example is the Web page pre-fetching. Pre-fetching Web pages can help users personalize their needs and reduce their waiting time. However it is only effective when the right documents are identified and user's moves are correctly predicted. This prediction heavily depends on the user's access history. If we can capture noticeable access patterns by clustering, we are able to do such prediction with increased confidence. Other applications are in collaborative filtering [18] and user communities [16].

In this paper, we present new clustering methods based on similarity measures of interests between Web visitors. We illustrate our clustering method with samples of similarity measures proposed for analysis Web visitation [10,20,22, 27,28]. In comparison with previous methods, our method is fast and robust. It is applicable to any similarity measure and it can dynamically track users with high efficiency. Next we expand on why it is difficult to use many of the clustering algorithms in the literature for segmenting visitation paths [13]. In Section 3 we describe our algorithm and provide the first mathematical proof of its time complexity and that it converges. In Section 4 we show experimentally the improvement that it represents a subquadratic algorithm. We also show that it does much better in the presence of noise than recent proposals. The last section summarizes our contribution.

2 The Challenge of Clustering Visitors

Clustering consists of grouping together a heterogeneous set $U = \{u_1, \ldots, u_n\}$ by some natural measure of similarity. The first challenge that lurks behind clustering Web-site visitors is to find this natural measure of similarity. The second challenge is that the clustering algorithms must be scalable to both, the size n of items to cluster and the computational requirements of the similarity measure (or distance between two items u_i and u_j). The third challenge is that the results must be of high quality in the presence of noise and outliers. There are three main types of clustering algorithms, and in our opinion, all previous attempts to use them for clustering user visitation paths are ineffective.

Hierarchical clustering. Typically, these algorithms cluster by bottom-up aggregation (merging) the most similar clusters, until there is a single group (although top-down partitioning is also possible). This family of algorithms presents results that are the size of the original input. For the applications that data mining applications have in mind, this is ineffective. They typically require quadratic time in the size of the input [14]. Perkowitz and Etzioni report [20] that Web-clustering with one algorithm from this family resulted in CPU-time requirements three orders of magnitude more than any other algorithm.

Euclidean or similar metric space clustering. These clustering methods demand that the information for a user u_i be supplied as an attribute-vector where each entry is a real-valued feature and that these vectors be distinguished by metrics like the Euclidean distance. This demands the identification of D features, and the use of a distance (typically the Euclidean distance) in $\Re^D$. This mapping to $\Re^D$ allows the use of data-structures and vector operations to create fast clustering methods. However, it raises modeling concerns in that, for example, the center of mass of a cluster as attribute-vector may not have the values of a prototypical item for that cluster.

More serious is that for measuring similarity between visitation paths, the resulting D may be very large. For example, one common mapping to attribute-vectors could be to transform a visitation path into a vector of frequency counts of pages visited and the time spent by the user in each page. This could force D to be twice the size of the universe of pages. Other transformations are even more complex. This rules out the use of data structures like R-trees (the base of DBSCAN [5]) or CF-Trees (as in BIRCH [30]). Also, it may not be possible to use meaningfully statistical indicators (like vectorial means in STING [26]). Not being able to treat attribute-vectors numerically rules out algorithms like k-Means [11] or Expectation Maximization [4], or its variants like fuzzy-c-means [9] or Harmonic-k-means [29].

Use the similarity matrix. The drawbacks of the previous alternatives resulted in methods that attempt to work with dissimilarities directly. These also face the problem of infeasible computational resources. First, for the applications like clustering visitors of a Web-site, similarity computation demands inspection of logs for the patterns of visitation and comparisons that require time at least proportional to the length of the visitation path. Even if we assume that the dissimilarity can be computed in constant time, these methods need to compute the dissimilarity between all pairs (u_i, u_j), which implies that they will require at least quadratic space and quadratic time to get started [10,20,22,27,28]. While these methods avoid using Euclidean space, they are all based on computing attribute-vectors of path features with positive entries and assessing the similarity between two users as the cosine of the angle between the corresponding vectors. The similarity is then a real value between 0 and 1. However, the computation of the similarity matrix makes the methods far from scalable and their proponents report experiments with 500 paths or at most around 1,000 paths.

Our approach is not to use means as the estimators of location of a cluster, but to use the more robust estimator, the median [21]. Statistically, this corresponds to clustering by minimizing a different loss function, rather than the sum of squared dissimilarities, we minimize the sum of dissimilarities. In fact, the squaring seems to be introduced historically in order to allow differentiation of the objective function.

Here, we present a general applicable method that is fast and robust with respect to an arbitrary measure of similarity defined by the data miner exploring the data. Our method calls on the computation of the dissimilarity only when it needs it. It is inspired on the iteration that occurs in k-Means, Expectation Maximization, fuzzy-c-means, and Harmonic-k-Means. However, although these iterative methods are the result of numerical optimization from the iteration of the necessary conditions for optimality in differentiation, not all of them have been proven to converge (and those for which such a proof exists, it usually involves rather daunting mathematics).

3   Clustering Algorithm

Consider the following optimization criteria for clustering.

$$\text{Minimize} M(C) = \sum_{i=1}^{n} d(u_i, rep[u_i, C]),\tag{1}$$

where $C \subset U$ is a set of k representatives, $rep[u_i, C]$ is the most similar representative (in C) to u_i and $d(\cdot, \cdot)$ is a measure of dissimilarity. We underline that $d(\cdot, \cdot)$ does not need to be a distance satisfying the axioms of a metric. In particular, while $d(u_i, u_i) = 0$ we do not require that $d(u_i, u_j) = 0$ implies $u_i = u_j$. Also, we do not require the triangle inequality, however, we do expect symmetry, that is $d(u_i, u_j) = d(u_j, u_i)$. This criteria is satisfied by all similarity measures based on computing the cosine of the angle between attribute-vectors of positive-valued features [10,20,22,27,28]. Note that these similarity functions $sim(\cdot, \cdot)$ have a range in $[0, 1]$ and the corresponding dissimilarity is $d(\cdot, \cdot) = 1 - sim(\cdot, \cdot)$, also in the range $[0,1]$. The clustering criteria in Equation (1) was brought over from statistics as medoid-based clustering [15]. However, Han and Ng proposed an algorithm CLARANS for this optimization that is a randomized interchange hill-climber in order to obtain subquadratic algorithmic complexity. CLARANS can not guarantee local optimality. The best interchange hill-climber [8] is the Teitz and Bart heuristic [25] which requires quadratic time. Only in restricted cases, the time complexity of this type of hill-climber has been reduced to subquadratic time (for example, $D = 2$ and Euclidean distance [6]).

Thus, we take the route of randomized variants of iterative algorithms [7]. The iteration is the familiar iteration found in k-Means, Expectation Maximization, fuzzy-c-Means and Harmonic-c-Means (refer to Fig. 1). The iteration alternates classification of data from a current model (classification step) and model refinement from classified data (reconstruction step). The parameter that defines the model is the subset C of k elements in U. We start with a random set C^0 of representatives, and we repeatedly apply the Iterative Step until convergence. At the t-th iteration, the classification step computes the representative of each data item u_i. Computing $rep[u_i, C^t]$ requires a simple pass through the data and $O(nk)$ computations of $d(\cdot, \cdot)$. This results in a temporary partition of U into k clusters $U_1^t, \ldots, U_k^t$. The reconstruction step computes a new representative for each group U_j^t amongst the items in the group ($j = 1, \ldots, k$).

Iterative Step$(C = \{c_1, \ldots, c_k\} \subset U)$

    Classification step(C)

        For $j = 1, \ldots, k$: find $U_j = \{u_i \in U \mid d(u_i, c_j) \le d(u_i, c_{j'})j' = 1, \ldots, k\}$

    new $C \leftarrow$ Reconstruction step

        For $j = 1, \ldots, k$: new $c_j \leftarrow$ new estimator of median for U_j

---

Fig. 1. Body of the iteration alternating between finding a classification for the data given a model, and finding a model given classified data.

To detail our algorithm further, we must describe how a new representative c_j^{t+1} is computed for each subset $U_j^t \subset U$. The algorithm we use is a randomized approximation of the discrete median that has complexity $O(\|U_j^t\|\sqrt{\|U_j^t\|})$ [7]. For this subproblem of approximating the discrete median we denote with $S = \{s_1, \ldots, s_n\}$ the set of elements (during the t-th iteration of the algorithm, when applying it to the j-th cluster, S is actually U_j^t). We also denote by OLD_MED(S) the previous approximation to the discrete median of S (during the t-th iteration, OLD_MED(S) is actually c_j^t).

First, recall that the discrete median of a set $S = \{s_1, \ldots, s_n\}$ is the element $x = med\_d(S) \in S$ such that $M(x, S) = \sum_{i=1}^n d(x, s_i)$ is minimum. Clearly, the discrete median $med\_d(S)$ can be computed in $O(\|S\|^2)$ computations of the dissimilarity $d(\cdot, \cdot)$ by simply computing $M(x, S)$ for $x = s_1, \ldots, x = s_n$ and returning the x that results in the smallest value. We will refer to this algorithm as EXHAUSTIVE. It must be used carefully because it has quadratic complexity on the size $\|S\| = n$ of the data. However, it has linear complexity of $\phi(d)$, the time to compute $d(\cdot, \cdot)$. Thus, our methods use randomization.

The first step consists of obtaining a random partition of S into approximately $r = \sqrt{n}$ subsets $S_1, \ldots, S_r$ each of approximately $n/r \approx \sqrt{n}$ elements. Then, algorithm EXHAUSTIVE is applied to each of these subsets to obtain $m_i = med\_d(S_i)$, $i = 1, \ldots, r$. These r items constitute candidates for the median of S. We compute $M(m_i, S)$ for $i = 1, \ldots, r$ and also $M(old\_med(S), S)$. The item that provides the smallest amongst these (at most $r + 1$) items is returned as the new approximation to the discrete median. The algorithm has complexity $O(\phi(d)\|S\|\sqrt{\|S\|})$ because EXHAUSTIVE is applied to $\Theta(\sqrt{\|S\|})$ sets, each of size $\Theta(\sqrt{\|S\|})$; thus this requires $O(\phi(d)\|S\|\sqrt{\|S\|})$ time. Finally, $M(m_i, S)$ requires $O(\phi(d)\|S\|)$ time and is performed $O(\sqrt{\|S\|})$ times. This is also $O(\phi(d)\|S\|\sqrt{\|S\|})$ time. These algorithms have been shown mathematically and empirically to provide robust estimators of location [7]. This is because randomization is not sampling. Sampling reduces the CPU-requirements by using a very small part of the data, and the accuracy suffers directly with the size of the sample. Randomization uses the entire data available.

We enhance the fundamental results of iterative clustering algorithms by proving that our algorithm converges. We prove this by showing that both steps, the classification step and the reconstruction step never increase the value of the objective function in Equation (1).

Lemma 1. Let $U_i^t, \ldots, U_k^t$ the partition of U after the classification step in the t-th iteration of the algorithm. Let $M(U_i^t, \ldots, U_k^t) = \sum_{j=1}^{k} \sum_{u_i \in U_j^t} d(u_i, c_j^t)$. Then, the value $\sum_{j=1}^{k} \sum_{u_i \in U_j^t} d(u_i, c_j^{t+1})$ of the objective function after the reconstruction step is no larger than $M(U_i^t, \ldots, U_k^t)$.

Proof. Since for each j, we have $\sum_{u_i \in U_j^t} d(u_i, c_j^t) = M(c_j^t, U_j^t)$, and the randomized algorithm for approximating the discrete median considers the old median estimate c_j^t amongst other $\sqrt{\|U_j^t\|}$ candidates, the new median estimate results in a smaller sum $\sum_{u_i \in U_j^t} d(u_i, c_j^{t+1})$.

Lemma 2. The value $M(C^{t+1} = \{c_1^{t+1}, \ldots, c_k^{t+1}\}) = \sum_{i=1}^{n} d(u_i, rep[u_i, C^{t+1}])$ after a classification step is no larger than the value $\sum_{j=1}^{k} \sum_{u_i \in U_j^t} d(u_i, c_j^{t+1})$ before such classification step.

Proof. Note that for data item u_i, its contribution to the sum before the classification step is $d(u_i, c_j^{t+1})$. The contribution of u_i to $M(C)$ after the classification is $d(u_i, rep[u_i, C^{t+1}])$. But $rep[u_i, C^{t+1}]$ is the item in C^{t+1} that produces the smallest value of $d(u_i, c_{j'}^{t+1})$ for $j' = 1, \ldots, k$. Thus, $d(u_i, rep[u_i, C^{t+1}]) \leq d(u_i, c_j^{t+1})$, from which the claim follows.

Theorem 1. *Our algorithm converges.*

Proof. The domain of the objective function has size $\binom{k}{n}$, since it consists of all subsets of size k of U. Thus, the objective function has a finite range. The algorithm can not decrease the value of the objective function continuously.

This result is in contrast to the problem of the continuous median in dimensions $D \geq 2$ and the Euclidean metric (the continuous Fermat-Weber problem) where fundamental results show that it is impossible to obtain an algorithm to converge [1] (numerical algorithms usually halt because of the finite precision of digital computers). Still, our method only guarantees local optima.

4   Experimental Results

Now we demonstrate empirically the virtues of our algorithm. First, we illustrate the much improved use of CPU-time, later we show that it actually produces better clustering quality. We will not argue on the techniques by which entries in an access log are converted to visitation paths. We adopt the conventional assumption [2,10,17,20,22,27,28] that each traversed link l_m from page p_u to p_v, has been identified in a session and to a visitor, and this is a component of a path. Paths are sequences $p_1, l_1, p_2, l_2, \ldots, l_{\rho-1}, p_\rho$ that indicate a visitor starting page, and ordered page trajectory by using specific links.

4.1   On the Scalability of the Methods

We reproduced to the best of our ability the implementation of the clustering algorithm by Xiao et al [27], which is an incarnation of the methods suggested by Shahabi et al [22]. We use the simplest of the similarity measures, since other measures require more computational time, and therefore, our algorithm would outperform the algorithms based on similarity matrices by a larger margin. Let $P = \{p_1, \ldots, p_m\}$ the set of pages, and let the corresponding usage-feature vector ACCESS_{u_i} of user u_i defined by

$$\text{ACCESS}_{u_i}[j] = \begin{cases} 1 & \text{if } p_j \text{ is accessed by } u_i \\ 0 & \text{Otherwise.} \end{cases}$$

Then, the Access Similarity Measure is defined as the cosine of the angle between the usage-feature vectors; namely

$$\text{ACCESS}(u_i, u_{i'}) = \frac{\text{ACCESS}_{u_i}^T \cdot \text{ACCESS}_{u_{i'}}}{\|\text{ACCESS}_{u_i}\|\|\text{ACCESS}_{u_{i'}}\|}.$$

We used the same data set of logs identified with visitor and sessions used by Xiao et al [27], Namely, we used the Web-log data sets publicly available from the Boston University Computer Science Department. Fig. 2 (a) displays the difference in CPU time between the Matrix-based algorithm detailed in Xiao et al [27] and our Medoid-Based algorithm. In fact, the Matrix-based algorithm requires over 18,000 CPU seconds (5 hrs!) with 590 users while our algorithm requires only 83 seconds (just over a minute). Fig. 2 (b) displays the difference in CPU time between the two algorithms again with synthetic data generated as it will be described in the next section. Again, the Medoid-based algorithms clearly outperforms the Matrix-based algorithm. This plot also displays 95% confidence intervals of the CPU time requirements over 5 runs for each algorithm.

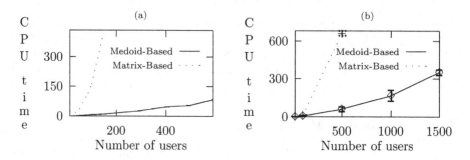

Fig. 2. CPU time comparison of Matrix-based algorithms and our Medoid-Based algorithms as a function of the input size.

Shahabi et al [22] attempted to cluster the rows of the matrix by k-means; however, this makes the algorithmic complexity quadratic, since the dimension of the vectors to cluster is also n.

4.2   On the Quality of Clustering

To evaluate the quality of the clustering one needs to compare the results of the algorithms with the true clustering. Typically, one generates synthetic data from a mixture or from a set of k representatives by perturbing each slightly. The clustering algorithm must retrieve as a group all items in the data that were generated from the same representative (or same component, in the case of a mixture). The error (as a percentage) in assigning items to their original representative is an indication of the quality of the clustering. Methods with larger error on the same synthetic data set are considered poorer quality methods.

We use Shahabi et al [22]'s strategy to generate our synthetic data. The Web pages of a site are nodes in a hypergraph (the pages can have links to themselves, or there could be two pages connected by two different links). The pages can also have links going out of the site, or links arriving from the outside. In this graph we pick k random walks of length ρ. These paths are the representatives and are called *nucleus paths* [22]. Another parameter of the generator is the *branching factor $br \in (0, 1)$*. Then, repeatedly, one nucleus path is selected at random, and a visitation path is constructed from it. At each node, the path-generator makes a random choice. While still following the visitation path, with probability $1 - br$, it continues to do so to the next node. With probability br, the path-generator branches randomly and uniformly to an adjacent node, and from

Table 1. Error rates in clustering with respect to generated data around nucleus paths.

n	Matrix-based	Medoid-based
100	34%	27% ±3.4
500	54%	27% ±3.4
1000	n/a	27% ±3.4
1500	n/a	27% ±3.4

there on it uniformly and randomly selects the next link for the current node (uniformly from those leaving the node) until completing a path of length ρ. (we also use $\rho = 8$ and $br = 0.05$ [22]). Table 1 shows that the randomized iterative Medoid-based algorithm we have proposed recuperates the class correctly for approximately 73% of the paths across the range of data sizes tested. This is much better that the Matrix-based algorithm. The Xiao et al algorithm is a hill-climber where each iteration costs $O(n)$ and thus, the $O(n^2)$ version of the algorithm can only evaluate $O(n)$ swaps of columns in the dissimilarity matrix. Better quality is to be expected in the Matrix-based algorithm if the hill-climber exhaust all swaps of columns, but then, the number of hill-climber iterations would be $\Theta(n^2)$ for a total cost of $O(n^3)$ of the algorithms, which is prohibitly large. We did not compare with the the the Matrix-based algorithm of Perkowitz and Etzioni, because it also requires $O(n^2)$ time and its goal is not to recuperate clusters, but to identify some high-density hot spots. This algorithm is thus incapable of recovering the components of a mixture.

5   Final Remarks

We have discussed why it is difficult to use most of the clustering algorithms in the literature for segmenting visitation paths. Simply, similarity between two paths is a high-dimension problem. The more features we consider to compare two paths (the pages visited, their order, the time spent on each page before using a link to the next, the commonality of sub-sectors, the commonality of sub-sequences) the larger the feature-vectors we have to handle. This has concentrated developments around matrix-based clustering. We have shown here that this is unnecessary. Randomization techniques combined with discrete optimization result in a subquadratic algorithm of the Expectation Maximization / k-Means family that converges and that is resistant to noise. Thus, improving the state of the art of categorizing visitors towards Web Usage Mining.

References

1. C. Bajaj. Proving geometric algorithm non-solvability: An application of factoring polynomials. *Journal of Symbolic Computation*, 2:99–102, 1986.
2. J. Borges and M. Levene. Mining assocaition rules in hypertext databases. R. Agrawal, ed., *4th Int. Conf. on KDD*, 149–153, NY, August 27-31 1998.
3. C. R. Cunha and C. F. B. Jaccound. Determining WWW user's next access and its application to prefetching. *Int. Symp. on Computers and Communication'97*, Alexandria, Egypt, July, 1997.
4. A.P. Dempster, N.M. Laird, and D.B. Rubin. Maximum likehood from incomplete data via the EM algorithm. *J. Royal Statistical Society B*, 39:1–38, 1977.
5. M. Ester, H.P. Kriegel, S. Sander, and X. Xu. A density-based algorithm for discovering clusters in large spatial databases with noise. E. Simoudis, et al eds., *2nd Int. Conf. KDD*, 226–231, Menlo Park, CA, 1996. AAAI Press.
6. V. Estivill-Castro and M.E. Houle. Robust clustering of large geo-referenced data sets. N. Zhong & L. Zhow, eds., *3rd PAKDD-99*, 327–337. LNAI 1574, 1999.
7. V. Estivill-Castro and M.E. Houle. Fast randomized algorithms for robust estimation of location. *TSDM2000*, 74–85, Lyon, 2000. LNAI 2007.
8. V. Estivill-Castro and A.T. Murray. Discovering associations in spatial data - an efficient medoid based approach. X. Wu, et al, eds., *2nd PAKDD-98*, 110–121, Melbourne, Australia, 1998. LNAI 1394.
9. I.B. Hall, L.O. Özyurt and J.C. Bezdek. Clustering with a genetically optimized approach. *IEEE T. on Evolutionary Computation*, 3(2):103–112, 1999.
10. T. Kato, H. Nakyama and Y. Yamane. Navigation analysis tool based on the correlation between contents and access patterns. Manuscript. http://citeseer.nj.nec.com/354234.html.
11. J. MacQueen. Some methods for classification and analysis of multivariate observations. L. Le Cam and J. Neyman eds., *5th Berkley Symp. on Mathematical Statistics and Probability*, 281–297, 1967. Volume 1.
12. B. Mobasher, H. Dai, T. Luo, M. Nakagawa, Y. Sun, and J. Wilshire. Discovery of aggregate usage profiles for web personalization. *WEB Mining for E-Commerce Workshop Web KDD-2000*, Boston, August 2000.
13. T. Morzy, M. Wojciechowski, and Zakrzewicz. Scalabale hierarchical clustering methods for sequences of categorical values. D. Cheung, et al eds., *5th PAKDD*, 282–293, Hong Kong, 2001. LNAI 2035.

14. F. Murtagh. Comments of "Parallel algorithms for hierarchical clustering and cluster validity". *IEEE T. on Pattern Analysis and Machine Intelligence*, 14(10):1056–1057, 1992.

15. R.T. Ng and J. Han. Efficient and effective clustering methods for spatial data mining. *20th VLDB*, 144–155, 1994. Santiago, Chile, Morgan Kaufmann.

16. G. Paliouras, C. Papatheodorou, V. Karkaletsis, and C. Spyropoulos. Clustering the users of large web sites into communities. P. Langley, ed., *17th Int. Conf. on Machine Learning*, 719–726, 2000. Morgan Kaufmann.

17. J. Pei, J. Han, B. Mortazavi-asl, and H. Zhu. Mining access patterns efficiently from web logas. T. Terano, et al, eds., *4th PAKDD*, 396–407, Kyoto, 2000. LNCS 1805.

18. D.M. Pennock, E. Horvitz, S. Lawrence, and C.L. Giles. Collaborative filtering by personality diagnosis: A hybrid memory- and model-based approach. *16th Conf. on Uncertainty in Artificial Intelligence*, 473–840, 2000. Morgan Kaufmann.

19. M Perkowitz and O. Etzioni. Adaptive web sites: an AI challenge. *IJCAI*, 16–23, Nagoya, Japan, 1998.

20. M Perkowitz and O. Etzioni. Adaptive web sites: Automatically synthesizing web pages. *15th National Conf. on Artificial Intelligence*, 727–732, 1998. AAAI Press.

21. P.J. Rousseeuw and A.M. Leroy. *Robust regression and outlier detection*. Wiley, NY, 1987.

22. C. Shahabi, A. M. Zarkesh, J. Adibi, and V. Shah. Knowledge discovery from users web page navigation. P. Schevemann, ed., *Int. Workshop on Research Issues in Data Engineering IEEE RIDE'97*, 20–31, 1997.

23. M. Spiliopoulou. Web usage mining for web site evaluation. *Communication of the ACM*, 43(8):127–134, 2000.

24. J. Srivastava, R. Cooley, M. Deshpande, and P.-N. Tan. Web usage mining: Discovery and applications of usage patterns from web data. *SIGKDD Esplorations*, 1(2):12–23, January 2000.

25. M.B. Teitz and P. Bart. Heuristic methods for estimating the generalized vertex median of a weighted graph. *Operations Research*, 16:955–961, 1968.

26. W. Wang, J. Yang, and R. Muntz. STING: A statistical information grid approach to spatial data mining. *23rd VLDB*, 186–195, Athens, 1997. Morgan Kaufmann.

27. J. Xiao, Y. Zhang, X. Jia, and T. Li. Measuring similarity of interests for clustering web-users. In M.E. Orlowsak & J.F. Roddick, eds., *12th Australian Database Conf. ADC 2001*, 107–114, Gold Coast, 2001. IEEE Computer Society.

28. A.M. Zarkesh, J. Adibi, C. Shahabi, R. Sadri, and V. Shah. Analysis and design of server informative WWW-sites. In K. Golshani, F.; Makki, editor, *6th ACM CIKM*, 254–261, Las Vegas, 1997.

29. B. Zhang, M. Hsu, and U. Dayal. *K*-harmonic means — a spatial clustering algorithm with boosting. *TSDM2000*, 31–42, Lyon, 2000. LNAI 2007.

30. T. Zhang, R. Ramakrishnan, and M. Livny. BIRCH: An efficient data clustering method for very large databases. *SIGMOD Record*, 25(2):103–114, June 1996.

Online Learning for Web Query Generation: Finding Documents Matching a Minority Concept on the Web

Rayid Ghani[1], Rosie Jones[1], and Dunja Mladenic[1,2]

[1] Carnegie Mellon University (USA),
[2] J. Stefan Institute (Slovenia)
{Rayid.Ghani, Rosie.Jones, Dunja.Mladenic}@cs.cmu.edu

Abstract. This paper describes an approach for learning to generate web-search queries for collecting documents matching a minority concept. As a case study we use the concept of text documents belonging to Slovenian, a minority natural language on the Web. Individual documents are automatically labeled as relevant or non-relevant using a language filter and the feedback is used to learn what query-lengths and inclusion/exclusion term-selection methods are helpful for finding previously unseen documents in the target language. Our system, CorpusBuilder, learns to select "good" query terms using a variety of term scoring methods. We present empirical results with learning methods that vary the time horizon used when learning from the results of past queries. Our approaches generalize well across several languages regardless of the initial conditions.

1 Introduction

In this paper we describe an approach for learning to automatically generate web queries to retrieve documents in a minority language. We explore different term selection methods and lengths for generating queries and use on line learning to modify the queries based on feedback by the language filter. We show that starting from a single document or a set of keywords in the target concept our methods can learn to generate queries that can acquire a reasonable number of documents in Slovenian from the Web and that our approach also generalizes to other languages that are also minority languages on the Web.

Glover et al. [7] use machine learning to automatically augment user queries for specific documents with terms designed to find document genres, such as home pages and calls for papers. Rennie et al. [9] use reinforcement learning to help a crawler discover the kinds of hyper-links to follow to find research papers. WebSail [4] uses reinforcement learning based on relevance feedback from the user. Our approach differs from WebSail in that we derive our learning signal automatically from a language filter, and does not require any user input. Boley et al. [2] proposed to use the most-frequent words for query generation for their WebACE system. However, they did not evaluate a system employing automatic

N. Zhong et al. (Eds.): WI 2001, LNAI 2198, pp. 508–513, 2001.
© Springer-Verlag Berlin Heidelberg 2001

query-generation. Ghani et al. [5] described an algorithm for building a language specific corpus from the World Wide Web. However, their experiments were limited to a small closed corpus of less than 20,000 documents, vastly limiting the generalization power of their results to the Web. They also did not investigate the use of learning.

2   CorpusBuilder Architecture

Our system, CorpusBuilder, iteratively creates new queries, in order to build a collection of documents in a single language. The target language is defined by one or more initial documents provided by the user, and the language filter. At a high level, CorpusBuilder works by taking as initial input from the user two sets of documents, relevant and non-relevant. Given these documents, it uses a term selection method to select words from the relevant and non-relevant documents to be used as inclusion and exclusion terms for the query, respectively. This query is sent to the search engine and the highest ranking document is retrieved, passed through the language filter and added to the set of relevant or non-relevant documents according to the classification by the filter. The process is then iterated, updating the set of documents that the words are selected from at each step.

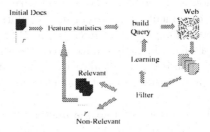

Fig. 1. System Architecture

We generate queries using conjunction and negation of terms. Query term selection methods were as follows. As a baseline we used *uniform* (UN) selecting k terms from the relevant documents, with equal probability of each term being selected. *term frequency* (TF) selects the k most frequent terms from the relevant documents. *probabilistic term frequency* (PTF) selects k words from the relevant documents according to their frequency and has been shown to perform better than simple frequency on a similar problem [5]. *rtfidf* (RTFIDF) selects the top k words ranked according to their rtfidf scores. *odds-ratio* (OR) selects the k terms with highest odds-ratio scores and has been shown to outperform other methods on document categorization when dealing with a minority concept [8]. *probabilistic odds-ratio* (PO) selects words with probability proportional to their odds ratio-scores.

We used van Noord's TextCat implementation [10] of Cavnar and Trenkle's character n-gram based algorithm [3] which was shown to be over 90% accurate on a variety of languages and document lengths.

3   Fixed Query Parameters

To understand the behavior of our term-selection methods we conducted exhaustive experiments for each length separately. These experiments used three different initial documents and the variance in the results was small. The evaluation measures we used were (a) percentage of documents retrieved in the target class and (b) percentage of web queries retrieving documents in the target class. Our experiments show that *odds-ratio* (OR) is consistently the best with respect to both evaluation measures. Different methods also varied in the query-length at which they attained their peak performance: *term frequency* with length 4, *probabilistic term frequency* and *odds-ratio* length 3 while *probabilistic odds-ratio* with length > 1 gives a very high number of rather strict queries for a very small number of target language documents. The detailed results are reported in [6].

4   Learning Query Parameters

As described in section 3, different methods excel with different query lengths. As we retrieve more documents our system may explore different parts of the Web and perform better using different querying mechanisms. This observation motivates a family of algorithms that have access to the same term-selection methods as before and can learn the ideal method and length at different points in time. We describe these learning algorithms in the next section and also report experimental results.

Our queries can be described by four parameters: two for Inclusion and Exclusion Term-Selection Method and two for Inclusion and Exclusion Length. Since we believe that the target concept is shifting and a query method that works well in the beginning in one part of the feature space may not work well later during the process, we incorporate some randomness in our learning methods. Instead of learning the four parameters for a query directly, we focus on learning the success rate for each term-selection method and length (0–10) and then by imposing a multinomial distribution over all methods and lengths (their probabilities being proportional to their success rates), we can probabilistically select the parameter values. We do not use the *uniform* term-selection method in our learning experiments, since it performed poorly during experiments not involving learning.

4.1   Learning Methods

We performed experiments varying the time horizon used in our on-line learning [1]: from all available history, to a time-decaying view of the past, to a learner firmly rooted in the present. Since our target concept at every step is previously unseen documents in the minority class, the set of target positive documents is reduced at every step. Thus more recent queries may be more relevant to the current best query. At the same time, the aggregated knowledge from past queries may prove invaluable for learning about the task as a whole. **Memory-Less Learning (ML)** was designed to permit a successful querying method to continue as long as it was finding positive documents. In this method, we pick the initial method uniformly and then continue with the successful method until it fails. On failure, we pick one of the other methods with uniform probability. **Long-Term Memory Learning (LT)** estimates each method's future probability of success based equally on all past performance. We used two kinds of updating rules: additive update (LTA) and multiplicative (LTM), Winnow-like update using $\beta = 0.5$. **Fading Memory Learning (FM)** bases some of the current performance on the past, but gradually reduces the impact of learning experiences further in the past.

4.2   Results for Learning Methods

Our first set of experiments compared different methods when using the same fixed length for both inclusion and exclusion terms. We found that the best performing length is 3–5, since length 3 or higher was the best in the percentage of the target class documents, while in the number of queries length 1–5 was the best. What happens is that shorter queries are more successful in getting documents but less accurate than the longer queries.

For each document-based experiment our system had access to one positive document in the target language (Slovenian, Croatian or Tagalog) and four negative documents in the other languages (Czech, Croatian, English, Serbian and Slovenian). Our hypothesis is that different learning methods will differ in their performance, since they use different time horizons in the on-line learning process. When comparing different learning methods, Long-Term Memory and Fading Memory learning perform better than Memory-Less (Figure 2). Long-Term Memory learning dominates both Fading Memory and Memory-Less in terms of number of documents retrieved, as well as queries issued. However, all learning methods underperform the best performing combination of parameters (*odds-ratio* using length 3–5) that we found by manually searching the parameter space exhaustively. In order to test the generalization power of our system for different target-languages, we performed experiments on two other natural languages, Croatian and Tagalog, which are also representative of minority languages on the Web. The results confirm that after 700–1000 documents and about 1000 queries issued, the methods start to differ on all three languages. The best performance is achieved by the Long-Term Memory methods.

5   Conclusions and Future Work

We found that our basic *odds-ratio* query construction method outperforms our other methods. *odds-ratio* picks inclusion query terms that are highly unique

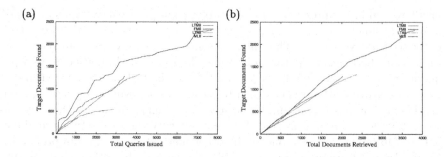

Fig. 2. Comparison of learning methods. (a) In Terms of queries Long-Term Memory using Winnow-like update performs the best. (b) In Terms of retrieved documents, after 700–1000 documents LTMII is again the best.

to the target language while excluding terms that are unique to non-relevant languages. Since this is the only method which uses both relevant and non-relevant documents simultaneously to select query terms, we believe that this property is the key to its success. *tf* picks terms that are frequent in the target language but not necessarily unique and hence results in queries that are not as precise as those generated by *odds-ratio*.

We also found that for experiments with learning query parameters Memory-Less learning (ML) performs worse than all the other learning methods over different natural languages. This was expected since ML is a naive algorithm which persists with a successful mechanism until it fails and then switches to another one randomly thus ignoring past knowledge of success rates. The best performance was achieved using Long-Term Memory learning LT with either a multiplicative or an additive update rule. It accumulates all the information from earlier queries by counting the successes and failures of individual mechanisms and updates their scores accordingly. It is interesting to note that Fading Memory learning FM, which relies more on recent information, performs worse than LT.

We tested the influence of changing the initial conditions for both fixed and learning query parameters and found that the variance in the results was small. We started the system using three different initial documents and, as an alternative, starting with nine lists each of words supplied by three native speakers of Slovenian (common, unique, useful for the task).

An interesting question for future work is how our results transfer to other target concepts such as collecting documents about a topic or documents that match a user profile. Using these techniques to augment existing techniques for developing a domain specific search engine is also an interesting future direction.

References

1. Blum, A. (1996). On-line algorithms in machine learning. *In Proceedings of the Workshop on On-Line Algorithms, Dagstuhl, 1996.*.

2. Boley, D., Gini, M., Gross, R., Han, E.-H. S., Hastings, K., Karypis, G., Kumar, V., Mobasher, B., , & Moor, J. (1999). Document categorization and query generation on the world wide web using webace. *AI Review*, *13*, 365–391.

3. Cavnar, W. B., & Trenkle, J. M. (1994). N-gram-based text categorization. *Proceedings of SDAIR 1994* (pp. 161–175). Las Vegas, NV.

4. Chen, Z., Meng, X., Zhu, B., & Fowler, R. H. (2000). Websail: From on-line learning to web search. *Proc. of the International Conf. on Web Information Systems Engineering*.

5. Ghani, R., & Jones, R. (2000). Learning a monolingual language model from a multilingual text database. *Proceedings of CIKM 2000*.

6. Ghani, R., Jones, R., & Mladenić, D. (2001). *Building minority language corpora by learning to generate web search queries* (Technical Report CMU-CALD-01-100).

7. Glover, E., Flake, G., Lawrence, S., Birmingham, W. P., Kruger, A., Giles, C. L., & Pennock, D. (2001). Improving category specific web search by learning query modifications. *Symposium on Applications and the Internet*. San Diego, CA.

8. Mladenic, D., & Grobelnik, M. (1999). Feature selection for unbalanced class distribution and naive bayes. *Proceedings of ICML 1999*.

9. Rennie, J., & McCallum, A. K. (1999). Using reinforcement learning to spider the web efficiently. *Proceedings of ICML 1999*.

10. van Noord, G. Textcat. http://odur.let.rug.nl/ vannoord/TextCat/.

A Formal Ontology Discovery from Web Documents

Norihiro Ogata

Faculty of Language and Culture, Osaka University
ogata@lang.osaka-u.ac.jp

Abstract. This paper defines a framework of formal ontology that is compatible with domain-specificity that Web documents has, and natural language structures. Furthermore, this paper investigates how to extract information about the formal ontology of the domain written in Web documents based on logics, Web technology such as XML and natural language processing.

Keywords: Web, formal ontology, XML, logic programming, NLP

1 Introduction

The huge amount of documents distributed over the WWW can be regarded as easily accessible resources of domain-specific knowledge. However users may also be annoyed with the quantitative enormousness, qualitative irregularity, and unfamiliarity of contents of the documents arising from easy accessiblity to specific domains and the unstructuredness of the WWW. One of the possible solutions to this problem is to specify and annotate the text structures and the semantic contents, i.e., *(formal) ontology* (in the sense used in Artifical Intelligence or knowledge engineering [5], i.e., *formal specifications of conceptualizations*) of each document by giving top-down definitions of their specifications using HTML, XML, and RDF (see [9]) such as OntoBroker[2], SHOE (Simple HTML Ontology Extensions[7]), XOL (an XML-Based Ontology Exchange Language [6]), OIL(Ontology Inference Layer[3]), and so on. However, their drawbacks are that total design, definitions, and consent formation of each domain, which can be frequently created and revised, high costs; and their non-flexiblity such that each user's preference cannot be reflected into the definitions. One of the other possible solutions is to extract and discover the ontological information of each of the WWW documents by giving only loose and general forms of ontology and text structures. This approach can not only handle the problem, but also makes possible an automatic acquisition of domain-specific knowledge. This paper will propose a formal basis and logic-, Web-technology- and Natural Language Processing-based system architecture of ontology discovery from WWW documents as an efficient utilization of Web resources in these senses.

N. Zhong et al. (Eds.): WI 2001, LNAI 2198, pp. 514–519, 2001.
© Springer-Verlag Berlin Heidelberg 2001

2   A Formal Ontology and FOML (Formal Ontology Markup Language)

A *formal ontology* $\mathcal{O}$ is a triple $\langle O, \mathfrak{C}_O, \vdash_O \rangle$, where O is a classification, $\mathfrak{C}_O$ a concept lattice generated by O, and $\vdash_O$ a set of Horn-constraints supported by O. A *classification* O is a triple $\langle Tok(O), Typ(O), \epsilon_O \rangle$, where $Tok(O)$ is a set of tokens, $Typ(O)$ a set of types, and $\epsilon_O : Tok(O) \times Typ(O) \rightarrow \{1, 0\}$. A *concept lattice* [4] $\mathfrak{C}_O$ generated by O is a pair $\langle C, \leq_C \rangle$, where C is a set of concepts generated by O, $\leq_C$ an order between concepts, i.e., $c_1 \leq_C c_2$ iff $tok_{c_1} \subseteq tok_{c_2}$ and $typ_{c_2} \subseteq typ_{c_1}$. A *concept* $c \in C_O \subseteq pow(Tok(O)) \times pow(Typ(O))$ over O is a pair (c_{tok}, c_{typ}) such that $tok(c_{typ}) = c_{tok}$ and $typ(c_{tok}) = c_{typ}$, where $tok(\alpha) = \{x \in Tok(O) | x \epsilon_O \alpha\}$ and $typ(x) = \{\alpha \in Typ(O) | x \epsilon_O \alpha\}$. A Horn-constraint $h \in vdash_O$ supported by classification O is a pair $\langle \Gamma, \varphi \rangle$ of types and a type such that for all $\alpha \in \Gamma$ such that $a \epsilon_A \alpha$, implies $a \epsilon_A \varphi$.

The concept lattice generated by a classification *classifies* the information on the hierarchical dependency of the concepts in the classification, whereas the local logic generated by the classification *classifies* the information on the specification and inference of the concepts.

To connect formal ontologies defined in the previous section and Web documents, this section introduces an XML-based markup language FOML (Formal Ontology Markup Language) which is sound to the definitions of formal ontologies in the previous section, as in the DTD of Appendix A. FOML is much simpler than the other markup languages such as SHOE, XOL, and OIL, and only reflects the information of formal ontology, i.e., triple of classification, constraints, and concept lattice. FOML can be considered as an XML intervening between an XML for natural language processing and other ontological XMLs.

3   Discovery of Classifications from XML(SNLP)

Suppose that we have an HTML document with some XML tags of shallow natural language processings such as part-of-speech tagging, partial parsing, and noun phrase-chunking, and call this an XML(SNLP) document. The XML(SNLP) document is supposed to have tags such as `<np>` (noun phrase), `<det>`, `<cn>` (common noun), `<prep>` (preposition), `<pn>` (proper name), `<pp>` (past participle), `<apposition/>`, `<comma>`, `<paren>` (parentheses), and so on. We can find ontological information from information in the XML(SNLP) document. For example, given a fragment of a biochemical document "fluoropyrimidines such as 5-fluorouracil and 5-fluorodeoxyuridine," this document can be processed as the following XML(SNLP) document:

```
<np><np nform="fluoropyrimidine">fluoropyrimidines</np>
    <prep>such as</prep> <np>5-fluorouracil</np>
    <conj>and</conj> <np>5-fluorodeoxyuridine</np></np>
```

and furthermore processed as the following FOML+XML(SNLP) document:

```
<np><ontology>
  <np nform="fluoropyrimidine">
  <type>fluoropyrimidine</type>
  fluoropyrimidines</np> <prep>such as</prep>
  <np><token ofType="fluoropyrimidine">5-fluorouracil</token></np>
  <conj>and</conj>
  <np><token ofType="fluoropyrimidine">5-fluorodeoxyuridine</token></np>
</ontology></np>
```

and as a result, we can find the following partial formal ontology:

```
<ontology>
  <type>fluoropyrimidine</type>
  <token ofType="fluoropyrimidine">5-fluorouracil</token>
  <token ofType="fluoropyrimidine">5-fluorodeoxyuridine</token>
</ontology>
```

Such rule-based discovery of ontological information can be formalized as in Appendix B.

4   Deductive Discovery of Constraints

An XML(SNLP) document with FOML tags except `<constraint>` can be mapped into (horn) clauses of logic programming, as follows:

```
F(<ontology><type>X</type>;Y+</ontology>)=("X:type.",F(Y)+)
F(<token typeof="Y">X</token>)="X:Y."
```

where X:Y means 'X is of type Y'. A discovery method of constraints from these clauses can be presented as the following logic program in a way basically similar to inductive logic programming [8], where X-->Y means a constraint.

```
body_make:- setof(X,type(X),C), powerset(C,B), asserta(body(B)), fail.
body_make:- true.
Types --> Type :- body(Types), type(Type), \+ member(Type,Types),
    \+ (member(X,Types), Token:X, \+ Token:Type).
```

5   Deductive Discovery of Concept Lattices

Concept lattices can be also discovered by logic programming, as follows:

(i) generation of concepts:

```
make_concept:- boy(Types), elements(Types,E),
        intersection_all(E,Tokens),
        asserta(concept0(Tokens,Types)), fail.
make_concept:-true.
concept(Tokens,Types):- concept0(Tokens,Types),
      \+ (concept0(Tokens,Types1), \+ Types1 == Types,
        sublist(Types,Types1)).
elements0(T,Elements):- setof(X,(X:T),Elements).
elements(Types,Elements):- body(Types),
        setof(X,(T (member(T,Types),elements0(T,X))),Elements).
```

(ii) inheritance from subtypes to their supertypes:

```
X : T :- subtype(T1,T), X : T1.
```

(iii) nonmonotonic subtyping:

```
subtype(X,Y):- must_subtype(X,Y), \+must_subtype(Y,X).
subtype(X,Y):- evidentially_subtype(X,Y), \+must_subtype(Y,X),
               \+evidentially_subtype(Y,X).
subtype(X,Y):- may_subtype(X,Y), \+must_subtype(Y,X),
               \+evidentially_subtype(Y,X).
evidentially_subtype(X,Y):- X:type, Y:type, most(X,Y),
               \+most(Y,X), \+must_subtype(Y,X).
most(X,Y):- elements(X,E1), elements(Y,E2),
               |intersection(E1,E2)| > (0.8 * |E1|).
```

(iv) generation of order:

```
subconcept(c(Tok1,Typ1),c(Tok2,Typ2)):-
    concept(Tok1,Typ1), concept(Tok2,Typ2),
    sublist(Tok1,Tok2), sublist(Typ2,Typ1).
```

where literal `may_subtype(Y,X)` is translated from FOML tag
`<subtype type="Y">X</subtype>`, affix `must_` expresses a *stable* proposition
and is used as background knowledge and user's prereference, `evidential_` is
used as an expected proposition from the data, `may_` expresses a *non-stable* proposition and is used as an expected proposition discovered from XML documents
by the rules in Appendix A and the mapping in the previous section. The non-
monotonicity of (iii) is implemented by the negation-as-failure.

6 Conclusion

We have seen a theory of formal ontologies based on classifications, their local
logics and their conceptual lattices, its XML implementation FOML, and its
discovery method implemented in logic programming which has an aspect of
nonmonotonic reasoning and an aspect of inductive learning. This system can
be refined as a practical knowledge acquisition and information retrieval system
on the WWW using the Java language. In fact, we have implemented Concept
Lattice Viewer and Constraint Viewer by Java, and FOML serves as their shared
data format, which can constructed from Web documents.

References

1. Jon Barwise and Jerry Seligman. *Information Flow: The Logic of Distributed Systems*. Cambridge University Press, Cambridge, 1997.
2. Stefan Decker, Michael Erdmann, Dieter Fensel, and Rudi Studer. Ontobroker: Ontology based access to distributed and semi-structured information. In R. Meersman et al., editors, *Semantic Issues in Multimedia Systems. Proceedings of DS-8*, pages 351–369. Kluwer Academic Publisher, Boston, 1999.

3. D. Fensel, I. Horrocks, F. Van Harmelen, S. Decker, M. Erdmann, and M. Klein. OIL in a nutshell. In R. Dieng et al., editors, *Knowledge Acquisition, Modeling, and Management, Proceedings of the European Knowledge Acquisition Conference (EKAW-2000)*, pages 75–102. Springer-Verlag, Berlin, 2000.
4. Bernhard Ganter and Rudolf Wille. *Formal Concept Analysis*. Springer, Berlin, 1999.
5. Tom R. Gruber. A translation approach to portable ontology specifications. *Knowledge Acquisition*, 5(2):199–220, 1993.
6. Peter D. Karp, Vinay K. Chaudri, and Jerome Thomere. XOL: An xml-based ontology exchange language. http://ecocyc.panbio.com/xol/xol.html, 1999.
7. Sean Luke and Jeff Heflin. SHOE 1.01: Proposed specification. http://www.cs.umd.edu/projects/plus/SHOE/spec.html, 2000.
8. Shan-Hwei Nienhuys-Cheng and Ronald de Wolf. *Foundations of Inductive Logic Programming*. Springer-Verlag, Berlin, 1997.
9. F. van Harmelen and D. Fensel. Practical knowledge representation for the web.

Appendix A: The DTD of FOML

```
<!DOCTYPE foml [
<!ELEMENT ontology   (domain*, type+, token*, subtype*, concept*, constraint*) >
<!ELEMENT domain     (#PCDATA) >        <!ELEMENT type       (#PCDATA) >
<!ELEMENT token      (#PCDATA) >        <!ELEMENT subtype    (#PCDATA) >
<!ELEMENT constraint (body, type) >     <!ELEMENT body       (type*) >
<!ELEMENT concept    (token*, type*) >
<!ATTLIST ontology   attr (partial|total) "partial">
<!ATTLIST domain     attr (simple|complex|undef) "simple">
<!ATTLIST type       alias (#PCDATA) #IMPLIED
                     morph (suffix|infix|affix|non|undef) "non">
<!ATTLIST subtype    attr (direct|nondirect|undef) "undef"
                     type (#PCDATA) #REQUIRED>
<!ATTLIST token      attr (direct|nondirect|undef) "undef"
                     ofType (#PCDATA) #REQUIRED>
]>
```

Appendix B: Transformation from XML(SNLP) to FOML+XML(SNLP)

INPUT	OUTPUT
Typing Context Rules	
`<np><det>;<cn>;<pp>X;<pn>;`	`<np>` `<ontology>` `<det>;<cn>` `<type>` `;<pp>X;<pn>` `<token>` `;` where X∈ {termed, called, designated, known as}
`<np><cn>;<apposition/>;<pn>;`	`<np>` `<ontology>` `<cn>` `<type>` `;<apposition/>;<pn>` `<token>` `;`

`<np><det>;<cn>;<comma>`
 `<p>X;<pn>;`
	`<np>` `<ontology>` `<det>;<cn>` `<type>` `;<comma>;<p>X;`
	 `<pn>` `<token>` `;`
	 X∈ {to be known as, to be called}

`<np><pn>;<comma>;<det>;<cn>`	`<np>` `<ontology>` `<pn>` `<token>` `;<comma>;<det>;<cn>` `<type>` `;`
`<np><pn>;<hyphen>;<det>;<cn>`	`<np>` `<ontology>` `<pn>` `<token>` `;<hyphen>;<det>;<cn>` `<type>` `;`
`<np><pn>;<paren><det>;<cn>`	`<np>` `<ontology>` `<pn>` `<token>` `;<paren><det>;<cn>` `<type>` `;`
`<np><pn>+;<conj>;` `<adj>other;<cn>`	`<np>` `<ontology>` `<pn>` `<token>` `+;<conj>;` `<adj>;<cn>` `<type>` `;`

`<np><det>;<cn>;<p>X;`
 `(<pn>;<comma>)+;`
 `<conj>;<pn>;`
	`<np>` `<ontology>` `<det>;<cn>` `<type>` `;<p>X;`
	 `(<pn>` `<token>` `;<comma>)+;<conj>;<pn>` `<token>` `;`
	 where X∈ {like, such as, except, other than}

where gray boxes mean added DOM nodes, and `<X><Y>` DOM node `<X>` subordinates DOM node `<Y>`, `<X>;<Y>` DOM node `<X>` and `<Y>` are subordinated to the same DOM node and `<X>` precedes `<Y>`, and X+ an $n(> 0)$-times occurrence of X.

The Variable Precision Rough Set Model for Web Usage Mining

V. Uma Maheswari, Arul Siromoney, and K.M. Mehata

School of Computer Science and Engineering,
Anna University, Chennai 600 025, India,
asiro@vsnl.com

Abstract. Web Knowledge Discovery and Data Mining includes discovery and leveraging different kinds of hidden patterns in web data. In this paper we mine web user access patterns and classify users using the Variable Precision Rough Set (VPRS) model. Certain user sessions of web access are positive examples and other sessions are negative examples. Cumulative graphs capture all known positive example sessions and negative example sessions. They are then used to identify the attributes that are used to form an equivalence relation. This equivalence relation is used for the β-probabilistic approximation classification of the VPRS model. An illustrative experiment is presented.

1 Introduction

The explosive growth and widespread use of the World Wide Web suggests the potential of data mining on the web. A broad overview of the techniques and tools for data mining on the web is presented in [1]. The World Wide Web can be modelled as a graph with the web pages as nodes and the links between pages as edges. The work currently carried out in web data mining fall into two broad areas of focus: (a) mining information from web pages (nodes) and (b) mining information from the link structure (graph).

A lot of work in mining information from the link structure is in mining web user access patterns. In this paper, the mining of user access graphs is considered as a classification problem. Certain user sessions of web access are taken as positive examples and others as negative examples of a user class. Classifying sessions as positive and negative examples can be based on criteria such as users with high purchase power, users from a particular site, users who are likely to visit a particular page, users with a specific area of interest, users who are likely to purchase a particular product, etc.

Rough set theory [2,3] defines an indiscernibility relation, where certain subsets of examples cannot be distinguished. A concept is rough when it contains at least one such indistinguishable subset that contains both positive and negative examples. The Variable Precision Rough Set (VPRS) model [4] is a generalized model of rough sets that inherits all basic mathematical properties of the original rough set model. It allows for a controlled degree of misclassification. Any

N. Zhong et al. (Eds.): WI 2001, LNAI 2198, pp. 520–524, 2001.
© Springer-Verlag Berlin Heidelberg 2001

partially incorrect classification rule provides valuable trend information about future test cases if the majority of available data to which such a rule applies can be correctly classified.

This paper

- uses cumulative graphs (that capture all positive example sessions and negative example sessions) to identify attributes that are used to form the elementary sets of rough set theory
- uses this preprocessing stage to define more meaningful attributes that reflect the data set better, by using the output of another decision making technique
- uses the Variable Precision Rough Set model to classify unknown sessions as positive or negative
- presents the results of an illustrative experiment

2   The VPRS Model and Web Usage Graphs

The basic notions of rough set theory are defined in [2,3]. Let U be a certain set called the *universe*, and let R be an equivalence relation on U. Equivalence classes of the relation R are called *elementary sets*. Let X be a certain subset of U. The β–positive region of the set X corresponds to all elementary sets of U that can be classified into the concept X with conditional probability greater than or equal to the parameter β. The conditional probability is the probability of occurrence of X conditioned on the elementary set. Similarly β–negative region of the set X corresponds to the elementary sets of U that can be classified into the set $\neg X$. The formal definitions are found in references such as [4,5] and are omitted here due to space constraints.

Now, let U be a universe of examples. Let a graph G_x be associated with every x in U. Let $G_U = (N_U, E_U)$ be a graph associated with the universe such that G_x, for every $x \in U$, is a subgraph of G_U. N_U is the set of nodes and E_U is the set of links of G_U.

Let us consider a particular set of Web pages and links between them [6]. Each node in N_U corresponds to one of these Web pages and each link in E_U corresponds to one of these links. A single session x when a user enters any Web page in N_U till the user finally leaves the set of Web pages in N_U is a subgraph of $G_U = (N_U, E_U)$, denoted by $G_x = (N_x, E_x)$, where a node in N_U is a node in N_x if the user visited it at least once in this session, and a link in E_U is a link in E_x if the user traversed it at least once in this session.

The universe U is considered to be the set of all such sessions. A session $x \in U$ is a positive example ($x \in X$) or a negative example ($x \in (U - X)$) based on some concept of interest (X). For example, the concept could be either all sessions where the user purchases some product, or all sessions of users with high purchasing power (determined from some other nongraphical data).

The use of cumulative graphs (that capture all known positive and negative sessions) for mining web usage graphs is introduced in [7].

Consider the set $X(\subset U)$ of positive examples, with $U - X$ corresponding to the negative examples. Let $x \in X$ and let G_x be the subgraph of G_U associated with x.

We define $Posgraph(X, U) = (N_P, E_P, W_P)$ as a weighted directed graph where a link $e \in E_P$ has the associated weight $w \in W_P$, where $w = w'/|X|$, and w' is the number of positive examples that have the link e in their associated graphs. $Neggraph(X, U) = (N_N, E_N, W_N)$ is defined in a similar manner using negative examples.

Let $K \subset U$ consist of known examples and $U - K$ consist of unknown future test cases. Let G_x be the graph associated with $x \in K$. Let there be two weights p_e and n_e associated with any link e in G_x. p_e (n_e) is the weight of e if present in $Posgraph(X \cap K, K)$ ($Neggraph(X \cap K, K)$) and is 0 otherwise. Consider three user defined parameters, *posthreshold*, *negthreshold* and *gapthreshold*. We associate the following attributes with each x.

Attribute 1: is set if there exists a link e in G_x such that $p_e > posthreshold$ and $n_e = 0$. In other words, this attribute is set if there exists any link in this session graph such that it is not traversed in any of the negative example sessions (i.e. $n_e = 0$) and is traversed in a sufficiently large number of positive example sessions (i.e. $p_e > posthreshold$, a user defined parameter).

Attribute 2: is set if there exists a link e in G_x such that $p_e - n_e > gapthreshold$. In other words, this attribute is set, if there exists any link in this session graph such that it is traversed in a sufficiently large number of positive example sessions, when compared to negative example sessions (i.e. $p_e - n_e > gapthreshold$, a user defined parameter).

Attribute 3: is set if there exists a link e in G_x such that $n_e > negthreshold$ and $p_e = 0$.

Attribute 4: is set if there exists a link e in G_x such that $n_e - p_e > gapthreshold$.

Attribute 5: is set if there exists a link e in G_x which does not satisfy all the four conditions stated above.

An equivalence relation is defined using these attributes. Every element $x \in K$ falls into an appropriate elementary set based on its attribute values. After one scan of the training set, we can compute the number of positive sessions and negative sessions in each elementary set. We note that the β–positive region consists of those elementary sets where the number of positive sessions divided by the total number of sessions(i.e the conditional probability of the elementary set) is greater than β. The β–negative region consists of the remaining elementary sets.

Consider a session $x \in (U - K)$ that is to be classified as a positive or negative example. The elementary set of x is determined by the values of the attributes of x. x is classified as positive if the elementary set is in the β–positive region and is classified as negative otherwise.

We note that the attributes are formed from $Posgraph(X \cap K, K)$ and $Neggraph(X \cap K, K)$. In other words, the raw data is preprocessed to determine the cumulative graphs that are then used to get the attribute values. Thus the elementary sets and the VPRS model are used as a postprocessing stage on the output of a preprocessing stage, rather than on the raw data directly. We see that only 5 attributes are used for classification.

3   Experimental Illustration

The dataset used in our experiment is taken from the website http://www.cs.washington.edu/research/adaptive/download.html and is the data set used in [6,8]. The data pertains to web access logs at the site http://machines.hyperreal.org during the months of September and October 1997. Each day of the month has a separate file. Each file records all the requests for Web pages made to the Web server on that particular day. Sessions with less than 3 edges or more than 499 edges were not considered.

The dataset (U) is divided into positive example sessions (X) and negative example sessions $(U-X)$. As an illustration, all sessions that had an access from www.paia.com are treated as positive examples and all sessions that had access from www.synthzone.com as negative examples.

A value of 0.5 is used for the threshold β in this experiment. This value of β assigns an elementary set to the β-positive region when the number of positive examples in that elementary set are more than the number of negative examples in that elementary set.

Ten fold cross validation was done by using days ending with 0, 1, 2, . . . 9 as the ten sets. The results of the ten fold cross validation are tabulated below.

Day	Positive examples				Negative examples			
	Training	Test	Correct	Wrong	Training	Test	Correct	Wrong
0	521	53	47	6	2084	294	284	10
1	531	43	39	4	2242	136	127	9
2	524	50	45	5	2163	215	205	10
3	503	71	56	15	2094	285	278	7
4	511	62	50	12	2159	220	214	6
5	512	61	54	7	2169	207	199	8
6	512	62	53	9	2083	295	286	9
7	522	52	51	1	2186	192	183	9
8	519	54	49	5	2174	205	187	18
9	511	63	59	4	2056	323	308	15
Avg	516.6	57.1	50.3	6.8	2141	237.2	227.1	10.1

The average results are tabulated below.

	Predicted Positive	Predicted Negative	Total
Actually Positive	50.3 (88%)	6.8 (12%)	57.1
Actually Negative	10.1 (4.3%)	227.1 (95.7%)	237.2
Total			294.3

It is seen that 88% of the positive test sessions were predicted correctly as positive and 95.7% of the negative test sessions were predicted correctly as negative. The average accuracy of prediction of this model in this experiment is 94.3%.

4   Conclusions

This paper uses the cumulative graphs of all known positive and negative sessions to identify the attributes used to form elementary sets. Thus attributes are not directly taken from the raw data. Domain relevant decision making techniques are used to formulate the attributes. The VPRS model is then used to classify the unknown sessions. The results of an illustrative experiment are presented.

Choosing attributes directly from the raw data, in applications such as web mining, generates a very large number of attributes. This results in too many elementary sets that do not have a meaningful number of training set examples. However, attributes formed after preprocessing the data are fewer in number. Also, since the attributes are formed from a domain relevant preprocessing stage, it increases the effectiveness of the overall knowledge discovery process.

Further work can be carried out to use the cumulative graph model in other applications. Further studies are to be done to extend the use of rough set techniques in the postprocessing stage of the knowledge discovery process.

References

1. R. Kosala and H. Blockeel. Web mining research: A survey. *SIGKDD Explorations*, 2(1), July 2000.
2. Z. Pawlak. Rough sets. *International Journal of Computer and Information Sciences*, 11(5):341–356, 1982.
3. Z. Pawlak. *Rough Sets — Theoretical Aspects of Reasoning about Data*. Kluwer Academic Publishers, Dordrecht, The Netherlands, 1991.
4. W. Ziarko. Variable precision rough set model. *Journal of Computer and System Sciences*, 46(1):39–59, 1993.
5. A. An, C. Chan, N. Shan, N. Cercone, and W. Ziarko. Applying knowledge discovery to predict water-supply consumption. *IEEE Expert*, 12(4):72–78, 1997.
6. J. Borges and M. Levene. Mining association rules in hypertext databases. In *Proc. Fourth Int. Conf. on Knowledge Discovery and Data Mining*, pages 149–153, 1998.
7. V. Uma Maheswari, Arul Siromoney, and K. M. Mehata. Mining web usage graphs. In *Knowledge Based Computer Systems (KBCS2000)*, pages 186–192. Allied Publishers Limited, 2000.
8. M. Perkowitz and O. Etzioni. Towards adaptive web sites: Conceptual framework and case study. In *The Eighth Int. World Wide Web Conference*, Toronto, Canada, May 1999.

Supporting Cooperative Consensus Formation via Ontologies

Kaoru Sumi and Riichiro Mizoguchi

The Institute of Scientific and Industrial Research, Osaka University,
8-1 Mihogaoka, Ibaraki, Osaka, 567 -0047 Japan
kaoru@ei.sanken.osaka-u.ac.jp

Abstract. In this paper, we propose the Discussion Board system to support the nebulous communication between the users who do not clearly express the concepts intended. This is achieved by indicating the conceptual differences between the users through the users' direct creation of the concepts as ontologies and by showing other concepts obtained from World Wide Web.

1 Introduction

When people communicate with each other, reaching a mutual understanding is often difficult. This can be caused by the misunderstanding of words, lack of knowledge, difference of viewpoints, and so on. For the participants, however, the cause of the misunderstanding is not clear. Even worse, people do not always have an explicit conceptualization of the world which might contribute to a resolution of a such misunderstanding. Under such circumstances, rather than resolving the problem, continuing the communication can cause more confusion. We believe a conceptual representation of the participants' topic of interest can help, since such information can provide an understanding of the conceptual structure of the topic and the cause of the misunderstanding.

An ontology, which is "an explicit specification of conceptualization" [1], is the backbone of the knowledge structure of a target world. One of the problems of ontology research is the difficulty of its development. How to design an ontology has been a key issue of ontological engineering[1]. One of the promising approaches to this problem is the use of Human-Computer Interaction (HCI) technology, which makes the interaction between the system and the developer, and the interaction between developers in collaborative development cases, more efficient [2] [3].

Ogino et al. reported on the activities of sharing ontologies, aiming at controlling the multilingual information between EDR dictionary and WordNet [4]. Aligning the ontologies without tools can be an extremely tedious and time-consuming process. Noy and Musen proposed a semi-automatic approach to

---

[1] A Step Towards Ontological Engineering (Translation of the paper presented at the 12th National Conference on AI of JSAI, pp.24-31, June, 1998)
http://www.ei.sanken.osaka-u.ac.jp/english/step-onteng.html

N. Zhong et al. (Eds.): WI 2001, LNAI 2198, pp. 525–529, 2001.
© Springer-Verlag Berlin Heidelberg 2001

ontology merging and alignment[2]. These efforts used already-made ontologies. Our aim is articulation of the tacit knowledge in the nebulous mental world[5]. In field of creativity support systems, what process of discussion changes the condition of conceptual difference to the condition of understanding or mutual consent, and how to support that has not been established.

We have studied the personalization of information using the model of conceptual structure according to each user's viewpoint by observing the user's behavior [6]. We also have developed the system which can compare the conceptual difference between a user and an expert [7]. In these researches, the system infers user's concept indirectly. The proposed method described in this paper is these combined approaches describing the concept directly by users, and inferring the user's concept indirectly by the system, (by helping users to construct the concept). When people find difficulty in mutual understanding, the system will ask each of them to build an ontology of the common target world, with some help functions, and then compares the ontologies built, and facilitating the discussion on the similarity and/or differences between them. This in turn should lead to a consensus or, at least, to a better understanding of why they cannot come to an agreement.

A beneficial aspect of our endeavor is that the use of an ontology does not require very rigorous definitions of concepts. What is mainly needed is a hierarchical structure of the key concepts and viewpoints associated with it. Using ontologies as a mediation tool has an implicit side effect, that is, we can expect a rough ontology on which the participants can agree when they happily come to a consensus.

Our long-term goal includes building a support environment for the resolution of misunderstanding, for facilitating creative thinking and for building an agreeable ontology using an ontology as a mediation tool.

2   Cooperative Consensus Formation System via Ontologies

With the proposed system, the Discussion Board, the scenario of the users' discussion will proceed as follows: (1)Having difficulty understanding each other. (2)Discussing the conceptual differences using the Discussion Board. (3)Discovering the conceptual differences. (4)Understanding each other and/or having mutual consent. (5)(Creating a new idea.)

We propose that the cause of conceptual differences encountered when people communicate are as follows: (1)Misunderstanding of same objects. (2)Viewpoint-differences of same objects. (3)Similar concepts of different objects. (4)Same term for different objects.

The Discussion Board displays an explanation of the conceptual differences between the users and visualizes the difference independently and relatively, allowing the users to discover the differences and understand each other and/or achieve mutual consent in the "Discovering the conceptual difference" step and the "Understanding each other and/or having mutual consent" step.

By showing the concepts of the others from the World Wide Web (WWW) in the "Creating new idea" step, users can be expected to obtain new knowledge and create a new idea. The others' conceptual structures are represented by the Document Object Model (DOM) tree structure of eXtensible Markup Language (XML) on WWW.

An object has some common concepts, but, at the same time, there are different concepts according to individual viewpoints, thus some conceptual differences present. This is the individual concept. Individual concepts have different elements, or structures, and weights. We treated the individual concept as an ontology, just as the common concept was treated as an ontology, because it is common within a field or generation. The Discussion Board supports blurred conditions caused by the difference between individual concepts.

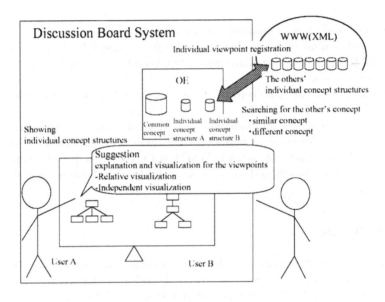

Fig. 1. System framework for Discussion Board

Fig. 1 is the framework of the Discussion Board. The users enter into a discussion by editing their own individual concept using the Discussion Board. The Discussion Board shows the individual viewpoint by explaining each viewpoint and visualizing the difference. The system uses the ontology editor system (OE) [8], an ontology editing tool, to store common concepts and individual concepts. The Discussion Board shows the individual concepts of others by searching for the similar or dissimilar concepts on the WWW according to similarity, and visualizing the differences of the concepts for comparison. The function of the Discussion Board system is as follows:

(1)Storing common and individual concepts.

This function can be used for searching the WWW and for operation histories.

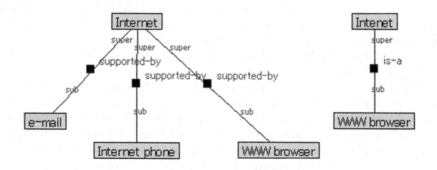

Fig. 2. Conceptualizations of Internet

(2) Searching similar or dissimilar concepts according to similarity.

This function illustrates whether the individual concept held by a majority or minority in the world, stimulate interest or knowledge [6] and prompt the user to create a new idea.

(3) Explanation and visualization of the concept differences relatively or independently.

For system explanation and independent visualization using each concept of the users, can be understood, at first site, the helping increase domain understanding. For relative visualization using WWW data, the difference of several others' concepts can be understood, at first site, the helping increase domain understanding.

3   Example

In Japan, we often encounter difficulties in communication caused by the difference of concepts. For example, when A said *Internet*, A may mean some application supported by Internet, but B does not understand which application A means. A assumes that the *Internet* is a WWW browser, but s/he can't explain this using a word that B will understand. Using the Discussion Board, A describes the concept of *Internet* as in the right of Fig. 2. If A can not express the concept exactly, s/he can request the Discussion Board system to show similar concepts of others from WWW data. B will explains the concept of Internet as in the left of Fig. 2. They understand and clarify the concept of each other by describing concept structures directly using the Discussion Board. After the discussion, A comes to an agreement with B and revises the concept.

The Discussion Board shows the relative visualization using the multidimensional scaling method. It displays in a two-dimensional space by matching the similarity of a pair of structures to the distance in the space. In this space, a pair of the structures which have higher similarity are located nearer, and a pair of the structures which have lower similarity are located farther. It can be seen quite obviously that the similarity of concepts.

The Discussion Board system is effective for the articulation of concept that we can not express completely of which, but, we have some information. We can clarify our knowledge and recognize what we need to know by using this system. It may also contribute to a clarification of our unconsciousness.

Expression using the Discussion Board clarifies our concept, and the visualization simplifies our understanding of other viewpoints of the concept and it's expression. We will view several concepts by searching the concepts of the others on the WWW. By comparing our viewpoint of a concept and with others, we determine whether we have the right or wrong answer, or a major or minor notion.

4   Conclusion

In this paper, we proposed the Discussion Board system for supporting the nebulous communication between who do not clearly express the concepts they intend. We expect the user to be able to understand each other's viewpoints and/or to reach a mutual consent, and to create new ideas by understanding the viewpoints of the others. We described the fundamental view of the Discussion Board system in this paper. We believe it will be a novel approach for articulation of the tacit knowledge in the nebulous mental world using a unification between ontology and HCI. We will verify some prototypes which is corresponding to several problems of communication difficulties.

References

1. T. R. Gruber. A translation approach to portable ontologies. *Knowledge Acquisition*, 5(2):199–220, 1993.
2. Natalya Fridman Noy and Mark A. Musen. SMART: Automated Support for Ontology Merging and Alignment. In *Twelfth Workshop on Knowledge Acquisition, Modeling and Management*, 1999.
3. Enrico Motta and John Domingue. Enabling knowledge creation and sharing on the web: Current and future aktions. In *12th International Conference on Knowledge Engineering and Knowledge Management (EKAW2000)*, 2000.
4. Takano Ogino, Hideo Miyoshi, Fumihito Nishino, Masahiro Kobayasi, and Jun'ichi Tsujii. An experiment on matching edr concept classification dictionary with wordnet. In *Workshop on Ontologies and Multiligual NLP (IJCAI 97)*, 1997.
5. Koichi Hori. A system for aiding creative concept formation. *IEEE Transactions on Systems, Man, and Cybernetics*, 24(6):882–894, 1994.
6. Kaoru Sumi. Intelligent tool for facilitating creative communication. In T. Nishida, editor, *Dynamic Knowledge Interaction*. CRC Press, 2000.
7. Kaoru Sumi and Toyoaki Nishida. Communication supporting system for ongoing conversations in users' background knowledge. In *Proceedings of IEEE KES2000*, volume I, pages 60–63. IEEE, 2000.
8. Kouji Kozaki, Yoshinobu Kitamura, Mitsuru Ikeda, and Riichiro Mizoguchi. Development of an environment for building ontologies which is based on a fundamental consideration of relationship and role. In *The Sixth Pacific Knowledge Acquisition Workshop (PKAW2000)*, pages 205–221, 2000.

Web-Based Intelligent Call Center for an Intensive Care Unit

Kyungsook Han and Dongkyu Lee

Department of Computer Science, Inha University, Inchon 402-751, South Korea
khan@inha.ac.kr

Abstract. This paper presents an intelligent call center, one that is a subsystem of a web-based monitoring system of an intensive care unit. Based on Computer Telephony Integration (CTI) technology, the call center attempts to efficiently and automatically send messages to patients' families, doctors, and other staff of the hospital via communication media suitable to the occasion. The problem of determining the appropriate media is complicated by the urgency of the message, calling time, and communication media available to the target person. The Dempster-Shafer theory is employed to determine the most suitable communication media in terms of rapid and safe transmission of the message. In addition, the calling process is performed through agent technology without requiring the intervention of the user of the call center. The call center enables message transfer through various communication media in an integrated environment, and relieves the ICU staff from the time-consuming and tedious calling task, which in turn will enable the ICU staff to concentrate better on their primary function, caring for patients.

1 Introduction

The Intensive Care Unit (ICU) provides special service for critically ill patients. While it may vary from unit to unit and hospital to hospital, there are restrictions imposed on visiting hours and the number of visitors for the safety and privacy of all patients in the ICU. At least one family member is required to be available in the waiting room around the clock to give consent for any emergency treatment required in case the patient is in critical condition. Maintaining a family member permanently stationed in the ICU for a long period is stressful for the patient's family members, especially those who live far from hospital. To reduce the inconvenience to patients' family members, we have developed a web-based real-time monitoring system and call center for an ICU. This paper describes the development of the call center and its experimental results.

In the ICU, there are many occasions requiring contact with medical staff members and patients' family members. Several communication media are available (telephone, cellular phone, pager, email, fax, etc.) and finding the most suitable one is important for effective and reliable message transfer but is not easy as the most suitable commu-

N. Zhong et al. (Eds.): WI 2001, LNAI 2198, pp. 530–539, 2001.
© Springer-Verlag Berlin Heidelberg 2001

nication media may vary from person to person and time to time. We have developed an intelligent call center using Computer Telephony Integration (CTI) and agent technology. The call center sends messages to patients' family members, medical staff members, and other staff members of the ICU through various communication media in an integrated environment without requiring intervention from the user of the call center. This call center relieves the ICU staff of the time consuming job of message transfer and thus allows the staff to concentrate on caring for patients. CTI provides enhanced, computer controlled, telecommunication services by integrating the call handling capabilities of private branch exchanges (PBXs) and the data processing capabilities of computers [1, 2, 3]. CTI has many applications, including call centers [4, 5, 6].

Agents have a variety of definitions and functions depending on application areas. An agent in general can be defined as a software package which functions continuously and autonomously in a particular environment, often coexisting with other agents and processes [7, 8]. The requirement for continuity and autonomy originates from the desire that the agent should perform the activities in a flexible and intelligent manner that is responsive to changes in the environment without requiring constant human guidance or intervention. Ideally, a self-learning agent that functions continuously in an environment over a long period of time would be able to learn from its experience. In addition, it is expected that the agent that inhabits an environment with other agents and processes will be able to communicate and cooperate with them, and perhaps in a mobile manner [9, 10, 11, 12]. The main benefits of using agent technology in the call center are the convenience and efficiency of message transfer. The only thing required for message transfer is to select the target person and the message. Agents take care of the rest — from updating the numbers of communication media and to determining the suitable communication media based on the urgency of the message, calling time, calling history, and communication media available to the target person.

As for the organization of this paper, the next section, section 2 presents a web-based intelligent call center, achieved by a combination of the CTI technology, agents, and an inexact reasoning method. Section 3 provides preliminary experimental results of the call center and the general lessons learned from this project are summarized in the final, Conclusion section.

2 Call Center for an Intensive Care Unit

The intelligent call center we have developed is intended for use by the ICU staff members. The ICU call center is composed of three parts: call engine, call agent, and database interface, as shown in Figure 1. The call engine consists of hardware to make a phone call and control software. It physically transfers messages through various media. The database interface provides an interface for patients' family members and staff members of the ICU to enter their contact information into the database within a web browser. The call agent reads the target person contact information from the database and decides the most suitable communication media to be used by the call engine. The call agent also analyzes the calling results for future calls. Each of the three components is described in detail below.

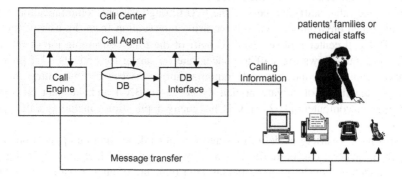

Fig. 1. Architecture of the call center

2.1 Call Engine

The call engine integrates a phone and a computer to transfer messages. This requires special hardware — either a voice modem or a voice-processing board. The former was used in this study to develop a prototype system of a call center. Messages and their priorities were determined in collaboration with the ICU medical staff at Inha University Hospital. An example of messages sent by the call engine is shown in Table 1.

Contact persons were classified into two types: hospital personnel and patients' family members. Hospital personnel were further divided into medical staff (attending doctor, resident, and intern) and ancillary hospital personnel. Communication media used by the call center to contact patients' family members include phone, cellular phone, fax, and email. To contact hospital personnel, a pager is used as well.

Table 1. Message types sent by the call center

Priority	Message	Contact person
1	Critical condition of the patient	Medical staff, patient's family
2	Arrival of a new patient	Medical staff
3	Request for discharge from the ICU by the family of the patient	Medical staff
4	Request for written consent	Patient's family
5	Order of patient transfer to another unit	Ancillary personnel
6	Notice of test results of the patient	Medical staff, patient's family
7	Notice of patient transfer	Patient's family
8	Issue of the medical certificate requested by the family of the patient	Patient's family
9	General notices	Medical staff, patient's family

When sending an urgent message, the call center delivers messages both to medical staff and the patient's family member via phone or cellular phone since the call center can confirm receipt of the message. Since a person may have more than one phone number, the call center scrolls through all numbers until it gets through to the target person.

When sending a non-urgent general message, the call center first attempts to contact the target person either at the home/work phone number or the cellular phone. If the first call fails due to busy line or no answer, then the call engine sends the message either by email or fax. When the target person has no fax or email, the call engine keeps calling until contact is made. During sleeping hours (11pm through 7am), a general message is sent either by email or fax if available.

2.2 Call Agent

The call agent is a software package that functions autonomously. Three types of call agents were employed in the system presented here — system agent, learning agent, and media decision agent. The system agent periodically performs time-scheduling functions by hourly activating the learning agent and then the media decision agent. Figure 2 shows the relationship between the system agent and other agents.

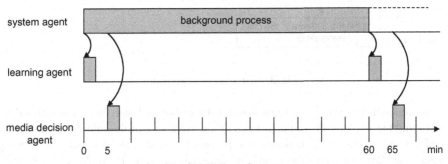

Fig. 2. Relation of agents

2.2.1 Media Decision Agent

The media decision agent uses an inexact reasoning method called the Dempster-Shafer theory [13] to determine communication media suitable to the calling situation and time, as shown in Figure 3. The media decision agent computes the probability of each communication media using the combination rule of the Dempster-Shafer theory as follows.

$$m_i \oplus m_b(z) = \sum_{x \cap y = z} m_i(x) \, m_b(y), \text{ for } i = 0, 1, 2, 3 . \tag{1}$$

$$\sum_{x \in U} m_i(x) = 1, \text{ for } i = 0, 1, 2, 3 . \tag{2}$$

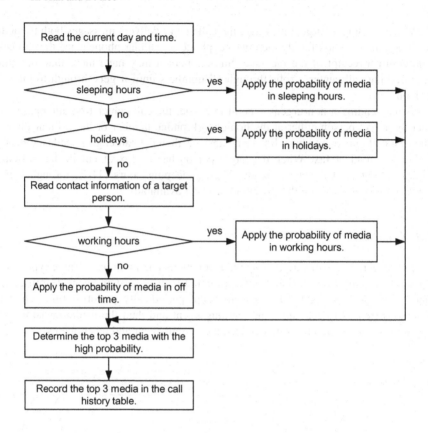

Fig. 3. Media decision procedure

In equation (1), the $\oplus$ operator denotes the orthogonal sum, which is defined by summing the mass product intersections on the right side of the rule. In equations (1) and (2) m_0, m_1, m_2, and m_3 denote the probability of successful contact at sleeping hours, holidays, working hours, and off time, respectively. Examples of such probabilities for patients' family members are shown in Table 2. In equation (1) m_b represents the basic probability to be used in the orthogonal sum. As shown in Table 3, the basic probability is equally 1/14 for each subset of communication media. If any of the communication media forms are not available, the learning agent updates the probabilities shown in Table 3 before applying the Dempster-Shafer theory, which is described later in section 2.2.2. After deciding the communication media, the media decision agent is deactivated. Equation (2) is a constraint enforced by the Dempster-Shafer theory.

The set U in equation (2) denotes a set of subsets of all communication media considered. In our call center, the subsets were limited to those with less than or equal to three elements for the efficiency of the system, as shown in equation (3).

$$U = \{\{H\}, \{O\}, \{C\}, \{S\}, \{H, O\}, \{H, C\}, \{H, S\}, ..., \{H, C, S\}\} . \qquad (3)$$

Table 2. Probability of a subset of communication media for each time (m_t)

	H	O	C	S	H, O	H, C	H, S	O, C	O, S	C, S	H, O, C	H, O, S	O, C, S	H, C, S
sleeping hours (m_0)	.1	.02	.04	.04	.05	.1	.15	.01	.02	.02	.1	.1	.05	.2
holidays (m_1)	.04	.02	.1	.04	.01	.15	.1	.02	.02	.05	.1	.05	.1	.2
working hours (m_2)	.02	.1	.04	.04	.05	.02	.01	.15	.1	.02	.1	.1	.2	.05
off time (m_3)	.1	.02	.04	.04	.05	.15	.1	.02	.01	.02	.2	.1	.05	.1

H: Home number of a family member
O: Office number of a family member
C: Cellular phone number of a family member
S: Second family member's home number

Table 3. Basic probability (m_b)

H	O	C	S	H, O	H, C	H, S	O, C	O, S	C, S	H, O, C	H, O, S	O, C, S	H, C, S
1/14	1/14	1/14	1/14	1/14	1/14	1/14	1/14	1/14	1/14	1/14	1/14	1/14	1/14

2.2.2 Learning Agent

The learning agent is always activated earlier than the media decision agent since the learning agent is required to compute the probability that is used by the media decision agent. Every communication media is originally assigned an equal value as its basic probability shown in Table 3. If a certain media x is not available to a person, the learning agent reduces the probability of x to zero and redistributes the reduced amount equally to other singleton sets that have only one element. For the subsets that have two elements with x being one of them, the learning agent reduces the probability of them by half and redistributes the reduced amount equally to the other subsets with two elements. Likewise, for the subsets that have three elements with x being one of them, the learning agent reduces the probability of them by one third and redistributes the reduced amount equally to other subsets with three elements.

The learning agent also changes the basic probability if a calling history for the target person is available. Whenever a message cannot be sent to the target person via a certain communication media, the learning agent computes the number of failures for the media and reduces the probability of the media by a constant fraction of the original probability. The reduced probability is redistributed to the other subsets as discussed above.

2.3 Database Interface

The call center decides the communication media to be used based on the calling time and the types of messages to be sent. Contact information for target persons may change over time, and thus the persons are allowed to directly enter and/or modify their own information within a web browser. The Extensible Markup Language (XML) was used to develop the database interface.

The call center maintains 6 database tables. (1) contact information of patients' family members, (2) contact information of attending doctors, (3) contact information of residents, (4) contact information of interns, (5) contact information of ancillary hospital personnel, and (6) call history. Tables for contact information contain communication media available and working hours of the target person. The call history table contains the order of communication media to try and previous calling results.

3 Implementation and Experimental Results

The call engine software was written in Inprise C++ Builder 4.0 and Asyncpro, which is a TAPI component of Turbopower Company. A voice modem was used as call engine hardware. The call engine sends a message via a communication media selected by the media decision agent. The call engine must be capable of detecting call failure such as busy line or no answer. A voice modem can detect a busy line but not the lack of an answer. So, a DTMF (Dual Tone Multi Frequency) event was used allowing a called person to press a special dial button on a line. If this event was detected, message transfer was considered successful. Figure 3 shows a graphic user interface of the call engine. For an urgent message of priority 1, patient names are listed first, and the operator selects one to transfer a message. For general messages, the operator selects the class of a target person and then a target person to send a message.

The call engine was developed in the form of Active X controls, and inserted to a Web page to make the call center an integrated environment. MS-Access databases were used to build the databases, which were accessed by the call engine using ODBC (Open Database Connectivity). The Paradox database was used to build the probability tables, which were accessed by the call agents using BDE (Borland Database Engine).

The agent was divided into 3 classes as mentioned earlier. The system agent functions as a background process of Windows 98. It is desirable to keep the agents in the Windows system tray area because they stay out of the way, letting the user concentrate on his or her work. Yet, the agents can still be easily located when the user needs to interact with them [14]. The system agent was developed in Microsoft Visual C++ 6.0 using Windows API. The API puts the agent in the system tray, and remains merely as an icon throughout its lifetime. It also provides a popup menu when the right mouse button is pressed over the agent's icon in the system tray. Figure 4(a) shows an icon representing the system agent just as it activates the learning agent. The

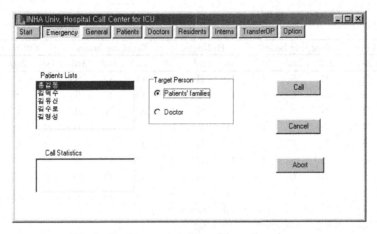

Fig. 3. Graphic user interface of the call engine

shape of the icon of the system agent changes after it activates the media decision agent as shown in Figure 4(b).

(a)   (b)

Fig. 4. System agent

The call center was tested on a Pentium PC running Windows 98. When a line was connected successfully, the voice modem played a wave file or sent a fax or email without any problem. When a line was not connected, the modem took some time to detect the failure since it had to wait on the DTMF for a while. Table 4 shows a test result of the media decision agent when a message was sent to a patient's family member. Table 4 shows the communication media chosen by the media decision agent for eight cases. The eight cases of family members can be classified into three types: (1) All communication media were available but no calling history existed (case 1), (2) Certain communication media was absent and no calling history existed (cases 2-5), and (3) All media as well as the calling history were available (cases 6-8). The test result shows that the media decision agent chose a suitable media for each case.

The time available to the call center that uses an agent for determining a suitable communication media remains nearly constant, irrespective of calling occurrences or contact persons. This is because the agent periodically updates and predetermines a suitable communication media based on calling history. Therefore, the call center with an agent exhibits relatively low performance with few calling occurrences but high performance when the calling occurrences are numerous and the situation is complex. In addition, the CTI system of the call center presented here was separated from its business logic, and thus it can be potentially applied to areas other than ICU.

Table 4. Test results of media decision

Time	Sleeping hours			Holidays			Working hours			Off time		
Case	1st	2nd	3rd	1st	2nd	3rd	1st	2nd	3rd	1st	2nd	3rd
1	H	S	C	C	H	S	O	C	S	H	C	S
2	S	C	O	C	S	O	O	C	S	C	S	O
3	H	S	C	C	H	S	C	S	H	H	C	S
4	H	S	O	H	S	O	O	S	H	H	O	S
5	H	C	O	C	H	O	O	C	H	H	C	O
6	H	S	C	C	H	S	O	C	S	H	C	S
7	H	C	S	C	H	S	C	H	O	H	C	S
8	H	O	S	H	O	S	O	H	S	H	O	S

Case 1: All media in Table 2 and 3 are available.
Case 2: home phone number is missing.
Case 3: office phone number is missing.
Case 4: cellular phone number is missing.
Case 5: second family member's home number is missing.
Case 6: home number fails once out of 5 calls.
Case 7: office number fails 7 times out of 9 calls.
Case 8: cellular phone number fails 2 times out of 4 calls.

4   Conclusion

This paper has described the development of a web-based intelligent call center for a hospital ICU. In the ICU, there are many occasions requiring contact with medical staff members and patients' family members. Selecting the best communication media under uncertain conditions is not easy and the calling process itself is often time-consuming and disruptive. Based on CTI technology, the call center attempts to efficiently and automatically send messages to patients' family members, doctors, and other hospital staff via communication media suitable to the occasion. The Dempster-Shafer theory is used to determine the most suitable communication media for the rapid and safe transmission of a message. In addition, an agent periodically applies the Dempster-Shafer theory to recent calling histories to perform the calling task automatically and efficiently. The experimental results of this study showed that the call center is capable of delivering messages through various communication media in an integrated environment. The call center is useful especially for a busy ICU with many calling occurrences and complex situations, and thus relieving the ICU staff from the time-consuming and tedious calling task.

Acknowledgments. This work was supported by the development program for exemplary schools in information and communication from the Ministry of Information and Communication (MIC).

References

1. Messerschmitt, D.G.: The Future of Computer Telecommunications Integration. IEEE Communications Magazine 34 (1996) 66-69
2. Asatani, K.: Standardization on Multimedia Communications: Computer-Telephony-Integration-Related Issues. IEEE Communications Magazine 36 (1998) 105-109
3. Nixon, T.: Design Consideration for Computer Telephony Application Programming Interfaces and Related Components. IEEE Communications Magazine 34 (1996) 43-47
4. Flegg, R.: Computer Telephony Architectures: MVIP, H-MVIP, and SCbus. IEEE Communications Magazine 34 (1996) 60-64
5. Glitho, R.H.: Advanced Services Architectures for Internet Telephony: A Critical Overview. IEEE Network 14 (2000) 38-44
6. Frank, D., Lucic, H., Opsenica, M., Puksec, L., Zic, M., Brajkovic, S., Maricic, V.: The EMA System: a CTI based e-mail alerting service. IEEE Communications Magazine 38 (2000) 122-128
7. Hayzelden, A., Bigham, J. (eds.): Software Agents for Future Communication Systems. Springer-Verlag, Berlin Heidelberg New York (1999)
8. Bradshaw, J.M.(ed.): Software Agents. The MIT Press, Massachusetts (1997)
9. Liang, T.-P., Huang, J.-S.: A Framework for Applying Intelligent Agents to Support Electronic Trading. Decision Support Systems 28 (2000) 305-317
10. Fazlollahi, B., Vahidov, R.M., Aliev, R.A.: Multi-Agent Distributed Intelligent System Based on Fuzzy Decision Making. International Journal of Intelligent Systems 15 (2000) 849-858
11. Xu, X., Guo, J., Chen, P., Kang, Y.: A Change Notification Framework Based on Agent for Information System. Proceedings of the 36th International Conference on Technology of Object-Oriented Languages and Systems (2000) 195-200
12. Cohen, P., Cheyer, A., Wang, M., Baeg, S.: An Open Agent Architecture. Working Notes of AAAI Spring Symposium on Software Agents (1994) 1-8
13. Shafer, G.: A Mathematical Theory of Evidence. Princeton University Press, New Jersey (1976)
14. Pallmann, D.: Programming Bots, Spiders, and Intelligent Agents in Microsoft Visual C++. Microsoft Press, Washington (1999)

Electronic Homework on the WWW[*]

Chunnian Liu, Lei Zheng, Junzhong Ji,
Chengzhong Yang, Jingyue Li, and Wensheng Yang

Dept. of Computer Science,Beijing Polytechnic University,Beijing 100022, China
Ai@bjpu.edu.cn

Abstract. This paper presents the design of an Intelligent Tutoring System (ITS) MathEH, that is a coached problem solving system, also called "Electronic Homework". In describing the main modules of the system, we emphasize its novel aspects: (1). Using Constraint Logic Programming (CLP) as the domain knowledge representation and automatic reasoning mechanism. (2). A method for probability propagation in Bayesian networks to achieve two adversary requirements: exact probability computation and real-time response. (3). The design decisions about how to deploy MathEH on the WWW.

1 Introduction

An Intelligent Tutoring System (ITS) [Mu99] is a combination of the traditional CAI, Artificial Intelligence (AI) and Cognition Science. ITS represents an important application area in Computer Science covering a big variety of research topics. We can roughly classify and characterize ITSs in several dimensions as follows:

- Target users: students/teachers
- Functionality: coached problem solving / teaching material understanding / learning by examples
- Domain subject: mathematics/physics/languages/…
- Environment: standalone/on the WWW

A coached problem solving ITS, also called an Electronic Homework (EH), helps students to do homework after attending their classroom sessions. We are developing MathEH, an electronic homework for high-school mathematics education. The novel features of this ITS system include: (1). Using constraint programming for automatic problem solving. (2). A method for probability propagation in Bayesian networks to achieve two adversary requirements: exact probability computation and real-time response. (3). Distributed environment, that is, to deploy MathEH on the WWW. In this paper we present these novel features of MathEH, especially the design of its deployment on the WWW.

As in most ITSs, MathEH contains four main modules. In the following, each section discusses one module, with the emphasis on the novel features of MathEH.

---

[*] This work is supported by the Natural Science Foundation of China (NSFC), Beijing Municipal Natural Science Foundation (BMNSF) and Chinese 863 High-Tech Program.

N. Zhong et al. (Eds.): WI 2001, LNAI 2198, pp. 540–548, 2001.
© Springer-Verlag Berlin Heidelberg 2001

2 Domain Knowledge and Automatic Problem Solving

A teacher knows his/her domain knowledge by heart. Given a problem in the domain, he/she can easily construct all the solution strategies. The challenge is how to coach students in one-to-one manner, considering the particulars for each student: how well the student understands the teaching materials? What is the cognitive characteristics of the student? Etc. A good teacher can do well, though decisions are made usually by intuition.

To mimic a human teacher, an ITS should be able to perform automatic problem solving, and this in turn requires that the domain knowledge must be represented in some formal way.

For example, ANDES system [ANDES00] represents domain knowledge in Horn clauses, so logic programming system such as Prolog can serve as the automatic reasoning mechanism.

On the implementation level, each rule (a knowledge element in the domain) is represented as a Strips operator (a classical AI technique, see[Nil98]). Each operator is specified by its name, preconditions (subgoals) and effects. The problem itself is represented by two dummy operators: *start* operator with the known part of the problem as its effects, and *finish* operator with the goal of the problem as its preconditions. The automatic reasoning can be carried out in either forward or backwards manner. The Current World Description (CWD) are maintained during the reasoning. Initially, CWD consists only of the known facts of the problem. As more and more rules (Strips operators) are introduced and executed during the reasoning, CWD will contain more and more facts. The overall aim is to satisfy the original goal of the problem by CWD. This mechanism can be implemented by Logic Programming systems.

However, like many other Strips-style planning systems, it poses two restrictions. First, initial known facts contains no logic variables (problem variables are regarded as "constants" in logic point of view, while a logic variable means "anything"). Secondly, the effects of any operator contain no logic variables other than those that appear in the preconditions of the operator. The results of these restrictions are that CWD contains only ground facts, and whenever all preconditions of an operator are satisfied by CWD (hence the operator is executed), its effects become ground facts too and are added to CWD. Finally, satisfaction of the initial problem goal by CWD means that CWD contains the goal facts. These restrictions may be too hard for representing high-school mathematics that is our domain knowledge in MathEH.

In light of above, we decide in MathEH to use a Constraint Logic Programming (CLP [Hen96]) system as the automatic problem solver. The novel points in this design are as follows.

(1) We use CLP programs to represent domain knowledge, and the problem is represented as a query of CLP. Because Logic Programming is a special case of CLP, the expressive power in our system will surely increase. CLP contains a logic inference engine and a constraint solver. The former can be used to generate the solution

graph of the problem, the latter can be used as a tool to solve the constraint set accumulated during reasoning and give the explicit solutions to the program. Of course constraint solving itself should not be the domain subject, because the solver works as a black box, so the student cannot learn much about constraint solving from this mechanism. For example, if the student is studying how to solve linear equations, he cannot expect that this CLP-based mechanism will be very much helpful. On the other hand, if the student is studying some other subject in which the problem can be reduced to solving linear equations, our mechanism can teach the student about the principles and skills of the reduction procedure, meanwhile providing an automatic tool to solve the resulting linear equations.

(2) The domain knowledge can be stored in constraint database [KLP00]. Constraint Databases (CDBs) are the combination of Constraint Logic Programming and database technology, naturally extending relational, deductive, or object-oriented databases by making feasible the use of constraints to represent possibly infinite but representable complex data. Our design will extend the application scope of CDBs.

As far as we know, there are no any other ITS systems using CLP technology.

3 Student Modeling

To achieve one-to-one coaching, the system must maintain a formal model for each student. Because MathEH is an electronic homework system, the student model must contain the solution graph for the current problem. The solution graph represents all solutions and all solution paths for the problem. Furthermore, the student model should also contain long-term knowledge assessment of the student (that is, the knowledge level of the student, indicated by his/her performance in solving previous and current problems). In [ANDES00], a student model is a Bayesian network. The nodes in the network are rules (knowledge elements), rule applications, the original goal, deduced subgoals and facts. The network is the solution graph augmented by probabilities for rule nodes and conditional probabilities for other nodes. The probability attached to a rule node indicates the level of the student's understanding of the rule (a knowledge element).

One of the most important operation upon the Bayesian network is to update the probabilities of rule nodes when a student action (such as writing an equation) is observed. The computational complexity of the probability propagation is definitely an issue, because the network is a fine-grained model and the computation must meet the real-time requirement. However, the exact probability propagation is NP-hard [Mi97], so ANDES system tried several approximate algorithms, such as *Gibb's* sampling [Hr90], logic sampling and likelihood sampling [Co93].

Based on the particular situation we have in a coached problem solving system, we use in MathEH a method that satisfies two adversary requirements: exact probability propagation and real-time response. We observe that, when the problem is proposed to the student, he/she may take several minutes to read and understand the problem, before he/she takes any observable actions. During this time, the system needs only to generate the solution graph and merge the graph with the existing student model consisting of the rules (attached with probabilities) used so far by the student. For the remaining time, the system is in the idle state (waiting for the student actions). [DP97] proposes a method for probability propagation in Bayesian networks that suits our situation very well. The method contains two steps: First translating the Bayesian Network into a semantically equivalent structure **Query DAG** (the computation complexity of the translation could be NP-hard in general), then the probability propagation can be carried out on the Query DAG (that is a linear algorithm and the result is exact). So, our system can utilize the idle time to do the translation, and use the linear algorithm to perform exact probability computation and produce response in real-time to the student actions.

As far as we know, there are no other ITS systems using Bayesian networks can achieve both exact probability computation and real-time response.

4 Pedagogic Decision Making

MathEH provides the student with two modes for problem solving:

• He/she can try to solve the problem by paper and pen in the usual way, then inputs the answer through the interface to the system. If the answer is not correct, the system will propose a sub-problem for the student to consider. If the student solves the sub-problem correctly (or wrongly), the system will propose a larger (or smaller) sub-problem for the student. This procedure will continue until the student solves the original problem. The system decomposes the original problem based on the student model, and the performance of the student in solving the (sub)problems is recorded in the student model.

• He/she can solve the problem directly in the student interface: defining variables, entering equations, drawing diagrams, etc. Whenever the student makes an error (say, entering a wrong equation), or asks the system for help, the system makes various pedagogic decisions based on the student model. The decisions include: the most probable place in the solution graph where the student is working, what knowledge elements the student does not understand well, what kind of hints should be generated and presented to the student, and so on.

5 Web-Based Student Interface

For the standalone version, the interface design presents no particular difficulty, except for the fact that we need matching the system-generated expressions and equations with the student-entered ones. In the following we will concentrate on the WWW version of the system.

There have been several efforts to deploy ITS on the WWW [BRS97, ASF98, OWK97]. The advantages of the Web version of MathEH are obvious. First, students can receive tutoring from anywhere they have access to the Internet. Secondly, the teacher knows each student's current knowledge level and position in the curriculum because all student models reside on the centralized server which the teacher can access to. Thirdly, Web-based ITSs with different purposes can interact and cooperate to achieve a better level of adaptability and intelligence.

The basic architecture for the Web version is the Browser/Server (B/S), where the kernel modules (domain knowledge, automatic reasoning, student models, pedagogic decision making) constitute the MathEH application server (there is also the standard HTTP Server). On the client side, the student can use any WWW browser.

In MathEH, we would like a more active and complex client side. This means that the student interface may be implemented in a Java applet executable in a standard Web browser, and the HTML page of MathEH incorporates the Java client applet, to be retrieved by students using the browser.

We will explain the main reasons for this design in the following subsections. The basic idea is that we need code running on the client, interacting with the student independently from the MathEH Server.

5.1   Complex Interactions and Quick Feedback

For example, to solve the following problem: "Given that the current population is m and the yearly increase rate is b, in how many years will the population reach n"? The related meta domain knowledge looks like:

```
operator(solveQfromE(E,Q),     %% Operator Name:  Solve Q from equation E
    [eqn(E),                   %% subgoal:  find an equation E
    contain(E,Q),              %% Precon:   E contains Q
    others(E,Q,Qs),            %% Precon:   find other quantities Qs in E
    all(Qs)],                  %% subgoals: every item in Qs is a subgoal
    [solved(Q)]).              %% effect:   Q can be solved by E
```

The automatic problem solver considers equation $Y=(1+b)^X$ (that is a particular piece of domain knowledge), verifies that the equation contains X (the required quantity of the problem – the number of years), and finds in the equation other quantities b and Y (a temporary variable). As b is a known quantity of the problem, the solver tries to solve Y (a temporary variable, and $m*Y=n$ is another piece of domain knowledge).

Based on this kind of reasoning, a solution graph is generated. On the student side, he/she is allowed to define problem variables X, b, Y, m, n, to enter the equation $Y=(1+b)^X$ and to highlight Y as the next quantity to consider (see Figure 1 for the snapshot of the student interface for this example).

Based on these observable actions, the system can judge better about the student's intentions, giving more accurate and real-time feedback. If we only allow the student to enter the final result, the system should guess a lot about the

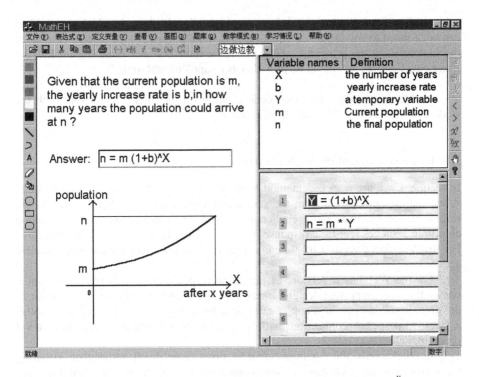

Fig. 1. The snapshot of the student interface for solving $n=m(1+b)^X$

understanding of domain knowledge and the problem-solving plan of the student (the guess involves a lot of computation and is not very accurate).

This kind of interactions (concerning intelligent selection of terms from equations and immediate feedback from the system) is too much for HTML. Code running on the client is needed. If we consider natural language interface (this feature will be added to MathEH in future), more computation has to be carried out "locally".

5.2 Supplemental Tools for Student to Solve Problems

In MathEH, we provide students with various tools for problem solving.

For example, we allow the student to draw draft diagrams on the interface window. (Draft figures can illustrate the problem that the student is solving. In future we will further establish the logic connection between diagrams and equations). To support this feature, simple drawing tools should be provided in the menu of the interface window.

Another example is the equation solver. As we mentioned before, if the student is studying how to solve linear equations, the system should not allow the student to use an automatic solver (otherwise the student cannot learn anything about the current subject). But if the student is studying some higher-level subject in which the problem can be reduced to solving linear equations, the main purpose of the system is to teach the student about the principles and skills of the reduction procedure, meanwhile the linear equations solver should be provided as a supplemental tool.

In these cases, we also need code running on the client, interacting with the student independently from the MathEH Server.

5.3   Response Time of the Web Version

In section 3, we use a special method to ensure the real-time response of the system. When the system evolves from the standalone version into the Web-based version, response time becomes more challenging. Even when the probability propagation algorithm achieves real-time response, there is still the issue of Web communication. For the Web-based version, all we can expect is "reasonable response time for student actions".

For the Web-based version, as far as the response time problem is concerned, one of the most important design targets is to speed up the communication as far as possible. In this aspect, Java applet can help a lot. Using Java applet we can establish a persistent socket connection with a persistently-executing application server program.

In other words, the communication becomes more direct, rather than restarting the server program each time a client request arrives. As results, we could achieve quicker communication and server responsiveness.

5.4   More Flexible and Enjoyable Interactivity

Our users are high-school students. The success of the system depends on whether the youngsters are eager to use and enjoy it. In Section 4, we mentioned that two usage modes are provided. The purpose is to avoid the tight jacket effect that would discourage students. Also, we need enjoyable interactivity. The interface should be visually interesting, incorporating animation, sound and other "funs". These features are not as serious as the core algorithms, but vital for the success of the system in real world distribution. Most work of this kind has nothing to do with the core computation on the server side, hence can be carried out on the client side. Here we see another reason for code running on the client.

5.5   Integrating Different ITSs over WWW

MathEH is not the only kind of Intelligent Tutoring System, neither its functionality is sufficient for the teacher to assess his/her students. We also need other kinds of ITS with different functionality: to support student's understanding of instructional materials, to help students in learning by examples, etc. While it is not practical to develop a comprehensive ITS system with all desired functionality, it is possible to deploy several ITS systems (each with some particular features) on WWW, and integrate them by model sharing, communication and cooperation. There are many deep issues to consider in this ambitious research area, but code running on the client is certainly more important than in the single MathEH system.

As a conclusion of Section 5, we would like to point out that code running on the client is necessary in the Web-based version of MathEH, as described in details in the above five subsections. We choose Java applet in the implementation mainly for the purpose of portability. Other programming tools will be considered as alternative or supplemental means. Especially, major DBMS providers have products related to their database systems (Sybase, Oracle, etc.), our choice of programming tools will partly depend on the database system that is really used in MathEH.

6 Conclusions

MathEH is a kind of Intelligent Tutoring System (ITS) supporting coached problem solving in high-school mathematics. The novel aspects in this system are:

(1) Using Constraint Logic Programming (CLP) as the domain knowledge representation and automatic reasoning mechanism.
(2) A method for probability propagation in Bayesian networks to achieve two adversary requirements: exact probability computation and real-time response.
(3) The design of the Web-based version of the system, allowing intelligent and enjoyable student interactions, providing supplemental problem solving tools, and ensuring quick response. It also has the potential to be integrated with other ITSs over the WWW in future.

The design of MathEH has been completed and the implementation work is underway. In few months time we would be able to report the results from implementation and initial application.

References

[ANDES00]   Schulze, K.G., Shelby, R.N., Treacy, D.J., Wintersgill, M.C., VanLehn, K., Gertner, A. 2000. Andes: An intelligent tutor for classical physics. *The Journal of Electronic Publishing, University of Michigan Press*, Ann Arbor, MI, 6:1;
http://www.press.umich.edu/jep/-06-01/schulze.html
[ASF98]   S. Alpert, M. Singley, P. Fairweather, 1998, AlgeBrain: Intelligent Tutoring on the Web, *RC 21358, IBM Research Division*
[BRS97]   P. Brusilovsky, S. Ritter, E.Schwarz, 1997, Distributed Intelligent Tutoring on the Web, *Proc. of the 8th World Conference of the AIED Society*
[Co93]   S. Cousins etc. 1993, A tutorial introduction to stochastic simulation algorithms for belief networks. *Artificial Intelligence in Medicine* 5:315,340
[DP97]   A. Darwiche and G. Provan, 1997, Query DAGs: A Practical Paradigm for Implementing Belief-Network Inference, *Journal of Artificial Intelligence Research,* 6: 147-176
[Hen96]   P. Van Hentenryck, V. Saraswat etc. 1996, Strategic Directions in Constraint Programming, *ACM Computing Surveys,* 28(4):702-726

[Hr90] T. Hrycej, 1990, Gibb's sampling in Bayesian networks, *Artificial Intelligence,* 46, 351-363

[KLP00] G. Kuper, L. Libkin, J. Paredaens (Eds), Constraint Databases, Springer-Verlag 2000

[Mi97] Tom M. Mitchell, 1997, Machine Learning, The McGraw-Hill Companies, Inc.

[Mu99] Murray, T. 1999, Authoring intelligent tutoring systems: an analysis of the state of the art, *International Journal of Artificial Intelligence in Education*, 10, 98-129.

[Nil98] N.J. Nilsson, 1998, Artificial Intelligence: a New Synthesis, Morgan Kaufmann Publishers, Inc.

[OWK97] Y. Okazaki, K. Watanabe and H. Kondo, 1997, An ITS (Intelligent Tutoring System) on the WWW, *System and Computers in Japan*, 28(9):11-16

The Shopping Gate – Enabling Role- and Preference-Specific E-commerce Shopping Experiences

Markus Stolze and Michael Ströbel

IBM Research, Zurich Research Laboratory, Säumerstrasse 4,
CH-8803 Rüschlikon, Switzerland
{mrs, mis}@zurich.ibm.com

Abstract. Customer relationship management, one-to-one marketing, recommendation systems, and real-time click mining are common means to create a personalised customer interaction in today's e-Commerce. However, one major aspect of customisation and adaptation has thus far been neglected – one buyer might assume multiple shopping roles. Searching for a present for an 11-year-old daughter leads to a different preference profile than evaluating workstations for the purchasing department.

This paper proposes the shopping gate – a site on the Internet where buyers can create and maintain different roles with specific preference profiles. Before going on an electronic shopping trip, a buyer can pass the shopping gate, choose the appropriate role and take the corresponding preference profile along to the merchants 'on the way', thus entering these shops with a role-specific 'skin'. Our prototype implementation of the shopping gate server, role representation, and protocol is based on open standards such as the platform for privacy preferences (P3P) and XML Schema.

1 Introduction

If a buyer returns to an e-Commerce shop she or he has visited before, different levels of personalisation (adaptation to the buyer profile) can be applied:

- A profile for this buyer is already available and can be used to recognise the buyer ('Welcome back Michael Ströbel...') and to retrieve historical information such as the order book, payment modes etc.
- On the basis of the past shopping behaviour and the click history, it is possible to customise advertising in order to promote, for instance, add-ons to past purchases ('great savings on the new MP3 plugin for your PDA...').
- The buyer might have been or is being classified and therefore recommendations based on the statistics of the identified buyer cluster can be made ('other people who bought this also liked...').
- If interviewing techniques ('is this PDA for business or for private use?') are used for filtering or preference elicitation, product offers can already be configured according to past answers.

N. Zhong et al. (Eds.): WI 2001, LNAI 2198, pp. 549–561, 2001.
© Springer-Verlag Berlin Heidelberg 2001

The goal of these personalisation measures is to support the buyer in finding the right product whilst also creating a lock-in situation, in which the buyer's motivation to switch to another merchant is reduced owing the burden of repeating the personalisation process.

Nevertheless, a problem arises if this time, the buyer, (Bob), is looking for a product in the e-Commerce shop from a different background than the previous times. There is no way for the merchant to detect whether Bob plans to purchase a product for himself or on behalf of somebody else [3]. We conceptualise the shopping background (needs, preferences, transaction history...) with the notion of a 'shopping role'. Bob might have, for instance, the role of an employee in the purchasing department, or the role of a father to a teenage girl (Alice). If personalisation measures assume the wrong role, the result can be annoying for the buyer. If Bob so far used an online book shop predominantly to buy books for Alice, but now tries to find work-related literature, recommendations and advertisements for the latest and greatest teenager entertainment will probably be less helpful if not downright irritating. Hence, the goal of supporting the user in the product selection is missed, and the effect of personalisation might even be reversed, increasing the likelihood of buyers switching to other merchants.

With real-time personalisation based on click-through clustering, this undesirable consequence can be avoided to some extent, but then historical data is not incorporated in the personalisation, and the adaptation is very vague and error-prone, at least at the beginning of a shopping session when only few characteristics are identifiable.

We therefore believe that the solution to this problem is that buyers themselves reveal their current shopping role: 'father of a teenage girl', 'agent in the purchasing department' etc. Unfortunately this is a very tedious task to perform every time the buyer enters a shop, and the means to enter a profile might vary from shop to shop. Hence, we propose the shopping gate to support a buyer in the task of creating, maintaining, and slipping into shopping roles.

The contribution of the shopping gate concept to web intelligence is two-fold. First, web-mining-based personalisation measures of sellers can be much more effective if correct shopping role specifications are available. Second, a rich shopping role specification, e.g. with fine-tuned evaluation criteria, enables the buyer to hand over structured shopping tasks such as matchmaking or ranking of offers to an autonomous agent, thus leaving the buyer more time for the actual decision making.

The remainder of this paper is organised as follows: in the next section, an informal usage scenario for the shopping gate functionalities is outlined. Section 3 briefly summarises the high-level requirements we identified for the success of the proposed solution. An overview of our work in progress regarding the prototype architecture, role representation, and suggested interaction protocol is provided in Section 4. Finally, the preliminary findings are discussed and evaluated in Section 5.

2   The Shopping Gate Scenario

We envision the shopping gate (ShoG) to be a site on the Internet run by a trusted third party. Buyers can open an account, which might host multiple roles, at the ShoG.

A role is defined by properties, preferences and a history of past transactions and clicks. Role properties comprise, for instance, the age or the sizes of the role owner. Preferences are either limited in their scope to one role or shared among several roles of the same user. Our hierarchy of preferences comprises:

- General tastes and high-level interests (horses, 70ies style, yellow).
- Needs in terms of product types (e.g. music CDs, books, make-up, attire).
- Essential attributes of these product types (e.g. fabric, number of pages).
- Preferred values or value ranges for these attributes (fabric = cotton, delivery time = 2 days)
- Evaluation criteria defined as utility functions for attributes.
- Relative importance of the evaluation criteria (e.g. price is much more important than delivery time).

2.1 Skin Shopping

Before visiting an e-Commerce shop, Bob will enter the ShoG and select the appropriate role for the shopping trip – or create a new one if no existing role fits the current background.

The role selected is rendered to a runtime specification and handed over to a mobile shopping companion, e.g. in the form of a conversational agent (c.f. [19]), which will follow Bob on the shopping trip. Whenever Bob enters an online shop the companion will inform the shop about the current role, its properties, associated preferences and the transaction history. This information can be used by the online shop to generate a role-specific shop presence. Not all information will be disclosed. Depending on the level of trust, evaluation criteria, for instance, may remain secret to the companion. In this case, the companion will evaluate suggested products on behalf of Bob and disclose this additional information for his eyes only.

For shops Bob will 'look', for instance, as a teenage girl with a preference for yellow clothes and horses, although he actually is a middle-aged purchasing agent. We borrow the metaphor of skinnable user interfaces (see MP3 players, Netscape 6 etc.) to express that the user is wearing a role-specific skin for the shopping trip.

The role representation in the companion is not static but subject to permanent feedback. If the seller wants to inquire about additional preferences of Bob (e.g. 'are you interested in Arabian horses?'), the companion may add the new elicited preference definitions to the current role. The same is true if the buyer rejects products although they seem to be optimal according to the current preference structure. In this case the companion will request the user to indicate changes to the current preferences, so that the actual choice argumentation is reflected correctly in the role definition. If transactions take place, the related details are added to the role history.

Whenever Bob decides to end the shopping trip or to assume a different role, he passes again through the ShoG, places the companion 'on the shelf', and the role data is updated.

2.2 Skin Hopping and Cascading

The shopping gate also provides the functionality of sharing a set of roles or preferences among ShoG users. Let us assume a scenario, in which so far, Bob used to buy books for Alice but one day his wife urgently needs a present for their daughter. In this case Bob could share this already fine-tuned shopping role (e.g. 'parent of a teenage girl') with his wife, who could then use this skin for a Christmas shopping trip.

Another option is that the ShoG itself offers several pre-defined skins, which could be based on collected statistical buying behaviour. This approach is already demonstrated, for instance, by the CNet Buying Advisor profile solution [6] (e.g. 'hardcore gamer'), which offers users pre-defined preference profiles to find the right desktop computers, or CDNOW's gift guide [8] (e.g. 'Teen Pop Princess').

To model the plausible real world scenario that Bob enters a shop together with Alice requires a different functionality – skin cascading. In the role representation, Bob uses the preferences of Alice regarding essential attributes etc. but overrides some attributes (e.g. the price domain) or the evaluation criteria (e.g. emphasising the quality). In the ShoG this is performed through a cascade of roles in which Bob's preferences overlay Alice's preferences.

3 Requirements

The primary requirement for the operation of the ShoG will be a network of e-Commerce shops supporting the shopping role specification data format and the ShoG interaction protocol. To support acceptance of the data format and the protocol, both should be based on open and accepted standards to the greatest extent possible, thereby also facilitating an implementation. The representation for the role specification also has to be rich enough to capture the most relevant elements of a shopping role, but still needs to provide clearly defined semantics and formalisms to support structured automated processing on the merchant side.

In addition to these essential 'critical mass' and 'formality' requirements, the ShoG architecture as well as the protocol defining the interaction between buyer, shopping gate, and merchant, have to ensure that uncontrolled access to the preferences of the buyer is not possible. Imagine what would happen if Bob's wife has access to one of his roles that specifies interest in women's shoes size 36, although she has 38? Performance, on the other hand, is also an issue that has to be considered. The ShoG intermediation should not add significant overhead to the buyer/merchant interaction, thus ruining the benefits of improved personalisation because of an unsatisfactory user experience.

The same applies to the user interface design of the ShoG, which has to balance the effort necessary for role creation and maintenance with the benefits achievable through centralised role handling. This involves different dimensions of trust: buyers need to understand that revealing their preferences can be beneficial (e.g. because they receive targeted recommendations) but also need to be sure that their preferences are represented correctly (this especially applies to evaluation criteria).

4 Prototype Overview

Our ShoG prototype is based on two emerging W3 standards: the platform for privacy preferences (P3P, [12]) and XML Schema [13].

P3P is an addition to the HTTP protocol for the exchange of privacy information between a HTTP server (an e-Commerce shop) and a HTTP client (a buyer's web browser). The main focus of P3P is to define a protocol that allows a client to specify which privacy guarantees or server certificates are required for supplying a server with a requested set of personal data, such as the birth date or a credit card number.

P3P already includes the abstract concept of a user having multiple 'personae', which implies that P3P profiles can hold information about multiple roles and might reveal information about different personae to different servers [4]. However, P3P does not specify how these personae can be managed (including issues such as sharing etc.) and how the personal data is actually structured and transferred. Therefore our ShoG prototype complements the P3P framework with additional persona or role management functions, a format for the structure of personal data, and an extended role data communication protocol.

XML Schemata specify classes of XML instance documents by describing the document structure in a much richer way than is possible on the basis of document type definitions (DTD) [5]. One of the primary advantages of using XML schemata compared to the DTD mechanism is that it is possible to express hierarchies of data types, which is used for the representation of ontology concepts in the role data definition (see Section 4.2).

The following sections describe how these two standards are used in the implementation of the ShoG prototype, which comprises the ShoG server, the role representation, and the ShoG protocol.

4.1 ShoG Server

The foundation for the implementation of the ShoG server is the WBI programmable web proxy [7]. The facilitation of P3P implementations through WBI was already demonstrated in the online privacy agent (OPA) project [14] at IBM's Almaden Research Center. In principle, our ShoG server is an implementation of a P3P user agent with additional persona or role management functionality. The operation of the ShoG server web-proxy functionality differs from a normal web-proxy in that it augments HTTP requests from buyer clients to merchant servers with additional P3P or shop-

ping role data and also may modify the responses. Buyers have their browser configured to use the ShoG as their proxy server, hence there is no need for downloads or
installations on the client side.

The ShoG functionality is implemented as a WBI plugin consisting of several
agents that monitor and edit outgoing HTTP requests and incoming HTTP responses.
WBI is complemented by a SQL database with native XML extensions, which functions as a role cabinet. Finally, the ShoG server also provides the additional management functionalities for skin hopping, cascading, etc.

4.2   Role Representation

Every ShoG user can create one or more shopping role specifications (SRS). An SRS
is organised in three main groups (see Section 2), each with a set of role elements. The
SRS relates to the general P3P data categories in the following way:

- SRS properties element group – P3P demographic data (gender, age…).
- SRS preferences element group – P3P preference data (likes and dislikes…).
- SRS history group – P3P transaction data (logs of activity, purchases made…)

An SRS is represented as an XML document. The structure of SRS XML documents is defined in the ShoG base schema with the namespace 'http://www.shog.ch'.
This schema defines the structure of the actual SRS data of buyers as well as the
structure of SRS proposals, generated by merchants (see next section).

For buyers the base schema is extended to allow also the expression of preferences
regarding the disclosure of the SRS data to merchants using the P3P preference exchange language (APPEL). To integrate the notations of APPEL and SRS, the declarations of the APPEL namespace and the ShoG base schema are imported into the
ShoG buyer schema using the XML Schema 'import namespace' mechanism:

```
<schema targetNamespace="http://www.shog.ch/buyer"
   xmlns="http://www.w3.org/2000/10/XMLSchema"
   xmlns:xsg="http://www.shog.ch
   xmlns:xsgb="http://www.shog.ch/buyer
   xmlns:appel="http://www.w3.org/2001/02/APPELv1"
   <import namespace=
      "http://www.w3.org/2001/02/APPELv1"
      schemaLocation=
      "http://www.w3.org/2001/02/APPELv1.xsd"/>
   <import namespace="http://www.shog.ch
      schemaLocation="http://www.shog.ch/shog.xsd "/>
   <element name="SRS" type="xsgb:SRS"></element>
   <complexType name="SRS" mixed="false">
      <sequence>
         <element ref="xsg:PROPERTIES_GROUP"
            minOccurs="0" maxOccurs="1"/>
         <element ref="xsg:PREFERENCES_GROUP"
            minOccurs="0" maxOccurs="1"/>
         <element ref="xsg:HISTORY_GROUP"
            minOccurs="0" maxOccurs="1"/>
```

```
<element ref="appel:RULESET"
    minOccurs="0" maxOccurs="unbounded"/>
  </sequence>
</complexType>
...
```

The additional declarations in the ShoG schema are based on representations used in our previous work in the area of buyer decision-making [15] and buyer/seller negotiation [17]. Formalisms for likes and dislikes are expressed as unary and binary constraints comparable to the approach undertaken with CCL in the domain of agent communication [20]. In addition, evaluation criteria based on multi-attribute utility theory [15] can be specified by the buyer.

The second building block for the role representation is an ontology. Ontologies are formally specified models of knowledge, which can be used to share semantics among a set of agents – in the ShoG scenario, buyers and merchants. The ShoG ontology defines a containment hierarchy of concepts (e.g. 'preferences' ⇨ 'likes' ⇨ 'taste') with properties such as 'colour' and respective property value domains ('yellow', 'green', etc.). The purpose of this ontology in the ShoG prototype is first to ensure that merchants generate requests for SRS data according to this ontology (thus requesting syntactically and semantically correct SRS elements), and second to guarantee that the SRS data provided by the buyers is 'understandable' for the merchants. Following the approach chosen in our SILKROAD project (see [17] for details), the ShoG ontology is also generated into an XML schema, which extends the ShoG base schema. To reduce the complexity of the ontology representation, it is possible to generate domain-dependent subset schemas, e.g. for the book or music domain. The final set of generated ShoG schemas can be accessed centrally on the ShoG server.

Before the ShoG user starts a shopping session with real merchants, the appropriate role has to be selected. The corresponding SRS data is checked out and used by the ShoG server for the consecutive execution of the ShoG protocol.

4.3 The ShoG Protocol

The ShoG protocol manages the interaction between the buyer's client, the ShoG server, and the merchant's server. It follows the interaction model of the P3P protocol, and therefore does not create any supplementary overhead in the sense of additional interaction steps.

After the role selection, buyers navigate with their browser to the desired web page in the same way as they would without the ShoG in place. The ShoG web-proxy receives the corresponding HTTP request, augments it with a ShoG header tag to indicate that this user is ShoG-enabled ('shogged'), and relays it to the target merchant server.

If the merchant is shogged as well, the server will answer with a P3P/SRS proposal. The SRS proposal specifies the SRS elements the merchant is interested in. To what extent SRS data is disclosed to the shop and for what intended purposes (P3P lists purposes such as 'customisation of site to individuals' or 'contacting visitors for marketing of services or products') depends on the P3P statements issued by the shop in the P3P policy file and on the preferences of the user stated in the APPEL section of the SRS. This negotiation is part of the standard P3P protocol. Upon fulfilment of the buyer's privacy preferences (P3P acceptance), the SRS proposal with the request for SRS data is processed.

Technically this SRS proposal is an XML document instance conforming to the ShoG ontology schema (see above), which is added as XML stream to the HTTP header information. The SRS proposal specifies all SRS elements the merchant is interested in with empty value domains (placeholders). The ShoG replaces the SRS proposal placeholders with the appropriate data (if available, see below). Next, the original HTTP request of the buyer is expanded again, this time with the SRS proposal data generated, and forwarded to the merchant's server.

Receiving this request, the merchant is enabled to use the included SRS data as input for personalisation measures, e.g. shop layout customisation, recommendations, or promotions – compliant to the usage statements committed in the shop's P3P policy. If the merchant is not shogged, the server ignores the ShoG header and the ShoG server will not receive a response with a P3P/SRS proposal but only the URL data originally requested by the buyer. During the entire session with the merchant, the ShoG continues to indicate that this buyer is shogged by adding the ShoG header to the buyer's requests.

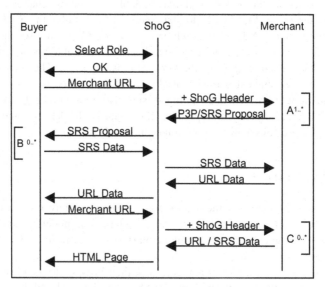

Fig. 1. ShoG protocol.

The ShoG protocol features several optional extensions. First of all the SRS proposal might request for data that is not available in the selected role. In this case, the ShoG server will relay the SRS proposal (rendered in HTML) to the buyer (see option 'B' in Fig. 1.). The buyer may complete the SRS data, which is then passed back to the ShoG server, where the new data is added to the current SRS in the role cabinet and forwarded to the merchant.

The second option is that the merchant server can at anytime (indicated with the 0..n possible repetitions of the SRS proposal step 'A' in Fig. 1.) answer the page request of a shogged user with a new SRS proposal, asking, for instance, for additional preferences. The ShoG server tries to serve this request with the available role data. If the requested data is not available, the SRS proposal is again relayed to the buyer. An alternative possibility for the merchant is to send a standard HTML page requesting SRS data with form fields, complemented by the SRS proposal in the HTTP header. If the ShoG server cannot supply the requested information, this option enables the ShoG to use the HTML page created by the merchant to request the data from the buyer instead of generating its own HTML-rendered SRS proposal. The benefit of this option for the merchant is that the ShoG interaction does not interfere with the merchant's user interface and navigation framework.

The third option may be used if the merchant learned something about the buyer and intends to feed this information back into the selected role specification. Often buyers will not immediately buy one of the products offered in the first view, and instead navigate the shop for a while, possibly answering additional questions about their needs and stating preferences for certain product features and feature ranges. As a result the merchant will learn more about the buyer and thereby is able to expand the role specification. This is also possible at anytime and initiated by the inclusion of the updated SRS data in the HTTP header (see option 'C' in Fig. 1.).

5 Discussion

This paper demonstrates how buyers themselves can reveal their current shopping role to one or more e-Commerce merchants in a managed and efficient way. The goal of the proposed solution, the shopping gate, is to avoid irrelevant or badly-targeted personalisation measures, such as recommending children books on horses to 40-year-old accountants because they once bought such a book for their daughter. To demonstrate our approach in more detail, we presented a ShoG prototype comprising the server architecture, role representation, and interaction protocol. In this final section, our approach is evaluated and compared with related research efforts.

5.1 Evaluation

The primary contribution of the ShoG from a merchant's perspective is that the proposed solution provides a finer-grained and more accurate foundation for web intelligence mechanisms. Upon first contact, the merchant may already receive a rich buyer specification including demographic data, preferences, and a transaction history. Furthermore, this specification represents the shopping background, the role selected by the buyer, which may vary from visit to visit and therefore is a critical input for personalisation measures. The advantage for buyers is first that they can create and maintain shopping role specifications in a centralised way rather than having profiles at several merchants. Second, they can explicitly reveal their current shopping background to a merchant, thus avoiding, for instance, irrelevant recommendations due to profile information situated in the wrong context.

Regarding the requirement of a 'critical mass', the advantage of the proxy-based solution is that it does not require specialised browser technology or extensions on the client's side. All web browsers that allow the specification of a remote proxy server can be used. If extensions on the client's side are not an issue, an alternative to the ShoG server mediating requests and responses between buyers and merchants is to run the proxy directly on the buyer's computer. This is also supported by the WBI architecture. For this scenario, the complete role specification has to be downloaded from the ShoG server to the user's computer. The advantage of this alternative is that the amount of traffic the ShoG server needs to handle is decreased, as it only has to serve users who want to change or update their currently active role.

On the server side however, several components are necessary for a merchant to be 'ShoG-enabled'. The e-Commerce systems of merchants must be not only P3P compliant but also have to parse incoming requests for the ShoG header and to react according to the specifications of the ShoG protocol. In addition, a merchant needs to 'speak' the ShoG SRS data format to request or use specific SRS elements.

The interaction defined by the ShoG protocol is compliant to the P3P interaction, and therefore aligned with an open standard. The SRS data specification, however, is currently proprietary. We are looking at emerging XML standards such as ebXML or dialects complying to the BizTalk framework, but thus far have not found any formalism for the specification of shopping preferences such as evaluation criteria.

To what extent we comply with the other requirements identified (see Section 3) can, as of today, not be answered convincingly – our ShoG design and implementation is still work in progress. We have not addressed security issues yet, and have not conducted comprehensive performance and usability tests.

5.2 Related Work

Seller role management is currently being provided by several e-Commerce merchants such as smarterKids (an Internet shop for educational toys [10]). At smarterKids, users can maintain a profile for each of the children they are buying gifts for. Based on the cognitive style associated with the child, different types of products will be offered. The main disadvantage from a user's perspective is that it is not possible to re-use profiles for shopping at other merchants. Also, at smarterKids, different users cannot access a profile generated by another person. If the father generated a profile for the daughter, the mother can only access the profile if she logs in under the same user name. Seller role management systems such as used by smarterKids can, in principle, be extended with role sharing, but then still cannot support cross-merchant role management.

The idea of 'cookie jars' could provide an alternative method for role management. Users could use a tool that allows them to maintain multiple, distinct, and named stores ('cookie jars') for the cookies they receive from the merchants. Associating jars with distinct roles would allow users to appear to the same merchant in different roles, depending on the cookie jar they select. The advantage of this solution is that it works without any extensions on the server side. The disadvantage is that users cannot share roles, because cookie jars are managed locally. Furthermore, users can also not re-use their role specification with other merchants either, because each merchant stores its own, merchant-specific cookies in the cookie jar. Thus, neither of these two discussed alternative solutions supports n:n role sharing between multiple buyers and merchants.

PrivacyBank.com [9] already offers many services comparable to the functionality envisioned for the ShoG. In addition to privacy protection, 'FormL' is a technology that takes new information typed into form fields at merchant sites and adds it to a central PrivacyBank.com profile, from where it can be dragged back into other forms. 'Info Sharing' is an additional service that allows PrivacyBank.com account holders to share information with other PrivacyBank.com members. In contrast to PrivacyBank.com, our ShoG architecture is based on open standards such as P3P and XML Schema, achieves seamless communication of role data, provides additional functionality such as the possibility for one user to create and maintain multiple roles, captures not only demographic data but also preferences, and is based on a shared ontology to guarantee syntactical and semantical consistency of the role data.

The notion of roles is also discussed in the area of computer security as part of pseudonym systems (see for example [2]). Pseudonyms are used to guarantee anonymity, for instance, during the shopping process, but can always be traced back to one unique identity. The main purpose of the shopping gate is to support personalisation measures, whereas pseudonym systems address trust issues in e-Commerce. Our approach also assumes the existence of one unique buyer identity, which is associated with one or more shopping roles. The concept of a unique identity becomes critical if merchants offer, for instance, discounts or promotions for buyers that can be exercised either only once or only on the basis of demographic characteristics (e.g. age). If a ShoG user assumed the role of student, a bookstore might offer special university discounts, although the buyer in reality is not a student.

5.3 Future Work

From a functionality perspective, our next planned extension is to use the WBI agent mechanisms (for an overview see [1]), especially the monitor, autonomous and generator agent types, to further assist the shopping process, thus creating a real shopping companion plugin for the ShoG according to our ShoG scenario. In one scenario, a monitor agent could record browsed product offers. When triggered by the user, an autonomous agent is then able to evaluate the recorded offers based on the role specification evaluation criteria, and a generator agent could pass the offer comparison back to the user.

Another extension would be to add more negotiation capabilities to the agents representing the buyer. Currently the negotiation capabilities are limited to the disclosure of role specifications according to the P3P protocol. As part of IBM's Zurich Research Laboratory's SILKROAD project (see also [18]) we developed several services that can be used to assist business negotiations in electronic markets. Adding these generic negotiation services (e.g. matchmaking, scoring or mediating) to the ShoG architecture opens up interesting opportunities for advanced buyer representation and autonomous shopping behaviour. Using the matchmaking service, for instance, the ShoG server could already pre-select the 'best' merchants for the buyer.

In addition to an ongoing search for alternative role data formats, we also monitor the efforts related to the Composite Capabilities/Preference Profiles (CC/PP) standard [11]. The goal of CC/PP is to define how client devices express their capabilities and preferences to the server that originates content, so that content can be delivered according to the capabilities of various client devices, such as mobile phones or PDAs. Device specifications are not only an interesting extension to our SRS format, but CC/PP could also evolve to an alternative implementation platform.

However, the most important task upon completion of the prototype is to evaluate the use of the ShoG concept in an experiment with real-world buyers and merchants.

References

1. Barrett R., Maglio P., Kellem, D.: How to Personalize the Web. In: Proceedings of the ACM CHI 97, Atlanta, GA (1997).
2. Berthold O., Köhntopp M.: Identity Management Based On P3P. In: Proceedings Workshop on Design Issues in Anonymity and Unobservability, International Computer Science Institute, Berkeley, CA (2000) 127-145.
3. Burke, R. : Integrating Knowledge-based and Collaborative-filtering Recommender Systems. In: Proceedings AAAI-99 Workshop (AIEC99), Orlando, FL (1999).
4. Clarke R.: Platform for Privacy Preferences: An Overview. Privacy Law & Policy Reporter Vol. 5, No. 2 (1999) 35-39.
5. Erdmann M., Studer R.: Ontologies as Conceptual Models for XML Documents. In: Proceedings of the 12th Workshop for Knowledge Acquisition, Modeling and Management (KAW'99), Banff, Canada (1999).
6. http://computers.cnet.com – visited 02-28-01.
7. http://www.almaden.ibm.com/cs/wbi/ – visited 02-27-01.
8. http://www.cdnow.com – visited 02-28-01.
9. http://www.privacybank.com – visited 03-05-01.
10. http://www.smarterkids.com/ – visited 03-05-01
11. http://www.w3.org/Mobile/CCPP/ – visited 03-05-01.
12. http://www.w3.org/P3P/ – visited 02-27-01.
13. http://www.w3.org/XML/Schema/ – visited 03-05-01.
14. Meyer J.: How to Manage, Negotiate, and Transfer Personal Information on the Web. Master Thesis, FH Hamburg, Germany (1999), available at http://wwwcssrv.almaden.ibm.com/wbi/p3p/.
15. Raiffa H., Keeney R.: Decisions with Multiple Objectives. Wiley, New York (1976).
16. Stolze M.: Soft Navigation in Product Catalogs. In: Research and Advanced Technology for Digital Libraries, edited by C. Nikolaou and C. Stephanidis, Lecture Notes in Computer Science Vol. 1513, Springer, Berlin (1998) 385-396.
17. Ströbel M.: Communication Design for Electronic Negotiations. In: Proceedings of the 10th International World Wide Web Conference, Hong Kong (2001) 9-20.

18. Ströbel M.: Design of Roles and Protocols for Electronic Negotiations. Electronic Commerce Research Journal, Special Issue on Market Design (2001 in press), manuscript available at http://www.zurich.ibm.com/~mis/SilkRoad/ECR_2001.pdf.
19. Trower T.: Creating Conversational Interfaces for Interactive Software Agents. In: Proceedings of ACM CHI 97 Vol. 2 (1997) 198-199.
20. Willmott S., Calisti M., Faltings B., Santiago M., Belakhdar O., Torrens M.: CCL: Expressions of Choice in Agent Communication. The Fourth International Conference on Multi-Agent Systems (ICMAS-2000), Boston MA (2000).

Building Reusable and Adaptable Web-Based Courses

Paola Forcheri, Maria Teresa Molfino, Stefano Moretti, and Alfonso Quarati

Istituto per la Matematica Applicata – Consiglio Nazionale delle Ricerche
Genova - Italy

Abstract. The high costs of production and maintenance of high quality web-based instructional material require to optimize its use, by means of methods and tools that allow, on one hand, to dynamically obtain a variety of courses starting from a set of contents and pedagogical objectives, and, on the other, to build personalised educational paths starting from a course and learner's needs. On this basis, we present an approach to the design and development of educational content aimed at tackling, in a uniform context, both problems of reusability and adaptability of web-based instructional material. The feasibility of our idea has been analysed via an XML-based application oriented to the training of adults (mathematics teachers and University students) on Game Theory. This application is an operative example of the power of XML technology for building educational web systems which satisfy both the author's need of reusing material and the learner's need to avail him/herself of effective educational resources.

1 Introduction

As several experiences show, high quality web-based instructional material seems to be a valuable vehicle to increase long life learning opportunities either if it is used as a support for (distant) classroom activities or as a tool to encourage self-learning, thus suggesting to study methods and to realise tools which help to widen its application field [10]. Within this context, two main research lines are followed. On one hand, methods are studied to enhance the possibilities of reusing material in a variety of educational contexts, according to various attitudes of teacher and different educational objectives [7, 8, 9]. On the other, attention is paid to the problem of providing autonomous learners with material endowed with the capability of adapting the content to be shown to individuals, taking into account their personal motivations, backgrounds, learning styles, attitude towards the topic [3, 4, 6].

Considering the above, we propose an approach to the organisation and structuring of educational content aimed at tackling both problems of reusability and adaptability of web-based instructional material. We realised this approach by means of XML technology [2].

Our proposal has been studied with reference to the development and delivery of Web courses, organised as electronic textbooks about a mathematics topic: Game Theory.

In the following, we will illustrate our work; a description of the XML implementation will be also given.

N. Zhong et al. (Eds.): WI 2001, LNAI 2198, pp. 562–567, 2001.
© Springer-Verlag Berlin Heidelberg 2001

2   The Course Model

The content. The content of the course is modelled by a set of *educational objects,* each one representing a concept according to one author's view and objectives. The educational objects are organised in basic components that establish the granularity of the content.

More formally, an educational object *EO* is defined as a collection of pairs $<wbc_1, wbc_2, .., wbc_n>$. Each pair wbc_i, called *weighted basic component*, comprises a *basic component identifier id_i* which identifies a basic component, and a *weight w_i*, that is its cognitive contribution within the context defined by the educational object. We call *absolute degree δ* of the educational object the maximum of these weights.

Two advantages derive from this approach. Firstly, the same basic component can be used to construct, in a modular way, a variety of educational object, that may be used in various courses. Secondly, the different weights that can be assigned to a basic component give us better control on the student. For example, the definition of limit of a function, which is a basic element in the formation of the concept of limit of a function, is referenced in the educational object that represents the concept of Taylor's series.

In our case, the educational objects present a 'regular' structure, which establishes an ordering relation on their basic components (definitions, theorem statements, proofs, intermediate text, exercises, examples,...). Thus, educational objects can be defined by using a grammar expressed by EBNF notation.

The structure. We define a course according to two different perspectives: *composition structure* and *pedagogical structure*.

The composition structure refers to the content organisation with respect to exposition needs, such as sequentiality or hierarchy.

The pedagogical structure logically partitions the content of a course in *L layers* on the basis of the cognitive difficulties and the pedagogical relevance for the expected users. For example, in our case (Game Theory) we can have different kinds of users, such as Mathematics students, and Economics students. The courses, at least in Italy, can be quite similar, but there are notable differences as to the examples and exercises. This means that, from a pedagogical point of view, the same content can pertain to different courses but in each of these it plays a different educational role.

More precisely, we represent the course as a structured list of pairs $[<EO_i, j>$: $i=1,..,n; j=0,..,L(C); L(C) \leq n]$, where EO_i is an educational object, and j is its *layer*. The layer represents the cognitive contribution of that object to the course. Let $D(C) = max(\{\delta(EO_k)+j : <EO_k, j> \in C\})$ be the *degree* of course C.

Personalizing the course. Given the above definition of pedagogical structure, a criterion is needed to establish accessibility, for an individual student, to the course content. A criterion can be, for example, to pass a set of tests; another one can be the content space already explored; or, it can be used a combination of these two cases.

Our approach allows the teacher to select case by case the most suitable criterion. This choice facilitates the reuse and the adaptability of a course to different educational contexts and individual needs.

Each *accessibility criterion* Π is represented by a set of *conditions* $\{p_0, p_1, ..., p_{D(C)}\}$ that have to be satisfied by a student, to go deeper into the course. These conditions state the accessibility to the content according to the following:

- if $p_{h,}$ $0 \leq h \leq D(C)$ is satisfied then wbc_i is *h-accessible*, $wbc_i = (id_i, w_i) \in EO$, $w_i = h\text{-}j$, $<EO,j> \in C$
- if $p_{h,}$ $0 \leq h \leq L(C)$ is satisfied then EO is *h-accessible*, $<EO,h> \in C$

Let us define the *knowledge state* of an individual student U with respect to a course C, as the tuple $<s,a,f>$, $0 \leq s \leq a \leq f \leq D(C)$ where s represents the initial knowledge of U, f is the target knowledge to be acquired by U and a is the *actual knowledge* of U. The actual knowledge a is given as follows: a student U of C moves from the knowledge state $<s,a,f>$ to the knowledge state $<s,a+1,f>$ *if and only if* $p_a \in \Pi$ is satisfied.

Accordingly, we can see *h-accessible* content (both base components and objects) as the knowledge that has to be acquired by a student before he/she may deal with *h+1-accessible* content.

3   The Model Implementation

The system realising the model relies on XML technology. This architectural and implementation choice derives from several considerations:
- The intrinsic XML capability of specifying and extending a language via a Data Type Definition, directly solves the problem of specifying the modular structure of the educational objects and of the course [1];
- XML realises a clear separation between data, modelled as XML documents and their representation, obtained via the association of XSLT stylesheets to them. Thus, it naturally reflects the need of modelling the content of a course independently of the different personalisation needs [5];
- There is a direct mapping of a EBNF representation into an XML DTD, that facilitates the realisation of tools aimed to support the authoring of educational content characterised, as in our case, by a regular structure;
- XML is a standard web technology, thus allowing us to construct and deliver a system that is really independent from proprietary/specific solutions hence portable to different platforms.

System architecture. The system presents the course material as HTML pages accessed via an extendible index that reflects the course structure. When the student asks for a page, its content is dynamically created, starting from the educational objects pertaining to the course and from the actual knowledge of the student himself (see Fig. 1).

The content creation process is managed by Java servlets that handle run-time information such as user state, style of presentation, etc. and create on-the-fly XML code (which assembles the content of other static XML files). This code is coupled

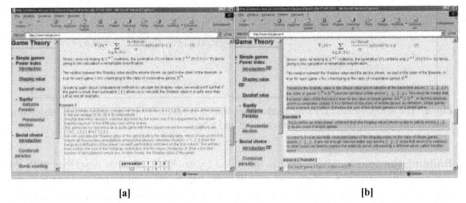

[a]   [b]

Fig. 1. Views of the course according to successive student's knowledge states

with the appropriate XSLT stylesheet file and processed by the Xalan XSLT processor of the Apache XML Project. The whole task is supported by Tomcat 3.2.1 servlet engine of the Apache Jakarta project which interoperate with the Web server to deliver the content.

This approach allows to handle contextually reusability, through modularization, and adaptability, via personalisation. In the following, we discuss these aspects separately.

Assembling the content. This task is accomplished by a XSLT style sheet on the basis of the course content stored into two kinds of XML files: the ones containing the educational objects and those containing the basic components. In this way we separate the structure of an educational object (given by the list of its children tag elements, i.e. weighted basic components) from its physical representation, thus allowing a basic components to be referred by different objects.

The 'glue' between the two kinds of files is given by two XML DTD features: the definition of external entities and the specification of ID type attributes associated, in our case, to the basic components. These features are at the basis of the reusability mechanism we adopt: via its identifier each basic component (or educational object) can be included in other objects.

Personalising the content. The content is selected starting from the actual knowledge state a of the user at hand. Via the weight associated to each basic component of an educational object, the system filters the a-accessible basic components. This is obtained through the use of XSLT template rules, like the one in Fig. 2 which shows the matching of each basic component's weight against the user state.

While filtering elements, XSLT allows us to easily vary the background colours associated to the children elements of an educational object according to their different weights, so emphasising their cognitive meaning (compare Fig.1 [a] and [b]).

```
<xsl:template match="thc[@weight&lt;=//user/@state] |
                      thp[@weight&lt;=//user/@state]>
.......................................
</xsl:template>
```

Fig. 2. The template rule relating to the selection of theorem 's claim and proof basic components component (through tag element `thc` and `thp`).

Building the course. The course is modelled by an XML file that describes both the composition structure, by means of the tag elements `paragraph` and `educationalobject`, and the pedagogical structure, by assigning the attribute `layer` to the element `educationalobject` (see Fig. 3).

```
<!ELEMENT course (paragraph|educationalobject)+>
<!ATTLIST course
       name     CDATA #IMPLIED
>
<!ELEMENT paragraph (paragraph|educationalobject)*>
<!ATTLIST paragraph
       name     CDATA #IMPLIED
>
<!ELEMENT educationalobject (#PCDATA)*>
<!ATTLIST educationalobject
       name     CDATA #IMPLIED
       eoid     CDATA #REQUIRED
       layer    CDATA #REQUIRED
>
```

Fig. 3. Excerpt from the course structure DTD.

The association of a style sheet to the XML file that models the course permits us to construct the course index that support the navigation.

To this aim, we act as follows. Each item of the index is given by the name of the corresponding educational object. When the student moves from a state $<s,k-1,f>$ to a state $<s,k,f>$ (for example because a test has been performed successfully) the system changes the course index as follows:
1. It turns the name of each k-accessible educational object into an active link;
2. All s-accessible objects (s<k) including k-accessible basic components are augmented with the icon 'new'.

This mechanism is realised, through XSLT statements, by using: the value of the layer; the value associated to the actual knowledge of the student; the degree D of the course; and the absolute degree δ of each educational object. All these parameters are mapped into XML-tagged structures.

4 Concluding Remarks

The production of web-based courses is a time-consuming and costly task. As a consequence, their diffusion is possible if teachers can avail themselves of already developed educational resources, and adapt them to their specific teaching objectives. This possibility is greatly increased by coupling the use of modelling standards for the educational process with the use of standard technologies.

Our proposal, which operatively analyses the potential of XML to realise educational systems which fit both authors' and users' needs, constitutes a contribution in this direction.

References

[1]   Bosak J. & Bray T. (1999) XML and the Second-Generation Web, *Scientific American*, May 1999.

[2]   Bray T., Paoli J., Sperberg-McQueen C.M. & Maler E. (eds.) (2000) *Extensible Markup Language (XML) 1.0 - W3C Recommendation (Second Edition)*, http://www.w3.org/TR/2000/REC-xml-20001006.

[3]   Brusilovsky P., Kobsa A. & Vassileva J. (eds.), (1998) *Adaptive Hypertext and Hypermedia Systems*, Kluwer Academic Publishers, Dordrecht.

[4]   Brusilovsky P., Stock O. & Strapparava C. (eds.) (2000) *Proceedings of Adaptive Hypermedia and Adaptive Web-Based Systems*, Springer-Verlag LNCS, Berlin.

[5]   Clark J. (eds.) (1999) *XSL Transformations (XSLT) Version 1.0 - W3C Recommendation* (16 November 1999), http://www.w3.org/TR/1999/REC-xslt-19991116.

[6]   De Bra P. (1998) Adaptive Hypermedia on the Web: Methods, Technology and Applications, *Proceedings of WebNet 98 - World Conference of the WWW, Internet & Intranet*.

[7]   Forte E., Haenni F., Warkentyne K., Duval E., Cardinaels K., Vervaet E., Hendrikx K., Wentland Forte M. & Simillion F. (1999) *Semantic and Pedagogic Interoperability Mechanisms in the ARIADNE Educational Repository*, ACM SIGMOD Record, Vol. 28, No. 1, pp. 20-25, March 1999.

[8]   IEEE Computer Society - Learning Technology Standards Committee (sponsored by) (2001) *Draft Standard for Learning Technology - Learning Technology Systems Architecture (LTSA)*, IEEE P1484.1/D7, 2001-03-11, http://ltsc.ieee.org/doc/wg1/IEEE_1484_01_D07_LTSA.doc.

[9]   Weibel S., Kunze J., Lagoze C. & Wolf M. (1998) *Dublin Core Metadata for Resource Discovery*, The Internet Society, September 1998. ftp://ftp.isi.edu/in-notes/rfc2413.txt

[10] Schreiber D.A., Berge Z.L. (Eds.) (1998) *Distance Training*, Jossey-Bass Publishers.

Group Learning Support System for Software Engineering Education – Web-Based Collaboration Support between the Teacher Side and the Student Groups –

Atsuo Hazeyama, Akiko Nakako, Sachiko Nakajima, and Keiji Osada

Tokyo Gakugei University, Department of Mathematics and Informatics
4-1-1 Nukuikita-machi, Koganei-shi, Tokyo 184-8501, Japan
hazeyama@u-gakugei.ac.jp

Abstract. Software development is knowledge-intensive work. In a software project, various types of problems need to be resolved. One approach to acquire necessary knowledge for software development in university education is for the students to experience project-based software development. For this kind of education to succeed collaboration is important, both between the teacher side (teacher and TAs) and student groups and within the group members. This paper proposes a collaborative software development learning environment that in particular focuses on supporting collaboration between the student groups and the teacher side.

1 Introduction

With the rapid permeation of information and communication technology such as the Internet into our society and with the ever-increasing advancement of user needs, the demand for software system development and for increasingly complex software systems is on the rise. This has created a need for capable persons who can design and implement software systems; thus the rearing of such persons has become a crucial point. Since software development is knowledge-intensive work, it is not easy to train persons to accomplish this kind of work. Furthermore, software projects give rise to a wide variety of problems that must be resolved. To solve these problems, software developers need to acquire not only theoretical knowledge pertaining to software engineering but also know-how and/or experience by putting this knowledge to practical use. One approach to acquiring the software development knowledge needed for university education purposes is for the students to gain experience in project-based software development. To enable students to gain such experience, our department has been and is now conducting a class in which the goal is the design and development of practical software systems [4].

For this kind of education to succeed collaboration is important, both between the teacher side (teacher and TAs) and student groups and within the group members. An example of such collaboration is the teacher side giving students directions, suggestions, or advice based on situations that the students are confronted with.

N. Zhong et al. (Eds.): WI 2001, LNAI 2198, pp. 568–573, 2001.
© Springer-Verlag Berlin Heidelberg 2001

Time constraints must be strictly adhered to in this kind of education. And since it is impossible for collaboration to be achieved in a face-to-face fashion each and every time, an effective and efficient collaborative learning environment is required.

This paper considers types of collaboration in software engineering education between the teacher side and a student group and proposes a Web-based system for supporting this collaboration.

2   Collaboration to Be Supported in Software Engineering Education and Requirements for Supporting It

In the class our department is conducting, the teacher side plays the roles of a client who orders software development, the manager of the group, and an adviser. These roles require collaboration between the teacher side and the student groups respectively as follows:
* the role of a client requires formal collaboration such as inspecting the adherence to requirement specifications and testing the acceptability of deliverables. From the viewpoint of the software life cycle process, acceptance testing is an activity to verify adherence to requirements
* the role of a manager requires inspection of artifacts created during the software development processes and management reports
* the role of an adviser requires answering questions from groups and/or making announcements to all students

To fulfill these requirements, the following functions are necessary:
* Inspection support
* Acceptance testing support
* Informal communication

These activities have been practiced in the class for several years. Based on the experience gained in these classes, we propose the below-listed functions specific to software engineering education.

Inspection support. Software inspection has been widely acknowledged as an effective technique for detecting defects in artifacts [1]. To date a number of inspection process support systems have been developed [2, 6]. These systems have provided solutions for various important aspects of inspection, including realization of paperless inspection, sharing of comments, and enabling inspectors to perform inspections on their workstation.

In education classes of this type, several groups do their exercises in parallel (in our case, around eight groups run in parallel each year) and each group creates several types of requirements and/or design specifications. The teacher side has to grasp the progress of each artifact of each group, and give comments and/or suggestions as necessary.

It is necessary to ascertain which artifacts each member of the teacher side has finished making comments on. Furthermore, inspections may be iterated a number of times for the inspection of an artifact to be completed. In such cases, inspections must be performed by referring to the comments which were made in the last meeting.

Acceptance testing support. In acceptance testing, the clients test the delivered system according to the scenario of practical usage. If problems are detected during the testing they request modifications be made, and the developer must then find a way to solve the problems. Problem management involves tracking the reported problems so that they can be completely eliminated. The goals here are to convey necessary information among participants promptly, to track the problems comprehensively, and to shorten the time needed to resolve them by, for example, retrieving similar problems. Several commercial problem-tracking products are now available; they support workflow by issuing problem reports for as long as necessary. In doing so, they provide several types of charts and reports.

Our experience in the education field has shown that problem-detecting ability differs significantly between students and the teacher side. To fill this gap in the issuing of problem reports, we provide viewpoint information based on quality attributes for a detected problem.

Informal communication support. Informal communication such as Q&A requires a central repository that manages data and shares information. In addition, it must be as easy to use as an ordinary E-mail system.

We intend to implement our system on the WWW because doing so will enable asynchronous collaboration in distributed environments to be realized easily and a uniform user interface to be provided.

3 Collaboration Support System

3.1 Overview

This section describes the collaboration support system we have developed for software engineering education, a system which satisfies the requirements described in the previous section. The functions outlined below are parts of the whole system that we have been developing [3, 5]. The system is composed of three sub-systems, one each for group organization, textbook creation, and development process support. The development process support sub-system is the main one; it supports template-based document creation, information sharing via a Web browser, collaboration, and collection of metrics data. Figure 1 shows the architecture of this sub-system.

These three sub-systems are integrated via DBs, and the system as a whole is implemented as CGI programs written in Perl programming language.

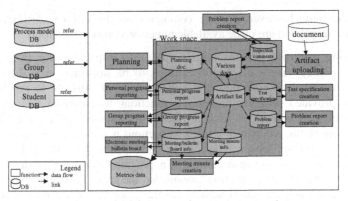

Fig. 1. Architecture of development process support sub-system

3.2 Inspection Process Support

Figure 2 shows how our system supports the inspection process. Prior to the inspection meeting, a group registers the artifacts to be inspected into the system. The system analysis and design specifications are usually created not only with texts but also diagrams, figures, tables and so on by using word processors, presentation tools, and drawing tools. The documents created by using the tools are uploaded into the system.

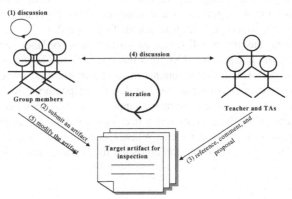

Fig. 2. Inspection process

Once a group selects the artifacts and requests inspection, a notification message requesting inspection is sent to the teacher side. When an inspector (a teacher or TAs) selects an artifact of the group, a window appears displaying the artifact and denoting comments. Each inspector can write comments independently, and can view the comments of other inspectors. After denoting comments the inspector decides whether re-inspection is needed or not. When all inspectors finished inspecting, the group is automatically informed of the results. An inspector who judges that there is no need for re-inspection does not have to participate in the next inspection meeting.

He or she may, however, provide comments on the artifact. Artifacts that have undergone inspection are made available to persons outside the group.

Monitoring progress. The teacher side performs inspections for all groups. Since each group may have a number of artifacts to be inspected, it is difficult for the teacher side to determine how the development of artifacts is progressing. We therefore provided progress monitoring functions to eliminate this problem. The progress of development of each artifact is represented by a value denoting the development status, and that of artifact inspections is represented by a state transition diagram. Values are assigned according to whether the artifact is "waiting for inspection", whether the inspection is "in progress", or whether the inspection is "finished". "Waiting for inspection" means that the group is creating or modifying the artifact and the teacher side is waiting for the group to request inspection. Once the group submits an artifact and requests that it be inspected, the status value is changed to "in progress". After all inspectors have written their comments and decided whether a re-inspection is needed, the status value reverts to "waiting for inspection" and the group is notified of the results. Once all inspectors have approved the artifact, the status becomes "finished". The system also shows the total number of inspections that were made.

Support of version management and configuration management. As the development of artifacts progresses, the artifacts (documents and/or programs) may need to be revised. This makes version management essential, particularly in the inspection process. The inspection results may indicate that new artifacts need to be created. This means configuration management is also required. In configuration management, the group must specify which version of which artifact is valid.

When required, the group will revise an artifact in accordance with the inspection comments from the teacher and TAs. In some cases re-inspection is required. When re-inspection is performed, the comments made during the first inspection need to be taken up at the next inspection meeting, so that the inspectors can use them to check the submitted artifacts. These comments cannot, however, be carried over when an artifact is registered in the system and a user can specify its file name. The system must therefore manage the file names. When registering an artifact, the system asks the user whether it is a revised version and what the version number is.

3.3 Problem Management

We also developed a problem management system that manages problems detected during the acceptance testing. This system includes the functions given below.
* A web-based template for submitting problem reports and having the developer return them to the persons who submitted them
* workflow management of each problem report
* notification via E-mail when counter-action is initiated
* data management
* information retrieval for each field and status information
* graphs that show details for each group and for the class as a whole

3.4 Q&A Bulletin Board

We also provided the system with BBS-based informal communication support with the following functions:

* Bulletin board systems (BBS) are provided for announcements and for Q&A sessions between individuals within a group, among groups, and between groups and the teacher side.
* The discussion history for each item can be viewed.
* Since the Web is essentially a pull-type system, it is important to issue notifications when collaborating with the Internet. When a message is submitted to a BBS, an E-mail message with its URL is automatically sent to notify the sender that it has been received. To avoid discussions of messages being carried out via E-mail, we use E-mail only for sending notification messages.
* When responses to a question or proposal are not submitted within a certain period of time (defined by the user), a message requesting a response is automatically sent.

4   Conclusion

This paper described types of collaboration in software engineering education between the teacher side and student groups and proposed a Web-based collaboration support system.

Acknowledgements. This study is supported by a Grant-in Aid for the Encouragement of Young Scientists (No. A 12780120) from The Ministry of Education, Science, Sports and Culture of Japan.

References

1. Gilb, T., Graham, D.: Software Inspection. Addison Wesley Publishing (1993)
2. Harjumaa, L., Tervonen, I.: Virtual Software Inspections over the Internet. Proc. of the Third ICSE Workshop on Software Engineering over the Internet (2000) http://sern.ucalgary.ca/~maurer/icse2000ws/ICSE2000WS.html
3. Hazeyama, A., Miyadera, Y., Xiangning, L. Yokoyama, S., Souma, T.: Development of Group Programming Support System. Proc. of the 7th International Conference on Computers in Education (ICCE99), IOS Press (1999) Vol. 1, 669 – 676
4. Hazeyama, A.: An Education Class on Design and Implementation of An Information System in A University and Its Evaluation. Proc. of the 24th International Computer Software and Applications Conference (COMPSAC2000), IEEE CS Press (2000) 21-27
5. Hazeyama, A., Osada, K., Miyadera, Y., Yokoyama, S.: An Education Support System of Information System Design and Implementation and Lessons Learned from Its Application. Proc. of the 7th Asia Pacific Software Engineering Conference, IEEE CS Press (2000) 392-396
6. Shoenig, S.: Supporting a Software Engineering Course with Lotus Notes. Proc. of the International Conference on Software Engineering Education and Practice, IEEE CS (1998)

The Intelligent Electronic Shopping System Based on Bayesian Customer Modeling*

Junzhong Ji, Lei Zheng, and Chunnian Liu

Dept. of Computer Science, Beijing Polytechnic University, Beijing 100022, China
ai@bjpu.edu.cn

Abstract. The rapid development of computer network technology makes the electronic shopping come into fashion. In this paper, first we analyze the common electronic shopping system and discuss the bottlenecks that restrict its development. To solve these problems, individual product information should be provided to customers. Then we propose a Bayesian customer model and apply it in our intelligent electronic shopping system, which can predict the requirements of customers and provide them with individual product information actively.

1 Introduction

In recent years, electronic commerce (EC) [5] has become the focus of the IT industry with the rapid development of Internet technology. EC is a conduct to support the decision-making of the manager by searching and obtaining information through Internet. Electronic shopping is a form that is the most common in EC systems and the most relevant to the daily life of people. Electronic shopping has surpassed several obstacles of traditional commerce, such as territory, time and the price comparison.

However, there are some bottlenecks that restrict the development of electronic shopping.

(1) The information of products usually takes the form of multimedia whose data are so immense that transferring information is confined by bandwidth.

(2) At present, most of commerce web sites show the same web pages to every customer, but the favorite issues and needs vary from customers, so it is hard to satisfy every customer.

To solve these problems, we suggest that merchants should actively provide individual product information for customers, which can save time and bandwidth. Nowadays, it is a significant task of IT industry to provide customers with indiv-idual information service, and the main idea of this paper is how to fulfill this task.

The remainder of this paper is organized as follows: section 2 introduces the structure of our electronic shopping system. In section 3, we discuss how to gain useful information in communicating with customer. We then show in section 4 how

---

* The work is supported by the Natural Science Foundation of China (NSFC), Beijing Municipal Natural Science Foundation (BMNSF) and Chinese 863 High-Tech Program.

N. Zhong et al. (Eds.): WI 2001, LNAI 2198, pp. 574–578, 2001.
© Springer-Verlag Berlin Heidelberg 2001

to predict customer's requirements in terms of Bayesian customer model. In section 5, finally, we present some conclusions.

2   Structure of the Electronic Shopping System

At present, there are three kinds of EC's management modes: B to B (business to business), B to C (business to consumer) and C to C (consumer to consumer). The development of B to B and B to C is very fast, and the Electronic Shopping System belongs to B to C. In our electronic shopping system, all purpose B/S (browser/server) structure is adopted. The subsystems of server-end are as follows:

- Application Server:

Application server acts as both business platform and certificate authority server (CA). It deals with business information, manages relational database, signs membership certification and maintains certification and blacklist.

- Web Server:

The merchant uses web server releasing information. In addition, a customer with a browser uses web server dealing with business.

With the help of this framework of the system, merchants are able to import thousands of merchandise information on their web server for attracting customers to compare, choose and buy goods on their web sites.

3   Data Mining in Customer Information

Taking advantage of customers' information, our electronic shopping system could provide customers with individual service. In this section we will discuss how to abstract useful customers information from commerce data.

As the commerce operation increasing, commerce data will increase remarkably. Discovering available information (pattern) and knowledge (rules) from these data could help the merchants to direct the management of market and provide the merchants with marketing strategies. The technology of data mining is useful to abstract valuable conclusive information from original data [10], and our electronic shopping system uses the data mining technology based on rule classification. The original data in the system include customer basic information (i.e. profession, age, gender, credit card number etc), customer behavior record and knowledge database. Here custom-er behavior record, which is changed frequently, refers to shopping record and logs generated when the customer browsing the web site. Knowledge database refers to the analytical rules database concerning consumption, which is used to analyze customer information and classify different consumptive colony. Data in knowledge database represent the professional knowledge that is a combination of the Consumption Psychology, Cognition Science and Artificial Intelligence. According to the knowledge in knowledge database, our electronic shopping system obtains the useful information by which we can predict the potential consumption (discuss in section 4), and then saves the information into the refined data database identified by customers' ID.

Because the customer information maybe is imperfect, a fuzzy method is used to classify customers and divide them into these categories: strong affirmation is 1, affirmation is 0.8, weak affirmation is 0.6, unclear is 0.5, weak negation is 0.4, negation is 0.2 and strong negation is 0. For example, the present attribute-values of a customer are: enjoying recreation (0.6), buying furniture (0.8), being a merchant (1), good income (0.8) and so on. At the same time, in order to analyze the relationship of these attribute-values and the merchandise requirements of this customer, the conclusion cannot be drawn simply based on several pieces of professional knowledge, because the relationship concerns many factors (habit, fashion, psychology). Therefore, we suggest Bayesian network modeling technology [1,2,3].

4   Bayesian Customer Model

A Bayesian belief network (BBN), represented by a directed acyclic graph, describes the joint probability distribution governing a set of variables by specifying a set of conditional independence assumptions, along with a set of local conditional probabilities [6]. The structure of BBN in our electronic shopping system is shown in figure 1, each node is a boolean valued variable, whose value can be obtained from refined database in data mining.

The main idea of modeling the BBN in figure 1 can be expressed as follows:

• Because customers purchase commodity frequently and periodically, our system may discover valued information from customers' regular records and history records.
• Some merchandise that a user has bought often raise his potential requirement for others, so our system could dope out his short-term life plan.
• User's requirement degree for some type of merchandise always depends on his interest and hobby.
• User's purchasing power is an essential factor that affects his requirement.
• User's consumption of some type of merchandise connects closely to special holidays and current fashion.

In figure 1, the links and the probability tables encode the probabilistic relations between merchandise and interest and life plan. The probability values of other nodes in the figure, for instance furniture & decoration, fishing gear and platina accouterment, are just the requirement degree that the electronic shopping system predicts. In figure 1, a conditional probability table is given for each variable with predecessors, describing the probability distribution for that variable given the value of its immediate predecessors, while a priori probability table is attached to each node without Predecessors. The probabilities in these tables are acquired in terms of experiential data and expert's estimation, and experiential data are obtained from the investigation of markets.

In light of above, we have presented a Bayesian customer model in our system. In the following, we will briefly discuss probabilistic inference process in our system.

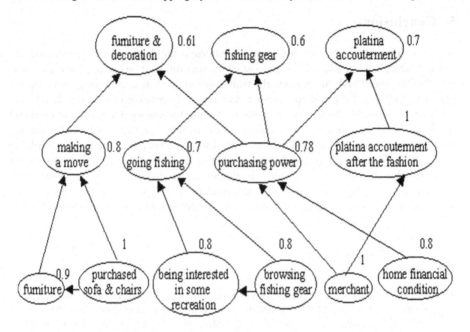

Fig. 1. The customer Bayesian model at some certain time

At first, the probability of each node in Bayesian model is initialized by the user data. For example, if a customer's occupation, purchased merchandise and the pursuing fashion are known, the values of these nodes are set as observed data and their probabilities are set to 1. Then, in terms of the initial (or priori) probability and conditional probability of each node, we use some probabilistic inference algorithm [7,8,9] to update the probability of each nonevidential node. In order to reduce the complexity of the algorithm, we choose a approximate algorithm called Gibbs Sampling [4]. The modification of these probabilities reflects how the evidential nodes affect other nodes (see figure 1). In this way, the probability of each merchandise, called requirement degree of some merchandise, can be calculated. In our experiment, the requirement degree of the furniture & decoration is 0.61, while fishing gear is 0.60 and platina accouterment is 0.7. If the requirement degree of some merchandise is over a certain threshold (for instance 0.6), the electronic shopping system will actively send the customer an electronic advertisement of this merchandise. The information of the merchandise whose requirement degree is slightly below the threshold is also saved in a database, because it is useful to generate the customer's individual web page.

According to what we discussed above, the Bayesian model can trace the thinking of customers, predict customers' potential needs, and send available information to customers in advance.

5 Conclusions

As a new form of trade, electronic shopping shortens the distance between the merchant and the customer, and lowers the cost of interaction, so it has an apparent advantage. On the other hand, the present electronic shopping system can not provide customer with individual information service, as a result its development is restricted. As BBNs have proven to be a very powerful technique for knowledge representation and reasoning under uncertainty, we designed an electronic shopping system based on Bayesian customer model, which could perform following functions: acquiring available information from user's original data, predicting customer's potential requirements with probabilistic inference, and actively suppling customers with individual service.

In summary, by means of BBNs the electronic shopping system could become more efficient, and the implementation of our system would be of great value in EC.

References

1. Chulani, S., Boehm, B., & Steece, B, (1999) Bayesian analysis of empirical software engineering cost models, IEEE Transactions on Software Engineering, 25(4), 573-583.
2. Conati, C., Gertner, A., Vanlehn, K., & Druzdzel, M. (1997a,). On-line student modeling for coached problem solving using Bayesian networks. Paper presented at the Proceedings of the 1997 User modeling Conference, Sardinia.
3. Conati, C., & Vanlehn, K. (1996a). POLA: a student modeling framework for Probabilistic On-Line Assessment of problem solving performance. In Proceedings of the Fifth International Conference on User Modeling , 75-82.
4. HRYCEJ,T. (1990). Gibbs sampling in Bayesian networks. Artificial Intelligence, 46, 351–363.
5. Kalakota, R., & Whinston, A.B. (1996). Frontiers of Electronic Commerce. New York: Addison-Wesley Longman.
6. Mitchell, T. (1997). Machine Learning. New York: The McGraw-Hill Companies, Inc.
7. Pearl, J. (1987). Evidential Reasoning Using Stochastic Simulation of Causal Models. Artificial Intelligence, 32, 245-257
8. Pearl, J. (1988). Probabilistic reasoning in intelligent systems, Morgan Kaufmann, Palo Alto, CA.
9. Pearl, J., & Fusion. (1986). Propagation and structuring in belief networks. Artificial Intelligence, 29, 241-288.
10. Silberschatz, A., Korth, H, F., &Sudarshan, S.(1999). Database System Concepts, Third Edition. New York: The McGraw-Hill Companies, Inc.

Leveraging a Web-Aware Self-Organization Map Tool for Clustering and Visualization

Sheng-Tun Li

Department of Information Management,
National Kaohsiung First University of Science and Technology,
2 Juoyue Road, Nantz District, Kaohsiung 811, Taiwan
stli@ccms.nkfust.edu.tw

Abstract. The self-organization map (SOM) neural network has been recognized as a successful paradigm for clustering and visualization in a large variety of real-world applications. There exist a number of useful stand-alone SOM tools, however, they cannot be adapted to the new-generation web environment. In addition, different user interfaces required for operation and the heterogeneity of platforms where the tools run on prevent them from appeal. In this paper, we propose a web-aware SOM tool which integrates the computationally powerful SOM_PAK and the vivid Nenet tools to augment the advantages of each. The proposed SOM tool is capable of delimiting the desired clusters by adopting two-level network topology and silhouette coefficients.

1 Introduction

The self-organization map (SOM) network [3] has been shown as the most successful paradigm in unsupervised neural networks. There exist diverse SOM tools as freeware, shareware, or off-the-shelf systems, each of which has its own merits and pitfalls [1]. However, most of the tools are stand-alone applications which cannot accommodate with the new-generation web and distributed environment. Besides, there are differences exist in the user interfaces of these tools thus it needs well-trained researchers to operate. A cost-effective approach to overcome such limitations is to integrate them in a web-based environment so that the features of each can be augmented and a unified GUI can be achieved. However, such an undertaking is a non-trivial task, in addition to the usual hustle, source code could be unavailable, utilities to be integrated may be implemented in different programming languages, and platforms on which they run may be also different. Recently, the development of interoperable architectures has paved a feasible way towards system integration under such considerations [5]. In this study, we propose a web-aware SOM tool, namely wSOM, which rejuvenates two "official" standalone SOM legacies, SOM_PAK and Nenet, in different platforms to highlight the distinguished features of computational power and vivid visualization, respectively. In addition to the original functionality of SOM, wSOM is enhanced with the capability of identifying the desired optimal clusters by

N. Zhong et al. (Eds.): WI 2001, LNAI 2198, pp. 579–583, 2001.
© Springer-Verlag Berlin Heidelberg 2001

adopting a two-level SOM architecture and by using the so-called silhouette co-efficients [2]. This paper is organized as follows. The underlying technologies for the proposed tool is presented in Sect. 2. The web-aware SOM tool is described in Sect. 3. In Sect. 4, the experiment result on the iris and air pollution data is discussed. Sect. 5 concludes the paper.

2 Underlying Technologies

In this session, we briefly review the underlying technologies used for developing wSOM. SOM_PAK includes four major utilities: (1) *randinit* for initializing the reference vectors of a Kohonen map randomly and defining its parameters, (2) *vsom* for facilitating the learning of SOM, (3) *qerror* for evaluating the learning performance, and (4) *vcal* for labeling the input data onto the neurons in the trained map. The output of SOM_PAK is the so-called *cod* file which contains the trained reference vectors with labels. In contrast to SOM_PAK, Nenet provides an Windows-based tool for the tasks performed in SOM_PAK. One of the signif-icant advantages of Nenet is the colorful generation of SOM visualization. Nenet has SOM_PAK-compatible file format which facilitates the potential integration with SOM_PAK.

Java RMI (Remote Method Invocation) is one of the major representatives of distributed object computing (DOC), which has demonstrated as an emerg-ing technology for dealing with heterogeneity issues in programming language, platform, and object model [5]. In RMI, a server-side service provider remotely defines interfaces to be invoked for an object, implements them in a Java appli-cation server, and generates the server skeleton and the client stub. The provider instantiates the remote object and registers it with the RMI bootstrap registry server to make it available for remote invocation. On the other side, a client locates a reference to the remote object by looking up the registry and calls a method on it. RMI is powerful enough as CORBA except that local and remote objects must be implemented in Java. Such limitation can be relieved by the ob-ject wrapper such as the JNI (Java Native Interface) or native process facility, which offers a subtle solution toward interfacing to a native system without re-engineering the source code. In addition, accompanied with an omnifarious set of Java APIs, thus RMI shows a greatly attractive solution and a flexible software infrastructure for developing secure and portable distributed applications. As a result, RMI is adopted as the DOC paradigm in this study.

3 Web-Aware SOM

The web-aware SOM tool, named as wSOM, is component-based system in na-ture. Fig. 1 shows the architecture of the proposed wSOM. It contains wSOM Client, Web Server, Clustering Component, and Visualization Component. The web server acts as an object repository for downloading wSOM client applet to eliminate the need for installing the component. Besides, it can overcome the shortcoming of stateless nature in HTTP/CGI so a wSOM client is allowed to directly interact with objects in the server. wSOM Client presents the GUI for accessing the back-end services of clustering and visualization. The end-user is granted to create a new spreadsheet or to import a local data file of interest to be explored via the HTTP protocol. Clustering Component takes in charge of clustering and is composed of several small components as follows. SOM_PAK Agent sequentially invokes the four major utilities in SOM_PAK, as mentioned in Sect. 2, which are wrapped as Java objects. It also records all transitional processing results and the final resulting object, a codebook file representing the "cod" file in SOM_PAK.

In contrast to the original SOM_PAK tool, the SOM_PAK component is enhanced to allow concurrent invocations. SOM_PAK Session Manager keeps the state of each invocation (session) by maintaining a session hash table. SOM_PAK RMI Registry is the bootstrap registry to make the clustering service available for remote invocation so that each wSOM client may locate and send service requests to. Since SOM_PAK and object wrappers are implemented in C and Java, respectively, SOM_PAK Component can run on any platforms where C compilers and JVM can be deployed to. For visualization, Visualization Component offers vivid graphic representation of internal structures of data explored. Nenet Agent invokes Nenet Object, an object wrapper for the Nenet tool on Microsoft Windows to initialize the color map with the codebook, generated by Clustering Component. Snapshot Generator is invoked to move and click a button to change the display into interpolate 2D Umatrix mode. Nenet Agent makes itself ready for service by registering to Nenet RMI Registry as in Clustering Component. In contrast to Clustering Component, the visualization component allows one connection session at a time since scraping the screen in Nenet is window oriented instead of command-line oriented; multiple concurrent displays might disturb the Nenet system.

It is of great necessity for a SOM tool to delimit regions on the map for supporting cluster analysis. There are a couple of different approaches toward deciding number of clusters in SOM [6]. The easiest way is to assign the number of neurons on the map to be equal to the number of expected clusters in the data set. This approach often results in the overestimated number of clusters for larger maps. In this study, we adopted a comprised approach, from a viewpoint of reusability in object-oriented information systems, the so-called two-level SOM. It augments the conventional SOM by an additional one-dimension Kohonen layer in which each neuron is connected to the ones in the previous Kohonen layer [4]. During training, the weight vectors on the first Kohonen layer are fed into the second Kohonen layer as inputs. Upon completing the training, each neuron on the new layer represents a cluster identified. The cluster validity of wSOM is evaluated by the silhouette coefficient [2]. Intuitively, S_i indicates how well data i is assigned to an appropriate cluster. The larger S_i is, the better clustering is achieved. At the extreme case, negative one of silhouette implies data i was misclassified whereas zero indicates that a clear determination could not be made. Therefore, the optimal number of clusters is k, which maximizes $\tilde{s}_k$, the average silhouette width for the whole data set.

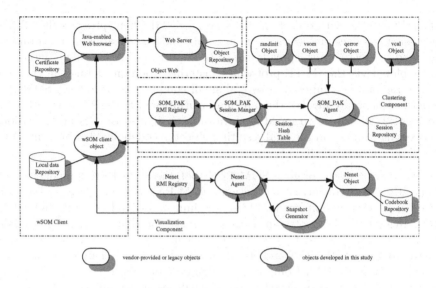

Fig. 1. The system architecture of wSOM

4 Experiments

In this section, we discuss the experimental results on the well-known Fisher's iris benchmark and a case study on discovering spatio-temporal patterns in air pollution data. The iris data set contains 150 flowers, labeled as three classes evenly. The SOM_PAK and Nenet components run in Solaris 7 on SUN Ultra80 with 1GB memory and Microsoft Windows NT 4.0, respectively. The Swing-based user interface of the client side allows one to enter and/or choose parameters as in SOM_PAK. In addition, users are granted to specify the range of the number of clusters to be explored. A new data table can be created as a spreadsheet. This GUI also provides importing local or remote data files thru the HTTP protocol to support a mobile decision-making environment. The codebook after training can be exported to a local file for further processing. To evaluate quantitatively the clustering performance for the experiment, a simple "voting" strategy is utilized in labeling clusters due to the availability of the class information in the data set. A cluster will be labeled as class c if its majority of the cluster belongs to class c in the iris data set. Therefore, the overall clustering performance can be formally justified by a cost function of misclassified rate. For determining an optimal number of clusters, numbers between three and nine have been tested in this experiment. Table 1 illustrates the clustering performance according to different clusters. It indicates that number eight is the optimal cluster numbers, which also achieves the minimal misclassified rate.

The wSOM tool was also applied to a case study in data mining whose goal is to help EPA (Environmental Protection Administration) in Taiwan, investigate the spatial variability of air pollutants associated with time. The mining result

Table 1. The clustering performance of iris data

Number of clusters	3	4	5	6	7	8	9
Silhouette coefficient	-0.136	-0.050	0.003	-0.017	0.004	0.0005	-0.0074
Mis-classified rate	0.16	0.11	0.04	0.03	0.02	0.02	0.03

confirms its effectiveness in discovering spatio-temporal patterns in temporal databases; a detailed discussion can be found in [4].

5   Conclusions

In this paper, we proposed a web-aware SOM tool, wSOM, in an interoperable environment by integrating two popularly-used stand-alone tools, SOM_PAK and Nenet. The design philosophy is on the basis of effectiveness in cost, reusability in existing components and rapid prototyping in system development. We applied the Java distributed object computing model to deal with issues of interoperability in heterogeneous languages, platforms, and visual object models. The resulting system highlights the computational efficiency attributed to SOM_PAK on UNIX and vivid visualization attributed to Nenet on Windows. It rejuvenates the original tools with the functionality of Web-aware, concurrent processing, and load balancing. In addition, the wSOM system is built upon a two-level SOM_PAK network to allow one to identify the resulting clusters. The optimal number of clusters is determined by silhouette coefficients. The experiment conducted on clustering the iris data and real-world air pollution data validates its usefulness. The overall benefit can be quite significant. The system may evolve with time by simply incorporating new components or adaptively modifying the current components.

References

1. Deboeck, G.: Software Tools for Self-Organizing Maps, In: Deboeck, G., Kohonen, T. (eds.): Visual Explorations in Finance with Self-Organizing Maps. Springer-Verlag London Limited (1998) 179–194.
2. Kaufman, L., Rousseeuw, P. J.: Finding Groups in Data: An Introduction to Cluster Analysis. John Wiley & Sons (1990).
3. Kohonen, T.: Self-Organizing Maps. Springer-Verlag Berlin Heidelberg (1997).
4. Li, S.-T., Chou, S.-W., Pan, J. J.: Multi-resolution Spatio-temporal Data Mining for the Study of Air Pollution Regionalization. Procs. of the 33rd Hawaii Int'l Conf. on System Sciences (2000).
5. Saleh, K., Probert, R., Khanafer, H.: The Distributed Object Computing Paradigm: Concepts and Applications. The Journal of Systems and Software **47** (1999) 125–131.
6. Vesanto, J., Alhoniemi, E.: Clustering of the Self-organizing Map. IEEE Trans. on Neural Networks **11:3** (2000) 586–600.

Experiencing NetPeas: Another Way of Learning

Eric Zhi-Feng Liu[1], Sunny S. J. Lin[2], and Shyan-Ming Yuan[1]

[1] Department of Computer and Information Sciecne, National Chiao Tung University,
Hsinchu, Taiwan 31151, R.O.C.
{totem, smyuan}@cis.nctu.edu.tw
[2] Center for Teacher Education, National Chiao Tung University, Hsinchu, Taiwan 31151,
R.O.C.
sunnylin@cc.nctu.edu.tw

Abstract. This study implement networked peer assessment in designing and, in doing so, develops a networked peer assessment model as well. Based on the proposed model, a networked peer assessment system is designed as its main frame in conjunction with an optional Vee diagram used as its interface to facilitate designing. In this system, students turn in their homework via a friendly web browser. Students assess each other's homework by offering comments through the Internet. Students then reflect and modify their homework based on those comments. This procedure is repeated for k (k≥1) consecutive rounds, based on the schedule. In this process, students act as an adaptive learner, author, and reviewer. This learning model allows students to further develop their critical thinking and problem solving skills. Results revealed that the networked peer assessment model facilitated students to continuously progress when learning to design work.

1 Introduction

Topping [7] defined peer as a student with the same academic background. For example, a course in which the participating students have very different backgrounds, such as mathematics and music majors, would hardly to implement peer assessment activities. Topping concluded that among the diverse subjects taught in higher education that adopts peer assessment include writing composition, civil engineering, sciences, electrical engineering, information, humanities, and social sciences. Topping also indicated that the computer-based peer assessment systems are few and worth to explore it's usefulness in educational practices.

Authors believe that peer assessment is most effectively implemented by using a user friendly web system as a medium, thereby eliminating communication restrictions such as time and location. The anonymity of networked environments, which include local area network and distributed web-based system, would somewhat avoid unfair peer assessment.

N. Zhong et al. (Eds.): WI 2001, LNAI 2198, pp. 584–588, 2001.
© Springer-Verlag Berlin Heidelberg 2001

Constructivism emphasizes the learners' active participation so that they actively engage in knowledge construction. From a constructivist perspective, learners must not only be aware of what they are learning, but also respond to the comments of other counterparts in terms of which new knowledge is reconstructed. Containing important characteristics of constructivism, a networked peer assessment model allows students to learn by submitting homework and receiving suggestions from peers to improve their work. In doing so, they can develop their critical thinking skills with the increasing number of repetitions of peer assessment (Liu *et al.* [4]).

Boud [1] recognized the gap between expectations of students in higher education and what is required in real life. He emphasized examining assessment practices to determine whether they are compatible with the goals of higher education. From his perspective, student assessment should focus on improving the quality of learning. Boud [1] viewed peer assessment as a cornerstone of improving the quality of learning. Moreover, Vee diagram (Novak and Gowin [6]), a heuristic strategy adopted in scientific exploration, allows learners to view the interaction between "relevant concepts" (thinking) and "practice of experiment" (doing). The Vee diagram can completely record an experiment-oriented work easily (e.g. designing a new artificial intelligence algorithm). In this study, authors have mainly focused on designing a networked peer assessment system (*Netpeas*) and an optional Vee diagram to be used as its interface to facilitate creative designing.

2   Networked Peer Assessment Model

The conventional means of grading homework consists of teachers assigning homework and students turning it in before the deadline. Teachers then grade the homework and return the assignments to the students. In this process, learning is limited to the experiences that students gain by doing their homework. Moreover, controlling and evaluating the process of doing the homework is difficult for instructors.

In contrast, this study, based on the work of Liu *et al.* [4], develops a networked peer assessment model to break up the conventional learning process into smaller categories. Certain arrangements are provided to increase the effectiveness of learning.

The networked peer assessment model comprises of the following steps:
1. Students and the teacher jointly discuss the homework project (in this case, designing a science activity for secondary students).
2. The science activity designed by each student is uploaded to the system.
3. The system randomly assigns m reviewers ($1 \leq m \leq n$, n is the maximum number of reviewers in an assessment procedure).
4. Reviewers grade the homework and comment on it.
5. The teacher grades each student's homework and observes the comments written by students without revealing the results.
6. Students are notified by the system of their grades and comments.

7. Based on the comments on each student's homework, they must modify the original homework.
8. Steps 2 to 7 are repeated k-1 (k≥1) times.
9. The teacher performs a final assessment.

After turning in their homework, the students are assigned homework to grade the assignments, as dispatched by the system. Each student is responsible for grading others' homework. The suggestions and grades evaluated by reviewers are then returned to the original author. The authors must correct their mistakes or modify their original work based on the suggestions of peer reviewers.

2.1 Goal of Persistent Progression

In our study, The entire learning process is achieved through several consecutive assessments plus the associated improvements. Our goal is to help students make progress in each round. Therefore, this system allows each student to look at his (or her) grades and comments after each round is completed in improving his (or her) homework. In order to make sure that each student does correct his (or her) mistakes or improve the weaknesses each round, a method is proposed to monitor the students. That is, the same reviewer is assigned to grade the same homework each round. The advantage of doing this is that the same reviewer can examine if the homework is modified or not according to his (or her) comments addressed previously.

3 Vee Diagram

Novak and Gowin [6] proposed using a Vee diagram as a heuristic strategy to explain the correlation between the structure of knowledge and the course of action in obtaining or expanding this structure. Restated, adopting the Vee diagram emphasizes the interaction between "knowing" (conceptual frameworks) and "doing" (methodological processes). Figure 1 presents the components of Vee diagram used in one of our studies.

The center is the starting point, i.e., a focus question to be explored. Along with the V shape up to the tip point are the events or objects that students must observe to explore the focus question. On the left hand side of the V shape are the general concepts and theories. The right hand side contains the observation procedures under the guidance or methods of exploring the focus question. In this study, students were asked to present their science activities through the interface of the Vee diagram. Peers further evaluated these activities according to the process of the networked peer assessment model.

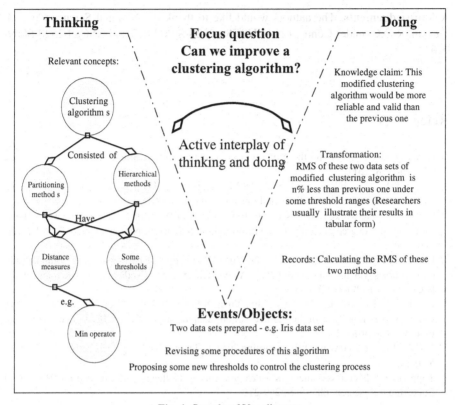

Fig. 1. Sample of Vee diagram

4 Conclusions

This study described the design experiences of developing a networked peer assessment system to facilitate instruction and learning. Based on our results, authors conclude that using a computer network to facilitate peer assessment has the following merits:

1. Increased freedom of time and location for learners.
2. Cross-platform tools for hypertext access.
3. Ability of students to modify their work efficiently.
4. Increased instructor-student and student-student interaction and feedback.
5. Higher degree of anonymity than traditional peer assessment.
6. Significantly lower transmission and delivery costs than traditional peer assessment.
7. Fewer limitations on transmission of data than traditional peer assessment.

Author's experiences [2-5] proved that peer assessment a teaching strategy that may be useful in improving student learning. Thus, it is our belief that peer assessment is not only an effective evaluation indicator, it is also an effective instructional strategy.

Acknowledgements. The authors would like to thank the National Science Council, Taiwan, R.O.C, under Contract Nos. NSC89-2520-S-009-013 and NSC89-2520-S009-016.

References

1. Boud, D.: Assessment and the promotion of academic values. Studies in Higher Education. **17** (1990) 185-200.
2. Lin, S.S.J., Liu, E.Z.F., and Yuan, S.M.: Web-based Peer Assessment: Attitude and Achievement, IEEE Transactions on Education, in print (2001).
3. Liu, E.Z.F.: Networked peer assessment system: an analysis of student segments. A thesis for the master degree of Computer and Information Science of National Chiao-Tung University (1999).
4. Liu, E.Z.F, Chiu, C.H., Lin, S.S.J., and Yuan, S.M.: Student participation in computer science courses via the Networked Peer Assessment System (NetPeas), Proceedings of the ICCE' 99, 1 (1999) 774-777.
5. Liu, E.Z.F., Lin, S.S.J., Chiu, C.H., and Yuan, S.M.: Web-based Peer review: An effective web-learning strategy with the learner as both adapter and reviewer. IEEE Transactions on Education, in print (2001).
6. Novak, J.D. and Gowin, D.B.: Learning how to learn. Cambridge University Press, New York (1984).
7. Topping, K.: Peer Assessment Between Students in Colleges and Universities. Review of Educational Research. **68** (1998) 249-276.

ITMS: Individualized Teaching Material System – Web-Based Exploratory Learning Support System by Adaptive Knowledge Integration –

Hiroyuki Mitsuhara, Youji Ochi, and Yoneo Yano

Dept. of Information Science and Intelligent Systems, Faculty of Engineering, Tokushima University, 2-1 Minamijosanjima, Tokushima, Japan
{mituhara, ochi, yano}@is.tokushima-u.ac.jp

Abstract. A problem in Web-based exploratory learning is the learning impasse caused by the content of a page. To enable learners to avoid the impasse, it is necessary for a system to adapt the content. We developed a Web-based exploratory leaning support system named ITMS, which belongs to the category of Web-based AES and has the following features: (1) it deals with the open Web, (2) it adaptively integrates the knowledge that they learned into an arbitrary page, and (3) it presumes their latest knowledge states from their knowledge reference.

1 Introduction

In the present situation that the Web is expected to be teaching material for school education and life-long learning, exploratory learning is surely shifting from stand-alone style to Web-based style.

A problem in Web-based exploratory learning is the learning impasse caused by the content of a page. Specifically, it occurs at the page that omits its related knowledge (explanations) and interrupts learners' understanding such a page. A search engine is one of the remedies. When falling into the impasse, the learners can utilize the search engine to find the related knowledge that exists somewhere in the open Web. However search engines often give them piles of pages. The piles interrupt their selecting a page. This situation is so-called information overload and indicates that the accuracy and the usability of search engines are not enough for educational usage. Web-based AES (Adaptive Educational System), which adapts the content, is the alternative to search engines. However the current Web-based AES mainly deals with the closed Web (inside one server) and does not support open-ended exploratory learning [1-4].

We developed a Web-based exploratory learning support system named ITMS (Individualized Teaching Material System), which has the framework of adaptive knowledge integration. This framework enables learners to avoid the impasse in the open Web by adaptively integrating the knowledge that they learned into an arbitrary page. A key feature of ITMS is to presume their latest knowledge states from their knowledge reference.

N. Zhong et al. (Eds.): WI 2001, LNAI 2198, pp. 589–595, 2001.
© Springer-Verlag Berlin Heidelberg 2001

2 Adaptive Knowledge Integration

The related knowledge that causes the impasse is divided into the knowledge that learners have never learned and the knowledge that they had leaned before but do not understand at present. We focus on the impasse caused by the latter and propose the framework of adaptive knowledge integration.

2.1 Framework

Learners will avoid the impasse by referring to the related knowledge that they do not understand. Hence our framework dynamically provides them with an adaptive repository. Specifically, it extracts the related knowledge automatically from a page by means of the keyword matching and integrates the related knowledge into the page on the basis of their knowledge states. Fig. 1 shows our framework.
(1) Closed Web
Learners learn knowledge through exploring the closed Web created by some teachers (a set of educational Web pages). Our framework deals with a fraction of the pages as a component of the knowledge, which is named a knowledge component. The knowledge components are structured appropriately.
(2) Open Web
The learners, who learned knowledge somewhat in the closed Web, stabilize their learned knowledge or learn new knowledge effectively through exploring the open Web that has various contents. The impasse frequently occurs in the open Web.
(3) Learner model
The element of the learner model is a learner's knowledge states. The learner model is built, based on his/her knowledge reference in the closed Web (See section 3).
(4) Adaptation filter
The adaptation filter, which is created on the basis of the learner model, selects the knowledge components that the learner does not understand from many knowledge components. Finally, the selected components are restructured and are integrated into an arbitrary page as a new page.

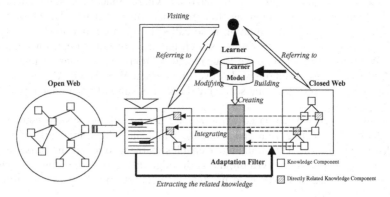

Fig. 1. The framework of adaptive knowledge integration

2.2 Knowledge Component

The knowledge component has the following features.
(1) Fine-grained content
This feature realizes fine-grained adaptation. The procedure for creating the knowledge components is shown below.

(i) A teacher creates the closed Web (educational pages).

(ii) He/she creates the knowledge components by fractionizing the pages, taking into account attributes of the components. For example, a page concerning "World Wide Web" is fractionized into its concept, history, mechanism, and application.

(iii) He/she creates the indexes of the knowledge components. The index is composed of KK (Knowledge Keyword) and KI (Knowledge ID). KK is used to extract the related knowledge from a page and KI is used as ID and the title of the knowledge component. He/she can designate some keywords as KK. For example, KK of the knowledge component of "World Wide Web" is as follows: "World Wide Web", "WWW", "Web", and "Internet". The indexes are directly described in the pages with HTML comments.

(2) Presentation using hierarchical stretch-text
The knowledge components are structured hierarchically. They can contain the knowledge components that are created by other teachers and are stored in distributed servers. This feature provides the learners with various kinds of knowledge that exist all over the world. The knowledge components are presented using hierarchical stretch-text, which is effective in improving information overload and disorientation (getting lost in hyperspace) [5]. When the learners refer to the knowledge, they click the title of the knowledge component and the knowledge component is immediately expanded beside the title. This knowledge presentation facilitates their knowledge reference.

2.3 Integration Process

When a learner visits a page in the open Web, the adaptive knowledge integration is performed along the following procedure.
(i) Extracting the related knowledge
Whether KK corresponds with words on the page is checked in order to extract the related knowledge from the page. If they correspond, all knowledge components with the same KK are extracted as the related knowledge.
(ii) Filtering
Whether the learner understands the extracted knowledge (component) is checked from his/her learner model. The knowledge that he/she does not understand is selected through the adaptation filter.
(iii) Integrating
If the knowledge components are embedded directly inside the page, its original layout alters notably and he/she will be confused. Hence our framework creates a new page with selected knowledge components.

3 Learner Modeling

We propose presuming learners' latest knowledge states from their knowledge reference in the closed Web. This method does not interrupt their exploration, since knowledge reference is based on their autonomy. In addition, they can easily refer to the knowledge presented using the hierarchical stretch-text.

3.1 Hypotheses

We simply classify the knowledge state into "understood", "vaguely understood", and "forgot (not understood)". Each knowledge component has one state. We consider that learners' knowledge reference is strongly associated with their knowledge states and set up the following hypotheses.
(a) The learners do not refer to the knowledge they understand.
(b) The learners actively refer to the knowledge they do not understand.
(c) The learners understand knowledge just after referring to the knowledge.
(d) While the learners do not notice knowledge, the state of the knowledge decline.

3.2 Knowledge State Presumption

On the basis of the above hypothesis (a), (b) and (c), the state of the knowledge (component) that the learners can directly refer to is always presumed to be "understood". In other words, under the situation they can see (click) the title of the knowledge component, the state of the knowledge is always presumed to be "understood". On the other hand, the state of the knowledge that they cannot directly refer to (It is named hidden knowledge. For example, the indirectly related knowledge is applicable to the hidden knowledge) cannot be presumed, since it is unknown whether they are aware of the hidden knowledge. For example, when a learner refers to K3 from K0 in Fig. 2 (a), although the states of K1, K2, K3 and K5 are presumed to be "understood", the states of K4, K6, K7 and K8 (hidden knowledge) cannot be presumed.

3.2.1 Support of Knowledge State Presumption
In order to presume the state of the hidden knowledge, it is necessary to make the learners notice the hidden knowledge. We realize it by highlighting the title or transferring the hidden knowledge component to the top layer. It is named hidden knowledge alteration. Fig.2 shows the outline of the hidden knowledge alteration.

Practically, the knowledge state is stored as a discrete value and is interpreted as one of the three according to thresholds. The discrete value indicates the number of times that the knowledge remains hidden sequentially. On the basis of hypothesis (c) and (d), the state of the knowledge with a low value is guessed to be "understood", and with a high value is guessed to be "forgot". Specifically, the state changes at the point that the value exceeds the thresholds.

3.2.2 Updating Threshold

Updating the thresholds depends on whether the learners refer to the altered knowledge. For example, when a learner refers to "forgot" knowledge, it can be thought to be that his/her state of the knowledge may have been "forgot" before the alteration. Accordingly, one of the thresholds is decreased and the next alteration is performed earlier. In the contrary case, it can be thought to be that the knowledge state is not currently "forgot". Accordingly, the threshold is increased and the next alteration is performed later. Briefly, the thresholds indicate the tendency of the knowledge state declines. The threshold with a high value indicates that the tendency is weak and the threshold with a low value indicates that the tendency is strong.

3.3 Creating Adaptation Filter

The adaptation filter is created on the basis of the tendency of the knowledge state declines. When the number of times that a knowledge component was extracted exceeds "forgot" threshold, the adaptation filter passes the knowledge component. Fig. 3 shows the relation between the tendency and the adaptive knowledge integration.

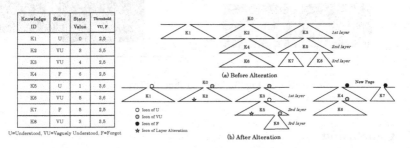

Fig. 2. The hidden knowledge alteration

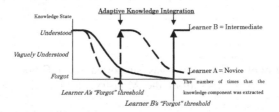

Fig. 3. Timing of the adaptive knowledge integration

4   Learning Example

Fig.3 shows an example of the exploratory learning in the open Web. The left page that a learner visited explains Ray Tracing Parametric Surface and requires a lot of the related knowledge on geometry from the learner. On the left page, we can see the words of "B-Spline surface", but there are not its detailed explanations. ITMS presents the right page with three knowledge components to the learner.

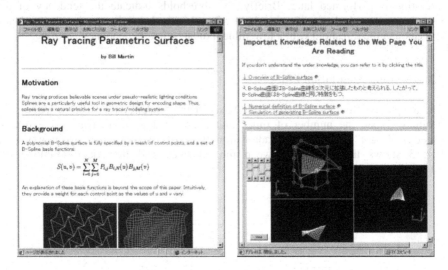

Fig. 3. A screen shot of ITMS

5   Conclusion

In ITMS, the usability of the knowledge presentation is especially important, since it is strongly associated with the learners' knowledge reference. We have obtained good results of the usability through experiments. Our important future work is to evaluate the validity of our learner modeling. We are planning to experiment on a large scale.

Acknowledgements. This work was supported by a Grant-in Aid for Scientific Research (B) No.13480047 from the Ministry of Education, Science Sports and Culture in Japan.
This work was supported in part by a grant to RCAST at Doshisha University from the Ministry of Education, Japan.

References

1. Kay, J. and Kummerfeld, R. J.: An individualized course for the C programming language, Proc. of Second International WWW Conference (1994)
2. Brusilovsky, P., Schwarz, E., and Weber, G.: ELM-ART: An intelligent tutoring system on World Wide Web, Proc. of ITS-96 (1996) 261-269
3. De Bra, P., & Calvi, L.: AHA! An open Adaptive Hypermedia Architecture, The New Review of Hypermedia and Multimedia, vol. 4 (1998) 115-139
4. Henze, N., Nejdl, W.: Adaptivity in the KBS Hyperbook System, Proc. of the 2nd Workshop on Adaptive Systems and User Modeling on the WWW (1999) 67-74
5. Höök, K., Karlgren, J., Waern, A., Dahlbäck, N., Jason, C.G., Karlgren, K., Lemaire, B.: A glass Box Approach to Adaptive Hypermedia, User Models and User-Adapted Interaction 6(2-3) (1996) 157-184

An Intelligent Sales Assistant for Configurable Products

Martin Molina

Department of Artificial Intelligence, Technical University of Madrid
Campus de Montegancedo s/n, 28660 Boadilla del Monte (Madrid), Spain
mmolina@fi.upm.es

Abstract. Some of the recent proposals of web-based applications are oriented to provide advanced search services through virtual shops. Within this context, this paper proposes an advanced type of software application that simulates how a sales assistant dialogues with a consumer to dynamically *configure* a product according to particular needs. The paper presents the general knowledge model that uses artificial intelligence and knowledge-based techniques to simulate the configuration process. Finally, the paper illustrates the description with an example of an application in the field of photography equipment.

1 Introduction

Some of the recent proposals in e-commerce have been oriented to improve the communication and the level of assistance to the consumer by providing more active web-based applications including semantic features. For this purpose, advanced techniques from different fields such as artificial intelligence (knowledge-based systems, natural language, etc.) and advanced user-system interaction (multimedia presentations, 3D graphics, etc.) are being applied [1]. For example, *Ebrain* uses rule-based knowledge representation and natural language techniques to guide visitors through a website explaining products and special offers. Another example is given by [2] that proposes virtual shopping advisor that makes recommendations after a cluster-based analysis of the customer.

To provide this type of support, these applications need to automatically interpret diverse and detailed knowledge about the products and their context. This is especially important in the case of markets of *configurable products*, i.e., products that need to be dynamically configured according to the needs of customers by assembly specific components. The complexity and diversity of knowledge for this type of applications requires appropriate technical solutions. In this context, this paper contributes with a general approach to this problem. The paper presents how this type of application can be supported by knowledge-based architecture using problem-solving methods from artificial intelligence and, the paper illustrates the description with an application that was developed in the field of photography equipment.

N. Zhong et al. (Eds.): WI 2001, LNAI 2198, pp. 596–600, 2001.
© Springer-Verlag Berlin Heidelberg 2001

2   The Knowledge Model for the Sales Assistant

In order to develop the web-based application, we followed the general idea of *intelligent assistant* [3], a type of software application oriented to help operators in making decisions. We followed this approach to design a system, conceived as a virtual sales assistant, with the following characteristics: (1) the system recommends candidate product configurations based on the interpretation of the customer needs, (2) the systems tries to justify the proposals with convincing explanations, and (3) the customer must be able of changing (total or partially) the proposals.

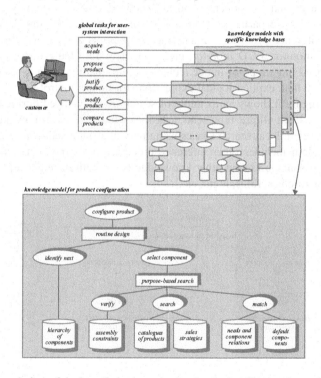

Fig. 1. General view of the knowledge organization for the intelligent sales assistant [4]

To provide this support the sales assistant must bring together different types of knowledge: (1) knowledge about *the products*, (2) knowledge about *the customer*, and (3) knowledge about *the company* interests. We designed a computer-based solution using knowledge-based techniques, following the recent trends in knowledge engineering techniques that apply a *model-based* view (CommonKADS [5] or Protégé-2000 [6]). Figure 3 shows a general view of the knowledge organization. The figure shows the main global tasks, which support the interaction with the customer, associated to the corresponding knowledge models. Details about this model can be found at [4].

3 Symbolic Knowledge Representation

The previous model includes a number of types of knowledge bases that, for instance, in a particular domain with 10 generic components, would produce a total of 37 specific knowledge bases. The particular software implementation requires to associate a particular symbolic representation and inference procedure for each knowledge base and to establish the corresponding control mechanisms for the execution of the global model. For this purpose, advanced knowledge engineering tools can be used such as the KSM environment [7], [8]. For example, the knowledge about relations between customer-needs and components, and the knowledge about assembly constraints can be formulated by a particular frame-based representation (figure 3) with a special matching inference procedure. Each frame represents a type of component (e.g., a color CRT monitor, LCD monitor, etc.) and each slot of the frame can be either a customer need (e.g., type-of-image: color-medium-quality) or an assembly constraint. In addition to that, explicit logical expressions formulate control knowledge for frame matching. Figure 2 shows an example of search tree developed during the configuration process. Each ellipse represents a task-execution that develops additional inference processes in local search spaces using particular knowledge bases. In addition to this, the system includes other inference processes for different functions (justification, comparison, etc.) using other knowledge bases with different representation formalisms (hierarchies, rules, logic, etc.).

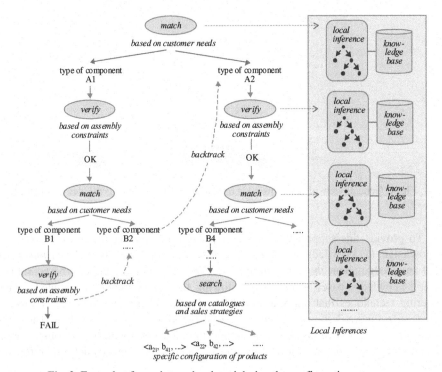

Fig. 2. Example of search tree developed during the configuration process.

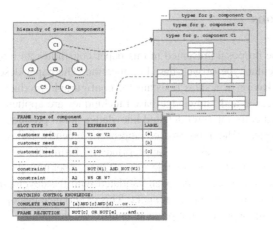

Fig. 3. Example of part of the symbolic representation for the intelligent sales assistant.

4 Application

Following this general approach, a system was developed for a real-world application in the field of photography equipment. A website prototype was developed to assist potential customers in buying equipment of photography. Figure 4 shows an example of some windows presented by the application in the website (Spanish language). In this case, according to the partial data about the customer, the assistant proposes an initial solution based on a compact camera and additional complements. The customer can ask for justification about this proposal and the assistant provides explanations based on the needs that were satisfied. The customer can also change the proposal asking for alternative products. In all these cases, the configuration process is repeated considering the new needs and constraints. In addition to that, the customer can express its level of satisfaction. With this information the system adapts the user preferences in order to propose more adequate answers.

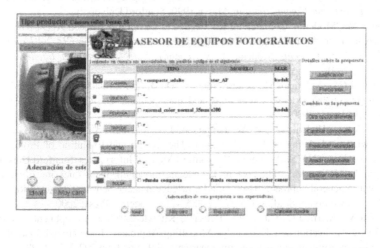

Fig. 4. Example of windows of the web-based application for photography equipment.

5 Conclusions

In summary, the proposal presented in this paper constitutes an innovative solution to develop a particular type of web-based application. The paper describes a solution to simulate the behavior of a sales assistant for configurable products. For this purpose, artificial intelligence and knowledge-based techniques are applied to explicitly represent and automatically interpret detailed knowledge about products, customers and the company strategies. The model-based approach, recently followed in the field of knowledge engineering, has been appropriate to formulate the different types of knowledge and the particular flexible and efficient operational implementation. The model described in the paper has been validated with the development of an application in the field of photography equipment. This experience has opened new possibilities for the development of future projects in different domains.

Acknowledgements. This work was developed in the Intelligent Systems Research Group (Dep. Artificial Intelligence, Tech. Univ. Madrid). Rocío Serna was in charge of the development of the web-based application for photography equipment.

References

1. Terpsidis I., Moukas A., Pergioudakis B., Doukidis G., Maes P.: "The Potential of Electronic Commerce in Re-engineering Consumer-Retail Relationships through Intelligent Agents". Roger J.Y. et al (Eds.). Advances in Information Technologies: The Business Challenge, IOS Press, 1997.
2. Urban G.L., Sultan F., Qualls W.: "Placing Trust at the Center of Your Internet Strategy" Sloan-Management-Review. vol. 42, No.1, pp. 39-48. ISSN 0019-848X, 2000.
3. Boy, G., Gruber T.R.: "Intelligent Assistant Systems: Support for Integrated Human-Machine Systems" Proceedings of 1990 AAAI Spring Symposium on *Knowledge-Based Human-Computer Communication*, March 1990, Stanford University.
4. Molina M. "Modeling Commercial Knowledge to Develop Advanced Agent-based Marketplaces for E-commerce" Proc. of the *Fifth International Workshop CIA-2001 on Cooperative Information Agents* Modena (Italy). *Lecture Notes in Artificial Intelligence* series, Springer. 2001.
5. Schreiber G., Akkermans H., Anjewierden A., De Hoog R., Shadbolt N., Van de Velde W., Wielinga B.: "Knowledge engineering and management. The CommonKADS methodology" MIT Press, 2000.
6. W.E. Grosso, H. Eriksson, R. W. Fergerson, J. H. Gennari, S. W. Tu, & M. A. Musen: "Knowledge Modeling at the Millennium (The Design and Evolution of Protege-2000)". Technical Paper No. SMI-1999-0801. Stanford Medical Informatics. Stanford University
7. Cuena J., Molina M.: "The role of knowledge modelling techniques in software development: a general approach based on a knowledge management tool" International Journal of Human-Computer Studies. No. 52. pp 385-421. Academic Press, 2000.
8. Molina M., Sierra J.L., Cuena J.: "Reusable Knowledge-based Components for Building Software Applications: A Knowledge Modelling Approach" International Journal of Software Engineering and Knowledge Engineering. vol 9, No. 3, pp 297-317., 1999.

Reconciling of Disagreeing Data in Web-Based Distributed Systems Using Consensus Methods*

Ngoc Thanh Nguyen

Department of Information Systems, Wroc•aw University of Technology, Poland
thanh@pwr.wroc.pl

Abstract. In a Web-based distributed system reconciling of disagreeing data is needed when a data conflict exists. A conflict of data is a situation in which some sites of the system generate and store different versions of data which refer to the same subject (problem solution, event scenario etc.). Thus in purpose to solve this problem one final data version called a consensus of given versions should be determined. In this paper we present a consensus system serving to representing data conflicts; the definition of consensus; the postulates for consensus choice functions and their analysis.

1   Introduction

The purpose of reconciling of disagreeing data is to make use of them. This ability should be one of features of intelligent Web-based distributed information systems. Distributed intelligent systems consist of autonomous sites and the autonomous feature is the resource of such kind of conflicts that the information generated by the sites on some matter may be inconsistent. Such information may include results of retrieval processes made by independent agents for the same user query, or solutions of the same task whose solving is entrusted to different agents. The problem is how to determine the final version of the inconsistent results for given query or different solutions of given task. Generally, this kind of situations is related with preserving of data consistency. It often happens that the environments occupied by distributed system sites overlap. The reason of this phenomenon is resulted from the needs of mutual verification and data replication in purpose to increase the computation efficiency and to relieve the Web. For example, the information about all borrowers is replicated in each site of the distributed system of a bank, or the regions occupied by different meteorological stations overlap. Thus we can assume that in different sites of a Web-based distributed system there may be stored and processed data referring to the same part of the real world. Because the data processing is made by each site in an independent way, particularly the data may be uncertain and incomplete (which for

---

* This work is partially supposed by Grant No. 331823 of Research Division, Wroclaw University of Technology.

N. Zhong et al. (Eds.): WI 2001, LNAI 2198, pp. 601–605, 2001.
© Springer-Verlag Berlin Heidelberg 2001

example come from observations), it is very likely that in the sites inconsistent information for the same subject can be stored. We call such a situation a conflict. Generally, such kind of situations can take place when the system sites realize a common task, or solve a common problem or gather information referring to a common world.

In this work we propose to use consensus methods for solving this kind of conflicts in distributed systems. We should show that this version which is the consensus of given versions, should be the most credible one. Consensus methods, firstly used in social and sociological science [1], are a very good tool for data reconciling and working out an agreement in solving conflicts [6]. These methods are particularly useful for these systems in which uncertainty of information is assumed but the decision making process is required. For conflicts in distributed systems (particularly in multiagent systems [4]) consensus methods are useful for their solving.

2 Conflicts in Distributed Systems

The simplest conflict takes place when two bodies have different opinions on the same subject. In work [7] Pawlak specifies the following elements of a conflict: a set of agents, a set of issues, and a set of opinions of these agents about these issues. The agents and the issues are related with one another in some social or political context. Each agent for each issue has 3 possibilities for presenting his opinion: (+) – yes, (–) – no, and (0) – neural. We say that a conflict takes place if there are at least two agents whose opinions on an issue differ from each other. Generally, the following 3 constrains of a conflict can be distinguished: *conflict body* specifies the direct participants of the conflict; *conflict subject* specifies to what the conflict refers and its topic and *conflict content* specifies the opinions of the participants on the conflict topic. In Pawlak's approach the body of conflict is a set of agents, the subject is a set of contentious issues and the content is a collection of tuples representing the participants' opinions. Information tables [8] should be useful for representing this kind of conflicts.

In this paper we define conflicts in distributed systems in the similar way. However, we will define a system which can include more than one conflict, and within a conflict the attributes representing agents' opinions are multivalue, which more precisely describe these opinions.

3 Consensus System

3.1 Basis Notions

We assume that a real world is described by means of a finite set A of attributes and a set V of attribute elementary values, where $V=\bigcup_{a\in A}V_a$ (V_a is the domain of attribute a). Let $\Pi(V_a)$ denote the set of subsets of set V_a and $\Pi(V_B)=\bigcup_{b\in B}\Pi(V_b)$. We assume that for each attribute a its value is a set of elementary values from V_a, thus it is a element of set $\Pi(V_a)$. By an elementary value we mean that one which is not divisible in the system, thus it does not have to be an atomic value.

We define the following notions: Let $B \subseteq A$, a tuple r_B of type B is a function $r_B : B \to \Pi(V_B)$ where $(\forall b \in B)(r_b \subseteq V_b)$. A tuple is elementary if all attribute values are empty sets or 1–element sets. Empty tuple, whose values are empty sets, is denoted by symbol ϕ. Partly empty tuple, whose at least one value is empty, is denoted by symbol θ. The sets of all tuples of type B and of all elementary tuples of type B are denoted by $TYPE(B)$ and $E\text{-}TYPE(B)$ respectively.

3.2 Definition of Consensus System

We assume that some real world is commonly considered by agents which are placed in sites of a distributed system. The subjects of agents' interest consist of events which occur (or have to occur) in the world. The task of the agents is based on determining the values of event attributes (an event is described by a tuple of some type). The system defined below should include this information.

Definition 1. *By a consensus system we call the following triple:*

$$Consensus\_Sys = (A, X, P)$$

where:

- A - a finite set of attributes, which includes a special attribute Agent; each attribute $a \in A$ has a domain V_a (a finite set of elementary values) such that its values are subsets of V_a; values of attribute Agent are 1–element sets, which identify the agents.

- X - a finite set of consensus carriers; $X = \{ \Pi(V_a) : a \in A \}$

- P - a finite set of relations on carriers from X, each relation is of some type A (for $A \subseteq A$ and Agent $\in A$).

The purpose of Definition 1 is relied on representation of two kinds of information: the first consists of information about potential conflicts in the distributed system, which require solving, and the second includes the information needed for consensus determining. We accept the following assumptions: Let $R \in P$ be a relation of type $A \subseteq A$ and $r \in R$, tuple r_B where $B = A \setminus \{Agent\}$ represents a set of events described by elementary tuples r' of type B where $r' \subseteq r_B$ (for each $b \in B$ $r'_b = \emptyset$ iff $r_b = \emptyset$). Relations belonging to set P are classified in such way that each of them includes relations representing similar events. For identifying relations belonging to given group the symbols "+" and "−" should be used as the upper index. If P is the name of a group, then relation P^+ is called a positive relation (contains positive knowledge) and P^-–negative relation (contains negative knowledge). If $r \in P^+ \subseteq TYPE(A)$ then we have the following interpretation: In the opinion of agent r_{Agent} one or more events included in r_B should take place. If $r \in P^- \subseteq TYPE(A)$ then we say that in the opinion of agent r_{Agent} none of the events included in r_B should take place. The same agent cannot simultaneously state that the same event should take place and should not take place. It means that the same event cannot be classified by the same agent into positive and negative relations simultaneously.

The structures of the consensus carriers should be defined. Because it is assumed that values of attribute a are not elementary values but subsets of set V_a for $a \in A$, as the structure of a carrier we will define distance functions between sets of elementary values. We have defined 2 general distance functions, namely δ and ρ [6]. These functions are the general forms of defined in the literature distance functions for such structures as rankings [1], semillattices [2], n-trees [3].

Definition 2. *For 2 tuples r and r' of type A the distance function φ assigns a number*

$$\varphi(r,r') = \frac{1}{card(A)} \sum_{a \in A} \partial(r_a, r'_a) \text{ where } \partial \in \{\rho, \delta\}.$$

3.3 Consensus Definition, Postulates, and Their Analysis

A consensus is considered within a consensus situation, which is defined as follows:

Definition 3. *A consensus situation is a pair $<\{P^+, P^-\}, A \rightarrow B>$ where $A, B \subseteq A$, $A \cap B = \varnothing$ and for every 2 tuples $r \in P^+$ and $r' \in P^-$ there should be held $r_A \neq \theta$ and $r'_A \neq \theta$.*

The first element of a consensus situation includes the domain from which consensus should be chosen, and the second element presents the subjects of consensus (i.e. set $Subject(s) \subseteq TYPE(A)$) and the content of consensus, such that for a subject e there should be assigned only one tuple of type B.

For given relations P^+ and P^- let us define relation $P^{\pm}$ (called complementary to P^+ and P^-) as the set of all non-empty elementary tuples which are not included in these relations. Thus relation $P^{\pm}$ contains all possible events which do not occur in relations P^+ and P^-. These events, therefore, should be treated as the uncertainty of agents.

Definition 4. *For situation $s = <\{P^+, P^-\}, A \rightarrow B>$ a pair $\{C(s)^+, C(s)^-\}$ where $C(s)^+$, $C(s)^- \subseteq TYPE(A \cup B)$, is called a consensus if the following conditions are fulfilled:*

a) *For any $r, r' \in C(s)^+$ tuples r_A and r_A' are elementary and if $r_A = r_A'$ then $r_B = r_B'$,*

b) *For any $r, r' \in C(s)^-$ tuples r_A and r_A' are elementary and if $r_A = r_A'$ then $r_B = r_B'$,*

c) *$C(s)^+ \cap C(s)^- = \phi$.*

Let relation $C(s)^{\pm}$ be complementary to relations $C(s)^+$ and $C(s)^-$. Relation $C(s)^+$ is called the positive component, relation $C(s)^-$—negative component and relation $C(s)^{\pm}$—uncertain component of the consensus.

Below we present 6 postulates for consensus, their formal forms and comments are presented in work [5]:

- **P1.** *Closure of knowledge*: The positive (negative) component of consensus should be included in the sum of positive (negative) elements of the consensus.
- **P2.** *Consistency of knowledge*: The common part of positive (negative) elements of consensus basis should be included in positive (negative) component and should not be included in negative (positive) component of the consensus,
- **P3.** *Consistency of uncertainty*: The common part of uncertain elements of consensus basis should be included in uncertain component of the consensus
- **P4.** *Superiority of knowledge*: If for given subject e only one agent generates opinion (positive or negative) and other agents do not, then the opinion of this agent should be in consensus for subject e.

- P5. *Impasse solving:* For any $e \in Subject(s)$ and $r \in E\text{-}TYPE(B)$ where $r \neq \phi$, if the number of tuples including r in $profile(e)^+$ is equal to the number of tuples including r in $profile(e)^-$, then r should be included in $C(s,e)^{\pm}$.
- P6. *Maximal similarity:* The distance between consensus $C(s) = \{C(s)^+, C(s)^-\}$ and the basis $\{P^+, P^-\}$ should be minimal.

Each of postulates P1, P2,... and P6 is a characteristic property of consensus functions and may be treated as a logical condition for candidates for consensus. The semantics of these formulas includes all possible consensus systems.

Theorem 1. *For any situation and any its consensus the following dependency is true*:
$$P6 \Rightarrow (P1 \wedge P2 \wedge P3 \wedge P5).$$

Theorem 2. *There exists a situation for which the consensus satisfying the following formula does not exist*
$$P1 \wedge P2 \wedge P3 \wedge P4 \wedge P5 \wedge P6.$$

The first theorem shows an important property of postulate P6, namely consensus satisfying this postulate should satisfy also postulates P1, P2, P3 and P5. The second theorem, on the other hand, shows that in general all the postulates may not be satisfied simultaneously.

4 Conclusions

In this work we present a consensus system which enables to store information about conflicts in Web-based distributed systems, and to solve these conflicts by determining consensus. The future works should concern the investigation of criteria, which allow to state if the chosen consensus is sensible for given situation, in other words, if this conflict situation is consensus-oriented or not.

References

1. Arrow, K.J.: Social Choice and Individual Values. Wiley New York (1963)
2. Barthelemy, J.P., Janowitz, M.F.: A Formal Theory of Consensus. SIAM J. Discrete Math. **4** (1991) 305-322.
3. Day, W.H.E.: Consensus Methods as Tools for Data Analysis. In: Bock, H.H. (ed.): Classification and Related Methods for Data Analysis. North–Holland (1988) 312–324.
4. Ephrati, E., Rosenschein J.S: Deriving Consensus in Multiagent Systems. Artificial Intelligence **87** (1998) 21–74.
5. Nguyen, N.T.: Using Consensus Methods for Solving Conflicts of Data in Distributed Systems. Lecture Notes on Computer Science **1963** (2000) 409-417.
6. Nguyen, N.T.: Conflict Profiles' Susceptibility to Consensus in Consensus Systems. Bulletin of International Rough Sets Society Vol. 5, No. 1/2 (2001) 217-224.
7. Pawlak, Z.: An Inquiry into Anatomy of Conflicts. Journal of Information Sciences **108** (1998) 65-78.
8. Skowron, A., Rauszer, C.: The Discernibility Matrices and Functions in Information Systems. In: E. S•owi•ski (ed.): *Intelligent Decision Support, Handbook of Applications and Advances of the Rough Sets Theory*, Kluwer Academic Publishers (1992) 331-362.

Web Based Digital Resource Library Tracing Author's Quotation

Youji Ochi [1], Yoneo Yano[1], and Riko Wakita[2]

[1] Faculty of Engineering, Tokushima University
2-1, Minami-josanjima, Tokushima, 770-8506, Japan
{ochi,yano}@is.tokushima-u.ac.jp
[2] Faculty of Education and Regional Studies, Fukui University,
3-9-1, Bunkyo, Fukui, 910-8507, Japan
oriko@cup.com

Abstract. In recent years, the researches about the learning environment using Web are increasing. In addition, in a classroom, some teachers prepare a Web based teaching materials on Web, and introduce them into their lesson. Moreover, since many of Web contents are exhibited on the Internet, some teachers use the contents as their teaching materials. However, a teacher may not aware existence the teaching-materials resource suitable for his needs. On the other hand, a student is often unable to look for suitable Web resource, either. We focusing on the features of Web that is easy information exchange in the distributed environment. We developed a digital resource library that supports to share of Web teaching materials using author's quotation. In this paper, we consider the use form of Web teaching materials from the viewpoint of a teacher and a student. Then we describe the outline of our approach and prototype system.

1 Introduction

The trial that uses WWW for education is now popular with the spread of the Internet in recent years. However, though many Web teaching materials are prepared, a student is often unable to look for suitable Web resource, either. Therefore, the framework that supports their search of Web teaching materials is needed.

The approach that supports to look for Web is divided into an information retrieval and navigation. A search engine is typical as a former. Many general search engines have a search environment based on keywords, and it tends to show many unnecessary reference results. Morimoto et al. [2] is developing the reference support system that derives the suitable keyword for the learner's purpose in use of a search engine. As latter approach, Okazaki et al. [3] is developing a user-side database that treats general Web contents as a teaching-materials resource. Takeuchi et al. [4] has realized the framework that two or more teacher's manage the structure of Web teaching materials. Moreover, Kashihara et al. [5] proposes the index of Web teaching materials corresponding to a student's study situation, and has realized navigation environment. It is good that the teaching-materials space is larger in order to realize the positive and

N. Zhong et al. (Eds.): WI 2001, LNAI 2198, pp. 606–611, 2001.
© Springer-Verlag Berlin Heidelberg 2001

discoverable education. However, if teaching-materials space is extended to general Web, it is difficult for a learner to select content in search by keyword-based search. In above-mentioned approach, it becomes difficult for a teacher to set up teaching-materials structure and the indexes beforehand. Then, in our research, we propose the framework grasps the structure of Web teaching materials from author's (e.g. a teacher) behaviors and support her/his search. We think that WWW is one huge Electronic Library that has an educational resource. Aizawa[1] has proposed 3-class model (Information Provider, Information Broker, User) as a model of the information circulation in an Electronic Library. We applied the model to an educational support system. The user is a student or a teacher and the information provider is a teaching-materials author. We think that the educational system as the Information Broker is important to search the teaching-materials. Then, we developed the digital resource library to search the teaching-materials on WWW that is suitable for user's (a teacher or student) various learning-needs. Our system has a new framework that traces author's quotation information to search the teaching-materials. In this paper, we describe the framework and a prototype system.

2 Proposal of "Educlusion"

2.1 Objective of "Educlusion"

We consider that the teaching material is a part of the author's knowledge that s/he selected from original knowledge in accordance with her/his educational purpose. We think that the following becomes original knowledge.

(1)   Original idea that a teacher has in her/his mind

(2)   The existing teaching materials (e.g. textbook, other teaching material)

Our research focuses on "Quotation" as a latter example. The remark-mentioned knowledge especially cannot be judged from teaching materials, unless an author writes it clearly. We think that the suitable knowledge for a student's needs may exist in the knowledge that the author did not select. In the information retrieval of Web, there is research [6] which searches for a Web page paying attention to the degree of quotation. However, since this research defines the hyperlink as quotation, it differs from our purpose.Our concept is based on "Transclusion" that Nelson [7] proposes, which is embedment from other contents. "Transclusion" aims at including the copyright and reorganization of an original portion. In our research, we propose "Educlusion (Educational Transclusion)" as Transclusion that treats an educational intention. In our research, a teacher creates teaching materials by combining with the quotation-contents of existing Web teaching materials or Web contents. The difference with a student's needs and teaching materials is the disagreement of the needs of a student and knowledge that the author's quoted. We consider that the suitable knowledge for a student may exist in an original content that author did not quote. Navigating from a quotation place to Web teaching materials of a quoting origin, the student leads to canceling the difference with her/his needs and teaching materials. When quotation is performed, a quoting origin has a high possibility of being the teaching-materials resource that has utility value as @teaching materials. As for showing a quoting origin to a teacher, s/he can acquire the expertise of teaching-materials creation. The contents of a quoting origin and a quotation destination are not often same, and a quotation part can be called new partial teaching materials processed by the author's educational view. Showing quotation action of other authors and some quotation parts lead to acquiring the expertise of the teaching-materials creating method to a teaching-materials author.

2.2   Merit of Searching WTM by Educlusion

Totaling the quotation information, user can know the feature and structure of the Web teaching materials based on the quotation direction or an intention. For example, looking for Web teaching materials that are tendency to be quoted, the user can search for the Web resource with abundant information. Moreover, indexing by quotation intention, a user can discover the contents with simple or detailed information.

3   Realization of Educlusion by a Software Agent

We propose a software agent that is called "Qgent(Quotation Agent)" as solution of the technical problem of the preceding chapter to construct the digital library tracing quotation information. Qgent is avatar of the user (student or author) in a digital library, and resides in each resource in a library permanently. Moreover, it pursues the following information.

1. Quotation origin
2. Quotation destination
3. Author of the Web material
4. Aim of quotation

Qgent supervises an author's quotation action (e.g. her/his copy and paste). When the author quotes a teaching material, Qgent checks the quotation portion and information. Then it embedded the information in the teaching material as quotation destination. At the same time, Qgent grasps a quotation portion, the URL and a quotation intention (simplification, circumstantiation) in the teaching materials. Then, it notifies quotation information also to Qgent as a quoting origin. About within teaching materials, Qgent embeds the information of the quotation portion in direct teaching materials. We propose a quotation-instance in order to write the quotation information on quotation origin. A quotation instance is the copy of the teaching materials. Qgent writes quotation information on it. Qgent can prevent an unjust alteration of original contents (WWW teaching materials) and manage quotation information by this framework.

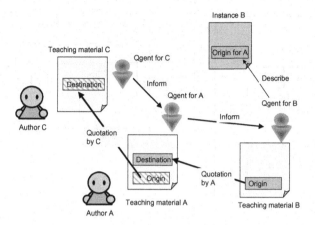

Fig. 1. Framework of Agent traced Quotation

In the case of searching teaching materials, Qgent utilizes the quotation information embedded to teaching materials and own quotation database in order to search the quoting origin and destination (Fig. 1).

4 Prototype System

We are developing a digital library that is called "QT-Library", in which the user can search Web teaching-materials by quotation information. This system has the following functions like a general digital library.

1. Registration of Web teaching materials
2. Reference of Web teaching materials
3. A classification and arrangement of Web teaching materials

We implement this system by the client/server system, and the server is using Web server as the base. The configuration of our system is shown in Fig. 2 and we describe each module below.

(1) Server Module
A digital library server and the quotation information DB constitute a server module. The quotation information DB is a relational database in which the quotation relation between pages is registered.

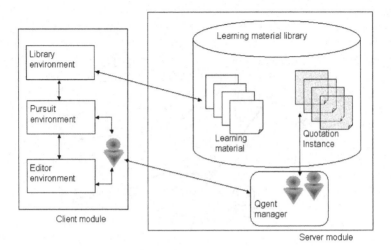

Fig. 2. System configuration

Fig. 3. Snapshot of our system

(2) Client Module

A library environment, an editor environment, and a quotation-tracing environment constitute a client module. Library environment has an interface similar to a general link collection, and Web teaching materials are managed hierarchical per user. Moreover, a user can also refer to the others' library and learn by Web teaching materials in this environment. Editor environment is used at the time of teaching-materials creation, and supports quotation work of the author. Qgent mounted in the editor accumulates and manages of quotation information. Quotation tracing environment supports the user to search of the quotation origin and a quotation destination from the information on Qgent. This environment visualizes the information on a quotation portion in the quoting origin and a quotation destination using dynamic HTML. Fig.3 depict the snapshot of client user-interface.

5 Discussions and Conclusion

In "Think Quest project"[8], a student arranges on the basis of teaching materials, and the situation to collect. If our approach introduces to the above case, it supports the student's discovery of the learning method and arrangement of knowledge. We think that the method of contents creation and learning of Web teaching materials are also refined by quotation trace. Navigating Web teaching materials based on quotation information can expect not only a dissolution of the difference with a student's needs and teaching materials by new teaching-materials presentation but discovery of the new knowledge (teaching materials) outside the category of the author's educational viewpoint. As a future works, we are researching the filtering algorism for the teaching-materials selection and the version management is mentioned. This work was supported by a Grant-in Aid for Scientific Research (B) No.13480047from tne Ministry of Education, Science Sports and Culture in Japan.

References

1. Morimoto, Y., et al.: A development of information retrieval support system for learning material on the Web, Trans. of Japanese society for Information and Systems in Education, Vol.17, No.3 (2000) 231-240
2. Okazaki, Y., et al.: Integrating existing WWW resources into a WWW courseware and its application in classroom lessons, Trans. of Japanese society for Information and Systems in Education, Vol.15, No.4 (1999) 285-292
3. Adachi, T., et al.: WWW based Learning System considering Reuse of Learning, Trans. of Japanese society for Information and Systems in Education, Vol.14, No.5 (1998) 201-210
4. Hasegawa, S., et al.: Reorganizing Learning Resources on WWW and Its Application to an Adaptive Recommendation for Navigational Support, Trans. of the Institute of Electronics information and communication engineers D-I, Vol.J83-D-I, No.6 (2000) 671-681
5. Aizawa, M., et al.: Using Digital Libraries as a Community Hall for Worldwide Information Spiral Development, Trans. of the Institute of Electronics information and communication engineers D-II, Vol.J81-D-II, No.5, (1998) 1014-1024
6. Fukushima, T.: WWW Information Retrieval Technologies and Evaluation Problems, Magazine of Information Processing Society of Japan, Vol.41, No.8 (2000) 913-916
7. T. H. Nelson: Literary Machines, Mindful Press (1991)
8. URL: http://www.thinkquest.gr.jp/

Author Index

Lecture Notes in Artificial Intelligence (LNAI)

Lecture Notes in Computer Science